Contents

D0002422

Maps

In memory of N. Keith Clifford

Preface

More than twenty years have elapsed since the completion of the last comprehensive history of Christianity in Canada. The three-volume *History of the Christian Church in Canada*, by H.H. Walsh, John Moir, and John Webster Grant, was a landmark study, representing the apex of a particular development in the historical study of Christianity in Canada. The focus of this development was, as Paul Dekar said in a 1980 presentation to the Canadian Society of Church History, the 'outer story' of Canadian Christianity, emphasizing the evolution of ecclesiastical institutions, the lives and work of church leaders, and the role of the churches in the public life of the nation. In addition, the *History of the Christian Church in Canada* reflected the ecumenical spirit of the 1960s and 1970s and the intense preoccupation with Canadian identity which was characteristic of that era: the use of 'church' instead of 'churches' in the title signalled the authors' commitment to the ideal of Christian unity; and one of their central concerns was to identify what was distinctively Canadian about Christianity in this country. The three volumes were originally planned as a contribution to Canada's centennial celebration of 1967, though their appearance was delayed by unforeseen circumstances.

While the strengths of the *History of the Christian Church in Canada* marked the successful culmination of years of research, its shortcomings helped to set the agenda for future work. A host of researchers set about filling the gaps in its treatment, and the two decades since its publication have been an especially fruitful period for the study of the history of Christianity in Canada. A wide assortment of books, articles, and postgraduate theses have substantially improved our knowledge and helped to correct imbalances in previous interpretations. Regional studies, for example, have compensated for the homogenizing and centralist tendencies inherent in any survey, and important works have appeared on particular denominations or religious communities that were previously badly neglected. The common thrust of much of this recent work has been to tell the 'inner story' of Christianity in Canada in a way that would complement the 'outer story' summarized in the work of Walsh, Moir, and Grant. Inherent in this overall effort has been greater attention to popular religion and the relationship between religion and social realities such as gender, ethnicity, and class. Patterns of religious practice among the general population and the social dimensions of religious experience have emerged to take their place alongside traditional topics such as the history of missions, church–state relations, and the development of ecclesiastical institutions. Valuable contributions have been made to the interpretation of social movements, such as the temperance crusades, that had deep roots in religion. Popular piety, including the role of voluntary associations in devotional life, has been a major focus of research. Efforts have also been made to assess the degree of lay conformity (or non-conformity) to clerical standards of observance at various stages of Canadian history. Patterns of religious affiliation and the role of religion in community life have been included as a prominent theme in major urban histories. Biographies have retained a prominent place, but increasingly they have embraced the role of religion in the private and family as well as the public life of their subjects. A great deal of important work has appeared on broad religious movements, such as the revivalist tradition in Canada, with the result that we now have a fuller and more nuanced understanding of such topics. The place of women in the church life, and the place of religion in the lives of women, has emerged as a major topic of inquiry. The study of religion has also been linked to material culture, as we have come to appreciate that church architecture and other forms of symbolic expression provide both a window on the inner spiritual life of believers and a witness to the place of Christianity in the cultural landscape of the nation. Christianity among the First Nations has been another area of major concern, but, in contrast to earlier works, recent studies have attempted to see this story from the perspective of native converts as well as white missionaries. At the same time, the resistance of the First Nations to proselytization and assimilation has begun to receive the serious attention it deserves.

Much of this recent work has appeared in major publishing projects such as the McGill–Queen's University Press series entitled *Studies in the History of Religion*, edited by the late George Rawlyk. Many important contributions are to be found as well in the *Dictionary of Canadian Biography*. The thirteen volumes of the *Dictionary* that have appeared to date contain numerous biographies of clergy and of lay people active in religious affairs; and many of these studies constitute the best or only treatments of their subjects. Regional series, such as the volumes published by Lancelot Press on behalf of the Atlantic Baptist Historical Association, also occupy an important place in this literature.

No new general history of Christianity has appeared, however, that effectively incorporates the results of these two decades of scholarship. The two most important new surveys—one by Robert T. Handy, the other by Mark A. Noll—attempt to encompass the whole of North America. This broad approach has the advantage of placing Canadian developments in a comparative framework, but in a single volume covering so much ground, the Canadian story can be told only in outline and is inevitably overshadowed by the American narrative. A recent collaborative work, *The Canadian Protestant Experience*, provides a valuable overview of Protestant denominations in Canada but omits by definition the Roman Catholic majority, including virtually the entire French-speaking population of the country. The multi-volume

Histoire du catholicisme québécois, edited by Nive Voisine, is a monumental contribution to the study of Quebec Catholicism, but again it is necessarily limited in scope, omitting by design both Protestants in Quebec and French-speaking Catholics in other parts of the country.

The pages that follow, therefore, are an attempt to fill a major void by providing an up-to-date and comprehensive one-volume history of Christianity in Canada, concise enough to serve as a student textbook but broad enough to be of interest to general readers. The work of five authors, it was planned from the outset to be an integrated history, bound together by common themes. While tracing the institutional development of Canada's major churches, each section focuses on five major topics: lay religious practice and outlook; relations between church and state; missionaries and prospective converts; inter-denominational relations; and the impact of Christianity on Canadian society and culture. We have sought to ensure unity and consistency through our emphasis on these common themes, but have made no effort to achieve uniformity of interpretation or standardization in style, preferring to allow each author his own voice.

The work is divided along linguistic rather than regional or denominational lines. Although it tries to take account of regional and denominational diversity, it deliberately seeks a high level of generalization by emphasizing the common experience of the churches. From our present vantage point, the elements of religious consensus and historical points of convergence stand out even more clearly than they did two decades ago; for even in the midst of rivalry and conflict, the churches have agreed more with each other than any of them could agree with the increasingly secular assumptions of contemporary Canadian culture. In the periodization of the material, we have looked not so much to milestones in general Canadian history as to events that had a direct and substantive bearing on religious life. Sometimes, as with the conquest of Canada by the British, the two converge, but in most cases they do not. For example, we have identified the flowering of the Ultramontane revival in French Canada (around 1840) and the final disestablishment of the Church of England in English Canada (1854) as more fundamental turning-points for the churches than Confederation (1867). In terms of chronology, we have followed the story in detail from the age of European exploration in the late fifteen century through to the period around 1960, when the decline in participation in organized religion became unmistakable. For the years from 1960 to the present, where proximity to the events makes precise historical analysis difficult, the Epilogue offers a briefer, more impressionistic reflection on major developments.

It is impossible to produce a survey of this kind without incurring innumerable debts to the scholars on whose original research one relies. We have tried to acknowledge our many debts in the notes, but there are several people who helped us directly by reading and commenting on portions of the text or by answering questions on particular matters of fact or interpretation. At the risk of inadvertently leaving someone out of the list, we would like to thank Phyllis Airhart, J.M. Bumsted, Louis Rousseau, Randi Warne, Luca Codignola, Olive Dickason, Brian Fraser, Claude Gilbert, Cornelius Jaenen, Ian Manson, Mark McGowan, Barry Moody, Elizabeth Profit, Matteo Sanfilippo, Neil Semple, Hans Rollmann, Phillip McCann, and Marguerite Van Die. We owe a special debt of gratitude to people associated with Oxford University Press, including the former Managing Editor, Richard Teleky, who first suggested this project, Phyllis Wilson, now Managing Editor, who has provided support and guidance almost from the outset, and Sally Livingston, who did more than we can adequately describe by way of hands-on developmental editing to shape and improve the text. The remaining flaws are entirely our responsibility.

We are also grateful to Alex Colville for permission to reproduce his work 'Visitors Are Invited to Register' on the cover, to Sandra Murphy for suggesting its use, to the various archives and museums that provided illustrations, and to Gary McManus and Clifford Wood of Memorial University of Newfoundland's Cartographic Lab (MUNCL), who drew the maps. The preparation of the maps was supported by a grant from the Publications Subventions Board of Memorial University of Newfoundland. The Jackman Foundation graciously provided a grant to support the translation of Chapter Two from the original French. The translation was carried out with exemplary attention to detail by James MacLean.

N. Keith Clifford was among the original collaborators on this project, but his untimely death prevented him from completing his part of the work. In appreciation of his role during the formative stages of the project and in recognition of his many contributions to the study of the history of Christianity in Canada, we dedicate this volume to his memory.

T.M.
January 1996

One

The French Regime to 1760

TERRY CROWLEY

BEGINNINGS TO 1659

Christianity arrived in Canada from Europe, but it made little impact during the first six hundred years of contact between the two continents. Norsemen sailing out of Greenland with Leif Eiriksson were the first to arrive, around AD 1000. Although the Norse settlement at L'Anse-aux-Meadows in Newfoundland was short-lived, European contacts with Baffin Island and Labrador were maintained over several centuries. Then, in the late fifteenth century, improved navigational devices and advances in ship-building permitted the establishment of new links. Sponsored by merchants in the English town of Bristol, Italian navigator Giovanni Caboto first explored Canada's Atlantic coast in 1497–8 in search of new fishing grounds and a westward route to China. Soon fishermen from France, Portugal, Spain, and Britain were visiting annually to exploit the North Atlantic's rich cod stocks, and, in the course of their sojourns on shore, trading for furs with the local native peoples.

We do not know whether any of these earliest visitors attempted to communicate their religious beliefs to the natives. The first explicit references to Christianity in the region that would be known as New France came during the voyages of Jacques Cartier. Cartier's goals were profit and glory, but he was a religious man who had committed parts of the Bible to memory and carried with him a work of popular devotional piety called *The Book of Hours*. At Gaspé in 1534 he and his men knelt down and prayed around a large cross they had erected. When the Iroquois chief Donnacona objected to this foreign intrusion, Cartier indicated that the symbol was only a sea marker intended to guide him on a return voyage. While he may have brought two Roman Catholic priests with him on his second trip in 1535, they evidently were no longer part of the expedition by the time it reached Stadacona (the future Quebec City). There Donnacona requested baptism, but Cartier was unable to oblige him in the absence of a priest. The natives at Hochelaga (site of the future Montreal) viewed Cartier as a healer with miraculous powers. When ailing villagers sought cures, Cartier recited the opening to the Gospel of St John, made the sign of the cross over them, and distributed tin *Agnus Dei* (Lamb of God) symbols. Back at Stadacona, where the French were struck with scurvy during the winter of 1535–6, a portrait of Mary was placed outside their fort, a mass was held, and intercessory prayers were offered for deliverance, with Cartier promising to make a pilgrimage if he were allowed to return to France safely. By May of 1536 the white-cedar brew provided by the Iroquois had cured the Frenchmen's disease and they were able to set sail for home. Before they left, however, gratitude did not prevent Cartier from seizing Donnacona and nine of his people. Taken to France, three of the captives were eventually baptized, including Donnacona, but none is known to have returned to North America.[1]

The goal of such expeditions was financial gain from the extraction of natural resources or the discovery of a new route to China. Little attention was therefore directed towards colonization or proselytism during most of the sixteenth century. In time, however, the growing success of the Spanish and Portuguese settlements in South America attracted the acquisitive interest of the monarchs in France and the British Isles, and towards the end of the century they began granting trading monopolies to commercial companies for specific areas of North America in return for undertaking settlements. Initial attempts at colonization were not promising. In 1598 a colony was begun by the Marquis de La Roche de Mesgouez on Sable Island, off Nova Scotia's southern shore, that lasted only five years; the one established in 1600 by Pierre Chauvin de Tonnetuit at Tadoussac, at the mouth of the Saguenay River, failed after one year, although the location remained a seasonal fur-trading post where goods were exchanged with the Montagnais people. Pierre Du Gua de Monts built a habitation that included a chapel on Île Ste-Croix, in the Bay of Fundy region, in 1604, but left it the next year for Port-Royal; when he lost his land grants and trade monopoly in 1607, that colony too was abandoned, at least temporarily. Not until 1608, when Samuel de Champlain established a post at Quebec, did permanent settlement start, a year after a commercial company had begun England's first lasting colony at Jamestown.

While Christianity figured only tangentially at the opening of Canada's history, it assumed greater importance in the early seventeenth century as colonization began and the country was identified as a Roman Catholic mission field. Behind these developments stood the legacy of Europe's Protestant Reformation and the Counter Reformation policies formulated by the Roman Catholic Church in the Council of Trent between 1545 and 1563. The influence of the new program was slow to be felt in France because of the religious civil wars that racked the country beginning in 1562. Peace returned only in 1598, when Henri IV promulgated the Edict of Nantes declaring an official policy of limited toleration for the Protestant minority, the Huguenots. French activities in the North Atlantic region reflected these religious antipathies, particularly as Huguenot merchants were heavily involved in the companies that sponsored the first bridgeheads in Canada. Conflicts resulted, notably in the 1604 expedition to Acadia. A Calvinist, de Monts chose both Protestants and Roman Catholics to accompany him, but relations between them were strained, and at Port-Royal a fist-fight broke out between one of the two Roman Catholic priests and the Protestant minister.[2] Similarly, the handful of permanent residents at Quebec included Huguenot involvement in the colony in the list of grievances they drew up in 1621.

While the Edict of Nantes had brought freedom of conscience for France's Protestant minorities, the older idea of the need for an all-embracing orthodoxy to ensure a country's internal stability did not die. By creating confessional states that acknowledged only one established church, European monarchs attempted to avert the disastrous consequences of religious disunity. Where better to begin than in the new societies then being established in the Western hemisphere? For this reason Cardinal Richelieu, Louis XIII's chief minister, took measures to strengthen Roman Catholicism in Quebec when, in 1627, a charter was granted to a new and financially stronger commercial endeavour designed to expand New France. By this agreement the Compagnie des Cent-Associés (Company of One Hundred Associates) was to settle only French Roman Catholics in the colony, and to treat aboriginal people converted to Catholicism as natural-born French. In addition, the church was placed on a stronger institutional footing by the requirement that the company fund the costs of Roman Catholic worship and provide support for three priests in each of the colony's settlements for fifteen years. Protestants still lived in and traded with New France, but their religious services were not tolerated, and Catholics would monopolize public offices and most professions during the French regime.[3]

The fervency of the renewed Roman Catholicism that accompanied the end of the religious wars in France profoundly affected French religious outlook and practice during the first half of the seventeenth century. Once the assembly of the French clergy adopted the reforms of the Council of Trent in 1615, the country that had stood apart from the Counter Reformation embraced it wholeheartedly in numerous pious activities at home and abroad. A renewed sense of spirituality gave rise to a host of charitable works associated with such people as Father Vincent de Paul; devotional writing flourished as the works of Bishop François de Sales and Cardinal Pierre de Bérulle gained popularity; new orders of religious men and women were established and older ones expanded; lay associations were formed to promote the faith, of which the

Compagnie du Saint-Sacrement, established in 1627, became the most influential; and interest in missionary work grew dramatically, especially among French women.

The missionary impulse was not new. Christianity had been mission-oriented since its earliest days, and proselytizing zeal was the natural result of faith in one God claiming the allegiance of all people. Many Christians steeped in eschatological expectations believed that neither the apocalypse nor the millennium would arrive until all humanity had been evangelized. But the fervour of the Counter Reformation provided a new stimulus, and if Spain and Portugal had led the field in missionary activity in the sixteenth century, after 1600 the church in France determined that it would direct a concerted campaign of evangelization towards the native people of Canada.

The first sacramental acts on Canadian soil that can be documented were performed by the Roman Catholic priest Jessé Fléché, a member of Jean Biencourt de Poutrincourt's colonization effort in Acadia, who in 1610 baptized the Micmac chief Membertou and twenty members of his family. However, Fléché did not know their language and hence could not provide instruction. Poutrincourt's son rushed the names of those who had supposedly received the sacrament back to France, in order to secure royal approval and financial backing for his father's enterprise. With the patronage of Antoinette de Pons (the marquise de Guercheville), the wife of the governor of Paris, the Jesuit fathers Pierre Biard and Énemond Massé arrived at Port-Royal in the following year. Aghast that baptism should have been performed without proper instruction, they referred Fléché's conduct to the theologians at the Sorbonne, who similarly condemned the administration of a sacrament without adequate preparation. To avoid such errors, Massé decided to live among the Micmac to learn their ways and their language. But he accomplished little before the New England marauder Samuel Argall captured Acadia in 1613. In the course of the battle, Brother Gilbert Du Thet became the first French Jesuit to die in Canada when he was shot while operating a cannon.

Meanwhile, Champlain had left Quebec for France in hopes of putting the colony on a more solid financial footing. In 1613 he engineered the creation of the Compagnie de Rouen et de Saint-Malo to provide new backing, to settle six families, and to support a resident clergy at Quebec in return for a monopoly of the trade in beaver pelts. Thus three priests and a brother from the Paris province of the Récollets—a reformed minor order of the Franciscans, who had been active as missionaries in the southern reaches of the hemisphere since 1500—arrived in New France in 1615. Superior Denis Jamet was based in Quebec, while Brother Pacifique Duplessis became responsible for the area from the St-Maurice River to Quebec, Father Jean Dolbeau used Tadoussac as his base, and Father Joseph Le Caron headed west for the territory south of Georgian Bay.

The peoples to whom the Roman Catholic missionaries would minister varied considerably in their social systems, political arrangements, and religious beliefs, but they are divided for convenience into two large linguistic and cultural groupings, Algonkian and Iroquoian. Algonkian-speaking peoples predominated along the Atlantic coasts and in the area of the St Lawrence valley. Nomadic hunters, gatherers, and fishing peoples, they included the Micmac of Acadia and Prince Edward Island, the Abenaki confederacy in Maine, and the Maliseet of the northern New Brunswick region. The Cree, Naskapi, and Montagnais (Innu) of the Saguenay, eastern Quebec, and Labrador inhabited the vast reaches of the Canadian Shield, while the Algonquin nation lived between Montreal and Ottawa, and the Ottawa, Nipissing, and Ojibwa/Cree occupied territories farther west and north. In the fertile areas of southern Ontario and upper New York state, by contrast, the Iroquoian peoples lived a more sedentary life based primarily on agriculture (corn, beans, and squash) and fishing. Here two confederacies predominated: the Huron around Georgian Bay, who consisted of the Deer, Rock, Bear, and Cord nations, and the Iroquois (or Five, later Six, Nations) composed of the Seneca, Onondaga, Cayuga, Oneida, and Mohawk, who were positioned closest to the French settlements. Finally, outside the confederacies but sharing common cultural and linguistic traits with the Huron and Iroquois were the Erie, Neutral, and Petun of southern Ontario.

The arrival of Europeans on the Atlantic coast had set in motion a process of change that would affect many native groups long before their first direct contact with the newcomers. Fifty years before the earliest permanent French or English settlement in North America, European goods had been traded and re-traded to peoples as far inland as the Seneca—the westernmost members of the Iroquois confederacy.[4] Equally rapid was the spread of European diseases against which the natives had no natural defences. Although precise figures are impossible to establish, epidemics clearly devastated native populations. Nor can there be any doubt that the fur trade proved ruinous for native social and economic organization. It would be a mistake, however, to assume that the aboriginal people were merely passive victims of the European invasion. Most were active participants in the new system. They welcomed the European goods they were offered in exchange for their furs, and they embraced their new trading partners as useful allies in war. In addition, some groups accepted the presence of French priests in their midst.

A number of native beliefs and practices had parallels in Christianity. Among eastern Algonkian groups, for instance, the 'master spirit' *kitchi-manido* stood, like the Christian God, above all creation. Like Christians, the indigenous peoples believed in an afterlife and treated their dead with solemn reverence. Both cultures attributed special significance to visions and dreams, and just as Catholics of the time sought to attain higher spiritual levels through

Native acceptance

contemplation, self-denial, and mortification of the flesh, native societies believed that spiritual guidance and protection could be obtained through observance of the proper rituals and purification ceremonies.[5]

In other respects, however, the differences were radical. Whereas the Christian missionaries regarded nature as intended by God for the use of humanity, native cultures believed that all living things were imbued with their own spirit, and stressed the continuity of human life with the rest of the natural environment. The Christian aims of transcending the world and attaining individual salvation were incomprehensible to aboriginal societies. Believing utterly in the truth of their mission, the priests for their part were incapable of seeing native spirituality as anything more than a body of superstitions held by people who stood in dire need of Christian instruction.

After one year the first Récollet missionaries concluded that the indigenous peoples were so different from Europeans that their entire culture would have to be altered if they were to become Christians. Recalling the Latin American model of the *congregación*, or gathering of native peoples into settled villages, they decided that French and natives would have to live together if the latter were to be assimilated to European ways. In 1616 the friars developed a three-pronged policy—settlement, recruitment of more missionaries, and dissemination of information to influence the Compagnie de Rouen et de Saint-Malo in their favour—that constituted the first religious and political program created in New France.[6] As the company's aim was profit, and as many of its traders were Huguenots unsympathetic to Roman Catholic priests, the basis was set for conflict between religious and economic objectives that would continue for many decades. Nevertheless, in 1618 the Paris Récollets obtained a charter from the papal nuncio that assigned them central Canada exclusive from other provinces in their order—though not from priests of other orders.

The Récollet missions were tied to the network of trading alliances that, stretching along the north shore of the St Lawrence and into southern Ontario, linked such geographically far-flung peoples as the Montagnais of the Saguenay, the Algonquin along the Ottawa River, and the Huron around Georgian Bay. These groups competed with the Iroquois nations, who traded first with the Dutch and later with the English at Fort Orange (Albany); each year bands of Iroquois travelled north to trade for furs with more distant groups. In 1615 Father Joseph Le Caron struck out for Huronia and made contact with the Petun, the Huron's neighbours, before returning to Quebec the next year. His colleague Guillaume Poulain was less fortunate in 1622 when, on his way to Nipissing territory, he was captured by the Iroquois and tortured; released in a prisoner exchange, Poulain eventually returned to his ministry. The following year two more Récollets, Gabriel Sagard and Nicolas Viel, determined to settle in Huronia, but the Huron agreed only after Champlain insisted upon compliance as part of their alliance with the French. Killed in a native attack near Montreal in 1625, Viel was proclaimed the first martyr to the faith in New France. (The death of the Jesuit Du Thet, twelve years earlier, was not considered a martyrdom since he died in a battle against the English.)

By 1620 the Récollets had secured enough financial backing to start construction of a residence at Quebec and a chapel at Cap Tourmente, downriver from the settlement. In their house they opened a school to assimilate Indian children and teach them Christianity. But the native youngsters could endure neither the European regimen nor the sedentary lifestyle, and the school closed within five years. Efforts by the Récollets to augment their limited numbers proved more fruitful in 1625 when the new viceroy of New France, the duc de Ventadour, sponsored three Jesuit priests and two lay brothers to go to Canada. While Énemond Massé, who brought prior experience in Acadia, remained in Quebec to help the Récollets complete their house, the thirty-three-year-old Jesuit Jean de Brébeuf left the settlement in 1626 to spend three years near Georgian Bay learning the Huron language. Recalled to Quebec in 1629, he returned to France along with other residents when the settlement was captured by the English Kirke brothers. Thus ended the first mission to the natives in central Canada, with experience gained but little progress made in terms of conversions.

Nor was much accomplished by early missionary efforts in Acadia, which was assigned to the Capuchins (another offshoot of the Franciscans). Theirs was the first mission established on Canadian soil under the authority of Rome's Congregation for the Propagation of the Faith, a new branch of the Roman Curia created to co-ordinate missions worldwide.[7] In 1632 the Capuchins accompanied Governor Isaac de Razilly to establish his new settlement at La Hève on Nova Scotia's south shore, where they constructed a chapel and boarding-school for native and French children. Moving their headquarters to Port-Royal, they erected the first church in the region in 1643 and the following year opened a small school for the Abenaki; run by the mother of one of the missionaries, it operated for eight years.[8] Although they received financial support from Cardinal Richelieu and members of the royal family, the Capuchins managed only to baptize a few dying infants and convert a handful of adults during their three decades in Acadia. Nevertheless, they expanded their purview after 1645 by establishing new centres on the Penobscot River in the Maine region (where the Jesuits had served prior to 1613), the Baie des Chaleurs, and Cape Breton Island.

Acadia was so accessible by sea that other religious orders ministered there as well. Four Récollets from the province of Aquitaine had gone to the region in 1619, but after the commercial company supporting them collapsed four years later, they sought refuge at Quebec in 1624. Three more Grey Robes—as the Récollets were called—returned to Acadia in 1630 to settle at Cape Sable in Nova Scotia where Charles de Saint-Étienne de La Tour ran a commercial company. Shortly afterwards, another trio established themselves on the St John River in New Brunswick and two friars began a mission at St Ann's Bay on Cape Breton. Jesuits also ministered on Cape Breton intermittently from 1629 to 1644 and, after settling at the Baie des Chaleurs in 1635, spread to Bathurst Bay and Miramichi.

When Quebec was restored to France through the Treaty of Saint-Germain-en-Laye in 1632, the monarchy accorded a monopoly of religious services in central Canada (New France) to the Society of Jesus. Not only did the Jesuits possess superior resources, but the Récollets were split by internal wrangling between the provinces of Paris, whose members had earlier served at Quebec, and of Aquitaine, which was already represented in Acadia. Although the Roman Congregation for the Propagation of the Faith concurred with granting New France exclusively to the Jesuits, the royal decision was controversial because, although the Jesuits were admired in some quarters, in others they were deeply mistrusted. Unlike other religious who swore vows of poverty, chastity, and obedience, the Jesuits were bound by a fourth vow, to the pope. Some people viewed the Society as the advance guard of the papacy and a threat to the Gallican liberties, the national rights of the Roman Catholic Church in France that had been acknowledged in the Concordat of 1516 between France and the papacy. Indeed, the Jesuits had been banished from France as enemies of the state in 1594, but Henri IV had allowed them to return in 1603 because their services to education were so highly valued.

The Jesuits were known for their teaching, street ministries, mission work, collective discipline, and rigorous spirituality based on the exercises of Ignatius Loyola, the priest who had founded the order in 1540. All their experience came into play in the North American mission field after 1632. Upon their return to Quebec the Jesuits had to rebuild the house of Notre-Dame-des-Anges that, six years before, they had constructed across the St-Charles River. In 1634 they joined French fur traders in creating a post upriver from Quebec at Trois-Rivières and established a mission for Algonkian nations at nearby Cap-de-la-Madeleine. In the same year they began the mission of Saint-Joseph in the village of Ihonatiria near Georgian Bay, adding a second in Ossossané, a settlement to the south, in 1637. At Quebec they opened the Collège des Jésuites in 1635 to provide elementary instruction for French boys and a year later they started a school for aboriginal youth, but it did not last even as long as its Récollet predecessor.

Initially the Jesuits believed that the nomadic Algonkian nations would not be fully converted until they adopted the sedentary life of agriculturalists. Starting in 1637, therefore, they devoted much of their attention to the community of Montagnais and Algonquin peoples they created at Sillery, just outside Quebec, which was patterned after the South American *congregación* and named for Noël Brulart de Sillery, the wealthy Frenchman who had provided funding for it. Intended as a model settlement—where, for example, residents would vote by secret ballot to elect magistrates and prayer captains—it also served as a centre for learning native languages and a base for 'flying' missions to the Montagnais such as the Holy Cross mission at Tadoussac. By 1645 Sillery counted 167 Christian converts, some of them undoubtedly attracted by the supplies that the Jesuits provided—an important consideration in the face of the disruption in their traditional economy. Although Sillery was the first reserve for native people in the country, the Jesuits originally held the title to the land on behalf of its residents.[9]

Even more ambitious was the mission begun in 1639 in the Huron territory near Georgian Bay. Located on the Wye River flowing into Midland Bay, Sainte-Marie-Among-the-Hurons was protected by stone bastions and log palisades, within which the Jesuits constructed a chapel, hospital, mill, stables, barns, and residences for priests and lay workers. Beyond the walls stood a Huron encampment with longhouses inhabited by converts. Up to sixty-five French resided at Sainte-Marie, most of them lay workers. Generally only three priests used the mission as their base, while eight to ten others ministered in various other locations.

Despite their distance from Quebec, the Huron were a logical choice for the largest and most concerted Jesuit program of evangelization. Wealthy intermediaries in the fur trade and firm allies of the French, they initially numbered twenty to twenty-five thousand people living in two dozen villages. In 1634, however, the first in a series of deadly epidemics began that by 1640 would halve the Huron population. Many naturally associated these dreadful events with the recent arrival of the men in black robes. Yet at the same time the epidemics made some Huron more vulnerable to priestly persuasion. As the Europeans enjoyed relative immunity to these diseases, they were able to care for the sick, carry food to the needy, and take advantage of various occasions to discredit the medicine of the shamans. The Jesuits used pictures to illustrate Christian conceptions; they impressed Huron society with the power of the written word as a means of communication and as a preserver of ancient truths; and they challenged the authority of their main rivals with their own shamanistic powers, not only forecasting an eclipse, but praying for rain and summoning wildlife with apparent success. Music and colourful Catholic liturgies were put to good use too; it was here that Jean de Brébeuf composed the country's first Christmas carol, *Jesus Anatonhia*. Religious medallions and rosaries were distributed, and coloured sticks were used as mnemonic devices for keeping track of sins as well as the church calendar.

Their beards and strange clothes—along with the fact that they showed no sexual interest in women—distanced the priests from the natives. However, unlike the Récollets, who had stayed on the outskirts of the villages, the Jesuits lived among the people. They also made determined efforts to master and record a language that was radically different from their own. There were no words in Huron for hell, faith, grace, or sin, and 'soul' had to be rendered as 'our medicine'. Even the parables missed their mark in a place where bread, mustard seeds, prisons, and kingdoms were unknown, and the idea of heaven meant little. Cultural taboos had to be respected as well. For example, since it was forbidden to speak of the Huron's dead kin, the common invocation was changed to 'In the name of our Father, and his Son, and their Holy Spirit.'

Yet even these efforts at adaptation did not prevent hostile reactions, particularly when the Jesuits attempted to stamp out traditional ceremonies or baptize the dying—a practice that incurred accusations of sorcery. In 1635 the people at Ihonatiria insisted that the priests remove the cross atop their residence as it was considered the source of the epidemic ravaging the village. Three years later a chapel was stoned and crosses were torn down. In 1640 three of the four Huron nations decided to expel the Jesuits and Governor Huault de Montmagny disciplined some members of the confederacy for the insults the priests had suffered the previous winter. Four years later, soldiers were sent from Quebec to protect the Jesuit establishments.

Conversions were few during the 1630s, but the numbers increased over time. That some priests were given Huron names suggests that perseverance did lead to acceptance. Isaac Jogues was called Ondessonk, or 'bird of prey', while Jean de Brébeuf was named Echon, after a tree with medicinal properties, and was even made a chief in 1638. Although conflicts with fur traders were common, the Jesuits were protected by their lay servants (donnés), who carried firearms as the priests could not. By 1642 there were two hundred Huron converts, and within a few years Huronia had seven churches.[10] Nineteen priests ministered in the region by 1649; 29 served in the mission at various times, and only one was ever rejected as unsuitable for the work because of his inability to learn the language and adjust to life in Huronia.

No real harm came to the priests when they were among allies, but caught by enemies they often met grisly ends. The first Jesuit death among the natives of central Canada occurred in 1642, when a large party of French and Huron heading for Georgian Bay were captured by the Iroquois and carried off to Ossernenon, south of Lake Ontario, where they were tortured. As the surgeon, René Goupil, made the sign of the cross over a child, one of the Iroquois killed him with a hatchet. Isaac Jogues had his fingers so badly mutilated that he was useless to the Iroquois woman to whom he was enslaved, and she exchanged him with the Dutch in New Netherlands. Four years later, when Jogues returned to the area, he too was slain along with Jean de La Lande, a servant in the Society's employ. In retaliation, the French captured the murderer of Jogues and, following baptism, put him 'to death in the sentiments of a true Christian'.[11]

Events such as these were a staple of the Jesuits' annual reports to France. Published from 1632 to 1673, the *Relations* were missionary propaganda intended to loosen the purse-strings of the faithful. Their dramatic tales and exotic appeal captivated the French reading public to such an extent that, during the first three decades in which they appeared, Paris publishers reduced their output of travel books about the Orient and the Middle East.[12] For modern readers, these inspirational accounts of a nascent church overcoming apparently insurmountable odds may seem to verge on hagiography. They also stand in marked contrast to the Jesuits' annual private journal and other contemporary texts not intended for publication.

Nevertheless, in disseminating information about Canada, prompting donations to undertake new initiatives, and motivating others to take up missionary work, the *Relations* provided invaluable assistance to the mission church in New France. When the Jesuits asked in 1635 that French noblewomen endow a convent at Quebec, a young widow named Marie-Madeleine de Chauvigny de La Peltrie responded. Suffering from a serious illness, she made a vow that if her health were restored she would build a house in New France and dedicate her life to teaching native girls. When she recovered, La Peltrie went to Tours where she persuaded Marie de l'Incarnation, assistant mistress of novices and instructor in Christian doctrine at the Ursuline convent, to join her. Having entrusted her young son to her sister and entered the convent following the death of her husband, the former Marie Guyart was deeply mystical in her religious practice. Although obsessed with fears inspired by the Jesuit accounts, she chose to give precedence to the religious glory that the missionary enterprise promised. Arriving at Quebec in 1639 with Mme de La Peltrie, two other Ursulines, and a young companion, Marie de l'Incarnation threw herself into her mission with a joyful enthusiasm that she conveyed to France in beautifully written letters. Within a few months she and the other nuns were teaching eighteen native girls, along with a few French children.

It was under the sponsorship of another noblewoman, Marie-Madeleine de Vignerot, duchesse d'Aiguillon, that three Augustinian Hospitalières, or nursing sisters, from Dieppe arrived in Canada on the same ship as the Ursulines. A smallpox epidemic raging among the local native people commanded their immediate attention. At Sillery the Hospitalières constructed a two-storey stone building and opened a small school to provide religious instruction to young girls. In 1642 alone the 'women in white', as they were known, cared for a hundred Montagnais, Algonquin, Abenaki, and Huron. However, two years later Iroquois incursions forced them to seek refuge at Quebec. The hospital they established there—called the Hôtel-Dieu because, as their constitution noted, in it they would serve 'Jesus Christ in the person of those afflicted with illness'[13]— was the first such institution in New France. The first Canadian-born nun, Marie-Françoise Giffard, was received into the Augustinians' novitiate in 1646.

Another important mission inspired, at least in part, by the *Relations* was the settlement of Ville-Marie on the island of Montreal. The idea for this venture started in France with a pious voluntary organization called the Compagnie du Saint-Sacrement. Composed of wealthy and influential people, this secret society sought to extend Christianity through evangelization, good works, and efforts to uphold public morality (the latter including spying on such questionable elements as actors). The Company's founder, the duc de Ventadour, had sponsored the Jesuits at Quebec, and another member, Sébastien Cramoisy, the publisher of the *Relations* and a political client of Cardinal Richelieu, had taken part in the discussions leading to the arrival of the Augustinian sisters. Through Jérôme Le Royer de la Dauversière, who was also influenced by the *Relations*, the Company spawned an auxiliary in 1639 that was called the Société de Notre Dame de Montréal pour la Conversion des Sauvages de la Nouvelle-France. Subscriptions were received and the island was purchased the following year. Because the new outpost was the closest yet to the Mohawk cantons, a well-connected career soldier, Paul de Chomedey de Maisonneuve, was appointed to lead the expedition.

The group's first mass on the island of Montreal was sung on 17 May 1642 by the Jesuit Barthélémy de Vimont, and the first baptism of an Algonquin child took place three months later. The nurse in the expedition, the thirty-five-year-old Jeanne Mance, began treating patients immediately, and with the help of a large donation from Angélique de Bullion, the widow of a former superintendent of finance, in 1645 opened the hospital that would become Montreal's Hôtel-Dieu. It did not receive that name, however, until it was taken over by the Hospitalières de Saint-Joseph in 1659, because, despite her personal piety, Mance did not belong to a religious order.

In this period the church of New France directed most of its efforts towards the country's aboriginal peoples. The natives were seen not only as humans capable of salvation, but as valuable tools in the fight against corrupt European Christian practices. Unspoiled by the Old World's institutions and untainted by its collective sins, the budding Christianity of New France extended the hope of a return to the church's pristine roots; as Marie de l'Incarnation wrote, 'the fervour of the primitive church has descended to New France and it illuminates the hearts of our good converts.'[14] In conceiving of their church as a return to the simplicity of the Apostles, 'a Jerusalem blessed by God and composed of citizens destined for Heaven',[15] the missionaries of early Canada cast the natives in a positive light as nature's people, *les bons sauvages*. This attitude invited a more receptive response among native people than did the Puritans' view of New England as the Devil's dominion prior to arrival of God's chosen, the English.

Over time, careful observation of aboriginal culture led the Jesuits to modify their approach to evangelization. Noting the reverence in which native societies held their elders, as early as 1639 they decided to abandon their original focus on children and instead concentrate their efforts on converting adult men. 'As God made man in order to make men God's', wrote a Jesuit superior, 'a missionary does not fear to make himself an Indian, so to speak, with them in order to make them Christians. . . . We must . . . follow them to their homes and adapt ourselves to their ways, however ridiculous they may appear, in order to draw them to ours.'[16] Christianity, a religion that had syncretized Hebrew and Greek beliefs at its origins and adapted elements from other belief systems as it spread, found new expressions among Canada's aboriginal peoples. Some traditional customs lent themselves to translation into Christian terms: for example, the native ceremony performed by the Montagnais and Algonquin, in which a deceased person was 'resuscitated' by giving his name and obligations to a promising kinsman, was easily incorporated into Christian practice: 'I take this resurrection of my nephew, that I now accomplish,' said a Christian captain at Sillery in 1648, 'as a symbol of the true resurrection to which we look forward.'[17] By this time, according to the Jesuits, neophytes in the faith were 'beginning to give quite a Christian character to the harmless usages that they have derived from their infidel ancestors'. However, formal instruction in the principal elements of the Catholic faith—a process that sometimes lasted up to three years—was still a condition of conversion and baptism. Catechumens taught by Jean de Brébeuf memorized the sign of the cross, the *Ave Maria*, the Ten Commandments, and the prayer to the guardian angel, as well as other brief prayers.[18] Brébeuf also had them commit to heart more gradually the fundamentals of Catholic doctrine, which he translated into Huron from a catechism that a Spanish Jesuit had written for children and other newcomers to the faith.

Among that minority in most native groups who listened to the priests—mostly men, since it was principally to them that the Jesuits directed their efforts[19]—baptism was accepted for a variety of reasons. Like many other peoples of the world (apart from adherents to such major religions as Islam and Christianity), the First Nations did not insist on spiritual exclusivity. Some were enticed by the material advantages—not only supplies but special trading privileges—bestowed by the French on Christians; some espoused the new beliefs in much the same way that they adopted European technology; and for some accepting Christianity represented less a rejection of traditional ways than a means of acquiring an efficacious new spiritual power to add to the powers they already possessed.

How well the 5,800 Huron that the Jesuits baptized up to 1649 absorbed Christian doctrine will always remain a subject of conjecture. Even though most Christian churches have never required tests of belief, accepting affirmations of faith as sufficient grounds for admission, scholarly debate has raged over the authenticity of the conversions recorded in New France. On the one hand are those who accept them as valid, since in most cases baptism was preceded by religious instruction. On the other are those who consider the baptisms largely a sham, either because syncretized native beliefs differed too greatly from the European model, or because the adaptations required to make the faith intelligible in aboriginal societies distorted its meaning.[20] This debate reflects two very different answers to the fundamental question of what it means to be a Christian. For their part, seventeenth-century Jesuits considered those who prayed regularly and observed the seven sacraments to be among the faithful, while Marie de l'Incarnation left such judgements to a higher authority: 'God is the master of men's hearts and he alone knows the moment of their conversion.'[21]

Equally contentious is the question of Christianity's contribution to the collapse of the Huron confederacy. By the 1640s the Iroquois were increasing the number and severity of their attacks on their northern adversaries. Peace talks in 1645 averted more extensive bloodshed, but in 1648 and 1649 massive incursions by the Five Nations destroyed Huronia. In June 1649 the priests burned the Sainte-Marie mission before fleeing with three hundred Huron to Christian Island in Georgian Bay, where they began constructing Sainte-Marie II. When, weakened by malnutrition, they were attacked again in 1650, Father Paul Ragueneau led them back to Quebec, where they established their own village on the Île d'Orléans. A second group of equal size moved from Manitoulin Island to the St Lawrence valley the following year. Among the victims of the conflict were five of the eight Canadian martyrs canonized by Pope Pius XI in 1930: Brébeuf, Antoine Daniel, Gabriel Lalemant, Charles Garnier, and Noël Chabanel. Their deaths were described graphically in the *Relations*.

Was Christianity, by creating new divisions among the Huron and weakening their response to aggression, largely responsible for their defeat and dispersion?[22] The Jesuits themselves blamed the numerical superiority in firearms that the Iroquois had acquired from Dutch traders. (French policy, instituted in 1641, had permitted only Christian natives to be outfitted with guns.) These crude instruments were not essentially superior to native weapons, but they did instil fear and panic. More important were the changes that European commercial arrangements had introduced in the nature of aboriginal warfare. Previously limited, for the most part, to petty vendettas with few casualties, warfare now assumed new proportions with destruction and subjugation as its objectives. Emerging initially simply as the pirates of the fur trade, the Iroquois were the first to adopt the new pattern. While some Huron Christians did stop fighting, seeking refuge and protection in their new religion, such conduct was probably not the determining factor: the almost simultaneous destruction of the Petun, who had received missionaries, and the Neutral and Erie, who had not, suggests that other causes were more important. As well, parties favourable and unfavourable to the French later emerged among the

Onondaga without significant effect. (Among the Iroquoian peoples such divisions were common, allowing those on opposing sides to negotiate with enemies to end hostilities without humiliation.) Finally, population decline must also be considered: the Five Nations had experienced epidemics in the late 1640s, but their numbers had not been reduced as drastically as those of the Huron. No doubt the Huron defeat was the result of the interplay of all these factors.

In Acadia European activity in this period was characterized by fratricidal commercial wars in which the clergy adopted sides and paid the price of protection. The Récollets linked themselves with La Tour and the Capuchins with Governor Razilly and his cousin Charles de Menou d'Aulnay. When d'Aulnay, who by now had replaced Razilly as governor, died in 1650 owing money to a French merchant, financial backers imprisoned some of the Capuchins; others fled to the woods or returned to France. The school that they had established for aboriginal children through a gift from the Queen of France was closed in 1652. Their weakened mission collapsed in 1655, the year after Port-Royal fell to the Massachusetts merchant Robert Sedgwick, and although Capuchin priests returned to Cape Breton between 1656 and 1658, their mission did not last long. Acadia would not be returned to France until 1670. For a time during the British occupation three Jesuits continued to serve French fishermen in the northern part of the region, but they finally withdrew, as the Acadian adventurer Nicolas Denys wrote, because 'there was nothing more to be done with these people whose frequent company with the ships keeps them in a state of perpetual drunkenness'.[23]

A similar problem plagued the Sillery reserve, where the proximity of European settlement permitted access to alcohol. Following an Iroquois raid in 1655 and, later, a fire that destroyed most of the buildings, Sillery was largely abandoned. By mid-century the Ville-Marie settlement was experiencing difficulties as well. With only fifty residents during its first decade, the community was able to maintain the communal lifestyle, strict religious observance, and high ideals with which it had begun. But in the absence of new recruits it stagnated, and Iroquois raids were so frequent that dogs had to be trained to serve as sentinels so that people could work in the fields. The Ursulines too faced recruitment problems: although they opened a novitiate in 1646, for the next two decades they had to rely on France for new members. The Jesuits saw their contingent reduced when eight of the thirteen priests returning from Huronia left immediately for France. However, a new opportunity appeared in 1653, when in the course of peace negotiations the Iroquois asked for priests to reside among them, and within three years, seven priests and fifty workers were living among the Onondaga (Iroquois) south of Lake Ontario.

While missions to the aboriginal peoples were the main concern of the early seventeenth century, the church of New France did not ignore the colony's small European population. In 1645 there were only six hundred French in Canada, but by 1663 that number had increased to approximately three thousand. The clergy in the settlements were so numerous in relation to the laity that an intense religious atmosphere developed not unlike that in early New England. In 1635, regulations against blasphemy and failure to attend mass on holy days were posted outside the church in Quebec on a pillar to which an iron collar (the Canadian stocks) was affixed. In the following year the Jesuits stopped a woman from presenting the bread for consecration, in a ceremony called the *pain bénit*, because they disagreed with her manner of dress. Celebrations associated with the church calendar enlivened the religious atmosphere enforced by company officials. Religious festivals were marked by processions through the streets in which notables carried a canopy over a litter bearing statues while the faithful, including native converts, paraded behind. The angelus rang three times a day from the steeple bell. Fireworks were displayed for the feast of St Joseph, bonfires were lit on the eve of St John the Baptist, and in the spring a maypole was erected outside the church, the centre of the community. Ville-Marie exemplified this idealistic intensity. Quebec, however, remained slightly more worldly, as evidenced by its popular entertainments. In 1640 a tragicomedy had been mounted in the warehouse of the fur-trading company of the capital; the play *Le Cid* was presented in 1646, and a ballet the following year.

Those with religious vocations gave full expression to the interiorization of faith that the Counter Reformation had assimilated from its Protestant predecessor. Contemporary trends towards mysticism and humanism also contributed to the new emphasis on individual unworthiness in the agonizing process of gaining personal salvation through God's grace, as did the example of medieval ascetics and the diffusion of Spanish practices through contact with Belgium and translations of devotional works. In working for the spread of God's glory and the triumph of the church in a hostile land, the clergy in Canada consciously identified their efforts with the lives of the saints and apostles. Before leaving Sainte-Marie in 1650, Paul Ragueneau carefully exhumed the corpses of Jean de Brébeuf and Gabriel Lalemant, had their flesh burned, and carried their charred bones back to Quebec, where he recorded testimony, under oath, that would later assist with their canonization. A prominent place in heaven as well as in history was eagerly sought, and self-sacrifice and martyrdom were constant themes.

Clergy and lay people alike engaged in practices intended to heighten spiritual attainment, and biblical precedents were followed in attaching religious significance to dreams and visions. Believing that the 'Devil . . . loves not the spirit of mortification',[24] many Christians pursued bodily abnegation. The Jesuit Énemond Massé wrote that complete spiritual attainment derived from sleeping on bare ground, saying mass in a hair shirt, chastising the body through daily self-flagellation, and fasting three times a week. He recommended that to atone for giving offence to another person, 'you shall gather up secretly with your tongue the spittle and phlegm proceeding from the mouths of others'.[25] As a young woman seeking her vocation, Marie de l'Incarnation wore a penitential shirt with thorns and knots, and rose at night to whip herself with thongs and nettles; on occasion she also burnt her flesh and ate bitter wormwood, although eventually her spiritual director curbed these practices. Marie said that in her conversion experience she had encountered Christ and been immersed in his blood. She also related having had a dream in which God took her to a country full of mountains, valleys, and heavy fogs. Similarly, Jean de Brébeuf believed he had been personally visited by Mary, Joseph, and angels and saints, but he kept such matters secret except from his own confessor. He too engaged in fasts, mortifications of the flesh, and vigils lasting long into the night.[26]

The power of the clergy in this early period derived partly from the spiritual authority that accompanied their religious functions and partly from their ability to deliver education, social assistance, and medical services; above all, however, the small number of colonists and the scarcity of educated talent among them made it inevitable that clerics would assume unusually prominent roles. It was a Récollet who carried the remonstrances of the colonists against company rule to France in 1621, and in 1650 the Jesuit Gabriel Druillettes became the colony's first foreign ambassador when he was delegated to the Confederacy of New England, a short-lived political arrangement among some of the British colonies, in an abortive attempt to forge an alliance against the Mohawk. After the trading monopoly passed from metropolitan control to local residents organized into the Communauté des Habitants in 1645, the Crown established an administrative structure assuring the clergy's political influence. In the first Council of New France in 1647, the superior of the Jesuits was accorded second order of precedence, after the governor-general. Although representation was broadened in the next year, priests continued to attend Council meetings until 1656, the year before formal clerical representation ended and the elective principle was instituted.[27] The Jesuit Jérôme Lalemant conducted business for the Communauté in France and Paul Ragueneau, superior of the society at Quebec from 1650 to 1653, after he returned from Huronia, assumed such prominence in public affairs that he incurred criticism from other clergy that ceased only when he was assigned to Trois-Rivières. Commercial companies also generously endowed the church with seigneurial land grants, although property was worth little as yet. By 1663 church institutions had received 16 per cent of the land conceded along both shores of the St Lawrence from Quebec to Montreal. Containing approximately one-third of the river frontage, those 1.9 million arpents[28] constituted some of the best land available. Sixty per cent of the church's holdings belonged to the Jesuits.[29]

A series of events at mid-century strengthened religious structures in the colony, particularly at Ville-Marie. The community had been so short of funds—and of new recruits to replace those who died or were killed in Iroquois attacks—that its mission appeared bound for failure. But Jeanne Mance obtained additional funding from her patron to keep the settlement going, and in 1653 Maisonneuve went to France, where he arranged for the immigration of over a hundred soldiers and settlers. The infusion of new blood relaxed the strict religious atmosphere that until then had prevailed, although it was still possible for a farmer to be fined by the courts, at the behest of a priest, for ploughing on a Sunday. After a temporary peace was reached with the Iroquois in 1653, the island became an international centre for the fur trade and larger numbers of Canadiens began to seek better bargains further inland. Although, in the course of this evolution from mission to trading centre, Ville-Marie came to assume the name of the island on which it was situated, its religious institutions were actually strengthened. When Marguerite Bourgeoys, an external member of the Congrégation de Notre-Dame in France, arrived with the contingent of 1653, she proceeded to have a new cross erected on the mountain; initially attending to the needs of other settlers, five years later Bourgeoys was given a stone stable to begin more formal instruction of young girls and boys. The ranks of male clergy were augmented in 1657 when four additional priests reached Montreal from the Compagnie des Prêtres de Saint-Sulpice (Sulpicians) in Paris, a new community of secular priests established by Jean-Jacques Olier, a cleric who had been associated with Montreal's beginnings through the Compagnie du Saint-Sacrement. In addition, Jeanne Mance secured the services of the Hospitalières de Saint-Joseph, whose members left France in 1659 to become the third female cloistered order in Canada. Finally, as the original society supporting the mission had collapsed, arrangements were made whereby the Séminaire de Saint-Sulpice became Montreal's new seigneur in 1663.

The end to Jesuit dominance in Quebec's religious affairs came in a series of petty ecclesiastical confrontations following the arrival of the Sulpicians. Although the archbishop of Rouen claimed Canada as an extension of his diocese, because people from his region had long sailed for Canadian waters, he could not administer an area so far away. Hence in 1649 he had delegated part of his ecclesiastical authority to the Jesuits so that they might supervise the female religious orders in the colony. However, he then accorded the same powers as vicar-general to the Sulpicians before they left France. Upon arrival in Quebec, the Sulpician superior Thubières de Levy de Queylus assumed control of the Jesuits' parish in the community, forbade Jesuit priests to perform services for the French outside their chapel, complained to France about their conduct, and took to the pulpit to satirize those he claimed to have monopolized both church and state in the colony. Similar critiques voiced by anti-Jesuit French administrators in the years following gave rise to Canada's unique 'black legend': that the clergy had exerted undue control over Quebec, and that the Jesuits were the chief offenders. In turn, priests belonging to the Society of Jesus let it be known that their rivals were 'more troublesome . . . than the Iroquois'.[30]

The dispute subsided when the archbishop of Rouen limited the Sulpicians' authority to the island of Montreal, where they were both seigneurs and parish priests. But enmity remained as each order sought to secure the appointment of its own candidate as the first bishop of Quebec. Despite these complications, the establishment of the country's first bishopric gave expression to a growing episcopal–royal alliance that sought to increase hierarchical authority in the Catholic Church as the monarchy tightened the reins of absolutism in government.[31] According to the Gallican liberties—concessions that the French monarchy and church had obtained from the papacy—the king of France possessed the right of nomination for a variety of ecclesiastical offices, including that of bishop, but the pope retained the power of appointment. The Sulpicians proposed de Queylus and secured the support of the assembly of the French clergy, but the Jesuits favoured François de Laval, a young secular priest and abbé awaiting episcopal posting to the Asian mission field, who had been educated at two of their best colleges, LaFlèche in Anjou and Clermont in Paris. Louis XIV also favoured Laval, but the archbishop of Rouen actively opposed the decision. Because of this imbroglio, Rome chose to appoint Laval vicar apostolic—a position that made him subordinate to the Congregation for the Propagation of the Faith—and titular bishop of Petraea, a former diocese in the Middle East that for centuries had been extinct because it was located in Muslim territory. So controversial was the move that Laval's consecration on 8 December 1658, in the Lady Chapel of the church of Saint-Germain-des-Prés in Paris, had to be performed in secret by the papal nuncio.

A PERIOD OF TRANSITION: 1659–1700

The church to which François de Laval sailed in 1659 was limited in clerical resources but immense in reach, stretching from the Atlantic ocean to the Great Lakes. With Acadia temporarily in British hands, the male clergy in Quebec consisted of only twenty-one priests belonging to religious orders (called regulars) and six lay brothers and secular priests (so named because they did not adhere to a communal rule). Thoroughly imbued with the moral outlook of the Counter Reformation and determined that the church he administered would not replicate the sins of the one he had left behind, the thirty-six-year-old vicar apostolic fitted most of his clergy like a glove. Whatever the similarities in ideals, however, priests and nuns were unprepared for the plans Laval envisioned or the presumptuous manner in which he behaved. To end the disputes that had prevailed in the colony, Laval created an *officialité* (ecclesiasti-cal court) to try conflicts involving the clergy, even though he would not pos-sess the formal power to do so until the pope created the diocese of Quebec in 1674 and appointed him its bishop. He also proceeded to apply a number of ideas gleaned from his earlier involvement with a secret devout association in France known as the Assemblée des Amis, or Bons Amis. Dedicated to per-sonal sanctification through prayer and charitable works,[32] in Laval's view its members represented the model for the entire clergy of New France.

It was another ideal of the Counter Reformation that priests should be bet-ter educated. In 1663, therefore, Laval created the Grand Séminaire de Québec. Unlike similar institutions then being established in France, it was subordinated to the Séminaire des Missions Étrangères in Paris, with which Laval retained personal links. Inspired by his involvement with the Bons Amis, as well as the Jesuits' accounts of their mission, Laval wanted to institutionalize the communalism that had animated the early Christian Church. More than a theological school, the seminary was to be the hub around which all would revolve: a true community of priests whose dedication to one another would ensure a heightened religious spirit. Drawing the seminary's first members from the Assemblée des Bons Amis, Laval also arranged for the tithe initiated after his arrival (which was carefully monitored by the state and levied only with its approval) to be paid to the seminary, to support the new community of priests.

In return, the Quebec seminary was to build churches and train and nurture the clergy throughout their lives, serving as both a retreat for spiritual renewal and a hospice for ailing and elderly priests. Fearing that permanent appoint-ment to isolated parishes might over time corrupt the morals and religious practices of priests—a common problem in France—Laval applied the Jesuits' flying-mission approach to francophone as well as native communities, sending priests directly from the seminary. In so doing he not only ensured the semi-nary's control over pastoral activities, but provided a practical solution to the problems posed by the dispersal of Canadien settlement and the limited num-ber of clergy. Thus the seminary and the diocesan clergy were one, and the entire diocese was to be run on missionary principles. When the first parish was erected according to canon law in the town of Quebec in 1664, the right of appointment of its priest rested with the seminary. This centralized system at once allowed for the more efficient use of limited personnel and gave expres-sion to Counter Reformation ideals that included the introduction of the Roman liturgy at Quebec.

Laval's religious devotion entailed such rigidity that it provoked bitter ani-mosities. In reorganizing the Jesuits' Quebec church (l'Église de l'Immaculée-Conception de Notre-Dame), he ended the practice of naming the governor an honorary member of its parish council and changed the former system of open election of churchwardens in favour of secret balloting by previous holders of the office. So contemptuous was the bishop of civilian authority that disputes arose with Pierre de Voyer d'Argenson, one of two governors whom he would help to depose. When Governor d'Argenson objected that Laval did not possess the power to create an *officialité* and had impinged on royal authority, the prelate remained intransigent. In 1660, d'Argenson wrote to his brother that 'a Bishop can do what he wants and threaten only excommunication', but he requested his own recall to France the next year.[33] Relations between Laval and d'Argenson's successor, Pierre Dubois Davaugour, were no better and he was recalled as well, even though the new governor increased the church's power by appointing the Jesuit Paul Ragueneau to preside over the Council of New France, which deliberated daily on colonial affairs.

More than any other question, the brandy trade with the natives divided church and state. While there has been a tendency among historians to play down the issue and regard the church as overstating the ravages of alcohol in order to excuse its lack of success in converting the First Nations, the severity of the problems related to drink through the centuries militates against such an interpretation, as does the fact that officials in the British colonies recorded similar experiences. The problems were real. Natives drank only sporadically, when they had the means to acquire alcohol, but when they did, it was most often to get dead drunk. Normally generous with material goods, they jealously guarded liquor, driving away additional bodies when there was not enough liquor for all to become intoxicated. For highly ritualistic societies living in close quarters, alcohol provided a means of escape, and as dreams played an essential role in aboriginal culture, brandy was valued for its hallucinatory properties. When violence, rape, and disorder resulted, the white men's drink provided a convenient excuse, relieving individuals of responsibility for their actions.

It was the brandy trade that first raised the question of whether temperance or prohibition is more effective in containing substance abuse. A seeping chancre since Champlain had forbidden the use of liquor as a trade good in 1633, the problem grew as competition increased with the Dutch and British to the south and fur traders moved farther inland. When a royal proclamation reinforced this prohibition in 1657, de Queylus became the first church official to attempt religious sanctions, declaring the sale of brandy to the Indians to be a mortal sin. Bishop Laval went further, excommunicating persons found to be involved. At first the state reinforced the church's position by having lawbreakers whipped, but in 1662, after Jesuits intervened on behalf of an accused woman to reduce her sentence because of her sex, Governor Dubois Davaugour reversed the government's position. Royal policy could not be implemented impartially, he concluded, and prohibition placed too severe a penalty on one side without deterring the other; instead, the governor preferred temperance. Laval sought confirmation of his stand from the theologians at the Sorbonne and went to France later in the year to plead his case. While on furlough, he secured Davaugour's recall as well as royal recognition of his own episcopal jurisdiction over Quebec.

These difficulties brought the attention of Louis XIV to Quebec at a time when his most powerful minister, Jean-Baptiste Colbert, was seeking at once to extend the monarchy's absolute sovereignty and to strengthen the royal finances. The decision to appoint a bishop at Quebec can itself be seen as part of a larger plan to shift the colony from company supervision to royal governance, for in swearing oaths of loyalty to the Crown and receiving government subsidies, bishops supported the principle of the absolute monarch's undivided sovereignty. In 1663 the institution of royal government ended the reign of the commercial companies over Quebec's affairs, but not the policy of according trading monopolies in beaver pelts to businesses in return for payments to the royal treasury. Henceforth Quebec was to be treated along the same lines as some of the French provinces, with a royal governor-general (and local governors), representing the king, responsible for military and foreign affairs, and an intendant responsible for justice, public policy, and finance. These two officials reported to the Secretary of State for the Navy and Colonies—one of Colbert's portfolios—and were themselves generally drawn from the army or navy. A Sovereign (later Superior) Council was also established as the colonial high court and the point of registry for royal decrees before they were enforced in the colony. Laval reached the pinnacle of his temporal power when he secured a seat on the court and shared its first appointments with the governor-general. However, while the clerical presence on the Superior Council would later be strengthened by the addition of a priest-councillor in 1703, it was seldom determining, particularly as bishops were frequently absent in Europe for long periods of time.[34]

The new constitutional regime added a range of perspectives that had previously been lacking. Colbert harboured anti-Jesuit sentiments, as did a number of the administrators sent to Canada, notably Louis de Buade, Comte de Frontenac, who would serve two terms as governor-general (1672–82 and 1689–98). The instructions prepared in 1665 for Jean Talon—the second intendant of New France, but the first to set foot in Canada—stressed the need to strengthen state power by establishing a balance between church and state in the colony. Five years later the Récollets were re-introduced to Quebec as a counterweight to the Jesuits. While they served primarily as garrison chaplains and parish priests, Bishop Laval assigned them missions at Gaspé, the St John River, and Fort Frontenac (Kingston), as well as at Trois-Rivières, where they also taught school. The Récollets had not been dissuaded from their long-standing belief in the need to assimilate the indigenous peoples to French culture. They found ready allies among the Sulpicians, who remained resolutely

French in outlook, and among state administrators who, for two decades after 1663, carried out royal policy aimed at increasing Canada's population through official encouragement of intermarriage. In 1668 Laval bowed to these currents by opening the Petit Séminaire de Québec—the seminary of the Infant Jesus—as a boarding-school for native and white boys who showed potential for becoming priests. It began with six Huron and seven French students, but as not one of the former went on to become a priest, Laval's experiment with creating a native clergy ended in 1673 as unsuccessfully as previous attempts to assimilate aboriginal children. No aboriginal man is known to have assumed a religious vocation during the French regime.

Although the Jesuits adjusted readily to the new constitutional order, their adoption of a more relativistic position, admitting some uniquely aboriginal elements into Christian practice, incurred criticism from other religious orders as well as government officials. As a result of this conflict over the missionary endeavour, together with general suspicion of the Society, the Jesuits were accused of trading illegally in furs. There was little foundation to these accusations, but as beaver pelts served as currency in early Canada, donations often took the form of fur pelts that had to be exchanged for specie.[35] Officials such as Frontenac and his rival François-Marie Perrot, the governor of Montreal, who were themselves fur-traders, proved all too ready to impute their own questionable conduct to members of the Society of Jesus. Against such accusations the Acadian missionary Antoine Gaulin retorted indignantly that a priest living among the natives was compelled to lead a life 'scarcely different from that of an animal . . . and that to snare beaver!'[36] Anti-Jesuit officials also backed the more compliant Récollets in dealings with the court at Versailles. So intense did the rivalry become that in 1691 a book appeared in Paris, under dubious authorship, advancing the Récollet position. Entitled *Premièr établissement de la foy dans la Nouvelle-France* and attributed to a Récollet priest named Chrestien Le Clercq who had ministered at Gaspé after 1675, the publication was largely a pastiche of material from other sources. Its creators were really two Frenchmen: Abbé Claude Bernou, who hoped to secure a bishopric in North America, and the editor of the *Gazette de France*, Eusèbe Renaudot.[37]

Since royal absolutism allowed no formal opposition, public debate occurred only within administrative structures. As a result, government in New France became a matter of warring factions based on patron–client relationships formed to further mutual interests. The colony emerged as a hornet's nest in which private profits and advancement were secured at the expense of honesty or the common good. These tendencies were exacerbated by the absence of a printing press in the colony and the restraints imposed on the published word in France by government censors. Public assemblies were banned, except when authorized by royal officials, and collective petitions were prohibited on the grounds that they were conducive to revolt against royal authority.

The consequences for clergy who dared to criticize the king's officials were shown clearly in 1674. At Easter High Mass in Montreal, the Sulpician François Salignac de la Mothe-Fénelon preached a sermon that alluded to abuses by officials, especially the burdensome statute labour (*corvée*) employed by Governor Frontenac to construct a fort at Kingston, where he was known to be trading furs for personal profit. Sitting in the congregation was René-Robert Cavelier de La Salle, Frontenac's partner in the fur trade and his client in political affairs, who stood up and drew attention to the gravity of the priest's accusations. Undeterred, Fénelon gathered signatures on a petition protesting Frontenac's imprisonment of Montreal's governor Perrot, even though the latter was just as rapacious a trader as his superior. Frontenac ordered Fénelon to appear before the Sovereign Council, but the court refused to hear the case and referred it to France. Although the governor-general was rebuked for his high-handedness, Fénelon was not allowed to return to Canada, and he subsequently left the Sulpicians.

In regard to popular norms, the church in New France acted as an independent moral force, but it soon abdicated this role where government was concerned. Laval trod warily between the demands of Rome and those of the French monarchy; the French church was too intricately bound to the state, especially in the financial support it received from government, to do otherwise. Quebec's first bishop learned the lesson of the Fénelon affair. When a Récollet had the temerity to allude publicly to divisions between the governor and intendant in 1681, Laval reprimanded him, and when the priest proved recalcitrant, forbade him to preach. The bishop did not always yield to the government: for example, when it wanted all its decrees read from the pulpits, Laval resisted, and instead had them posted on local church doors. But his successor complied. The nature of the colony's political system obliged church officials to pursue their objectives through the process that we have come to know as élite accommodation, interacting with government officials on a personal level.

Nowhere was government intervention more eagerly sought than in dealing with the Iroquois, for the peace of 1653 did not last long. In 1656 the Mohawk had resumed their raids, attacking the Huron residing on the Île d'Orléans. Two years later, when Jesuit missionaries living among the Onondaga, to the west of the Mohawk cantons, learned that a Mohawk attack was imminent, they held a great medicine or 'eat-all' feast for the natives, and when their guests had gorged themselves, the priests slunk away under cover of darkness; thus ended the first significant mission to the Iroquois. Soon the resumption of guerilla-style attacks on the settlements created a panic among the colonists that bordered on hysteria. Although these actions amounted to little more than harassment, the French were so fearful that they prepared for a siege of Quebec. After no attacks occurred in 1660, clerical chroniclers proclaimed the avoidance of the Armageddon to be a miracle, which they attributed to a combined French, Huron, and Algonquin expedition that had encountered the Iroquois at the Long Sault on the Ottawa River. By the end of a week-long siege, all the Frenchmen involved—including their leader, a young man named Adam Dollard des Ormeaux—had been killed: martyrs, in the view of the Jesuits and Marie de l'Incarnation, to their Catholic faith.[38]

At first the mother country paid little attention to these troubles, being more concerned with establishing its new colony at Placentia, on Newfoundland's south shore, to exploit the lucrative North Atlantic fishery. Finally, in 1665, it dispatched the Marquis de Tracy and the Carignan-Salières regiment to Quebec to subdue the Iroquois. Told that their campaign was 'a holy war, in which [was] involved only the glory of God and the salvation of souls',[39] the troops were given scapulars (badges of devotion) to wear into battle and emphasize the pious nature of the enterprise. Their impact on Quebec, however, was far from holy. The soldiers were a rough crowd—upheavals and courts martial resulting in death sentences had attended their recruitment in France—and their numbers overwhelmed the small settlement at Quebec. Contemporary clerical chroniclers were not inclined to complain, but the Sulpician François Dollier de Casson alluded to the 'vices which have, in fact, arisen since [the soldiers arrived], along with many other troubles which had not up to that time made their appearance here'.[40] So many of the soldiers were Protestants that clerics were kept busy catechizing and securing abjurations from heretic belief.

When the French invaded Mohawk territory in 1666, they planted a cross that symbolized the close association between religion, culture, and the force of arms. The temporary peace that resulted was vital to the colony's demographic expansion. The cold climate and hostilities with the natives had created such a negative image of Canada in France that in 1663 the mother country began assisting immigration, sending women in particular to right the gender imbalance in the colony's population. Roughly half of these *filles du roi* were former inmates of a Paris hospice for people in abject poverty. Like many of the soldiers of the Carignan-Salières regiment—a third of whom decided to settle in the colony—a few of the female immigrants were former Protestants, but they had been required to abjure before embarkation.

The diversity of its new inhabitants transformed New France, doubling its population to 7,605 by 1673, when assisted immigration ended. The liberalizing influence of the newcomers could be seen in the raucous popular entertainments during the carnival that preceded Lent in 1667. When Bishop Laval denounced some women belonging to a pious religious association who had joined in the celebrations, the Sovereign Council ruled that such festivities might not be condemned. Nevertheless, some two-thirds of the fifteen thousand people who came to the country in the seventeenth century remained only temporarily.[41]

Some of the changes introduced into the religious life of Canada during the second half of the seventeenth century were permanent and others were not. In a series of difficult adjustments, the principal structures of Roman Catholicism had been established. The appointment of a bishop and the addition of new religious orders had ended the Jesuit monopoly in matters of worship, but they had also created internal divisions. In raising the Catholic Church to the pinnacle of political power during the 1660s, royal policies set the basis for its increasing subservience to the state, and by the end of the century, the government would begin restricting the operation and expansion of the colony's religious orders. At the same time, the larger and more diverse population required greater government financial support to extend the medical, social assistance, and educational services run by the church. The needs of the rapidly expanding Canadien population came to demand a greater share of clerical attention. But even though, after 1700, the missionary enterprise would be eclipsed by service to the European population, the numbers of priests would still prove inadequate to meet the religious needs of the colonists.

In terms of popular religious beliefs and practices, the latter half of the seventeenth century proved transitional. Although mystical practices came to be questioned in some quarters as early as the 1670s, for the time being they continued unabated. The case of Marie Barbier, the first Montreal woman to enter the Congrégation de Notre-Dame, was illustrative. She thought that an intervention from the Virgin Mary had saved her from an attempted rape prior to entering the order as a novice in 1679. Offering special prayers to the Infant Jesus, Marie Barbier entered into such constant dialogue with the Holy Child that her spiritual director claimed she was able to achieve miraculous feats: multiplying food in times of scarcity, putting out fires, and curing the sick with bread made in Christ's honour. Those with religious vocations were not the only ones to sublimate the self in order to achieve higher spirituality. Jeanne Le Ber, the colony's best-known recluse, was a merchant's daughter who lived in complete seclusion under a priest's direction from the age of seventeen until her death in 1714 at the age of fifty-two. Natives such as Kateri Tekakwitha (1656–80), the first aboriginal North American to be named venerable by the church, emulated the practices they observed or were told of.

Asceticism reinforced the link between religious fervour and supernatural beliefs among the early Canadiens. Even people devoted to Christianity saw no contradiction between the two. In a world that could not explain the origins of disease or deformities, the reasons for natural terrestrial or celestial phenomena, or the sources of mental illness or depression, magic readily formed a continuum with religion, just as it did in the Christian Scriptures. Recourse to either religion or magic might be sought to avert human disaster. Still, the church distinguished between those expressions that were officially sanctioned and those that were not. In part, of course, this distinction was based on the fact that while both religion and magic are predicated on belief in the powers of the supernatural, the former is supplicatory, calling on divine power through prayers and other devotions, while the latter is manipulative, depending on personal power to command the supernatural. At the same time, however, the church was well aware that every claim to special powers or divine intervention was fraught with danger, since false attributions might discredit it at least as effectively as any Protestant effort to portray Catholic beliefs as superstition.[42]

A cult of relics flourished in seventeenth-century Canada. Churches displayed bodily fragments in elaborate reliquaries and paraded them on ornate litters in processions, while individuals wore and traded them. In 1666 so many people crushed into the Ursulines' church to see specimens from saints recently arrived from Europe that the floor collapsed and many individuals were thrown into the vault below. Nor were saints necessarily imported: they were also actively sought among the faithful departed at home. Bodily parts from such people were so highly prized that organs were often willed to one institution and other remains to a second. Bishop Laval returned to Quebec from France bringing the heart of Canon Jean Dudouyt; as first procurator of the Séminaire de Québec, Dudouyt had been highly esteemed. The hospital nun and mystic Catherine de Saint-Augustin pulverized some of the bones of Jean de Brébeuf and fed them in a drink to a recalcitrant Protestant soldier of the Carignan-Salières regiment to secure his conversion.[31] Catherine Gandeacteua, an Erie who had been largely responsible for founding the mission that later became Kahnawake, was considered so highly that in 1689 a quarrel developed over her final resting-place; in the end her remains were left at the mission. Following a Christian practice dating from late antiquity, the Ursulines in 1663 exhumed the body of Marie de Savonnières de la Troche from the garden where it had been buried eleven years before. As she had been one of the original founders of the order at Quebec and had lived an exemplary life, de Savonnières's remains were examined closely for the odour of sanctity, the sweet bodily fragrance associated with saints. When her flesh was found to be milk-white, and her brain and heart still entire, some of the nuns undertook to wash the bones. 'Neither the sight nor the handling of the bones nor the white mass caused us any fear as do ordinarily the corpses of the dead,' Marie de l'Incarnation wrote, 'but they filled us rather with the feelings of union and love with the deceased. Everyone strove to kiss the bones and to be the first to render this final duty.'[44] When the Quebec Hospitalières performed a similar exhumation, the two communities exchanged relics.

Similarly, supernatural powers were imputed to religious images and other objects. In 1707 a likeness of the Virgin Mary placed on a patient in Quebec's Hôtel-Dieu was held to be responsible for his recovery and confession. The hospital's superior, Jeanne-Françoise Juchereau de la Ferté, introduced devotions to the sacred heart of Mary there in 1690, and a dozen years later began the practice of kissing the hands and feet of the Virgin's statue. Bishop Laval had a large portrait of the holy family placed on the steeple of his cathedral when the expedition of New Englander William Phips threatened the citadel in 1690, and after the enemy was repulsed, the name of a church then under construction in the Lower Town was changed to Notre-Dame-de-la-Victoire, a designation that would be pluralized following Sir Hovenden Walker's failure to conquer Quebec in 1711. Blessings with holy water—of fields, animals, and harvests—were common.

Miracles constituted as much a part of officially sanctioned religious life as devotion to saints and religious representations. According to Quebec's second bishop, Jean-Baptiste Saint Vallier, saints' relics should be venerated because 'their bodies have been temples of the Holy Spirit, they have served as instruments for good works, and God uses them to perform several miracles.'[45] The prelate himself became an active propagandist in favour of canonization for the Récollet Didace Pelletier after he attributed his own recovery from a serious illness to the dead priest's intercession. Although a study of the Quebec region during the French regime has uncovered one hundred and forty-four accounts of miracles, the Jesuits were more discreet than other orders in describing such events as 'marvels' or 'wonders'. Attributions of miracles tended to be associated with the dangers that men faced in their daily lives as woodsmen and sailors. Thus the perils of navigation and the intercession of Saint Anne led to the creation of a shrine at Beaupré, a site below Quebec, where the treacherous waters of the St Lawrence narrowed, that long had been venerated by indigenous peoples as spiritually significant—a 'power spot'. A sailors' chapel constructed there in 1658 was followed two years later by the first church. By 1665 Marie de l'Incarnation reported miracles at Beaupré where the 'paralysed [were] seen to walk, the blind to recover their sight, and those sick with various maladies their health'.[46] Priests soon began to record such events, and the church became a pilgrimage site, as did L'Ancienne Lorette and the convent called Notre-Dames-des-Anges outside Quebec. Natives passing by made gifts of pelts that were sold to decorate the buildings, and *ex-voto* religious paintings, so called because they were commissioned in fulfilment of a vow following miraculous recovery, were donated as well.

Throughout the Western world, religious faith was underpinned by fear: in particular, the dread of not dying a 'good death', united with God. Personal conversion to Christ and regular observance of the sacraments were not enough, for salvation was God's alone to bestow, and the unredeemed faced eternal damnation. The church's interpretation of natural calamities reinforced the terror of divine retribution: fires, droughts, famines, insect infestations, and even the devastation of war were judged to be either indications of God's displeasure or the work of the devil, demonstrating the deity's special providence more clearly than the normal course of events. When an earthquake struck the St Lawrence valley in 1663, settlers thought the tremors augured the end of the world and the day of judgement. The writer of the Jesuit *Relations* reported the appearance of intertwined serpents flying on wings of fire during the autumn of 1662; another night, a great globe of fire was visible at Quebec and Montreal. Three suns were said to have appeared on the horizon on 7 January 1663; a priest at Trois-Rivières saw a monster on a moat and communicated with the spirit of Jean de Brébeuf; and at Quebec in February the mystic Catherine de Saint-Augustin envisioned four demons shaking the town as one would a carpet, as an expression of God's wrath at the colony's sins. The first tremors hit shortly afterward, and Marie de l'Incarnation reported seeing 'fires, torches, and flaming globes, which sometimes fell to the earth and sometimes dissolved in the air . . . Terrible spectres were also seen.'[47] Tremors continued for seven months in 1663 and were felt again in 1665, when they were also preceded by the augury of three suns in the sky.

The striking similarities between the supernatural imagery of Canadien Catholics and New England Puritans during this period derived from common religious and social-psychological origins. The gospels of Mark and Matthew had incorporated Jewish apocalyptic themes in forecasting the second coming of Christ after lightning, earthquakes, falling stars, and eclipses, while the book of Revelation saw the voice of God expressed even more dramatically.[48] Thus religious minds were predisposed to interpret inexplicable happenings as portents, a tendency reinforced by oral traditions circulating the accumulated lore of centuries past. It is also possible that food mould, especially in rusty wheat, may have produced hallucinations. However, the 'augury' of the three suns was simply a natural occurrence in North America's cold winter weather.

Such visions and fears belong to the world of popular religion, a term originally coined by medieval historians to denote the difference between official Christian beliefs and those held more commonly. No strict divorce between the two was evident in New France: laity and clergy alike participated in the world of wonders. Nevertheless, church practices and structures in the colony—in particular, the flying-mission approach favoured by Laval—placed a degree of constraint on the clergy. That some did mix folk beliefs and religion was clear as late as 1742 when, after a soldier named Beaufort was convicted of attempting to extort money through divination involving a crucifix, the latter became an object of veneration among Quebec's hospital nuns. But the rarity of official records on behaviour of this kind suggests that such tendencies were minimal. By contrast, in places such as Ireland, priests living in isolated areas, far from the control of central authorities, often shared their parishioners' superstitions.

Only five cases of sorcery were ever brought before the courts in Quebec, and of these only one resulted in death.[49] The victim was a former Protestant, a miller named Daniel Vuil, who was executed for witchcraft in 1661. Sailing to Quebec in 1659 on the same ship that carried François de Laval—who persuaded him to abjure his Protestant faith—Vuil had fallen in love with a fourteen-year-old girl travelling with her parents. Unfortunately, fears of witchcraft were rampant at that time as a result of a trial in which Maisonneuve had blamed sorcery for the impotence of Montreal's first altar boy after his marriage. When, a year later, Vuil was rebuffed by the girl who had smitten his heart aboard ship, he was accused of resorting to witchcraft to infest her house with demons. Priests were dispatched to conduct an exorcism, Vuil was arrested, and the girl was held at the hospital under the care of Catherine de Saint-Augustin—who, according to Father Pierre Chastellain, appeared every morning with her arms black as ink from the devil's blows. Laval had Vuil tried in the ecclesiastical court, where he was found guilty of witchcraft. Turned over to civilian authorities for execution, Vuil was shot in 1661.

The high drama of this singular event underscores the contrast between the experiences of the French and English settlers in their adjoining colonies. In New England during the half-century following 1647, sixty-one people were brought to trial for witchcraft and fourteen were executed, with events at Salem in 1692 commanding the greatest attention.[50] With a population of 15,000 at the end of the century, compared with New England's 100,000, New France recorded proportionally only half as many witchcraft trials, and many fewer deaths. Two sets of circumstances, one social and the other doctrinal, may account for New France's relative freedom from religious hysteria. First, unlike the Puritans who migrated in groups during the decade following 1632, the colonists arriving in New France and Acadia came as individuals or in families from various regions of the mother country over a longer span of time. They settled not in villages, as the New Englanders did, but on farms dispersed along waterways. This relative isolation, together with the diversity of their customs and dialects, produced new francophone cultures without the cohesive social outlook characteristic of village life in New England. Second, the Puritan emphasis on human depravity and the individual's inability to obtain salvation created an anxiety about God's intentions that could not be assuaged. By contrast, Catholic doctrine, while it too stressed humanity's fallen, sinful state, offered believers greater hope of helping themselves. Those who could not satisfy divine justice might have to expiate their shortcomings in purgatory, but the additional grace attained by Christ and his saints was available to the faithful. Works of supererogation beyond regular charitable or religious activities were rewarded with indulgences that might be used to compensate for sins; one Quebec bishop recommended to confessors that such activities be undertaken as penance to atone for the sins of avarice, theft, and the sale of brandy, or by those who could not observe fasting regulations or required marriage dispensations. Even if salvation was not guaranteed,

Catholic believers could at least take comfort in the certainty that, as the prelate wrote, only 'those who have filled their days with good works will be saved'.[51] Differences in what the two branches of Christianity chose to emphasize, as well as contrasts in immigration and settlement patterns, help to explain why witchcraft figured more prominently in New England than in New France.

In any case, by the late seventeenth century church officials were coming to view exaggerated claims of various kinds, even in the service of religion, with increasing suspicion. The glowing accounts of missionaries' success in acculturating native children subsided, and the Jesuits stopped publishing their annual accounts in 1673. The appearance in 1671 of Paul Ragueneau's biography of Catherine de Saint-Augustin brought to light such excesses in the search for spiritual attainments through mysticism that, when asked for her opinion, Marie de l'Incarnation demurred: 'persons of knowledge and virtue are withholding their judgement and remain in doubt, not daring to trust in extraordinary visions of this nature'.[52] This shift in perspective paralleled developments in France. In 1660 the French government banned the secret meetings of the Compagnie du Saint-Sacrement in an attempt to quash what it interpreted as dissent. Prosecution for witchcraft was officially ended in France in 1682, although such cases were still heard intermittently at Quebec, and in 1691, after three priests lent credence to the visions of the Montreal nun Marguerite Tardy, two of them were quickly recalled to Paris. The third, Étienne Guyotte, was similarly disciplined three years later because he had denounced some women as witches and refused communion to others on account of their jewellery and cosmetics.

At the same time the church developed various means of channelling religious fervour. Among these were the pious lay religious associations called confraternities, which made their first appearance in 1652 and proliferated over the next few decades. The confraternities appear to have counted large memberships—although, as overzealous priests sometimes enrolled entire parishes, their numbers are not entirely to be trusted.[53] Superseding the craft confraternities that had typically celebrated the feast days of their patron saints with mass and noisy socializing, the new associations were subject to closer clerical supervision. While open to all believers, some were segregated by sex: the Confrérie de la Sainte-Famille, for example, admitted only women, while the Congrégation des Hommes de Ville-Marie was restricted to men. Membership entailed regular observance of the sacraments, participation in religious services and processions, private prayer, the upkeep of chapels, and, in some cases, visits to the sick or prison inmates. In return for such activities, the church offered indulgences whose weight varied with the merit of the works undertaken. Another innovation of the latter half of the seventeenth century was the nine-day prayer vigil known as the novena.

Missions continued to spread as New France expanded to the west and south. But missionary authorities were increasingly hampered by the scarcity of personnel, despite the priests provided by the Quebec seminary. The mission to the Iroquois that had ended in 1658 was revived in 1661, when Father Simon LeMoyne was invited back by the Onondaga, and soon there were six Jesuits working within the Confederacy. Their task was complicated, however, by defeated Huron among the Iroquois who resurrected past conflicts with the missionaries. Gaining acceptance was difficult, alcohol was a constant problem, and the work proceeded at a snail's pace. The superior of the missions, Father Jacques Bruyas, who had arrived south of Lake Ontario in 1667, did not see any conversions until nine years later; it was only then that he finally felt sufficiently secure to erect a statue of the Virgin Mary. In 1668 the Sulpician order established a mission to the Cayuga on the Bay of Quinte on Lake Ontario's northern shore, and one of its members ministered as far west as the future Port Hope. But this effort did not last long, and by 1686 the other Iroquois missions had been abandoned as well, even though they had made considerable progress in evangelization. When the War of the League of Augsburg erupted in 1689, two-thirds of the Mohawk moved closer to the French settlements in the St Lawrence valley.[54] The peace of 1701 that ended the French and Iroquois wars led the Jesuits to return south of the lake the following year, but beginning in 1704 the Iroquois also accepted Anglican priests sent by the Society for the Propagation of the Gospel, and in 1709 the Jesuits withdrew to Quebec for the duration of the War of the Spanish Succession (1702–13).

Meanwhile, the western Great Lakes had become a new focus of activity. The Jesuit Father Claude Allouez attempted to proselytize among the Ottawa in 1665, but when they spurned him, he went on to establish one mission (Saint-Esprit) on the south shore of Lake Superior and another at Green Bay on Lake Michigan, and travelled as far as Sault Ste Marie. In twenty-four years of missionary work, Allouez came into contact with twenty-three different peoples, including the Sioux and the Nipissing, and baptized some ten thousand people. By contrast, the reputation of the renowned missionary-explorer Jacques Marquette was based on a much shorter period of activity. In 1671 he founded Saint-Ignace at Michilimackinac, the site that would be the base for Jesuits working in the immense upper Great Lakes region, and two years later he accompanied Louis Jolliet down the Mississippi as far as the Arkansas River. The following year he opened a mission (Immaculée-Conception) for the Kaskaskia people in the Illinois country, a nation that Allouez had served before him. While he did touch a number of peoples, including Petun, Ottawa, Ojibwa, Miami, Fox, Sauk, Sioux, and Cree, before his death in 1675, many have charged that Marquette's reputation has been overblown.[55]

Further activity by the Society of Jesus was constrained not only by Governor Frontenac's anti-Jesuit policies but also by his cohort La Salle, who reserved the southern region that he had explored for the Récollets. Frontenac and La Salle joined with individuals like Antoine Laumet de Lamothe de Cadillac, the military commandant at Michilimackinac and future founder of Detroit, in using their offices to profit from the brandy trade and other illicit practices. After a general assembly of twenty leading colonial residents, dubbed the 'Brandy Parliament', was convoked to make recommendations to the government, in 1679 Louis XIV ruled that traders might not sell liquor in the aboriginal villages, although natives could purchase moderate amounts in the French settlements. As brandy might also be carried west for personal use, the door was left open for resumption of the trade, much to the displeasure of the Jesuits who were the missionaries in the west.

When Acadia was reoccupied by France in 1670, it too was placed under royal government, but it did not benefit from an infusion of state aid, and as a result it languished both materially and spiritually. In 1641 the white population in Nova Scotia numbered barely seventy-five families, although there was also a significant Métis element. The Récollet priest Claude Moireau was appointed the sole missionary for the entire region that is now New Brunswick and Nova Scotia in 1675. The following year the Séminaire de Québec sent Louis Petit to re-establish services in the small community of Port-Royal, which two years later was erected into a parish called l'Assomption. Having little contact with Moireau, who was based in Beaubassin (Amherst, NS) and travelled extensively, Petit ministered alone to the Acadians and the various native nations in the region, although he did maintain a teacher to instruct boys. In 1684 the Quebec seminary dispatched a second missionary, Louis-Pierre Thury, to minister to the Maliseet, Micmac, and Penobscot of Maine; to make sure that these peoples remained loyal to France, Thury accompanied many of their war parties against the English. A year later, Petit was also able to secure the services of a nun from Montreal's Congrégation de Notre-Dame to direct a boarding-school for girls. Nevertheless, when Laval's successor visited the area the following year, he found it so deprived of clergy that he left behind two Sulpician priests. Soon both secular and regular clergy from various orders were ministering from centres in Beaubassin and Grand Pré. However, conflicts with government were common,[56] and as the priests were still forced to divide their time between whites and natives, they occasionally incurred criticism from Acadians for neglecting their needs. Because settlement was dispersed and the number of clergy small, people sometimes baptized their own children and did not hurry to obtain the formal rite. Little respect was accorded religious holidays: Acadians worked, danced, and held social evenings, and taverns stayed open.

When Laval retired in 1685, his successor was also a nobleman chosen by Louis XIV. Jean-Baptiste de La Croix de Chevrières de Saint-Vallier set out on a determined course to remould the diocese according to his own views, but his rigid adherence to increasingly outmoded Counter Reformation ideals combined with his personal hubris and obstinacy to create severe divisions both within the clergy and between clergy and laity. Although his arrogance was perhaps understandable in such a young man—he was only thirty-two when he assumed office—it continued throughout his long tenure (1685–1727), centring on two convictions: that a recurring thought must be a divine inspiration, and therefore should be followed, and that a bishop need accept advice from no one but the king.[57] Where conciliation was needed, Saint-Vallier responded with confrontation. In 1694, in response to disputes over precedence, he placed the Récollets' Montreal church under interdiction, and when, their appeals unheeded, the Récollets began to hold services nevertheless, he did the same to the priests themselves. Saint-Vallier also completed the dismantling of Laval's plan for the diocese, a process that had begun in 1679 when Louis XIV decreed that tithes would be paid to parish priests instead of the seminary, and that laypersons might become patrons of local churches by assisting in their construction. After a ferocious battle, Saint-Vallier secured the separation of the parishes from the seminary in 1692.

The new bishop brought from France strong views concerning the need to separate the sacred from the profane. By insisting on political and social obedience rather than emphasizing the doctrine of faith, hope, and love, Saint-Vallier's catechetical teaching translated religion into a kind of moral book-keeping. He offended the Jesuits by ordering them to withdraw from the primary school they had been operating in the town of Quebec and forbidding them to allow theatricals or debates among the students in their college. In order to prevent a production of Molière's *Tartuffe*, a dramatic satire on hypocritical piety, he bribed Governor Frontenac in 1694 and later demanded that the government repay him by deducting the amount from the governor's salary![58] When he counselled priests to refuse absolution to women wearing dresses with breast supports, the Intendant Jean Bochart de Champigny referred the matter to the French clergy, who brought pressure to bear on their Canadien counterparts to adopt a more tolerant attitude. Yet Saint-Vallier persisted in his heavy-handed moralism, in 1700 exhorting confessors not to allow dancing or social gatherings where the sexes mixed.

Saint-Vallier was equally determined to extend the church's control over social welfare. In France, until the second half of the seventeenth century, attempts to deal with poverty had generally been limited to driving beggars out of the towns. Beginning about 1650, however, royal policies in the mother country tended toward the establishment of government-sponsored poorhouses staffed primarily by religious orders. Colonial officials had first attempted the former solution in 1677, but it had not worked. Hence in 1686 Saint-Vallier purchased a house in Quebec for the Sisters of the Congrégation de Notre-Dame to run as a providence mission, instructing young women and sheltering unfortunates when asked; as a teaching order, though, the Sisters did not want to move beyond these simple acts of charity. Two years later the Sovereign Council addressed the problem of indigence by creating poor boards in Quebec, Montreal, and Trois-Rivières; each was placed under the direction of three laypersons and a local parish priest. As these depended on voluntary contributions from the public, laywomen solicited alms door-to-door, and some court fines were made payable to the boards.[59]

Thus church and state entered into competition in providing services to the poor. Nevertheless, Bishop Saint-Vallier was adamant that religious institutions were better equipped to cope with the problems created by poverty. He envisioned the creation of a hospice, or poorhouse, like the one he had established in France before leaving for Canada. Although the intendant Jean Bochart de Champigny thought the money would have been better spent on placing priests in rural parishes, Saint-Vallier persisted, and in 1692 he secured a royal proclamation establishing the Quebec hospice (the Hôpital-Général) under the direction of a board made up largely of laypersons but on which he also had a seat. After purchasing the former Récollet convent outside the town of Quebec, the bishop entrusted the new institution to the Augustinian nuns of the Hôtel-Dieu in 1693. However, when Saint-Vallier's addition to their duties extended into a plan for them to create a separate order to run the hospice, the Sisters objected. They feared the town could not support additional services and they did not wish to depart from their medical role in order to care for the destitute, the blind, the insane, orphans, and other unfortunates. But Saint-Vallier proved too skilful both for the nuns and for those advocating secular control of the poorhouse. After guaranteeing it an annuity, the bishop took over responsibility for the institution in 1698, despite lay opposition, and in the following year separated the nuns of the hospice from those of the Quebec Hôtel-Dieu. When the Sisters protested, the local government annulled his decision.

Saint-Vallier pulled out all the stops. Breaking into tears as he attempted to cajole the Augustinians, he later manipulated the elections for their mother superior to deny the office to its incumbent.[60] Temporary calm was restored only through the mediation of the retired bishop Laval before Saint-Vallier left for France in 1700, hoping to influence the court in his favour. He succeeded, but the government required financial guarantees before it would officially recognize the new religious order. Accordingly the bishop, together with wealthy merchants such as Charles Aubert de La Chesnaye, made large contributions, and the Sisters of the Hôpital-General de Québec were granted official recognition in 1701. Quebec's hospice thereafter remained Saint-Vallier's pet charity, receiving one-tenth of the approximately six hundred thousand *livres* that he donated to the church.[61] Providing shelter to between forty and fifty individuals each year, the hospice also housed some eighteen pensioners, particularly disabled soldiers. A separate pavilion was constructed for the insane of both sexes and in 1717, at the bishop's urging, Father Charles Plante fitted out another house that the Sisters of the Hôpital-Général ran to reform prostitutes.

The Ursulines too extended their activities in this period: concurring with Saint-Vallier that Trois-Rivières was too small to support a teaching order alone, they agreed to care for the sick when they opened their new convent there in 1697. In addition, two new male religious communities were established. In 1686 Maturin Rouillé and six unmarried Montreal men formed a lay community of school teachers known as the Rouillé Brothers; however, despite the financial support they received from the Sulpicians, debt caused them to fold in 1693.[62] The efforts of a former merchant named François Charon de la Barre were somewhat more successful. Following his recovery from a serious illness, Charon rallied other entrepreneurs to help him begin construction of a hospice in Montreal in 1692. Two years later Saint-Vallier allowed the Charon Brothers to live as a community under the name Frères Hospitaliers de la Croix et de Saint-Joseph and to care for destitute men. Royal authorization and subsidy for the institution followed, but as the government was determined to restrict the number of religious orders and their size, the Minister of the Navy and Colonies resolutely refused to recognize the Frères Charon as a religious community.

In addition to promoting institutional growth, Saint-Vallier published three books: in 1688 an account of the church in New France, and in 1702 and 1703 a catechism and a book of rites, the latter two volumes being amalgams of other manuals current in France. The catechism had little effect in his diocese, however, as the major shipment was captured by the British—along with the bishop himself—on his return voyage to New France in 1704. Thereafter Saint-Vallier was detained first in England and later in France for nine years in all, partly at the behest of Louis XIV, who viewed him as a disruptive influence in the colony. As for the book of rites, it was seized on by the Jesuits, who took advantage of a number of small printing errors to retaliate against their adversary on doctrinal grounds. Charged with being a follower of Cornelius Jansen, a bishop whose austere theology of pietistic appeals directly to God had been condemned by the pope for downplaying the importance of the sacraments, Saint-Vallier was forced to seek advice from theologians at the Sorbonne. When the charge was not proven, a revised edition of the rites was published later the same year. In fact, it was rigorism rather than Jansenism that characterized Saint-Vallier's religious practice and rule. The bishop was so sensitive to the issue that in 1694 he had had one of his protégés sent back to France following accusations of Jansenism from other members of the clergy.[63]

A MISSION CHURCH IN DECLINE: 1700–1760

The recurring wars between France and England that began in 1689 occasioned profound changes as the increased scale and frequency of military conflict fostered a closer identification between church and state. In addition, missionary activity was affected as French imperial policy shifted with the establishment of Louisiana, the conclusion of peace with the Iroquois, and the loss of most of Acadia under the Treaty of Utrecht (1713). New colonies, and their missions, came to be regarded as military establishments positioned to forestall British expansion by containing the British colonies between the Appalachian mountains and the Atlantic ocean. Throughout the continent, garrisons were added to missions and new military forts were built to which Roman Catholic chaplains were posted. In the Great Lakes region and the upper reaches of the Mississippi valley, native villages grew up outside these forts, with their own chapels separate from those for white soldiers and fur traders.

The new military exigencies aggravated the chronic shortage of clergy in remote areas, and even eastern missions were not always well served after 1700. Although the Jesuits had six members ministering to Maine's aboriginal peoples by 1699, and maintained a mission at Meductic for the Maliseet of the St John River valley, the vast northern part of Acadia and the lower St Lawrence saw clergy only intermittently. Following the death of Father François de Crespieul in 1702, the Montagnais went without a priest for eighteen years; when a Jesuit re-opened the mission in 1720 the only vestige of Catholicism he found was that a few of the people were able to recite a jumble of the Lord's Prayer and the *Ave Maria*. Drunkenness was rife, polygyny common, and despite the presence of missionaries, the Micmac of Île Royale found it so difficult to cope with the disorder in their midst that in 1739 they asked French military officials to establish regulations for social behaviour.[64]

The flying-mission approach favoured by Bishop Laval was abandoned and sedentary missions became the norm. Not only were the clergy tired of endless trekking, but they wanted to isolate the native people from the debilitating effects of white influence. As a result, the distinction between missions and reserves—always weak in New France because the royal grants of land for reserves had been made to missionaries for the benefit of the natives—came to mean less than ever.

These settlements provided a refuge from starvation, disease, and the conflicts that by the end of the seventeenth century were no longer simply commercial but increasingly imperialistic in nature. But they were not without problems. At La Prairie, on the south shore of the St Lawrence across from Montreal, the village established in 1668 for the Mohawk and Oneida soon experienced such severe trouble because of alcohol that it was forced to move several times before coming to rest at Kahnawake (the mission of Sault-Saint-Louis; also known as Caughnawaga) in 1714. One French governor, aghast at the independent ways of people there, proclaimed in 1741 that the settlement 'has become a kind of republic'.[65] Jesuits like Pierre de Lauzon and Jean-Baptiste Tournois, who ministered at Kahnawake, were so protective of the Iroquois that they incurred criticism from government officials, and in 1751 Tournois was expelled to France for condoning their illegal trade in furs with the English, which he felt was preferable to maintaining frequent contact with the French traders of Montreal. The Sulpicians, for their part, had established what was initially a true reserve for Christian Huron at La Montagne, outside Montreal, in 1676, but it was indicative of how little they had learned from their predecessors that they also settled Iroquois there, some of whom were ransomed captives. Burned by drunks in 1694, the village moved twice before settling in 1721 at Oka (Kanesataké), at the confluence of the Ottawa and St Lawrence rivers. A new Jesuit mission at St-Regis (Akwesasne), near the future Cornwall, Ontario, was begun in 1755.

Interest in the Illinois country and the vast Mississippi region increased at the turn of the eighteenth century. The colony of Louisiana was established in 1699 and New Orleans named its capital in 1718. While the Jesuits had been accorded the Illinois country as a mission field by Bishop Saint-Vallier in 1690, eight years later he gave the Quebec seminary permission for its priests to work among the Tamaroa, a tribal division of the Illinois peoples who lived on the east bank of the Mississippi River, opposite present-day St Louis. The dispute that erupted was so furious that it ended only with the king's decision in support of the prelate in 1701. The Jesuits' Louisiana initiative was independent of the northern Great Lakes (or Ottawa) mission, each operating under the authority of a priest named vicar-general by the bishop of Quebec. Following the death of Claude Allouez in 1695, the Ottawa mission effectively ended with the Jesuits' decision to burn their mission at Michilimackinac in 1705. Although the Capuchins served New Orleans and the area up to the Arkansas border, the Jesuits would remain the foremost missionaries in the Mississippi region until 1762, when the Society was suppressed by the government of France during another fit of anti-Jesuit fervour.[66]

After 1717 the American mid-west was administered as part of Louisiana and the Capuchin superior at New Orleans was appointed as vicar general, but the region remained part of the Quebec diocese. In 1727 Ursulines from France began the first girls' school in New Orleans and the Jesuits established a residence there. The mission of the priests from the Séminaire de Québec to the Tamaroa at Cahokia on the Mississippi River failed when their numbers and preparation proved inadequate to the undertaking. One of them, Abbé Jean-François Buisson de Saint-Cosme, a former parish priest whose temperament was clearly unsuited to such work, concluded in 1704 that it 'would be necessary first to make these barbarians into men and then they could be made Christians'.[67] As in the early days of New France, many priests lost their lives in the new mission field, among them Gabriel de la Ribourde in 1680, Nicolas Foucault in 1702, Buisson de Saint-Cosme in 1706, and Jean-Pierre Aulneau in 1736. In 1707, the Tamaroa were reported to have considered the death of the Quebec missionary Marc Bergier 'a cause for triumph. They gathered around the cross he had erected, and there they invoked their Manitou, each one dancing, attributing to himself the glory of having killed the missionary, after which they broke the cross into a thousand pieces.'[68]

In Atlantic Canada, France lost peninsular Nova Scotia and the colony of Placentia in Newfoundland but kept Cape Breton Island under the Treaty of Utrecht. However, the British permitted Roman Catholic priests to continue their ministry to Acadians and native people in the forfeited area of the mainland. Shifting its attention to the territories it retained under the Treaty, France immediately began construction of a walled city at Louisbourg on Cape Breton (which was renamed Île Royale), to serve as a base for the fishery, a transportation centre for intercolonial trade, and the first line of defence for New France, and in 1720 it initiated settlement of Île Saint-Jean (Prince Edward Island), where a permanent mission was established five years later by the Récollet Félix Pain. Antoine Gaulin, a priest from the Séminaire de Québec who had been sent to Acadia to assist Louis-Pierre Thury in 1698, continued the missionary practice of inciting the region's native peoples against the English, but he was initially unable to get the Micmac to move to Île Royale. Between 1717 and 1720 he created a large Micmac mission at Antigonish, still on British soil but close to French territory. Finally, in 1723 during Dummer's War (1722-6)—a conflict between New England and the native peoples of Nova Scotia and Maine—the Micmac did move to the island, settling at Mirliguèche, on the west side of Bras d'Or Lake, where a church and presbytery were built in 1726. Gaulin's most important successor, Pierre Maillard, who arrived in Île Royale directly from France in 1735, became a specialist in the Micmac people's language and wrote informatively about their way of life. In 1750 Maillard moved his headquarters from Mirliguèche to Île de la Sainte-Famille (today Chapel Island) in the south of Bras d'Or Lake; today the Micmac still gather annually at this site to celebrate St Anne's Day (26 July).

The inroads made by such missionary efforts have been judged by some scholars to represent the most momentous of all the changes experienced by the continent's indigenous peoples.[69] In fact, however, the missionaries' success varied with time, place, clerical resources, and individual First Nations. For those groups living closest to European settlements, the changes in all aspects of their lives were so profound as to defy any attempt to separate religious from secular causes. By contrast, native people in more remote areas made no significant changes in their customs, despite innovations such as the appointment of native lay assistants (*dogiques*) of both sexes and adjustment of the religious calendar to suit the seasonal nature of native life.

The strength of various peoples' attachment to the new religion varied as well. The Micmac, Maliseet, and Abenaki remained so firmly Catholic that attempts at Protestant evangelization by the New England Company, between 1717 and 1720, failed completely. The Montagnais of the Saguenay and the Algonquin, some of whom were centred at Oka, also became at least nominally Catholic. But the Iroquois nations, who identified religion with trade, accepted the ministers of those allies who offered the greatest advantages; the most significant advances were made among the Mohawk, with Catholicism prevailing in the St Lawrence valley and the Church of England dominating south of Lake Ontario. Most of the peoples surrounding the Great Lakes acquired some familiarity with the Christian religion. In general, though, knowledge of the faith remained as imperfect as it was among most Canadiens, and both syncretism and dimorphism—the simultaneous assent to both old and new ways—were common.

In their private correspondence missionaries were forthright about the difficulties they faced. Pierre Maillard, who became known as the 'Apostle to the Micmac', noted that after a century and a half of evangelization, the people continued to associate the Great Spirit with the sun. Buisson de Saint-Cosme wrote from the southwest in 1702 asking for a servant capable of 'standing up to the most impertinent barbarian because it is unseemly for a missionary to have to punch a barbarian'. From Acadia, the missionary Jean-Louis Le Loutre observed in 1738 that under 'the eyes of their missionary, they [the natives] could be taken for saints. At church they are angels in their modesty, subservience to their patriarchs, and submission to what they are told, but it is fleeting. All evaporates when they go on hunts.' What pastor serving a European population might not have noted a similar contrast between the Sunday face and everyday behaviour? Thus the largely uncorroborated claims of the early records, intended for publication, must be weighed against the informal observations written without any such intent. In their private writings, priests admitted that to be accepted they had to conform to indigenous ways. 'Our Indians would have difficulty understanding what was said to them,' the missionary Sébastien Rale informed his brother in 1723, 'and they would be inattentive if we did not conform to their manner of thinking and expressing themselves.'[70]

Among the Canadien population the difficulty of the transition to a new era at the turn of the eighteenth century was evident in Marguerite Bourgeoys, who died in 1700, and in Bishop Laval after he had left episcopal office. Both had played formative roles in establishing the country's religious institutions, and neither welcomed the changes they observed. In her advanced years Bourgeoys, who would be canonized in 1984, indicted her community for abandoning the simple life and strict rule of the early days, entrenching class divisions, and indulging in such comforts as mattresses. Laval, saddened by Saint-Vallier's destruction of his grand design, gave away all his property and devoted himself to prayer, mediation, charity, and his seminary until his death in 1705. At his funeral people pressed prayer books and chaplets to his body; others stole bits of his clothing as relics. Bishop Saint-Vallier, for his part, continued to embody the rigorous ideals of an earlier time until his death in 1727, but royal and clerical opposition combined with the vicissitudes of war to keep him away from Canada for sixteen years of his episcopacy (1687–8, 1691–7, 1704–13). Until the appointment in 1741 of the last bishop of Quebec during the French regime, Henri-Marie Dubreil de Pontbriand, his successors made little impact on religious life because they were either unwilling to go to Canada in the first place or were absent in France.

The spectacular fertility rates in both Acadia and New France beginning in the latter half of the seventeenth century caused an expansion in the population with which the church could not keep pace. After 1700 the ranks of the male clergy, which had increased by a factor of five in the previous half-century, declined slightly and then stagnated. The principal causes were a drop in ordinations and declining interest in the colony on the part of France as the expanding sugar-and-rum economy of the West Indies outstripped Canadian enterprises apart from the fishery. Having assumed responsibility for missions in Santo Domingo and Martinique, as well as Istanbul and China, the French Jesuits augmented their ranks in Canada with Belgians. But the deficit continued, and Canadian-born priests were not able to make up the difference, although their presence did grow among the secular clergy from 15 per cent in 1700 to 46 per cent in 1755. Even so, the priest-to-people ratio diminished from 1:18 in 1635–40 to 1:184 by 1760. Despite its imposing presence, the Roman Catholic Church remained a mission institution dependent on material support and priests from overseas.

Just as serious as the shortage of priests was their uneven distribution within the diocese. Both Quebec and Acadia were predominantly agricultural societies in which incomes were sometimes supplemented by seasonal employment in the fur trade. Yet despite the preponderance of the rural population, most of the clergy served in the towns or in missions; in 1712, only 46 priests (36 per cent) were ministering in the countryside. The towns were equipped with an impressive array of religious institutions, but the outlying settlements, with three-quarters of the population, saw priests only rarely. By 1713 the priest-to-people ratio in urban areas stood at 1:83; elsewhere the ratio was 1:289. This problem was not new. 'Three-quarters of the inhabitants of Canada do not hear mass four times a year [and] often die without sacraments', wrote the intendant Jacques de Meulles in 1683. 'They are no more educated in our religion than the Indians.'[71] Although the numbers of priests grew over time, in rural areas the proportions of priests to people (1:464 in 1754) remained low by French standards, and 41 per cent of the male clergy were still based in urban centres. The situation in Acadia was much the same. There too the population was highly mobile, and priests were scarce. Even a seasoned veteran like François-Marie Perrot, who became governor of the region in 1684, had characterized Acadian life as 'dissolute, libertine, and vagabond'. Not only did Acadians tend to move away from settlements to escape regulation by authorities,[72] but clerical resources were unable to match the growth in their numbers, to some ten thousand by 1755. Few Acadians assumed a religious vocation; only a dozen have been found among the clerical ranks during the French regime, and eight of those were nuns.

Although Saint-Vallier had created more parishes and appointed more resident parish priests than Laval, their numbers were still too few to give parochial organizations the important place in social and religious life that they would later acquire. Episcopal authority had been extended in 1699, when Saint-Vallier secured a government decree according to the bishop, rather than the seigneurs, the right to locate and build churches, but no significant effort was made to establish parish boundaries until the governor and intendant decided to do so in the 1720s. Many rural churches were so inconveniently located that people found access difficult, and by the 1730s four-fifths of the one hundred parishes in the Quebec colony still did not have resident priests.[73] The absence of clergy suited many who were not eager to pay the tithe that supported them; however, even parishes that were visited only infrequently could not always avoid paying this tax. Contentious from the moment it was introduced by royal letters patent in 1663, the payment was reduced in 1667 from one-thirteenth of the fruits of human labour and production from the soil to one twenty-sixth of the grain harvests, but it would continue to cause disputes long after the end of the French regime. Clerics complained that the amount was too low and that people cheated in their calculations. While the government supervised and enforced payment when necessary, it also censured priests who attempted to increase the rate.

Most of what we know about local religious life during the French regime derives from church-owned seigneuries or the towns. Parish councils elected church wardens to conduct financial business, but many merely signed the annual accounts, leaving the direction of parish affairs to their priests. Geographical dispersion along the St Lawrence and other waterways created distances that made it difficult for many people to avail themselves of religious services, although parish priests commanded great moral authority because they knew so many families and were among the few who were able to read and write. In 1743 parishioners in the Jesuit-owned seigneury of La Prairie even thought that the vicar-general would send their parish priest the powers necessary to get rid of the grasshoppers that ravaged crops that year. The towns presented a contrasting picture. Social prestige was attached to the rental of pews that were reserved for the wealthy and passed between the generations through the payment of a mutation fee. Together, pew rentals and burial fees brought in more revenue than Sunday collections and the special donations in honour of the Infant Jesus received during the Christmas season.[74] Thus a relatively small number of people accounted for the bulk of the church's local revenues, and by the end of the French regime, half of the colony's parishes were still not self-supporting.

The availability of church-run medical, social, and educational services was similarly limited in rural areas. However, by 1700 an impressive array of facilities had been established in the major towns. In the near-total absence of professional physicians—New France had only four between 1608 and 1760—the hospitals run by the Augustinians in the town of Quebec and the Hospitalières de Saint-Joseph in Montreal were important sources of medical care. And while the state-sponsored poor boards withered, the hospices run by the Frères Charon in Montreal and the sisters of the Hôpital-Général in Quebec served an essential function in providing shelter for those unable, for whatever reason, to support themselves.

A major part of the church's attention was devoted to education. The Frères Charon and the Congrégation de Notre-Dame instructed children in Montreal and its environs, but the nuns extended farther afield, sending representatives to the Maritimes as well. Both the Récollets and the Ursulines ran schools in Trois-Rivières, while the Ursulines' mother house in Quebec operated a combination boarding- and day-school. Although it appears to have attracted principally the offspring of the nobility, business people, and artisans, it continued to enrol native girls up to 1725—much longer than any other school. The Sulpicians in Montreal and the Jesuits in Quebec also operated elementary schools at various times, and the Petit Séminaire de Québec, which served primarily as a boarding-school, accepted many charity cases. The intellectual standards at the Collège des Jésuites in Quebec, the highest in the colony, were reputed by historian Pierre-François de Charlevoix to be comparable to those of its provincial counterparts in France early in the eighteenth century. The Grand Séminaire de Québec accepted all boys regardless of social background, but fewer than one-quarter of the eight hundred and fifty students enrolled during the French regime stayed long enough to graduate, and only about half of those became priests.[75]

Education revealed more fully than any other area the fundamental problems that church institutions faced as the population grew. The rapid drop in literacy rates in both New France and Acadia during the eighteenth century suggests that immigration almost inevitably meant mortgaging the literacy of the next generation. The ability to read and write declined so severely in Acadia that by 1745 no bride or groom at Port-Royal was able to sign the marriage register (the standard means by which historians measure these skills).[76] Similar, if slightly less dramatic, trends in Quebec made that region backward in comparison with most of the British colonies to the south. New England was exceptional in the emphasis it placed on education, but literacy rates in Canada were low in comparison even with those in Pennsylvania and southern Appalachia. So few parishes in the St Lawrence valley expressed any interest in education that by the end of the French regime there were still only twenty elementary schools in Quebec, half of them in the towns. Of the rural residents who constituted three-quarters of the population, only one-tenth were literate. These inadequacies stemmed from the rapidly increasing population, insufficient resources, and the class orientation of many religiously-based educational institutions, which often charged fees. While literacy rates in the French colonial towns were comparable to those in France, the Canadiens as a whole were less well-educated than most of their counterparts in the mother country.

Whereas male vocations stagnated after 1700, the numbers of women in religious life continued to grow. In 1715, when its total population was only fifteen hundred, Montreal counted one hundred women in religious orders. Female orders expanded by 2.3 per cent annually during the first quarter of the eighteenth century; by 1725 there were over 260 nuns in New France as a whole, almost all of them born in Canada, belonging to either the secular Congrégation de Notre-Dame or one of the cloistered orders: the Hospitalières de Saint-Joseph in Montreal, the Augustinian Hospitalières de la Miséricorde de Jésus and the Sisters of the Hôpital-Général, both in Quebec, and the Ursulines in Quebec and Trois-Rivières.[77]

Class distinctions between these communities mirrored the hierarchical structures both of the Catholic Church itself and of society at large. Whereas the nuns of the Hôpital-Général drew their members from the upper echelons of Quebec society, the Augustinians of the Hôtel-Dieu relied largely on young women from rural areas, and the Congrégation de Notre-Dame recruited from a broader social spectrum. Among the cloistered orders internal organization also reflected class distinctions. While choir nuns, who devoted themselves to religious duties, tended to come from notable families, plain sisters came from a lower level on the social scale; to them were imparted life's drudgeries, duties they shared with servants and slaves.

The largest community was the Congrégation de Notre-Dame, a secular teaching order that served not only Montreal but outlying and remote parishes as well. Its Providence houses offered a few scholarships for charity cases, but, as in the schools run by male religious, most students had to pay fees. Although the education that the Sisters offered young women was still narrowly defined—religion, reading, writing, and domestic skills formed the core of elementary instruction—the few who mastered French and Latin might advance to study arithmetic. That literacy rates for women in some parts of

New France were higher than those in the mother country attests to the Sisters' success in teaching basic skills.[78]

The Ursulines too were dedicated primarily to education, but all the other communities devoted themselves to caring for the sick and needy. Medical work was the most arduous, and nuns engaged in it tended to die younger than others. Hospitals were not necessarily houses of death (90 per cent of those treated at Quebec's Hôtel-Dieu during the French regime were later released), but those who could afford to pay a physician or surgeon generally avoided such institutions. Hence the nuns' ministry was directed principally towards the poor and members of the military. Regarding their work as offering a path to salvation through emulation of Christ, hospital nuns ministered to the soul as well as the body, counselling their patients on the need to confess, take the sacraments, and die in the faith and the love of Christ. Religious instruction was offered daily, and mass was said regularly in hospital chapels.[79]

In addition to opportunities for education and work, religious life offered a degree of self-direction that was not otherwise available to most women. But the autonomy of female communities was far from complete. Although Christianity posited the spiritual equality of all people, for centuries it had assigned women to an inferior station in life—a station exemplified by the image of Mary as little more than Joseph's demure companion. In the seventeenth century, as the number of women religious expanded during the Counter Reformation and many more women became nuns, a subtle shift in symbolism occurred: Mary came to be portrayed as the embodiment of virginal purity, in stark contrast to the increasingly popular figure of Mary Magdalene.[80] Together, these powerful symbols—the virgin and the repentant whore—created the diptych within which the patriarchal church sought to confine all women, lay and religious alike. All female communities accepted the spiritual direction of a priest, and the Council of Trent had strengthened the church's control by placing them under the watchful eyes of local bishops, rather than permitting them to group houses together under a superior general. It had also demanded enclosure for all women's orders. However, the expansion of women's communities that began with the Counter Reformation was most rapid among secular nuns, who remained uncloistered and took vows that the church considered simple rather than solemn. These distinctions subverted the intention of the Council of Trent but allowed increasing numbers of women to assume a religious life.

With this flowering of female vocations, some male clerics became anxious to contain women's activities lest they threaten male powers and prerogatives.[81] Thus the Sulpician superior François Dollier de Casson opposed the old French customs of allowing women to distribute bread that had been blessed and to take up the collection during services; Bishop Laval curbed sung services among the Ursulines (he believed that singing contributed to vanity in women), tried to change their constitution and make them a more contemplative order, and denied canonical recognition to the secular Congrégation de Notre-Dame; and Bishop Saint-Vallier, in addition to meddling with the Augustinians' elections, not only tried to enclose the Congrégation, but obliged them to accept the dowry system that had previously been restricted to cloistered communities.

Such interference notwithstanding, the women's religious orders did establish a measure of autonomy within the church, in the process eroding the long-standing view that virtue could be associated with men alone. Their right to catechize had been accepted since the first nuns arrived in New France, even though it was still questioned in the mother country.[82] On occasion, they united in the face of external pressures or used divisions among ecclesiastical authorities to their advantage. The Ursulines managed to stymie Laval's proposed changes to their constitution through their own resolve and the diplomacy of Marie de l'Incarnation. And when Saint-Vallier tried to enclose the Congrégation, the nuns enlisted the support of the Sulpicians in Montreal and Paris to quash his initiative. Finally, the state both at home and abroad provided other avenues that women's communities were sometimes able to pursue. When Laval denied recognition to the Congrégation, for example, in an effort to unite them with the Ursulines, Marguerite Bourgeoys travelled to France and obtained royal letters patent for her order in 1671.

In fact, while church and state in New France had been closely identified from the beginning, the state increasingly became the dominant partner in the relationship. The subordination of institutional religion to government reflected the 'divine right' of the absolute monarch. Ecclesiastics might reign in matters of Christian faith, but the king, as yet unimpeded by doctrines of natural rights, enjoyed ultimate authority over the realm. The Gallican liberties, which had given the French church a large measure of control over its internal affairs, outside Rome's direct purview, fostered an even closer identification between church and state as the king nominated candidates for vacant ecclesiastical offices, and papal decrees had to be registered within the country before they were legally enforceable. At the same time, Catholicism supported monarchical government through its moral teachings, although the intendant and other officers of the colonial commissariat bore the legal responsibility for public order. Obedience to authority, both civil and religious, was thought to be the principal virtue holding society's thin tissue together and preventing anarchy.

The church served the interests of the state by acting as an agent of colonization, an instrument of governance, and a source of conservative social values. Having learned from the Fénelon affair in 1674, clerics always spoke in favour of authority, even though they were sometimes placed in awkward positions. In 1704, during the War of the Spanish Succession, François de Vachon de Belmont found himself peering over the gates of Montreal's fortifications at an angry mob protesting the prohibitively high price of salt that was a result of hoarding. As superior of the Sulpician seminary and hence the island's seigneur, Vachon counselled prudence and then attempted to secure a more equitable distribution of salt at a lower price. Visibly shaken, he had a statement read in the churches:

> Sedition is a blind fury which, without fearing the justice of God or the King that it offends equally, nor foreseeing the fratricide it risks among co-citizens, favours the designs of our enemies and places the native land that we share in danger of losing the faith and the king's protection.[83]

'Religion should have made them remain silent,' the priest of Batiscan maintained during a trial that concerned the verbal abuse heaped on him by the seigneur Madeleine de Verchères and her husband, 'but rage, passion, overtook and blinded them.'[84] In a circular in 1742, the last bishop of Quebec during the French regime went so far as to maintain that those who passed the limits of legitimate authority were condemned to eternal damnation.

In return for its support of government, Roman Catholicism derived great benefits. Through legislation regulating public morality, for instance, government upheld the church's teachings as well as its views with respect to gender roles. Blasphemy constituted a crime punished by the state through public humilation, fines, and sometimes exile to the galley ships plying the Mediterranean. Church and state held similar ideas about the nature of society. Families, not individuals, were conceived as the basis of society, while the social orders (or estates) of the realm—among which the clergy constituted the first rank—figured more prominently than social classes. When enshrined in law, these principles placed men at the pinnacle of the family unit, restricting the freedom of male children up to the age of twenty-five and of women throughout their lives.[85] Civil marriages were not recognized, and under canon law men needed the permission of their parents to marry before the age of thirty. In accordance with the patriarchal principles of both the monarchy and the church, marital laws disadvantaged women in favour of men in the family— although not as severely as in the British possessions.

The intimate association between church and state opened the door for government to regulate minor matters of religious observance. Early in the eighteenth century, when priests proved unresponsive to popular requests, the colony's intendant ordered the church in Quebec's lower town to offer mass on Sunday mornings so that elderly people would not have to climb the hill that divided the town. Other ordinances banned dogs from services and enjoined men not to smoke at the back of the church during sermons. In 1739 the intendant Gilles Hocquart upheld the Catholic character of the colony by deporting Esther Brandeau, a young Jewish woman who had lived disguised as a boy.

In addition, government officials ensured that Protestants in the colony made no public professions of their faith. Proof of adherence to Catholicism through baptismal attestations was required for state appointments, while professions such as that of notary were closed to Protestants. As we have seen, the government also served as arbiter in the internecine disputes that too frequently divided the church.

Financial considerations weighed heavily in the intricate interplay between church and state. Every edifice in the ecclesiastical structure was subsidized from the state treasury, which by 1700 accounted for forty per cent of church revenues. By 1760 the church had acquired eight seigneuries constituting one-quarter of all the land granted by the Crown. Its buildings were among the most impressive in the colony, and it functioned as the major patron for the arts, commissioning sculptures, paintings, and music. Yet this wealth was by no means equally distributed. While the Sulpicians at Montreal and the Récollets in the Atlantic region were frequently accused of returning surplus income to France, other groups struggled to survive. Quebec's hospital and hospice showed operating deficits in most years, which the nuns managed only by borrowing.[86] By 1734 the finances of the Quebec seminary had deteriorated to the point that one-quarter of its income went to service debts. After Montreal's hospital was destroyed by fires in 1695, 1721, and 1734, the Hospitalières de Saint-Joseph suffered years of privation. All the nuns in the colony tried to supplement their incomes through handiwork and manual labour.

Nor was this close partnership with the state without hazards. While the church's wealth in the principal settlements exposed it to criticism, bishops and clergy contributed to the problem by allowing themselves to be used as instruments of state policy—most obviously, perhaps, when they held services to celebrate the birth of an heir to the throne or the victory of the king's arms in battle. Clerics were characterized as insatiable in their desire to acquire property, a situation 'very contrary to what they always preach to the people by inspiring in them a detachment from worldly possessions'.[87] State support also implied a sometimes stifling control. Royal officials ensured that clergy became neither too numerous nor too rich: religious communities were not permitted to exceed the limitations prescribed in the letters patent obtained from the king, and notaries were forbidden to transact contracts conveying property to church institutions without state permission. In 1722 a royal edict increased the dowries required from women wishing to become nuns to encourage them to marry and produce children instead (ten years later, when this regulation proved too restrictive, the amounts were lowered). State officials investigated church finances, and when they encountered opposition, the Superior Council supported their legal right to do so. In 1732, following an incident at Fort Niagara, the government even withdrew the church's customary right of providing asylum.[88]

In the part of Acadia ruled by Britain, the church's relations with the civil power assumed a different character. Escalating international tensions intensified the Roman Catholic clergy's identification with France. But diocesan officials soon learned to cope with their alien rulers, and clerics came to play increasingly important roles as politicians and diplomats when the British tried to force the Acadians to swear an oath of allegiance. Among the mediators were Fathers Noël-Alexandre de Noinville and Charles de La Goudalie, who in 1730 negotiated an agreement whereby the Acadians swore to remain neutral in conflicts between France and England. A few priests, however, following the warrior-missionary tradition established by Thury in Acadia in the late seventeenth century, encouraged the native people to fight the British. Although they themselves did not take up arms, both Sébastien Rale, a Jesuit ministering to the Abenaki, and Jean-Louis Le Loutre, a Spiritan missionary who actively incited the Micmac to oppose the British, had prices put on their heads; Le Loutre spoke of his own single-minded devotion to saving the 'many souls entrusted to his care . . . who would have been inevitably perverted if the English had been able to win them.'[89] Other missionaries including Antoine Gaulin and Pierre Maillard identified no less passionately with their country's cause, but adopted a more moderate course. Priests tried to restrain the use of torture; they also ransomed prisoners who were then returned to the British, and paid the bounty on scalps (for which they were reimbursed by French authorities).

In addition to using missionaries to extend its influence among the native people of Acadia, France provided financial aid to establish religious institutions in areas of recent settlement such as Île Royale. Three sisters from Montreal's Congrégation de Notre-Dame, who opened a girls' school in Louisbourg in 1727, did not manage to obtain such favour until 1754. But subsidies were given to the Récollets based in Louisbourg, who served as parish priests and garrison chaplains, and to the Frères de la Charité de l'Ordre de Saint-Jean de Dieu, who operated the one-hundred-bed royal hospital. Neither the dedication of Louisbourg's male clergy nor its inhabitants' zeal for religion matched this government support. No parish church was ever constructed—services were held in chapels—and there were even fewer priests per capita than in rural Quebec. As a tithe was not imposed, voluntary donations of fish emerged as the standard form of lay support for the clergy, but such gifts often became the subject of dispute (as they did with the Anglican clergy in Newfoundland). Fishermen worked on Sundays and taverns served as the primary social centres for working people, while the private libraries of the upper classes typically contained more secular than religious volumes.[90]

This laxity in religious observance was perhaps not surprising, given Acadia's chronic shortage of priests. Yet after 1700 even New France began to witness a decline in the church's influence that reflected developments in

Europe. While historians of eighteenth-century France have spoken of de-Christianization and laicization, perhaps 'secularization' better describes the subtle shift in emphasis that was now occurring. Since the latter part of the seventeenth century, European intellectuals had been seeking to devise a political system without divine sanction, a religion without mystery, and a morality without dogma.[91] As such thinkers struggled to place humanity rather than God at the centre of rational explanation, religious or supernatural interpretations were gradually supplanted in some quarters by scientific ones. These trends were reflected in the writings of Baron Lahontan and Thomas Pichon, two Frenchmen whose accounts of New France and Acadia, respectively, were so scandalous in their pre-Enlightenment anti-clericalism and scepticism of religion that they had to be published outside France.[92] Deriding Catholic belief in original sin and the incarnation, Lahontan also prefigured Jean-Jacques Rousseau in portraying the 'noble savages' as living in a egalitarian state of nature uncorrupted by the vicious self-interest and ambition rampant among Europeans.

The force of increasing secularism was evident early in the eighteenth century. The state began to extend its purview in a number of areas during the War of the Spanish Succession (1702–13), but there was no corresponding expansion in the church's role. When, in 1706, the intendant assumed responsibility for abandoned children, the state entered the arena of social welfare previously left exclusively to the church. Government also assumed a more interventionist role in regulating the wheat trade and resisting the movement of rural people to the towns when harvests failed, notably in 1737–8 and 1742–4. Although the bishop seconded these efforts through a public pronouncement in 1742, the government could not rely on the church's moral authority to ensure compliance, and in the end it used troops to commandeer grain. Far fewer confraternities were established than in the previous century, and enrolments fell off greatly in relation to the growing population. That fewer cases involving blasphemy reached the courts in New France suggests that offences of this nature were now considered less serious; yet beginning in 1723, petty criminals guilty of such minor crimes as salt-smuggling were deported from France to Quebec and Louisbourg. Inventories of estates taken after death in Montreal, Quebec, and Louisbourg showed that few people possessed religious objects or books. Charitable bequests declined as those directed for the celebration of masses increased,[93] while voluntary donations in Quebec and Montreal parishes were no higher by the end of the French regime than at the close of the previous century, despite inflation and population growth. Artisans' apprenticeship contracts rarely mentioned religious duties or provisions for observance of Sundays and religious holidays.

The perennial shortage of priests meant that more and more people were being raised outside religious parameters. The numbers of premarital sexual

liaisons increased,[94] and the times at which people married came to be determined largely by seasonal patterns of life rather than the church calendar. The
church's prohibitions on sexual intercourse during Lent were not observed,
while Mardi Gras became the social high point of the year. Taverns emerged as
the hubs of many communities. In neither Atlantic Canada nor the St
Lawrence valley were authorities able to enforce regulations requiring drinking
establishments to close during the hours of religious services on Sundays and
holidays. When priests preached against dancing and gambling, many people
turned a deaf ear despite sanctions including ostracism from confraternities.
Even specifically religious occasions, such as local celebrations of a church's
patron saint, came to be characterized by excessive imbibing and other activities upon which the clergy frowned. In the 1720s, two cousins wishing to
marry in Louisbourg maintained that they did not need church dispensation
because they lived 'among infidels and barbarians and ignorant Catholics with
little instruction in Religion'.[95] Equally tellingly, a second earthquake in the St
Lawrence valley in 1732 was not accompanied by the supernatural interpretations seen in the previous century, although church congregations continued to
swell with wavering believers whenever war or natural disasters threatened.

Even among the clergy, the high standards of the previous century were
beginning to erode. Education for the priesthood deteriorated as the teaching
ranks at the Collège des Jésuites came to be filled by men with few accomplishments, many of them exhausted missionaries. Not many Canadiens
joined the Sulpicians, and none of the three known to have been admitted to
the Society of Jesus returned to the colony. Instruction in theology at the
Grand Séminaire de Québec paid too much attention to externals, such as the
administration of the sacraments, and too little to intellectual development.
Pedagogy was interpreted as memorization and repetition. 'You are inflicting
on this Church a serious wound that may have difficulty healing,' the seminary's Paris affiliates wrote colleagues in Quebec in 1704, 'in raising to the
priesthood so many youth who have only a smattering of theology. Such
dunces will not do a great deal of good and are at risk of doing a lot of damage.'[96] Communal life at the seminary withered as well: income was no longer
held in common, and priests took their meals in town. After the boarding-
school at the Collège des Jésuites closed, the Petit Séminaire accepted scholars
who had no intention of entering holy orders, and in 1706 Bishop Saint-Vallier
charged that the school was preparing boys for everything except the priesthood, training those aged ten years and above 'to be carpenters, sculptors,
organists, etc., but not for studying'.[97] Rural priests, who used to visit the seminary now and then for spiritual replenishment, were no longer welcomed
because the seminary's directors considered them a bad influence on students.
In addition, antagonisms developed between the Quebec institution and its
affiliate, the Séminaire des Missions Etrangères in Paris, over the appointment

of Canadiens to positions of responsibility. Although the Parisians expressed willingness to appoint colonials, they worried that Quebec's priests might become a burden because of their limited wealth, and as a result the direction of the colonial seminary remained in French hands.

Decline was evident in other segments of the clergy as well. When nuns from the Hôpital-Général de Québec began escaping cloister to attend dinner parties, some among their number were so disturbed that they approached the bishop, who denounced such conduct and threatened to reduce the size of the community. Much of the humble physical labour that in Marguerite Bourgeoys's time had been performed by nuns was now given to servants. Marie Barbier, the successor to Bourgeoys as superior of the Congrégation de Notre-Dame, contrasted the conditions she had known as a novice, beginning in 1679, with those prevailing near the end of her life, some sixty years later. 'I cannot understand how, being young and weak as I was,' Barbier wrote, 'I could have undertaken all the work that I did. I had the care of two cows that I milked and made butter from. . . . I carried wheat to the mill on my shoulders and brought back flour the same way.'[98]

Episcopal authority managed to contain the occasional alcoholic priest or womanizer, but the Récollets at Louisbourg presented a larger problem. Ecclesiastics repeatedly reproached this order, whose members after 1730 were drawn exclusively from the province of Brittany, for lax religious conduct and loose morals. In 1726 Bishop Saint-Vallier's plan to reform Récollet practices ran into trouble when the secular priest he sent to Louisbourg unceremoniously deposed his predecessor at a Sunday service. The local outcry that resulted, together with the shortage of priests, ensured that the Récollets were allowed to remain, but priests from outside the order were often appointed to serve as their superiors. In the face of new realities, the ideal of unbending adherence to strict moral standards gradually became more accommodating. Thus when a superior of the Quebec seminary died in 1747, he was eulogized as having been 'sweet and affable with a lively and discerning mind, [with] great judgement and a similar prudence that always made him equable and steady'.[99] Apart from occasional clerical condemnation of social mores, the moral rigour that had characterized the seventeenth century was almost extinct.

Paralleling contemporary trends in South America and France, only one new religious order was established in Quebec during the first half of the eighteenth century. In 1737 Marguerite Dufrost de Lajemmerais, the wealthy widow of François-Madeleine d'Youville, and three companions in Montreal founded a lay association devoted to serving the poor. The following year they secured a house large enough to live in communally and to take in unfortunates, but their enterprise was challenged when two brothers-in-law of d'Youville joined other townspeople in signing a petition against the Sulpicians' alleged plan to put the women in charge of Montreal's hospice, in the place of the Frères Charon. Rumours spread about their conduct, and some, remembering the d'Youville family's association with the brandy trade, called them *les grises*: tipsy women. Family squabbles and religious rivalries were the source of these aspersions, but they also reflected public scepticism about the respectability of women who would abandon their middle-class comforts to take on more prominent roles, however selfless. Undeterred even by a fire that destroyed their house in 1745, d'Youville and four associates formalized their relationship. In a deed written later that year they professed their desire 'to quit the world and renounce all that we own', declaring their purpose to be directed 'to the greater glory of God, for the salvation of our souls and the relief of the poor'.[100] Marguerite d'Youville negotiated adroitly through complicated legal and political proceedings to assume responsibility in 1747 for the Montreal hospice, which following the death of François Charon, in 1719, had ceased to provide adequate care. Receiving royal acknowledgement in 1753, the Sisters became the Soeurs de la Charité de l'Hôpital-Général de Montréal. However, playing on the other meaning of their sobriquet, they adopted a grey habit, and in time became popularly known as the Soeurs grises, or Grey Nuns.[101]

Soon after the formal establishment of the Grey Nuns, New France became embroiled in the international conflict that brought its end. Indeed, even before the Seven Years' War began in Europe, fighting had erupted in the Ohio valley and Acadia, and in 1755 the British government in Nova Scotia had begun deporting the Acadians to its colonies. Attempting to escape, many sought refuge in the remaining French possessions of Île Saint-Jean and Île Royale; others ended up as refugees in the French West Indies or the ports of France. Although the fighting initially went well for New France, after the formal declaration of war in 1756, British arms swept from Louisbourg in 1758 to Quebec the next year, and finally proved triumphant with the fall of Montreal in 1760.

The Roman Catholic Church faced these momentous events with grave uncertainty. On the most immediate level, it had sustained serious material losses in the war as many of its buildings were damaged or destroyed. It also had good reason to fear the victors' reaction to the fact that a small minority of priests (about ten per cent) had played active roles in the conflict; and although most participation had been limited to providing intelligence, the Sulpician missionary François Picquet had gone so far as to lead Iroquois warriors in the battle that the French won at Carillon (Ticonderoga, NY) in 1758. The broader picture was no more encouraging. The church could not fail to realize that religious fervour had disappeared in many quarters, along with hopes for the evangelization of all North America's peoples. Natives were not formally prohibited from joining the priesthood (as they had been in South America since 1555), and female religious orders included a number of native women: Geneviève Skandudharoua was accepted as a full member by Quebec's Hôtel-

Dieu, as were Marie-Barbe Atontinon and Marie-Thérèse Gannensagouas by Montreal's Congrégation de Notre-Dame. Nevertheless, the absence of even a single indigenous male clergyman remained a telling indictment of cultural chauvinism and residual racism, and while women had gained new importance in religious life generally, they had not seriously challenged the prevailing patriarchy. Nor had the church as a whole outgrown its dependence on France for money and personnel. Although most of the women in religious orders were Canadian-born, as were the graduates of the Séminaire de Québec who predominated in the secular priesthood, the majority of priests and brothers were of European origin.

The British adhered to the same principles of the confessional state that had characterized the French regime. Fortunately, however, through their long involvement with Acadia, Roman Catholic officials had developed the diplomatic skills required to save the heart of their church. Counselling moderation to all who came in contact with the new rulers, Bishop de Pontbriand wrote to the first British governor in 1759 that he intended to conduct himself as did 'all bishops whose dioceses reside under two sovereigns, and if some of the clergy deviate from these principles, I will be the first to remedy it.'[102] Such prudence permitted the close association of church and state to continue, with the British military respecting church property and personnel. The generals also granted free exercise of religion, although when Montreal capitulated in 1760, guarantees were not provided to the male religious orders. Whether the British government would affirm this limited tolerance, or whether Roman Catholics in Canada would suffer from the same liabilities imposed on those in Nova Scotia and Newfoundland, remained to be seen.

Opposite: MISSIONS IN NEW FRANCE

SOURCES: Adapted from W.C. Sturtevant and W.E. Washburn, eds, *Handbook of North American Indians IV* (Washington, D.C.: Smithsonian Institution, 1988), 466; J. Axtell, *The Invasion Within: The Contest of Cultures in Colonial North America* (New York: Oxford University Press, 1985), 63.

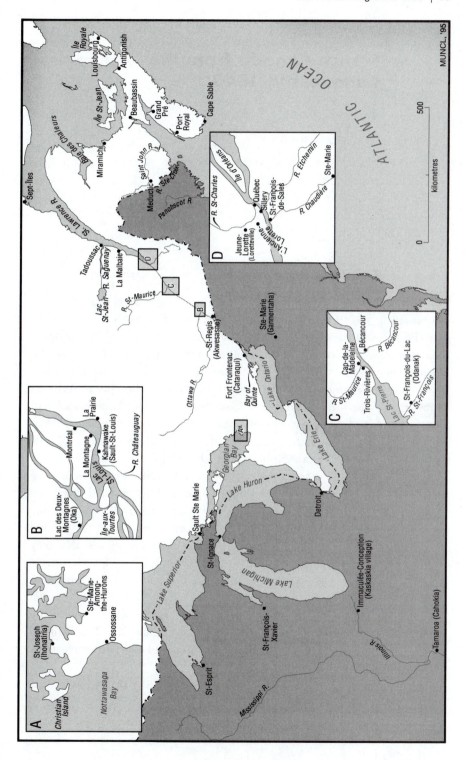

MUNCL, '95

ATLANTIC OCEAN

Île Royale
Louisbourg
Antigonish
Beaubassin
Île St-Jean
Grand Pré
Port-Royal
Cape Sable
Miramichi
Baie des Chaleurs
Saint John R.
Sept-Îles
St. Lawrence R.
R. Ste-Croix
Meductic
Penobscot R.
Tadoussac
La Malbaie
R. Saguenay
Lac St-Jean
R. St-Jean
R. St-Maurice

D
R. St-Charles
Île d'Orléans
Québec
Sillery
St-François-de-Salès
R. Etchemin
Ste-Marie
R. Chaudière
Jeune-Lorette (Loretteville)
L'Ancienne-Lorette

C
St-Régis (Akwesasne)
Ste-Marie (Gannentaha)
Fort Frontenac (Cataraqui)
Bay of Quinte
Lake Ontario
Ottawa R.

B
Montréal
La Prairie
La Montagne
Kahnawake (Sault-St-Louis)
R. Châteauguay
Lac des Deux-Montagnes (Oka)
Lac St-Louis
Île-aux-Tourtes

C
Cap-de-la-Madeleine
Bécancour
R. Bécancour
Trois-Rivières
R. St-Maurice
Lac St-Pierre
St-François-du-Lac (Odanak)
R. St-François

A
Georgian Bay
Lake Huron
Sault Ste Marie
Lake Superior
St-Ignace
Detroit
Lake Erie
Lake Michigan
Immaculée-Conception (Kaskaskia village)
St-François-Xavier
St-Esprit
Tamaroa (Cahokia)
Illinois R.
Mississippi R.

A
Christian Island
St-Joseph (Ihonatiria)
Ste-Marie-Among-the-Hurons
Ossossane
Nottawasaga Bay

kilometres
0   500

Two

French Canada from the
Conquest to 1840*

GILLES CHAUSSÉ

THE CONQUEST AND ITS AFTERMATH

The Seven Years War, which brought France and England into conflict beginning in 1756, spilled over into North America. In fact, the rivalry between
New France and the thirteen colonies was just as intense as that between
their mother countries in Europe. Peaceful coexistence was hardly possible
between two colonies that shared the same dreams of expansion and development. Bitter enemies since the failed attack on Quebec by Sir William
Phips in the previous century, the Canadiens and the 'Bostonians' had
already begun to fight two years earlier, in 1754. Following an unequal struggle, the French and Canadien troops were defeated on 13 September 1759, at
the Battle of the Plains of Abraham, and Montreal fell a year later, on 18
September 1760. From then on the two main cities of New France were occupied by British troops, until the end of hostilities in Europe could determine
the colony's fate. Canada was lost and its people humbled. 'If you could see
the poor people,' wrote Louis-Joseph Godefroy de Tonnancour, 'they would
bring you to tears. Could the Canadiens possibly have imagined that they
would be abandoned and delivered to their enemies? . . . we are utterly
ruined.'[1] The future was uncertain for the 70,000 people of New France,[2] for
whom the memory of the Acadians' deportation, five years earlier, was still
fresh. Indeed, in 1756 the bishop of Quebec, Henri-Marie Dubreil de
Pontbriand, had warned of the dangers the colony would face if the English
were to win the war: 'Their treatment of the people of Acadia foretells what
we have to fear.'[3]

Much to the surprise of the Canadiens, however, the British authorities
treated them with benevolence and consideration, for the new governor of

* Translated by James MacLean

Quebec, General James Murray, realized that in this way he could earn their respect: 'The Canadiens have been taught to look upon [us] as barbarians whose only view was their destruction; hence the obstinate resistance they have made, and the eagerness they shewed to take up arms against us. They begin now to be astonished with our conduct, [and] will soon be convinced that there was no deceit in it . . .'[4] With London's approval, this astute policy would be followed until the signing of the Treaty of Paris in 1763 formalized the definitive transfer of New France to the British Empire.

The treaty that was signed in Paris on 10 February 1763, ending the Seven Years War, did more than close a chapter in Canada's history: as the historian Guy Frégault has written: 'After the battle for Quebec a book was closed. History did not go on, it started anew.'[5] The Canadiens had lost everything: the war, their homeland, their ties with their mother country, and their military, economic, and political leaders. Before long, when the Royal Proclamation of 7 October 1763 set up the administration of the new territories, their country would be known as the 'Province of Quebec'. Responses ranged from resignation to the deepest sorrow. 'The peace we wished for for so long, but that has been made under conditions so contrary to our wishes,' wrote the Ursulines of Quebec, 'has brought us unspeakable distress.'[6] The Récollet Théodore wept bitter tears as he sang the *Te Deum* ordered by the grand vicar of Quebec, Jean-Olivier Briand, after the signing of the Treaty.[7] Henri-François Gravé de la Rive, one of the directors of the Séminaire de Quebec, summarized the general feeling: 'How sad we are.'[8] Yet in the midst of this collective ordeal there remained one consolation and hope: the Canadiens had not lost their religious leaders. In future they would look to these leaders and cling to their church with fierce determination.

However, that institution itself was in an extremely precarious situation. Within five years the numbers of male clergy had shrunk from 196 secular and religious priests in 1759 to 137 by the end of 1764, or one priest for every 500 Catholics, compared to one for every 350 in 1759. Of the 59 lost, 39 had died, while another 20—all but two of them French—had left, either by choice or by force, for France. The consequences for the missionary enterprise were particularly serious: the vast Illinois region was left with only three priests, the Great Lakes region with only two, and in Acadia not a single missionary remained after the death in 1762 of Abbé Pierre Maillard. The only source of comfort for the church in Canada was the relatively low average age—46.3 years—of its priests, of whom 56 per cent were Canadian-born.[9]

In addition to losing a third of its priests, the church had suffered a serious blow with the death of Bishop de Pontbriand on 8 June 1760. This was an irreparable loss, especially since no priest was now allowed to come from France. Governor Murray had been explicit on this point, informing the superior of the Sulpicians 'that he would never tolerate any French priest coming to

Canada as long as he was governor.'[10] Moreover, the British authorities had forbidden both the Jesuits—whom Murray particularly distrusted, regarding them as ill-humoured schemers—and the Récollets to accept any new members. This measure meant the definitive closing of the country's only *collège classique*, the Collège des Jesuites, which had already been converted into military stores in October 1759. It also meant that these two religious communities, which in 1764 had 16 and 22 members respectively, were doomed in time to disappear.[11] On the other hand, the Sulpicians, the seigneurs of the island of Montreal since 1663, were tolerated until such time as London could determine the validity of their property rights.

Only the communities of religious women, which at the end of 1760 had more than two hundred members, were treated leniently by the British authorities. There were five such communities: the Hospitalières of the Hôtel-Dieu in Montreal (26 members); the Grey Nuns of the Hôpital-Général in Montreal (15); the Hospitalières of the Hôtel-Dieu (26) and the Hôpital-Général in Quebec City (22); the Ursulines in Quebec (30) and Trois-Rivières (15); and the Sisters of the Congrégation de Notre-Dame in Montreal and rural areas (70). That these communities were left undisturbed can probably be explained by the essential nature of the services they delivered to the population, especially in the field of health care. They were, of course, subject to requisition, as in the case of Quebec's Hôtel-Dieu, which was reserved almost exclusively for the use of the English until 1784, and Ursuline convent, which was converted into a courthouse in 1763. Nevertheless, these arrangements allowed the communities to survive, since the English paid generously for the services they provided.

With respect to material conditions, the church had suffered greatly from the ravages of the war. More than 30 of the 140 churches in the St Lawrence valley had been destroyed or damaged, and 16 of 110 presbyteries burnt down.[12] In addition, the church was now deprived of the 8,000 pounds that the King of France had paid annually to the Quebec chapter, as well as the 5,000 to 6,000 pounds of revenue that used to come each year from the Abbey of Maubec in France and from several priories.[13] These losses were considerable, representing more than half of the church's annual income.

The institution's legal status was no more enviable. Having lost the support of the state, the church was entering a new phase in which the religion of the majority was not that of the ruling élite. Although Article IV of the Treaty of Paris granted freedom of religion in the colony, it included the restrictive clause 'as far as the laws of Great Britain permit'. In fact, Catholicism was not an authorized religion in Great Britain in the eighteenth century, and even if the militant anti-Catholicism of the Elizabethan era was past, Catholics did not enjoy the same rights as other citizens. Futhermore, the instructions received by Governor Murray on 13 August 1763 and 7 December 1763 took care to specify that these laws prohibited 'absolutely all Popish Hierarchy in any of the Dominions belonging to the Crown of Great Britain' and could 'only admit of a Toleration of the Exercise of that Religion'. Murray himself was to 'watch the Priests very narrowly' and to deport any who attempted to move outside their proper domain and involve themselves in civil matters. The governor was also to work towards the establishment of the Church of England 'in both principle and practice', and to persuade the Canadiens 'to embrace the Protestant religion, and to raise their children in it.'[14] Applied literally, these instructions could only put the survival of the Canadian Catholic Church in jeopardy. At best tolerated with suspicion, and with very little room to manoeuvre, it was indeed 'a Church under the iron rule of the conqueror'.[15]

Under these circumstances, Catholic leaders were determined to do everything possible to please the governor and win the favour of the British authorities. The outcome of the mission undertaken by Étienne Charest, seigneur de Lauzon, in October 1763 would be a sharp reminder of the situation. When he was entrusted with the task of going to London to defend the Sulpician Étienne Montgolfier, who in September 1763 had been elected by the Quebec chapter to succeed Bishop Pontbriand, Charest met with no success. The British authorities were not moved even when Montgolfier himself travelled to London in February 1764. His appointment was opposed by Governor Murray, who considered him haughty and imperious.[16] The future bishop of Quebec could be selected only with Murray's agreement, and the only candidate he would accept was Jean-Olivier Briand.

Dean of the Quebec chapter in the absence of Canon Joseph-Marie La Corne, who had been living in France since 1750, Briand was chosen titular bishop of Quebec by his fellow priests in September 1764.[17] A level-headed man, and not overly ambitious, he enjoyed Murray's respect. The governor favoured the establishment of a national clergy, and he saw in Briand a man who had consistently conducted himself with candour and moderation;[18] in his view, no clergyman in the province was more worthy of royal favour.[19] Although Briand arrived in London in November 1764, it was not until the autumn of 1765 that he received authorization to go to France to be consecrated, and even then only on condition that the ceremony take place without any splendour or publicity. Briand had managed to overcome the opposition of the archbishop of Canterbury in particular, who was calling for the Protestant evangelization of Canada by Huguenot ministers from France. Although he had to be satisfied with the title 'Superintendant of the Romish Church', on 16 March 1766, in the chapel of the château of Suresne, just outside Paris, Briand received the episcopal anointing at the hands of the bishops of Blois, Rodez, and Saintes. The presence of a bishop was ensured; the Catholic Church in Canada had taken an important step towards ensuring its own stability and survival.

Briand's return to Quebec on 28 June 1766 was triumphant. Murray, who was leaving Canada for London the same day to defend himself against a petition of British merchants in the colony demanding his recall, was anxious to convey to the bishop the satisfaction he felt: 'I have ardently wished to take you by the hand and sincerely congratulate you on your Promotion, an event which has made me very happy, as I did every thing in my power to contribute to it both by my public letters to the Kings, Ministers, and my private solicitations to my friends. . . .'[20]

The jubilant crowd acclaimed their bishop to the sound of church bells. 'It was a touching thing', the Quebec *Gazette* wrote, 'to see [the people] expressing their joy to each other everywhere they met, and repeating over and over: So it is true, we have a bishop! God has had mercy on us.'[21] Three weeks later Bishop Briand officially took over his episcopal see in the chapel of the Séminaire de Québec, which was then serving as the cathedral. Vicar-General Joseph-François Perreault greeted the new bishop with these words: 'Our gracious Sovereign has now brought us this great comfort in giving you to us, according to our wishes. What strong love and loyalty we must have for the best of kings! But at the same time, what gratitude and devotion we must have for the Holy See, which consented to confirm our happy choice.'[22]

The Canadiens were convinced that they had won an important victory in being recognized as a distinct group; from now on religion would be a rallying point and a rampart against the absolutism of the occupying power. Turning out in great numbers to welcome the bishop, in effect they elected him their official spokesman in dealings with the British authorities. 'In acclaiming their new bishop, the head of the most powerful community organization over which they retained control,' writes the historian Michel Brunet, 'the Canadiens flaunted their Catholic faith in defiance of the Protestant conqueror, while at the same time asserting their collective will to survive.'[23] A special relationship had been formed between the Canadiens and their church, a symbol of their resistance and an affirmation of their collective identity. In the absence of their former political leaders, who had returned to France, the bishop became the people's sole representative with the British authorities. He had established himself as both a religious and a political leader.

Some historians have accused Bishop Briand of servile compliance with the English.[24] Such judgements are unfair to a man who had no personal ambition and was trying only to spare his people the unhappy fate of the Acadians a few years earlier. In agreeing to collaborate with the British authorities, he was merely following the path laid down by his predecessor, who had recommended to the clergy complete submission to established authority, even if it was English and Protestant.[25] 'Since the King of England is now, through conquest, the sovereign of Quebec,' Bishop Pontbriand had written after Wolfe's capture of Quebec, 'we owe him all the respect that the apostle Saint Paul speaks of.'[26] The same policy had been adopted by the bishops of Quebec in the case of Acadia after 1713, when the Treaty of Utrecht made this territory an English colony, and indeed Bishop Briand would reproach the Acadians in 1766 for their lack of loyalty towards the British authorities, and for having 'strayed from those wise Christian teachings' that would have spared them many hardships.[27]

The need to maintain cordial relations with the new rulers, together with Briand's own conception of church and society, made it entirely natural for him to seek the support of the state. Soon after the Treaty of Paris he had exhorted the faithful, in the name of religion, 'to carry out the duties of loyal subjects devoted to their prince'.[28] It mattered little to the bishop that the king was a Protestant: the people owed him loyalty and obedience as long as nothing contrary to their religion was required of them. Earlier Bishop Briand had written to General James Abercromby: 'I beseech you, Sir, to maintain your protection of the Church; I would almost dare to say that you must do so, just as the Church must respect you.'[29] True to this principle, Briand did not hesitate to appeal to Murray—in effect, inviting the state to act as the secular arm of the church—when in 1774 two priests, Gravé de la Rive and Joseph-André-Mathurin Jacrau, challenged his authority concerning Notre-Dame de Québec, the church that he wanted for his cathedral. Such was eighteenth-century Catholic theology, which considered civil and religious authority to be closely bound, and taught that the faithful must obey their legitimate rulers, even those who had become so through the right of conquest. It was a theology based on the teaching of the apostles Peter and Paul, whom Bishop Briand did not fail to cite when he ordered a *Te Deum* to mark the coronation of George III: 'Saint Peter, the Prince of the Apostles, orders us in his First Epistle to be subject to the king and to all who share in his authority. He stipulates that we must pay him every kind of tribute and respect. The Apostle Paul goes into even greater detail about these same duties.'[30]

In return for the protection of the church and the religious freedom of Catholics, Bishop Briand was prepared to guarantee the support of the clergy and the submission of the people. In taking this stance, he was not only ensuring the preservation of Catholicism in Canada, but 'efficiently serving the interests of the community' for which he was then the principal spokesman.[31] However, not all segments of that community approved of the bishop's actions. Among the critics was Michel Chartier de Lotbinière, a member of the Canadien nobility who may be considered one of the first champions of lay interests in French Canada after the Conquest; he judged the church and its leaders very harshly, charging them with servility and opportunism in appropriating a political role that was not properly theirs.[32] No doubt part of this reaction can be traced to the fact that he had been removed from power and deprived of some of his land by the British government without compensation.[33]

In addition, though, Chartier de Lotbinière reflected the views of a group that rejected the new post-Conquest social order. For their part, the British governors of Quebec hoped to keep the new colony in the Empire by forging an alliance with the same socially conservative forces that ruled England at the time: the church and the aristocracy. Convinced that the people would blindly follow their social betters, they vastly overestimated the bishop's influence over his flock, especially in temporal matters. The governors also incorrectly assumed that, as landholders, the seigneurs were the Canadien equivalents of the British nobility. Flattered by this attention, the seigneurs and the higher clergy fully endorsed the governors' plans to rule the colony through them and without an elected assembly. In this they were motivated both by the hope of obtaining long-term concessions in matters of religion and law and by their attachment to a conservative ideology stressing hierarchy, deference, and respect for authority. Their policy of collaboration—which would be scrupulously followed by Catholic leaders well into the nineteenth century—helped to consolidate British power and effectively meant that both the church and the seigneurs served as instruments of British power.

In voicing his opposition to this policy, Chartier de Lotbinière aligned himself with a minority of Canadiens, mostly small merchants and professionals, who rejected the social compact from which they were excluded and who called instead for popularly elected institutions. Influenced by currents of liberal thought that had surfaced during the Enlightenment, they were generally sympathetic to the ideals of the American and French revolutions. In their view, the church was not only impeding the intellectual, moral, social, and material progress of the times, but actively collaborating with the British to keep the Canadiens in a state of subjugation. These men were the forerunners of the professional bourgeoisie that, as we shall see, would emerge at the end of the century and effectively challenge the church's authority.

POPULAR RELIGION AND CULTURAL DIVERSITY

The nature of popular faith and religious practice in this period is difficult to determine. In the absence of sociological surveys, we have to depend on the accounts of the religious leaders, and these are often ambiguous if not contradictory. Thus it is not uncommon to see Bishop Briand praising the people's religious fervour and in the next breath denouncing their loose behaviour.[34] We should not be surprised. Usually speaking through official pastoral letters marking special occasions, such as jubilees and visitations, the bishop would naturally tend to exaggerate any lapses that he observed, to urge the faithful on to ever-greater efforts.

What is clear is that Canadiens in general were still practising Catholics with an undeniable affection for their bishop and priests, the majority of whom had come from their ranks. Religion had shaped their entire history for 150 years. Surrounded by a clergy that was both numerous and demanding, they had been deeply affected by the Counter Reformation and brought up in a strict, even austere religion. The clergy in the cities was composed mainly of French priests, such as the Sulpicians, the Jesuits, and the priests of the Séminaire de Québec, who had received their training in France. The clergy in the countryside, however, was made up of secular priests, most of them Canadiens, trained at the Séminaire de Québec. These clerics watched carefully over the people's moral behaviour and did not hesitate to order interdictions, excommunications, and public penances when they judged the situation sufficiently serious. In addition, they encouraged the laity to join confraternities, 'to strengthen and channel [their] piety' and 'to achieve through these associations better moral supervision of the members'.[35] In this homogeneous society where non-Catholics and non-churchgoers had no place, not only Sundays but some twenty holy days of obligation were faithfully respected, along with seventeen other feasts of devotion.

Alongside the prescribed religion—the religious practices officially sanctioned and codified by the Catholic Church and its spokesmen—existed a religion of everyday life, a folk religion that derived directly from the people and eluded clerical control. Under this heading belong the most spontaneous expressions of popular faith, such as visits to pilgrimage sites and the erection of crosses along the roads, especially between Quebec and Montreal. (After the Conquest an English soldier, Thomas Anbury, lamented the frequent stops made by carriage drivers in order to recite what he considered very long prayers.[36]) Other aspects of this folk religion, however, are subject to speculation. Some historians have written of serious irregularities in religious practices, a utilitarian approach to religion, and even a 'fetishist religion, not at all thought out, made up as much of superstition as of authentic devotions, in a word, a religion-as-insurance'.[37] Were there in French Canada, as in some remote regions of France, traces of pagan practices that had escaped the control of the clergy? Certainly the rural population, and to some extent the urban residents of the three large towns, Quebec, Trois-Rivières, and Montreal, whose mental world and religious practices had changed little from those of the countryside, still lived on 'the tales of evening-party storytellers, on their customs from another age and on their own myths'.[38] On the other hand, the grip of the clergy on French Canada was too strong to allow superstitious practices to take firm root. The pious practices of Canadiens appear to have been less dubious, in the eyes of the church, than those of their counterparts in France, their popular religion more tame. Hence in this period we find no so-called witchcraft, magic, or charlatanism.[39] In short, we may conclude with the historian Pierre

Hurtubise that popular religion 'included a very significant folk element; that on the whole the clergy were able to put up with this element, . . . and that if they never intervened (or almost never) it was most likely because they considered it quite peripheral and therefore not very dangerous'.[40]

Yet if Catholicism was still the norm in French Canada, the erosion of religious commitment that had begun earlier in the century continued after the end of the French régime. In 1769 Bishop Briand expressed his dismay at the 'great many' people who 'profess their religion . . . only outwardly so they will not seem to be separate from the others. They are Christians who still proclaim their Christianity with their mouths but who contradict it with their behaviour, and have renounced it with their spirit and their heart.'[41] In particular, Briand accused the people of abusing alcohol, ignoring the church's laws on fasting and abstinence, and failing to observe Sundays and holy days: 'People avoid going to hear the word of God, they do their manual labour without permission or any need to do so, they go to taverns, they have dinner parties, they go on day outings, they spend the afternoon gambling, all things that are contrary to the respect due to these holy days, to God's law and to the decrees of the Church.'[42] Four years later he again denounced inadequate church attendance: 'In the summer they say it is too hot, in the winter it is too cold. False excuses! It is not the poor climate that is stopping you, it is the indifference of your heart for God.'[43] Among the other ongoing problems that the bishop lamented over the years were drunkenness, disobedience, immodesty, public cohabitation, and incest, as well as insults and affronts to priests.[44]

Nor were the laity particularly generous towards their church. They were often quite miserly when it came to providing for the material welfare of their pastors, and if they agreed to pay the tithe, which then usually amounted to one twenty-sixth of the harvest, and which the Quebec Act made compulsory for all Catholics as during the French regime, most did so grudgingly. According to Bishop Briand, 'People here like to be well served, without any cost to themselves.'[45] By contrast, the English took pride in paying their Protestant ministers well.[46] Catholics were likewise reluctant to pay the fees required at marriage for dispensations from banns and impediments, which they claimed were just an opportunity for the bishop to amass wealth, although in fact the money collected was usually distributed to the poor. It is true that the people were hardly wealthy, having suffered significant material losses immediately after the Conquest, but still Briand could not help condemning their indifference and apathy towards ensuring the future of their religion.

The Canadiens were frequently reproached for their spirit of independence. Often they listened to the words of their clergy with unbelief, and openly disregarded laws that they considered too restrictive. Neither was it uncommon for the faithful to appeal to the governor and civil officials to obtain a judgement against their bishop. In 1792, fifty-three parishioners of L'Ancienne Lorette petitioned the governor to replace their priest, Charles-Joseph Brossard Deschenaux, against whom they had numerous grievances.[47]

If the final years of the French regime were to some degree marked by an uninterested or indifferent attitude towards religion, however, by 1771 Bishop Briand could note in a pastoral letter that the country had none 'of those supposedly bright minds who blaspheme all the mysteries, and who want nothing to do with an imposed and indispensable religion'. Indeed, he declared; 'We acknowledge, to the glory of our God, that among our flock we find a large number whose regular attendance at the various services, and whose frequent participation in the sacraments create for us the greatest comfort we could feel, and very often make us shed tears of joy.'[48] Even in his private correspondence—perhaps a more reliable reflection of reality—the prelate expressed satisfaction: 'There are doubtless bad Christians, there is dissolute behaviour, there is licentiousness, but I do not think there is any more than there was fifteen or twenty years ago, and I am not without consolation as far as this is concerned.'[49]

All things considered, there can be no doubt that following the Conquest the people of Quebec constituted a community of practising Catholics who meant to remain faithful to their religious origins. This did not mean that they had become model believers (as can be seen in the bishop's statements), but they remained for the most part sincerely attached to their faith and their clergy. As Brunet has clearly pointed out, this special attachment was not unrelated to the exceptional circumstances of that era:

> Deprived of a civil government serving them as a distinct ethnic group, unable to rely on an élite of completely free lay people working through institutions under their exclusive authority, Canadiens developed a very particular kind of attachment to the Church, clergy and ecclesiastical organization. Their religious faith inspired them, that is certain. But they were also driven in this direction by powerful worldly incentives. Their group interests played a greater role in this matter than previously. . . . The union between the Canadien population and the Church took on a social, economic and political character that it did not have in the days of New France.[50]

When he became bishop of Quebec in 1766, Briand took jurisdiction over the whole of North America, with the exception of Newfoundland and the British colonies in America, which came under the authority of the vicar apostolic in London, and of Louisiana, which France had ceded to Spain in the secret treaty of 1762. The heart of the diocese consisted of 113 parishes, most of them spread along the St Lawrence. Equally important, however, were the native missions scattered across the huge diocese. The latter part of the

French regime had been marked by a decline in missionary zeal that continued after the Conquest as the numbers of priests and religious decreased and the Jesuits gradually disappeared. Yet Bishop Briand had a genuine concern for the natives' spiritual well-being. At times he could be firm, as when in 1767 he threatened to recall the missionary from Kahnawake (Sault-Saint-Louis) if the natives did not mend their ways. But as he wrote in 1766 to the vicar-general of Trois-Rivières, concerning the Abenaki of Saint-François-du-Lac (Odanak): 'These are souls redeemed by Jesus Christ who have been entrusted to me just like the others, and I must undertake everything possible to save them.'[51]

In 1766 the diocese had only six aboriginal missions with a priest in permanent residence: Lorette, a suburb of Quebec; Bécancour, Saint-François-du-Lac, Kahnawake, and Saint-Regis (Akwesasne) on the St Lawrence River; and Lac-des-Deux-Montagnes (Oka), on the Ottawa River. With the exception of the latter, which was assigned to the Sulpicians, all were served first by Jesuits and later by secular priests. In addition, the nomadic peoples who came to spend the summer or part of the winter on the shores of the St Lawrence were ministered to by the priests of neighbouring parishes such as Maskinongé, Trois-Rivières, and Trois-Pistoles. Finally, there were the annual flying missions to the north shore, from Tadoussac to Sept-Îles and Mingan, along the Saguenay, Saint-Maurice, and Ottawa rivers and, after 1830, to the Témiscamingue and Abitibi regions. Two natives would accompany the priest on these expeditions, one to serve as interpreter and the other as catechist.[52] To the east, the native people of Acadia did not secure a replacement for Abbé Maillard, who had died in 1762, until 1768, after repeated requests to the British government. This replacement was Abbé Charles-François Bailly de Messein. Ironically, the authorities in London not only allowed Catholic missionaries into the Maritimes—after initially being reluctant to do so—but supported them financially, in order to keep the natives loyal to the British Crown.[53]

That the First Nations were generally devoted to Catholicism and wanted to have missionaries with them is clear from the approaches that the Huron chief of Lorette made to Murray in September 1760, as well as those made to the Council in Halifax by the Micmac chief of La Hève in 1762, and by the chief of the Saint John River Maliseet of New Brunswick.[54] Few adopted Protestantism, despite London's support for conversion efforts and, after 1811, its attempts to replace Catholic with Protestant missionaries.[55] They respected the Catholic missionaries, and when they did complain of occasional authoritarianism and long absences, the problem was usually corrected.[56]

The missionaries, for their part, wrote approvingly of the natives. 'They are intelligent, obedient, respectful towards their priests, and good Catholics. They pray often, eagerly listen to the word, and display tender and loving devotion,'

observed Bishop Jean-François Hubert in 1794.[57] Another churchman, Abbé
Luc Aubry, wrote in 1836, following his mission to the King's posts on the
north shore: 'They are very attached to the Catholic religion, respectful and
obedient to their missionary, and comply with what he prescribes.'[58] While
continuing to espouse the long-term goal of acculturation, the missionaries did
not interfere in the day-to-day life of native societies. They respected the aboriginals' cultures and encouraged the publication of prayer books in their languages.[59] They also tried to keep them as far away as possible from the
corrupting influence of white society. In 1816 Bishop Joseph-Octave Plessis
would write:

> We did not think that in order to civilize them it was appropriate to lead them
> away from their usual way of running their families. Here we generally find that
> their morals are more pure than the Europeans'. It seemed even less wise to teach
> them foreign languages, as experience in the villages near Canadien towns has
> shown that the natives readily adopt the vices of every nation whose language
> they learn, and that their young women (who unfortunately are too often sought
> out by whites) are much more easy to seduce when they understand the language
> of their seducers.[60]

In addition, on several occasions the missionaries interceded with the
British authorities on behalf of the natives. For instance, writing in 1832 to a
Captain M. Cullock, Abbé Joseph Marcoux, who for thirty-six years had been
a missionary at Kahnawake, forcefully reminded the captain that Governor
Murray's promises had gone up 'in smoke, like everything promised to the
natives by every governor of the country'.[61]

One factor, however, was a cause of distress for the missionaries: dependence on alcohol. In this, of course, the natives were no different from the
whites who were responsible for the brandy trade. From the beginning the
bishops of Quebec had condemned those who procured alcohol for the natives
in sufficient quantities for them to get drunk, and had made this offence a
'reserved case' in which only the bishop could grant absolution.[62] But such
sanctions had little effect. Writing from Halifax in 1769, Bailly de Messein said
that he had 'only one major enemy to fight on [the natives'] behalf, and that is
drunkenness'.[63] In 1784 Bishop Briand was still urging the people of
Kahnawake to imitate the virtues of the first converts of their nation, compared with whom 'you have utterly degenerated, abandoning yourselves to
drunkenness and the impurity to which it gives rise.'[64] And in 1788 Bishop
Hubert, who had worked as a missionary for several years, took a pessimistic
view: 'In general there is very little that can be done for the salvation of these
barbarians, as every day the abuse of intoxicating drink makes them likely to
commit serious crimes.'[65]

On the whole, the attitude of both the higher clergy and the missionaries was one of benign paternalism. Despite scarce human resources, they provided the native peoples with more or less continuous spiritual care, even in the remotest corners of the colony. They fought the ravages of alcohol, learned native languages, published devotional and doctrinal works in those idioms, and adapted their pastoral efforts to the specific ways of life of various groups. Yet the missionaries still believed that the key to the natives' survival was sedentarization and acculturation to the European way of life. Ignoring the causes of the breakdown of the native social fabric, they combatted only the symptoms of that breakdown, above all alcoholism. Ultimately, they believed that they knew what was best for the natives, and this attitude could only create a barrier between them and the people they served.

Also included under the bishop of Quebec's jurisdiction was the extensive though sparsely populated territory of Acadia. There were still only a few villages in this region, since the resettlement of the Acadians, who had been dispersed since the *Grand Dérangement* or Deportation, had begun only with the end of hostilities. In 1763 the Acadian population stood at about 4,700: 2,500 in mainland Acadia (New Brunswick), 1,800 on the peninsula (Nova Scotia), and 400 on Île Saint-Jean (Prince Edward Island).[66] Instead of returning to their traditional lands, which in the meantime had been occupied by English colonists, they settled in areas far from historic Acadia, around St Mary's Bay, Chéticamp, and Île Madame in Nova Scotia; in the Caraquet and Saint John River districts of New Brunswick; and in the Malpeque region of PEI. Establishing a new French Acadia would be a formidable challenge in a colony that now considered itself firmly Protestant and English-speaking. Moreover, deprived of their civil and political rights,[67] the Acadians had been without any missionaries since the death of Abbé Maillard, and the British authorities were reluctant to accept the presence of Catholic priests. The first missionary appointed by Bishop Briand for the native peoples and the Acadians, Bailly de Messein, was received by the latter as a saviour in 1768. 'With great joy and great zeal,' wrote the historian Henri-Raymond Casgrain in 1888, 'did they take from their hiding-places their liturgical objects, church ornaments, chalices, ciboria, etc. A rustic altar was set up in one of the least poor cottages. Then everyone gathered together to attend mass and receive the sacraments. The children were baptized; many of them, born more than twelve years earlier, had never seen a priest. Many kind words were exchanged, many tears were shed.'[68]

Although he was treated with respect by Nova Scotia's governors Michael Francklin and Lord William Campbell, the Abbé had to contend with the intolerance of the British population and the mistrust of some politicians who hampered his work. Shortly before returning to Quebec in 1772, Bailly regretted that because of the suspicion he incurred he had been unable to do more for the Acadians:

At present everything in the government seems to work against having more Catholic missionaries. This opposition comes entirely from the Presbyterians and the people from New England. . . . The governor continues to grace me with his protection, as do the chief clerks. But in an American government it is not the head but the lesser members that are in charge. They all mean well with respect to the Catholic religion, but the population is fanatic. Two Presbyterian ministers have preached against me in public. I have been mentioned in the newspapers. It is said that if the king is allowed to put a priest in Nova Scotia, he will have to allow one in Boston. The appointment of a priest in Nova Scotia is a disgrace: that summarizes their objections.[69]

If the concern of the bishops of Quebec for the welfare of the Acadians is not to be doubted, the fact remains that Bishop Briand and his successors, as Léon Thériault puts it, 'regarded them almost as if they had become genuine British subjects'.[70] Thus in 1796 Bishop Hubert went so far as to ask London for Irish priests, emphasizing that the Catholics in the Maritimes were 'almost all English, Irish, Scots and Acadians who have a good knowledge of the English language'.[71] In 1807 Bishop Plessis suggested to the vicar apostolic in Newfoundland, Bishop Patrick Lambert, that he extend his jurisdiction to the whole of the Atlantic region;[72] fortunately for the Acadians, Lambert refused. Nevertheless, as Thériault emphasizes, despite their mistaken perception of the Acadian reality, the bishops of Quebec continued 'sending French-speaking priests to Acadia, even well after the Maritime provinces had themselves been established as dioceses'. And when the time came, in 1835, it was 'the ecclesiastical authorities of the province of Quebec who were most sympathetic to the appointment of Acadian bishops and the development of community cultural institutions.'[73]

In the thirty years that followed the Conquest the Acadians had only sporadic contact with missionaries. In 1781 there were only three for the whole of Acadia: James Macdonald, who in 1772 had settled on Prince Edward Island with about fifty Scottish families; Joseph-Mathurin Bourg, who, having been expelled from Acadia with his family in 1755, became in 1772 the first Acadian to be ordained to the priesthood, and the following year replaced the Jesuit Jean-Baptiste de la Brosse, visiting the Acadians from his base in Tracadièche (Carleton, in the Gaspé); and Thomas-François Leroux, the first resident priest in an Acadian parish, appointed to Memramcook in 1781. Despite their lack of contact with missionaries, the Acadians were no less deeply attached to their church, at least in the opinion of Abbé Bailly: in 1771 he reported that their religion was 'in no way lost' and they were 'very devout'.[74]

One of the first consequences of the Conquest was the arrival of English-speaking immigrants from Britain, and especially the American colonies, in the St Lawrence valley. Numbering 450 in 1765, according to General Murray, and settling primarily in the towns, they belonged to the Anglican and Presbyterian churches, and at first had military chaplains as their ministers. Before long, however, London decided to send bilingual ministers to the new colony, both to serve Protestants, whether English- or French-speaking, and to convert Catholics. Thus by 1768 three French Huguenot pastors attached to the Society for the Propagation of the Gospel—David-François de Montmollin, Leger-Jean-Baptiste-Noël Veyssière, and David Chabrand Delisle—were serving the Anglican communities of Quebec, Trois-Rivières, and Montreal, respectively. Their efforts at proselytism had limited success: by 1771 only two conversions to Anglicanism had been recorded in Montreal. But relations between the two communities were good, and Anglicans in Quebec and Montreal were able to use Catholic churches as places of worship. The only real problems arose on the rare occasions when young Catholic women renounced their faith in order to marry Protestants.

RELATIONS WITH CIVIL AUTHORITIES

The harmonious relations that the bishop of Quebec had cultivated with Governor Murray continued with his successor Guy Carleton, a former officer with General James Wolfe who arrived in Quebec in September 1766. Having already met Bishop Briand in London and promised his full co-operation, Carleton did not share the anti-Catholic prejudices of the new attorney general, Francis Masères, an English lawyer of Huguenot descent. He understood all the advantages of the compromise reached by his predecessor with Bishop Briand. To impose the authority of Great Britain on the newly conquered colony and maintain the strict obedience of the population, the governor depended on the support and collaboration of the religious leaders who were the only ones with any real influence over their compatriots. This was all the more important in view of the increasing discontent and defiance in the thirteen colonies since the imposition of new taxes in 1765. Anger was brewing among the Americans, and the prospect of a revolt was more likely each day. In addition, Carleton still feared a renewal of hostilities by the French, who looked forward to exploiting the American situation to their own advantage and whose spies had already been at work since 1764. Under these circumstances it was essential that Carleton gain the support of the Canadiens through conciliatory policies towards the people and cordial relations with Bishop Briand.

It was not long before the bishop had become not only Carleton's friend but one of his most trusted advisers. As a result, the governor rejected the idea, advocated by the archbishop of Canterbury, of converting French Canada to Protestantism. Briand had nothing but praise for Carleton, who had succeeded in making the people forget the harshness of the Conquest and the precarious situation of the Catholic Church, which still had no official status. 'Here we enjoy perfect peace,' wrote Briand, 'under the government of one of the most amiable of men. Religion is practised here in complete freedom, and in many cases more fervently than ever.'[75] 'We hardly notice,' he remarked in another letter, 'that we are under a Protestant prince. It must be admitted that no nation is as humane as the English one, and that it possesses all the virtues that flow from this.'[76] The two men came to collaborate very closely. Thus on the matter of choosing a coadjutor bishop for Quebec, Carleton favoured the appointment of the parish priest of Saint-Pierre, Louis-Philippe Mariauchau d'Esgly. With his consecration on 12 July 1772, the delicate question of episcopal succession was settled. Henceforth there would be two bishops at Quebec: a titular bishop and a coadjutor with the right of succession. 'In this way,' explained Briand, 'if one of the two should die, the other will immediately choose, with the approval of the government, a coadjutor; he will submit his nomination, receive his bulls from Rome, and consecrate the new coadjutor, and so it will continue without cost and without any need to travel to Europe.'[77] The elevation of d'Esgly, the first Canadien to become a bishop, marked the beginning of the Canadianization of the Catholic Church in the colony. This was what the governor wanted, in order to expedite the breaking of the remaining ties between French Canada and its former mother country.

In the meantime, in August 1770, Carleton had returned to London to brief the British authorities on the situation in Canada and explain his policy of tolerating Catholicism. Anxious to do justice to the country's people, and convinced that he needed to win the confidence of its ruling classes to ensure their loyalty, he condemned the unrealistic assumptions of the Royal Proclamation of 1763, which had ignored the people's rights and grievances especially with respect to French laws and access to civilian employment. After four years of laborious negotiations his point of view finally prevailed when, on 22 June 1774, George III gave royal assent to the Quebec Act, which re-established French civil law, extended the borders of the country, exempted Canadiens from the oath of the Test Act, and officially recognized the Catholic religion by allowing the church to collect tithes. It is true that the Act contained serious restrictions, forbidding the bishop to correspond with Rome and giving governors the right to oversee the appointment of parish priests and the selection of new ordinands. In practice, however, the governors never objected to the bishop's forwarding his mail to Rome through the intermediary of France, and they accepted the lists of new parish priests and ordinands that the bishop sent them each year. Overall, the Quebec Act was a victory both for the Catholic Church and for the Canadien people.

Of course the motives behind this liberal legislation were not entirely disinterested. Carleton had witnessed the growing unrest to the south, especially since the Boston massacre of March 1770, and had counted on the Quebec Act to gain French Canada's co-operation in stemming any American revolt. Recognizing this intention, the inhabitants of the thirteen colonies considered the Quebec Act to be one more in the series of intolerable laws that followed the Boston Tea Party of 1773. Reactions were very strong. There was talk of a pact between George III and the pope to sell out the Americans. Josiah Quincy exclaimed: 'What! have we Americans spent so much of our blood and treasure in aiding Britain to conquer Canada, that Britons and Canadians may now subjugate us?'[78] And Alexander Hamilton declared:

> The affair of Canada, if possible, is still worse [than that of Boston]. The English laws have been superseded by the French laws. The Romish faith is made the established religion of the land. The free exercise of the Protestant faith depends on the pleasure of the Governor and Council. . . . Does not your blood run cold, to think that an English Parliament should pass an act for the establishment of arbitrary power and Popery in such an extensive country? . . . They may as well establish Popery in New York, and the other colonies. . . .[79]

The English who had settled in Quebec and Montreal since the Conquest–mostly merchants and government officials–had also reacted with anger to the proclamation of the Quebec Act, which refused them the elected assembly on which they had counted to establish their dominance over the Canadiens. Without guarantees for either their property or their religion, the anglophone community expected dire repercussions.[80] Petitions to the king, the House of Lords, and the Commons demanding repeal of the Quebec Act were in vain. Sharing the indignation of their counterparts in the thirteen colonies, the English inhabitants of Quebec were forced to recognize that their cause was virtually hopeless.

This is the background to the American invasion that would have important repercussions for the Catholic Church and for Canadien society. On 26 October 1774, the General Congress of the colonies, meeting at Philadelphia, approved a letter to be sent to the people of Canada inviting them to side with the rebel colonies. In a tone that was conciliatory, for recent enemies, the letter strongly condemned the Quebec Act, claiming that far from being liberal, it in fact reduced them to slavery by depriving them of their most basic rights. It then invited the Canadiens to join their rebellion and send a delegation to the next Congress, to be held on 10 May 1775. The letter did not have the desired effect, for scarcely had it been made public when another document drafted by the congress arrived in the province. Entitled *Address to the people of Great Britain* and dated 21 October 1774, this document spoke in disparaging terms of the morals and religion of Canadiens. A third letter from the Congress, dated 29 May 1775, did not succeed in dispelling the suspicions aroused by this double-dealing. The Canadiens had just received their first lesson in democratic government.

Indeed, the invasion of Canada had already begun with the capture of Fort Ticonderoga on 10 May and Crown Point, on Lake Champlain, two days later. Benedict Arnold's incursion into Saint-Jean on 18 May demonstrated the threat hanging over Montreal. Bishop Briand, who was more than happy with Carleton's attitude towards the church and the advantages granted by the Quebec Act, considered it his duty to intervene and warn the people against the Americans' policy of friendly co-operation. He also mistrusted the American rebels, who in his view were seeking the Canadiens' support only in order to subjugate them the more easily later. Nor was the bishop unaware that antipapal prejudices were still widespread in the thirteen colonies; in fact, the proposed alliance was nothing more than a massive fraud: 'No other sect has persecuted Catholics as the Bostonians' has. None has insulted priests, desecrated churches and the relics of saints as it has, none has attacked the confidence of Catholics in the protection of the Saints and the Holy Mother of God with more horrible blasphemies than it has.'[81]

On 22 May 1775, in response to a request from the governor, Bishop Briand addressed a solemn pastoral letter 'to all the peoples of this colony' and not simply, as was the custom, 'to all the faithful of this diocese'—as if at this grave moment he was conscious of making a historic gesture. In it he recalled the church's official doctrine with respect to obedience:

> Your oaths and your religion impose on you the essential obligation to defend your country and your king with all your power. Close your ears, therefore, dear Canadiens, and do not listen to these seditious men who seek to make you unhappy, to extinguish the feelings of submission to your legitimate superiors that your upbringing and religion have engraved on your hearts. Carry out with joy everything you are told to do by a beneficent governor whose only care is for your interests and your happiness.[82]

The bishop's pastoral was soon followed by a circular letter from the vicar-general of Montreal, Étienne de Montgolfier, in support of Governor Carleton's proclamation re-establishing militias in the parishes.[83] But the response to these efforts on the part of the religious leaders was far from satisfactory: the people were not at all enthusiastic about defending the interests of Great Britain. Bishop Briand, whom some suspected of collusion with the governor, was unable to hide his surprise and disappointment: 'My pastoral was read, and the nonsense spoken on that occasion was pitiful; it presupposes a serious lack of religious spirit.'[84] The Canadiens displayed the same neutrality during the invasion of their territory by American troops in the autumn of 1775. By the time of the unsuccessful attack on Quebec of 31 December 1775, many even secretly wished that the city would fall into American hands. Nevertheless, despite the sympathy they showed for the invaders, very few

Canadiens–500 at most–joined their ranks, and 'most of them,' claimed Bishop Briand, 'were just poor wretches, beggars and drunkards.'[85]

In truth, the Canadiens were scarcely more fond of the Americans than of the British. The failure of the attack on Quebec City had cooled the enthusiasm of quite a number, and they distanced themselves even further from the Americans when, in the final weeks before leaving Canadian soil, the latter behaved more like enemies than liberators. The Bostonian cause had been so compromised that when, in April 1776, a group of Americans led by two members of Congress, Benjamin Franklin and Samuel Chase, and including Charles Carroll and his cousin, the former Jesuit John Carroll, travelled to Montreal to win Canadien support, the mission went by unnoticed. Father Carroll, on whom the Congress was counting to gain the support of the clergy, was politely received by Vicar-General Montgolfier. But the only other member of the clergy he met was the Jesuit Pierre-René Floquet, with whom he had several meetings. When the Americans left Montreal at the end of May, the friendship and neutrality that the congress had so earnestly sought were, in Trudel's words, 'lost for good'.[86]

Even so, Bishop Briand had many reasons to be shocked and disappointed. Canadiens had shown very little desire to obey the governor's orders and come to the defence of their territory. Some had even fought side by side with the Americans. Others had blatantly ignored the instructions of their bishop and taken the liberty of handing over priests to rebel leaders because they were preaching in favour of the English. Finally, several had 'hoped that the Bostonians, those despicable highwaymen and bandits, would prevail'.[87] Briand must have realized that his authority was no longer respected as it once had been. At the beginning of the hostilities he had confided to Montgolfier: 'The situation of the colony seems dismal and its future highly uncertain. . . . I write and I punish, but what do people say? They say that the priests and I are afraid. . . . There should be troops; they would be more persuasive than the Word of God that we proclaim to them.'[88] He made the same admission of impotence to the priest of Montmagny: 'My authority is not respected any more than yours. Like you, I am called an Englishman. . . . I should put all the churches, even most of the diocese, under interdict.'[89] It was no coincidence that Briand considered it advisable in June 1776, when the American troops withdrew, to publish an unusually long and extremely harsh pastoral letter in which he reminded the Canadien rebels of the gravity of their crime: 'What an abyss of sin you have plunged into. . . . How many sins you have committed before God! . . . It is clear that all, or almost all, those who refused to listen to their priests when they received instruction, either from the pulpit or in court, and who were not willing to follow their teaching, have fallen into schism and separated themselves from the Church.'[90]

For the first time since the Conquest Canadiens had resisted the orders of their bishop, who had intervened on six occasions during the American invasion. After this episode Bishop Briand could no longer be considered the undisputed leader of the nation. The gulf between the clergy and the people had widened, even if the latter had not intended to call into question their adherence to Catholicism. A breath of freedom had touched them. The letter of 26 October 1774 from the American Congress, and the appeal for liberty issued on 28 October 1778 by the Comte d'Estaing, vice-admiral of the squadron sent by France in support of the rebel colonies, had given Canadiens their first taste of democracy and freedom. From then on they would always be reluctant to come to the defence of the king or British interests, or to follow the instructions of their religious leaders in this regard.

Briand retired in 1784, and his successor, Bishop d'Esgly, died four years later. Yet the bishop of Quebec remained the principal intermediary between the people and the British authorities. Thus it was Bishop Jean-François Hubert who was called upon in 1789 by Judge William Smith, president of the Commission of Education set up by Carleton (now Lord Dorchester) to report on the education system in the province. Smith wanted the bishop's advice on a reform plan that would provide for the establishment of a school in every parish and a model school in each district, to be overseen by a mixed university at Quebec to which both Catholics and Protestants would be admitted. This plan was not without merit in a province where scarcely 4,000 people out of 140,000 knew how to read and write. But Hubert vigorously opposed it: he saw nothing in the plan to protect the faith and morals of Catholics, and above all he feared interference from the state. Faced with these objections, the reform plan was abandoned. In the course of this debate Bishop Hubert was taken to task by his coadjutor, the former missionary Bailly de Messein; known as the 'priest of the English' because of his friendship with Dorchester, Bailly had been imposed on Bishop Hubert as coadjutor only months before.[91] Trained in France and sympathetic to the ideas of the French Revolution, the coadjutor bishop was known for his spirit of toleration. Unlike Hubert, he had no objection to the future university's being run by the state, nor to the establishment of a public education system in the province. For Bailly, the only role of the bishop should be the one 'that every university accords to people of knowledge and merit'.[92]

THE CHALLENGES OF LIBERALISM AND ANGLICANISM

At the same time political debate was raging over the establishment of a legislative assembly. The arrival in Quebec of more than 5,000 Loyalists following the American Revolution had prompted the British authorities to proceed with a plan of institutional reform that would culminate in the creation of Upper and Lower Canada under the Constitutional Act of 1791. Canadiens were divided on this issue for various reasons. The Montreal *Gazette*, which had already condemned the obscurantism of Bishop Hubert in the matter of a mixed university, campaigned in favour of a legislative assembly. The Catholic clergy did not take part in the debate. However, Bishop Hubert felt uneasy about the advent of parliamentary government. He had not failed to notice that 'the spirit of liberty and independence' had developed considerably among Canadiens following 'the circulation of American manifestos' that had incited them to revolt in 1775; and that this taste for liberty and independence had spread through the proliferation of newspapers and free conversation about political matters.[93] Henri-François Gravé de la Rive of the Séminaire de Québec expressed similar concerns about the establishment of a parliamentary regime: 'People I consider to be thoughtful are very angry with this change, for there are a few of our Canadien braggarts and many English admirers of the national assembly who are already talking about the rights of man as a basis for laws.'[94]

What especially worried the religious leaders was the growing public infatuation with the ideas of the French Revolution. Already the most educated Canadiens were avidly reading the works of the Enlightenment philosophers—Voltaire, Montesquieu, Diderot, Rousseau—many of which were available in the public libraries of Quebec and Montreal (established in 1779 and 1796 respectively). A mood of rationalism was spreading among the intellectual élite of French Canada, as it had already done among liberal Protestants in the country's English-speaking communities. Men like Pierre du Calvet, Valentin Jautard, and Fleury Mesplet made no secret of their enthusiasm for the ideas of Voltaire. Though few in number, in 1778 these liberal intellectuals had founded the Académie de Montréal in his memory, and they took it as their task to combat superstition, 'more dangerous than the most fearful plague'.[95] As they moved away from the church, they attempted to discredit the clergy and hold them up to contempt.[96]

The bishops of Quebec had already warned the faithful against reading the 'impious' books then circulating in the diocese, and against associating with people who were only nominally Catholic, 'as libertine in spirit as in the heart'.[97] According to Bishop Hubert, 'Canada is not completely sheltered from the spiritual evils that are afflicting Europe.[98] Indeed, the French Revolution was inspiring unparalleled fervour in every class of society, especially among the intellectual élite (judges, lawyers, notaries, doctors) and a certain number of educated merchants and artisans in the towns. City-dwellers in particular were well informed of the events unfolding in France, as from 1789 to 1792 the Quebec *Gazette* and the Montreal *Gazette* reported on the development of the Revolution with unconcealed enthusiasm.[99]

The importance of the press in the dissemination of political ideas during this period cannot be overemphasized. Although their circulation was limited, newspapers still reached the less educated and provided them with information. Modelled after the British press, the Quebec *Gazette*, founded in 1764, always displayed a marked sympathy for the French revolutionary movement. Critical of Rome, whose reactionary attitude it condemned, it 'allowed news to be printed that was truly daring for the Catholic community in Canada'.[100] The Montreal *Gazette*, founded in 1778 by Fleury Mesplet, went a step further. Influenced by the ideas of Voltaire, and decidedly anticlerical, it did not stop at making positive commentaries on the progress of the Revolution. It took advantage of what was happening in France to intensify its own struggle against the seigneurs, whom it held guilty of opposing plans for a legislative assembly, and the clergy, whom it accused of keeping the people in ignorance and servitude. As the voice of revolutionary intellectuals and republicanism in Montreal, the *Gazette* went so far as to call for a social revolution in Lower Canada as in France. 'The kind of man we need in 1790,' wrote Mesplet, 'is the kind who knows the rights given to him by nature, and who knows how to enjoy them and defend them.'[101] Both newspapers would maintain their sympathy for the French Revolution until the end of 1792, when it began to take a new, distinctly more radical direction. This was also the time when France, which had just deposed its king, was preparing to declare war on England. As a result, the British press stopped backing the revolutionary movement in France, and under these circumstances it was difficult to be openly in favour of the Revolution in Lower Canada.

Catholic leaders in Canada were not unconcerned about these events, which directly affected the status of their church in France. They reacted strongly to the Revolution's repressive measures: the nationalization of church property, the creation of a national church with the Civil Constitution of the Clergy, the persecution of priests who refused the oath to the latter and remained loyal to the Church of Rome, and the massacres of September 1792, which boded ill for the future course of the Revolution. Bishop Hubert was also worried about revolutionary propaganda in Lower Canada and the enthusiasm that greeted revolutionary ideas among the élites in particular. However, until this point no public condemnation had been issued by the bishop, and the excitement about the Revolution had not gone beyond the stage of talking. No revolutionary movement was in sight in Canada. Only in the autumn of 1793, therefore, did Bishop Hubert feel the need to intervene publicly.

In the meantime the population had been won over by pro-revolutionary feelings. Despite the declaration of war between Great Britain and France at the beginning of 1793, Canadiens remained deeply attached to their former mother country; many secretly hoped for the victory of the French armies over the British. The presence of French emissaries in Lower Canada encouraged those who wished to see France re-establish a foothold in North America and free them from English domination. For example, in June 1793 the French minister Genet, an envoy to the Philadelphia Convention, sent the Canadien people a letter entitled 'The Free French to their Brothers in Canada' in which he encouraged them to follow the example of the Americans and French and free themselves from British control:

> Man is born free. . . . It is up to you to stamp again on your brows the original dignity that nature gave to man and that slavery erased. . . . Everything around you is leading you to freedom. The country you inhabit was conquered by your forefathers. It owes its prosperity only to their care and to yours. This land belongs to you. It must be independent. Break then with a government that has become the most cruel enemy of the freedom of nations.[102]

This call to insurrection made a deep impression, especially as at the same time rumours were circulating of an imminent invasion by France. On 4 October 1793, Genet did indeed order the Santo Domingo fleet, stationed in Chesapeake Bay, to go and destroy the Newfoundland fishing ports, seize the town of Halifax, and travel up the St Lawrence to sound out the mood of the people and incite them to revolt. Now, at the governor's suggestion, the bishop of Quebec decided to intervene. On 9 November Bishop Hubert addressed the people to remind them that their ties to France had been definitively broken at the time of the Conquest, and that from that time on they owed loyalty and obedience to the king of England. In addition, he noted that the oath to the British sovereign sworn by Canadiens bound them 'in such a way that they could not violate it without being guilty of a grave sin before God Himself', and that 'the greatest misfortune that could befall Canada would be to fall into the hands of these revolutionaries'.[103] Although the invasion never took place—the fleet chose to return to France before winter set in—Hubert was justifiably worried about the future. In the spring of 1794 he told Father James Jones of his fears: 'It is impossible to overstate the respect that we owe to his majesty's representatives, since they are sufficiently cautious not to demand anything that goes against our conscience. In addition, the surprising restlessness that the revolution in France is creating in the popular mind makes co-operation between the Empire and the priesthood more necessary.'[104]

That many people did not share the bishop's view was evident in May 1794, when a draw was held in the Quebec region to select militiamen for a force of 2,000 men: a mutiny erupted and one of the leaders cried out, 'Long live the French!'[105] 'Love for France and hatred of the occupier,' writes Michel Brunet, 'made working class Canadiens forget the questionable aspects and abuses of the French Revolution.'[106] The religious leaders were all the more anxious to reassure the British authorities. Invited to deliver the funeral oration for Bishop Briand, who had passed away shortly after this incident, the parish priest of Quebec, Abbé Joseph-Octave Plessis, reaffirmed the loyalty of the people and the clergy:

> Forgive that initial mistrust by a people who did not yet have the good fortune of knowing you; and if, after thirty-five years of your gentle rule, there are still some among us who are sufficiently blind or ill-intentioned to keep their resentment alive and suggest to the people the criminal desire to return to their former masters, do not ascribe to all what is only the vice of a few.[107]

Still the agitation continued, especially in the Montreal area. Here, in the autumn of 1796, a new document was circulating in which the French representative in the United States, Citizen Adet, assured the Canadiens that they would soon be delivered from the yoke of the English.[108] At the same time Governor Robert Prescott informed the Duke of Portland, in London, that news of the presence of a French squadron on the coast had been welcomed by many Canadiens, encouraging unrest in Montreal.[109] This report was confirmed by Hubert's coadjutor, Bishop Pierre Denaut, who wrote from his presbytery at Longueuil, on the outskirts of the city:

> It appears that we are on the verge of a revolution similar to the one in France. Every day since Sunday large crowds of residents from almost every locality have been forming. . . . They say that they will gather together again tomorrow in even larger numbers. They will probably be several thousand. . . . Revolution, history has said, begins with a crowd of hungry women; how much more should we fear determined men![110]

As in 1793, Bishop Hubert intervened again in 1796 to remind the people of 'the principles of loyalty, obedience and fidelity' they owed the government and to condemn the ideas of rebellion and independence that for several years had been wreaking such havoc.[111] The previous year, in August 1795, an unsigned 'Letter from the Canadiens to Consul of the French Republic in New York' had declared that their countrymen 'all love France, hate the English and fervently desire to be reunited with the mother country from which they have been separated too long'.[112] In fact, a revolution could have occurred in French Canada if leaders had come forward to carry it through. But the new Canadien politicians, who were just beginning to participate in parliamentary institutions, were loath to engage in such radical action. Strong admirers of British institutions, they intended rather to use the forum of the Legislative Assembly to publicize their demands. Moreover, they held very harsh opinions of the 'second French Revolution' of 10 August 1792, which they believed opened 'the way to anarchy, disorder, murder, pillage, and the tyranny that destroys freedom and property',[113] and of Napoleon Bonaparte, 'that destructive genius threatening all the nations of Europe'.[114]

The unrest in Canada really came to an end only in 1797, when the British authorities, who thought they had discovered a huge plot hatched by French agents, carried out the exemplary execution of David McLane, a revolutionary who was more of a madman than an anarchist. Until then, the religious leaders lived in a state of considerable apprehension. They developed an instinctive mistrust of liberal and democratic ideas, and never missed a chance to reaffirm their loyalty to the British Crown. Thus the coadjutor bishop, J.-O. Plessis, would point to the British victory over the French fleet at Aboukir, in 1798, as proof that the British Conquest had indeed been a godsend for French Canada: 'How fortunate for us that Providence separated us from France before she abandoned herself to this terrible blindness, and instead subjected us, through a kindness that we did not deserve, and for which we cannot be too grateful, to the generous and beneficent government of His Most Gracious Majesty, the King of Great Britain.'[115]

Yet these repeated declarations of loyalty on the part of religious leaders did not protect the Catholic Church from London's efforts to subjugate it. A religious crisis began in 1793 that was to last for a quarter of a century. It coincided with the appointment of the first Anglican bishop of the diocese of Quebec, Jacob Mountain. The new diocese, which since 1787 had been under the Anglican bishop of Nova Scotia, Charles Inglis, included both Upper and Lower Canada. At the time of Mountain's arrival on 1 November 1793, the Anglican diocese of Quebec was in a precarious position, having a total of only twelve ministers and missionaries. Of these, the three French-speaking ministers had never enjoyed the respect of Canadiens or even of some among the British, who accused them of insufficient mastery of the English language and, in the cases of Veyssière and Montmollin, immoral conduct.[116]

For Bishop Inglis, who made a pastoral visitation to Quebec in 1789, it was not surprising that the rate of conversion to Catholicism in Lower Canada was twenty times that of conversion to Protestantism.[117] Continuing a policy initiated by Inglis, Mountain decided to replace the three French-speaking ministers with English-speakers. From then on the Church of England gave up the attempt to convert French-speaking Catholics and concerned itself only with the English-speaking Protestants of the colony. This was especially urgent because, according to Charles Morgan, the investigator sent to report on the situation, Methodists, Baptists, and other evangelical groups were moving in from New England and undertaking a dangerous program of proselytism. As proponents of a more democratic and egalitarian Protestantism, these ministers, in their 'Cunning and perseverance', represented a real threat to the Anglican Church, which was jealous of its status as the official church.[118]

As the king's bishop, moreover, Mountain was frustrated to see that Hubert, the pope's bishop, enjoyed greater esteem. Resolving to make the Church of England the colony's established church in fact as well as in law, and to restrict the power of the Catholic bishop, he claimed that the latter was assuming an authority incompatible with the statutes of Great Britain and the instructions that had been given to the governors since 1763. His views were shared by Attorney-General Jonathan Sewell and Civil Secretary Herman Witsius Ryland, who detested papists and their religion, 'which sinks and debases the human mind, and which is a curse to every country where it prevails'.[119] He could also count on the support of the new lieutenant-governor, Sir Robert Shore Milnes, whose administration from 1799 to 1805 was characterized by a large-scale offensive designed to make the colony British in every respect: political, economic, social, cultural, and religious.

On the social and cultural level, the Royal Institution for the Advancement of Learning, founded in 1801 to promote the Anglicization and Protestantization of Canadiens, was one of the main components of a comprehensive program developed by Milnes and his officials. In the area of religion, Milnes had denounced 'the predominance of the Roman Catholic religion' and 'the independence of the clergy' in a report dated 1 November 1800:

> This independence, I find, goes considerably further than what was intended by the Royal Instructions wherein it is particularly declared to be His Majesty's Pleasure 'that no Person whatsoever is to have Holy Orders conferred upon him, or to have the Cure of Souls without a License for that purpose first had been obtained from the Governor' &c. But this Instruction has hitherto never been enforced, by which means the whole Patronage of the Church has been thrown into the hands of a Roman Catholic Bishop, and all connexion between the Government and the People through that Channel is cut off, as the priests do not consider themselves as at all amenable to any other Power than the Catholic Bishop.[120]

To remedy this situation, Milnes suggested to Portland that a closer relationship with the Catholic bishop be developed by raising his annual salary, which was then 200 pounds sterling. In return the bishop would give up certain prerogatives, such as the appointment of parish priests and admission of candidates to holy orders. Portland accepted the proposal: 'The resumption and exercise of that power by the Governor and the producing such a Licence requisite for admission to Holy Orders, I hold not only to be of the first importance, but so indispensably necessary, that I must call upon you to endeavour to effect it by every possible means which prudence can suggest.'[121] But Milnes had no intention of rushing things, preferring to use caution and diplomacy. No doubt he remembered the indignant protest of Bishop Denaut following the government's attempt to substitute the Protestant for the Catholic Bible in the courts in 1795. Denaut had not had kind words for Attorney-General Sewell, 'who will rapidly take us to the point where we will be completely dominated', or for Milnes, whose actions seemed ambiguous: 'I do not like these encroachments by the government. It moves one step at a time, but I know that it means to lead us in a dangerous direction.'[122]

The lieutenant-governor had a first opportunity to carry out his plans in 1801 when the churchwardens of the Catholic parish of Montreal requested the letters of amortization for the Maison Vaudreuil, which had been acquired in 1773 to house the college established by the Sulpicians. Consulted by Milnes, Sewell replied that the state recognized property rights only over church buildings, and that it was essential to put a stop to the claims of the Catholic bishop:

> The general system of the Church of Rome is an Imperium in Imperio. And the present situation of the church in Canada is preeminently such. It is with us a distinct body from the state, an ecclesiastical authority without a shadow of temporal influence and as such an increasing evil highly dangerous to the Government. Yet in the present situation of Canada, where nineteen twentieths of the inhabitants are Catholics, the subject is a matter of great delicacy. Something however it is evident must be done.[123]

A second opportunity presented itself to Milnes in 1805, when a man named Bertrand-Lavergne, a resident of a newly erected parish at Rivière-du-Loup who refused to pay the tithe on the pretext that the parish did not legally exist, brought his case before the courts. Emphasizing the advantages that official recognition by London would have for the Catholic Church, Milnes urged Bishop Denaut to request this formally in exchange for certain concessions. These included making parish assignments permanent and acknowledging the king's right to veto the appointment of priests and the selection of candidates to the priesthood. Although wary of the risks involved in such a move, Bishop Denaut was persuaded by the arguments of his coadjutor, Bishop Plessis, who was obsessed by the desire to 'get the Church out of the humiliating situation it found itself in' and to 'secure the favour of the government'.[124] In addition, such an undertaking might hasten the legal recognition of the parishes founded since 1722, which the British government considered illegal. Thus in July 1805 Bishop Denaut presented two petitions: one, addressed to the king, requesting official recognition of the Roman Catholic Church and its head in Lower Canada; the other asking the lieutenant-governor to plead the cause of the petition before the king.

The Catholic Church was in a perilous situation, but circumstances worked in its favour. Milnes departed for England in the summer of 1805, and Bishop

Denaut died a few months later, in February 1806. His successor, Bishop Plessis, was able to take advantage of the favourable attitude of Thomas Dunn—the president of the Executive Council who, in the absence of a governor, was serving as civil administrator of the province—to swear the oath of loyalty to the king in his capacity as 'Bishop of Quebec' and to have Bishop Bernard-Claude Panet accepted as coadjutor. Mountain remarked bitterly at that time that Dunn had 'grievously disappointed my hopes & fatally thwarted my plans'.[125] Finally, although the judgement in the Bertrand-Lavergne case proved unfavourable to the church—the plaintiff was not forced to pay the tithe—the appeal court refused to rule on the legality of the parishes. Hence there was no longer any immediate danger to the Catholic Church in Canada. Even so, this episode clearly demonstrated that Bishop Denaut was justified in his concern for the future.

The arrival of Governor-General Sir James Henry Craig in 1807 brought a new development in the religious crisis. Craig shared the views of Jacob Mountain, observing that the Catholic bishop of Quebec, although not officially recognized, exercised 'a much greater degree of authority than he did in the time of the French Government'.[126] Like Milnes, he wished to reduce that authority by securing recognition of the king's right to make parish appointments. To this end he had three rather stormy discussions with Bishop Plessis in May and June 1811, in which he pointed out that in Lower Canada the Catholic religion was merely tolerated. He also reminded Plessis of the fate of a Catholic bishop in Havana, who had been expelled from the country because he continued to appoint priests despite the ban on this practice by the governor. To this Plessis retorted, 'I would rather accept being put aboard a warship than betray my conscience.'[127] In the end, this firm attitude, together with a political situation that prompted Craig's recall to London before the year was out, prevailed over the governor's desire to exert more control over the church. The new secretary of state for the colonies, Lord Bathurst, even referred to Plessis as the 'Catholic Bishop of Quebec' in a letter to Craig's successor as governor, Sir George Prevost, on 2 July 1813. Although it would be years before this title was officially recognized, Mountain despaired, immediately writing to Bathurst: 'From a vain hope of conciliating and an ill-founded fear of offending, we have given them [the Canadiens] everything.'[128]

Throughout this difficult period the Catholic Church had been unable to prevent a dramatic drop in the numbers of its clergy. From 1759 to 1791 the number of priests had declined from 196 to 146, while in the same period the French-speaking population had doubled from 70,000 to 140,000. The ratio of priests to believers, which had been 1:350 in 1759, fell to one to 1:1,000. Of the 133 parishes in the diocese, 75 were without a pastor. However, the situation became more hopeful in 1793 with the arrival of 22 priests from France, including 12 Sulpicians driven out by the Revolution.

The decline in numbers of priests was accompanied by a further weakening of the faith and increasing religious indifference. In 1787 Bishop Hubert had declared that 'faith, the primary and most essential virtue of Christians, has died in more than one heart', 'piety has all but disappeared', 'crime has taken off its mask', and 'impiety and irreligiousness have taken root'.[129] His assessment was equally severe seven years later. In a report on the Diocese of Quebec prepared for the Congregation for the Propagation of the Faith, Hubert condemned the principal evils afflicting church and society in French Canada: mixed marriages, which though few in number were giving rise to religious indifference; the distribution of immoral books, which were still flooding the country and destroying Catholics' faith; licentiousness; and dishonesty in business, where the good faith, honesty, and mutual trust of earlier times had given way to distrust and deception, and usury was rampant. 'Some rude peasants,' wrote the bishop, 'who are ignorant of everything else, know all about haggling, and are intent on winning whatever the cost. They evade their tithes and seigneurial duties as long as there is a way of doing it with impunity. That is why innumerable lawsuits are continually blocking the courts, why there is hatred between neighbours and relatives, and why lawyers have such astonishing prestige.'[130]

The lack of devotion at church on Sundays and holy days was another subject of complaint among the clergy. People talked during services, while men gathered in large groups at the doors of the church as to discuss their affairs. Referring to this matter in July 1810, André Doucet, the parish priest at Quebec, stated that it was not uncommon to see 'three or four hundred people gathered together playing games, quarrelling, and planning unspeakable orgies'.[131] Irregularities on holy days were also condemned by the bishop: 'These days are almost always profaned either by doing some hired labour, or by deplorable idleness, or by dances, feasts, overindulgence and scandals of every kind.'[132] In this context it is not surprising to see Antoine Tabeau, the priest of Boucherville, note in 1818 that participation in religious confraternities had declined, that some had simply been forgotten while others hung together by only a few rare meetings.[133] In fact, the confraternities would not experience a revival until 1840.

Nevertheless, according to Hubert, licentious behaviour was not as widespread in the country as in the cities of Quebec and Montreal, where moral corruption had for thirty years wrought 'terrible destruction'. At the root of this phenomenon, he believed, were the population's idleness and extreme poverty, as well as the proximity of aboriginal nations to Montreal and the presence of foreign soldiers and sailors at Quebec. One social class, however, shunned 'any kind of depravity',[134] and their conduct was a comfort to the clergy. This was the emerging class of artisans and shopkeepers, the product of the expansion of the towns serving markets both inside and outside the colony.

Their behaviour reflected the growing emphasis they placed on bourgeois values such as thrift, diligence, and self-discipline.

In Hubert's view, licentious behaviour was most evident among the rising professional class—mostly lawyers, doctors, notaries, and small businessmen—who were coming into their own following the establishment of the Legislative Assembly. In the past this class had been excluded from power by the dominant conservative social forces, notably the seigneurs and the upper clergy, who unswervingly supported British rule. But now, as the Quebec economy diversified, the number of professionals was growing, along with their influence. These men would soon become supporters of liberal and democratic ideas that reflected their own ambitions for power and social prominence. They would also become critical of the bishops' unquestioning support for Britain, and of the power that the upper clergy wielded.

In a society where religious values were no longer passed down as before, it is not surprising that vocations to the priesthood had little appeal for young people. In 1791 the principal of the Collège de Montréal (founded in 1767 by the Sulpician Jean-Baptiste Curatteau) told Bishop Hubert that among the students there was 'a great deal of laziness and very little religion'.[135] The bishop himself noted with regret the students' 'lack of interest in the clerical state', as well as the disturbing inroads that 'spirit of independence and libertinism' was making among them.[136] At the same time Hubert lamented the low quality of the candidates for the priesthood produced by the Séminaire de Québec. Few completed more than two years at the Grand Séminaire, and even during that time they were often employed as teachers or supervisors in the colleges, to the detriment of their theological education. (This situation would improve somewhat in 1825, when Jean-Jacques Lartigue, the auxiliary bishop in Montreal, set up the Séminaire Saint-Jacques in his residence to provide a stronger background in theology.)

Despite these educational deficiencies, however, Bishop Hubert saw no reason to suspect any priest of heresy. Coming from all social classes, but mainly from the common people, they led well-ordered lives and diligently carried out the duties of their office. A foreign observer, John Lambert, would say in 1818 that the priests rarely exhorted the faithful to do what they themselves did not.[137] They lived in a simple manner, according to Bishop Briand, who set an example for his clergy;[138] to a parish priest who complained of his material conditions, the bishop replied: 'Is it appropriate for priests not to want to share in the misery of the people?'[139] Periods of acute food shortages, as in 1784 and 1789, provided opportunities for the clergy to draw closer to the people, whom they generously assisted.[140] Even the anticlerical Louis-Antoine Dessaules, mayor and seigneur of Saint-Hyacinthe, admitted that the priests were noted for their 'courtesy and refined manners'.[141] Finally, with respect to the moral behaviour of the clergy, Bishop Hubert wrote that 'in general there prevails among them great attachment to decency, at least outwardly.'[142] For the period 1760–1840 the historian Lucien Lemieux has found little evidence of alcoholism among the clergy and few cases of priests summoned before the courts. The occasional instances of worldly behaviour that he does report appear relatively minor: attending dances and parties, gambling, practising medicine, owning romantic and frivolous books, running small businesses, and going hunting.[143] On the whole, the Canadien clergy appear to have been distinguished by their sobriety, dignity, and selflessness.

No doubt there was considerable exaggeration in the portrait that Bishop Hubert drew of the religious and moral behaviour of the general population. Faith may have been dormant in this period, but it was not dead. The people's indifference to religious matters reflected the profound changes that their society was undergoing. The Catholic Church was no longer revered as it had been, for the most part, during the early years of the British regime, and even Governor Craig remarked to Bishop Plessis in 1811 that an acquaintance who had known the country very well for a long time assured him that religion was dropping off significantly.[144] That the people were losing confidence in their episcopal leadership had been evident ever since they ignored Bishop Briand's instructions during the American invasion. Under these circumstances, the influence of the liberal ideas transmitted by agents of the revolutionary Directory in France spread rapidly, with the result that for fifty years, from 1791 to 1840, the church was to experience a period of hibernation.

CLERICAL CONSOLIDATION

Regarded with suspicion by the British authorities and ignored by an increasingly large number of the people, the Catholic Church also found itself called into question by the new lay élite. Now that the Legislative Assembly provided a forum where they could make themselves heard, these men supplanted the religious leaders as spokesmen for the Canadien community. Although they had turned their backs on the revolutionary adventure, their political goals still alarmed the religious leaders. From 1806 on these deputies—who by now were known as the Parti canadien—forcefully demanded measures that they claimed followed naturally from British constitutional law, notably ministerial responsibility and an elected legislative council. At the same time they condemned the government's unjustified expenditures, its practice of allowing members of the bench to hold legislative or executive office, and the corrupt behaviour of certain senior officials. All this provoked a bitter struggle between the Legislative Assembly, which was dominated by the Parti canadien, and Governor Craig. Disinclined to support the democratic aspirations of the popular assembly, Bishop Plessis deplored the growing influence of the Parti canadien's newspaper, *Le Canadien*, among the people and even the clergy, declaring that it would 'destroy every principle of subordination and set the province ablaze'.[145] When, fearing 'a general uprising', the government had the offices of the paper searched in March 1810, Plessis expressed his concern 'that a large number of priests were encouraging the publication of *Le Canadien* by their subscriptions' and that 'its ideas were praised in and around the presbyteries'.[146]

This situation clearly illustrates the dilemma faced by the church. On the one hand, the religious leaders distrusted the new politicians who had over-shadowed them and who spoke out in a way they considered audacious and dangerous. On the other hand, the lower clergy, who were recruited from all classes of society, could not help standing by their compatriots and supporting the struggles of the Parti canadien with the British administration, while the higher clergy recognized the threat presented to the church by the bill propos-ing the union of Upper and Lower Canada in 1822.

The news of the introduction of this bill in the London parliament was greeted with disbelief throughout the country. On 7 October 1822 a huge protest meeting was held in Montreal that, according to *Le Spectateur canadien*, was destined to be 'epoch-making in the history of Canada and Canadiens'. Like the political leaders who anticipated disastrous consequences for their compatriots, the new auxiliary bishop in Montreal, Jean-Jacques Lartigue, was deeply concerned by this 'iniquitous measure', which had to be stopped at all costs: 'Besides the harm in the civil domain that this proposed bill would cause us as Canadiens, it would oppress us even more as Catholics by a clause [clause 25] that establishes the spiritual supremacy of the king over our Church, and that would have the appointment of all parish priests in Canada depend on the favour or whim of a Protestant governor.'[147]

In December 1822 the clergy joined other Canadiens in signing a petition to the king demanding withdrawal of the Union proposal. The newspaper *Le Canadien* hastened to applaud this gesture which, it said, demonstrated the 'reli-gious and patriotic zeal' that the parish priests had always manifested.[148] Bishop Lartigue later wrote of this event: 'Did we not see the pastors united with their flock when they demanded only fair treatment, and when they demanded it in the proper manner? Did not the whole Catholic clergy walk hand-in-hand with the Canadien people when they effectively opposed the much-vaunted union of the two provinces of Canada?'[149]

In thus taking a stand in a conflict between the Legislative Assembly and the imperial government, the religious leaders departed from their cherished principle of political neutrality. No doubt the gravity of the situation explains their intervention; but it was an exceptional gesture. The parliamentary crisis of 1827, when Lord Dalhousie dissolved the Assembly for its refusal to vote a limited budget and then, when the new Assembly met, attempted to veto the choice of L.-J. Papineau as speaker,[150] gave the religious leaders an opportunity to clarify their thinking on this point. Writing to J.-B. Keller, the parish priest of

Sorel, whom certain newspapers had accused of supporting candidates of the Parti canadien during the election campaign, Bishop Lartigue said:

> The clergy has to be very careful not to take part in any of these election quarrels, which would gradually cause them to lose the influence they need in order to carry out their ministry fruitfully and to promote the devotion of our fellow subjects to the government; that has always been our course, ever since the Legislative Assembly was established, and to behave otherwise would be both contrary to our duty and detrimental to our religion.[151]

It was wise of the bishop to advocate political neutrality. Aware that the church was caught 'in the crossfire because of the quarrels between the Administration and the Legislative Assembly', and that each of the two parties was trying to gain the clergy's support, Lartigue considered it essential that in this crisis 'all the clergy exhibit uniform and consistent behaviour, and that they be more united than ever so as not to lose any of their influence'. 'I believe that our course should be not to sign anything that will be sent to England by either side and to involve ourselves as little as possible in these discussions.'[152] Moreover, the bishop was confident that the people would understand that it was in the church's interest not to attract the animosity of the British government at a time when it was still exposed to the hostility of anti-Catholics in Lower Canada. Nor would London be taken in by the silence of the religious leaders; in fact, their political neutrality deceived no one. The Montreal nationalist newspaper *La Minerve* also emphasized in favourable terms the 'independent position' adopted by the clergy during this crisis: 'The Canadien people will perhaps be persuaded by this that the Catholic religion is not an intolerant, persecuting religion, that it can easily ally itself to a freedom which is just, and that to stay strong it has no need of a mutual offensive or defensive pact with the temporal authorities.'[153]

What was the situation of the Catholic Church while this political struggle was unfolding in Lower Canada? By the end of the War of 1812 it had managed to avert the threat that had been hanging over it since 1793. In the course of the war, Bishop Plessis and his clergy had urged the Canadiens to be faithful subjects of the king. A number of Canadiens had taken part in the fighting, and some priests had served as chaplains in the army. Having intervened repeatedly to encourage the people's loyalty and zeal, the bishop greeted the end of hostilities with joy and declared that 6 April 1815 would be a day of thanksgiving for this happy event.[154] As a reward for his loyalty during the conflict, in 1818 the British government had recognized Plessis as the 'bishop of the Roman Catholic Church of Quebec', with the right to sit in the Legislative Council. Pleased with this triumph, the bishop immediately wrote to Rome: 'Here for the first time the Catholic episcopate of Canada has been recognized and acknowledged in my person by the British government, and I have reason to hope that my successors will be recognized as well.'[155]

After the legal and material insecurity of the preceding years, this recognition, even if it applied only to Bishop Plessis personally and not to his successors, represented an enormous step towards freedom for the Catholic Church. Yet many points remained undecided, including the civil recognition of parishes, the title deeds of educational institutions, and the question of the property of Saint-Sulpice, which the British government still coveted. Furthermore, the bishop of Quebec was unable to take any important initiative without the agreement of the British authorities. Confident, however, after this first victory, Bishop Plessis travelled to London and Rome to arrange for the division of his diocese, which was much too large for a single bishop. This idea was not completely new. Bishop Hubert in 1789 and Bishop Plessis in 1806 had already considered it, but circumstances had prevented them from carrying it out. The situation in 1819 was much more favourable. In London the bishop nevertheless came up against the ill humour of Lord Bathurst, secretary of state for the colonies, who was annoyed by the fact that the year before Rome had raised Plessis to the rank of archbishop without first consulting the British authorities. For them, such an appointment was unthinkable, given the presence in Quebec of an Anglican bishop who now found himself occupying a lower rank than the pope's bishop. After being assured that Plessis would give up the idea of bearing the title 'Archbishop', Bathurst agreed in September 1819 to the appointment of new bishops, on the understanding that they would be subordinated to Bishop Plessis.

In 1818 Rome had appointed Alexander Macdonell and Angus Bernard MacEachern both as vicars-general and as auxiliary and suffragan bishops[156] of Quebec for the districts of Upper Canada and Prince Edward Island. In addition, Plessis secured from Rome the creation of two more districts, as well as the appointment as bishops of Jean-Jacques Lartigue in Montreal and Joseph-Norbert Provencher in the Red River district to the west. There were now five ecclesiastical divisions—Quebec, with 200,000 Catholics; Montreal, with 200,000 as well; Upper Canada, with 15,000; Prince Edward Island, including New Brunswick and Cape Breton Island, with 15,000; and the Red River colony, with 3,000[157]—while for the territory of Nova Scotia, with 10,000 faithful, Rome had appointed a vicar apostolic in 1817 in the person of Edmund Burke.

Burke's and Macdonell's own negotiations with the British and Vatican authorities were not without influence on their appointments in the Atlantic region. The long memorandum that Burke presented to the Congregation for the Propagation of the Faith, in 1815, calling for the Maritimes to be separated from Quebec and assigned to the care of English-speaking bishops, had been well received by the Vatican authorities, who were now on good terms with

London.[158] Similarly, the plan submitted by Macdonell to the British authorities during his trip to Europe in 1816–17, proposing the creation of two new dioceses—one at Charlottetown, the other at Kingston in Upper Canada—had strongly influenced the decisions of London and Rome.[159] In particular, Macdonell had informed the British authorities of his fear that Bishop Plessis would propose French-speaking candidates to head these two dioceses if London did not act quickly. He was supported in this by MacEachern, who also believed that the diocese of Quebec should be split up, and who, like the other English-speaking priests of the diocese, had 'a sense of alienation from the Canadian hierarchy'.[160]

The Acadian population was growing significantly in this period. Numbering roughly 10,000 in 1806—nearly one-tenth of the region's population—they would increase to 30,000 by 1830. Their civil and political rights were expanding as well. In 1783, in response to pressure from Irish Catholics, the legislature of Nova Scotia had allowed public Catholic worship without restrictions. In the same year the legislature also amended the law of 1758, which had seriously limited the property rights of Catholics, and it no longer tried to hinder Catholic missionaries since Abbé Joseph-Mathurin Bourg had managed in September 1778 to persuade the natives of the Saint John River valley to back the British rather than the Americans. The situation in 1783 was thus very different from the one that had prevailed twenty years earlier, when Catholic priests were in theory banned from Nova Scotia on threat of imprisonment. Similarly, in 1786 a more tolerant law was passed by the legislature of Nova Scotia allowing the creation of Catholic schools, and three years later Nova Scotia granted Catholics the right to vote. (New Brunswick would not follow suit until 1810.) But the right to sit in the legislature was not granted to Catholics until 1830, soon after the Emancipation Act recognized Catholicism in Great Britain and abolished the oath of the Test Act.[161] In the same year, the Assembly of Prince Edward Island adopted a law granting the emancipation of the island's Catholics.

By the beginning of the nineteenth century, therefore, an Acadian church was in the process of formation. An important factor in this process was the arrival of a dozen missionaries who had been driven out of France by the Revolution, among them Father Jean-Mandé Sigogne, one of the most notable missionary figures of the period. As a result the number of Acadian parishes grew in the three principal areas where Acadians had settled: Arichat (1786), Pointe-de-l'Église, or Church Point (1799) and Chéticamp (1801) in Nova Scotia; Memramcook (1781), Caraquet (1788), and Saint-Basile (1792) in New Brunswick; and Rustico (1800) in Prince Edward Island. By 1815 the Acadians had received five pastoral visits from bishops of Quebec, in 1795, 1803, 1811, 1812, and 1815.[162] The visit of 1803 was particularly moving at Pointe-de-l'Église, which was receiving a bishop for the first time: 'The whole village, with Father Sigogne at the front, was waiting for him on the beach, their hearts beating and tears in their eyes.'[163]

The Acadian church nevertheless remained fragile. Rome's creation of the vicariate apostolic of Nova Scotia in 1817 meant that the Acadians of mainland Nova Scotia were now separated from the mother church in Quebec and placed under the authority of an English-speaking bishop, Edmund Burke. The Acadian community of Nova Scotia had good reason to consider this decision unfair, even though there had been no Acadian priest since the death in 1797 of Abbé Bourg. The Acadians of Prince Edward Island felt similarly offended when the diocese of Charlottetown was established in 1829 despite the opposition of the bishop of Quebec, Bernard-Claude Panet, who considered the separation of Charlottetown from Quebec untimely. Bishop Plessis's attempts several years earlier, in 1820, to bring the apostolic vicariate of Nova Scotia back under his own control by joining it to the episcopal district of Prince Edward Island on the death of Bishop Burke had proven equally vain.[164] It is understandable that in 1829 Bishop Panet had pity on those 'good Acadians'[165] whose relations with the English-speaking bishops were rather strained. The parish priest of Shediac, Abbé Antoine Gagnon, whom Bishop Joseph Signay would propose to Rome as successor to Bishop MacEachern at Charlottetown in 1835, had already confided to Plessis that he did 'not like either the Scots or the Irish. They have ways that are theirs alone and that are difficult, if not impossible, to accept.'[166] Bishop Signay would gladly have had the diocese of Charlottetown joined to the diocese of Quebec.

Nor was the Acadian church's transition from a missionary enterprise to an established institution entirely smooth. The arrival of resident priests disturbed the people's deep-rooted habits. The Acadians had never known a truly omnipresent church. Accustomed to carrying out themselves a number of ecclesiastical functions when missionaries were not there,[167] and not having had to look after the needs of their priests for long periods of time, the Acadians experienced some difficulty in adjusting to the new reality. Between 1763 and 1840 there was 'a kind of power struggle between the missionary and the lay person' that gave rise to many 'quarrels over questions like tithing, pews in the churches, weddings, the construction and repair of churches and presbyteries, [and] also over such practices as baptising infants immediately after birth.'[168] More than once Acadians rebelled against the instructions of their new pastors. The residents of Pointe-de-l'Église, for instance, found it difficult to accept the authoritarian attitude of Father Sigogne. But they still expressed an unswerving devotion to this missionary who served as a guiding spirit for 45 years, from 1799 to 1844.[169] Furthermore, Father Sigogne, while reproaching these 'quarrelsome, hard to please people' for their stubbornness and spirit of independence, could still praise 'their good nature and good will'.[170]

Meanwhile, more than 2,500 kilometres west of Montreal, near Fort Douglas (Winnipeg) on the Red River, a new Catholic community was being established under the direction of Bishop Norbert Provencher, who in 1820 was appointed auxiliary bishop to the bishop of Quebec and at the same time the prelate responsible for the new episcopal district. Entrusted in 1818 with the task of establishing the Catholic Church in this region, Provencher had in the mean- time built a chapel dedicated to St Boniface. The new bishop became responsi- ble for a vast territory inhabited by Scottish, Irish, and Métis settlers and stretching as far as the Rocky Mountains. The plan to transform the mission into an episcopal district was not carried out without difficulty: it ran into oppo- sition from both the directors of the Hudson's Bay Company (who were less sympathetic to the Catholic religion since the death of Lord Selkirk in 1820) and the managers of the North West Company, the HBC's rival, who were clearly averse to Catholicism. Provencher also had to confront the hostility of the Anglican minister John West, who had arrived in the settlement in August 1820 and was fiercely anti-Catholic. Provencher was nevertheless well received by the interim governor of Assiniboia, Andrew H. Bulger, when he returned from Lower Canada, where he had been consecrated bishop in May 1822.

Bishop Provencher had four objectives in his apostolic work: educating young people, helping with settlement, improving the moral behaviour of whites, and converting the natives.[171] In 1819 he set up a boys' school in St-Boniface, and ten years later he entrusted a Métis woman, Angélique Morin, with responsibility for a girls' school. With respect to agriculture, he encour- aged cultivation and cattle-breeding, and in 1838 he set up an industrial school to make use of bison hides as well as the wool from sheep. In the realm of pas- toral care, Bishop Provencher fought alcohol abuse and encouraged Canadien men to regularize their marriages with native and Métis women. However, with the exception of the efforts of Abbé Sévère Dumoulin in the Pembina (North Dakota) region between 1818 and 1823, evangelization really began only in 1831 with the arrival of Abbé George-Antoine Bellecourt, who under- took a mission among the Saulteaux Chipewyan (Dene) west of St-Boniface on the Assiniboine River. To help him achieve his objectives, Bishop Provencher never had more than four or five priests at a time; altogether, thirteen mission- aries assisted the bishop in the period up to 1843.

Despite these modest beginnings, the Catholic Church was well established in St-Boniface by 1830. Relations between Bishop Provencher and the gover- nors of the Northern Division of the Hudson's Bay Company had definitely improved. From 1825 on, he even received a subsidy from the company, which was regularly increased. And, beginning in 1837, he was admitted as an adviser to the meetings of the Assiniboia Council, where he had considerable influ- ence. Provencher could now envisage making his episcopal district an autonomous ecclesiastical territory. To this end, in 1835 he made a trip to

Rome, whose eventual success, nine years later, would play an important part in ensuring the future of the Catholic Church in the Northwest.

The voyage of Bishop Plessis to Rome and London in 1819–20 had represented an important advance for the church in Canada. Although he probably did not obtain everything he wished, the results were positive. From this point on Plessis was assisted by four auxiliary bishops enjoying considerable administrative autonomy in their respective districts of Upper Canada, the Northwest, the Maritimes, and Montreal. In the long term, the presence of auxiliary bishops, especially in the cities where there were large numbers of Protestants, facilitated the establishment of permanent dioceses. This was particularly true for Montreal, where the Protestants, numbering roughly 6,000 represented a third of the population. Louis-Joseph Papineau was among those who considered it very good,

> to lend more weight to the Canadien clergy, to see a man in the purple robe frequently strolling the streets of Montreal. As the Protestants become accustomed to seeing this robe without feeling irritated, will not the administration, in which they will always be numerous and influential, remove all the sooner its opposition to letting the bishop exercise his authority to establish new parishes? Will it not more quickly agree to the creation of suffragan bishoprics to that of Quebec?[172]

Similarly, Bishop Provencher believed that his presence as auxiliary bishop could only be beneficial to the church in the Northwest by giving 'more weight to religion'.[173] In fact, it would not be long before all four of these districts were made bishoprics: the dioceses of Kingston in 1826, Charlottetown (including Prince Edward Island, New Brunswick, and the Îles de la Madeleine) in 1829, Montreal in 1836, and the vicariate apostolic of Hudson Bay and James Bay in 1844.

In 1819, when London and Rome authorized the division of the diocese of Quebec, the church was preparing to launch a vast campaign in Lower Canada that would coincide with the appointment of Jean-Jacques Lartigue as auxiliary bishop in Montreal. This highly cultivated man was profoundly attached to the church and to the person of the pope. Vigorously opposed to Gallicanism, which advocated the independence of local churches from the Holy See, and a staunch defender of the absolute authority of the pope and the primacy of the Church of Rome, he was one of a generation of great Ultramontane bishops who would openly assert the supremacy of the church within civil society. In the course of his nineteen years at Montreal, first as auxiliary bishop, from his consecration in 1821 to 1836, and then as titular bishop, from 1836 to 1840, Lartigue was to play a dominant role in the church's efforts to create a model Christian society in French Canada.

In particular, this social project comprised plans for the church to control the field of education and take responsibility for the whole area of social welfare. The church had played a dominant role in education ever since the first schools were founded in the seventeenth century by the Ursulines at Quebec and by the Sisters of the Congrégation de Notre-Dame at Montreal and in rural areas. In 1820 there were more than a hundred educational institutions in Lower Canada, including 32 parish schools, 11 girls' schools, four convents, and three *collèges classiques* run directly by the clergy and religious communities. These schools compared favourably with the 37 schools managed by the Royal Institution, and with the 25 private schools founded by lay associations or teachers. A little more than 2,000 pupils out of an estimated total of 4,000[174] attended the church-run schools. These figures, however, represent only a small proportion of the school-age children in Lower Canada, who at that time numbered 70,000; in 1821 the newspaper *Le Canadien* called attention to 'the almost total lack of elementary schools' in rural areas.[175] As L.-P. Audet observed, 'the first twenty-four years of the nineteenth century remain a very dark period in the history of education in Lower Canada.'[176]

The first school legislation in the province that was favourable to the Catholic Church was the law of 1824, which established parochial schools under the direction of parish priests. Believing that education belonged by right to the church, Bishops Plessis and Lartigue gave as much encouragement as possible to the growth of these schools. By 1830 there were 68 of them, in addition to the 14 schools run by the Sisters of the Congrégation de Notre-Dame in rural areas. As Lartigue wrote to Panet, in 1829: 'We ought to urge parish priests, through a pastoral letter, to set up parish schools. In this way we can show the Protestants, who are always accusing us of discouraging education, that in fact we are the only ones who are promoting it in an effective manner.'[177] Indeed, this would be the final recommendation of Bishop Lartigue in 1839, in a pastoral issued shortly after the arrival of four Christian Brothers (Frères des Écoles Chrétiennes): 'If all your children could be educated, from their tender years, by the Christian Brothers and the Sisters of the Congrégation de Notre-Dame, as a number have had the good fortune to be in our episcopal city, how happy the results would be for your families.'[178]

If education was the cornerstone of this social project, however, the church also intended to have a strong presence in the field of health and welfare. Since the arrival of the Hospitalières at Quebec and Montreal in the seventeenth century, the church had taken responsibility for helping the sick and the indigent. In 1820 Lower Canada had five hospitals to care for the sick and the elderly: the Hôtel-Dieu and the Hôpital-Général in Quebec, run by the Hospitalières de la Miséricorde de Jésus; the Ursuline hospital in Trois-

Rivières; and the Hôtel-Dieu and the Hôpital-Général in Montreal, managed by the Hospitalières de Saint-Joseph and the Grey Nuns, respectively. The poor and the indigent, whose numbers were continuously on the rise, in the cities especially, were taken into the care of the religious communities and other church organizations. The persistence of poverty, which had been continuous in Lower Canada since the Conquest, was attributed in large part to periodic natural disasters such as floods, which were common in the Montreal area, and fires of the kind that reduced more than half of the city of Montreal to ashes in 1765 and 1768; occasional food shortages caused by poor harvests, as in 1788–9, 1813–17 and 1830–7; frequent epidemics, like that of the (probably syphilitic) disease that swept the Baie-Saint-Paul region for thirteen years, from 1773 to 1786, and the cholera epidemics that struck twice and spared no area of the province in 1832 and 1834; and, finally, the arrival, starting in 1820, of large numbers of impoverished Irish immigrants. The deplorable hygienic conditions under which the latter arrived were undoubtedly a factor in the huge epidemic of 1832, which left hundreds of orphans for the religious communities to care for. In that year a Catholic orphanage was founded in Montreal, with the encouragement of the Sulpicians, which soon took in approximately forty children.

The realization of the church's social project depended to a great extent on the activism of a small number of outstanding women, both lay and religious. The pioneer in this respect was Marguerite d'Youville, whose Grey Nuns shunned traditional religious life behind a cloister in favour of an enduring commitment to the poor. In the early nineteenth century, however, as Montreal and Quebec City began to industrialize, other, more direct forms of social intervention were required. Inspired by the example of St Vincent de Paul, in the late 1820s a number of wealthy laywomen formed volunteer charitable organizations known as the Dames de Charité. They collected funds for the poor, visited them in their homes, established soup kitchens, sheltered orphans and physically dependent women, and found work for domestic servants. Eventually specializing in particular services, these groups were the crucible in which many female religious communities with a distinctive social commitment were later formed. In 1843, for example, Émilie Gamelin, née Tavernier, who as a young widow of twenty-seven had begun working with elderly and disabled women, founded the Institut des Soeurs de la Charité de la Providence (Sisters of Providence). Similarly, the widow Rosalie Cadron-Jetté started out caring for unwed mothers in her own home before founding the Institut des Soeurs de Miséricorde in 1846. Alongside the older communities dedicated to teaching and nursing, lay and religious women alike established new forms of social intervention between 1760 and 1840 that laid the foundation for the remarkable flowering of female religious life that would occur in the period after the Union.

PROTESTANTISM AND REVOLUTION

During the 1830s the Catholic Church was thus deeply involved in the areas of both social welfare and education. In making these the main priorities of their social project, the bishops of Quebec and Montreal were reacting to a twofold danger: Protestant efforts to convert Catholics and the plans for a lay society put forward by the leaders of the Legislative Assembly.

Only in 1815 did Protestant proselytism begin in Lower Canada, when the Bible societies engaged in a promotion campaign to win Canadien converts. By 1817 Bishop Plessis was already deeply concerned about 'the great harm done by the bibles distributed by the Protestant societies in the province', especially the Methodist groups in Montreal and the Ottawa valley. To refute Protestant claims that the Catholic Church did not allow its faithful to read the Bible, he planned to publish a French edition of the New Testament.[179] Although, when the bishop consulted him on this matter, the superior of Saint-Sulpice replied that 'the fervour the Protestants show for the Bible is not yet cause for alarm',[180] Plessis immediately embarked upon his project with the help of Jean-Jacques Lartigue, who was then attached to the Séminaire de Saint-Sulpice. Lartigue pursued this work on an occasional basis until Plessis's death in 1825; but he did not consider it a priority, feeling that the zeal of the Bible societies had slackened considerably in the Montreal region. Nevertheless, in 1826 he condemned the use of Royal Institution schools, as well as some Protestant schools (in Quebec City, Trois-Rivières, Terrebonne, Chambly, and Rigaud), for the purposes of Protestant proselytism. 'It is a critical time,' he wrote to Bishop Panet. 'If these Protestant schools get hold of our youth, there may be no remedy.'[181] The existence in Lower Canada of some Protestant private schools that were open to both English- and French-speaking pupils had aroused the fears of Bishop Plessis in 1822: 'These attempts of the Protestant clergy to work their way in everywhere and take over public education are truly alarming. It is the duty of parish priests to hinder them by any means that zeal suggests and prudence allows.'[182]

Protestant efforts to open schools and convert Catholics would not bear fruit, however, until after 1834, when the first French-speaking evangelists arrived from Switzerland. Sent by the Evangelical Mission Society of Lausanne, Henri Olivier, Henriette Odin, and Louis Roussy settled first in the Montreal region, where they opened a meeting hall and three small schools. When, after a few months, the inhabitants of Montreal proved hostile to any kind of conversion activity, Olivier returned to Switzerland while Odin and Roussy withdrew to Grande-Ligne, an area about fifty kilometres south of Montreal that had recently opened to settlement. Shortly after, the first French Protestant church in Canada was established at Grande-Ligne. But the results remained modest despite the support of two apostate Catholic priests, Louis-

Léon Normandeau and Hubert-Joseph Tétreau, as well as Doctor Cyrille-Hector-Octave Côté, a well-known Patriote. Indeed, many more Protestants were converted to Catholicism; the district of Montreal alone saw roughly a hundred such conversions between 1816 and 1836.

A more serious threat for Bishop Lartigue came from the new lay intelligentsia, which did not disguise its admiration for the Enlightenment. Inspired by the ideas of the French Revolution, the leaders of the Assembly, particularly the Montreal leaders of the Parti canadien, were developing a vision of society that ran directly counter to that of the Catholic Church. Beginning in 1829, they set out to redefine Canadien society in secular terms, advocating separation of church and state and firmly asserting the rights of lay people against what they called the encroachments of the clergy. Two measures in particular were intended to limit the influence of the clergy and transfer to the state the control that until then the church had exercised over schools, hospitals, and parish councils: the Assembly Schools Act of 1829, and the Parish Councils (or Notables) bill of 1831.

Condemning the role traditionally played by the church in the field of education, the political leaders wished to give the Assembly the ultimate responsibility for education and create a system of state-run schools to operate alongside the church-controlled schools created in accordance with the school acts of 1824 and 1827. To accomplish these aims, in 1829 they adopted the Assembly Schools Act. Modelled after legislation in the state of New York, this law entrusted the organization of schools, under the supervision of the Legislative Assembly, to trustees elected democratically in each parish. This measure would result in a significant rise in the rate of school attendance in Lower Canada. In the very year of the law's adoption, 262 trustees' schools were added to the 206 existing schools. By 1830 they constituted 752 of the province's 981 schools, and the number of pupils had gone from 18,401 to 41,791. In 1832 their total reached 872, or more than two-thirds of the 1,216 existing schools. And by 1836, when the law expired and was not renewed, their number had risen to 1,200.[183]

Whatever the undoubted merits of this law, it is nevertheless the case that through it the political leaders had, as Bishop Lartigue said, sought to 'paralyze the moderate influence' of the church in this field, by transferring the parish priests' responsibility for schools to elected trustees. Just as the bishop had fiercely opposed any collaboration of the church with the Royal Institution, so he strongly condemned the law of 1829 and encouraged the clergy to take advantage of the school acts of 1824 and 1827 to create schools managed by parish councils. A few years later, in 1836, when the law establishing normal schools was passed, he reiterated his concerns to Bishop Pierre-Flavien Turgeon: 'What the bill of 1829 did to weaken our primary schools and take them out of the hands of the clergy so they could be handed over to lay people, the normal schools are going to do with respect to the formation and education of our schoolteachers in the whole province.'[184] Thus responsibility for education was at the heart of the controversy that set the church against the leaders of the Assembly. When, in 1836, the Legislative Council refused to renew the 1829 law, Bishop Lartigue considered it a 'valuable and perhaps unique opportunity' for the church to take back control of education through the creation of schools in each parish under the direction of its priests, and thereby 'rescue the future generation from an abhorrent system of education'.[185]

The second measure that divided the church and the leaders of the Assembly was the controversial Parish Council, or Notables, bill of 1831, which stipulated that all 'notables' (landowners) would participate in meetings of parish councils. By refusing to take into consideration a petition from the clergy opposed to the measure, the Assembly leaders elicited the condemnation of religious authorities such as Bishop Lartigue, who denounced the bill as 'an ill-conceived monstrosity':

> I am very angry at the result of our attempts to obtain justice in the Chamber, but I am not surprised. The abominable ideas about the Church that certain members are trying to establish, followed only too blindly by this race of sheep, show us what to expect if we do not oppose their projects as zealously as they will promote them. . . . It is one thing for the Church to let herself be plundered when she cannot prevent it; another to aid in her own enslavement.[186]

For Lartigue, there was no doubt about the goal of the Assembly leaders: they intended to introduce into the meetings of churchwardens the democratic practices used in the Legislative Assembly and thereby lessen the influence of the clergy in the running of parish councils and among the people, with a view eventually to gaining the upper hand over the church. The debate lasted several months and provoked some extremely sharp verbal exchanges, both in the newspapers and in the Legislative Assembly. Louis-Joseph Papineau claimed that the Act of Supremacy adopted in England gave the government control over all the temporal affairs of the church. Speaking of the clergy's petition in the legislature, he declared:

> In spite of your splendid robes, your petition is, without exception, the least excusable one that has ever been submitted to the Legislature. You are incapable of seeing or feeling, yet you claim a divine right to control everything. Can anything be more anti-national, more anti-patriotic? You are men of paradox who think you are living in [some earlier] century, when the Church took control of temporal goods and authority. . . . You may well exercise a dangerous influence over the people; but your initiative at this time is indiscreet and your conduct extremely ill-considered.[187]

In response, Bishop Lartigue declared that these remarks reflected 'the present attitude of old France' and were not only useless but harmful to the Canadien cause: 'Papineau and several others have conducted themselves in a shameful manner on this question, and they could do no better thing to please our enemies than to drive a wedge between the clergy and the Assembly.'[188] The leaders of the Assembly had declared war on the church, and the latter had to fall back on the Legislative Council, made up mainly of English-speaking Protestants, in order to have the bill defeated. A profound difference of opinion on the direction that Canadien society should take divided Bishop Lartigue and his cousin Papineau, who accused the church of wanting 'to form within the state, within civil society, among citizens all subject to the laws, an independent, privileged order'.[189] A power struggle had been set off between the two institutions, and they were to confront each other even more furiously after 1832.

Although the radicalism of the Assembly leaders had long worried the religious authorities, it was an article in *La Minerve*, the Patriote newspaper of Montreal, that particularly aroused their fears. On 16 February 1832 *La Minerve* published a passionate article openly advocating revolt and the separation of Lower Canada from England. Arguing from the principle that 'the greatest hardship for a politician is to have to obey a foreign power', the anonymous author continued:

> Our country finds itself in very critical circumstances, and we may need a revolution to put it into a more natural and less precarious situation. . . . Immediate separation from England is the only means of preserving our nationality. Later, when immigration will have made our enemies equal to us in numbers, more daring and less generous, they will deprive us of our liberties or we shall suffer the same fate as our unfortunate compatriots, the Acadians. Make no mistake, that is the fate that awaits us if we do not soon make ourselves independent.

This revolutionary article created a sensation in Lower Canada. It was symptomatic of the profound discontent that had overtaken the political milieu. Since 1827, when Dalhousie attempted to veto the choice of Papineau as speaker, the radical leaders of the Assembly had been deeply disappointed by the constitution of 1791, which in their view was 'only a deceptive shadow of the English constitution'.[190] Exasperated by London's systematic opposition to their demands, they had lost all admiration for British institutions and hardened their attitude towards the authorities in London. Strongly influenced as well by the July Revolution of 1830 in France, on which the Canadien newspapers reported at length, they decided that the time had come for a major confrontation with London. At the same time, seditious meetings in various places encouraged resistance and insubordination to the established authorities.

In 1834 Louis-Joseph Papineau, the unchallenged leader of the Patriote party, declared: 'The people want nothing more to do with the present system, which has only been an unfortunate experiment, accompanied by forty years of injustice and suffering.'[191] In the same year the legislature adopted a series of resolutions reiterating all the grievances accumulated over the years of parliamentary struggle.

The political situation in Lower Canada was becoming explosive. It was very troubling for the moderate leaders of the Parti canadien in the Quebec City region, who disagreed with the uncompromising policy of the radical Montreal leaders. The religious authorities too were alarmed by the revolutionary climate that was beginning to overtake Lower Canada. Bishop Lartigue feared the worst. Two days after *La Minerve* published the revolutionary article of 16 February, he wrote to Bishop Panet:

> Now our Canadien papers are becoming more revolutionary than ever. . . . Revolution is openly called for and high treason is revealed without pretence. . . . Is there no one who will charitably warn the governor that it is his duty to see that the authors of such writings are prosecuted without hesitation by the solicitor general, if he does not want it to be too late when he does try to silence them?[192]

The power struggle that had now begun between the church and the political leaders would reach its conclusion in 1837. In the meantime, Governor Archibald Acheson Gosford's attempts to initiate a dialogue with the Legislative Assembly proved fruitless. Indeed, the legislature persisted in its refusal to collaborate, and unrest continued to grow in Montreal and the neighbouring Richelieu valley. At a protest meeting held at Saint-Ours on 7 May 1837, the political leaders openly defied the British authorities. Strongly condemning the Russell resolutions of 6 March 1837, which permitted the governor to draw on the public treasury without the authorization of the Assembly, they passed a declaration that, without specifically calling for armed revolt, urged their compatriots to boycott English products (which through customs duties provided an important source of revenue) and take up smuggling. Canadiens now had their own Declaration of the Rights of Man. Bishops Signay and Lartigue, extremely worried at the spread of revolutionary ideas, could not be indifferent to these exhortations to violate the laws of the land. At the risk of disappointing those who considered him a great patriot, Lartigue, who had become the titular bishop of Montreal the previous year, resolved to intervene. He took advantage of the presence of more than a hundred and fifty priests who had come to attend the consecration, as his coadjutor, of Bishop Ignace Bourget on 25 July 1837. Expounding his thoughts on the political situation, he reminded them that it is 'never permissible to revolt against legitimate authority, nor to transgress the laws of the country, in particular those which outlaw contraband'.[193] This intervention provoked a controversy in the newspapers between defenders and opponents of Papineau's extremist politics. For *L'Ami du Peuple*, in its edition of 29 July 1837, the bishop was trying 'to bring to their senses a peaceful and fortunate people, a people being drawn by foolhardy men into the horrors of revolution and civil war'. Yet the spirit of rebellion continued to spread, especially in Montreal, where on 22 October 1837 more than twelve hundred Patriotes paraded in front of Saint-Jacques church to protest against Lartigue's intervention.

A turning-point in the development of the revolutionary movement was the Assembly of Six Counties, attended by more than six thousand people at Saint-Charles-sur-Richelieu on 23 October 1837. Those who spoke made it clear they were prepared to resort to arms to further their cause. The parish priest of Saint-Charles, Abbé Magloire Blanchet, was greatly impressed by the size of the gathering and the determination of the Patriote leaders. Sympathetic to the cause of the Patriotes and aware that they could no longer be considered merely a noisy minority, he appealed to his superiors to act with great caution: 'One must be very careful now when speaking of a man of the people [L.-J. Papineau]. I believe that it would be best for the clergy, at the present time, to remain silent so as not to leave themselves open to rejection; I am referring to those who have always been obstinately opposed to the Patriotes.'[194]

The message reached Montreal too late. On 24 October, considering it his duty to act even if he could not expect much success, Bishop Lartigue addressed a pastoral letter to the faithful of his diocese in an effort to warn them against the deceptive speeches of the agitators and dissuade them from taking up arms. Deploring the events that had been taking place in Lower Canada for several months, the bishop justified his intervention on strictly moral, non-political grounds. To the question 'What are the duties of a Catholic toward the duly constituted civil power in each state?' the bishop replied that the scriptures and the teaching of the church were unambiguous: Catholics were forbidden to oppose with force the legitimate authorities, to whom they owed respect and obedience.[195] Underpinning the church's teaching on this point was the doctrine of the divine right of kings, according to which the authority of sovereigns was conferred upon them directly by God.

This doctrine, which had first appeared in England during the reign of James I, and had been adopted by the celebrated theologian Bossuet at the time of Louis XIV, had been reiterated on many occasions by Pope Gregory XVI, notably in the encyclical *Mirari Vos* of 15 August 1832, and in the brief *Superiori Anno* of 29 June 1832, to the bishops of Poland. It did not, however, have the support of all the thinkers in the church. Some, like Félicité de Lamennais and Abbé Maret, professors of theology at the Sorbonne, appealed instead to a tradition going back to Cardinal Bellarmin and the Spanish theologian Francisco

Suárez in the sixteenth century. In contrast to the theory of the divine right of kings, this tradition held democracy to be of both divine and natural origin, since God had given power directly to the community, to the people and to the nation, and not to the king.[196] (This was the view of the Catholic bishops of Belgium who had supported the Liberals in their struggle against William I of the Netherlands, during the revolution of August 1830.)

Behind the moral question raised by Lartigue's pastoral was an implicit warning against the unbridled ambition of political leaders who claimed the right to power in the name of the sovereignty of the people, but who in reality were using the people to attain their own ends. In fact, in his view their policy of confrontation was suicidal and could never succeed. On this point the bishop had the support of the moderate Patriote leaders of the Quebec City region, who similarly questioned Papineau's leadership and the recourse to arms. *Le Canadien* made its view plain on 6 November 1837:

> The question of armed resistance against the colonial authority has been dis-
> cussed only against the will of the great majority of the people. Although the peo-
> ple want reform, they never intended to obtain it through brute force, but
> through legal, constitutional and peaceful means. In short, all those who have
> gone beyond these limits have either misjudged the feelings and the mood of the
> people, or replaced the people's will and desires with their own.

In the Montreal and Richelieu regions, where revolutionary agitation had reached fever pitch, Bishop Lartigue's pastoral was not well received. In sev-eral churches large numbers of faithful walked out as the pastoral was being read. The Patriote press referred to collusion between the bishop and the gov-ernor to crush the revolutionary movement. According to *La Minerve*, the bishop had shown in this situation 'as little discretion and foresight' as he had shown at the time of his coadjutor's consecration: '. . . as little discretion, because he abandons the livery of the Gospel in order to put on that of the political partisan; as little foresight, because he is doing harm to his clergy, who have been nourished and sustained by the people, not to hear them preaching absurd obedience but to listen to the precepts of a religion whose founder was put to death when the priests of his time accused him of sedition.'[197]

Later the Patriotes would even accuse him of having betrayed his country, and his pastorals of having caused bloodshed.[198] Lartigue was not surprised; he had predicted such reactions: 'They will probably tell many lies about this as they do about everything else in the public press, and there is nothing I can do about it.'[199] The moderate voices of less extremist papers like *L'Ami du peuple* and *Le Populaire* could hardly make themselves heard: 'What he meant to preach was submission to the laws; respect for princes and charity among their sub-jects. That is what the bishop of Montreal has done, and it will earn the head of our clergy the gratitude and respect of all good citizens; it will also be of no small help in undoing the plans of our revolutionaries.'[200]

The bishop's intervention triggered a real crisis of conscience among the priests of the diocese. Although only one, Abbé Étienne Chartier of Saint-Benoît, publicly dissociated himself from Lartigue, several were deeply torn between their attachment to the bishop and their feelings of solidarity with the people. For example, when the parish priests of the Richelieu valley gathered for a meeting at the Collège de Saint-Hyacinthe on 4 November 1837, they respectfully expressed to Bishop Lartigue their concern over the October pastoral and requested that he intervene with the British authorities on behalf of the rights of the people: 'This petition would only be an act of justice toward the people after the pastoral letter that Your Grace has deemed appropriate to address to them, prescribing their obligations, since, if they alone were reminded of their duty, these people would be entitled to say that the Gospel must be preached to the great as to the humble, and that kings themselves must obey its laws.'[201]

Visibly distraught by the turn of events, Bishop Lartigue agreed to the priests' request. A petition was immediately drafted in which the clergy of Lower Canada earnestly beseeched the British authorities to take into consideration the needs of the people. Signed by the priests of the Montreal area, the petition encountered some opposition from the bishop and clergy of Quebec City, who feared that it might be interpreted by the British authorities as support for the revolutionary cause. Bishop Signay wrote to Bishop Lartigue: 'In general this undertaking will be considered political. The ultra-nationalist patriotes will certainly see it as such. Far from recognizing in it our spirit of intercession . . . some will think that we are encouraging further unrest, since the people will then be able to say: "The clergy themselves proclaim the reality of our grievances and in fact do not disapprove of our agitation".'[202]

Faced with Quebec's opposition, Lartigue abandoned this attempt at conciliation. In the meantime events began to move faster, and, despite the appeals for calm issued by the moderate wing of the Patriote party, violence broke out in the Montreal region. After an incident on 17 November which the Patriotes attacked the soldiers who had come to arrest two members of their group, there were bloody confrontations at Saint-Denis on 23 November, Saint-Charles two days later, and Saint-Eustache on 14 December. Poorly armed and incompetently commanded, following a first, unexpected victory at Saint-Denis the Patriotes were forced to admit defeat. The suppression was particularly violent in the Richelieu and Deux-Montagnes areas, where the rebellion had originated, and the Patriote leaders ended up either in exile or in jail. Fearing a coercive bill that would bring unbearable misery to the population, the clergy of the Montreal region sent a message to Queen Victoria in which they expressed both their unassailable devotion to her and their wish 'that the fortunate inhabitants of this colony not be deprived, on account of the crimes of a few, of the advantages and privileges' that until then they had always enjoyed under British rule.[203]

The fears of the Montreal clergy and their bishop were justified. In February 1838 Governor Gosford was recalled to England and the Constitution of 1791 was indefinitely suspended until the conclusion of an enquiry headed by a special commissioner, Lord Durham. Meanwhile, on 8 January 1838 Bishop Lartigue addressed a second pastoral to the faithful of his diocese encouraging them 'publicly to make amends to God for all the sacrilege, murder, pillage, treason and other crimes committed in this district during the insurrectional crisis':

> What misery and what grief have been spread in much of your countryside since the scourge of civil war has ravaged this beautiful and fortunate land where prosperity and joy, order and security once reigned, before bandits and rebels, through sophistry and lies, led a portion of the people of our diocese astray. . . . Now you can easily distinguish your real friends, the true patriots, those who wish you well, from the ones who were seeking only to elevate themselves, to hold sway in a fanciful new state, and to take the place of those whom they might drive from office.[204]

Unlike the first pastoral of 24 October and the one issued by Bishop Signay on 11 December 1837, this pastoral specifically instructed the clergy that rebels who did not publicly retract were not to be admitted to the sacraments of the church, and were to be denied Christian burial if they died without disavowing their actions. For many these sanctions seemed too harsh. 'Far from reconciling these people with the clergy,' the Sulpician Pierre Rousseau would later write, 'it drove them away.'[205] But Lartigue was not greatly concerned; he had intervened because it was his duty and his conscience had urgently compelled him to do so.[206]

In the short term, the bishop's intervention caused a large number of Catholics to break with their church. Nevertheless, soon after this painful episode, the church recovered the authority and influence it had enjoyed before the advent of parliamentary institutions in 1791. The leaders of the rebellion had been thoroughly discredited by the failure of their endeavour. Bishop Lartigue firmly believed that, were they to become independent, the Canadiens would run the risk of becoming the puppets of their American neighbours: the huge American population 'would swallow them up perhaps a hundred years earlier than the British population of Europe could'.[207] Furthermore, the church's support for the unfortunate people who filled the prisons after the failure of the second rebellion of 3 November 1838—when the authorities made more than seven hundred arrests—as well as the frequent interventions of Lartigue and his coadjutor Bourget with the British authorities against the union of the two Canadas proposed in the Durham Report, succeeded in reconciling the people to their religious leaders. 'Through its good deeds,' wrote Bishop Bourget, 'the Church managed to restore that trust in their clergy which the people had lost for a while.'[208] As Michel Brunet puts it: 'In those tragic hours of collective humiliation, when their principal lay leaders, those who had benefited from their blind trust, had fled, the people spontaneously turned to their clerical leaders.'[209]

The Catholic Church was now re-established in its pre-1791 position. It was able to fill a vacuum, once again becoming a political force that the province's new political leaders had to reckon with. By 1840 it had also acquired a freedom that would not be challenged again by the British authorities. The attitude of its leaders during the insurrection of 1837–8 made the church less suspect in the eyes of London. Sir John Colborne, who had taken charge of the country's administration in February 1838, even described the superior of Saint-Sulpice, Joseph-Vincent Quiblier, as 'the saviour of Canada', saying that he had 'done more to crush the rebellion than all his [own] regiments'.[210] From this time on the British authorities would give free rein to the bishops, allowing them to establish new dioceses and bring priests and religious communities from France. Nor would they put any obstacle in the way of Rome's creation, on 9 June 1844, of the first ecclesiastical province in British North America. Under the jurisdiction of the archbishop of Quebec, it included the dioceses of Quebec, Montreal, Kingston, and Toronto. For its part, the church in Acadia, separated from the church in Quebec since 1829, entered a period of consolidation with the creation of a diocese for New Brunswick at Fredericton in 1842 and the diocese of Arichat in Cape Breton in 1844. The Acadianization of the church in the Maritimes was well under way, even though the formation of an Acadian clergy would take time and the first Acadian bishop, Édouard LeBlanc, would not be appointed until 1912.

Finally, 1840 saw the beginning of a major campaign by the church to create a true Christian society in French Canada and make a fresh start after forty years of democratic and revolutionary agitation. In fact, this campaign, which would blossom in the Ultramontane revival of mid-century, had been initiated by Bishop Lartigue at the time of his appointment in 1820, although unfavourable circumstances had prevented him from carrying it through. Even if an increase in religious practice and a significant rise in the number of priestly vocations had been noticeable since 1820, however, to ensure the predominance of the Catholic Church, two obstacles still had to be overcome: Protestant efforts at proselytism and the activities of those liberals who had not abandoned Papineau's dream of establishing a secular society in Lower Canada.

Proselytism by Protestants was by 1840 becoming more and more threatening. Swiss evangelists from the Grande-Ligne Mission, working mainly in the

Montreal region, hoped to take advantage of the unpopularity of the Catholic clergy who had opposed the rebellion of 1837–8. Now they worked even more zealously to convert Catholic Canadiens. 'One of the fortunate repercussions of this war,' noted Henriette Odin Feller, 'is that it has broken the priests' yoke: they have exerted no influence on the rebels, whom they tried to hold back with threats of excommunication; but nobody has taken any notice of them. . . . The time is come; Canada is open.'[211] In addition, the French Canadian Missionary Society, a new evangelical organization with objectives closely related to those of the Grande-Ligne Mission, had opened in Montreal in February 1839. Bishop Lartigue did not take this threat at all lightly, especially in view of the growing numbers of young people attracted to Montreal's only university, the English-speaking Protestant institution founded in 1821 and named for James McGill. Meanwhile, the liberals who wanted to revive Papineau's project regrouped around the Institut Canadien, founded in 1844 in Montreal, which became the centre of a struggle that would continue throughout the episcopate of Ignace Bourget.

These threats notwithstanding, by 1840 the Catholic Church had once again become a respected institution in French Canada; after turning their backs to it for a time, the Canadiens returned and dutifully let themselves be formed into a Catholic society that would last more than a century. The same year marked the beginning, in Montreal, of the French Bishop Charles de Forbin-Janson's Great Mission, a vast revival campaign, ardently promoted by Bishop Bourget, that would soon spread to the whole of French Canada. A new chapter was beginning for the Canadian Catholic Church, which from now on would become increasingly Roman and Ultramontane.

Opposite: THE UNITED PROVINCE OF CANADA, c. 1850.

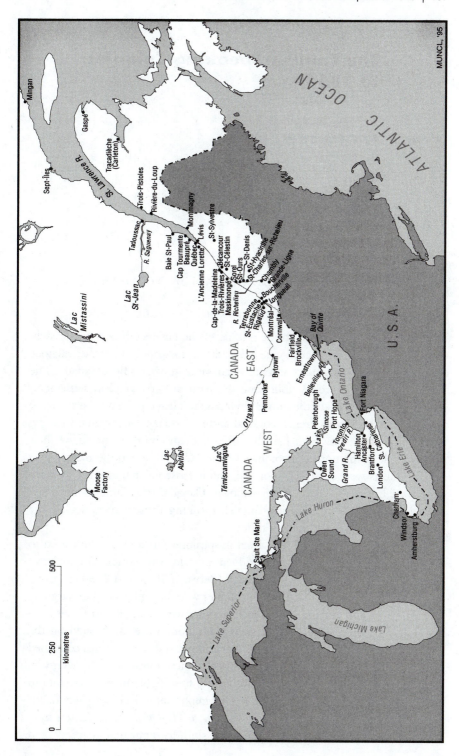

MUNCL, '95

Three

The English-Speaking Colonies to 1854

T E R R E N C E   M U R P H Y

ORIGINS AND FORMATION TO 1815

THE EMERGENCE OF ENGLISH-SPEAKING CHURCHES

From the early seventeenth to the middle of the eighteenth century, French-speaking Roman Catholicism enjoyed a virtual monopoly over the religious life of both European settlers and native converts in what is now Canada. The English-speaking churches, following the path of early English settlement, established themselves in the future United States, leaving the northern part of the continent mostly to French colonial and missionary endeavours. In a few exceptional cases, however, British and American churches did make their presence felt in the northern colonies before 1750. Although these early missionary efforts were too brief, sporadic, and inconsequential to serve as foundations of English-speaking Christianity in Canada, they faintly anticipated later developments by bringing English-speaking Protestant and Catholic clergy into the region for the first time.

The earliest examples of such English-speaking missions can be traced to the colonies established by private adventurers in Newfoundland and Nova Scotia in the early seventeenth century. Between 1610 and 1630—approximately at the same time that English colonies were being founded in Virginia, New England, and Guiana, and French colonies were being organized at Port-Royal and Quebec—a number of such plantations were established on the Avalon peninsula.[1] The royal charters that authorized these ventures contained provisions for missionary and ecclesiastical undertakings, and the clergy in England were enlisted by the civil authorities and highly-placed investors to help promote the cause of colonization. One important piece of propaganda for Newfoundland settlement, *A Plaine Pathway to Plantations*, was written by a Somerset parson, Richard Eburne, who skilfully appealed to piety and patriotism in attempting to persuade potential colonists to risk emigration.[2] Such works seldom failed to cite the spread of the Gospel and the conversion of 'infidels' as motives for overseas settlement. In practice, however, the main goal was the exploitation of natural resources, and little or no provision was made for organized religious life.

There were important exceptions to this rule. An Anglican clergyman named William Leat served in Newfoundland sometime before 1622, probably at John Guy's settlement at Cuper's Cove (Cupids).[3] If one assumes, as seems probable, that Leat arrived in Newfoundland before 1621, he ranks as the first English-speaking missionary to reside in what is now Canada. After a brief tenure, he returned to England, whence he made his way to Virginia. More clergymen came to the island with the launching of a plantation at Ferryland by Sir George Calvert (later Lord Baltimore) in 1621. Baltimore's Avalon colony foreshadowed the policy of religious toleration that would later be introduced by his son in Maryland. Settlers were of mixed religious background, and they were served by both Anglican and Roman Catholic clergy. A total of seven missionaries officiated in the colony during the 1620s: the Anglicans Richard James and Erasmus Stourton and the Roman Catholics Thomas Longville, Anthony Pole, Alexander Baker, Lawrence Rigby, and Anthony Whitehair, known as Father Hacket.[4] Although the principle of toleration was hard to put into practice—bitter conflicts developed between the Anglican and Roman Catholic clergy, and Calvert was accused by Stourton of favouring his rivals—its introduction at Ferryland marked a clear departure from Old World precedent.

In the same period, Sir William Alexander attempted to establish a Scottish colony, which he called Nova Scotia, in the territory that the French had occupied under the name of Acadia. His first, ill-fated expedition of 1622–3 included an unnamed missionary, possibly an Episcopal Church of Scotland minister, who died in Newfoundland when the settlers were forced to seek shelter there.[5] When Acadia passed temporarily into British hands in 1629, Alexander launched further expeditions, establishing short-lived colonies at Port-de-la-Baleine in Cape Breton and at Port-Royal. The former settlement, consisting mostly of recruits from England, included six to eight families who were zealous adherents of the 'Brownist' movement,[6] a Congregationalist community who wished to separate from the Church of England, but there is no evidence that they were accompanied by a minister.

Attempts at organized settlement in seventeenth-century Newfoundland and Nova Scotia were extremely tenuous and ultimately unsuccessful. Alexander's settlers were driven out of Cape Breton by French forces in 1630 and were compelled to withdraw from Port-Royal two years later, when Nova Scotia was returned to French rule by the treaty of Saint-Germain-en-Laye. Meanwhile, attempts at permanent settlement in Newfoundland faltered, and for more than a century the island remained little more than a station for the migratory fishery. This fact was reflected in the purely occasional presence of missionaries between 1630 and 1700 as naval chaplains, a handful of wandering friars from Ireland, and a few dissenting Protestant clergy visited the coast from time to time; the latter included Puritan preachers from New England and two female Quaker missionaries, Hester Biddle and Mary Fisher, who preached on board ships in St John's harbour in 1656 and 1659.[7] A tentative step towards a more stable ministry occurred in 1701 when John Jackson, an Anglican clergyman, arrived in Newfoundland in response to a petition from the small permanent population of St John's. Two years after his arrival, Jackson began to receive support from the newly-founded Society for the Propagation of the Gospel (SPG). Although the SPG had already sponsored two missionaries in the American colonies, its support of Jackson marked the beginning of what would become a long and decisive involvement in the northern provinces. Its early impact in Newfoundland was limited, however, since Jackson's immediate successors were few in number and came at irregular intervals, often leaving the island without a single resident missionary.[8]

Early exploration of the northwest provided another preliminary opening for English-speaking missionaries. In 1577, an Anglican chaplain accompanying Martin Frobisher evidently celebrated the eucharist on Baffin Island in the presence of Frobisher's men and a number of aboriginal people.[9] After the Hudson's Bay Company received its charter in 1670, one or two chaplains served briefly under its auspices. For example, an unidentified chaplain was living at Albany Fort when the French attacked in 1686;[10] Henry Sergeant, governor of the fort, employed him as an intermediary in arranging peace talks with the enemy.[11] Although the efforts of such chaplains are shrouded in obscurity, they were probably confined to company staff. Substantial missionary endeavours in the Hudson's Bay territory did not begin until the early nineteenth century.

The British Conquest of Acadia in 1710 and Quebec in 1759 meant the appearance in these former French colonies of Protestant military chaplains. Troops advancing on Port-Royal, Louisbourg, Quebec, and Montreal were accompanied by either Anglican or Congregationalist chaplains, depending on whether the expedition consisted mainly of British or colonial forces, and the thanksgiving services they conducted to celebrate the victory of British arms usually marked the first recorded Protestant worship in each case. Anglican chaplains who remained in the conquered territories, such as John Harrison at Port-Royal and John Brooke at Quebec,[12] organized rudimentary congregations among government officials and soldiers stationed in the garrison, but these were tiny islands of English-speaking Christianity amid populations that were overwhelmingly French-speaking and Roman Catholic.

When discussing the origins of English-speaking Christianity in Canada, therefore, an important distinction has to be made between the mere presence of clergymen who officiated briefly among small pockets of English-speaking inhabitants and the real beginnings of a continuous institutional presence for the principal denominations. The real foundation of the English-speaking churches depended not on the transient presence of clergy or the formal transfer of the colonies from French to British rule, but on large-scale migration to the colonies from Britain and the future United States. From this point of view, the middle of the eighteenth century was the true turning-point, especially in the Atlantic region.

It was only after 1750, for example, that Newfoundland began to make an appreciable transition from a fishing station to a resident colony, as the permanent population significantly increased. This demographic change was accompanied by the development of institutions, including religious institutions, appropriate to permanent settlements. The island's population, which came mainly from the Southeast of Ireland and the English West Country, included Anglicans, Roman Catholics, and Protestant dissenters (i.e., Protestants who did not adhere to the established Churches of England, Ireland, or Scotland). By the 1780s, when the total number of year-round inhabitants exceeded 10,000,[13] viable Anglican missions had been established at St John's and Harbour Grace; a resident prefect apostolic had been placed in charge of the Roman Catholic population; a dissenting congregation had been organized at St John's; and Methodism had gained a foothold in Conception Bay. A party of German and English Moravians, departing from London, had also founded a mission among the Inuit of Labrador.

Meanwhile, as a result of a conscious change in imperial policy, Nova Scotia was transformed from a British colony *de jure* to a British colony *de facto*. Hitherto British officials and soldiers had lived in the midst of a mainly French-speaking and Roman Catholic population; but in 1749 more than two thousand British settlers arrived at the new garrison town of Halifax, to be followed a year later by nearly three thousand 'foreign Protestants' from Germany, Switzerland, and Montbéliard. The foreign Protestants, mostly Lutherans or German Reformed, stayed briefly in Halifax before resettling in Lunenburg, where the SPG provided them with French- and German-speaking missionaries.

The expulsion of the Acadians in 1755 opened the way for migration from the American colonies. Between 1760 and 1765, approximately eight thousand 'Planters'—New Englanders attracted by the promise of free passage and lands, as well as the guarantee of religious toleration for Protestant dissenters—settled in the Annapolis valley, along the Bay of Fundy, and in the southwestern portion of the province. Soon economically motivated immigrants from the British Isles, including Ulster Presbyterians, Highland Scots (both Catholic and Presbyterian), Yorkshire Methodists, and Irish Catholics, had also established communities in Nova Scotia and Prince Edward Island. By the time of the American Revolution, the total population of the Maritime colonies had reached seventeen or eighteen thousand.[14] The influx of civilian Loyalists and disbanded soldiers that followed the Revolution more than doubled this number within a decade. The Loyalist migration not only greatly increased the density of the population in Nova Scotia but opened New Brunswick to large-scale settlement, paving the way for its establishment as a separate colony in 1784. Since a significant minority of the newcomers were either freed blacks or the slaves of Loyalist masters, the Loyalist migration also laid the foundation of the region's black community.

The English-speaking populations in Quebec and the future Ontario began their growth more slowly than did their Atlantic counterparts, although they eventually outstripped the latter by a wide margin. Initially, a handful of merchants joined soldiers and government officials to form small pockets of anglophones in such strategic centres as Montreal, Quebec, and Trois-Rivières. In religious matters they were served mostly by the Anglican garrison chaplains, although in 1765 a Church of Scotland minister, George Henry, organized a Presbyterian congregation at Quebec.[15] In 1773 a small group of mostly Scottish Catholics were led to Montreal via New York by an Irish priest named John McKenna. (Some members of this group later resettled in the Glengarry region of Upper Canada, southeast of the future Ottawa.) It was the Loyalist migration, however, that marked the beginning of a new era. Although in absolute terms fewer Loyalists moved to Canada than to the Maritimes, their relative impact on the region was greater. Their arrival opened up settlement in the western districts and led in 1791 to the division of the old province of Quebec into Upper and Lower Canada. Of diverse ethnic background, including Germans, Dutch, Highland Scots, Americans of New England stock, and native peoples, the Loyalists settled along the St Lawrence, at Kingston, in the Bay of Quinte region, on the Niagara peninsula, near the western end of Lake Erie, and, in the case of the Six Nations people, also along the Grand River.

The Loyalist migration proved to be merely the first wave in a rising tide of settlers from the United States. A much larger number of Americans poured into the Eastern Townships of Lower Canada and into Upper Canada as part of a general westward migration at the turn of the century. By 1812, these pioneers had boosted the English-speaking minority of Lower Canada to almost thirty thousand (10 per cent of the population),[16] while in Upper Canada Loyalist and post-Loyalist settlers had combined with small numbers of immigrants from the British Isles to produce a total population of nearly eighty thousand.[17]

In Lower Canada the range of denominations was relatively narrow, the English-speaking population being divided at this stage mainly between Anglicans, Methodists, Congregationalists, and Presbyterians. The denominational spectrum of Upper Canada, by contrast, was the widest in British North America even by 1815. It included not only Anglicans, English-speaking Roman Catholics, Methodists, Lutherans, Presbyterians, Baptists, and

Congregationalists, but also sectarian communities of German-speaking Mennonites and the closely-related Tunkers, as well as Moravians and Quakers. Although Moravians had established an isolated mission in Labrador and Quakers had briefly maintained a presence in Nova Scotia, the relative importance of denominations from outside the mainstream was greater in Upper Canada than in any other British North American colony. The religious profile of Upper Canada also differed from that of other colonies because of the overwhelmingly American origins of its early inhabitants. As many as eight out of ten settlers had come to Upper Canada from the United States, a much higher proportion than in the Maritimes, and they brought with them distinctively American forms of particular denominations.

The influx of new settlers between 1750 and 1812 gave rise to drastic changes in the religious life of the colonies. A shift occurred not merely from predominantly French-speaking to predominantly English-speaking forms of Christianity, but also from a high degree of religious and ethnic homogeneity to a situation of considerable diversity and complexity. Compared with twentieth-century Canada, characterized by secularity and multiculturalism, the diversity of the British North American population was very limited: most settlers were Christians by background, and the majority of churchgoers were associated with a handful of Protestant denominations. Compared with New France, however, where after 1627 the Roman Catholic Church had enjoyed a virtual monopoly, the arrival of new settlers of distinct religious and ethnic backgrounds marked a sharp change.

At the same time, the introduction of denominations with little or no previous foothold in the British North American colonies required major institutional adjustments. English-speaking settlers had to build up their churches almost from scratch, and the vast majority arrived without the benefit of clergy; only the minority involved in group migration brought ministers with them. Moreover, assistance from missionary agencies was largely restricted at first to the activities of the SPG, although a handful of preachers were sent out by the interdenominational London Missionary Society (founded 1795) and the Society for the Furtherance of the Gospel (founded 1741), which supported Moravian missions in Labrador.

Religious development was also limited by the relatively primitive conditions that prevailed in British North America.[18] With the partial exception of Quebec (Lower Canada after 1791), British North America consisted of widely-scattered and thinly-populated colonies. Most settlers were recent immigrants engaged in subsistence agriculture or fishing. Commercial activity flourished in towns such as St John's, Halifax, Quebec, and Montreal, as well as some smaller ports, but urban centres were few in number and limited in size. Communication and transportation were poor; there was little contact between small provincial capitals and the agricultural hinterland or coastal outports; and social institutions were at a very early stage of development. Frontier conditions put major barriers in the path of institutional Christianity. In addition to practical obstacles, such as the difficulty of travel, the clergy had to overcome less tangible problems, including the tendency in new and isolated communities to let go of traditional social restraints. Clergy sent to British North America gave full and plaintive accounts of the difficulties they encountered.

The situation was exacerbated by the fact that, whereas in both New France and New England institutional Christianity had developed as part of organized colonization programs, migration to British North America was largely unplanned. The lack of co-ordination meant that the initial impulse for the formal religious activity had to come mainly from the settlers themselves. Forced to rely on their own resources, many communities organized rudimentary public worship with respected lay people leading prayers and reading from either the Bible or books of worship. As the occasion required, they also baptized infants, witnessed marriages, and officiated at funerals. Sometimes they persisted in carrying out these functions even after the arrival of authorized clergymen: in Conception Bay, Newfoundland, for example, SPG missionaries complained in the 1760s and 1770s that 'common fishermen', both English and Irish (i.e., both Protestant and Catholic), performed baptisms, marriages and funerals, not only usurping the clergy's prerogatives but depriving them of an important source of income. The missionaries appealed to the civil authorities, and in 1779 Governor Richard Edwards ordered the justice of the peace to enforce the necessary restrictions.[19]

As a rule, reliance on lay readers was a temporary expedient rather than a conscious act of defiance. A more common and important form of local initiative was the recruitment of resident clergy by lay spokespersons or activists. Without waiting for help from external ecclesiastical agencies, many communities raised private subscriptions, constructed churches, and enlisted the services of clergy. This occurred not only among denominations (such as Congregationalists and Presbyterians) where it was standard practice for local congregations to issue a 'call', but also among those (such as Anglicans, Methodists, and Roman Catholics) whose clergy were usually appointed by central authorities. Local initiative of this kind was crucial to the early development of religious institutions in British North America. Its importance can be measured by the fact that the first SPG missionary and the first Methodist preacher in British North America, the first Presbyterian clergyman in the Atlantic region, the first English-speaking priest in the Maritimes, the priest who established Roman Catholic church government in Newfoundland, the first Lutheran minister in Upper Canada, and the first Dutch Reformed clergyman all came to their positions in response to petitions or invitations from local inhabitants.[20]

In the towns, lay leadership came mainly from merchants and other representatives of the 'middling' classes, such as shopkeepers, professionals, minor government officials, and independent artisans. A common pattern was for such people to form a committee to raise funds, build a church, recruit a clergyman, and manage parish affairs. As men of property, they were attracted by the task of building up the parish fabric and by the enhanced social status that the role of patron brought them. Their contributions usually earned for them the distinction of serving on the governing boards of their local churches. Anglican lay leaders held office as vestrymen, Presbyterians as elders, Roman Catholics as lay wardens, Methodists as trustees or stewards, and Baptists as deacons. Prosperous members of most denominations also bought or rented pews, assuring themselves a place of honour during religious services. But personal prestige was not the only attraction. Aspiring community leaders were convinced that organized religious life was essential to an orderly and stable society, and that religious belief was the foundation of ethical conduct. The social values of the 'respectable' class combined with genuine religious commitment to make the lay committee one of the driving forces in the early development of the colonial churches.

One example of this form of lay initiative can be found in Nova Scotia in the years following the American Revolution. As we shall see, Maritime Methodism generally traces its origins to a community of Yorkshire immigrants to Cumberland and especially to William Black, a farm boy from this district who emerged as a charismatic itinerant preacher in the 1780s. Equally important, however, if until recently less well-known, was a circle of merchants who came to Nova Scotia as part of the Loyalist migration[21] and settled mostly in Halifax or the Loyalist town of Shelburne. Together they formed a vibrant activist community linked by overlapping business, family, and religious connections. (Many were former members of the Methodist John Street Chapel in New York City.) They maintained close ties with British Methodism, corresponding with its founder John Wesley and with leading Methodist clergy in England after Wesley's death in 1791. The circle included active lay preachers, such as Robert Barry and John and James Mann, but only the Mann brothers proceeded to ordination; the others contented themselves with their roles as lay leaders and founding fathers of the Methodist societies in Halifax, Shelburne and neighbouring communities, and Liverpool. Philip Marchinton leased the building in Halifax where local Methodists held their early prayer meetings and in the spring of 1786 built a chapel to hold 1,000 people. Robert Barry brought William Black to preach in Shelburne, and participated in the construction of chapels at Shelburne, Barrington, Sable River, and Liverpool. Simeon Perkins played a major role on Methodist lay committees in Liverpool, including the one responsible for the building of the first Methodist chapel.[22]

Another form of lay initiative was for settlers to follow or to choose preachers from their own ranks. This approach, more common in the Atlantic colonies than in the Canadas, occurred not only where licensed ministers were completely lacking but also where incumbent clergymen were found wanting by their congregations. One example of this kind can be seen among the community of dissenters in St John's that took shape in the late 1770s in response to the preaching of the army paymaster John Jones. After his own conversion from a life of profligacy, Jones preached successfully to both fellow soldiers and civilians and soon moulded his followers into a viable congregation, much to the chagrin of Edward Langman, the Anglican missionary in the city, his successor Walter Price, and the Newfoundland governor. Jones initially carried on his ministry without any specific authorization. Only after he had established himself as a successful preacher did he return to England for ordination.[23]

A second example occurred among the German Reformed settlers of Lunenburg who, not content to be included in the Anglican parish established for them and other 'foreign Protestants' by a French-speaking SPG missionary, withdrew to form a separate congregation and arranged the ordination in 1770 of one of their own number, a devout fisherman named Bruin Romkes Comingo. Carried out by a specially constituted presbytery of Presbyterian and Congregationalist ministers, this was the first Protestant ordination in what is now Canada.[24]

The black settlers, including Anglicans, Methodists and Baptists, who entered Nova Scotia and New Brunswick as part of the Loyalist migration faced special difficulties. In white churches they occupied a distinctly second-class status, symbolized by the fact that they had to remain in segregated galleries during worship. Of the black preachers who began to arrive in the region from the United States during the 1780s, the most important was the Baptist David George,[25] who had already established the first continuing black Baptist congregation in the United States at Silver Bluff, South Carolina.[26] Proclaiming a message of freedom and equality before God,[27] he organized black congregations first at Shelburne, where 1,500 black Loyalists had settled, and later at Saint John, Fredericton, and Preston (near Halifax). In 1792, however, George joined a large portion of the region's black population in emigrating to Sierra Leone. After his departure, John Burton, a Baptist preacher from England, did his best to provide pastoral leadership for the black community, chiefly by including many blacks in his Halifax congregation and by treating them in a less discriminatory way than other white clergymen. This was not a satisfactory long-term solution for black Christians, because it failed to give them control of their own affairs; but Burton was able at least to provide a bridge between the work of George and later, more lasting attempts to establish African Christian congregations.[28]

For many denominations, the relative importance of external missionary agencies increased in the closing decades of the eighteenth century. The SPG, which had already been active in the Atlantic region, was able after the American Revolution to strengthen its efforts by redirecting resources from the United States to the loyal colonies. When the end of the war made it possible to cross the border again, American Methodists, Baptists, and Lutheran bodies all restored or developed links with British North America. For the Protestant churches of Upper Canada, American ecclesiastical bodies were a natural source of aid, since the colony was in many ways a geographic and demographic extension of the northern United States.

External missionary agencies possessed financial and human resources that far exceeded those available to local communities, and without their involvement institutional Christianity in British North America could never have grown at the pace it did. Even so, the results they achieved were mixed. The SPG, one of the strongest of the missionary societies, had great difficulty in persuading Anglican clergy to move to frontier regions such as Upper Canada.[29] Moreover, not only individual clergymen but sometimes entire agencies were reluctant to take charge of colonies that seemed too remote or peripheral to justify the allocation of scarce resources. The American Methodist Episcopal Church, for example, though initially providing support to the Maritime Methodists, soon lost enthusiasm for this project.[30] Largely because of the inadequate supply of preachers from the United States, the Maritime Methodists turned to the British Wesleyans for support in 1800. The British Conference was somewhat more willing than the Americans to accept the responsibility, but it did so at the cost of depriving Maritime Methodists of any hint of self-government for the next half-century.

Roman Catholics meanwhile were severely hampered by the cultural and linguistic barriers separating Irish and Scottish immigrants from the clergy of Quebec. Even the best efforts of French-Canadian bishops were woefully inadequate to the needs of the newcomers, and there were strict limits to what the latter could hope for from the churches in their homelands. Scottish Catholic bishops, initially inclined to regard overseas Highland settlements as extensions of their domestic mission, soon began to resent and resist the demands they placed on their overtaxed resources.[31] In light of all such limitations, plenty of scope was left for local initiative. As in the case of the Protestant churches, external agencies provided some assistance, but growth always depended in part on the development of indigenous resources.

Little was done before 1815 to promote missions to the First Nations. The formative years of the English-speaking churches fell between the so-called 'heroic age' of French Catholic missions in the seventeenth century and the flowering of evangelical benevolent associations that characterized the middle of the nineteenth century. Only a few voluntary societies included in their mandates the conversion of aboriginal peoples, and their missionary efforts were often haphazard and inconsequential. The SPG, through the isolated efforts of Thomas Wood in Nova Scotia, and the New England Company, which moved from the American colonies to New Brunswick after the Revolution, both undertook limited work among the Micmac.[32] The latter, however, had already formed a deep attachment to Roman Catholicism, which seemed only to deepen as English settlement threatened them with assimilation.[33]

Neither the severe shortage of Roman Catholic priests nor the official support enjoyed by Anglican clergy altered this fact. Wood was a personal friend of Abbé Pierre Maillard, the 'Apostle to the Micmac', and attended him at his deathbed in 1762, where he read in French the office for the visitation of the sick. Following Maillard's death, which left Acadia without a Catholic missionary for six years, Wood claimed to have been personally authorized as his successor in the native missions. But even with this endorsement he had little success in attracting Micmac believers to the Church of England. The efforts of the New England Company, which included both schools at Sussex Vale and a scheme to apprentice Micmac children to white families, at first appeared more promising. They were eventually exposed as fraudulent and exploitive, however, and Anglican missions to New Brunswick were severely compromised.[34]

In Upper Canada, early English-speaking missions to the native people were even less impressive. The first Protestant native communities, which consisted of the Anglican Mohawk at the Grand River and the Bay of Quinte and Moravian Delaware at Fairfield, were established as the result of immigration rather than successful proselytism.[35] Once these Christian communities had moved into the region, Anglican and Moravian missionaries worked among them on a limited scale. But the largest group of native people in Upper Canada were the Ojibwa, and until the 1820s they remained largely untouched by Christian evangelism.

In Newfoundland no systematic efforts were made to promote the conversion of the indigenous Beothuk. Despite early contact with Europeans along the coast, in the seventeenth century the Beothuk had adopted the defensive—but ultimately unsuccessful—strategy of withdrawal to the interior of the island, where they lived in relative isolation for more than a century.[36] The whites, on the other hand, even after penetrating the inland hunting grounds of the Beothuk in the mid-eighteenth century, made only limited and belated efforts to establish friendly relations with them.[37] By the time any serious initiatives were taken, the Beothuk were well on their way to extinction.

The situation in coastal Labrador was radically different. When Labrador was transferred to British control in 1763, both the Board of Trade and Governor Hugh Palliser of Newfoundland, wishing to ensure co-operation with British fishing and trade in the region, lent their support to the plan of the Danish-born Moravian Jens Haven to establish a mission among the native

Inuit.[38] Building on the experience of Moravian missions in Greenland, Haven made an exploratory trip to Labrador in 1764, and in 1769 the Moravians obtained a land grant of 100,000 acres in Esquimaux Bay (Groswater Bay). With the support of the London-based Society for the Furtherance of the Gospel, they dispatched a party of fourteen German and English missionaries who established a mission settlement at Nain in 1771.[39] From this base Moravian missions expanded to Okak in 1776 and Hopedale in 1782.

Like so many missionaries working among indigenous peoples, the Moravians were determined to gather their converts into carefully regulated villages, separating them so far as possible from non-Christian natives and rapacious white traders. This widespread missionary strategy was reinforced by the Moravians' own experience of communal living, for they wanted to recreate the Moravian City of God in the Labrador wilderness.[40] The local climate ruled out sedentary agricultural villages, considered the cornerstone of acculturation in most other regions, but the Moravian program was nonetheless assimilationist. Besides emphasizing the importance of obedience to the civil government, they inculcated the values of hard work, punctuality, thrift, and prudence. Meanwhile, they openly attacked Inuit religion, depicting it alternately as the work of the Devil and as a sham.[41] Even native converts resisted the challenge to their traditional way of life, wanting to incorporate elements of their own customs with the new ways introduced by the missionaries. The Moravians strongly discouraged such syncretism. Nevertheless, significant numbers of Inuit embraced Christianity, and the Moravian mission continued to prosper. By the end of the century 26 missionaries were living at the three stations along with 228 resident Inuit, half of whom had been baptized.[42]

By the closing decades of the eighteenth century, local denominational structures had begun to emerge, though the pace of development varied considerably from one denomination and region to another. Among Roman Catholics, Newfoundland was established as a separate ecclesiastical jurisdiction, under the immediate authority of the Holy See, with the appointment of James Louis O'Donel as prefect apostolic in 1784. In 1796 O'Donel was raised to the episcopate and his position elevated to that of vicar apostolic. In the remainder of British North America, Roman Catholics continued for the time being under the jurisdiction of the bishop of Quebec, but the supervisory powers that the latter entrusted, in the early part of the nineteenth century, to Edmund Burke in Nova Scotia, Alexander Macdonell in Upper Canada, and Angus MacEachern in Prince Edward Island were steps towards the eventual creation of separate dioceses.

For Anglicans, the turning-point was the appointment in 1787 of Charles Inglis as bishop of Nova Scotia. As the first Anglican bishop in the American colonies, Inglis initially presided over all of British North America. In 1796, with the appointment of Jacob Mountain as bishop of Quebec, a second

Anglican diocese was created incorporating both Lower and Upper Canada. Methodists and Protestant dissenters made slower strides toward the organization of local structures, but even in their cases a measure of progress was discernible. Methodists, still in the process of separating from the Church of England, held an unofficial conference in Nova Scotia in 1786 that stationed six preachers on four circuits, while in Upper Canada they were organized in 1794 as a separate district of the New York Conference. Meanwhile, Secession Presbyterians, who had separated from the established Church of Scotland in 1733 in protest against lay control of clerical appointments, organized two presbyteries in Nova Scotia, the Burgher Presbytery of Truro in 1786 and the Anti-Burgher Presbytery of Nova Scotia in 1794. The designations 'Burgher' and 'Anti-Burgher' reflected internal divisions among Secession Presbyterians in Scotland that would soon become irrelevant in British North America, but the more fundamental distinction between Secessionists and the Church of Scotland retained its importance as the two groups long remained separate denominations even in the New World. While the Church of Scotland was slower than the Secessionist group to establish local structures, it eventually became a major force in the religious life of the colonies, especially in the Canadas. Like the Church of England, the Church of Scotland felt that its privileges as a religious establishment ought to extend to the colonies. While it did receive a measure of special treatment from the civil authorities, it failed to achieve co-establishment in British North America.

The main problems of the period before 1815 were common to all the churches. At the root of most difficulties was a chronic shortage of clergy, as increases in the numbers of missionaries failed to keep pace with the rapidly expanding population. Furthermore, so long as there was a problem with the quantity of clergymen, there was also a problem with quality. Given the urgent need for recruits, proper examination of candidates' credentials was not always possible; and ecclesiastical authorities outside the country, seeing the chance to rid themselves of inferior or troublesome subjects, were sometimes less than scrupulous in deciding whom to recommend.

Such problems were exacerbated by the fact that the bishops and superintendents responsible for incoming clergy often had vast territories entrusted to their care. They could seldom keep a close watch over missionaries in the field, and the latter risked becoming demoralized through isolation, loneliness, and the hardships imposed by primitive living conditions. Every denomination included some clergy who were guilty of drunkenness, neglect of duties, sexual misconduct, or financial chicanery. These represented only a minority, but they were numerous enough to have a significant impact on the young colonial churches. The task of bringing them to order drained energies that could have been devoted to more constructive projects, and their involvement in public scandals threatened to bring all clergy into disrepute.

Religious commitment among the laity was another major concern of the pre-1815 era. On the one hand, the major role played by the laity in organizing worship, founding congregations, and recruiting clergy demonstrates that some people were determined to make formal religous practice a part of their lives. On the other hand, the clergy frequently complained about low standards of religious observance. The discrepancy can be explained partly by class differences, since lay activism in religious matters, at least in towns, often originated among the 'middling' classes. Merchants, independent artisans, professionals, and government officials had both the means and the motive to promote the cause of institutional Christianity. Believing that organized religious life was essential to the creation of a stable and prosperous society, they had the skills required to form new congregations and the money to purchase land, erect buildings, and support clergymen. Though constituting a small portion of the population, they played a crucial role in creating the institutional framework for colonial religious life.

Many of the settlers arriving in British North America, however, had only a very loose connection with institutional Christianity. Hard data are difficult to obtain, but a few examples allow us some insight into the dimensions of the problem. In 1803, John Langhorn, a pioneer Anglican clergyman in Upper Canada, arranged for a religious census of his mission. In Ernesttown (later Bath), one of the principal settlements under his care, he found that of a total population of approximately 2,100 people, 688 (32 per cent) could not easily be identified with a particular denomination.[43] This was not merely a question of denominational loyalties' being in a state of flux (though this was also true): a significant portion of the population fell largely outside the orbit of official Christianity. While most of these people had probably been baptized, and while they may also have sought out the clergy for other rites of passage such as marriages and funerals, they had no routine contact with any church. Few opportunities existed for the clergy to teach them essential doctrines or inculcate habits of regular worship. Furthermore, other evidence, admittedly incomplete, indicates that the situation in Ernesttown was not an aberration. In the very year of Langhorn's census, for example, John Strachan, the future Anglican bishop of Toronto, reported that a great part of the population of Cornwall had no religion at all.[44]

Even among settlers who could be identified with a particular denomination, standards of religious conduct were often low. Clergymen of virtually all denominations complained of ignorance of basic doctrines, erratic attendance at worship, irreverent or inattentive behaviour when people did come to church, reluctance to participate in the sacraments, and disregard for the sabbath. Failure to provide adequate support for the clergy was another common criticism. The reasons behind such withholding of support may have included genuine poverty, the expectation that missionaries could obtain government stipends, and dissatisfaction with particular clergymen; however, religious indifference was undoubtedly a contributing factor.

In evaluating the religious conduct of the laity, it is necessary to bear in mind that the reports of missionaries are virtually our only source of information on this topic, and that the picture that emerges may be biased accordingly. The clergy may have had unrealistic expectations, or they may have exaggerated their plight among a godless people in order to garner sympathy and support from ecclesiastical superiors. Even so, the complaints of missionaries are too frequent and too consistent to ignore. Clearly, a large portion of the population had not formed the habit of regular religious observance. Nor was it merely that traditional patterns of observance were disrupted in the process of resettlement. The behaviour of British North American settlers reflected to a large extent prevailing standards in their countries of origin. As late as the eighteenth century, lay religion in most European countries, especially outside the towns, was governed more by folk customs than by official norms. Rural clergy were poorly trained, and ecclesiastical organization was often very weak in sparsely populated regions. Popular conformity to official standards was achieved only as communications improved and the institutional presence of the churches in the countryside was strengthened. The challenge for clergy in British North America, therefore, was not dissimilar to that in more established societies. While frontier conditions and the impact of resettlement may have complicated the task considerably, they were not the root of the problem. Success in the colonial missions, as elsewhere, depended largely on institutional growth. The other essential ingredient was to deliver the message of the Gospel in ways that spoke to people's existential needs.

TENDENCIES IN RELIGIOUS LIFE

When the English-speaking churches were establishing roots in British North America, the intellectual life of Europe and America was dominated by the Enlightenment, with its emphasis on the supremacy of reason and on emancipation from the constraints of tradition and authority. The impact of rationalism on religious thought was profound and took many forms, including atheism (which denied the existence of God), deism (which accepted the existence of a Supreme Being but rejected revelation and mystery), and rational supernaturalism (which attempted to show that nothing essential in Christianity was contrary to reason). Atheism and deism represented the views of a radical minority that included John Toland in England and Voltaire in France. Rational supernaturalism enjoyed a wider influence through the works of men such as John Locke and John Tillotson. These thinkers, while exalting the human intellect, retained a place for revealed truth by insisting that revelation was above but never contrary to reason. Their mediating position between extreme rationalism and conventional orthodoxy had considerable appeal to those who sought a modern formulation of authentic Christian belief. On the other hand, many churchmen openly resisted the advanced ideas of the age, which they saw as a threat to faith. This group clung to a frankly supernaturalistic view of the world and to the orthodox doctrines of the Reformation or Counter Reformation.

Not everyone fitted neatly into rigidly defined schools of thought, however, and the influence of the Enlightenment was reflected in many shades of opinion. One of the ways in which rationalism influenced even the most conservative divines was in the tendency to intellectualize faith. In Enlightenment theology, religion was above all a matter of the mind, and faith was identified closely with adherence to formally defined doctrines. Among many enlightened theologians, moreover, there was a strong inclination to distinguish between essential and non-essential teachings. Reacting against the sectarian strife of preceding generations, many churchmen preferred to emphasize a limited number of truths on which all reasonable people could agree, especially if those truths were conducive to morality. The list of essential doctrines included the existence of God, the divinity of Christ, the divine creation of the universe, the immortality of the soul, the providential ordering of history, and the certainty of punishment for sin and reward for virtue. Individual denominations might preserve their peculiar principles, but fine doctrinal distinctions must not be allowed to become a source of controversy. Reason fostered restraint and moderation, and there was a deep distrust of religious enthusiasm, which was associated with fanaticism and conflict.

Generally, the missionaries who came to British North America as representatives of the major churches espoused the standard doctrines embedded in the traditions of their respective denominations. There were few, if any, advanced thinkers among them. The tenor of their theology and piety nevertheless reflected some of the major tendencies of the Enlightenment, including its moralism and intellectualism. One encounters representatives of all the older denominations who took a distinctly practical view of Christianity, emphasizing virtuous conduct over doctrinal subtleties and advocating moderation and tolerance in their dealings with fellow Christians. Piety among such people was undemonstrative, preaching was formal and intellectual, and worship was usually plain and decorous.

Conflict between denominations was not unknown in British North America before 1815, and there were one or two spectacular cases of acrimonious debate. Most notable of these was the vituperative pamphlet war in Nova Scotia between the Roman Catholic Edmund Burke and the Presbyterian Thomas McCulloch, sparked, somewhat ironically, by Burke's attack on the Anglican Bishop Inglis. The tone of the discussion is clear from the titles of the two treatises produced by McCulloch for the occasion: *Popery Condemned* and *Popery Again Condemned*. But such outbursts were the exception that proved the rule. Normally a spirit of harmony and restraint prevailed even between Catholics and Protestants, and the strongest condemnations were reserved for evangelical enthusiasts whose emotional expressions were considered evidence of excessive zeal.

A good example of the irenic tendencies of the age can be found in Newfoundland. When sectarian tensions between Roman Catholics and Protestant dissenters in St John's threatened to erupt in 1785 (partly as a result of the jealous meddling of the Anglican missionary Walter Price), James O'Donel and John Jones, pastors of the two congregations, hastened to co-operate in restoring peace. The conciliatory letters that the two exchanged vividly demonstrate their mutual conviction that Christianity in any of its diverse forms would promote morality, peace, and public welfare. 'It is true,' Jones wrote to O'Donel, '[that] you and I differ in Theological Points, but I hope we are jointly influenced by the same pious and benevolent motives so strongly recommended in the precepts and examples of our common Lord.' O'Donel replied that 'he who is an observant Christian of any denomination is not only a better man, but also a better neighbour, a better subject to his King, and a truer friend than he that is not so.' He continued: 'From what I here advance I hope you will do me the justice to believe I bestowed more of my time these Twenty Eight years past on the study of Philanthropy than Party and that I cannot be so foolish as to fall out with a man for not saying his prayers in the manner I do . . .'.[45]

While the intellectual principles of the Enlightenment fostered religious tolerance, the practical challenges posed by frontier conditions also encouraged co-operation among the churches. Competition between denominations was a fact of life, but such rivalries were often overshadowed by outstanding examples of good will and reciprocal support. These ranged from simple practical gestures, such as temporary agreements to share church buildings for divine worship, to formal assurances of mutual respect between clergymen of different denominations working in the same community. We have already seen the friendship between Thomas Wood and the Abbé Maillard, and many similar examples of co-operation can be cited. The Anglican rector in Halifax in the 1750s offered the use of his church on Sunday afternoons to the dissenting congregation of the town until their meeting-house was completed.[46] When Jacob Mountain arrived as first Anglican bishop of Quebec in 1793, the Roman Catholic clergy shared with him first the Récollet and later the Jesuit chapel.[47] In Montreal, during the first decade of the nineteenth century, Anglicans were permitted to worship in the Gabriel Street Presbyterian Church.[48] William Bulpitt, one of the earliest Methodist preachers in Prince Edward Island, reported that the Anglican incumbent allowed him to preach in his church and was generally a great friend to him.[49] The customary deference of British Wesleyans to the Church of England no doubt helped to make such benevolence possible, but underlying all these examples of co-operation was a commitment to common goals. The shared task of promoting Christianity in communities where organized religion was still not on a secure footing often took precedence over denominational rivalries.

The tolerant attitude of the clergy was echoed and even amplified by the laity. Resettlement in the New World, far removed from the scene of old controversies, helped to promote an atmosphere of friendship and collaboration among people of different religious backgrounds. Even more important, it promoted a sense of mutual involvement in the formation of a new society. Laity of the 'middling' classes, so instrumental in the foundation of religious institutions, were united to their counterparts in other denominations by common values and social aspirations. Congregational life was one of the principal arenas in which they could achieve social prominence, and the importance of organized religion was taken for granted in their efforts to build viable and stable communities. Examples of practical lay ecumenism abounded, including cases in which Protestants contributed to the church building funds of Roman Catholics.[50] It was also common for members of one denomination to attend the worship of others, especially—but not only—when services by their own clergy were unavailable.

Closely related to the irenic spirit of the Enlightenment was the stress placed in the eighteenth century on the social utility of religion. Christians were expected to contribute to the welfare and stability of society by obeying the civil authorities, whose powers were said to derive ultimately from God. Such assumptions were set within the framework of a static conception of the universe. The social order, like the natural creation, was thought to be arranged in an unchangeable pattern of higher and lower forms, each subject to the one above it. Confident of the harmony between religion, nature, and society, eighteenth-century churchmen actively encouraged acceptance of the status quo.

Conservative social doctrines were profoundly reinforced by the outbreak of revolution in America in 1776 and France in 1789. The spread of democratic principles, the real or potential damage to the interests of the British Crown, and the threat to the established social order all fostered a spirit of reaction within the traditional churches, the effects of which were soon felt in British North America. Rebellion against duly constituted authority was widely attributed to religious apostasy. The American Revolution was blamed on the influence of dissenting or sectarian forms of Christianity; the French Revolution was identified with atheism and free thought. There was a general sense of living in dangerous times, and many people sought in religion a bulwark against sudden or violent change.

A typical expression of this attitude was contained in the 1804 letter of instruction to Roman Catholic missionaries published by Edmund Burke, vicar-general for Nova Scotia. Referring to St Paul's insistence, in the Letter to

Titus (3:1), that Christians must be subject to the princes and powers, Burke declared:

> At no time since the establishment of the Christian Church was a strict obser-
> vance of this injunction of the Apostle . . . more indispensably necessary than in
> these unhappy days. . . . A spirit of insubordination, of independence, of revolt,
> the fruit of irreligion and immorality, pervades all ranks and extends its baneful
> influence to the extremities of the earth.[51]

While all the traditional churches espoused conservative social doctrines, the Church of England played a unique role in promoting counter-revolutionary ideology in British North America. As the established church of the mother country, it was identified absolutely with the British Crown. Especially after the American Revolution, the conviction grew among government officials and Anglican clergy that to bolster the loyalty of the remaining British colonies it was necessary to create a church establishment mirroring that of England. Already in 1758 the Church of England had been legally established in Nova Scotia.[52] In the wake of the Revolution, Loyalist clergy, supported by influential figures in London, campaigned successfully to strengthen this largely nominal establishment by the creation of a colonial bishopric.

It was their efforts that led to the appointment in 1787 of Charles Inglis, former rector of Trinity Church in New York City, as first bishop of Nova Scotia with jurisdiction over all of British North America. Charged with building up popular support for the established church as a way of strengthening the imperial connection, Inglis proved to be a man of indifferent abilities and limited imagination, especially when it came to adapting traditional Anglican forms and rituals to New World conditions.[53] Ideologically, however, he was perfectly suited to his mission, for he was convinced that church and state were the twin pillars on which a stable society must rest. 'There is a close connection,' he once said, 'between that duty which we owe to God, and the duty which we owe to the King, and to others in authority under him. So intimate is this connection, that they can scarcely be separated.'[54]

Four years after Inglis's appointment, steps were taken to bolster Anglicanism in the Canadas. In contrast to the situation in Nova Scotia, the Church of England had never been formally established in the province of Canada. In 1791, however, the Constitutional Act provided for one-seventh of all Crown land grants to be reserved for the support of the Protestant clergy (assumed by Anglicans to refer exclusively to them), and the erection of endowed Anglican rectories. Anglican clergy also had the exclusive right to perform marriages by licence and enjoyed a monopoly of military chaplaincies. These provisions for the Church of England amounted to *de facto* establishment, however limited in scope, and they were followed two years later by the appointment of Jacob

Mountain as bishop of Quebec. Mountain's powers exceeded those of Inglis inasmuch as he was accorded the title of 'Lord Bishop', which automatically entailed such temporal privileges as a seat on both the Executive and Legislative councils.

Believing with equal fervour in a close partnership between church and state, both Mountain and Inglis tried to advance the cause of Anglicanism as a means of strengthening attachment to the Crown. Though Inglis had to compete mainly with the influence of Protestant dissenters and Methodists, while Mountain worked in the midst of an overwhelmingly French-speaking Roman Catholic population, their common ambition was to make the Church of England the unifying force in a loyal British society founded on respect for tradition and authority.

The inflated aspirations of Inglis, Mountain, and the Anglican élite they represented were doomed to failure from the outset. Leaders of the Church of England, hopelessly one-sided in their understanding of the time and place in which they lived, failed to take serious account of religious and cultural forces that fell outside their narrow purview. The formative period of the English-speaking churches in British North America coincided not only with the reaction against the American and French revolutions but also with the evangelical revival. The latter was an international movement of religious renewal that swept many of the Protestant churches of Germany, Britain, and North America, sometimes transforming them from within and in other cases giving rise to new religious communities that broke or drifted away from the parent organization. Animated in part by a sense of spiritual decay, evangelicals reacted against the rationalism and moralism of eighteenth-century Christianity as well as the frivolity and luxury of secular culture. As an alternative to conventional religious life, evangelicalism offered a less intellectualistic, more affective style of preaching and worship, intended to speak to the hearts of sinners and bring about conversion. The result was a series of intense religious 'awakenings': periods of spiritual ferment and revitalization affecting large regions that often extended over several years. Such awakenings were promoted and sustained partly by local revivals, or rituals of mass conversion led by charismatic preachers whose impassioned oratory struck a responsive chord in people longing for a more vital religious experience than they could find in the formal worship of the day. In contrast to proponents of natural religion and glib moralism, evangelicals re-asserted the centrality of biblical revelation and the classical Protestant doctrine of justification by faith alone. Justification was to be attained, however, through the 'new birth', usually conceived as a distinct moment of conversion and often part of a deeply emotional experience or event.

Evangelical revivals took different forms, depending largely on the context in which they occurred. In the unsettled frontier conditions of the late eighteenth and early nineteenth centuries, they were intensely emotional, often boisterous affairs in which the experience of conversion was frequently attended by such physical manifestations of spiritual travail as swooning, trembling, and the temporary inability to speak. The preaching of evangelists was reinforced by lay participation, as people who experienced spiritual rebirth testified, sang, and exhorted those around them in the hope of bringing about further conversions. Such gatherings defied the usual standards of ecclesiastical decorum. Established religious institutions were in some instances augmented by new forms of association more conducive to vital religion, while in other cases they seemed to dissolve altogether in favour of invisible bonds of spiritual fellowship. Non-evangelicals, threatened by such changes, saw evangelicals as a danger not only to sound religion but also to order and stability in society.

At the popular level, evangelicalism could take an anti-intellectual form, and its enemies routinely denounced it as irrational and fanatical. This was a caricature. Experiential religion was not inherently irrational. The relationship between evangelical religion and the prevailing ideas of the eighteenth century was more complex than a simple reaction against the exaltation of the powers of human reason. John Wesley, the founder of Methodism, one of the most important branches of the evangelical movement, was an avowed disciple of the rational empiricism of John Locke, and like Locke he supported supernaturalist beliefs with empiricist arguments. While promoting an intensely personal form of religion, he regarded as anathema any hint that reasoned argument should be overturned by merely interior and subjective insights. He shared also the moral optimism of the Enlightenment, which was reflected not only in his confidence that human beings had the capacity to respond to divine initiative, but in his teachings about the holiness or perfection to be achieved by converted sinners. At the same time, there were important respects in which Wesley parted ways with rational supernaturalism. When Locke appealed, as he did in *The Reasonableness of Christianity*, to the supposedly empirical evidence of miracles and prophecies as proof of revealed truth, he confined such supernatural mysteries safely to the past. But for Wesley they were present realities, and he believed that God remained willing and able to grant new revelations and to intervene in the course of nature. His world-view was far closer to traditional supernaturalism than to modern, scientific rationalism.

The composition of the evangelical movement was no less complex than its intellectual roots. Though bound together by common themes and characteristics, it contained within itself a variety of forms, different enough from one another to come into conflict on occasion. The two most important manifestations of evangelicalism in eighteenth-century British North America were Methodism and the New Light movement within Nova Scotia Congregationalism. Methodism itself was a diverse phenomenon, incorporating not only the British Wesleyans but also American Methodist Episcopals and many smaller groups, mainly Calvinist, such as Lady Huntingdon's Connexion. Especially in its Wesleyan form, Methodism combined traditional elements such as sacramental worship and the services of professional clergy with such innovations as class meetings (regular gatherings of small groups of believers), extemporaneous prayer, itinerant ministers, and the use of lay preachers in local societies or congregations. In the long run, organization and discipline were as important to its success as were spontaneous outbursts of spiritual excitement. The New Lights, on the other hand, departed sharply from conventional church order and relied heavily on exuberant revivals led by unauthorized itinerant evangelists. Their leader, Henry Alline, flatly denied that he needed formal training or ordination in order to exercise his ministry, and he openly disparaged 'mere externals' such as baptism by water. British Wesleyan Methodists regarded the radical, spiritualizing tendencies of the New Lights with grave suspicion and frequently accused them of antinomianism, a contempt for the moral law stemming from the belief that, once saved, the 'saints' would persevere in their sanctity regardless of their actual conduct.

Evangelical influences entered the British North American colonies by various routes. Methodism—at that time still an evangelical movement within the Church of England—was introduced to Newfoundland by Laurence Coughlan, an ordained Anglican clergyman who came to the island in 1766 as an SPG missionary in response to a petition from local merchants.[55] While carrying on a regular Anglican ministry, Coughlan also preached an unorthodox form of Methodism, too 'enthusiastic' and emotional to retain John Wesley's support.[56] His evangelical message met with little response at first, but after three years of effort it sparked an intense revival among the common folk of Conception Bay. Following Coughlan's departure in 1773, Methodism on the island underwent significant changes, finally being brought under the direct supervision and moderating influence of British Wesleyanism. Nevertheless, the excitement caused by Coughlan's preaching marked the beginning of the movement in Newfoundland.

In Nova Scotia the evangelical movement, though strongly influenced by American developments, was a largely indigenous phenomenon, led initially by Alline, an Annapolis valley farm boy who had come to Nova Scotia with his family in the 1760s as part of the general migration of New England Planters.[57] Raised as a Congregationalist, Alline suffered a long period of anxious soul-searching and self-doubt that culminated in an emotional experience of conversion in 1775. Soon after, on the strength of an inner call to preach, he began an itinerant ministry among the out-settlements of the Maritime colonies, where he gained a hearing mainly among his fellow New England immigrants. Waves of revival, known as the Great Awakening in Nova Scotia, spread throughout the region, bringing into existence the loosely organized New

Light movement that supplanted traditional or Old Light Congregationalism. After Alline's premature death in 1784, the movement was kept alive by a cluster of successors, including his brother-in-law, John Payzant, and one of his early converts, Thomas Handley Chipman.[58] At the turn of the century it was transformed from within into an indigenous Baptist denomination.[59] This new denomination placed more emphasis on ecclesiastical order and formal standards of membership than had the vehemently anti-traditional New Light movement.

A few years after Alline began his ministry, another spontaneous revival broke out in Nova Scotia, this time among the Yorkshire Methodists who had settled in Cumberland near the present Nova Scotia–New Brunswick border. Among those converted in the course of the revival was young William Black, who like Alline soon began to preach throughout the region.[60] Black's travels took him not only throughout the Maritime colonies but also to Newfoundland, where he helped to sustain the Methodist movement inaugurated by Coughlan and to bring it closer to British Wesleyan norms.[61] In Nova Scotia Black was assisted at first mainly by American Methodist preachers, including the outstanding revivalist Freeborn Garretson,[62] but in 1800 he turned to the British Wesleyans as his principal source of support.[63] Although Methodism attracted fewer converts in the Maritimes than did the New Light/Baptist movement, it was nevertheless an important element in the overall spread of evangelical religion in the region.

In the case of central Canada, identifying individual founders of the evangelical movement is somewhat more difficult. Revivalism entered the Canadas chiefly from the United States through the influence of Baptists, evangelical Presbyterians and Congregationalists, and especially American Methodists. Loyalist families, led by the Emburys and the Hecks, who had been instrumental in founding Methodism in New York, organized the first Methodist society in Upper Canada in Augusta township (in the region of the future Brockville) at the end of the 1780s.[64] The first authorized Methodist preacher in Upper Canada was William Losee of New York, who made his first tour of the area in 1790.[65] Dozens of Methodist itinerants followed him across the border, preaching to a population that was also mainly of American origin. Garretson, who also served in Nova Scotia, was in charge of sending the early itinerants to Upper Canada. Among the most noteworthy of these preachers were Darius Dunham, Henry Ryan, and William Case.[66] Nathan Bangs, an Anglican from New England who was converted to Methodism after coming to Upper Canada, preached not only there but also in Quebec and Montreal.[67]

Methodism had been carried to Lower Canada first by lay preachers attached to British regiments; one of them was John Tuffy, who in the 1780s preached to both military and civilian audiences. From about 1800, the American Methodist Conference began to send missionaries. The visits of these itinerants, who included, besides Bangs, Joseph Sawyer, Thomas Madden, and Samuel Coate, were short and unrewarding. In Upper Canada, however, Methodism quickly became the fastest-growing and most dynamic denomination. Because American Methodism was more unreservedly revivalistic than its British Wesleyan counterpart and distinguished itself more clearly from the Church of England, Methodism in Upper Canada took on a different colouring than it did in Lower Canada or the Atlantic region. Its vitality and innovative character were well-suited to the pioneering element in Upper Canadian society.

Some historians have argued that religious awakenings often occurred at times of cultural crisis brought on by rapid social change. As traditional assumptions collapsed, revivals fostered a reorientation of communal values and the birth of a revised world-view capable of giving order and meaning to new experiences. The precise social context of particular revivals depended on local circumstances. In late eighteenth-century British North America, economic deprivation, political unrest, and the social dislocation associated with migration all played a part (sometimes in combination with one another) in setting the stage. Common to all such awakenings, however, was the fact that the preaching of revivalists spoke directly to the existential needs of communities in crisis.

In Newfoundland, Coughlan's followers were mostly common fishermen and their wives, trapped in near servitude to the island's merchant élite. His message transformed their lives, helping them to overcome self-destructive forms of behaviour such as alcoholism and to break the pattern of abject economic dependence by climbing out of debt.[68] In Nova Scotia, Alline provided his fellow New England settlers with a religious justification for their neutrality during the American Revolution. Rejecting politics as a 'worldly' concern, he created an image of Nova Scotia's Yankee population as a faithful remnant of New England Puritanism, spared the ravages of war and blessed with spiritual gifts as a sign of God's special favour.[69] In Upper Canada, itinerant preachers from neighbouring American states carried the message of the 'new birth' to a population of recent immigrants still in the process of forming viable communities. For many settlers, the cathartic experience of conversion seemed to ease the anxieties associated with resettlement, and the spontaneous sense of community generated by camp-meetings and similar religious gatherings helped to overcome the isolation of the frontier.

Although a few prosperous merchants took leadership roles among the Methodists, the members of the early evangelical movement were mostly common folk such as farmers and fishermen in rural districts and artisans in the towns. The colonial élite were identified with the older denominations, especially the Church of England and Church of Scotland. In this sense, the distinction between evangelical and non-evangelical religion tended initially to emphasize social divisions. Within the voluntary fellowship of believers, how-ever, inclusive and egalitarian forms of organization, based on spiritual accom-plishment rather than power or wealth, replaced patterns of authority determined by social rank. Women, children, and the economically disadvan-taged acquired a new status by virtue of their spiritual rebirth. This fact often led to dramatic role reversals, as women exhorted their husbands to repent or children led their parents to conversion. Women were disproportionately rep-resented among converts, and their role as instruments of conversion increased their spiritual authority in the home, where they assumed much of the responsibility for leading their children to a godly life. Women could even take on a formal leadership role, such as that of class leader in Methodist soci-eties. In the earliest phase of Wesleyan Methodism some women in England had also preached, but this practice had been severely restricted by the time Methodism took root in the colonies, and among most of the evangelical groups of British North America preaching was initially entrusted almost exclusively to men. There were a few exceptions, though, among the American Methodist Episcopals of Upper Canada.[70] For example, in the sec-ond decade of the nineteenth century Ellen Bangs (a sister of Nathan Bangs), who married the Methodist itinerant Joseph Gatchell, used her considerable gifts to supplement her husband's efforts in the pulpit 'very much to the satis-faction of the people'.[71]

Early evangelical preachers often lacked formal theological training and were generally people of modest social origins. This fact was the source of end-less complaints from the clergy of the traditional churches, who were offended by the notion that humble folk with limited education should presume to preach the Word of God with authority. The truth is that the traditional clergy had a tendency to exaggerate the gap between their own educational attain-ments and those of the evangelicals; but this did not prevent them from denouncing their rivals as 'ignorant sectaries' or 'fanatical enthusiasts' who swarmed across the countryside misleading a supposedly gullible populace. For the common people, on the other hand, the experience of hearing the Gospel proclaimed in a popular idiom by preachers who were often their social equals had enormous benefits in raising their self-esteem. Not the least impor-tant feature of the evangelical movement was that it provided a religious sanc-tion, and a channel of expression, for an autonomous popular culture.

Ridicule was a common weapon used by the 'respectable' clergy against evangelical groups. Such derision masked a deep concern over the impact of these movements, whose success in attracting new members outstripped that of the Church of England and other more established denominations. Evangelical groups were perceived as a threat to the established order in both church and state. Religious radicalism was widely identified with political extremism and the desire to overthrow civil authorities. The Anglican clergy, attributing to revival movements an inversion of their own church–state doctrines, were especially vociferous in denouncing Methodists and New Lights as republicans and democrats.[72]

The accusation that evangelical groups were politically disloyal was plainly untrue. Early evangelical preachers were far more likely to urge their followers to focus their attention on spiritual matters than on 'wordly' politics. The firm distinction that they drew between spiritual and temporal affairs usually resulted in the kind of mystical quietism promoted by Henry Alline or the apolitical loyalism espoused by the British Methodists. Even American Methodists, undoubtedly champions of egalitarian values, refrained from overtly political actions except when the need arose to protect vital denominational interests. William Black, leader of the Wesleyan revival in the Atlantic region, spoke for many others when he asked: 'What have the ministers of Christ to do with the administration of civil government? Christ's kingdom is not of this world. We are neither magistrates nor legislators.'[73]

Inasmuch as such attitudes led to passive acceptance of the existing political order, they were profoundly conservative. Whatever desire the first generation of British North American evangelicals had to improve the material conditions of their followers was to be fulfilled through the transforming power of spiritual rebirth, not by political agitation. As for specific questions of church and state, the evangelicals had in these early days little incentive to challenge the status quo, since the special status enjoyed by the Church of England clearly did not prevent them from achieving their spiritual objectives. Relying on direct appeals to the people, they had little need of state support or official recognition. Not until after 1815 did evangelical leaders enter the political fray to challenge Anglican privileges.

While the accusation of political disloyalty was misplaced, however, there was a deeper sense in which the Anglican clergy and other members of the colonial élite were right to see in revival movements a challenge to the existing social order. As a vehicle of popular and egalitarian culture, evangelicalism may not have advocated immediate or overt political action, but it did pose the threat of a transformation of values. Élite conceptions of society rested on distinctions of rank, deference to authority, the power of coercive institutions, and the obligation to obey traditional norms. Evangelical religion encouraged individual self-assertion, voluntary association, the definition of status in terms of virtue and achievement rather than birth and inheritance, and the maintenance of order through popular consent. Revival movements offered not only an alternative view of the world but autonomous forms of corporate organization and bonds of social cohesion that were outside the control of the governing classes. Their effect was not to destroy the fabric of society but to guarantee religious and cultural diversity. The goal of the Anglican leadership had been to make Anglicanism the basis of social unity in British North America. The success of evangelical groups ensured that no one denomination could exercise such cultural hegemony.

Just as Anglicans never achieved a controlling influence over the culture of British North America, they also failed to attain all the legal and constitutional privileges they sought. While the anti-revolutionary mood of the times favoured a renewed emphasis on order and authority in church and state, demographic and political realities made it impossible to achieve this stability through an exclusive church establishment. The government had to fashion a religious policy that would win the support of the majority of the colonial population. Since Anglicans comprised only a small minority, this meant extending a variety of rights and privileges to competing denominations.

Although Methodists and Protestant dissenters did suffer some serious restrictions and disabilities, including severe limitations on their right to perform marriages and exclusion from higher education, they were granted basic religious freedom throughout British North America. Not only were they free to worship according to the rites of their own churches, but they were exempt from any obligation to contribute financially to the established church. In fact, in addition to guaranteeing such exemptions, the government in some cases offered financial support to non-Anglican churches, especially Presbyterians. Usually paid in the form of stipends for individual clergymen, such awards fell far short of the substantial sums allocated to the Church of England; furthermore, they were made on a case-by-case basis and implied no formal recognition of the denominations concerned. Nevertheless, they illustrate the government's willingness to sacrifice a strict understanding of church establishment in order to achieve its own goals. Colonial administrations, while paying lip-service to the exclusive privileges of the Church of England, were willing to support within limits any church whose principles were considered conducive to good order and the preservation of the status quo.

The legal situation of Roman Catholics in British North America, though considerably more complex than that of Protestant dissenters and Methodists, further illustrates the limitations imposed on the Anglican establishment by the exigencies of colonial politics. In the Canadas, where Roman Catholicism was originally identified with the French-speaking population, government policy had been shaped by the need to secure the loyalty of the recently conquered Canadiens. This had resulted first in a simple policy of toleration toward Catholics, legally embodied in the Treaty of Paris of 1763, and reinforced in practice by the tacit arrangement that permitted French Canadians to have their own bishop. In the 1770s, however, when the threat of revolution in the thirteen American colonies made it even more necessary to reconcile the inhabitants of Quebec to British rule, the Quebec Act had granted the Roman Catholic Church not only religious freedom but also the legal right to collect tithes from its adherents, a prerogative normally reserved to established churches. The liberties bestowed on the Quebec Catholic Church were more precarious than at first appeared. The Treaty of Paris contained an ambiguous phrase stating that such liberties were granted only 'as far as the laws of Great Britain permit'. Freedom of worship was guaranteed, but the instructions to the governors as well as the Quebec Act made the exercise of Roman Catholic ecclesiastical jurisdiction subject to the royal supremacy. In theory, this provision placed control over the appointment of clergy in the hands of the Protestant civil authorities, leaving Catholics extremely vulnerable to interference from hostile or overzealous governors. For the time being, though, toleration was assured, and the accommodation with French-speaking Catholics had important consequences for the English-speaking churches. On the one hand, Anglicans were profoundly jealous of the prerogatives accorded to Roman Catholics, which seemed in practice to exceed their own privileges. On the other hand, English-speaking Catholic immigrants arriving in Canada from Scotland and Ireland found themselves exempt from the sort of anti-Catholic legislation that they had known at home. The Constitutional Act of 1791, which divided Upper from Lower Canada, did not alter this fact. Both French- and English-speaking Roman Catholics in the future provinces of Quebec and Ontario continued to enjoy religious liberty.

The situation of Catholics in the Atlantic colonies was less straightforward. They did not benefit from the tolerance extended to the Catholics of Quebec, and were in fact subject initially to penalties and disabilities similar to those imposed on the Catholics of the British Isles. The substance of these restrictions, as well as the precise manner in which they were introduced, differed with local circumstances, ranging from a simple exclusion of Catholics from the general provisions for religious liberty in the Royal Instructions to the Governor (Newfoundland) to a fairly elaborate body of anti-Catholic legislation enacted by the colonial legislature (Nova Scotia). Basically, all the Catholics of Atlantic Canada were to one degree or another denied religious liberty. In the worst instances, this meant that Catholic clergy were officially forbidden to exercise their priestly functions and that Catholics in general could not purchase or inherit land, operate schools, vote in elections, be called to the bar, or be elected to government office.

In most cases, however, these restrictions on Catholics were honoured more in the breach than in the observance.[74] (Newfoundland, as we shall see, was a partial exception.) Colonial governments were aware of the need to reach a pragmatic accommodation with the rapidly expanding Catholic population of the Atlantic region, and they recognized the Catholic clergy as important allies in their efforts to inculcate respect for established authority. Ignoring the law against priests, they not only permitted but actively encouraged Catholic missionaries to come to the region and in some cases awarded them government stipends, similar to those paid to Presbyterians. Moreover, the immigration of

Irish and Scottish Catholics to Atlantic Canada coincided with the dawn of Catholic emancipation in Britain, and the progressive relaxation of the penal code by the imperial parliament was soon reflected in the Atlantic colonies. The process of reversing anti-Catholic provisions began as early as 1779 with changes to the Royal Instructions to the Governor of Newfoundland.[75] The Maritime colonies gradually followed suit by repealing local statutes and (in the case of Nova Scotia) by appealing to London for further concessions to Catholics. By 1786, all restrictions, save those excluding Catholics from the political process, had been dismantled. By 1830, Catholics had also received the vote and the right to sit in local legislatures where these existed.[76]

The liberal concessions made to competing denominations meant that the actual advantages enjoyed by the established church were relatively few. Aside from the fact that the Church of England received the lion's share of government funding for religious purposes, its privileges were limited to the exclusive right of its clergy to perform marriages by licence, the sole right of its parishes to form corporations for the purpose of holding property, and the controlling voice that Anglicans enjoyed in the formation of educational institutions. These privileges were real enough, and they often proved inhibiting and irksome to other denominations; but they fell far short of constituting a strong or dominating church establishment. Furthermore, such advantages were purchased at the cost of government interference. Anglican bishops, in sharp contrast to their Roman Catholic counterparts, could not even station their own clergy without the consent of colonial governors. It is hard to avoid the conclusion that Anglicans lost more than they gained by state support. The stifling effects of their church's subordination to the state more than outweighed the limited benefits of official recognition; and Anglican energies were too often dissipated in trying to defend privileges that were ultimately untenable in a pluralistic society.

In spite of all the ways in which Anglican ambitions were frustrated, it is important to stress that what one witnesses in British North America is not the triumph of one form of Christianity over another. The Church of England, though subject to many limitations, remained, along with other traditional churches and the newer evangelical denominations, an important force in religious life. The situation was far too complex to be reduced to a simple contrast between polar opposites. Denominational relations were characterized not by categorical divisions but by a complex pattern of overlapping affinities and enmities. Depending on the precise issue at stake, the line was drawn sometimes between Anglicans and non-Anglicans, sometimes between Protestants and Catholics, and sometimes between traditional and evangelical denominations. Before 1815, the cleavage between what William Westfall has called the 'religion of order' embodied in the older churches, and the 'religion of experience' promoted by the revival movements was the most important in terms of its impact on society and culture.[77] In the next generation, however, changing external circumstances and new developments within the denominations would shift the focus to the conflict between the Anglican establishment and the rights of other churches.

GROWTH AND EXPANSION (1815–1840)

RELIGIOUS RENEWAL AND INSTITUTIONAL DEVELOPMENT

The circumstances of the British North American churches changed dramatically in the second decade of the nineteenth century. The War of 1812, combined with a sharp increase in immigration from the British Isles after 1815, resulted in fundamental changes to both the demography and the ideological climate of the colonies. First, the war drove a wedge between the British colonies and the United States and promoted among British North Americans a growing sense of their own identity. Especially in Upper Canada, where ties to the United States had previously been very strong and where the impact of the war was greatest, people increasingly rejected American values and influences and defined themselves as other than American. While this was a peculiarly negative form of self-definition, it signalled a resurgence of Loyalist and anti-republican ideals and marked the faint beginnings of national consciousness. Second, armed conflict disrupted the flow of people across the border, and immigration from the United States was relatively less important after the restoration of peace. On the other hand, the end of the Napoleonic Wars opened the seas to emigrants from the British Isles. Rapid social and economic change at home and the prospect of achieving prosperity in the New World spurred tens of thousands of Scots, Irish, English, and Welsh to cross the Atlantic in search of new opportunities. Landing in British North American ports, these newcomers not only swelled the population of individual colonies but also lent them a more decisively British character. In the Maritime colonies, their arrival reinforced the trend away from American to British immigration that had begun even before the French wars. In Upper Canada, it marked a radical shift as a population once overwhelmingly American in origin soon became predominantly British, although that designation included a variety of ethnic groups. Indeed, British immigrants often tied their identity closely to religious affiliation; Irish Catholics, Ulster Presbyterians, evangelical Irish Anglicans, Irish Methodists, Scottish Presbyterians and Baptists, and Highland Catholics were either distinguished from their compatriots by religion or set apart from their co-religionists by nationality and by the peculiar tenor that national traditions lent to their religious attitudes and convictions.

Consistent statistical information about the flow of immigrants is impossible to obtain, but enough figures are available to see clearly the dramatic pattern of growth and its implications for the churches. Between 1815 and 1839, before the rate of emigration had even reached its high point, nearly half a million people left the United Kingdom for British North America.[78] Although many of these subsequently moved on to the United States, those who remained in the British colonies were sufficient to raise their permanent populations to unprecedented numbers. The rate of increase caused by this influx of settlers varied from one region to another, but all of the colonies expanded rapidly. The population of Newfoundland, probably about 50,000 in 1815, rose to approximately 80,000 in 1840.[79] That of Prince Edward Island grew from less than 20,000 to almost 50,000 in the same period.[80] New Brunswick, which had perhaps 70,000 residents in 1815, rose to roughly 90,000 in 1827 and 170,000 in 1840.[81] Nova Scotia, the fastest-growing of the Atlantic colonies, jumped from an estimated 80,000 in 1815 to more than 120,000 in 1827 and exceeded 200,000 by 1838.[82] The total English-speaking population of Lower Canada, for which early figures are not available, totalled approximately 150,000 in 1838.[83] The most dramatic gains occurred in Upper Canada. From an estimated 90,000 people in 1817, the figure rose to 150,000 in 1824 and by 1842 had more than tripled to 487,000.[84] Besides increasing the population of established colonies, immigration also opened new areas to English-speaking settlers. The most important of these was the Red River colony, established in 1811 by the Scottish philanthropist Lord Selkirk in what is now the province of Manitoba.

The influx of British settlers coincided with and partly accounted for important social and economic changes in the colonies.[85] The sharp increase in population led to the clearance and occupation of an increasing portion of the most arable land. Villages began to spring up in the countryside and transportation between one settlement and another gradually improved. Expanding British markets, combined with a system of protective tariffs, stimulated the exploitation or cultivation of such staples as timber and wheat. A competitive market economy emerged, surpassing subsistence agriculture as the mainstay of economic life. Many settlers carried on with traditional farming, but there was a growing tendency for such people to supplement their incomes with some form of wage labour. For the churches, the long-term result of these changes was that they had to pursue their mission in a significantly different social environment from the one that had existed before 1815. The changing social context presented fresh challenges and new opportunities for the churches to exert a formative influence on British North American culture.

In immediate terms, the explosion of population affected the churches in three important ways. The first, and most obvious, effect was that it placed an unprecedented strain on their human and material resources. Still in the very early stages of development, colonial churches suddenly faced the task of ministering to thousands of newcomers. More churches and clergymen were urgently needed, and it was not immediately clear where they would come from. A second, related consequence was that the beginning of English-speaking settlement in the West broadened missionary horizons and presented a new challenge, especially to the Protestant churches. A third effect was that immigration altered the denominational balance in individual colonies. In Upper Canada in 1815, for example, Methodists were easily the single largest denomination, while the Church of England, despite its claims to pre-eminence, represented only a small minority of the population; but by 1842, Anglicans had been catapulted into the leading position, surpassing the second-place Methodists by more than 25,000.[86] In the process, the Church of England had ceased to be the denomination mainly of a small élite and had acquired a genuinely popular basis.

The growing predominance of British over American settlers strengthened the ties between colonial churches and parent organizations in the United Kingdom. Since most of these were more conservative than their American equivalents, the effect was to reinforce moderate tendencies in British North American religious life. This had especially important consequences for Methodists, Presbyterians, and Congregationalists, who either veered in a strongly British direction or found themselves torn apart by competition between British, American, and indigenous forces. Among Baptists, on the other hand, British influence was not so pervasive. In southwestern Upper Canada, where they were relatively numerous, Baptists retained their strongly American character, while in the Maritimes they emerged from Henry Alline's New Light movement to form an indigenous denomination under local leadership. In the Ottawa valley and Montreal, British (especially Scottish) influences did predominate, but the efforts of the Montreal Baptists to provide leadership for their brethren in Upper Canada met with little enthusiasm, and even the Ottawa valley Scots gradually loosened their ties with Montreal in favour of closer ties with Upper Canadian Baptists of American origin.[87] In all other major denominations, though, British influences proved crucial. Moreover, by far the largest group among British immigrants were the Irish. This caused a sharp increase in the English-speaking Roman Catholic population, where Irish soon outnumbered Highland Scots, but it also had a major impact on Anglicans, Presbyterians, and Methodists, especially in Upper Canada where the majority of Irish immigrants were Protestant.[88]

Gradually the denominational pattern of British North America became more complex. Although the vast majority of church members still adhered to a handful of denominations, several new religious bodies (some from the United States) made their appearance after 1815. Included in the list were Mormons, Universalists, Unitarians, Disciples of Christ, and the Catholic Apostolic Church ('Irvingites') who together took their places alongside the existing smaller denominations such as Quakers and Mennonites. In Upper

Canada, a local movement known as the Children of Peace developed under the leadership of David Willson after the latter had split with the Quakers. The Children of Peace combined elements from Judaism and Christianity and, in sharp contrast to Quaker plainness, celebrated elaborate rituals, incorporating rich imagery and stirring music, at the Sharon Temple, the symbolic centre of the movement, north of present-day Toronto.[89]

Equally important was the arrival of new branches of familiar denominations. To well-known forms of Presbyterianism, such as American Presbyterians, Scottish Secessionists, and the Church of Scotland, were now added groups such as the Reformed Presbyterian Synod of Ireland, which formally established itself in the Maritimes in 1832, and the United Secession Church of Scotland, whose representatives formed the Mission Presbytery in Upper Canada in 1834. Even wider variations were found among the Methodists. In 1828, as part of the reaction against American influences following the War of 1812, the separate Methodist Episcopal Church in Canada was formed under the leadership of William Case. Soon afterward a short-lived splinter group, known as the Canadian Wesleyan Methodist Church, was formed under Henry Ryan. In 1833 the Canadian Methodist Episcopals united with the British Wesleyans under the name of the Wesleyan Methodist Church in Canada, but an unhappy minority of Canadians disavowed this union and carried on independently as the Methodist Episcopal Church. Three new Methodist denominations from England also entered the colonies during this era: the Methodist New Connexion, the Bible Christians, and the Primitive Methodists. These new Methodist groups had been formed largely in reaction against the growing conservatism of the Wesleyan Conference in Britain. They accorded a larger role to lay people and sought to recapture the simplicity and spontaneity of early Methodism. Their impact was felt mainly in Upper Canada, but the Bible Christians also enjoyed a measure of success in Prince Edward Island. Meanwhile, Maritime Baptists were divided into Calvinist Baptists and Free Baptists. The Calvinist Baptists were the dominant party, but the Free Baptists constituted a significant minority, and were especially influential in New Brunswick.[90]

At the same time that massive immigration from the British Isles was transforming the context of colonial religious life, important internal changes were also reshaping the churches. The bloody events of the French Revolution and the turmoil of the Napoleonic era had shocked the older churches out of their complacency. The self-satisfaction that had characterized them in the eighteenth century gave way to a renewed zeal and activism. After an initial period of reaction, new and creative impulses made their influence felt as the traditional churches embarked on conscious efforts at renewal. Though still wary of revolutionary change, they were increasingly sensitive to the need for adaptation and more and more optimistic about the possibilities of the new age. The signs of religious revival included the proliferation of religious voluntary organizations, heightened missionary zeal, vigorous institutional growth, the increasing formative influence of religion on the lives of individual believers, and the development of programs to promote social reform under religious auspices. Not all of these trends were immediately evident in British North America, especially among its Roman Catholic minority, but their impact increased steadily over the first half of the nineteenth century.

Among Protestants, religious renewal found expression chiefly in the evangelical movement. Previously identified mainly with revivalist groups such as Methodists and New Light Congregationalists, evangelical impulses became increasingly evident after the turn of the century in the older, more established denominations. Evangelical parties among Anglicans and Presbyterians grew in strength, bringing a new emphasis on spiritual rebirth and the value of experiential religion. Revivalist forms of expression, comparable to those among Methodists, American Presbyterians, and New Lights, became common among evangelicals in the Church of Scotland, where they were linked to the Scottish 'long communion'—a three- or four-day outdoor gathering that combined evangelical preaching with the mass reception of the Lord's Supper.[91] Dating from the early seventeenth century, it spread to British North America with Highland immigration, and played a crucial role in Presbyterian revivals of the nineteenth century.[92]

This new openness to the place of emotion in religious life was moderated by the fidelity of the older denominations to traditional forms of worship and established ecclesiastical structures, and in the case of Presbyterians by Calvinist theology. A significant portion of Anglicans resisted the evangelical trend and continued to deplore anything that smacked of 'enthusiasm'. The spread of the evangelical spirit did, however, soften the antagonism between the older, more formal and new, experiential approaches to religion that had characterized the period before 1815. The dominant motif of the early and mid-nineteenth century was the quest for more vital forms of Christianity.

The evangelical movements of the eighteenth century were also experiencing important changes. While they continued to stress the life-transforming experience of conversion as the cornerstone of religious life, and most conversions continued to occur in the context of emotional revival meetings, the revivalist denominations also began to edge their way closer to churchly norms in ministry, worship, and ecclesiastical discipline. We are dealing here with incipient tendencies rather than mature developments, and several decades would pass before emerging patterns of institutionalization reached their conclusion. Nevertheless, it is clear that by the early decades of the nineteenth century, Methodists and New Lights were each in their own way entering a period of transition. Changes in the social context, including the development of more mature, settled communities, called for different responses than had the fading pioneer environment.

The pace and exact nature of the change varied from one region and denomination to another. Methodists, with their roots in the Church of England, already possessed many of the ingredients of traditional ecclesiastical life and needed only a re-orientation to emerge as a stable denomination. In the Maritimes they came under the control of the conservative Wesleyans as early as 1800, and this resulted immediately in more conventional piety, restraint of emotional excesses, better-educated clergy, political conservatism, and stricter church discipline.[93] The large and boisterous revivals characteristic of the early days of Maritime Methodism were banned in 1820 by the District Meeting. In the 1830s, Wesleyan authorities relented to the point of allowing 'protracted meetings' to take place, but these indoor revivals were by definition more orderly and restrained than outdoor camp-meetings. The first camp-meeting among Maritime Methodists did not occur until 1850,[94] by which time the control of the British Wesleyans was beginning to slip. Camp-meetings were by then becoming less spontaneous and more sedate.

The Wesleyans also gained a strong foothold in Lower Canada after the War of 1812. British Methodism was re-organizing its missionary efforts and devoting more financial and human resources to overseas colonies. Lower Canadian Methodists, who had received inadequate support from the American church, were eager to accept help from Britain. A growing number of Wesleyan missionaries entered the region, where they engaged in sometimes bitter conflict with their American brethren. In 1820, an agreement was worked out designating Lower Canada as an exclusively Wesleyan mission field and reserving Upper Canada for American Methodist itinerants.[95] This uneasy truce meant that Lower Canadian Methodism took on a decidedly conservative hue.

Upper Canadian Methodists differed sharply from their brethren in the Maritimes and Lower Canada. With their deep roots in the American Methodist Episcopal Church, they resisted incursions by the English Wesleyans and kept the fires of frontier revivalism burning more brightly. But even they were not immune from change. By the late 1820s, they were attempting to raise the educational standards of their clergy and making admission to the ministry contingent on successful completion of a basic examination;[96] and, as we have seen, having achieved independence from the Americans in 1828, they entered into a fragile union with the Wesleyans in 1833. This union facilitated and reflected the Methodists' integration into the general life of the province. It encouraged conservatism in politics and paved the way for the acceptance of government grants.

The New Lights of the Maritimes underwent a more radical transformation than the Methodists.[97] Between 1790 and 1810, a Second Great Awakening occurred that resulted in a reconstitution of the movement,[98] as bonds of fellowship resting on common spiritual experience were increasingly channelled into formal structures. Among the factors that combined to foster this change was an outbreak of antinomianism, attended by various excesses and irregularities, in the early 1790s that caused a strong reaction in favour of order and discipline. This trend was reinforced by a growing desire among some New Lights for respectability and status in the community, if only as a means of defending their rights in matters such as the laws regulating marriage. In Baptist polity, under the leadership of men such as Edward Manning, they found the stability they were seeking. The influence of the Calvinist Baptists of neighbouring New England was crucial in this respect. In 1800 a Baptist Association was formed, incorporating most of the New Light congregations, although a few later withdrew. A loosely connected spiritual fellowship that had consciously rejected 'mere externals' such as sacraments was thus transformed into a conservative denomination with adult baptism as its standard of membership and a policy of 'close communion' as the basis of ecclesiastical discipline. The ethos of the Maritime Baptists remained emphatically evangelical, but in Nova Scotia (and to a lesser degree in New Brunswick) evangelical zeal was tempered by denominational norms and structures.

The conservative trend was strengthened in 1825 when a number of socially prominent Nova Scotians, including the future premier W.J. Johnston, left the Anglican for the Baptist fold as the result of a split between evangelical and non-evangelical factions at St Paul's Church in Halifax. This group of former Anglicans was instrumental in pushing for a more educated clergy among Maritime Baptists, a concern that eventually contributed to the founding of Acadia College. They also transformed the politics of Baptists, leading them away from the Reform camp into the arms of the Conservative party.

Coupled with the profound changes under way in the older churches, the tranformation of evangelical movements narrowed the gaps between the Protestant denominations. Profound doctrinal, philisophical, and political differences remained, and it would be premature to speak of an evangelical consensus at this stage. But the areas of agreement were expanding as a growing body of opinion coalesced around shared assumptions. The contrast between revivalist and traditional approaches to Christianity had never been absolute in any case, and the spirit of the new century allowed common elements to come increasingly into focus.

The evangelical outlook, which emerged as the dominant religious ideology of the century, consciously harked back to the central principles of the Reformation, emphasizing the reality of sin, the absolute need for atonement through Christ, and the sole authority of the Bible as the source of saving truth. Also in keeping with classical Protestant doctrine, evangelicals emphasized human depravity. Yet their position on the question of free will differed from the classical view by allowing for at least a degree of human initiative and co-operation with the grace of God. Conversion was expected to bear fruit not only in individual regeneration but also in collective efforts for the improvement of society. Ethical conduct was emphasized over sectarian doctrine, often taking the form of service to the community through philanthropy, missionary endeavours, and agitation for social reform. A strong ecumenical impulse can also be detected in nineteenth-century evangelicalism, although this tolerant spirit did not extend to the Church of Rome. Evangelical piety was simple and usually unpretentious. It emphasized prayer, preaching, hymn-singing and Bible-reading over elaborate sacramental rituals. The spiritual development of an evangelical believer was mapped out in stages beginning with the conviction of sin and progressing through repentance and conversion to justification and regeneration. Various methods were used to propagate and sustain evangelical principles, but perhaps the most important was the dissemination of vast quantities of religious tracts and devotional literature. Also crucial was the emphasis placed on the home as a centre of religious life. The domestic basis of evangelical religion proved one of its great strengths. Lay participation and activism were encouraged, not only in explicitly religious matters but also in the benevolent undertakings to which the evangelical movement gave rise.

Evangelicals combined commitment to philanthropy and proselytizing zeal with a genius for new forms of corporate endeavour. Non-evangelical organizations such as the SPG and the Society for Promoting Christian Knowledge (SPCK) had already done a great deal to promote missionary work and religious eductaion. As a result of evangelical efforts, however, an ever-increasing assortment of voluntary associations dedicated to missionary, educational, and philanthropic purposes came into existence after 1790. Many evangelical organizations, such as the London Missionary Society, the Religious Tract Society, and the British and Foreign Bible Society, were interdenominational. Others, such as the Anglican Church Missionary Society (CMS) and the Church of Scotland's Glasgow Colonial Society, were the creations of the evangelical wings of particular denominations.

Yet even the members of different denominational organizations were united by common values and goals, and they often showed themselves open to co-operation. Indeed, the purposes of the various voluntary societies often overlapped, and the same people were frequently members of several organizations at the same time. Clergymen sent out by the London Missionary Society were often active in the Bible Society. The Bible Society, in turn, usually worked closely with the Religious Tract Society, as evangelical religious propaganda was distributed hand in hand with copies of the Scriptures. The Bible Society also co-operated closely with charity schools, including those sponsored by its sister organization the British and Foreign School Society. Literacy was promoted in part to raise standards of religious knowledge, while a favoured method of teaching poor children to read was to use cheap editions of the Bible. Together, evangelical voluntary associations formed an interlocking network of missionary and philanthropic organizations whose impact was heightened by the co-ordination of efforts on several fronts.

Besides its distinctive forms of piety and specific organizational patterns, the new evangelicalism was associated with particular social values. For men, these values included hard work, sobriety, and self-discipline. Diligence and frugality were part and parcel of the evangelical call to seriousness, and prosperity was interpreted as a sign of God's blessing. The evangelical ethos was well-suited to the changing economic circumstances as a society based largely on subsistence agriculture gradually gave way to a competitive market economy. The evangelical emphasis on industry, perseverance, and thrift was highly conducive to success in such an environment.

For women, the evangelical view of life also had important social implications. The available evidence—admittedly anecdotal—suggests that more women than men were drawn to evangelical religion. Though young women may have outnumbered men among the adherents of non-evangelical churches as well, the conspicuous role that they played in the evangelical revival helped to reinforce the notion that women were 'naturally religious'. Exemplary piety was part of an idealized conception of womanhood that also included purity, submissiveness, and domesticity.[99] The impetus for this view did not come only from evangelical sources, but there was a close harmony and reciprocal influence between evangelical assumptions and emerging social norms. As the development of a commercial economy encouraged a greater separation between the roles of men and women, the responsibilities of women came to be more exclusively identified with household duties, motherhood, and the nurture of children.[100] Children themselves were gaining a heightened moral status and were gradually becoming the focus of family life. Both parents, but especially mothers, were charged by evangelical clergy and educators with transmitting religious knowledge to the young and inculcating high moral standards. Mothers were also expected to provide a model of virtue and integrity for the rest of the family and to make the home a shelter from the allurements and vicissitudes of the world. The virtuous mother was crucial to the evangelical conception of family life, and it became a familiar refrain in evangelical literature for upright and respected men to acknowledge with gratitude the formative influence of their pious and self-sacrificing mothers.

The emphasis on domesticity, the notion of female submissiveness, and the myth of moral superiority all served to inhibit women from venturing beyond their narrowly circumscribed domain. Actual experience did not always correspond to the evangelical ideal, and it is important not to confuse an ideology with the reality of everyday life for women of all social stations. Still, the evangelical model of womanhood became a widely accepted norm among men and women alike, especially in the more prosperous segments of society, and it had a profound impact on standards of conduct and patterns of self-understanding.

In many ways it was prescriptive and constraining and placed severe limits on the types of activity and forms of expression available to women.

Yet the evangelical movement also offered women modest opportunities to expand their horizons psychologically and socially.[101] Religious conversion, following a period of anxious introspection and self-examination, involved a process of personal re-integration and self-affirmation. It also opened the way to emotionally intimate relationships outside the home, especially with ministers and other women who had embraced the faith. At crucial points in their spiritual development, women often depended heavily for guidance on male clergy or older women, their 'spiritual fathers' and 'spiritual mothers'. This reliance often resulted in deep and lasting friendships that provided continuity and comfort in lives often disrupted by the death of children, immigration, or early widowhood.

Evangelical piety was highly introspective and fostered a culture of self-examination. The habit of constantly reviewing one's spiritual progress, deeply rooted in Puritan tradition, was often associated with the keeping of private journals, which in many cases led to the publication of religious diaries and autobiographies. One such diary, written by Eliza Ann Chipman of Cornwallis, Nova Scotia, offers a valuable glimpse into the religious life of an evangelical woman living in a rural community in the first half of the nineteenth century.[102] From the time she was a teenager, Chipman was absorbed in a highly self-critical quest for conversion and regeneration. A preoccupation with her own mortality and the mortality of others inspired her to eschew frivolous activities and to struggle for freedom from worldly attachments. 'O how mean and unsatisfactory,' she wrote in a typical diary entry, 'do all temporal concerns appear to the heaven-born soul, who views them in their proper light and holds them at loose ends.' Chipman experienced conversion at the age of sixteen, after which she professed her faith before the minister and deacons of the local Baptist church. A few years later she married her first cousin William Chipman, a widower with eight children, two of whom were older than she was. Her husband, who was already a deacon and lay preacher, proceeded within two years of their marriage to the ordained ministry. Thereafter Eliza Ann Chipman's life was dominated by the concerns of marriage and motherhood. She bore twelve children of her own, eight of whom survived. From the time of her marriage until her death in 1853, at the age of forty-six, she continued to keep a careful private record of her spiritual progress, not revealing the existence of this journal to her husband until she was on her death-bed.[103] Although she remained highly self-critical, often reproaching herself for ingratitude and a lack of growth in the faith, she also found consolation and emotional gratification in her spiritual life. The Bible and sermons based on scriptural texts provided a framework within which she interpreted her own experience. At times of tragedy, such as the death from scalding of one of her children, she found solace in her faith. 'God has seen fit in his wisdom to hand me the cup of affliction to drink of,' she wrote, '. . . and although I have found it, and do still find it hard to be reconciled to this my lot, yet I know my dear Redeemer has chastened me for my profit, for he scourgeth every son whom he receiveth, and he hath in faithfulness afflicted me.'[104] Occasionally she displayed frustration or resentment over her circumstances, especially when domestic obligations distracted her from the cultivation of spiritual values. She was, she said, too much like Martha in the Gospel story, when she wished to be more like Mary. She clearly saw the inculcation and maintenance of moral values in the home as one of her principal responsibilities, and frequently worried that she had failed to instil religious commitment in her children. Outside the home she participated not only in Sunday worship but also in prayer meetings, auxiliary missionary organizations, and religious tract and Bible societies. In addition, she supported efforts to develop Baptist educational institutions, including Acadia College, although she played no direct role in such projects. On two occasions, one before her marriage and another after it, she even expressed a longing to participate actively in the foreign missions. But she made no effort to act on this fond wish, concluding that she must 'check . . . the ardent desires of a roving mind, and endeavour in whatever situation I am in therewith to be content'.[105]

The emergence of evangelical voluntary associations was crucial to the institutional growth of the British North American churches. Just as rising immigration was beginning to place new demands on the meagre resources of the colonial churches, the new missionary, educational, and philanthropic societies began to furnish increased assistance from overseas. A common pattern, which began to take shape in the early decades of the nineteenth century, was for local supporters to form auxiliary or affiliated branches of parent organizations. These local societies raised money and facilitated the reception of external aid that could take many forms: sponsored missionaries, funds and teachers for new schools, Bibles in English, Gaelic, French, and native languages, or mass-produced religious tracts for distribution among the populace. Some of the older, non-evangelical organizations also broadened their operations. Beginning in 1813, for example, substantial parliamentary grants enabled the SPG to support many more clergymen in the colonies.[106] Sometimes, when the efforts of old and new organizations overlapped, disedifying rivalries developed. Moreover, high Anglicans were generally opposed to interdenominational organizations, if only because co-operation with other denominations seemed to compromise the Church of England's claims to special status.[107] But despite such tensions, the material and human resources of the churches expanded rapidly, and regular services were provided to a growing proportion of the burgeoning population.

Internal developments in the churches also contributed to institutional growth. Local denominational structures were beginning to take shape, although at varying rates. One of the earliest milestones was set by Maritime Presbyterians, who in 1817 formed the United Synod of Nova Scotia, an independent body consisting initially of twenty-nine congregations in three presbyteries and embracing not only Secessionists but also some of the Church of Scotland clergy then serving in the province. This new body was a striking example of an ecclesiastical organization formed with New World rather than Old World circumstances in mind, and its success was only partly vitiated by subsequent competition from the Church of Scotland (the Kirk). Methodists were slower to move toward independent forms of organization. In the Atlantic region they were thoroughly dependent on the British Conference, and the control that the latter exercised was strengthened by the formation of the Wesleyan Methodist Missionary Society. In the Canadas Methodists continued as part of the Genesee Conference of New York, with separate districts for Upper and Lower Canada, until 1815, when British Wesleyan missionaries entered the region, challenging the monopoly previously enjoyed by their American counterparts. In 1820, however, an agreement was reached whereby Lower Canada would be reserved to the British while Upper Canada would remain under American jurisdiction.[108] Almost at the same time, the first steps were taken toward the formation of an independent Canadian conference, a goal that was realized in 1828.

Canadian Baptists, whose supply of preachers from the United States was badly disrupted by the War of 1812, began to form local organizations soon after the restoration of peace. A precursor of these was the tiny Thurlow Association, formed in 1802, which later became the Haldimand Association.[109] In 1816, the Clinton Conference was established by churches of the Niagara peninsula and the Lake Erie district. This effort proved short-lived, but by 1833 so much progress had been made that three associations— the Eastern, Western, and the Haldimand—came together to create the Baptist Missionary Convention of Upper Canada. An Ottawa Valley Baptist Association followed not long afterward.[110] Baptists in the Maritimes had formed a regional association as early as 1800, but partly because of rapid growth this was subdivided into separate associations for Nova Scotia and New Brunswick in 1821.

A similar process of elaboration and subdivision can be observed in other denominations. In 1821 and 1825 respectively, the vast Anglican dioceses of Quebec and Nova Scotia were organized into archdeaconries, and in 1827 the archdeaconry of York, which originally embraced all of Upper Canada, was further divided with the creation of the archdeaconry of Kingston. Similarly, the Presbytery of the Canadas, formed in 1818 by Presbyterians of diverse backgrounds, was divided into separate presbyteries for Upper and Lower Canada. In 1831 a new Secession synod, called the United Synod of Canada, was formed, and at almost the same time the Synod of the Presbyterian

Church in connection with the Church of Scotland was established. Kirk synods were organized in both Nova Scotia and New Brunswick in 1835. These local administrative developments sometimes anticipated and sometimes built upon the gains made through the intervention of missionary societies.

Important new organizational initiatives also took place among black Christians in British North America, whose numbers increased sharply during this period. Approximately two thousand black refugees arrived in Nova Scotia from the southern United States after the close of the War of 1812, more than compensating for the Loyalists who had removed to Sierra Leone; and by the 1820s fugitive slaves had begun to trickle into Upper Canada. Increased numbers, combined with the persistence of racist attitudes in white churches, reinforced the trend towards the formation of independent black congregations. Richard Preston, a former slave who arrived in Halifax in 1816, apprenticed as a preacher under Richard Burton in Halifax and eventually led a group of followers out of Burton's racially mixed but increasingly divided congregation.[111] In 1832, Preston organized the African Baptist Chapel in Halifax, which became the 'mother church' for about a dozen more black Baptist congregations in the region. The same tendency towards independence was evident in Upper Canada, where the history of African Christian churches began with the formation in 1820 of Salem Chapel in St Catharines.[112]

Of all the changes in ecclesiastical organization, perhaps the most significant were those that occurred among Roman Catholics in predominantly English-speaking regions. The creation of basic parochial structures in many centres between 1780 and 1815, and the sharp rise in Irish and Scottish migration after the close of the Napoleonic wars, fostered a new confidence and desire for independence among Catholics of British background. No longer content with their position as peripheral missions in the vast diocese of Quebec, they began to campaign for the creation of their own dioceses. Senior clergymen in the Maritimes and Upper Canada, sometimes acting through influential Irish or Scottish intermediaries, gradually persuaded the ecclesiastical authorities in Rome to remove the English-speaking colonies from Quebec's jurisdiction.

The first step in this direction was the erection of mainland Nova Scotia as a vicariate apostolic under Edmund Burke, who in 1817 became the first English-speaking Catholic bishop in British North America apart from Newfoundland. In 1818, the Scottish priests Alexander Macdonell of Upper Canada and Angus MacEachern of Prince Edward Island were also raised to episcopal status. Initially they remained under the authority of the bishop of Quebec, to whom they were appointed auxiliary bishops, but in 1825 Macdonell was named bishop of Kingston with jurisdiction over Upper Canada, and in 1829 MacEachern was appointed bishop of Charlottetown with responsibility for Prince Edward Island, New Brunswick, Cape Breton, and the Magdalene Islands. Separation from the diocese of Quebec established Irish and Scottish Catholics as a distinct and substantial ecclesiastical body.

Fundamental to the institutional growth of the churches was the rapid increase that took place in the total number of clergy. Missionary agencies brought scores of new preachers to British North America, while at the same time the colonial churches began training their own candidates for the ministry. One method used in the early stages of development was for senior clergymen to take young men into their own homes to complete their studies and prepare for ordination.[113] Another was for candidates to be trained in the field under the direction of experienced missionaries.[114] Between 1815 and 1834, the SPG alone provided scholarships to 29 students apprenticed to ordained clergymen in the Canadas.[115] Although opportunities for ministerial candidates to study in more formal, institutional settings were still extremely limited, in the Maritimes some preliminary steps were taken toward the establishment of seminaries. By 1840 Anglicans, Presbyterians, and Roman Catholics in the Atlantic region had all established colleges, and Methodists and Baptists were not far behind. Some of these institutions enjoyed an uncertain existence in the early years, but they laid the groundwork for the training of local clergy. The best-endowed and most stable of these institutions was the exclusively Anglican King's College in Nova Scotia, which graduated 158 students between 1802 and 1835, of whom 58 became clergymen.[116]

Comprehensive statistics for the number of clergy in the whole of British North America are not available, but an impression of the general rate of growth may be gained from individual examples. There were, for instance, 44 authorized clergy of all denominations serving in Upper Canada by 1812;[117] by 1830, there were that many Anglican missionaries alone.[118] Even so, the greatest increase in Church of England clergymen in Upper Canada came in the next decade, when the total more than doubled from 44 to 91. Meanwhile, the number of ministers serving other denominations in Upper Canada also increased substantially. Most dramatic was the surge in Church of Scotland representation, the result of aggressive activity by the Glasgow Colonial Society (founded 1825). The Kirk, which had only a single missionary in the region in 1818, counted 60 by 1840.[119] Major advances were made by the principal denominations in the Atlantic region as well. Maritime Baptists, who at this stage did not require formal qualifications of their pastors, ordained 47 local candidates between 1828 and 1845.[120]

Of course the population of British North America was also growing rapidly, and despite the increase in the total number of clergy, many lay people were still left without consistent pastoral care. Innovative methods were adopted to improve the situation. Both Anglicans and Presbyterians, who traditionally relied on resident pastors, appointed clergy to itinerate in neglected districts on the understanding that within a specified period they would organize settled congregations. Among Anglicans, the Upper Canada Travelling Missionary Fund and the Upper Canada Clergy Society were established for the express purpose of supporting such initiatives.[121] Roman Catholic missionaries were usually stationed in the towns and larger villages, but from these centres they served a number of satellite communities until the latter were able to support their own priests.

Within narrow limits, female preachers also played a part in the general expansion of the churches in the early nineteenth century. Developments in the Methodist Church, where women were generally accorded a greater public role than in other denominations, illustrate clearly the nature of their contribution as well as the constraints placed upon them.[122] Wesleyan Methodists had already abandoned the use of female preachers and increasingly relegated women to such ancillary roles as fund-raising, teaching in mission schools, and the religious instruction of children at home. While such activities were by no means insignificant, they reflected the prevalence of the notion of woman as 'helpmate'.

American Methodist Episcopals, however, who were generally more progressive than the Wesleyans, still employed a few female preachers in British North America, among them Eliza Barnes. Following in the footsteps of women like Ellen Bangs, Barnes began her work in Upper Canada around 1827, preaching to both whites and native people. Her extraordinary talents were widely acknowledged, and her efforts led to at least one major revival. But she faced opposition to female preachers from many of her male counterparts, including her future husband, William Case, and after her marriage in 1833 she conformed—'settled down', as contemporary sources said—to the role of minister's wife, teaching household and domestic science in the native missions to which he was appointed.[123] Only the new Methodist denominations such as Bible Christians and Primitive Methodists continued to employ female preachers until the middle of the nineteenth century. A number of female preachers associated with these denominations, such as Elizabeth Dart Eynon, Jane Woodill, and Ann Vickery, came to British North America where they achieved considerable recognition.

With institutional growth and the development of denominational structures, the general population came to conform more closely to official standards of Christian belief and practice. A growing number of people had regular contact with an expanding contingent of preachers and ministers who in turn had increased opportunities to instruct them in the faith and encourage regular religious observance. More was involved than mere external conformity. Zealous missionary activities and the combined efforts of a growing array of religious organizations promoted personal conversion, a deepening of religious commitment, and a genuine transformation of values in countless individuals. Institutional growth and spiritual awakening went hand in hand and were mutually reinforcing, although, as usual, the pace of development differed significantly from one region to another. New agencies, while vastly increasing the resources of the churches in established mission fields, also entered previously neglected territory and areas of recent settlement, where they found conditions similar to those encountered a generation or two earlier in older districts.

Cape Breton affords an excellent example of a remote corner of one of the older colonies where organized Christianity had made only slight progress before 1815. Settled largely by Highland Scots who faced enormous hardship and trauma in the process of resettlement, the island was for a long time no more than a peripheral mission. It suffered from a chronic shortage of clergy, glaring examples of misconduct among the few missionaries who did come to the island, and the lack of an effective parochial system for either Catholics or Presbyterians. Laymen, especially schoolmasters, were often the only ones available to conduct worship and provide rudimentary religious instruction. The bulk of the population remained ignorant of basic doctrines and religiously indifferent. Marriages were contracted without the blessing of clergy; the illegitimate children who were born of these marriages sometimes remained unbaptized; and many people died without the consolation of the church.

The creation of a vicariate apostolic in Nova Scotia in 1817, and the appointment in 1826 of William Fraser, a Scot residing in eastern Nova Scotia, as Edmund Burke's successor in this post, provided a fillip to Roman Catholic missions. Both the number and the overall quality of priests stationed on Cape Breton rose significantly.[124] At about the same time, the Nova Scotia Bible Society, founded in 1810 as an auxiliary branch of the British and Foreign Bible Society, began work among the Presbyterians, distributing Gaelic translations of the Scriptures and other religious literature. By 1825 a change was evident. New settlers began to arrive from the Hebrides who had been influenced by the evangelical revival in their homeland.[125] The newcomers acted as a leaven, raising religious consciousness on the island as a whole. Not content to be without the services of clergy, they began to petition for ministers from Scotland, and their pleas were answered in the first instance by the Glasgow Colonial Society. The real breakthrough, however, came with the involvement of its affiliate, the Edinburgh Ladies' Association. Under the leadership of Isabella Gordon Mackay, this organization adopted Cape Breton as its special cause, sending significant numbers of both clergymen and schoolmasters to the region. Among the most important of the former was the energetic James Frazer, who travelled all over the island, not only preaching and baptizing but promoting religious instruction, often through the agency of parents, and encouraging family worship.[126]

In the same period the first resident clergy were arriving in the West. The French-speaking Métis population were entrusted to the care of Roman

Catholic missionaries from Quebec, the first of whom was sent out in 1817, while the English-speaking settlers, both whites in the employ of the Hudson's Bay Company and the half-caste country-born inhabitants, fell initially under the Church of England.[127] In 1820 the evangelical Church Missionary Society sent John West as its first missionary to the Red River settlement.[128] West was soon followed by David Thomas Jones and William Cockran.[129] These men were confronted by a rude and unruly society, in which remoteness from centres of civilization and the wandering life-style associated with the fur trade had given rise to local customs plainly at variance with the standards of the church. They immediately embarked on a campaign of reform, regularizing marriages between company officers and native or mixed-blood women by forcing the couples to formalize their vows, baptizing the children of these marriages, appealing for strict observance of the sabbath, and denouncing drunkenness. Determined to impose new precepts of social behaviour, especially on the country-born, they tied their evangelism inseparably to the notion of 'civilizing' the inhabitants.

The focus of this civilizing mission was the crusade to promote a sedentary, agricultural life among people accustomed to a semi-nomadic existence. But commitment to this goal was not always compatible with the interests of the fur trade, and it resulted in friction between missionaries and Company officials. Blinded by cultural imperialism, the clergy also seemed at times to imagine that they could recreate English country parishes in the North American wilderness. Nevertheless, some of them were able to provide practical guidance that would prove helpful in confronting the vast social changes to come in the next generation. William Cockran, who had worked in agriculture before his ordination, established a model farm at Upper Church (later St John's) on the Red River in 1827 where he taught his country-born parishioners the technical and economic skills necessary for this way of life. A few years later, he repeated the experiment at nearby Lower Church (later St Andrew's).[130]

Especially in communities lacking mature social institutions, such as Cape Breton and Red River, the role of the clergy often went well beyond religion. Missionaries acted not only as administrators, financial advisers, and intermediaries in family disputes, but as moral police regulating a host of social offences. Illicit sex and the abuse of alcohol were among their favourite targets, but they were also instrumental in controlling violent feuds. To enforce their code of conduct, they relied on both spiritual sanctions, such as refusal of the sacraments, and the co-operation of the civil authorities who willingly supported them as agents of social control. Without a doubt, they contributed in many ways to the achievement of more stable, orderly, and cohesive societies. This was especially true in regions, such as Cape Breton, that enjoyed a high degree of ethnic and cultural homogeneity. In areas characterized by sharp racial and social divisions, however, the clergy sometimes had quite a different impact. In the Red River colony, where whites occupied a superior position to aboriginal people and half-breeds, and the latter were sub-divided into the English-speaking Protestant country-born and the French-speaking Catholic Métis, the Anglican clergy identified with the white élite. Their attitude towards non-whites was benevolent but condescending, and served to emphasize distinctions of status and race.[131]

Throughout British North America, the evangelical movement gave a new impulse to missionary work among the First Nations. Reduced to a relatively insignificant portion of the total population by the post-1815 tide of immigration, native people in the older colonies were steadily being pushed off their land to make way for agricultural settlement. The disappearance of game, alcohol abuse, and the spread of contagious disease accelerated the pace of social disintegration and rendered aboriginal people increasingly dependent on whites. The English-speaking churches, previously slow to undertake native missions, now entered the field with alacrity, believing that only a program of adaptation through Christianization and civilization could save the First Nations from extinction.

The favourite method of achieving this goal was the creation of model villages, complete with churches and schools, where missionaries and teachers could instruct native converts in the Christian faith, teach them agricultural skills, introduce them to European customs, encourage abstinence from alcohol, and promote literacy. In a characteristically evangelical fashion, the spirit of the missions was philanthropic. Native people were no longer seen merely as souls to be redeemed from heathenism but also as unfortunates in need of relief and protection. Colonial governments worried that natives would become a burden on the state, and encouraged the churches' efforts to ameliorate their living conditions. Many native people, convinced of the need to adapt, were receptive to such initiatives, and native leaders often took the lead in recruiting missionaries to work among their people.[132]

Examples of this new concern for the welfare of the First Nations can be seen in all parts of British North America. In Newfoundland and Labrador, the Moravians continued to expand their mission to the Inuit, and last-minute efforts were made to halt the decline of the Beothuk. Unfortunately, these inadequate attempts came too late, and with the death of Shawnadithit, in 1829, the Beothuk were extinct. In the Maritimes, the New England Company, though tainted with scandal, continued its work among the Micmac until 1826, and Walter Bromley, a Methodist reformer, established a Micmac agricultural village at Shubenacadie.[133] Roman Catholic authorities, who saw Bromley's project as a challenge to the Catholic allegiance of the Micmac, responded by founding two agrarian communities of their own, one at Tracadie, Nova Scotia, under the Trappist Father Vincent Merle, and the other at Bear River, under the Abbé Sigogne.[134] In the West, CMS missionaries concentrated at first on the white and half-breed populations, so that missions to native people *per se* got off to a slow start. Still, in establishing the Red River Academy, John West laid the foundation for a native ministry.[135] And William Cockran, encouraged by his success in promoting agriculture among the country-born, launched a similar project for a neighbouring Saulteaux band in 1832.[136]

The greatest advances of this period, however, occurred in Upper Canada, where a sudden flurry of missionary activity contrasted sharply with the relative neglect of the preceding decades. Methodist Episcopals, Wesleyan Methodists, Anglicans, and Baptists were all involved in these new efforts. Missionary work was promoted by a growing number of newly-established agencies, both local and external.

Of the various groups involved in missionary enterprises, the most spectacular results were achieved by the Methodists, especially in their work among the Ojibwa. One factor in their success was that Methodism offered converts the prospect of immediate personal transformation; for destitute and demoralized aboriginal people it had something of the same appeal as for socially marginalized whites. Another consideration was the Methodists' use of native contact persons and preachers.[137] Peter Jones, a mixed-blood Mississauga who was converted at a now famous camp-meeting at Ancaster in 1823,[138] became leader of a band of Ojibwa converts at the Credit River and the most effective of a group of ordained native preachers that also included John Sunday, Peter Jacobs, George Copway, and Peter Beaver. Other communities of Christian Indians were soon established at such locations as Grape Island, Rice Lake, and Lake Simcoe.[139] There were also important examples of resistance to Christianity among native traditionalists, such as Chief Kanootong of Bear River, who believed that natives must honour their own religion.[140] Yet by 1828, through the combined efforts of white missionaries and their native assistants, 1,200 of the 5,000 aboriginal people living near settlements in the southern portion of Upper Canada had received religious instruction from the Methodists.[141]

Optimism ran high among both missionaries and native converts in the heyday of Methodist missions in Upper Canada. Conversion to Christianity held out the prospect of immediate material assistance, successful adaptation to a changed environment, escape from self-destructive patterns of behaviour, and renewed self-esteem. But high hopes soon gave way to bitter disillusionment. The assimilationist program of the missionaries, however well-intentioned, was fatally flawed. In the first place, it was no easy matter, even with the active co-operation of converts, suddenly to replace centuries-old customs with a new way of life.[142] Native converts, though willing and eager to adapt, did not necessarily want to do so at the cost of their native identity.[143] Nor did acceptance of change bring all the benefits that the missionaries promised. Even Christian aboriginals had to contend with racist attitudes and discriminatory government policies. There was little point, for instance, in becoming an efficient farmer if one was unable to secure title to one's own land.[144] As disillusionment grew, native resistance increased, and governments and churches responded with coercion. The prospect of co-operative ventures between First Nations and whites, so real in the 1820s, was virtually dead by 1840.

Meanwhile, the strengthening of ecclesiastical institutions among the European population continued. One important effect of this process was to increase the formal authority of the clergy over the laity in matters of church governance and the control of higher ecclesiastical authorities over local congregations. In most areas, the loose and fluid arrangements of frontier missions was replaced by the order, discipline, and systematic supervision of regular church life. But this is not to say that the transition was always rapid or smooth. The laity in many denominations, having often been left to their own devices, were slow to relinquish the autonomy they had acquired in the process of shaping their own congregations. At the same time, new factors, including the spirit of democratic reform that was spreading through the colonies by the second quarter of the century, often reinforced their determination to control the government of their churches.

The most striking illustration of this point is the series of bitter 'trustee' conflicts that racked Roman Catholic congregations in many centres. Despite the authoritarian character of Roman Catholic church government, lay trustees, who had often been instrumental in forming organized congregations, had gained a large measure of control over the affairs of local churches in cities such as St John's, Halifax, Saint John, and York (Toronto). Basing their claims to authority on their legal ownership of church property and on their position as the founders and benefactors of their congregations, they tried to regulate the temporal and even spiritual affairs of their churches. Drawn as a rule from the more prosperous segment of the Catholic population, they consciously imitated Protestant laymen who served on the governing bodies of their churches and parishes, wishing to achieve the social prestige enjoyed by Anglican vestrymen, Presbyterian elders, Baptist and Congregational deacons, and Methodist trustees and stewards. Often they acted in concert with, or were manipulated by, renegade priests such as William O'Grady at York and Charles Ffrench at Saint John, both of whom openly defied episcopal authority.[145]

The result was that painful schisms developed as episcopal and antiepiscopal parties were formed within congregations and trustee and antitrustee factions took shape around rival candidates for pastor. Such divisions were invariably exacerbated by extraneous factors. Depending on local circumstances, political conflict, class tensions, and ethnic rivalry all contributed to trustee controversies. All the congregations in question were predominantly Irish, and in many cases they found themselves at odds with Scottish or French-Canadian bishops. The underlying issues, however, were local autonomy versus submission to central authority, and participatory democracy as opposed to clerical autocracy. Episcopal control triumphed only around mid-century, when charismatic Irish prelates, garnering immense support from the Catholic rank and file, were able to reduce middle-class lay activists to a plainly subordinate role in church affairs. A decisive step in this process was the formation of diocesan corporations for the purpose of vesting church property entirely in the hands of bishops. This arrangement effectively deprived trustees of the legal basis for their pretensions and translated into civil terms the monarchical powers that Roman Catholic bishops enjoyed under canon law. Lay activism survived among Roman Catholics, but after 1840 it was channelled away from parochial administration and into clerically-controlled devotional and philanthropic associations.

RELIGION, SOCIETY, AND POLITICS

Voluntary associations continued to proliferate among evangelical Protestants as the benevolent impulses that had characterized the movement from the outset developed increasingly into active programs of social reform. Throughout the English-speaking world, committed Protestants campaigned for causes ranging from the abolition of slavery to strict observance of the sabbath and abstinence from strong drink. Convinced that social evils were the product of the perverted human will, rather than of defects in the social environment, they strove to alleviate poverty, illness, violence, and crime through the conversion of individual sinners. British North American Protestants reflected the humanitarian and meliorist tendencies that were already blossoming among their British and American counterparts, but the focus of their efforts was initially somewhat narrower. Slavery was never the major concern that it was in Britain and the United States. Nor did strict sabbath observance immediately become the object of great public agitation. Before 1840, the issue that attracted most of the attention and energy of evangelical reformers was temperance.[146]

The first temperance societies in British North America were founded at the end of the 1820s,[147] and soon local societies sprouted up in dozens of communities. During this formative stage of the temperance crusade, American influences were crucial, though once under way it was reinforced by British examples. The temperance movement limited itself at first to restricting the use of 'ardent spirits'; wine, beer, and cider were considered acceptable for moderate use. Governments were lobbied to increase duties on imported spirits while controlling licences for liquor outlets. For the most part, though, early temperance advocates relied on moral persuasion. Temperance meetings were held throughout the country, resembling in many ways religious services or revival meetings. After vivid and emotional descriptions of the baneful effects of alcohol, members of the audience were invited to take the temperance pledge. Intemperance was so plainly depicted as a form of moral turpitude, and sobriety so closely identified with religious regeneration, that the temperance crusade became in effect an instrument of proselytism for evangelical denominations.[148] It is impossible to tell how many hardened drinkers were reformed by the movement, but temperance societies certainly attracted large memberships, in some communities amounting to a quarter of the adult population.[149]

The social dimensions of the temperance movement were complex. It cut across social groups and flourished in both urban and rural settings. The limited research that has been done into the topic in British North America suggests certain tendencies, but these can by no means be seen as fixed rules. In some cities, such as Saint John, leadership of the early temperance societies came from members of the colonial élite, including wealthy merchants, Crown officials, and professionals, who manifested a paternal concern for the welfare of the broader population.[150] As, in time, the movement turned from moderation to teetotalism, these patrician elements dwindled and the initiative passed to people of humbler station, including minor merchants and unskilled workers,[151] and especially tradesmen and artisans.[152] This shift suggests that less-compromising forms of the temperance crusade may have reflected a rejection of the values and hegemony of the ruling oligarchy.[153]

No doubt the motives behind the temperance movement were complex as well. Commercial growth in British North America created unprecedented opportunities for the rising generation, but success depended on industry, and industry depended on sobriety.[154] Reflecting the optimistic, entrepreneurial spirit of the times, temperance propaganda seldom failed to mention the economic, medical, and social benefits of abstinence, promising increased prosperity, better health, and happier families. At the same time, some temperance advocates may have used the movement as a way of making employees, servants, and apprentices more reliable and productive.

Yet any interpretation of the temperance movement that reduces it to an instrument of 'social control' is a gross oversimplification.[155] Given the complexity of human nature, it is not surprising to see religious commitment linked to social and economic concerns, or to find altruism mixed with elements of self-interest. The abuse of alcohol, much more widespread in pioneer than in contemporary society, was a real social evil, not only in itself but also because of its connection to family violence, crime, and poverty. Evangelical crusaders, though not always so disinterested as they liked to think, had a genuine desire to alleviate hardship. If they are to be condemned, it is as much for naïveté as hypocrisy. They imagined that alcohol-related problems could be overcome by a simple act of will without any prior changes in the social environment, and they tended to see abstinence as the solution to all social problems. Still, there was a truly progressive element in their efforts, and they were often active in the cause of political reform as well.[156] Their attempt to reshape prevailing social values through voluntary action was a threat to the oligarchies who had hitherto ruled the colonies through more élitist and coercive institutions. Members of the poorer classes who joined the movement cannot be written off as passive dupes of manipulation by their social superiors. Many of them recognized the tangible benefits of sobriety and related ideals in helping them adjust to a new social and economic order. Economic change held out opportunities for people of limited means as well as those with greater advantages, and modest gains could be achieved through self-improvement, thrift, and diligence.

Another major project of the evangelical movement was the establishment of Sunday schools. Founded in England in the 1780s, the Sunday-school movement had made inroads in the Maritimes by the turn of the century.[157] It spread to regions such as Upper Canada in the 1820s, and quickly became a standard ingredient in humanitarian programs of reform. Part of a broader effort to provide for the moral protection and physical well-being of children,[158] its initial goals were not explicitly religious. The first Sunday schools in Britain were intended to teach basic literacy to children of the poorer classes on their one day free of work. From the outset, however, moral instruction was part and parcel of the training.[159] The Bible was used to teach reading, and children were warned against hazards in the social environment that might lead them astray, including drink, bad companions, and unsuitable books.[160] At first many schools were interdenominational, especially in rural areas, but even in the towns, where they tended to be run under denominational auspices, the overall effort was co-ordinated by ecumenical Sunday-school unions. Anticipating the common schools of mid-century, they claimed to teach the Bible and basic Christian values while eschewing sectarian principles. British research has shown that Sunday schools inculcated middle-class social values, such as moral discipline and orderly behaviour, calculated to ensure respect for authority. But Sunday schools, no less than temperance societies, wielded a double-edged sword. On the one hand, they helped to nurture reliable and compliant workers; on the other, they gave people the means to achieve greater independence and social status.[161]

The co-operation of the churches in temperance crusades, Sunday-school unions, and other evangelical enterprises was offset to some extent by the growing political conflict engendered by the privileged position of the Church of England. This conflict was a crucial step on the way to establishing in British North America the sort of voluntarist and broadly democratic principles with which evangelical Christianity was closely associated. It was also in large measure the almost inevitable result of the progress that non-Anglican churches were making in the years following 1815. The increasing importance of the Church of Scotland, the advances made by older forms of dissent, and the institutionalization of revivalist groups combined to heighten active opposition to Anglican privileges.

While these privileges had never been sufficient to check completely the progress of rival denominations, the more non-Anglicans succeeded in developing their own institutions and resources, the more they resented the obstacles that remained in their way. Growing concern for such matters as the training and support of indigenous clergy and the acquisition and ownership of church property brought mounting pressure for change. The clergy reserves (which were rising in value), exclusive education policies, restrictions on the right to perform marriages, and legal barriers to the formation of parish corporations all came under attack. In the process, the Methodists in particular became—at least temporarily—overtly political and increasingly identified with the cause of constitutional as well as social reform. Church–state quarrels replaced the antagonism between traditional and evangelical religion as the main source of conflict among the British North American churches, although in some cases the two issues were closely related.

In Upper Canada, the challenge to Anglican privileges came from several quarters. Both political reformers, bent on overturning the rule of the local oligarchy, and spokesmen for non-Anglican denominations denounced the favoured status of the Church of England. Even within ecclesiastical circles, there were two distinct types of opposition. The first was associated with the traditional wing of the Church of Scotland, and took the form of a demand for co-establishment; the second was frankly voluntarist, and called for the separation of church and state. But many shades of opinion could be found between these two extremes. Some denominations had no clear church–state doctrine and were inclined to alter their position with the vagaries of the political situation.

The Anglicans continued to defend their special status by claiming that the stability of the social order, the good government of the colony, and the continuation of the imperial connection all depended on maintenance of the church establishment. The leading spokesman for this view in Upper Canada was the redoubtable John Strachan, named archdeacon of York in 1827 and bishop of Toronto in 1839.[162] Strachan was uncompromisingly loyal to the British Crown and a tireless defender of a conservative social order, whose energy, ability, and service to the province during the War of 1812 had earned him a place in the ruling élite known as the Family Compact, as well as seats on both the Executive and Legislative councils. From this position of privilege he defended the rights of the establishment while disparaging rival 'dissenters and sectaries' as uneducated, disloyal, and fanatical. In 1826, after Strachan had voiced such sentiments in a sermon at the funeral of Jacob Mountain, he was publicly challenged by Egerton Ryerson, a twenty-three-year-old Methodist probationary preacher.[163] Ryerson not only defended the province's Methodists but launched a vigorous attack on the sort of political high-churchmanship that Strachan typified, including the tendency to reduce the church of Christ to a tool for political preferment. Arguing that there was no basis in Scripture for formal ties between church and state, he insisted that such a union degraded Christianity by obscuring and perverting its spiritual mission.[164]

The battle between friends and enemies of the established church intensified thereafter. A broad alliance took shape between those who opposed the Anglican ascendancy mainly on religious grounds and those who opposed it primarily for political reasons. In 1827 a new grievance was added to the list when Strachan obtained a charter and financial support for King's College, York. While the charter required no religious tests of students except those in divinity, and its regulations were more liberal than those at King's College, Nova Scotia, the proposed college was nevertheless to be firmly under Anglican control and was clearly intended largely for the training of Anglican clergy and the inculcation of Anglican social philosophy.[165] Strachan was named its first president. The chorus of protest against these arrangements was so loud that the newly appointed lieutenant-governor of Upper Canada, Sir John Colborne, postponed the opening of King's and redirected efforts to the founding of a new grammar school, Upper Canada College.[166] Meanwhile, the 1828 election returned a majority of reformers, bringing to the legislature so strong a Methodist influence that it was dubbed the 'saddle-bag' parliament, and in 1829 Ryerson was appointed editor of the new Methodist newspaper, the *Christian Guardian*, giving him a prominent platform from which to promote his cause.

Strachan and the other defenders of the establishment were losing ground rapidly. In 1828, Methodists had obtained the right to hold church property corporately through the formation of circuit corporations,[167] and in 1831 their right to perform marriages was also recognized.[168] Furthermore, a reform parliament had also been elected in Britain and had announced its intention of phasing out grants to the SPG. This made the clergy reserves more important than ever to the Church of England in the colonies at the very moment when they were becoming harder to defend. A victory for the establishment occurred in 1836 with the creation of forty-four endowed rectories, but this measure, while providing new sources of revenue, also called forth another round of protests, and more setbacks followed. The substantial salary that had been paid to the bishop of Quebec was discontinued upon the death of the incumbent, Charles James Stewart, in 1837.[169] Two years later, when the diocese was divided and Strachan was appointed bishop of Toronto, he was not awarded a stipend and had to retain his position as rector and archdeacon in order to support himself until alternative arrangements were made.[170] Strachan was also pressured into resigning the seat on the Executive Council that he had held since 1817, managing only to cling to his position on the Legislative Council until the union of the two Canadas in 1841.[171] In addition, in 1837 the charter of King's College (which still had not opened) was revised in a manner that drastically reduced Anglican control.[172]

Ironically, the forces of dissent were softening their position at the same time. One reason for the change was the return to Upper Canada of the conservative British Wesleyans, who had withdrawn after their 1820 truce with the American Methodist Episcopals. The renewed activities of the Wesleyans led to the 1833 union between the British Conference and the Canadian Methodists (who had achieved independence of the Americans in 1828). Equally important was the feeling that many battles had been won and that the struggle against discrimination was less urgent.[173] Some Methodist spokesmen seemed suddenly to lose their enthusiasm for reform, and indeed Ryerson, who had completed the negotiations for the union with the Wesleyans, began to regard the moderate reformer Robert Baldwin's advocacy of responsible government as a threat to British constitutional principles and the imperial connection. With the same energy that he had previously devoted to demanding change, he now began to defend the existing order.[174]

In the meantime, the government of Upper Canada offered financial assistance to several major denominations, including the Church of Scotland, Presbyterian Seceders, Roman Catholics, and Methodists.[175] This paved the way to a proposed solution of the clergy-reserves question. In 1840, on the initiative of the new governor, Charles Poulett Thompson, a law was passed in the British House of Commons that divided the proceeds of the reserves among several churches.[176] The division was not equitable: the Church of England, with about a fifth of the population in Upper Canada, received nearly half of the benefits. Considering that they had previously received all the benefits, however, the 1840 law struck a major blow to Anglican exclusiveness. The other principal denominations seemed happy for the moment to accept the new revenues. The Wesleyan Methodist Church in Canada, product of the 1833 union of British and Canadian Methodists, did so with a measure of embarrassment, but the influence of British Wesleyans, who were not opposed in principle to state support, outweighed the Canadians' reservations about accepting government aid.[177] Among the major churches in the Canadas, only the Baptists, with their long voluntarist tradition, steadfastly remained outside the settlement. The new arrangement did not prove to be a lasting solution to the issue of the clergy reserves, but it marked the end of a distinct phase of church–state relations in Upper Canada. It also revealed a trend in British North America towards the division of state support, as opposed to an American-style 'wall of separation' permitting no state support for religious bodies or institutions.

In the Maritime colonies, church–state controversies took a somewhat different form. The absence of extensive clergy reserves, combined with the early establishment of the exclusively Anglican King's College at Windsor, Nova Scotia, meant that education rather than land endowments was the focus of concern. But the underlying issues were the same, as an increasingly defensive

Anglican establishment tried to fend off claims to fair treatment from churches representing the majority of the population.

The struggle began in 1816 when Thomas McCulloch, the leading Secession Presbyterian clergyman in Nova Scotia, established the Pictou Academy. The Academy soon became a rival to King's, offering a broader curriculum and inviting participation from all denominations. Members of the Anglican-dominated Halifax establishment resisted the challenge with all their might. Acting through the province's governing council, they attempted to thwart McCulloch's intentions by restricting membership on the college board to Anglicans and Presbyterians, refusing to confer degree-granting status on the institution, and consistently turning back attempts by the liberal Assembly to endow it with a permanent annual grant.[178] While successfully inhibiting the development of the college, however, the Council's obstructiveness also invested it with a broader political significance. Divisions between the Council and the Assembly spilled over into the wider constitutional question of the relative powers of the two branches of government. The Assembly, led by reform-minded politicians, not only supported McCulloch's educational goals but increasingly questioned the Council's right to veto money bills initiated by the Assembly. The Pictou Academy became a leading symbol of the struggle for religious and civil liberty, and McCulloch emerged as a major critic of the politico-ecclesiastical system that had gripped the province since the Loyalist era.

McCulloch also challenged Anglican exclusiveness on other fronts. In 1819, he organized the non-Anglican clergy, including Baptists and Methodists as well as Presbyterians, to petition the government for the right to perform marriages by licence. The Nova Scotia legislature passed a law that satisfied their request, but the imperial government disallowed the legislation, largely as a result of the efforts of John Inglis, Anglican bishop of Nova Scotia. McCulloch took up the cause twice more in the following decade, each time without success. For him, the marriage-licence issue was for the most part a way of rallying dissenting forces and attracting support for his educational ventures.[179] Through correspondence with men such as Edward Manning, a leading Baptist preacher, he earned a lot of good will, but it had few practical consequences: other dissenting denominations sent few if any students to the Pictou Academy.

The situation of the college worsened with the passage of time. In 1817 Lord Dalhousie, the governor of Nova Scotia, took the first steps towards establishing a college at Halifax that, though associated with the Church of Scotland, would be open to members of all denominations.[180] Dalhousie did not oppose the continuation of the Pictou Academy but resisted conferring degree-granting status upon it. Meanwhile the Secessionist McCulloch, who had been instrumental in the formation of the Presbyterian Church of Nova

Scotia, found himself locked in controversy with clergy from the rival Church of Scotland who were making strides in eastern Nova Scotia through the newly formed Glasgow Colonial Society. His chief opponents on this front were Donald Allan Fraser and John Kenneth MacKenzie, for whom the very existence of an academy training local clergy for the Presbyterian Church of Nova Scotia posed a threat to the privileged status claimed by the Kirk. In 1828, McCulloch failed to obtain the annual grant on which the academy depended, and in 1832 the government restructured the institution, placing four members of the Church of Scotland, hostile to the Secessionist McCulloch, on its board and reducing it eventually to the status of a grammar school. In 1838 McCulloch accepted the presidency of Dalhousie College. Recognizing the irony of this turn of events, he declared: 'God has given me to possess the gate of my enemies.'[181] Although the new institution was officially non-sectarian, the board of governors imposed a strong Presbyterian character on it, again thwarting McCulloch's desire to include other Protestants. McCulloch, whose ecumenical spirit did not extend to Roman Catholics, rejected a plan to appoint one of their leading clergymen to the faculty. Soon Baptists, Methodists, and Catholics, having been effectively excluded from Dalhousie, established their own colleges, placing higher education in Nova Scotia on an entirely denominational footing.

If the dream of creating a single non-sectarian university failed, however, the Anglican monopoly of higher education was broken. Not only did other denominations establish their own colleges, but in the meantime the statutes of King's were revised, removing religious tests for students in the arts.[182] Furthermore, the other churches were making significant inroads against Anglican exclusiveness in other areas as well. In 1828, the Nova Scotia legislature authorized all churches to form corporations for the purpose of owning property.[183] The same concession was thereafter gradually introduced in New Brunswick and Prince Edward Island. Between 1832 and 1834, all three Maritime colonies extended to dissenting clergy the right to perform marriages by licence. In 1835, in Prince Edward Island, lands previously ceded to the established church were re-appropriated for general use.[184] The Church of England in the Maritime colonies retained for the moment its status as the ecclesiastical establishment, but as its privileges were whittled away this status became increasingly meaningless in practice. It was only a matter of time before the law would catch up with the realities of the situation.

The emancipation of Roman Catholics in the Maritime colonies took place in the same period that saw Protestant dissenters achieve religious equality. In contrast to the Canadas, the Maritimes, especially Nova Scotia, had initially subjected Catholics to a variety of civil disabilities. Most of these restrictions, never strictly enforced in any case, had been removed during the 1780s; the only major issue remaining was the right of Catholics to participate in the political process. In 1789 Nova Scotia admitted Catholics to the franchise, and in 1810 New Brunswick followed suit.[185] Yet they were still denied the vote in Prince Edward Island, and in all three colonies Catholics were effectively excluded from the legislature by the requirement to swear the State Oaths and Declaration against Transubstantiation—oaths involving disavowal of the alleged political pretensions of the Holy See and rejection of Roman Catholic teaching regarding the Eucharist.

The barriers began to fall in 1820, when Cape Breton was reunited with Nova Scotia. Largely populated by Highland Scots and Acadians, Cape Breton elected a Catholic named Laurence Kavanagh as its representative to the Nova Scotia assembly. With the support of both the governor and legislature, Kavanagh was permitted to take his seat without swearing the obnoxious oaths. The Nova Scotia Assembly then tried to extend this privilege to all successful candidates, but full emancipation had to wait upon the course of events in Britain. When the Catholic Emancipation Act was passed in the imperial parliament in 1829, colonial legislatures were ordered to enact similar provisions. The Catholics of Prince Edward Island were at last included in the franchise and Catholic candidates became eligible for election in all three Maritime colonies.

In Newfoundland, as in other British North American colonies, church–state controversies centred on the struggle against the ascendancy of the Church of England. But the precise shape that this struggle took differed somewhat because of the peculiarities of the Newfoundland context. The gradually increasing resident population consisted of Anglicans, Roman Catholics, Methodists, and a small community of Congregationalists. Although the Church of England was not formally established, it enjoyed a privileged position *de facto*. Protestant dissenters and Roman Catholics were guaranteed religious liberty but had to struggle for their rights against prejudicial treatment by the authorities.[186] The deep social cleavage between the island's merchant and labouring classes followed religious lines, with Catholics in particular overrepresented among the poor. In sharp contrast to other colonies, Newfoundland had no local legislature through which non-Anglicans could express their grievances and campaign for reform.[187] Financial discrimination, attempts to prevent dissenting clergy from performing marriages, and the exclusion of Catholics from the Executive Council combined to create an atmosphere of mounting denominational tension. When an assembly was finally established in 1832 and the colony held its first election, these tensions exploded. The election was fought largely along religious lines, setting a pattern of rampant sectarianism that would become the bane of Newfoundland politics. Antagonisms were kept within manageable bounds only by instituting a system of proportionate denominationalism, whereby government patronage was handed out in accordance with each major church's share of the population.[188]

In all the British North American colonies, the assertion of the rights of Protestant dissenters and Roman Catholics steadily reduced the prerogatives of the Church of England. Die-hard defenders of church establishment, such as John Inglis and John Strachan, bitterly resisted the tide, but as time passed it became obvious even to them that they were fighting a rearguard action. By the 1830s, while still proclaiming establishmentarian principles, they were taking practical steps to adjust to new realities.[189] Cutbacks in SPG funding, the reduction of provincial grants, and the division of the clergy reserves made it necessary to look for alternatives to government support and endowments.

The solution was found largely in the formation of church societies, representative bodies that actively involved the laity in fund-raising. Diocesan church societies were formed in New Brunswick in 1836,[190] Nova Scotia in 1837,[191] Newfoundland in 1840,[192] and in Quebec[193] and Toronto in 1842.[194] They contributed substantially to the payment of clergy, the building of churches, the maintenance of church schools, and the support of theological students. In some cases they took over the functions of overseas missionary societies, such as the distribution of religious tracts, as well.[195] A step in the direction of independence from the parent church in Britain, church societies also paved the way for increased lay involvement in Anglican church government. While formal ties between church and state remained, voluntarist principles were making headway even within the ecclesiastical establishment.

MATURITY AND REORIENTATION (1840–1854)

NEW INFLUENCES FROM THE OLD WORLD

The year 1840 had marked a watershed in the history of British North America, and the following decade and a half would see even more profound transformations in religious life, carried out against a background of changes in society. Political, economic, and demographic developments resulted in the British colonies' becoming more independent, more populous, and, at least in the case of the Canadas, more prosperous than ever before. Upper and Lower Canada were joined in a legislative union in 1841. Political reformers achieved responsible government. The market economy that had developed after 1815 continued to grow, but patterns of commerce gradually shifted from the transatlantic trade to a continental economy. The first steps were taken toward industrialization. From the seed planted in 1812, nationalism began to emerge as a serious force. And the flow of immigration from the British Isles, more or less continuous since 1815, reached new heights. One reason for further increases in immigration was the Irish potato famine of 1845-9. In 1847, the worst year of the famine, over 100,000 people embarked at British ports for British North America. A large portion died in transit or moved on to other destinations after their arrival, but many remained and their impact was deeply felt, especially in the urban centres of Canada East and Canada West. The famine migration, however, was only one part of a broader story of transatlantic resettlement.

The wave of immigrants who entered British North America in the generation after 1830 virtually completed the settlement of the eastern colonies. Each of the Atlantic provinces grew significantly, most by approximately one-third.[196] The previously small English-speaking population of Canada East rose sharply to a quarter of the total.[197] In a single decade (1841–51) the number of people in Canada West more than doubled, from 455,688 to 952,004.[198] Just as important as the growing numbers was the changing social environment made possible by much greater concentrations of population. Except in the West, which was still in the embryonic stages of development, the middle decades of the century witnessed British North America's final transition from frontier conditions to stable and relatively densely populated communities.[199]

Developments within the major religious denominations reflected the growing maturity of the society. Building on the accomplishments of the preceding generation, during the middle decades of the century the churches continued their pattern of institutional growth and progress toward independence. Even if we limit ourselves to the period 1840–54 (the year of the secularization of the clergy reserves) we can identify a number of important trends. Church buildings increased in number, size, and quality; the total complement of clergymen rose significantly; ancillary agencies and institutions multiplied; and denominational structures continued to expand. In addition to new dioceses, districts, and associations, broader, more comprehensive umbrella structures were created to co-ordinate the increasingly diverse range of denominational activities. Sunday schools grew, Bible classes were organized, voluntary agencies proliferated, religious book rooms and lending libraries were established, the first 'home' missions were launched, and family worship was widely promoted. Religious newspapers, the first of which had made their appearance in the 1820s, became more numerous and more successful. Distributed to a growing number of homes and manses, these journals helped to keep religious issues in the forefront and to cement denominational loyalties. Church-sponsored colleges also entered their heyday in the middle decades of the century. More than a dozen denominational colleges were established, allowing lay students to study in a thoroughly religious environment while furnishing a much-needed supply of locally trained clergy.

The net result of these developments was to extend the influence of organized religion into almost every branch of life. Gone were the days when large portions of the population could be described as 'unchurched'. The major denominations had succeeded in establishing comprehensive networks of ecclesiastical institutions and incorporating within them the vast majority of the population.[200] Census returns (admittedly fragmentary) show steady growth in the proportion of people adhering to one or another denomination, and a corresponding decline in the fraction declaring no specific religious affiliation.[201] In response to this shift, the churches began to redefine their mission. Hitherto their main concern had been to reach out to the spiritually destitute. Now, with that goal substantially accomplished in the older areas of settlement, they began to concentrate on the nurture of those under their pastoral care and on the moral transformation of society.[202]

The geographical expansion of the churches' mission also rose in importance as the British North American churches launched their first 'home missions'. These were directed partly toward French Canadians, whom Protestant missionaries hoped to redeem from 'popish' tyranny and superstition, and partly towards the West. In 1840, the Wesleyan Methodist Missionary Society obtained permission from the Hudson's Bay Company to send missionaries into its territory. The arrival of James Evans, a veteran of the Upper Canadian missions, together with three Wesleyan preachers and two native assistants, marked the end of the monopoly that the Church of England had thus far enjoyed over Protestant missions in the region.[203] The first Presbyterian minister, John Black, arrived in 1851 in answer to a request from the Kildonan Scots, descendants of Lord Selkirk's original settlers.[204] The Church of England mission in the West, which until now had been run essentially as a foreign mission by the London-based Church Missionary Society, was also undergoing a change. The support of the CMS and other external agencies remained important, but a huge step towards independence was taken in 1849 with the establishment of the diocese of Rupert's Land. Beginning with five clergymen, four churches, and eight parish schools under his jurisdiction, the first bishop, David Anderson, was able gradually to build up the resources of the new diocese. One of his main initiatives was the acquisition of the Red River Academy, which he quickly converted into St John's College.

If the middle decades of the century were a time of increased maturity for the churches, however, they were also a period of reorientation. While growing self-reliance meant that they depended less on Britain for clergy and money, theological ideas and religious currents continued to flow from overseas. At least three major new developments spread across the Atlantic in the mid-nineteenth century: the Ultramontane revival among Roman Catholics, the Oxford movement in the Church of England, and the evangelical fervour of the Free Church created by the Great Disruption of the Church of Scotland. All three had profound effects not only for individual denominations but for the broader pattern of religious life in the colonies. The Free Church brought added dynamism to the evangelical movement, reinforcing its position as the dominant religious ideology. On the other hand, Ultramontane Catholicism and the high Anglicanism of the Oxford movement introduced strong counterbalancing forces. The influence of the new movements increased the vitality of the churches and at the same time contributed to rising sectarian tensions.

The first of the new forces was Roman Catholic Ultramontanism, whose sweeping influence had profound effects in both the French- and the English-speaking regions of British North America. The movement had grown up in Europe as part of the reaction against the French Revolution and was in large measure a rejection of the old alliance between throne and altar in favour of a new emphasis on the spiritual authority of the church, expressed primarily in the papacy. While increasing the power of the pope at the expense of national governments and hierarchies, it also brought about a general Romanization of the Catholic Church, encouraging authoritarian conceptions of church government and the spread of distinctly Italian forms of piety.

Ultramontanism made its way to the anglophone portions of British North America by way of Ireland, where its basic tendencies had converged with indigenous developments to produce a powerful movement for religious reform. The seeds of reform had been planted in the late eighteenth century, but they blossomed after the potato famine of the 1840s, when massive demographic changes, a sharp increase in the resources of the church, and the leadership of the Rome-educated Paul Cullen, archbishop of Dublin, combined to set a pattern of change. The thrust of reform was to bring popular religious practice into line with official Catholicism as defined by the Council of Trent, while discouraging or suppressing the folk religion associated with Gaelic culture. Irish wakes, funerals, and pilgrimages to holy wells declined, while the rate of attendance at Sunday mass, previously rather low, rose sharply. At the same time, a host of papally-approved devotional practices, such as veneration of the Sacred Heart and recitation of the rosary, were promoted among the laity. Pious confraternities, especially successful in attracting female members, were instrumental in effecting this transformation of popular piety.

The spirit and forms of Ultramontane Catholicism were carried overseas by lay immigrants and clergy who had been shaped in the new religious environment of Ireland. Since the pace of reform in that country differed according to region, spreading outward from the anglicized towns of the south and southeast to the Gaelic-speaking rural districts of the northwest, the rate of transmission to the New World depended on the origins of immigrants and the time of their arrival. In Atlantic Canada, pre-famine immigrants already reflected some of the new trends, while the Canadas were not deeply affected until the famine migration began. Over time, Irish Catholic communities in British North America mirrored their counterparts at home. Religious confraternities (such as the Confraternity of the Sacred Heart) and philanthropic associations (such as the St Vincent de Paul Society) were established in colonial towns and cities, providing an important focus for community life, promoting regular church attendance, and helping to disseminate the devotional practices associated with the Ultramontane revival. By the 1840s, for example, Halifax counted at least seven Catholic voluntary associations. These organizations did not act in isolation from one another but formed an interlocking network of agencies whose functions often overlapped. The proliferation of voluntary associations among Roman Catholics was analogous to the growth of similar organizations among evangelical Protestants. As Catholics developed their own societies, they created a comprehensive alternative to Protestant social institutions, facilitating greater independence and helping to ward off attempts at proselytization. A separatist mentality developed that reflected not only growing self-reliance, but also a suspicious, even hostile, attitude towards the outside world. Ultramontanism fostered a spirit of intolerance and intransigence among Catholics that helped to destroy the hitherto largely peaceful relations between Catholics and Protestants.

A new breed of senior clergymen also emerged among Catholics. More authoritarian than their gentlemanly predecessors, these new clerical leaders—Michael Anthony Fleming in St John's and James Dunphy in Saint John are good examples—attracted immense support from rank-and-file Catholics. In some respects they personified the communal aspirations of Irish Catholic immigrants. While asserting clerical authority within the Catholic community, they also championed the cause of Catholics in society at large. Their appearance on the scene marked the demise of the lay trustees who had played such a leading role in the formative years of colonial Catholicism. Episcopal authority was asserted over congregational autonomy, and the politics of accommodation, by which trustees had sought to ingratiate themselves with 'respectable' Protestants, gave way to a more forceful and public assertion of Catholic rights. In its extreme form, this became open antagonism toward non-Catholics.

An important part of the Irish Catholic revival, both at home and abroad, was the new pride and self-confidence it engendered. Strength came with numbers as the tide of immigration increased the Irish Catholic population; but there was also a new optimism about the prospects of advancement and collective self-improvement through common action. This was evident not least in the Catholic temperance clubs that grew up in conscious imitation of the work of the Irish crusader Father Theobald Mathew. Parochial total-abstinence societies had been established at a number of centres in the Atlantic region by the 1840s, and they spread to the Canadas in the 1850s. Like Protestant temperance associations, they sought to inculcate not only sobriety but also the related social values of self-discipline, self-help, and industriousness as a way of facilitating adjustment to an urban environment and commercial economy and of overcoming the very real social problems caused by the abuse of alcohol in the immigrant community. Such a reshaping of popular mores had added meaning for Irish Catholics in that it meant dispelling the reputation they had acquired as drunken ne'er-do-wells. Temperance societies worked alongside nationalist societies, another important vehicle of Irish Catholic self-assertion, and seized upon opportunities to demonstrate publicly the change that abstinence had wrought in the Catholic community. In Saint John, for example, on Saint Patrick's Day 1842, a thousand men gathered for morning mass, after which they paraded the city streets carrying aloft the banners of Father Mathew, Saint Michael, and Saint John. In Protestant temperance circles this display, despite its 'Romish' trappings, earned for them the admiration they sought; in other quarters, such as the Orange Order, it was seen as an ominous show of Catholic strength.[205]

The second major new religious influence of the mid-nineteenth century was the Oxford movement. Also known as Tractarianism (from the *Tracts for the Times* produced by the English leaders of movement, including John Keble and John Henry Newman), the Oxford movement was a new expression of the 'high church' tradition in the Church of England. The older high churchmen, well-represented in the colonies since the Loyalist era, derived the authority of the church largely from that of the state, whereas the Tractarians insisted on the church's apostolic origins and hence on its spiritual independence. Along with this insistence went a new emphasis on the authority of bishops, supported by the doctrine of apostolic succession: bishops were depicted as the successors of the apostles, and their powers were said to be transmitted in an unbroken line through the ages. The movement also introduced a new spirit to Anglican devotional life. In conscious opposition to the 'high and dry' rationalism of the eighteenth century, Tractarians, under the influence of the Romantic movement, extolled the place of emotion and aesthetic judgement in authentic Christian piety. Cultivating a sense of mystery and awe, they promoted personal holiness, sacramental devotion, and dignity and decorum in worship. Enthusiasm for the gothic revival in church architecture, as well as 'ritualism'—the desire to introduce more elaborate ceremonies into Anglican observance—were further expressions of the new religious sensibility.

Tractarian principles were introduced to the Atlantic colonies by English clergy who arrived after 1840. Noteworthy advocates of the new high churchmanship included Bishop Edward Feild of Newfoundland (1844–76), Bishop John Medley of Fredericton (1845–92), and Bishop Hibbert Binney of Nova Scotia (1851–87). The situation in Canada West was somewhat different. While newcomers from England had some success in spreading Tractarianism, the high-church party was mainly of local origin. Bishop Strachan, still the leading high churchman, showed a growing tendency to emphasize the church's independent authority,[206] but this shift in his views was tied up not so much with Tractarian ideals as with the pragmatic conviction that the colonial church had to become self-governing and self-reliant. Strachan's new perspective owed as much to American as to British sources, especially to the ideas of his friend John Hobart, Episcopalian bishop of New York.

Tractarianism was overwhelmingly the work of the clergy, but a significant minority of lay people gradually came under its spell, and, despite the strong countervailing influence of Anglican evangelicalism, the movement established pockets of strength in most parts of British North America. Wherever its influence was felt, it brought visible changes in daily religious life. Surplices replaced Geneva gowns in preaching, *Hymns Ancient and Modern* or Gregorian chant supplanted the singing of metrical psalms, daily rather than weekly services were introduced, holy days were observed, frequent communion became the norm, and elevated altars were decorated with lighted candles.[207] People knelt during prayers, bowing their heads at the mention of the name Jesus.[208] Hundreds of gothic churches were built, replacing or overshadowing earlier neoclassical or vernacular-style structures.[209] The new buildings included such impressive stone cathedrals as Christ Church in Fredericton[210] and St James in Toronto. Gothic church architecture eventually became standard among all the major denominations, but Anglican high churchmen led the way in promoting it. As in the case of the liturgy, these architectural reforms were pursued not as ends in themselves, but for their capacity to inspire devotion.[211] Vaulted arches, stained-glass windows, and dimly lit sanctuaries fostered feelings of awe, reverence, and serenity, lifting people above mundane experience and promoting a religious frame of mind.

At the same time that Ultramontanism and Tractarianism were transforming Roman Catholicism and Anglicanism, evangelical Protestantism in British North America also received a major new impetus with the arrival of the Presbyterian Free Church.[212] The Free Church was formed in Scotland in 1843 as the result of the Great Disruption within the Church of Scotland in which its evangelical wing, led by Thomas Chalmers, withdrew from the parent body over the questions of lay patronage and government interference in ecclesiastical affairs. The issues at stake had no immediate relevance to British North America. But evangelical Presbyterianism was well established in the colonies as a result of the efforts of the Glasgow Colonial Society,[213] and the cause of the Free Church was well promoted by delegates from Scotland such as Robert Burns, longtime secretary of the society, and by the journalists Peter and George Brown in Canada West, who used their newspaper the *Banner* for this end. Local events made colonial Presbyterians receptive to the Free Church message. When the Presbyterian Church in Canada was formed in 1840 by a union of the Church of Scotland Synod and the United (i.e., Secession) Synod, the wording of the legislation had raised fears that the government might try to interfere in church affairs.[214] After the Great Disruption, the new Canadian synod at first voted to support the principle of non-intrusion without actually joining the Free Church.[215] Not satisfied by this compromise, a minority withdrew to form a British North American Free Church synod. Within a generation, the Free Church had replaced the Church of Scotland as the pre-eminent form of Presbyterianism in Canada West. It also established an institutional presence of varying strength in all the other colonies. In Nova Scotia, it joined with the Secession churches in 1860 to produce the Synod of the Lower Provinces, whose members outnumbered the Church of Scotland's by more than three to one.

The Free Church was staunchly conservative in its approach to both doctrine and worship, but it brought to Presbyterianism a renewed missionary zeal and a powerful evangelical vision. This vision hinged on the concept of the 'headship of Christ': the obligation of nations to acknowledge their duty before God. While rejecting the intrusion of the state into religious affairs, Free Churchmen did not immediately repudiate the principle of establishment. Their main concern was that covenanted peoples should govern according to biblical precept. Activist in spirit, they were quick to enter the political arena, usually on the side of reform. They were also zealous promoters of programs aimed at moral reform, including the temperance movement, sabbatarian crusades, and efforts to stamp out vices such as dancing and theatre. They became a major source not merely of support but of leadership for such causes, repeatedly appearing on the executives of interdenominational organizations. Like evangelicals in other churches, they had no trouble co-operating with like-minded individuals from other denominations, and often found themselves closer to evangelical Anglicans, Methodists, or Baptists than to their rivals within the Presbyterian fold.

CONSENSUS, CONFLICT, AND COMPROMISE

In the midst of the cross-currents introduced by Ultramontane Catholicism, Tractarianism, and Free Church Presbyterianism, the evangelical movement remained the single strongest force in colonial religious life. Already powerful before 1840, it continued to gather momentum as the incipient evangelical consensus began to blossom into a full-scale coalition. The triumph of evangelical principles among a majority of Presbyterians, and their continued influence among a significant portion of Anglicans, was matched by a steady shift among Methodists, Baptists, and other descendants of eighteenth-century revivalism towards more churchly values.[216] Such changes continued to narrow the gap between revivalist groups and traditional churches and paved the way for even greater interdenominational collaboration.

The moral thrust of evangelicalism remained much the same as before, but there was an increase in the range of specific issues it addressed. Sabbatarianism and anti-slavery crusades were added to efforts to promote temperance, as the early stages of industrialization brought new threats to the observance of the Lord's Day and as harsh new legislation in the United States raised concerns over the plight of American blacks. The campaign against strong drink, meanwhile, took on a more uncompromising character. Attempts to eliminate all alcoholic beverages through legal prohibition replaced voluntary abstinence from ardent spirits as the movement's goal. This shift was encouraged by newly-founded fraternal orders such as the Sons of Temperance, which spread to British North America from the United States in the late 1840s. Although the new approach was resisted by many older temperance advocates, by mid-century it had become the standard policy of the movement.

The changes among revivalist denominations that facilitated the growth of the evangelical consensus had begun in the preceding generation, but they intensified after 1840. Success in propagating their beliefs and progress in the building up of denominational structures, along with the growing material prosperity of many of their adherents, brought gradual accommodation to prevailing social norms and an increased concern for social acceptance. Evangelical religion was becoming less a form of self-expression for the alienated or marginalized and more a vehicle for earnest believers in pursuit of social respectability. In the process, a significant proportion of members came to regard the unrestrained emotionalism of the early revival movement as a source of embarrassment, and sought ways to ensure moderation. Among Canadian Methodists, this tendency was reinforced by the mounting influence of the conservative Wesleyans, who were reunited with the Canadian conference in 1847. Ministers were urged to preach with dignity and decorum, showing restraint in their gestures and expressions, while the laity were advised to refrain from unseemly outbursts during worship.[217] The old concern for the sudden conversion of sinners declined in favour of a new preoccupation with the spiritual nurture of people born into the faith. Sunday schools grew in importance, and changed from interdenominational organizations for promoting literacy to denominational agencies for the religious instruction of the young.[218] The founding of denominational colleges reflected a desire to raise the educational level and social status of clergy.

These changes did not spell the end of revivalism. As a form of piety stressing the priority of the conversion experience, revivalism long outlasted the particular techniques used in frontier days to bring about that conversion.[219] Members of revivalist denominations continued to see the Christian life as a sequence of dramatic stages: conviction of sin, life-transforming conversion, and the quest for personal holiness. The methods used to achieve such results were modified as these denominations matured, but change was subtle and gradual, and it did not always occur at an even pace. Methodist camp-meetings actually increased in number in the 1850s before eventually going into decline.[220] Nevertheless, revivalism was increasingly institutionalized.[221] Camp-meetings came under stricter clerical control, protracted meetings (introduced in the 1830s) were continued, revivals occurred in denominational colleges,[222] professional evangelists were employed to complement the work of full-time pastors,[223] and the experience of conversion was gradually worked into the context of regular church life and family spirituality.[224]

Voluntary organizations remained among the chief tools of evangelical Protestantism, increasing in both number and scope in the middle decades of the century. Several new agencies promoting specific reforms joined the many already in existence. There were few general organizations devoted to further-ing intra-Protestant collaboration, but one notable exception was the Evan-gelical Alliance founded in Toronto in 1847. Although it did not succeed in creating a united front, it did promote interdenominational co-operation.

Militant evangelicalism was sustained by a profound belief in providence. In working for the conversion of sinners and the transformation of social life, fer-vent evangelicals believed that they were actively co-operating in God's plan for the world. This conviction was a version of the Victorian doctrine of progress. Evangelical Christians, however, understood progress in terms not of material improvement but of the gradual triumph of Christian moral values. Their goal was to build a truly Christian society, one in which evil would be vanquished and spiritual values would triumph. Evil was identified with crass materialism on the one hand and the teachings of the Church of Rome on the other. Confident of ultimate success against these two deadly enemies, evan-gelicals struggled to build the kingdom of God on earth.

Part of what set evangelicalism apart from competing religious ideologies was the degree of support it enjoyed. It brought together so wide and coherent a body of opinion that it could aspire to define standards not only for its own adherents but for the community at large. The more the evangelical consensus grew, the more adherents began to think of their principles as normative for everyone. It was this conviction that, despite the voluntarist principles of evan-gelicalism, allowed demands for legislation to replace persuasion as a means of achieving moral reform. From the evangelical point of view, there was a world of difference between church establishment and legislation to prohibit alcohol and ensure the observance of the Lord's Day. In the first case, the civil author-ities were bestowing privileges and unfair advantages on one church to the exclusion of others; in the second, they were translating into law widely-held community ideals.

In retrospect, the presumption and self-deception in all this is obvious. Evangelical Protestantism was indeed the dominant expression of Christianity in British North America, but the consensus on which it rested was not all-encompassing, even in the predominantly English-speaking colonies. Consensus was offset by conflict, both within and between denominations, and religious pluralism was too deeply entrenched to be swept away by a single uni-fied vision. Ultramontane Catholicism and high-church Anglicanism both commanded the allegiance of significant minorities, and a host of smaller denominations still fell outside the evangelical mainstream. Moreover, the evangelical world-view was narrow from a linguistic and ethnic point of view. Closely tied to incipient Canadian nationalism, it linked the future of British North America to the advance of English-speaking, Protestant culture. Evangelicals took little account of either French Canadians or First Nations, apart from their efforts to convert and acculturate them.

A good illustration of conflict within a denomination during this period can be seen in the Church of England, where the Tractarian movement came into direct confrontation with evangelical forces. With a strong footing in many parts of the colonies, the low-church party was strengthened significantly by Irish Protestant immigration in areas such as New Brunswick and especially Canada West. Indeed, the influx of members of the Church of Ireland—including the future evangelical bishop of London, Benjamin Cronyn—made the western portion of Canada West an evangelical stronghold. In the Maritimes the leading spokesman for low-church views was probably John W.D. Gray, the long-time rector of Trinity Church in Saint John, who in 1850 founded an evangelical newspaper, the *Church Witness*, which he used largely to attack his Tractarian adversary, Bishop Medley.

Conflict between evangelicals and Tractarians affected nearly every aspect of ecclesiastical life from worship and church-building to finances, polity, and education. Individual controversies reflected underlying theological divisions that were further complicated by ethnic distinctions between Irish and English. The low-church party, insisting on the priority of personal conversion brought about by hearing the Word of God, rejected the Tractarian emphasis on outward observance and grace-dispensing sacraments. The elaborate rituals that in the Tractarian view enriched the life of the church, restoring its ancient glory, seemed to evangelicals only so much 'popish' superstition. Evangelicals were also suspicious of the Oxford movement's glorification of the office of bishop, which in their eyes raised the spectre of abusive ecclesiastical authority. Fears of a 'Romeward' drift were greatly exacerbated when the English Tractarian leader John Henry Newman was converted to Roman Catholicism in 1845. The shocking news of Newman's desertion caused the evangelicals to intensify their resistance to Tractarianism, more convinced than ever that the enemy was within the gates.

The anti-Catholic element in evangelical opposition to Tractarianism was symptomatic of a much wider problem. The ecumenical spirit that had often characterized Catholic–Protestant relations before 1840 was fast disappearing, and anti-Catholicism was emerging as a major social force in British North America. The change had begun with the granting of Catholic emancipation. The political empowerment of Roman Catholics had led to a backlash in Great Britain, the repercussions of which were soon felt in the colonies. Thereafter, the increasing militancy of Roman Catholics, the arrival of thousands of famine Irish, and the fears of a papal conspiracy raised by the Tractarian movement combined to produce a groundswell of religious bigotry. As popular prejudice was channelled into organized 'no popery' crusades, anti-Catholicism began to replace earlier tensions between conventional and experiential religion, and between Anglicans and non-Anglicans, as the principal divisive influence in colonial religious life.

Newfoundland was the first colony where the changing mood was evident, largely because of its particular religious and social conditions.[225] Although Catholics composed nearly half the island's population, they were, as we have seen, disproportionately represented among the poorer classes, who were in turn blatantly exploited by the merchants. When Catholics attempted to assert their political rights, especially after the granting of representative government in 1832, their efforts were met by a Protestant backlash. In the other British North American colonies, the reasons behind sustained outbursts of anti-Catholicism (mainly after 1840) were also partly political. Rapidly increasing numbers of Catholics, armed with the franchise, were seen as a threat to Protestant hegemony. This fear was greatly exacerbated by the legislative union of Upper Canada and Lower Canada in 1841. Forced to reside in a single state with their French-speaking neighbours in Canada East, the English-speaking Protestants in Canada West imagined that a solid block of Catholic votes controlled the affairs of the entire province.[226] Even in Nova Scotia, where Catholics comprised only a quarter of the population, alarms were raised about Catholic control of the political process.[227]

Social factors also played a large role in the spread of anti-Catholicism. Tens of thousands of Irish famine migrants poured into the colonies after 1845, many of them destitute and disease-ridden, and some bringing along other problems such as drunkenness, crime, and violence. The refugees were perceived as a major threat to the stability of colonial society. Established residents resented the risk of contagion and felt that an intolerable strain was being placed on their philanthropic resources. Although the plight of the Irish was tragic, it often did more to confirm Protestant prejudices than to inspire Christian charity. Arriving at a time of economic change, the famine Irish became easy scapegoats for every unfavourable turn of events. The Protestant majority, uncertain of achieving the material progress that was the ideal of the age, tended to project their fears onto the immigrants, who were depicted as passive, docile, and backward.[228]

The most virulent expressions of prejudice against Irish Catholics often came from Irish Protestants. Hitherto the two groups had shown a considerable ability to co-operate, often banding together in benevolent societies and ethnic associations to provide mutual aid and celebrate their common Irish heritage. Co-operation of this sort began to break down as Irish nationalism became more and more exclusively identified with Roman Catholicism, but the final blow to Irish unity came with the famine migration. Irish Protestants found the starving refugees a great embarrassment and struggled to disassociate themselves from them.[229] As the Orange Order, already established in some of the colonies, grew rapidly in numbers and influence,[230] Irish Catholics organized themselves into rival societies, and violent confrontations became almost a routine feature of annual festivals such as St Patrick's Day and the Twelfth of July. Ironically, the result was to reinforce prejudice against all Irishmen, who were blamed for introducing endemic violence into colonial society.[231]

Although battles between Catholics and Protestants were played out on the local stage, anti-Catholic ideology remained for the moment a largely derivative affair. Non-Catholic immigrants brought prejudices with them from home, and both American and British propaganda was transmitted quickly through colonial newspapers and missionary journals.[232] British North Americans were well aware of American nativist principles extolling the rights of the established population over those of newcomers, and many accepted the notion that immigrants were a threat to cherished indigenous traditions. They also kept up-to-date with each new British 'no popery' outburst, and slavishly echoed such protests. Catholics were denounced from pulpits and lecture platforms as well as in the press, the charges against them conforming to a familiar and well-worn pattern. Besides gross superstition, they were condemned for political treachery, moral corruption, and economic backwardness.[233] Protestant propagandists appealed to prurient interests with bogus revelations of what transpired in Catholic confessionals and with spurious publications such as *The Awful Disclosures of Maria Monk*, a widely circulated book that purported to relate the experiences of a young woman in a Montreal nunnery.[234] A handful of ex-priests travelled from city to city giving sponsored lectures in which they claimed to expose the follies of their former faith.

Anti-Catholic agitation reached a crescendo in 1850, when Nicholas Wiseman, newly appointed archbishop of Westminster, triumphantly proclaimed the restoration of the Roman Catholic hierarchy in England. The British uproar over this 'papal aggression' found an immediate echo in the colonies. George Brown, now editor of the *Globe*, vociferously denounced the pretensions of the Catholic clergy, somehow managing to entangle the whole affair with the politics of the united Canada.[235] There were thoughtful people on both sides who recognized that no good could come of such recriminations, but their voices were drowned out. Indeed, discord was increased by two incidents that occurred shortly afterward in Canada East. In 1853, lectures by an Italian ex-priest, Alessandro Gavazzi, gave rise to violent disturbances at Quebec and Montreal, the latter resulting in the deaths of several members of the audience. Two years later, Robert Corrigan, an Irish convert to Protestantism, was murdered at Saint-Sylvestre, and the culprits were acquitted by an apparently partisan judge and a Catholic jury. Hostile Protestants were quick to cite the incident as proof of Catholic intolerance and treachery.

One outraged observer predicted that the murder of one Protestant would lead the way to further butchery.[236]

Sectarian strife of this sort clearly placed strict limits on the degree of religious consensus that could be reached in British North America. Another limiting factor was the presence of a number of smaller denominations whose peculiar principles differed significantly from those of the mainstream churches. They included groups already established in the colonies, ranging from Mennonites and Quakers to Primitive Methodists and the Catholic Apostolic Church, as well as new religious movements such as the 'Millerites', founded by William Miller, an American Baptist who predicted on the basis of Scriptural calculations that Christ would return in 1843. Together minor denominations comprised a small fraction of the population, but each one, guided by its own peculiar traditions and principles, brought an added dimension to the religious life of British North America. The broad spectrum included the communal life of the Mennonites, the mystical 'inner light' of the Quakers, the rationalism of the Unitarians, the glossolalia and elaborate rituals of the Catholic Apostolic Church, the ideal of a divinely ordered society among the Mormons, the optimism of the Universalists with their belief in the salvation of all, and the longing of the Disciples of Christ for the restoration of pure New Testament Christianity.

Generalizations about the small denominations are next to impossible. Judging by numbers alone, the definition of 'small' would have to include not only groups clearly outside the mainstream but also Lutherans and Congregationalists, neither of which had a large following in the British colonies. Furthermore, small denominations often differed as much from one another as they did from the major churches, and they were neither static nor immune to outside influences. Aggressive evangelicalism had penetrated both the Mennonites and Quakers, producing tensions and indeed schisms as some members urged change and adaptation, while others clung tenaciously to traditional patterns.[237]

Nevertheless, a common characteristic among many of the minor denominations was their rejection of prevailing cultural norms. Whereas the dominant evangelicalism worked actively and optimistically for the integration of religion and culture, the smaller religious bodies tended to be more pessimistic about the prospects of secular society. Their rejection of conventional standards took various forms, including separatism, communalism, and heightened eschatological expectations. Millennialist groups such as the Irvingites (Catholic Apostolic Church) and especially the Millerites enjoyed considerable success in Canada West in the middle decades of the century. They predicted not only that Christ would soon return to earth but that the coming of the Kingdom would be a cataclysmic event, overturning rather than fulfilling the existing order.[238] They made inroads among Methodists, Anglicans, and other denominations, posing a serious challenge to the assumptions of the dominant evangelicalism. The threat was taken seriously enough to call forth polemical responses from mainstream churches.[239]

Also falling outside the mainstream, though for very different reasons, were black Christians. The small black population of British North America experienced a significant increase around mid-century, largely because of a sharp increase in the number of fugitive slaves who made their way to Canada West via the underground railway. Evangelical Protestants responded to their arrival in typically philanthropic fashion, providing material aid and launching projects to facilitate resettlement. The most noteworthy of these ventures was the assisted black colony established by William King near Chatham in 1849 with the support of the Free Church. Managed by the Elgin Association, a stock company formed specifically for this purpose, the settlement provided land, education, and Christian nurture to freed black slaves. The religious and educational aspects of the settlement were supported by the Presbyterian Church and organized as the Buxton Mission. During the relatively brief history of the community these former slaves achieved considerable success in commercial ventures including a brick factory and a gristmill. Generally, though, blacks were still accepted into white churches on very unequal terms, and the trend continued towards the establishment of separate African Christian denominations. The African Methodist Episcopal Church entered from the States in 1838, and the Amherstburg Baptist Association was founded in Canada West in 1841. In the Maritimes, where African Baptists had already set up their own network of congregations, events followed a similar course. The African Methodist Episcopal Church established a presence, and in the late 1830s or early 1840s Jesse Coleman, a fugitive slave from Baltimore, founded the similarly named but distinct African Methodist Episcopal Zion Church. By 1854, five sister congregations had grown up at other centres.

The final thread in this pattern of persistent diversity was Christianity among the First Nations, which continued to develop and expand during the middle decades of the century. New initiatives in the Hudson's Bay territory, undertaken chiefly by Anglicans and Methodists, marked the beginning of a new phase in Protestant proselytizing efforts among the indigenous peoples. Although the Saulteaux showed little enthusiasm for Christianity, Cree and later Dene peoples embraced it willingly.[240] Not always waiting for missionaries to arrive among them, some native people travelled great distances to seek out clergymen. Others learned of Christianity from other natives who had become enthusiastic if unofficial converts. Within a matter of decades, communities of native Christians extended across the vast northwest. As in the eastern colonies, receptiveness to the new faith owed something to the expectation that conversion would bring access to the material benefits of white society. But it was due as well to an extraordinary spiritual ferment among the aboriginal population of the region.[241] Reports of innovations in the rituals of the shamans seem to indicate that a search for new sources of religious power was already under way when Christianity began to extend its influence. A new system of belief seemed necessary to explain a rapidly changing world, and since the changes were largely the result of contacts with whites, the religion of the whites appeared to offer the most potent and compelling alternative.

Native responses to Christianity cannot always be divided simply into rejection and acceptance. External conformity sometimes masked internal resistance, while by the same token outward opposition might conceal a hidden desire to appropriate parts of what the new religion had to offer. This point is well illustrated by the succession of indigenous prophetic movements that swept the northwest in the nineteenth century.[242] Usually based on claims of special revelations through dreams and visions, these movements were openly hostile to whites (especially missionaries) and called for the rejection of European ways. Millennial in spirit, they looked forward to an idealized future existence, defined in terms of traditional native values and customs and reserved exclusively for indigenous people. In anticipation of the new age, they often called upon followers to destroy valuable property; the destruction of dogs (introduced by whites) was a recurrent phenomenon. Yet such movements were plainly syncretistic, incorporating a number of ingredients from Christianity. One of the most remarkable native prophets, the Cree Abishabis, who actually called himself 'Jesus', derived some of his inspiration from Methodist hymns and is credited with promoting sabbath observance.[243] Rather than outright rejections of Christianity, therefore, such indigenous movements of spiritual renewal may have been attempts to appropriate the new faith on aboriginal terms.[244] Although they were extremely heterodox, no picture of Christianity among the First Nations is complete without them.

If changes in native society brought religious ferment, then religion in turn promoted changes in native society. On this score, developments in the West differed somewhat from those back east. Western missionaries began their work with the standard assumptions about the need to 'civilize' while Christianizing, and early ventures in the Red River district included the usual agricultural settlements of native converts. As missions expanded into the Northwest, however, missionaries were forced to change their approach. The northern landscape, inhospitable to farm animals and crops, made it impossible to impose a sedentary, agrarian way of life, and a measure of accommodation to native customs became a necessity. Missionaries relinquished none of their faith in the superiority of European culture, but they did make a few pragmatic adjustments. The modification of missionary methods can be seen in the translation of Scripture and hymns into the aboriginal languages of the Northwest. Early translations into Cree, such as those produced by the Anglican James Hunter and his wife Jean Ross, were done in Roman script, largely to facilitate a subsequent transition to English.[245] The Methodist James Evans, building on his earlier work among the Ojibwa of Canada West, developed a simple and easily memorized syllabic script that allowed Cree to emerge in its own right as a vehicle of written communication.[246] After initial resistance, Evans's syllabary was adopted by the Anglicans, and the Roman Catholic Oblate missionaries not only used it for Cree but adapted it to other languages. Although the introduction of writing in any form can be construed as a threat to the oral culture of the First Nations, syllabics played an important part in the preservation of their languages.[247]

Innovations of a less positive nature were occurring in the eastern colonies, where natives were no longer valued as trading partners. Marginalized by demographic and economic changes, they had come to be seen as obstacles to agricultural settlement and a drain on the public purse. Civil officials, who had assumed responsibility from the military for relations with indigenous peoples, were seeking solutions to the native 'problem', which in essence meant more effective ways of assimilation. Partnership between government and the churches was still considered essential in this enterprise, and conversion to Christianity was still linked to church-run programs of education and acculturation. The traditional day schools, however, were increasingly regarded as a failure, and their lack of success was blamed largely on the continuing influence of native parents on their children.

Encouraged by the Bagot Commission of 1842–4, a shift occurred from day to residential schools in which native youths were taught the 'three Rs' and practical skills in an atmosphere free from the countervailing influence of their families and villages. The avowed aim was to break down their native identity and bring about complete assimilation. The methods were essentially coercive. Teachers insisted on European standards of dress and hygiene; it became common practice to forbid the use of native languages; and students who ran away in protest were forcibly returned. The wishes of native people were never taken into account: missionaries and government officials simply assumed that they knew best. Moreover, these developments in education were part of a broader pattern that included legislation for the so-called protection of native lands and the Gradual Civilization Act of 1857. Without consulting the First Nations, these acts defined who was or was not an 'Indian' and introduced the notion of 'enfranchisement', a process to be achieved precisely by giving up Indian status.[248]

When one takes a broad view of religious life in the predominantly English-speaking colonies, the pattern that emerges shows measures both of consensus and of conflict. Strong pressures for conformity stood in constant tension with an equally strong pull towards diversity. The homogenizing tendency of the evangelical movement was counterbalanced by the determination of a wide variety of religious groups to maintain their distinctive principles. Compromise was not impossible, but the process of arriving at a *modus vivendi* was often difficult, and the confrontation between opposing points of view introduced considerable strains in social and political life.

Nowhere did such tensions surface more clearly than in the evolution of British North America's school system. Efforts to establish common elementary schools supported by compulsory taxation, a trend in all of the colonies after 1840, brought into sharp focus the struggle between uniformity and diversity. In Canada East the English-speaking minority had to rally to protect its rights in the face of an overwhelming French-speaking Catholic majority. Elsewhere the shoe was on the other foot, and Roman Catholics and other minorities had to defend themselves against pressures from the Protestant majority. Common schools in the English-speaking colonies were supposed to be non-denominational, but this was in no way intended to mean free from religious influences. Evangelical forces, which played a leading role in the development of the system, insisted that the new schools should inculcate the basic, shared principles of common Christianity, which they seldom thought to distinguish from their own peculiar tenets. In some regions, such as Newfoundland and Prince Edward Island, the focal point of evangelical efforts was the campaign to secure the use of Authorized Version of the Bible in the schools.[249] Catholics, who regarded the Vulgate edition as authoritative and who discouraged the independent reading of Scripture, regarded this goal as totally unacceptable.

Though initially open to the principle of non-denominational education, therefore, Catholics strenuously resisted this attempt to impose evangelical Protestant values and demanded schools of their own. In the early stages of the controversy, this was a more or less pragmatic stance, designed mainly as a necessary 'protection from insult'. But the growing influence of Ultramontanism, which proclaimed the subordination of the state to the church in such religiously sensitive areas as education, hardened the Catholic position, and soon Catholics were demanding separate schools as an 'inalienable right'.[250] Their demands were eventually met, and Catholic schools were provided either by law, as in Newfoundland and the united Province of Canada, or by custom, as in the Maritime colonies. High Anglicans also tried to obtain their own schools, but in their case the reasons had more to do with the traditional privileges of the Church of England, and their efforts were less successful. Only in Newfoundland did they ultimately secure the creation of a separate Anglican school board.[251]

While the evangelical majority failed to achieve the degree of uniformity they hoped for, their influence on the emerging school systems of the English-speaking colonies was enormous. The vast majority of pupils attended non-denominational schools steeped in the ethos of evangelical Protestantism, which in turn was tied to an unshakeable belief in the superiority of English-speaking culture. Evangelicals were developing a sense of national mission, the essence of which was the determination to keep British North America loyal to the Crown and predominantly Protestant and English-speaking. This mission bore some resemblances to the role that the Church of England had defined for itself after the American Revolution. But whereas the Anglican design rested on coercive institutions reflecting the privileges of a religious minority, the evangelical mission relied on voluntary institutions supported by the common ideals of the majority of the population. Evangelicalism, voluntarism, and nationalism were inseparably linked in a common front that aimed to break down exclusive structures and embrace everything within a comprehensive vision.

This unified vision provided much of the impetus behind the final assault on church establishment in British North America. In the late 1840s and early 1850s, evangelical ideals combined with voluntarist principles and the advancing tide of political reform to remove the last vestiges of the confessional state. The clergy reserves were secularized, acts of disestablishment were passed, Anglican colleges lost their preferential status, and Anglican bishops who still enjoyed government salaries or the right to sit on legislative councils lost those privileges. Not only external pressure but internal changes in the Churches of England and Scotland contributed to this process. Both the Tractarian movement and the emergence of the Free Church signalled a rejection of the Erastian ideals of the eighteenth century, which subordinated the church to the state, in favour of a new emphasis on the spiritual authority of the church. While the most intransigent spokesmen for the Church of England resisted the separation of church and state until the bitter end, a growing number of Anglicans thought the change was for the best. The Free Church progressed even more rapidly. Although it rejected from the outset the interference of the state in church affairs, it did not at first give up the principle of state support. Within a few years, however, it had for all practical purposes joined the ranks of the voluntarists. In fact, the Free Church principle of the 'headship of Christ', by which covenanted people lived in accordance with biblical precepts, was an important bridge between old and new conceptions. It opened the door to disestablishment without sacrificing the ideal of a Christian society.

In Canada West, the main issue in church–state relations remained the clergy reserves. The compromise of 1840, which had divided proceeds from the reserves unevenly among the various denominations, had been intended to resolve the question once and for all. In reality, it had succeeded only in creating a plural establishment that satisfied no one. The Church of England still received a disproportionate share of benefits (with 20 per cent of the population, it got 42 per cent of the revenues from the reserves), and voluntarists and reformers continued to feel that the reserves ought to be used for the public good, probably in the area of education. The election in 1848 of a reform government under

Robert Baldwin and Louis-Hippolyte Lafontaine raised hopes for a new settlement. Pressure mounted for the repeal of the imperial legislation of 1840 and the enactment of a new measure by the colonial legislature.

Only a small minority defended the status quo, the balance of opinion being divided between a larger minority favouring a revised scheme of denominational division and the majority supporting secularization. An Anti-Clergy Reserves Association (later renamed the Anti-State Church Association) was formed to promote the latter cause. Finally, after the passage of enabling legislation by the imperial parliament in 1853, the legislature of the united Canada passed a law that became the last word on this vexed topic. The reserves were to be sold and the proceeds deposited in the Municipalities Fund, from which they would be distributed annually among the various urban and county municipalities on a per capita basis. Those clergy who were currently receiving stipends from the reserves could either continue to collect them for life or have them commuted and invested in the name of ecclesiastical corporations that would then pay the stipends but hold the investments in perpetuity. Since most clergy were persuaded to choose the latter course, these commuted stipends became sizeable permanent endowments, especially for the Church of England. Even at the moment of effective disestablishment, therefore, a way was found for the Church of England to preserve something of its financial advantage over other denominations.

While the clergy reserves were the key church–state issue in Canada West, the role of the churches in higher education was also important. An 1837 reform of the charter of King's College, Toronto, had already reduced Anglican control of the institution, but without destroying its denominational character. Pressure for further changes increased in 1843, when King's, which had hitherto existed mainly on paper, actually began operations. A number of other denominational colleges, including Queen's (Church of Scotland), Victoria (Wesleyan Methodist), and Regiopolis (Roman Catholic) had come into existence in the meantime, and the question was how or whether they would receive fair treatment. A number of schemes were advanced, all of which wavered between two basic alternatives. One was to divide the King's endowment among the denominations in a manner reminiscent of the 1840 clergy-reserves settlement; the other was to amalgamate the various colleges into a single university, leaving the endowment intact but extending its benefits to everyone. Bishop Strachan fought hard for the first of these options, since he wanted to preserve the Anglican character of King's. The second option, creation of a single university, was promoted by a coalition of reformers and voluntarists, including Baptists, non-Wesleyan Methodists, Congregationalists, and the Free Church.

After several failed attempts to legislate a solution, Baldwin managed to pass a universities bill in 1849. This act completely secularized King's College, reconstituting it as the University of Toronto, removing all religious tests, and specifically excluding clergymen from the offices of chancellor and president. The other colleges were to be loosely affiliated with the new university without receiving any portion of the endowment; the hidden agenda was to starve them out of existence and create a centralized provincial monopoly over higher education. But Victoria and Queen's decided to carry on, and the redoubtable Strachan began to raise money and support for the creation of a new Anglican college. In 1851, he laid the cornerstone for Trinity College.

Meanwhile, Baldwin was replaced as leader of the reform party by Francis Hincks, who fashioned a compromise between the plan for a centralized and secularized university and the continued existence of denominational colleges. This compromise was implemented through the 1853 Universities Act, which separated the teaching college of the University of Toronto from the examining university with which all colleges were affiliated. In principle, any surplus in the university's funds could now be paid out to the church colleges—although the university usually made sure that no such surplus was allowed to accumulate. In addition, substantial legislative grants were paid to denominational colleges on an annual basis, but these ceased in 1868, causing considerable hardship. Despite the financial constraints placed on denominational colleges, they were recognized as an integral part of the provincial system of higher education. The Anglican monopoly had been overturned without excluding the churches from higher education.

In the Maritimes, where there were no systematic land endowments for the Church of England, higher education was even more central to church–state controversies. The failure to establish Dalhousie College as an all-encompassing, non-sectarian university in Nova Scotia, and the gradual emergence of Baptist, Methodist, and Roman Catholic colleges had placed higher education squarely on a denominational footing. Government financial support for King's College was gradually reduced, and the Board of Governors, previously composed of government officials, was replaced in 1854 by a board elected by alumni of the college. The change helped to place King's on the same footing as other denominational colleges. Meanwhile, another King's College had emerged at Fredericton in 1829 from foundations laid by the College of New Brunswick. Opposition to its privileged status culminated in an 1845 amendment to the charter that opened membership on the college council to representatives of other denominations. Fourteen years later, the college was completely secularized and transformed into the non-sectarian provincial University of New Brunswick.

The relations between church and state in the Maritimes also differed from those in the Canadas inasmuch as the Church of England had been formally established by acts of the local legislatures. With the spread of voluntarist sentiment and the progress of political reform, such legislation seemed at best an anachronism, and it was only a question of time before it was dismantled. The Nova Scotia Act of Establishment, originally passed in 1758, was overturned in 1851, and the equivalent legislation in New Brunswick, enacted in 1786, was repealed in 1854. Only Prince Edward Island was slow to change. Not until 1879 would the Island legislature reverse its 1802 act of establishment, though by that time the law was such a dead letter that its repeal encountered little or no resistance. The rescinding of the acts of establishment in Nova Scotia and New Brunswick marked a real and definitive change in the position of the Church of England. Whereas in the past the Church of England had so dominated public offices that its bishops were members of the governing councils, in 1851, when the newly appointed Bishop Binney claimed a seat on the Nova Scotia council *ex officio*, he was told by Earl Grey, the colonial secretary, that the seat held by his predecessor was a personal appointment and would not be continued. The naming of Bishop Medley to the New Brunswick council encountered so much resistance that in 1856 he was forced to resign.

The exclusion of Binney and Medley was part of a new pattern for Anglican bishops. (The case of Bishop Strachan was somewhat different: he had been dropped from the council of Canada West at the time of the legislative union in 1841, and had been appointed in the first place for his political services before he was raised to the episcopate.) The first resident bishop of Newfoundland, Aubrey Spencer, never sat on the council, nor did George Jehoshaphat Mountain, Bishop Charles James Stewart's successor in Quebec. Soon after being dropped from governing councils, colonial bishops also ceased to be appointed by the Crown or to receive British salaries. Their changing status signalled a fundamental shift in Anglican church government that would soon lead to the formation of diocesan synods, one function of which was to elect local bishops.

Together with the secularization of the clergy reserves, the ending of the Anglican monopoly in higher education, and the disestablishment of the Church of England in the Maritimes, the transformation of the Anglican episcopate removed the last substantive manifestation of the confessional state from what is now Canada. The separation of church and state marked the death of a tradition that reached back not just to the beginning of the British era but to the origins of New France. From the inception of organized European settlement in the northern colonies, the civil government, whether French or English, had assigned special privileges to one form of Christianity. In the 1850s formal church–state connections were finally severed. The Church of England might enjoy some residual financial advantages, and in English-speaking Canada it might continue to expect a degree of symbolic public recognition. Legally, however, all religious denominations were now on an equal footing, and voluntarism had replaced ecclesiastical establishment in principle as well as in practice.

This watershed in church–state relations coincided with turning-points in virtually every aspect of religious life. In less than a century, the British North American churches had evolved from struggling and scattered missionary outposts to mature ecclesiastical institutions. Dependence on parent organizations had given way to self-reliance, and the chronic shortage of trustworthy clergy had been largely overcome by the establishment of denominational colleges and seminaries. With the framework of regular ecclesiastical life securely in place, the churches had begun to turn from the struggle to establish basic institutions to more ambitious enterprises. The launching of home missions, both in the West and among French Canadians, was one sign of this new stage of development.[252]

In most parts of British North America, the time had passed when a large number of people were completely beyond the influence of the churches. Church membership had grown rapidly, outstripping the general rate of population growth, and formal membership seemed to a large extent to reflect genuine commitment. The churches had increased not only their institutional strength but also their formative influence on people's lives. Having gathered the majority of people within the corporate structures of Christianity, they turned their attention to consolidation, nurture, and expansion.[253] They also demonstrated a mounting concern with the transformation of society. Of course social reform was already a well-established element in the churches' mission. But by mid-century they had reached the stage where they no longer had to struggle under unfavourable conditions to reach the spiritually destitute or awaken the indifferent. Now they could concentrate on working from within to transform community life and shape a social environment that would reflect fundamental Christian values.

Opposite: ATLANTIC CANADA, NINETEENTH CENTURY.

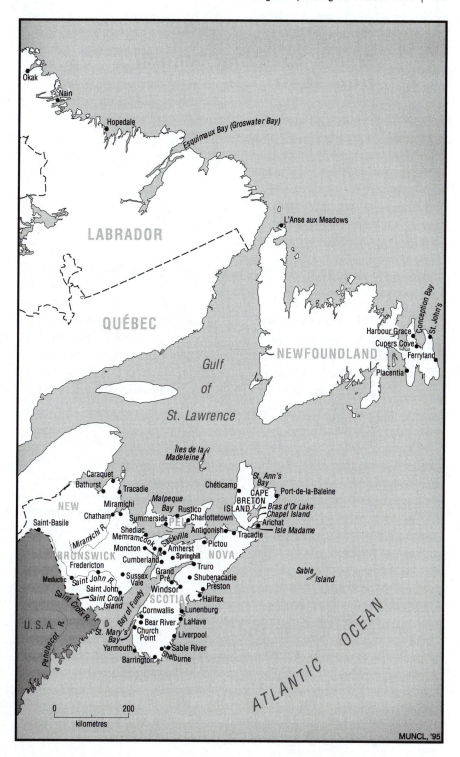

Okak
Nain
Hopedale
Esquimaux Bay (Groswater Bay)
L'Anse aux Meadows
LABRADOR
QUÉBEC
Harbour Grace
Cupers Cove
Conception Bay
St. John's
NEWFOUNDLAND
Ferryland
Placentia
Gulf
of
St. Lawrence
Îles de la
Madeleine
St. Ann's
Bay
Caraquet
Bathurst
Tracadie
Chéticamp
Port-de-la-Baleine
CAPE
BRETON
Miramichi
Malpeque
Bay Rustico
ISLAND
Bras d'Or Lake
Chapel Island
NEW
Saint-Basile
Chatham
Summerside
P.E.I.
Charlottetown
Arichat
Isle Madame
Miramichi R.
Shediac
Memramcook
Antigonish
Tracadie
BRUNSWICK
Moncton
Sackville
Pictou
Fredericton
Cumberland
Amherst
Springhill
NOVA
Meductic
Saint John R.
Sussex
Vale
Grand
Pré
Truro
Shubenacadie
Sable
Island
Saint Croix R.
Saint John
Saint Croix
Island
Windsor
SCOTIA
Preston
Halifax
U.S.A.
Cornwallis
Lunenburg
Penobscot R.
Bay of Fundy
Bear River
LaHave
St. Mary's
Bay
Church
Point
Liverpool
Yarmouth
Sable River
Barrington
Shelburne
ATLANTIC OCEAN

0   200
kilometres

MUNCL, '95

Four

French-Speaking Canada from 1840

R O B E R T O   P E R I N

RELIGIOUS REVIVAL (1840–1920)

Winds of change began to blow over the French-speaking peoples of Canada in the 1840s. For the next seven decades, but especially in the last third of the century, demographic and economic pressures would force them in ever greater numbers to seek out new areas of settlement or new forms of labour (see Table 4.1). They were people on the move. Acadians began to leave the coastal regions of the Maritimes where they had drawn their livelihood from the sea. They opened up new districts in the interior, along the Gulf, in the lower St Lawrence region and along the north shore, practising non-commercial agriculture. Similarly, French Canadians were leaving traditional settlements along the St Lawrence and Richelieu rivers in search of livelihoods in the largely marginal farmlands of the Eastern Townships, the regions south and north of the island of Montreal, the Ottawa valley, and the Charlevoix, Lac St-Jean, and Gaspé districts. Some crossed the Ottawa River into the counties of eastern Ontario, while a smaller number merged with an older French-Canadian agricultural community in the southwestern part of the province. In the early twentieth century, yet another wave would be drawn to northeastern Ontario, where they combined marginal farming with work in extractive industries, such as mining or lumbering.

The French-speaking population of the Prairies, at first composed of Métis, increased somewhat after Confederation when Canadian immigration agents operating in New England repatriated a number of French Canadians and Acadians and helped them settle in the West. Although this plan was partly successful, a greater number of French Canadians from Quebec headed south in search of prime farming land in the American midwest. Nevertheless, the French-Canadian communities of the West did grow, and they were able to attract small numbers of immigrants from France and Belgium arriving at the turn of the century.

Many French Canadians and Acadians, however, could not eke out a decent existence from the farm. As a result, they turned largely to unskilled wage employment in the cities both in Quebec and in New England. At first these workers, many of whom were women, went as sojourners. But the prospect of relatively good wages and steady employment turned a temporary phenomenon into a permanent one, involving the migration of entire families and even communities. Rural migrants to Montreal would have encountered freshly arrived immigrants from Europe and Asia, some of whom, such as the Italians and the Christian Arabs from what is now Lebanon, integrated with the French-speaking population. A larger wave of French Canadians bypassed the cities of Quebec altogether and settled in the United States. Exact statistics on the number of such immigrants are not available. But there is no doubt about the scale of the movement: it is estimated that one million French-speakers left Canada for the southern republic in the century after 1840, of whom as many as one hundred thousand may have been Acadian.

TABLE 4.1:   GROWTH AND DISTRIBUTION OF THE POPULATION OF FRENCH ORIGIN, 1840, 1870, 1900[1]

	1840	1870	1900
Acadians	approx. 50,000	86,000	139,020
French Canadians			
Quebec	approx. 550,000	929,817	1,322,513
Ontario	13,969	75,383	161,181
West			45,039

PROTESTANTISM: THE CHURCH MILITANT

In 1840 French Canadians and Acadians were all, nominally at least, Catholic. But this situation was about to change somewhat. Early defections from the ancestral faith occurred in the climate of emotional crisis following the crushing of the uprisings of 1837–8. A number of Patriotes whose ideological choices had distanced them from the institutional church including some who considered themselves deists, were forced into exile in the United States. Like some early French-Canadian immigrants to the United States, they readily equated the material progress of the republic with Protestantism and drew unflattering comparisons with conditions in Catholic Quebec. Moreover, the defeat of their political ideals, and their bitterness over the Catholic Church's collaboration with the British authorities, left them open to alternative forms of religious experience. Whatever the reason for it, conversion was a profoundly emotional experience in which aspirants acknowledged a sense of emptiness and meaninglessness in their lives, joyfully embracing the new faith. Such was the case with the Patriotes Dr C.H.O. Côté and J.B. Boucher-Belleville, who became Baptists, and Amand Parent, a convert to Methodism.[2]

The broader movement towards Protestantism in Quebec, however, is largely attributable to the French Canadian Missionary Society, an interdenominational body (excluding the Anglicans) that stepped up its work following the repression of the insurrections. While its efforts never had the official blessing of British authorities, they were consistent with London's long-term objective of assimilating the French Canadians.[3] Significant financial backing came from American sources.[4]

But money alone was not enough. Proselytism seems to have been more successful in new areas of settlement where the Catholic Church was institutionally weak, migrants were adapting to a new environment, and French Protestant missionaries were already active. It is no coincidence that, after the failure of missionary efforts in Montreal in the 1830s, mission stations were established at Grande-Ligne (inland from Laprairie on the south shore of Montreal) and Pointe-aux-Trembles (on the eastern tip of the island of Montreal), which served the adjacent areas on the north shore of the St Lawrence. Within a short time, French Protestant churches, usually paid for by foreign sources, were built in these new areas of settlement. Missionary efforts extended to the new districts along the Ottawa River in the following decade.[5] Evangelists also worked in the remoter parts of the Eastern Townships along the borders of Maine and New Hampshire, and by the 1870s French Presbyterians were active even in the more ethnically homogeneous areas of the Lower St Lawrence, as well as in northern New Brunswick and among the Acadians of Nova Scotia. The fact that all these were subsistence settler economies, heavily dependent on mutual aid,[6] made it easier for evangelists to penetrate them, particularly if they could offer schooling or medical services, as the physician Côté did.

Laymen and ordained ministers, coming at first from France and Switzerland, and then increasingly from Quebec, were the shock troops of the missionary movement, distributing Bibles and tracts door-to-door. (This activity was known even in English as colportage; those who performed it were called colporteurs). They were often courageous, persistent, and at times aggressive, not hesitating to challenge their listeners' convictions or the claims of the local parish priest. They welcomed doctrinal debates with the Catholic clergy, especially if an audience could be found—this was never hard, since French

Canadians relished oratorical confrontations. But for all the effort it took, colportage brought minimal results.[7] French Canadians still tended to mistrust Protestant proselytizing, and for that reason missionary work focused especially on school-age children. The Baptists, Presbyterians, Anglicans, and Methodists all established residential schools for boys and girls[8] that Catholic children could attend free of charge. As well, day schools were organized in many areas.

In other cases, Protestant missionaries were able to exploit divisions within Catholic communities. In 1869, for instance, the Iroquois at Kanesatake (Oka) demanded that the Séminaire de St-Sulpice recognize aboriginal claims to the old seigneury. When the Sulpicians refused, a number of natives, led by their chief, became Methodists. Aided by an Iroquois interpreter, Amand Parent ministered to them for a time in French. He also had a chapel built on the disputed land, much to the horror of the Sulpicians who successfully appealed to the courts to have it removed.[9] Other disputes among Catholics arose over the location and construction costs of new parish churches. In extreme cases, parishioners who rejected the bishop's judgement either left the church voluntarily or were forced out. One such confrontation occurred at Maskinongé in 1892, when despite canonical sanctions, a number of families refused to submit to the bishop's decision concerning the site of the new parish church; they held religious services without a priest until Baptists arrived and converted two dozen people. In Bonnyville, Alberta, dissension around unspecified causes in the 1910s led a local French Canadian to invite a Presbyterian compatriot to become the pastor of their congregation. A place of worship was soon erected, which, according to the minister, was the first French Protestant church west of the Great Lakes. Ten mission stations serving ethnically mixed communities were subsequently established.[10]

The success of Protestant missionary activity is difficult to judge in the absence of hard statistics. One source estimates that 2,000 conversions had been achieved by 1850, and that the readership of the French Protestant bimonthly newspaper *Le Semeur canadien* (founded 1851) numbered 650 in that decade. At its peak in 1900, French Protestantism was scattered throughout the Quebec countryside with 65 churches and mission fields served by 60 ministers and evangelists. This presence was more rural than urban, although congregations were solidly established in Montreal, Ottawa, St-Hyacinthe, and Joliette. The Presbyterians alone claimed a total of 12,000 French-speaking members in Canada at the turn of the century.[11] It is possible, then, that by that time French Protestants numbered nearly 20,000 and constituted slightly more than one per cent of the total French-speaking population. This suggests that Protestant numbers increased far more rapidly than the overall French-Canadian population.

Two figures stand out in the expansion of nineteenth-century Protestantism. The first is the notorious ex-priest Charles Chiniquy, who probably did more than anyone else to advance the fortunes of Presbyterianism in Quebec, both materially and spiritually. Although he was an aggressive, and at times outrageous, anti-Catholic evangelist, Chiniquy's arguments were not without intellectual appeal. The scholar, author, and Baptist clergyman Jean Charlemagne Bracq[12] attributed his conversion to Chiniquy, as did Amédée Papineau, son of the leader of the 1837 insurrection.

The second notable figure was Henriette Odin Feller. Born in Switzerland in 1800 to a bourgeois family, she was the backbone of Baptist missionary work in Quebec from her arrival in Lower Canada in 1835 until her death in 1868. It was largely through her efforts that Grande-Ligne emerged as an active centre of French-Canadian Protestantism. A woman of boundless energy, Feller found no task too trivial or too exalted. She had remarkable fundraising abilities, a good basic knowledge of medicine, and a profound spirituality. A story is told of how one day a former priest, Louis-Léon Normandeau, went to Grande-Ligne seeking spiritual guidance from the pastor, who happened to be absent. When Feller offered to help, Normandeau wondered how a woman could enlighten him on religious matters. But in fact she was instrumental in his conversion. Feller oversaw all aspects of daily life at Grande-Ligne, from care of the livestock to building repairs; she looked after all the correspondence and expected to be kept minutely informed about all aspects of the community's life when she was away.[13]

Protestant commentators agree that the missionary movement in Quebec was largely a failure. One reason was the hostility of the Catholic population. In the early days of proselytism, one pastor in the course of his rounds found his horse's mane and tail shaved off—a mark of disdain and ridicule. Some forty years later, police in Quebec City arrested officers and soldiers of the Salvation Army for boisterously proclaiming their message in the streets. For their part, Catholic clergy organized public burnings of Protestant versions of the Bible. Converts to Protestantism were often ostracized or boycotted—an unsuccessful Liberal aspirant to the Legislative Assembly was completely cut off from his family after he embraced the new religion—and neighbours frequently refused to have any personal or business dealings with converts. Other expressions of disapproval included barn burnings, contamination of animal fodder (with crushed glass), and *charivaris*—noisy, sometimes menacing rituals carried out in the middle of the night.[14] Most observers point out, however, that such tactics were not an ongoing problem: rather, they were used to prevent the introduction of Protestantism in a given community. It is unlikely that older and more established French Protestant congregations faced persistent harassment.

A second reason for the evangelists' relative failure in Quebec was emigration. Protestantism had its greatest successes in areas of settlement that were by nature unstable, with a high turnover of population. Local Protestant congregations tended to be so small that the departure of one or two families could mean the difference between having a resident pastor or merely an itinerant, between a local school and an expensive residential establishment. There is no doubt that the economically-motivated population movement following the First World War had a profoundly disruptive effect on Protestant congregations. At times, French-Canadian Protestant emigrants were numerous enough to recreate their religious structures in a new environment. This was the case of a number of Presbyterian families who settled in Huron County, Ontario. Others, such as those who emigrated to New England, were likely to join already established French congregations. In both cases, though, it was only a matter of time before they lost their cultural distinctiveness and blended into the English-speaking Protestant world. And this brings us to a third important obstacle to the spread of Protestantism in French Canada.

One historian of French-Canadian Protestantism firmly maintained that conversion did not lead to loss of national identity among French Canadians: 'L'Évangile ne dénationalise pas,' insisted Rieul Duclos. Yet even in Quebec, the problem of linguistic assimilation was ever present among French-Canadian Protestants. It is true that they worshipped in a French environment. The first hymnal was published in Quebec in 1844, and another, used extensively by various Protestant denominations, appeared with musical scores in 1857. But it is also true that congregations and individuals relied heavily on English-speaking Protestants for moral and financial support. French-Canadian Protestantism did not develop indigenous structures and was never more than an adjunct of the various denominations' missionary boards. The leaders of the main Protestant denominations were not always keen on proselytizing French Canadians, and it appears that those involved in such work were constantly obliged to justify it. Duclos for one felt that history might have taken a different turn had the Reformed Church of France directed missionary efforts in Quebec.[15]

The boundaries between French- and English-speaking Protestants were much more permeable than those separating their respective linguistic communities. Not only were the governing structures of their churches English-speaking, but in order to support themselves ministers often served both French and English congregations at the same time. A number of clergymen had English-speaking wives and most did their theological training in English-Canadian or American institutions, although McGill's Theological Faculty did have a French Department that offered courses in that language. As well, the French Protestant educational system was geared to bilingualism. Residential schools welcomed English-speaking students, and although they provided instruction in both languages, English became predominant in the upper grades. As for those students not attending residential schools, a Baptist minister admitted: 'Many of our young people have of necessity attended English schools, have there made friends and have drifted into English churches.'[16]

It would be difficult enough in such circumstances to maintain a distinct sense of identity. But in the climate of ethnic and religious confrontation that characterized Canada in the half-century after Confederation, French-Canadian Protestants were confronted with a Kierkegaardian dilemma: was it possible to be both French-Canadian and Protestant, or did one have to choose between culture and faith? Calvin Amaron, son of one of the first French Presbyterian missionaries in Quebec and editor of the Protestant weekly *L'Aurore*, illustrated the problem. Because the Catholic Church had obstructed 'the commercial, intellectual and moral life of the nation' for so long, he advocated a national system of education that would make students into British citizens first and foremost.[17] This view was supported by a leading Baptist minister, A. de L. Therrien, who stated:

> so long as he [the French Canadian] denies the state any voice in the education of his children, so long will he refuse to unite with his English brother in a system of national schools. This will largely account for the separation of the nationalities and the breeding of distrust which is responsible for the lack of cohesion between Quebec and the other provinces.[19]

These men expressed ambiguous feelings about their cultural identity. In the conflict over denominational education that divided Canadians for more than half a century, they spurned the opinions of French Canada and aligned themselves with the English-Canadian Protestant majority in advocating an end to Catholic education.

CATHOLICISM: THE CHURCH TRIUMPHANT

The rise of Protestantism notwithstanding, the vast majority of French Canadians and Acadians, even among those who left their traditional areas of settlement, remained firmly attached to their ancestral practices. As we have seen, since the beginnings of French settlement, religion had always been a profoundly social phenomenon. Celebrating rites of passage, building a parish church, and regular attendance at mass brought the community together, consolidating social ties and shared values. This pattern remained intact in the British period, although certain changes were observed as the constitutional struggle intensified under the parliamentary institutions established by the Constitutional Act of 1791. Some expressions of popular piety, such as devotional confraternities, virtually ceased to exist. Church precepts were more loosely observed by the popular classes, while the faith of the professional élite cooled. As the insurrections of 1837–8 neared, popular fervour was channelled into mass movements pressing for fundamental constitutional and social change. Because of their attachment to 'legitimate authority', religious leaders were increasingly isolated from the rest of the population.

The crushing of the insurrections, however, marked a new era in religious practice. In the atmosphere of despondency that hung over French Canada, church leaders reached out to the Patriotes, actively seeking reconciliation. These former enemies joined together several months later in an unsuccessful campaign to defeat the projected Union of the Canadas, which was widely expected to sound the death knell of the French-Canadian nationality. This agitation introduced church leaders to the strategies of mass mobilization perfected a few years earlier by the Patriotes. Through its actions, the Catholic Church was rehabilitated as a national institution.[19] To a people who had suffered the defeat of their revolutionary aspirations, it offered hope in the form of an alternative vision of national development: one that would not run afoul of the established authorities and would make the French Canadians a truly distinct people in North America. Religion was to be the vehicle of this distinctiveness. But unlike the traditional religion, this one would see personal spirituality find its ultimate expression in mass movements.

The church's vision was sustained by the rise of Ultramontanism in Europe. Under the authority of the papacy, the Holy See was seeking to centralize ecclesiastical power in Rome, instil uniform liturgical and devotional practices throughout the Catholic world, emphasize Catholic dogmas in opposition to Protestantism, and impose ideological conformity based on a rejection of revolution and liberalism. Although Ultramontanism spread to Catholic populations throughout Canada, the Ultramontane program was especially well suited to the new social, political, and cultural realities affecting French Canada in the Union period.

Popular piety

In the religious revolution that followed the 1841 Union, piety in French Canada became Roman.[20] It was more fervid, ostentatious, and public; it expressed itself more often than in the past and in a myriad of different ways. Women were at the centre of this devotional revolution, supporting it through assiduous practice. Many devotions were specifically directed to them and they transmitted the new piety both in the family and in the schools. Indeed, the trend towards female primary-school teachers, a key factor in the spread of mass education during this period, was a powerful stimulus to the religious revolution.

Although unaffected by the insurrections and the Union, Acadia was also swept up in the devotional upsurge. Religion had been a focal point of communal life after the Deportation of 1755–63. Despite the organization of Maritime Catholicism under prelates of British origin, a process largely completed by the 1840s, a number of Acadian communities were served by French-speaking religious from France, Quebec, or Acadia itself, who encouraged the spread of Roman devotions. They found fertile ground among a people who, like their French-Canadian cousins, were engaged in a struggle for cultural survival and expansion. In ethnically homogeneous areas of Acadia in particular, the family, the parish, and, where possible, the school transmitted the new practices. This pattern was replicated among French-Canadian emigrant communities throughout Canada and the United States. Although not all French Canadians outside Quebec had access to their own parishes and schools, where such institutions did exist, Roman spirituality flourished. As a result, most French Canadians shared a common religious expression wherever they might find themselves in North America.

Some practices dating from the time of settlement, such as the erection of wayside crosses, were revived;[21] others, including devotions originating in Counter-Reformation Europe, were introduced. These focused mostly on the central figures of Christianity, Jesus and, especially after her apparition at Lourdes in 1858, his mother Mary. Frequent public recitation of the rosary was particularly stressed. Some pastors gave lengthy meditations on the life and sorrows of Jesus or Mary during recitations in church. One popular object of veneration was the Blessed Sacrament. The Forty Hours devotion, begun in sixteenth-century Italy, took hold in Montreal in 1850 and within twenty years had spread throughout the province.[22] A particularly baroque variation of the latter was the Perpetual Adoration of the Blessed Sacrament, in which members of a confraternity took turns worshipping the host twenty-four hours a day, every day of the year.

Among the many religious communities that came to Canada after the Union were some that specialized in particular devotions. The Redemptorists fostered the veneration of St Anne; for the Holy Cross Fathers it was St Joseph; for the Oblates, the Virgin; for the Franciscans, St Francis and St Anthony; for the Precious Blood Sisters, the Passion of Christ. Private expressions of such devotions often included reciting special prayers, wearing a scapular, or displaying images of the object of veneration in one's home or workplace. Prominent or wealthy French Canadians obtained from the Holy See the favour of a private altar in their homes. Public displays involved celebrations of the saint's day or month, processions, novenas, and pilgrimages. Such activities were reinforced by the founding of confraternities, sodalities, and other such associations encompassing people sometimes of similar, sometimes of different, ages, genders, trades, and social or regional origins.

Actively encouraged by the Holy See throughout the Catholic world, the devotional revolution was by no means peculiar to French Canada. But whereas in the rest of Catholic North America this phenomenon found expression in ethnic sub-cultures, in Quebec it became an intrinsic part of the majority culture. This process was set in motion by a series of revivals initiated by Charles de Forbin-Janson in 1840–1.[23] A reactionary French aristocrat, named bishop of Nancy by Charles X, Forbin-Janson was forced to flee from his diocese during the July Revolution of 1830. He was a tall and elegant man who possessed extraordinary oratorical abilities, irrepressible energy, and a keen sense of theatre, which he put to good use both in France and in North America.

Assisted by teams of priests who heard confessions and gave communion to thousands of people, the French prelate preached at retreats in Quebec City, Trois-Rivières, Montreal, Ottawa, and their surrounding areas, as well as in Acadia. Possessing 'a marvellous knack for capturing the imagination and profoundly stirring the heart by impressive ceremonies',[24] Forbin-Janson made sure that every aspect of his missions was minutely planned. His powerful sermons focused on the depravity of sin, the catharsis of conversion, and the joy of salvation. Abandoning their normal lives for days at a time, the faithful often travelled considerable distances, staying in strangers' homes or camping in barns. No doubt the fact that such experiences were a dramatic departure from everyday routines heightened their emotional intensity. Conversion was not simply a personal matter but a mass event, finding expression in public reception of the sacraments and pledges to join temperance societies. In Montreal it took four priests two hours to give communion to the women of the parish following one of Forbin-Janson's retreats; in Trois-Rivières 10,000 people committed themselves to temperance; and a similar number crowded the churches of Quebec City to hear sermons given twice a day for two weeks.[25]

The Forbin-Janson missions were designed in part to counter the proselytizing efforts of Protestant evangelists. It seems no coincidence that Terrebonne, already the target of colporteurs and the site of the first French Protestant school (founded in the 1830s), was the first stop on the French bishop's tour of the Montreal area; or that the retreats preached in the district of Montreal ended with the erection of a 100-foot cross atop Mont Saint-Hilaire on the south shore of the island—a cross that would have been visible to Grande-Ligne and the Protestant communities that had begun to sprout on the south shore of the St Lawrence.

Not one to underestimate the importance of spectacle in rekindling religious sentiment, Bishop Ignace Bourget of Montreal continued these regional missions in his diocese after Forbin-Janson's departure. Clearly, though, the parish clergy could not keep pace with the strenuous physical and emotional demands that such revivals placed on them. The coming of the Oblates in 1841, a French community recently founded to re-Christianize the masses after the ravages of the French Revolution, relieved parish priests of such duties. Eventually, religious communities that specialized in conducting retreats, such as the Redemptorists and Assumptionists, as well as the Dominicans and Franciscans, would see to it that the flame lit in 1841 continued to burn.

Bourget capitalized on the popularity that temperance campaigns suddenly acquired in the 1840s. He and other bishops recruited charismatic clergymen, including the same Charles Chiniquy who later became a scourge of the Catholic Church, to preach at mass meetings modelled on retreats. Between 1848 and 1851 Chiniquy's powerful sermons prompted some four hundred thousand people in Canada East to sign the pledge. Those who promised to foresake their addiction to alcohol were given large black crosses which they proudly displayed in their homes. Local temperance societies proliferated all over French Canada under the leadership of parish priests.[26]

Liturgy was essential in sustaining the new spirituality. Bishop Bourget considered it so important that he spent the better part of two years in Italy, studying Roman liturgical practices. He published a voluminous work on the subject and then pressured his episcopal colleagues to reform Quebec's liturgy so as to reflect the Roman model in every detail. 'The faithful are wonderfully uplifted by the splendour of divine worship since it is conducted as much as possible according to Roman forms,' he reported to the Holy See in 1863.[27] The conservative press often commented on the magnificence of religious ceremonies in the diocese of Montreal. Planning his ceremonies down to the smallest detail, Bourget is even said to have taken time from his frenetic schedule in order personally to instruct young mass attendants in the new practices. Every aspect of worship was designed to make it a sensuous experience: candles, flowers, sumptuous vestments, incense, music, rich ornaments, and elaborate ceremonials heightened religious sentiments. This form of worship set French Canada apart from the rest of North America where, even in Catholic churches, a less elaborate liturgy prevailed.

Nor were ceremonies confined to the churches: processions brought religion into the streets. Popular spectacles meant to affirm the community of faith, they afforded French Canadians the opportunity to appropriate spaces dominated either demographically (as in Montreal in the 1840s) or economically (as in Quebec City and Trois-Rivières) by the British. Naturally Protestants were not pleased, but Bishop Bourget disregarded their objections as well as calls to caution and austerity by the Sulpicians, who did not want to offend the British majority's sensibilities.[28] Processions were also a visible sign of the order and authority of the Catholic Church. Each participant had an assigned place: children wearing their Sunday best or special costumes (some of which could be highly theatrical), the female and male members of confraternities with their banners and insignia, the church band and choir, members of religious communities, and finally the presiding clergyman. Spectators lining the streets or from their flag-bedecked balconies joined in the prayers and hymns.

In addition to Sunday worship and the feast days that marked the liturgical calendar, special occasions were used to strengthen the people's bonds to their religion. The return of a diocesan bishop from the Holy See, the arrival of a relic from Rome, or a visiting ecclesiastical dignitary would be an occasion to celebrate. Thousands of people flowed into the streets to witness events such as the magnificently stage-managed departure of the zouaves who left Montreal in 1868 to defend Rome against the forces of Italian unification,[29] the crowning of the statue of Notre-Dame-du-Cap in 1904, the opening of the Plenary Council of the Canadian Church in 1909, and the Eucharistic Congress the following year.

Statues, images, and relics were tangible objects of veneration that reinforced ties between French Canada and Rome; indeed, a number of Italian artists, some in Quebec, some in the home country, filled artistic commissions for parish churches. Contacts were also developed between local clergymen and dealers in the relics purportedly found in Roman catacombs during the extensive excavations carried out during the first half of the nineteenth century. A pastor on the Île d'Orléans brought his parishioners a relic of Philomena, a saint 'discovered' earlier in the century who caught the imagination of the entire Catholic world. And the rector of a parish near Trois-Rivières, Calixte Marquis, was a redoutable stalker of relics; he returned from Europe with no fewer than 6,200 of them, including the forearm of St Anne, a fragment of which he donated to the shrine of Ste-Anne-de-Beaupré.[30]

Relics attracted pilgrims and pilgrimages became an integral part of the devotional revolution. Wealthy patrons and even some parish priests visited such centres of devotion as Lourdes, Rome, and Jerusalem. The majority of French Canadians, however, made their pilgrimages at home. After falling into near ruin, old shrines, such as Notre-Dame-de-Bonsecours in Montreal and Notre-Dame-des-Victoires in Quebec City, were refurbished in mid-century. In addition, new centres of pilgrimage soon emerged. The high point was reached in the decade after 1873, when twelve shrines were established out of a total of twenty for the entire century. These reflected the spirituality promoted by the Holy See at the time: six were dedicated to the Virgin; two to her husband, St Joseph; three to her mother, St Anne; and one to the Sacred Heart of Jesus. It was no coincidence that this last shrine, intended for the atonement of all the affronts directed against Jesus, was situated near the French Presbyterian residential school at Pointe-aux-Trembles. Very few of these pilgrimage centres honoured particular saints outside of the Holy Family. Mary, in her many guises, dominated the devotional landscape of the second half of the nineteenth century.[31]

Interest in pilgrimages did not emerge spontaneously among the faithful: to some extent it was orchestrated by the clergy. There are examples of enterprising, if not entrepreneurial priests who built not only vast shrines, but the transportation facilities they required to attract the faithful, such as docks and railway stations. Two particularly successful clerical promoters of shrines were Luc Désilets and Calixte Marquis. Though sworn enemies in the complex ecclesiastical politics of the day, they had very similar ideas when it come to firing the popular imagination.

At Cap-de-la-Madeleine, construction of Désilets's new parish church could not begin in the winter of 1877–8 because the St Lawrence did not freeze over that year and building materials were stranded on the opposite side of the river. Prayers were said before the statue of the Virgin and Désilets promised her that the old church would not be torn down if she intervened. Suddenly, late in the season, when the thaw usually occurred, an ice bridge formed and held for a week, just long enough for materials to cross the St Lawrence. A few years later, the same statue opened its eyes to Désilets and two colleagues whose fortuitous presence allowed them to corroborate his story. As a result, Notre-Dame-du-Cap could be promoted as doubly miraculous, and it fast became the largest pilgrimage centre in North America.

Marquis's relics, for their part, were said to have produced two miracles in New York on their way to Quebec from Europe. In 1898, when his shrine at St-Célestin was being built, workers were in need of water for their construction materials. But the nearby well contained only mud, and the labourers returned empty-handed. Unperturbed, Marquis ordered them to return to the site, where this time they found water as pure as a crystal spring. From then on, this water was used only for curative purposes.

In order to flourish, however, a pilgrimage centre needed the unflagging activity of priests dedicated to publicizing its attractions. In fact, many of the *Annales*, or monthly bulletins put out by various shrines, had larger circulations than the most popular daily newspapers. Clerical publicists often embroidered the original wondrous stories connected with the centre's establishment, recounted miracles occurring there and elsewhere through the saint's intercession, and generally kept up the faithful's devotion to the saint. Shrines were also promoted through the sacred oil or water that was distributed to pilgrims seeking cures of one sort or another: hence the importance of natural springs in close proximity to the pilgrimage site. The more successful shrines also developed what can only be described as theme parks reproducing famous places or objects of veneration, such as the grotto of Lourdes, the *Scala Santa* (the marble stairs from Pilate's palace that Jesus is said to have descended after his condemnation to death), or life-size stations of the cross. Since management of the shrines attracting the most visitors was beyond the physical and material resources of individual priests, the most successful ones were taken over by religious communities. Ste-Anne-de-Beaupré (founded 1658), Notre-Dame-du-Cap (1883), and St Joseph's Oratory (1904) attracted hundreds of thousands of pilgrims not only from French Canada but from all over North America.

In some instances the church hierarchy actively encouraged the veneration of a particular saint, as when in 1877 it proclaimed Saint Anne the patron saint of Quebec. Similarly, the Jesuits prompted the Iroquois at Kahnawake to venerate the seventeenth-century Mohawk Kateri Tekakwitha, in order to hasten her beatification in Rome. A shrine might attract pilgrims because Rome or the local bishop bestowed indulgences upon the faithful praying there. Yet pilgrimages were not simply the result of clerical manipulation. Even if the meaning that pilgrims attached to such devotions remains unclear, and we can only speculate about motivations and the extent to which these coincided with the clergy's expectations, pilgrimages were clearly a popular phenomenon.[32]

Institutional support for popular piety

The devotional revolution was reinforced by the increasingly complex institutional network controlled by the Catholic Church. No doubt the most fundamental institution in this regard was the parish. While its importance in rural French Canada has long been recognized, the function it served in the cities has been much less clear. A recent study, however, has highlighted the crucial role it played in acculturating the thousands of rural migrants who moved to urban areas each year in search of a better life. A variety of devotional societies, together with numerous religious and more broadly social services dispensed by urban parishes, helped to cushion the shock of an alien environment. The parish provided a high degree of social and cultural cohesion, a link with the rural past, and a structure that eased the process of integration into city living.[33]

Beyond the parish level, the church came to play an ever more prominent role in public education, hospital care, and social services, as well as in some economic and professional organizations. This was in sharp contrast to the increasing secularization of other Western societies, where such responsibilities were assumed either by the state or by private institutions. Nevertheless, the degree of institutional completeness[34] that French-Canadian communities enjoyed under the aegis of the church varied widely. Certainly in Quebec's urban centres the fullest range of social and cultural services was available. Rural dwellers, however, tended to be less advantaged.

The situation was even worse outside Quebec, especially in the field of education. Catholic schooling was restricted in various ways in all three Maritime provinces around the time of Confederation, as well as in Manitoba and the Northwest at the turn of the twentieth century. In the Prairies and Ontario the use of French in public life and in schools was almost completely eliminated in these latter years. Only in the ethnically homogeneous areas of New Brunswick could Acadians boast levels of service similar to those enjoyed in rural Quebec. Elsewhere the availability of services depended on restrictive provincial legislation and the ethnic allegiance of the local bishop—which helps to explain why episcopal succession became such a hotly debated issue in this period. In most ethnically mixed communities, it became increasingly difficult for French Canadians to develop their identity within institutions that they could call their own.

Inside Quebec, by contrast, the role of the church in education was unequivocal, and female religious communities were particularly important in this regard. The Sisters of Providence and the Grey Nuns established a number of day-care centres in the latter half of the nineteenth century, largely to help working-class parents earn a family wage. In Montreal over 60,000 pre-school children attended these centres in the years 1858 to 1922. Inspired by modern European principles of child-care—though these had to be diluted over time because of over-crowding—nuns instilled in their charges the importance of prayer, introduced them to Bible stories, plied them with holy pictures, and promoted loyalty to the papacy: to this end, one kindergarten even re-enacted a battle between papal zouaves and Garibaldi's forces.[35]

Religious instruction began in earnest in the primary grades, since children had to know the catechism by heart before making their first communion at the age of ten. Hence parish priests became active promoters of public instruction, often chastising parents for lack of interest in their offspring's education and threatening to deprive children of first communion unless they went to school. The first Council of the ecclesiastical province of Quebec sought to institute a common catechism in 1851. But Bourget, the instigator of the idea, considered the new *Petit catéchisme de Québec* to be too vague, unintelligible to children, and ill-adapted to a country with a Protestant majority. His proposal to amend it caused such a stir in the episcopate that Rome had to intervene to restore order. Finally Louis-Nazaire Bégin, future archbishop of Quebec, produced a catechism that was adopted in 1888 and continued in use until 1951. This version was very close to the Baltimore catechism, used by Catholics throughout the United States.[36] In the archdiocese of Ottawa at the turn of the century, the catechism was taught in school twice a day, mornings and afternoons. Archbishop Thomas Duhamel reported that children also received religious instruction at church on Sunday afternoons, during *la belle saison* in the countryside, and throughout the year in the urban areas.[37] Parish priests provided intensive instruction in the weeks before the children's first communion.

In the late nineteenth century, approximately two-thirds of male and one-quarter of female teachers in Quebec were religious. It is not surprising, then, that schools served as vehicles for the new piety. Apart from the prayers that began and punctuated the day, students were introduced to particular devotions at special times of the year in the hope that they would continue such practices throughout their lives: October was dedicated to the Rosary, November to the dead, March to St Joseph, and May to Mary. During the month of Mary, teachers in some rural areas led their classes to wayside crosses which they would adorn with flowers.[38] After 1905, when Pope Pius X lowered the age for first communion from ten to six and urged frequent reception of the sacraments, children were encouraged to attend mass and benediction, as well as to take communion on the first Friday of the month in honour of the Sacred Heart. Schools also became recruitment centres for pious societies such as the Children of Mary, through which students were introduced to the life of confraternities.

In convent schools and academies, which catered not only to the daughters of the wealthy but to farm and working-class girls as well, religious instruction continued to be an important component of the curriculum, accounting for two-and-a-half to four hours per week. In the archdiocese of Ottawa, French catechisms such as those by Jean-Joseph Gaume and the Abbé Ambroise Guillois were in use at the turn of the century. On a more personal level, each student had a spiritual director, made an annual retreat in the fall, and received the sacraments at least once a month before Pius X's reforms promoting their more frequent reception.[39]

The regimen in the *collèges classiques* was even more exacting. Founded to prepare young men for the priesthood, these university-level residential establishments in fact became training-grounds for French Canada's professional élite. Students spent eight years under the constant surveillance of teachers who throughout the nineteenth century tended to be young ecclesiastics preparing for ordination. Although courses in religion or theology were not offered, church history, doctrines, discipline, and practices found their way into the curriculum, and in most institutions, attending mass and reciting the rosary were daily obligations. Young men were encouraged to examine their consciences frequently and to develop other forms of private and public spirituality. Sundays were largely taken up by high mass, vespers, and benediction. The *collèges* discouraged contact with the outside world: students were allowed to see their parents only once a week; correspondence was received and read by the superior of the *collège*; newspapers were generally forbidden; and relations with the opposite sex were limited to the immediate family.[40] This regimen would also apply to the first *collège classique* for women, the École d'Enseignement Supérieur pour les Filles, when it opened in 1908.

At the beginning of the twentieth century, the *collèges* were fertile ground for the development of Catholic Action, a concept that originated in France with social Catholicism. Especially after the Paris Commune of 1870, which had pitted workers against the forces of social conservatism, including the Catholic Church, this movement tried to develop concrete responses to the economic, social, and political problems of the modern world through the application of Christian principles rather than secular ideologies. Catholic Action was introduced to French Canada by the Jesuits, who wanted the public sphere—the world of politics, work, and public morals—to reflect the spirituality of the devotional revolution. They responded to the new secularism by creating *cercles d'étude* (study groups) for serious students in order to deepen their spirituality, their consciousness of contemporary problems, and their commitment to change. These groups were the forerunners of the Association Catholique de la

Jeunesse Canadienne Française (ACJC), launched in 1903. The event was made to coincide, fittingly, with the inauguration in Montreal of a monument to Bishop Bourget, who had died in 1885 and was regarded as a champion of Catholic Action. Nor was the role of women ignored in the crusade for the Christian regeneration of industrial society: the first women's *collège*, although not under the Jesuits' direction, also had its study group.[41]

Apart from education, the church also controlled a wide range of institutions, including foundling homes, orphanages, and hospitals; institutes for the mentally and physically disabled, the destitute, the aged, and the infirm; and shelters for prostitutes and unwed mothers. In fact, Quebec had the highest level of institutional care in Canada at the turn of the twentieth century.[42] Religious communities also provided direct service including home visits to the sick, the needy, and the dying; they distributed food, clothing, and money to the indigent in their homes, visited prison inmates, and provided job information. The number of religious engaged in these activities, most of them women, multiplied by thirteen between 1840 and 1871 in response to the new social context created by industrialization.

Generally, those who dispensed such services considered religion to be, if not a cure, at least a consolation for affliction, and reminders to that effect were never far away. Encouraged to keep themselves occupied, the female inmates of some establishments made scapulars, rosaries, reliquaries, and other articles in support of the devotional revolution. People requiring home care received comfort and admonishments couched in spiritual terms, as well as edifying literature and objects of piety. While it seems improbable that anyone was refused help because of religious indifference, the quality of care in some cases did depend on evidence of good morals.[43]

Despite the growing clericalization of society, the extension of the church's institutional control was also actively encouraged by a significant number of lay people in accordance with their social rank. Wealthy diocesans, for example, contributed large sums to many of Bishop Bourget's projects. The man familiarly known as his finance minister, businessman Olivier Berthelet, gave more than $500,000, an astronomical sum in the nineteenth century, to various works for the poor. There is hardly a religious community in Montreal that did not benefit from his generosity. Berthelet's sister Thérèse was an equally active philanthropist, as was his son-in-law François-Alfred-Chartier LaRocque. The Jesuits, for their part, were assisted in their educational works by a businessman and philanthropist of Italian descent, John Donegani. Lay women were indispensable in the founding and expansion of female religious communities dedicated to the care of the more vulnerable members of society. The 'complicity' between nuns and feminists, observed by historians studying the early part of the twentieth century,[44] was rooted in an older tradition. As the early history of the Sisters of Providence shows, lay women offered administrative acumen to their sisters in religion, organized bazaars to help pay for many of the charitable works, and financially supported some of the inmates of these establishments. In the archdiocese of Ottawa, volunteers belonging to the St Elizabeth and St Jerome Emiliani societies gathered twice a week in the fall and winter at the Hôpital-Général to sew clothes for the poor. The archbishop proudly reported that in 1885 their work helped out 175 needy people.[45]

The St Vincent de Paul Society, founded in France in 1833 by Frédéric Ozanam, was another important manifestation of the laity's collaboration with church. Sections of the Society were established in Quebec City and Montreal in the the late 1840s and were based on the parish. Made up mostly of workers, the organization was involved in a wide range of activities. Members founded savings banks to 'teach the poor to save' their earnings. Following St Vincent's own example, they lobbied for prison reform and worked to rehabilitate prisoners and delinquents. They also provided funds for a number of hospitals and social-service institutions, with which they worked closely, and cared for and educated homeless children. Fifty years after its establishment, the Society had 5,000 members and more than one hundred sections in Canada.[46]

If the church wished to remain a pivotal institution in French-Canadian society, however, new forms of social intervention were required, forms suggested by industrial society itself. The papal encyclical *Rerum Novarum*, published in 1891, encouraged such activity. In calling for the establishment of a new Christian social order based on justice and co-operation among the social classes, Leo XIII sought to reverse the de-Christianization of the European working class. Beginning with Archbishop Bégin's arbitration of the strike by Quebec City shoemakers in 1900, the church made sporadic attempts to come to grips with industrial society. There was an awareness that a new social order would not come about by papal fiat but by organizing—as workers were already doing. Yet the very nature of trade unionism presented obstacles. In the church's eyes, unions were based on materialism and class antagonism, principles that stood in conflict with *Rerum Novarum*'s objectives. In addition, they brought Catholics into contact with Protestants, and it was feared that such contact would encourage religious indifference. Hence new forms of workers' associations were required. Priests who had studied in Europe and had some familiarity with social Catholicism led the way, forming groups of clergymen and workers to study the workplace and its problems from a Christian perspective. In the first decade of the new century, some of the unions that had been excluded from the Trades and Labour Congress in 1902 associated themselves explicitly with the church and requested chaplains. These clerics in turn formed more study circles. Together with voluntary organizations such as St Vincent de Paul Society, study groups of students and workers inculcated values conducive to industrial society, including thrift, diligence, self-discipline, and punctuality.

The Jesuits gave a focus to all this disparate activity when in 1911 they founded the École Sociale Populaire for the study and spread of social Catholic doctrine. Nevertheless, social Catholicism still needed a mass base, and it was the young Jesuit Joseph-Papin Archambault who suggested the means of developing it: the closed retreat. Intense spiritual exercises conducted by clerical mentors and directed at lay men and women of similar social or professional backgounds who lived together for three to seven days away from their work and home, usually in bucolic surroundings, such retreats attracted an estimated 60,000 people between 1909 and 1923. Among them was Alfred Charpentier, future president of the Confederation of Canadian Catholic Labourers, founded in 1921 in Hull, Quebec. Through Archambault's efforts, Charpentier and other labour leaders met with trade-union chaplains and clerical activists, studied social Catholicism, and 'converted' to Catholic unionism.[47] Other groups were organized along similar lines: travelling salesmen, for instance, formed the Association des Voyageurs de Commerce under the guidance of Samuel Bellavance and other Jesuits. In this way the church exercised a considerable influence over such apparently secular organizations as trade and other professional unions, student associations, and women's groups.

Clearly, then, the Catholic Church had a massive presence in French-Canadian society. The question that remains is how faithfully people actually practised their religion. It cannot be answered in full without taking into account such factors as class, gender, and region, and research to date does not allow for a very sophisticated reply. We do know that the revival inaugurated by Forbin-Janson produced results over the long term. Statistics from the Montreal area indicate that whereas only 60 per cent of the faithful performed their Easter duty in 1836, that number rose to 95 per cent in 1881. This growth was almost linear over time, and the figures in other parishes are equally high.[48] Of course, receiving the sacraments once a year was the minimum required to remain a member of the church. Nevertheless, Henri Smeulders, a papal envoy sent to Quebec in 1883, gave a favourable report: 'How strong is the faith in the heart of the Canadiens', he wrote, 'how great is their attachment to the Holy See.' Some twenty years later, the first permanent apostolic delegate to Canada, Diomede Falconio, was impressed by the depth of faith that characterized the laity and observed: 'In general, these are truly practising Catholics.'[49]

On the other hand, many observers over time pointed out the laity's general ignorance of church dogma. Protestant proselytizers in the 1840s and 1850s claimed that French Canadians personally shunned theological debates and were unprepared to defend Catholic teachings on the virgin birth or the existence of purgatory, or the practice of granting indulgences.[50] At the beginning of the twentieth century, Archbishop Falconio, the apostolic delegate, reported in a similar vein that the Irish, while less demonstrative in their faith than the

French, were better able to defend their church against attacks on its doctrines. Another outside observer bluntly added: 'Faith looks a little like superstition in the lower classes and is very superficial in the upper classes.' He added sombrely: 'It is not strong, the people seem to me to be flighty, their behaviour does not correspond to their godliness.'[51] The fact that the commentator was a member of the Capuchins, the strict branch of the Franciscan order, may help to explain the sternness of his judgement.

But moral and religious laxity drew the ire of parish priests as well. Given that women were generally more assiduous in performing their devotions, such censure was generally aimed at men. In rural areas especially, clerics complained of men who arrived late for mass and left early, stood at the back of the church, went outside for a smoke, or fell asleep during the sermon.[52] In urban and country settings alike pastoral reports invariably deplored their parishioners' love of luxury, inordinate fondness for alcohol, neglect of the laws of fasting, failure to repay debts, and fascination with unedifying forms of entertainment. In many instances, the clergy's admonitions said more about their own rigorism than about the laity's depth of faith or religious commitment. Parish priests tended to have an austere conception of how the faithful should spend their time and money. In the countryside, dances, corn-shucking, and sugaring-off parties were considered occasions for sin, inviting alcohol abuse and intimate contact between the sexes.[53] In the cities, theatres, cinemas, popular newspapers and novels were regularly denounced. The frequency of clerical reprimands clearly indicates that the laity made up their own minds about the way they spent their leisure time.

Nor did they hesitate to challenge the clergy when their own interests were threatened. In every part of French Canada the division of parishes gave rise to fierce disagreements over such issues as property values.[54] Similar confrontations occurred over church taxes and marriage dispensations. Outside Quebec, French-speaking lay men and women often came into conflict with their English-speaking bishops over schools and pastoral care, and at times French-speaking prelates in Ontario and the Prairies even collided with their compatriots over related matters.[55] Such clashes were often exacerbated by financial questions, especially in times of economic downturn.

All over Canada, politics was a frequent subject of contention between French Canadians of every social origin and their clergy. Marginal farmers in Charlevoix county walked out of church in 1876 to protest a Sunday sermon that they regarded as scarcely-veiled political propaganda. On occasion laymen were ready formally to accuse the clergy of political interference. This occurred in a number of counties in Quebec after passage in 1874 of the federal law on undue electoral influence, and even led to court cases invalidating elections in some constituencies in subsequent decades. The 1896 federal election caused unrest in Acadian parishes in the diocese of Antigonish as well as in

French-Canadian areas of Manitoba.[56] Abstract issues such as political freedom were by no means the only reason behind these conflicts. The long arm of patronage reached the remotest communities as well as the highest levels of society, and gave people a stake in ignoring or downplaying the teachings of the church. Parishioners could blithely set aside the Quebec hierarchy's fulminations against Catholic liberalism if they expected that support for doctrinally questionable candidates would bring them material benefits. At times, politicians who failed to win the church over to their side actually encouraged the laity to challenge the clergy's authority.

The stereotype of traditional French Canadians as blindly following their priest's every whim is deeply rooted in the popular mind. The large families that once characterized French Canadians were attributed to priestly admonitions to be fruitful and multiply, while their economic inferiority was seen as the result of the church's teachings against the accumulation of worldly goods. As we have seen, however, in such diverse matters as partisan politics, school and parish questions, manners and morals, they were not simply meek followers of the clergy. In general, French Canadians of all social classes were more than willing to stretch the boundaries separating the spiritual from the temporal realm to suit their interests. In fact, they would not hesitate to fight, challenging ecclesiastical authority before the civil courts or the Roman Curia if necessary. The laity were neither fools nor empty vessels passively awaiting the clergy's direction. They had minds of their own and they did not do a cleric's bidding simply because they were told to.

Does this mean that popular religion in French Canada resembled its European counterpart, a phenomenon that some specialists have set in opposition to the religion of the clergy? Although historians disagree on this question,[57] serious empirical studies are virtually non-existent. Superficially, at least, it seems that religious practice in French Canada was quite orthodox and that pagan vestiges were not an organic part of it. There may certainly have been some affinities between the two: no faith, no matter how divinely inspired, can claim to be totally removed from the archaic roots of religion. Because French Canadians and Acadians lived in an overwhelmingly rural society, at the mercy of the elements, they often turned to prayers and other devotions in an attempt to ward off natural disasters. Similarly, most pilgrimages were made not for some spiritual purpose, but to obtain a temporal favour related to health, well-being, work, or the family.[58] People often used holy water, oils, or scapulars to effect some miraculous change. Religion tended to be immediate and concrete. Yet this spirituality still seems to be far removed from that of the Mediterranean peasant.

The French Canadians' God was immanent. Their religion tended to be more Christ-centred than its Mediterranean counterpart; it was not peopled by powerful mediators, such as village or regional saints, who alone could approach the distant deity. Nor does it appear that for the French Canadians, novenas, pilgrimages, or scapulars would necessarily bring about the sought-after goal; the link between cause and effect was much less immediate than in Mediterranean-style Christianity. The high rates of participation in parish missions, temperance crusades, confraternities, and exercises such as the Forty Hours devotion also suggest that personal improvement occupied an important place in the French Canadians' religion.[59]

Religious communities: Missions and education

In order to sustain the devotional revolution, the church needed a far more sophisticated structure than it had had before the Union of the Canadas. By the 1840s even the British authorities recognized that the day when one bishop could administer the affairs of the Canadian church, with the assistance of priests from the seminaries of Quebec and Montreal and the five female religious congregations, was clearly past. However reluctantly, in 1836 London had allowed the creation of a second diocese, at Montreal. Four years later the British authorities lifted their prohibition on the recruitment of priests and religious in Europe and formally recognized the Sulpician community's property rights, which had been in doubt since the Conquest.

One man who understood the full import of these changes and possessed a vision of what the church's role might be under the new social and political order was Montreal's Bishop Ignace Bourget. The bishop pushed for the creation of an ecclesiastical province that was finally established in 1844 against the wishes of the prelate who became its first metropolitan, the timorous Archbishop Joseph Signay of Quebec. Bourget was also the one who called for the convening of a council of the whole British North American church, which took place, albeit on a reduced scale, in 1851. It was essential for the institution to have such structures if it was to act as an effective body throughout the vast expanse of Canadian territory. The American Catholic Church, by contrast, had held provincial councils on a regular basis since 1829.

It was Bourget who gave impetus to the expansion of religious communities, both male and female, in Canada during the Union period. He personally recruited many from Europe and helped to found Canadian ones in order to meet the new social needs caused by migration, industrialization, and urbanization. Mass education required a rapid increase in the numbers both of teachers and of specialized schools. Bourget placed vocational and special education for boys in the hands of the Clerics of St Viateur, a French congregation. He also brought over teaching communities dedicated to educating the children of the social élite.[60] In the cities, indigence, social deviance, dependency owing to age, health or disability, and calamities such as epidemics and fires were reaching previously unknown levels. The bishop turned to female religious, both foreign and domestic, for social assistance.[61] Bourget also looked beyond his diocese to the missionary church in the vast expanses of the Hudson's Bay Company lands. He persuaded the Oblates of Mary Immaculate to direct the campaign to proselytize the First Nations. Other bishops took advantage of these initiatives by inviting the newly established orders into their dioceses. There is little doubt that wherever they went these communities energized the older ones and gave them a new sense of mission.[62]

In the new climate of religious revival, 57 new female communities emerged between 1837 and 1914. Of the 29 originating in France, 22 arrived around the turn of the twentieth century in reaction to the secularist policies of successive French governments.[63] Of the 26 founded in Canada, 11 were established between 1837 and 1860, during the period of greatest activity, and eight in the decades straddling the turn of the twentieth century; two others originated elsewhere in Europe. The numbers of religious women rose dramatically, from 650 to 13,579, between 1850 and 1920, while the ratio of nuns and sisters to the overall adult female population increased sevenfold.[64] The arrival of some 1,000 nuns and sisters from France at the beginning of the twentieth century, the greatest influx of foreign female religious in French Canada, accounted for part of this remarkable growth.

The numerical increase among religious women outside Quebec was per-haps even more spectacular. In 1850 there were only two communities and 23 religious affiliated to mother houses in Quebec. After the First World War, 27 congregations boasted a total membership of 5,760 women;[65] however, since a considerable number of them were posted in the United States, it is difficult to tell how many worked in Canada outside Quebec. Certainly we know that French-Canadian sisters played a crucial role in the survival of Acadian culture in New Brunswick. Despite restrictions on Catholic education, they worked within the public system and at the same time founded a number of private schools that gave students access to provincial teacher-training in their own language. Had these convents and academies not existed, young Acadians would have been forced to take their diplomas in English, to the detriment of their communities.[66]

Religious women were in the vanguard of the Canadian missionary effort at home and abroad. In 1844 four Grey Nuns left Montreal for Red River. On arrival, after a journey that had required seventy-eight portages, they immedi-ately set to work teaching Métis and native children. This was the beginning of a movement that saw different branches of the order establish schools and hos-pitals throughout the continent. Already by 1867, after an eleven-month trip from Montreal, seven nuns were ministering to the Dene in the Lake Athabaska–Great Slave Lake area. The Sisters of St Anne, established on Vancouver Island in 1858, would eventually extend their missionary endeav-ours to the Yukon and Alaska.[67] Working in the wilderness was in itself an exceptional enterprise for nineteenth-century women. But frontier conditions offered some of them even greater opportunities. In addition to their tradi-tional activities, sisters in isolated regions doubled as doctors, surgeons, den-tists, artists, musicians, carpenters, and fishers. By 1885, there were almost as many religious women (164) as religious men (121 priests and 66 brothers) in Manitoba and the North-West Territories, and as French-speaking settlements of immigrants from Europe and other parts of North America developed, indigenous foundations sprang up alongside the older Quebec communities to meet growing educational needs.[68]

But home missions could not contain the zeal of some women. On their way home to Montreal from Oregon in the early 1850s, four sisters ended up in Chile, where they obtained permission to remain; twenty years later others were working in Ecuador and Peru. At the end of the century others still were active in India and South Africa.[69] Finally, a French-Canadian community specifically created for the conversion of non-Christians was founded in Montreal by Délia Tétrault. In 1909 the first recruits left for China and a short time later the community set up a hospital and a trilingual school (French, English, and Chinese) to serve the Chinese of Montreal.[70] The new ethic associ-ated with these intense missionary impulses was demonstrated by Anne-Marie Florina Gervais, founder of a community created expressly for the conversion of the Chinese, who insisted that proselytism should be respectful of indigenous cultural traditions and wary of Western pretensions to superiority.[71]

In the past, historians tended to regard religious life as an impediment to the development of women's consciousness and their movement out of traditional roles; in the case of French Canada specifically, the tasks performed by nuns and sisters were thought to have blocked lay women's access to the profes-sions.[72] Recent scholarship, however, has considered nuns and sisters as women first and foremost, and according to this view, religious life offered women interesting career possibilities outside of marriage and motherhood.[73] Of course only a minority of sisters tended large institutions, managing big budgets and exercising a degree of administrative autonomy in a society where such activities were normally exclusive male preserves.[74] For every nun active in what was then considered a man's role, there were hundreds of others who provided cheap labour in Quebec's nurturing institutions. But even these women found in religious life job security and stability that they would not otherwise have enjoyed.

In some respects, the apparent autonomy of religious women was limited by the same gender relations that operated in the wider society. A female religious community was subject to the authority of the local bishop, who appointed its chaplain to serve as his eyes and ears in its daily operations. As well, the order's constitution had to be submitted and approved by male bureaucrats in Rome. Nevertheless, when their interests were in jeopardy religious women did not hesitate to question the authority of their male superiors. In 1883, for example, a conflict erupted between the Hôtel-Dieu Sisters and the bishop of Montreal, Charles-Édouard Fabre, over the Sisters' contractual obligations towards a medical school. Goaded on by the archbishop of Quebec, Fabre threatened the Sisters with excommunication if they refused to sever their ties with the institution. The women appealed to Rome and the bishop's arbitrary actions were overturned. Similarly, the superior of the Hôtel-Dieu Sisters in Tracadie, New Brunswick, complained to the apostolic delegate in 1902 that the community's long-serving chaplain, who enjoyed the local bishop's utmost confidence, was meddling in their affairs and undermining her authority. The apostolic delegate ordered an investigation and the chaplain was eventually removed.[75]

Female congregations worked actively with lay women to challenge the rigid division of gender roles. It was against the ferocious opposition of men both inside and outside the institutional church that Sister Sainte-Anne-Marie of the Congrégation de Notre-Dame lobbied successfully to create the *collège classique* for young women. The École d'Enseignement Supérieur pour les Filles, of which she was the first director, included chemistry and law in its curriculum and took a special interest in the social problems arising from industrialization. Students were encouraged to read the writings of French social Catholic thinkers including Lacordaire, Ozanam, and Lammenais. Not surprisingly, many of its graduates were in the vanguard of the movement for social regeneration. Sister Sainte-Anne-Marie went on in 1916 to found a training-school, the Institut Pédagogique, for women teaching at the university level.[76]

Nor were religious women immune from French-Canadian nationalism. The Grey Nuns in Red River regarded Louis Riel, whose sister was a member of their community, as the saviour of his nation.[77] That his cause received powerful support in Quebec likely reflects in part the nuns' close contacts with the mother house in Montreal. Ethnic allegiances bitterly divided many female congregations at the turn of the twentieth century, particularly in Ontario and New Brunswick.[78] French-Canadian nuns and sisters undoubtedly identified with the cause of their compatriots in these provinces, whereas their Irish counterparts believed that the interests of religion required them to accommodate to the British majority. There was an explicit connection between the École d'Enseignement Supérieur pour les Filles and the nationalist clerics Émile Chartier, Philippe Perrier, and Lionel Groulx, who were all on its staff. One of its first graduates, Marie Gérin-Lajoie, was not only thoroughly familiar with the writings of the economic nationalist Errol Bouchette, and the activities of Alphonse Desjardins, founder of the *caisses populaires* (credit unions), but later wrote for the nationalist periodical *L'Action française*.

If nuns and sisters reflected the ethnic tensions of the wider society, did convents also replicate class cleavages, as some historians have maintained? The differentiation between plain and choir sisters is often cited as proof of such social distinctions. While the former attended only certain religious services and performed the more menial tasks in the community, the latter had to be present at all offices and were the only ones who could elect their superiors. However, recent research shows that at the turn of the twentieth century only 20 per cent of all religious women were plain sisters. They represented only a fraction of nuns and sisters of modest birth and educational levels. Whatever the reasons for denying plain sisters a voice or positions of responsibility within the community, they had nothing to do with social or educational status.[79] Class cleavages undoubtedly existed in the convent, but they were not revealed at this level.

The number of men in religious life also increased dramatically after the Union. Whereas in 1840 there were 464 secular and religious priests, in 1920 this figure had risen to 3,263. In the same period the ratio of priests to faithful went from 1:1,185 to 1:578, peaking in 1880 at 1:570.[80] Of course these ratios varied according to area: dioceses in the ecclesiastical province of Montreal were somewhat more favoured than those in the ecclesiastical province of Quebec. It also seems that some regions contributed more to priestly vocations than others. When the archbishop of Ottawa called for the erection of a new diocese at Joliette that would be detached from Montreal and annexed to his ecclesiastical province, Archbishop Fabre countered that it was precisely from that district that his archdiocese drew many of its priests; without it, Montreal would have a deficit, rather than a surplus, of clerics.[81]

Priests in religious communities (regulars) always comprised a mere fraction of the total clergy in Quebec: in 1850, for example, they were only 10 per cent of the total. But by 1920 this figure had doubled. In the same period brothers saw their numbers swell from about 170 to 3,270. Whereas nuns and sisters comprised a minority of female teachers, male religious monopolized higher education in French Canada and accounted for the bulk of men teachers at the end of the nineteenth century.[82] As a result of the French government's secularist policies, male religious life in French Canada took on a distinctly French colouration at the beginning of the twentieth century with the arrival of one thousand regulars and seculars from the republic. Taken together, the total number of religious men (brothers as well as secular and regular clergy) went from 788 to 6,536.

Like their female counterparts, many male religious communities experienced ethnic tensions within their ranks. The problem of Canadianizing foreign-based congregations was particularly acute for the Sulpicians. A community of secular priests, and as such not a religious order, the Sulpicians recruited their members directly from France. They viewed Canadians with a mixture of contempt and suspicion, and discouraged them from joining their ranks. The community's administration was firmly in the hands of Frenchmen throughout the nineteenth and early twentieth centuries. Another community of secular priests, the Jesuits, had been attached to the province of New York since their re-establishment in French Canada in 1842, and French Canadians feared that this structure would lead to the anglicization of several young novices. Belgian control of Quebec Redemptorists and tensions within the Christian Brothers among French, French-Canadian, and Irish members created problems similar to those experienced by the Sulpicians.[83] On the other hand, some communities, such as the Clerics of St Viateur, rapidly established Canadian roots, and as a result were spared such tensions.

Outside Quebec, and not necessarily serving French-Canadian communities, French-speaking priests numbered approximately 870 by 1920, of whom a majority (485) were members of religious orders. If brothers are added to this figure, the number of men in religious life amounts to almost 1,200. The Oblate order accounted for a significant proportion of this total, with 307 members (242 priests and 65 brothers).[84] From their arrival in the Northwest in 1845 to the early years of the new century, the Oblates organized the life of the church both on the Prairies and in mainland British Columbia. Most came from France, although there were also French Canadians and Belgians. Through their control of the episcopate, they recruited priests, brothers, and sisters, mostly from Quebec and Europe. Subject to Rome's approval, they established administrative structures from parishes to ecclesiastical provinces and in addition organized social services, provided spiritual care to Catholic settlers and migrant workers, and acted as missionaries to First Nations.

Indeed, it was this latter aspect of their work that had brought them to Canada in the first place. Oblate attitudes towards the indigenous peoples differed little from those of earlier missionaries. Aboriginals were considered 'savages' not, as Bishop Alexandre Taché explained, because they were inherently barbarous or violent, but because they had no organized social structures, whether religious, political, or economic.[85] As a result, proselytism went hand in hand with persuading native people to abandon their nomadic way of life. The Oblates encouraged them to build permanent settlements and supported the reserve system as a means of achieving this objective. They wanted natives to take up farming or skilled trades and, above all, to send their children to residential schools. The missionaries believed that if aboriginal children were removed from their parents when they were young enough, they could be brought up as whites, without reference to native culture or language. Schools could divest young aboriginals of all that made them socially inferior, including their aboriginal names.[86] They would be Europeanized and eventually made to function normally in 'civilized' society.

This was the missionaries' objective. All too frequently, though, reality intruded into this ideal world. Rather than practice agriculture, for example, many natives preferred to find short-term jobs that brought them into contact with the most undesirable elements of white society. Recognizing the danger in this, the missionaries readjusted their sights and tried to isolate First Nations from the European population, encouraging them to recover the traditional ways of life they had abandoned.[87] In this respect, much has been made of the *réduction* system (known in Spanish as the *congregación*) introduced into a few British Columbia native communities and refined by Bishop Paul Durieu of New Westminster. Modelled on the Jesuit experiment in seventeenth-century Paraguay, this regime has been regarded as a major factor in the destruction of native culture, imposing 'a rigid and totalitarian system of social and spiritual control administered through a network of native church chiefs, watchmen, and spies, all reporting to the priest, who ruled like a monarch over the mission village and its people'.[88] Yet if, once again, a distinction is made between the ideals informing the system and the reality of missionary work, it becomes apparent that the Oblate presence in itself was much less disruptive than was once thought for either the material or the spiritual life of aboriginal people.

The Oblates were certainly part of a process that sought to undermine the identity and culture of the First Nations. But other important factors were also at play, including the prior integration of many aboriginal people into the white man's economy; socially disruptive forces such as epidemics and alcoholism; and government actions, such as the establishment of reserves and the crushing of the Riel uprising of 1885.[89] Although the Oblates co-operated with the government in seeking the assimilation of First Nations, the two parties did not necessarily agree on how best to achieve this goal. For example, in promoting residential schools, the Macdonald government wanted to isolate the children altogether from their parental and linguistic environment. The Oblates may have thought this was a worthy objective, but it proved an obstacle to their primary goal of conversion. They consequently violated government regulations by teaching catechism and printing primers in native languages, and by encouraging frequent contact between parents and students, contrary to their earlier insistence on separation.[90] Like the Jesuits in the seventeenth century, the Oblates came to regard the use of native languages as essential to their proselytizing efforts. Some even published grammars and dictionaries in the languages of the Cree, Blackfoot, Saulteaux, and Assiniboine nations. Thus there were aspects of native culture that missionaries unwittingly preserved.

Still, for the most part missionaries took a condescending view of natives. Father Morice, who ministered to First Nations in the northern interior of British Columbia over the last quarter of the nineteenth century, described these people as debased creatures, more like children than adults, possessing neither the former's innocence nor the latter's mastery of the passions. He concluded that they should be treated with firmness, prudence, and foresight.[91] Missionaries often emphasized the natives' child-like love of the tangible aspects of religion, ignoring the fact that adults of European origin too were attracted by the external manifestations of the Catholic faith. Clearly, though, aboriginal people had their own reasons for accepting or rejecting the new religion. Generally those whose economic situation was stable shunned it altogether during the period in which French-speaking Oblates were dominant. Others adopted it for motives other than spiritual. Some natives bluntly told missionaries that, although they were impressed by the externals of the 'French religion', their economic and political interests led them to adopt the 'English' one.[92] The fact that natives were ordained earlier and more frequently in the various Protestant denominations may also have worked to the Catholic Church's disadvantage. Even among those who did convert, many remained attached to the old ways, resisted sending their children to residential schools, and followed syncretic practices.[93] They also continued to take part in spirit dances and potlatches, to observe ancestral taboos, and to consult shamans. To the missionaries, such behaviour appeared inconstant, unpredictable, frivolous, and shallow.

The First Nations were in effect living in two different material and spiritual worlds. Schoolchildren were instructed in catechism and church history, and made to observe religious obligations. Boys were introduced to devotions such as the Sacred Heart, of which the Grey Nuns were particularly fond, while girls joined the Legion of Mary, and both were encouraged to make novenas. On the first Friday of each month they attended benediction wearing the ribboned medals that marked their particular devotions. Special events were always opportunities for celebration, as in 1915 at the Lake Athabasca convent, when the statue of the Immaculate Conception brought from France many years before was crowned in 1915; in other cases the occasion might be the anniversary of the Grey Nuns' arrival in the Northwest or the jubilee of the local school's founder.[94] Once at home, however, these children joined in their parents' rituals and festivals. Their native identity was effectively reinforced and a tradition of resistance to assimilation developed.

The control of the western church by French-speaking Oblates ensured that immigrant groups arriving at the turn of the century from continental Europe would not have to fight to be served in their language. The local bishops, unlike their American counterparts, made an honest effort to respond to the pastoral needs of Catholics of German, Hungarian, Italian, Polish, Belgian, and Dutch origin. The Ukrainians were a special case because of the distinct rite that their Orthodox ancestors kept in 1595 when they entered into communion with Rome: while a few French-speaking priests changed from the Latin to the Eastern rite, it was only with the appointment in 1912 of a Ukrainian bishop in Canada that these immigrants began to receive adequate pastoral care.[95]

Male religious played a larger and more vital role in the life of French-Canadian communities outside Quebec than within it. Their manpower and financial resources gave them a distinct advantage over individual parish priests in providing spiritual care and community services. The Oblates, for instance, were active not only throughout the old North-West, but in eastern Ontario and western Quebec. In addition to their missionary and parish work, they established and ran the University of Ottawa (chartered in 1866). The Jesuits, for their part, provided quality higher education at the Collège de St-Boniface, an institution serving all Prairie francophones. They did missionary work among the natives and founded a number of parishes in northern Ontario, many of which were eventually ceded to secular priests. But the Jesuits retained some parishes in the major towns and also offered pastoral services to the army of migrant workers who opened up the area to white settlement.[96] In 1913 they founded and ran a *collège classique* in Sudbury that was eventually absorbed into Laurentian University.

The situation was much the same in the Maritimes. The first Acadian *collège classique*, a bilingual degree-granting institution at Memramcook, New Brunswick, opened in 1864 under the Holy Cross Fathers. Its graduates would include many of the lay and religious leaders of the Acadian renaissance that began in the 1880s. The Eudists, a community that fled France in the late nineteenth century, were also key players in Acadian higher education. As well as serving a number of Acadian parishes and doing missionary work among First Nations in northern Quebec, they founded the Université Sainte-Anne at Pointe-de-l'Église, Nova Scotia, in 1890 and a *collège classique* at Caraquet, New Brunswick, a few years later. The initiative for these establishments came from enterprising local parish priests who often met with resistance from their English-speaking bishops. The most famous example of such conflict was the Collège St-Louis-de-Kent, an all-French institution established by the parish priest and closed after eight short years. The plan to create a similar institution at Arichat, Cape Breton, was stillborn, in part because of episcopal opposition. Church-run colleges were vital to Acadian national life because in many places government regulations restricted access to French public education in the name of cultural homogenization.[97]

Ethnicity and conflict

French Canadians and Acadians were the backbone of Canadian Catholicism, never constituting less than 70 per cent of the overall Catholic population in the period 1870 to 1920 and reaching a high of 75 per cent in the 1901 census. In the Maritimes, Acadians were the majority of Catholics by 1920, largely because of their spectacular increase in New Brunswick, where they made up 71 per cent of the Catholic population. In Nova Scotia and Prince Edward Island, Acadians accounted for about one-third of Catholics. In Ontario, French Canadians held their own at 41 per cent of the Catholic population in 1921, and in the Prairie provinces they represented roughly one-quarter of Catholics.[98]

Not only were French Canadians numerically preponderant, but they took the initiative in defining the structure and forms of Canadian Catholicism. The ecclesiastical province of Quebec, which included the Canadas and the Hudson's Bay Company lands, but not the Maritime colonies (the bishops of that region preferred to have a separate province[99]), gave the Canadian church coherence and drive. Seven councils were held between 1851 and 1886, the year in which the dioceses of Quebec were grouped into the separate provinces of Quebec, Montreal, and Ottawa. These synods brought together bishops and theologians who studied questions of dogma, defined discipline, promoted Catholic education, and standardized the liturgy, the catechism, and the religious calendar.[100] After participating in four Quebec synods, the Ontario dioceses, except for Ottawa, established their own ecclesiastical province in 1870, largely at the insistence of the English-speaking hierarchy. That same year, St-Boniface too was detached from Quebec and became a metropolitan see covering all western dioceses except Victoria, which was part of the province of Oregon. Despite these changes, Quebec remained Canada's most active ecclesiastical province, and the only one to hold councils on a regular basis as required by the sixteenth-century Council of Trent.

In addition, French Canadians contributed significantly to the development of the church throughout Canada. The first pastors in a number of parishes outside Quebec, they were also the first incumbents of many dioceses in Ontario and the West. French Canadians in religious communities set up and administered hospitals, schools, and other social-service establishments not only in French-speaking parts of Canada, but in English-speaking regions as well. The prominence and the activism of French Canadians in church matters contrasted sharply with their inferior position in the economic, social, and political realms. As English-speakers, the Irish and Scots bishops of Ontario and the Maritimes felt that they were better suited to represent the interests of Catholicism to the Protestant majority. They resented the association between the Catholic religion and the French language, arguing that English was the means to bring about the conversion of North America and Great Britain, and accused their French-speaking co-religionists of advancing their own narrow (some might have said tribal) interests.

This antagonism did not usually involve inter-communal strife except in areas of mixed population in the Maritimes and in parts of Ontario and the Prairies where communities, frequently French-speaking and Irish, fought to have parishes, schools, and pastors reflect their respective cultures. More often, ethnic conflict took an institutional form. For example, self-consciously Irish ethnic leaders demanded that the University of Ottawa, which had functioned as an English-speaking establishment in the latter part of the nineteenth century, rid itself of its French Oblate administrators and become a national English Catholic institution, like the Catholic University of America in

Washington. The Acadians, for their part, often unsuccessfully fought the Scots and Irish episcopate to obtain the appointment of Acadian pastors to their parishes, the use of French as a language of instruction in their schools, and the publication of pastoral letters and other episcopal documents in French. The hierarchy often responded to these demands with learned discourses on the universality of the church while privately expressing their belief in the futility of perpetuating French as a public language. Undaunted, Acadians raised the question of episcopal nominations, an issue that transcended the Maritimes and divided the entire Canadian Catholic Church. After years of agitation, Acadians finally got their bishop in 1912 when Édouard Le Blanc was named to the diocese of Saint John. The overwhelmingly Acadian diocese of Chatham (later Bathurst), however, had to wait until 1920 to have an Acadian at its head.[101]

The question of episcopal nominations in Ontario set the bishops of Quebec against those from the ecclesiastical province of Toronto. Since the erection of the province in 1870, Archbishop John Joseph Lynch and his suffragans had fought hard to have the diocese of Ottawa, which straddled the Quebec–Ontario border, incorporated into their jurisdiction on the grounds that the nation's capital should have an English-speaking bishop. In response, the Quebec hierarchy pointed out that French Canadians were the majority of the Catholic population even in the Ontario portion of the diocese. The issue became more clearly ethnic when Ottawa was raised to an ecclesiastical province in its own right in 1886, and it came to a head over the succession to Archbishop Thomas Duhamel, who died in 1909. Conceived as a compromise, the appointment of an English-speaker of French-Canadian origin, Charles-Hugh Gauthier, fooled no one, least of all the French-speaking diocesans. Having experienced the same problems as the Acadians in obtaining pastoral and educational services in their language, they demanded episcopal nominations in dioceses where they formed a sizeable portion of the population, namely Alexandria, Sault-Ste-Marie, and London.[102]

At the turn of the twentieth century, episcopal nominations in the West were a particularly contentious issue. Demands grew stronger for an end to the Oblate monopoly of hierarchical appointments as clergy and laymen from diverse ethnic backgrounds argued that French-speaking prelates were ill-suited to oversee the absorption into Canadian society of the immigrants who were flooding into the Prairie provinces. The Oblates were also accused of not catering to the specific needs of their English-speaking flock, notably in Winnipeg. The head of the ecclesiastical province of St-Boniface, Archbishop Adélard Langevin, replied that since English-speaking priests were almost always unilingual, he preferred to recruit multilingual clerics to serve Prairie Catholics, the majority of whom, even in Winnipeg, were not of British stock. Langevin firmly believed that the maintenance of the Catholic religion depended on preservation of the language of origin. Past experience in the Maritimes and Ontario indicated that if episcopal appointments went to English-speakers, Prairie Catholics would be forced into an English linguistic and cultural straitjacket and eventually become Protestant. But the archbishop's hope that all immigrants and their offspring would preserve their native tongues was clearly in vain, and in any case the size and diversity of Catholic settlement in the West were quickly expanding beyond the resources of the Oblate order.

In the event, the ecclesiastical map of the Prairies was completely redrawn in the 1910s and the status of St-Boniface—at the beginning of the decade the seat of a huge ecclesiastical province—declined precipitously. In 1912 Edmonton became an ecclesiastical province encompassing the diocese of Calgary and the vicariates of Mackenzie and Athabaska. When Langevin died in 1915, Regina was raised to archdiocesan status with Prince Albert as a suffragan see. At the same time Rome effectively reduced St-Boniface to half its size by creating the new archdiocese of Winnipeg.[103] One by one, western sees fell away from Oblate hands and were taken over by English-speaking incumbents: Vancouver in 1910, Calgary in 1912, Winnipeg in 1915, and Edmonton in 1920.

When Prince Edward Island joined Confederation, in 1873, there were eight French-speaking and nine English-speaking titular bishops in Canada excluding the diocese of Victoria. By 1920, each linguistic community had seventeen bishops. But this rigorous pursuit of equality in numbers could not conceal the Vatican's sympathy for the argument that English-speakers were better equipped to represent Catholicism. Inside and outside Quebec, Rome followed a conscious policy of excluding from the hierarchy clerics identified as French-Canadian nationalists. At least twice, for example, Philippe Perrier, a close colleague of Abbé Lionel Groulx, was passed over as a candidate for the episcopate. In the case of Édouard Le Blanc, the Holy See appointed a complete stranger to the Acadian national movement as the first French-speaking bishop in the Maritimes. On the other hand, Rome seemed to accept the idea that English-speaking bishops were best able to direct urban sees with large immigrant populations. Between the multicultural vision of the church espoused by French-speaking prelates and the melting-pot model advanced by their English-speaking colleagues, the Vatican opted for the second.[104]

From the very beginning, French-Canadian bishops were in the front-line of defence of denominational and linguistic rights.[105] Nor was it merely ethnicity that determined this course, for in the early years of Confederation French-speakers formed no more than a fraction of the Catholic populations of Ontario, New Brunswick, and the Northwest. At the end of the century, when linguistic rights were being assaulted, these bishops defended the sound principle that children should be given religious instruction in their native language. Yet in English-speaking Canada they were widely depicted as nationalist zealots whose behaviour alienated the Protestant majority and imperilled the position of the Catholic Church in Canada. Concerned about the effects such actions would have on its relations with the Canadian, British, and American governments, the Vatican was inclined to support the stance taken by the English-speaking hierarchy. The latter displayed a general indifference to Catholic rights outside their diocese or region, and most firmly believed that English should quickly become the common language of Catholics outside Quebec. In fact, the Holy See's position hampered the efforts of activist French-Canadian bishops and unwittingly contributed to the erosion of French and Catholic rights in Canada.[106]

The church and French-Canadian society

Clerical intervention in political issues has long been a subject of controversy in French Canada.[107] In the Union years, such intervention was really an extension of the historic antagonism between the church and the Patriote movement. In a number of pastoral letters, for instance, Bishop Bourget publicly condemned the liberal principles espoused by the distinctly French-Canadian anti-clerical party known as the Rouges, which flourished briefly in the greater Montreal area before Confederation.[108] In this, the bishop reflected the belief of Pope Pius IX (1846–78) in the fundamental incompatibility of liberalism and Catholicism, which was widely shared by Catholics throughout the world.

At Confederation the issue took another twist as important elements in the Quebec clergy began to express their frustration with George-Étienne Cartier's Conservatives. In 1871, Bourget and his ally in the Quebec hierarchy, Louis-François Laflèche of Trois-Rivières, openly endorsed the *Programme catholique*, a manifesto in support of conservative principles that had been drawn up by self-professed Catholic journalists during the provincial election campaign of that year. A short time later, in partial reaction against a Quebec bill of 1874 providing for the invalidation of elections on the grounds of undue clerical interference, Bourget persuaded the Quebec hierarchy to write a joint pastoral letter formally condemning Catholic liberalism. The bishop personally repeated this condemnation two years later as a campaign was launched by laymen and clerics opposed to this joint episcopal initiative.[109] Finally, just before the federal elections of 1896, the episcopate issued a joint pastoral obliging Catholics in conscience to vote for candidates favouring the re-establishment of Catholic education in Manitoba.

In Quebec, as elsewhere in Canada, there were partisan clergymen, including bishops, who thought nothing of abusing their office to advance the electoral fortunes of their favourite party. Some Quebec bishops and priests even had close relatives or friends who were leaders in federal and provincial politics. But a distinction must be made between this phenomenon and the Quebec hierarchy's public pronouncements, which appear to have been inspired by a legitimate desire to advance the rights of the church and its members.[110] Bourget's open letter of support for the *Programme catholique* referred to 'the true conservative party'. But if the bishop had simply wanted to back George-Étienne Cartier's Conservatives, he would not have used the word 'true'.[111] Indeed, the manifesto specifically denounced laws on marriage, education, civil registers, and parishes that the Conservatives had passed or refused to amend. In their criticism of education policy, proponents of the *Programme* were referring not only to the extravagant concessions made by the Quebec government to its Anglo–Protestant minority, but to Ottawa's failure to re-establish the Catholic school system abolished by the New Brunswick legislature in 1870.

Most clerics agreed that these measures were inimical to the church's interests, but not all Catholics were willing to do something about them. By promoting the election of avowedly Catholic candidates, the *Programme* was clearly differentiating between the latter and Cartier's followers. Thus the document was directed less against the Liberals than the Conservatives, who were also chastised for not granting an amnesty to the leaders of the Red River insurrection of 1869, Louis Riel and Ambroise Lépine. Many French-Canadian clerics regarded the Métis leaders as defenders of Catholic educational rights in Red River.[112] Bourget for one was so unhappy with the government's policies that in 1873 he seriously considered formally condemning the leading French-language Conservative organ, *La Minerve*, for spreading Catholic liberalism. In fighting the Rouges and Cartier's Conservatives, the bishop was not attacking a particular party, but a set of political principles hostile to the church's interests. Similarly, in the Manitoba Schools Question the church was primarily seeking not to defeat the Liberals,[113] but to get the new government, whatever its affiliation, to restore the rights of Manitoba Catholics to their schools.

The Quebec church's position on intellectual inquiry and freedom of expression has also provoked strong reactions. Attention has focused on Bishop Bourget's handling of the Institut Canadien, a literary society founded in 1844 to promote public learning through lectures, and the establishment of a library and reading room.[114] Although such institutes existed in other parts of the province, only the Montreal society was a stronghold of secularism and liberalism. The bishop pressured Catholic members to withdraw from it in the mid-1850s. While some heeded Bourget's call, a majority steadfastly refused. When further attempts at conciliation failed, Rome placed the Institut's 1868 yearbook on the Index of prohibited books and Bourget took advantage of this action to condemn the society outright. At that point one of its members, Joseph Guibord, died. In light of Bourget's condemnation, the parish priest refused Guibord burial in consecrated ground. Leading members of the Institut fought this decision right up to the Judicial Committee of the Privy Council, the Empire's highest court of appeal, which in 1874, five years after Guibord's death, ordered that his body be interred in Montreal's Catholic

Bishop Laval administering confirmation
in 1676. This ink and wash sketch
(c. 1686) by the Jesuit missionary Claude
Chauchetière is one of ten accompanying
his 'Narration annuelle de la mission du
Sault depuis sa fondation jusqu'à l'an
1686'. 'On donne la confirmation la
1re fois'; ARCHIVES DÉPARTEMENTALES DE
LA GIRONDE, BORDEAUX, FRANCE.
PHOTO: PATRICK ALTMAN.

The Great Feast of the Dead of the Huron
and Iroquois peoples. Illustration from
'Moeurs des sauvages ameriquains' (1724),
by the Jesuit missionary Joseph-François
Lafitau. METROPOLITAN TORONTO
REFERENCE LIBRARY.

'Jesuit Martyrs. Death of Father Antoine Daniel and Father Charles Garnier', c. 1680. A graphic representation of the death in 1648 of Daniel, the first Jesuit killed in Huronia. His colleague Garnier suffered the same fate the next year, although this work depicts the two events as one. LOMMELIN; INK, PAPER; 27.8 CM X 18.3 CM. MCCORD MUSEUM OF CANADIAN HISTORY (MONTREAL)/M2210.

Anonymous, 'Ex-voto of Madame [Angélique] Riverin and her children' (1703). Such paintings, commissioned in fulfilment of religious vows, were a familiar feature of Counter-Reformation piety. PAINTING; 53.5 CM X 61.5 CM; MUSÉE DE SAINTE-ANNE-DE-BEAUPRÉ/1994X.128. PHOTO: GUY COUTURE.

A wayside chapel on the Île d'Orléans, one of many that dotted the Quebec landscape. GOUVERNEMENT DE QUÉBEC, MINISTÈRE DE LA CULTURE ET DES COMMUNICATIONS, DIRECTION DE QUÉBEC/78.96.2(35).

Marguerite Bourgeoys (1620–1700), founder of Montreal's Congrégation de Notre-Dame, one of the several female communities that assumed much of the responsibility for social institutions in New France. NATIONAL ARCHIVES OF CANADA/C8986.

'The Baby Jesus', folk art attributed to Sister Marie Barbier of the Congrégation de Notre-Dame. CENTRE MARGUERITE BOURGEOYS, LES SOEURS DE LA CONGRÉGATION DE NOTRE-DAME, MONTREAL.

The Cathédrale Saint-Jacques in Montreal, built by Bishop Lartigue in 1825. The building in the foreground is likely his residence; to the right, the school he founded. ARCHIVES NATIONALES DU QUÉBEC, FONDS ARMOUR LANDRY/P97.

Joseph-Octave Plessis (1763–1825), Roman Catholic bishop of Quebec (1806–25), the first prelate of the post-Conquest era to have his episcopal status recognized by the British authorities. ARCHIVES NATIONALES DU QUÉBEC, FONDS FAMILLE BOURASSA/P266,S4,P95.

Jean-Jacques Lartigue (1777–1840), Roman Catholic auxiliary bishop (1821–36) and later first titular bishop (1836–40) of Montreal, was known for, among other things, his determined opposition to the liberal ideas of the Parti Canadien. ARCHIVES NATIONALES DU QUÉBEC, FONDS CHARLES PHILLIPS/P148,S2,P20.

Louis-Joseph Papineau (1786–1871),
speaker of the Legislative Assembly of
Lower Canada and Patriote leader, whose
revolutionary politics posed a threat to
both the British authorities and the
Catholic Church in Quebec.
NATIONAL ARCHIVES OF CANADA/C5435.

Jacob Mountain (1749–1825), the first
Anglican bishop of Quebec (1793). His
appointment signalled an effort to
strengthen the Church of England and
limit the influence and prerogatives of the
Catholic Church in Quebec.
THE ANGLICAN CHURCH OF CANADA,
GENERAL SYNOD ARCHIVES,
TORONTO/P7518-29.

The Séminaire de Saint-Sulpice in
Montreal. The figure in the foreground is
a detail of the Maisonneuve monument
on the Place d'Armes. ARCHIVES
NATIONALES DU QUÉBEC, FONDS
ARMOUR LANDRY/P97.

Henry Alline (1748–84). This portrait, based on a description of his physical appearance, was painted by Mrs Eva Scott to commemorate the bicentennial of his death. REPRODUCED BY PERMISSION OF ACADIA DIVINITY COLLEGE (HALIFAX).

Bruin Romkes Comingo, the first Protestant minister to be ordained in Canada (1770). Selected by his fellow Lunenburg settlers, he was ordained by an *ad hoc* presbytery of two Congregational and two Presbyterian clergymen. PUBLIC ARCHIVES OF NOVA SCOTIA/N-3100.

Laurence Coughlan (d. 1784), the Anglican clergyman who introduced Methodism to Newfoundland with his revivalistic preaching among the common folk of Conception Bay. COURTESY DR HANS ROLLMANN.

Peter Jones, or Kahkewaquonaby (Sacred Feathers) (1802–56), Methodist missionary to the Ojibwa. The most famous of the many native contact persons and preachers employed by the Methodists, he was converted at a camp meeting in 1823. PETER JONES COLLECTION, VICTORIA UNIVERSITY LIBRARY (TORONTO).

John Strachan (1778–1867), archdeacon of York (1827) and later first Anglican bishop of Toronto (1839), the leading spokesman for the prerogatives of the Church of England in Upper Canada. METROPOLITAN TORONTO LIBRARY BOARD.

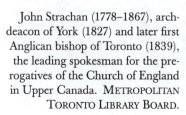

Egerton Ryerson (1803–82),
Methodist preacher and editor of the
Christian Guardian (from 1829).
Ryerson was the nemesis of John
Strachan and the chief proponent of
religious equality in Upper Canada.
METROPOLITAN TORONTO LIBRARY
BOARD.

Thomas McCulloch (1776–1843), the
Secession Presbyterian clergyman
who, as founder of the Pictou
Academy (1816), was the principal
advocate of non-denominational
higher education in Nova Scotia. He
became president of Dalhousie
College in 1838. PUBLIC ARCHIVES
OF NOVA SCOTIA/N1216.

King's College, Windsor, NS. This engraving
by R.W. Rutherford was published in the
Canadian Illustrated News, 8 September 1877.
COURTESY CHARLES DEVOLPI COLLECTION,
SPECIAL COLLECTIONS, DALHOUSIE
UNIVERSITY LIBRARIES (HALIFAX).

In 1820 the Church Missionary
Society sent John West as the first
Anglican missionary to the Red
River colony. PROVINCIAL
ARCHIVES OF MANITOBA, JOHN
WEST I COLLECTION/N221.

William Case, shown here with his
wife, Eliza Barnes Case, formed the
Methodist Episcopal Church in
Canada in 1828. UNITED CHURCH
ARCHIVES, VICTORIA UNIVERSITY
(TORONTO)/76.001P/937 N.

Ignace Bourget (1799–1885), Roman Catholic bishop of Montreal (1840–76) and leader of the Ultramontane revival in Quebec. NATIONAL ARCHIVES OF CANADA/C49514.

The following three scenes are from the International Eucharistic Congress held in Montreal in 1910, from a commemorative volume (*Le XXIe congrès eucharistique international, Montréal*) published the following year.

The papal delegate, Cardinal Vannutelli, and Archbishop Paul Bruchési of Montreal.

Mohawk representatives from Kahnawake.

The Blessed Sacrament in procession.

The Cathedral Basilica of Saint-Jacques-le-Majeur (Marie-Reine-du-Monde), Montreal (1870–94), modelled on St Peter's in Rome and intended by Bishop Bourget as a symbol of Quebec's loyalty to the Vatican. (*Le XXIe congrès eucharistique international, Montréal*, 1911).

Quebec's Premier Maurice Duplessis kisses Cardinal Villeneuve's ring during the Eucharistic Congress of 1938. (*Le premier congrès eucharistique national du Canada*, Quebec, 1938).

At St Joseph's Oratory in Montreal, an invalid is presented to the statue of Notre-Dame-du-Cap, on its way to Ottawa for the Marian Congress of 1947. PHOTO: ROGER ST-JEAN, *LA PRESSE*, MONTREAL.

The Dionne quintuplets, Émilie, Marie, Cécile, Yvonne, and Annette, at the Marian Congress. KING FEATURES SYNDICATE, NEW YORK.

'Camp Meeting Scene', by E.S. Shrapnel, from *Upper Canada Sketches* (1898) by Thomas Conant, reflects the continuing vitality of this form of revivalism in the late nineteenth century. ONTARIO ARCHIVES/S13885.

George Monro Grant (1835–1902), principal of Queen's University (1877–1902), was an advocate of historical criticism and religious toleration. NATIONAL ARCHIVES OF CANADA/C37819.

The best-selling novels of Charles W. Gordon (1860–1937), published under the name Ralph Connor, combined adventure, melodrama, and 'muscular' Christianity.

Salem Bland (1859–1950), one of the more radical proponents of the social gospel, was the author of an influential book entitled *The New Christianity*. UNITED CHURCH ARCHIVES (TORONTO), ACC. NO. 76.001 P489.

Nellie McClung (1873-1951) advanced both the social gospel and the cause of women's rights through her popular novels and many speaking tours. NATIONAL ARCHIVES OF CANADA/ PA30212.

The social reformer and Methodist minister J.S. Woodsworth (1874–1942), at a public meeting. After leaving the ministry on account of his pacifism and persistent doubts regarding central Christian doctrines, he became the first leader of the CCF in 1932. NATIONAL ARCHIVES OF CANADA/C55451.

cemetery.[115] Refusing to have the state dictate his course of action in a matter that was essentially ecclesiastical, Bourget deconsecrated the grave. Little more than a decade later, support for the Institut had dwindled to the point that it ceased to exist.

This incident is merely the most notorious of the Quebec bishops' actions against freedom of expression, which included perennial condemnations of the liberal press.[116] It is important, however, to situate Quebec within the wider Catholic culture. The fact is that the world born of the French Revolution and especially its intellectual dimensions were largely alien to that culture. The encyclical *Quanta cura* and its accompanying Syllabus of Errors, published by Pius IX in 1864, perhaps best symbolize the clash between the church and secular society with their categorical condemnation of a plethora of modern 'isms'. But other papal encyclicals, especially Pius X's *Pascendi* (1907), which condemned Catholic modernism, also helped to create an atmosphere of dogmatism and rigid conformity.[117] Meanwhile, the periodically revised Index of forbidden books set precise boundaries on intellectual investigation by the laity. Especially before the First World War, the Catholic mind was confined to a ghetto that refused to admit advances in many branches of science, literature, or political and social theory. Thinkers who attempted to build bridges to the modern world felt the full weight of ecclesiastical authority. The Catholic Church was then and still is an authoritarian institution. In this sense, then, the Quebec hierarchy's actions were not out of step with what was happening in the broader Catholic world.

In Canada, a country with a Protestant majority, the church certainly did not have the means to prevent intellectual inquiry as such. But it could force those who insisted on the untrammelled pursuit of this right to choose between their intellectual and religious convictions, as it did in its conflict with the Institut Canadien. The choice facing intellectuals was scarcely an easy one: since the first option entailed excommunication, in the overwhelmingly Catholic culture of French Canada it generally meant being cut off not only from the church but from the society. Unlike thinkers elsewhere who crossed that Rubicon, Quebec's aspiring intellectuals tended to opt for outward conformity to their faith. (One might well ask why the supposedly secular intellectuals of the Institut Canadien insisted on burial in a Catholic cemetery.) The forces of religious conformity were bolstered by the Union of the Canadas and Confederation to the extent that these developments left the Church as the sole institutional bulwark of French-Canadian culture.[118] But if such structural constraints explain the general climate making intellectual activity difficult in Quebec, they do not absolve individual thinkers who suppressed or abandoned their cherished ideas. A fair assessment of the issue of freedom of expression must take into consideration both the broader political and institutional context and the timorous nature of Quebec's aspiring intelligentsia.

Certainly the church did play a tangible role in what remained of Quebec's intellectual life. As part of their campaign to counter the influence of liberalism and secularism, the clergy sponsored a number of initiatives directed at the same professional groups attracted to the Institut Canadien's activities, including public lectures, night courses, and evenings of music, literature, and drama. In Montreal, still without a French-speaking university, the 1850s and 1860s saw the founding of various libraries, reading rooms, and literary, historical, and debating societies, as well as newspapers and periodicals. The Sulpicians were particularly active in this regard, although their rivals the Jesuits also promoted a number of similar societies for students. The Séminaire de St-Sulpice founded a parish library in 1844 that soon surpassed the Institut Canadien's holdings, and in the next decade they established the Cabinet de Lecture, housed in a four-storey building (one storey more than the Institut's three) containing an 800-seat lecture hall, a separate library, and a newspaper and periodical reading-room. The Cabinet also had a journal that published, among other things, the lectures presented there.

Needless to say, these activities were heavily circumscribed by the clergy. Parish libraries tended to specialize in devotional literature and saccharine works of edification, of which there was no dearth in the nineteenth century. Church-controlled newspapers offered biased, often totally inaccurate reporting, and lectures at the Cabinet did not allow for discussion. Once again, however, these facts should not be taken out of context. While nineteenth-century Canadian Protestants were fond of contrasting the enlightenment of their culture with the obscurantism of its Catholic counterpart, it is unlikely that local libraries in Ontario and the Maritimes were shrines to scientific and literary innovation either. Nor did the Mechanics' Institutes that flourished in these provinces stray much beyond the local community's values and culture, which tended to reflect conservative religious opinion. Perhaps at this level, then, one person's enlightenment was not so far removed from another's obscurantism.

The problem of creating structures truly transcending the insularity of both cultures is illustrated by the attempt to found a public library in Montreal at the turn of the century. In the absence of a consensus between the two communities about what such a library should contain, the linguistic and denominational structures that had been set in place at the time of the Union, and reinforced by Confederation, prevailed, and the Sulpicians opened a 200,000-volume library to serve the French-speaking Catholic population. The orthodox collection of this institution would certainly not have stifled intellectual inquiry, but it must have had a limiting effect.[119]

The church was a significant player in French Canada's economic and social life as well. Parish priests and their bishops had an immediate interest in the economic development of their local communities. The Quebec clergy lobbied for railways, bridges, public utilities, and the other essentials of an industrial infrastructure; promoted manufacturing, rural credit, and scientific, market-oriented agriculture; participated in municipal councils and school boards; and encouraged cordial relations between capitalists and workers. Acadian priests were no less active in their communities. In the absence of local leadership—and to the dismay of their English-speaking bishops—some were heavily involved in entrepreneurial activities, borrowing and lending money, building gristmills, sawmills, and local factories, and establishing credit facilities for their cash-starved and exploited parishioners. They encouraged co-operatives, and helped to extend agricultural frontiers and expand mutual aid through the all-Acadian Mutuelle de l'Assomption, founded in 1903.[120]

Evidence on the position occupied by the church in the social and economic spheres is still fragmentary and somewhat contradictory. Some ecclesiastical bodies wielded considerable economic and social power. The Sulpicians, for instance, though certainly not a typical community, were seigneurs of the entire island of Montreal and of two large seigneuries in the surrounding area. After the Union freed them from the legal constraints of the British period, the Messieurs, as they were known, zealously pursued their role as large landlords. The Sulpicians' relations with their tenants appear to have been thoroughly hard-nosed and business-like: they went after poor peasants who had evaded paying their seigneurial dues during the difficult 1830s. Yet they were lenient with entrepreneurs who wished to alter their feudal obligations to them. The Sulpicians' close connections with the political élite (George-Étienne Cartier was the solicitor for both the Messieurs and the Grand Trunk Railway) ensured that, when the seigneurial system was abolished in 1854, they were handsomely compensated. The enormous amount of capital accumulated was invested in railways, urban speculation, and other entrepreneurial ventures. Nor was the Seminary alone in courting and being courted by the economic élite. Other male and female religious communities, as well as episcopal corporations, supported and invested in development schemes, particularly railroads, while the Catholic press kept its primarily clerical readership abreast of economic news and served as a vehicle for civic or regional boosterism.[121]

In the diocese of Trois-Rivières there were parish priests who collected tithes from the faithful with the same ardour as the Sulpicians. Although generally avoiding civil suits, these clerics did not hesitate to threaten, cajole, and haggle with their parishioners. For them, financial matters were an important part of parish administration and pastoral care. Some enterprising parish priests, especially in times of scarcity, even speculated on the produce that the faithful gave them in payment of the tithe. In a number of cases, the incomes of pastors were among the highest in their parishes. One estimate suggests that it cost French Canadians more to support their priest and parish council than to administer both the local municipality and the school board.[122] In the relatively remote community of Chicoutimi, the Eudists, like the Sulpicians, apparently applied a double standard to the faithful. They cultivated their relations with local capitalists, showering them with honours and defending their interests, while training the lower orders to be a productive and sober workforce. Strikes and unions were rigorously condemned.[123]

Still, it would be misleading to generalize on the basis of such evidence. Parish income varied widely in Quebec, as did clerical attitudes towards parish debtors. Furthermore, any discussion of income must take into account actual income, as well as expenditures. In Quebec, the tithe owed to the pastor was one twenty-sixth of the wheat harvest or its equivalent. Yet in a working-class Montreal parish run by the Oblates, the tithes actually collected never amounted to more than one-quarter of what was due. At the same time, regular Sunday collections netted only small amounts, since on average only a third of the parishioners contributed. Hence the Oblate province was forced to provide funds to liquidate a debt that threatened to become a permanent burden on the parish. The order also helped to make up the deficit that was accumulating on the local school they established.[124] Similarly, while as seigneurs the Sulpicians received considerable privileges from the French Crown, their obligations were equally extensive. They spent more than any other religious community on social-service institutions, on the communities administering them, and on religious works across Canada and abroad.

Such activities may have helped to keep the lower orders in their place; there is no doubt that the Catholic Church, in French Canada and elsewhere, was intrinsically part of a conservative social order. If oppression were its only role, however, it is not conceivable that French Canadians could have remained so attached to it for so long. In fact, we have seen many examples of the church's efforts to assist the oppressed. Although some of the solutions it proposed may, in hindsight, appear inadequate or ill-advised, the concrete assistance it provided must have helped to create a sense of cohesion and solidarity between the church and its people. No doubt this solidarity helps to explain the centrality of religion in French-Canadian culture.

A PERIOD OF TRANSITION (1920–1960)

French-Canadian population growth was moderated in this period by generally difficult economic conditions (see Table 4.2). Recovery following the First World War was slow, particularly in the primary sector where French Canadians and Acadians were over-represented. As a result, some 130,000 French Canadians and an indeterminate number of Acadians, mostly from Nova Scotia and Prince Edward Island, emigrated to the cities of the United States in the 1920s. But the advent of the Depression brought this movement to an abrupt halt, and in the 1930s even peripheral regions of Quebec witnessed short-lived attempts at agricultural settlement as people sought shelter from the effects of economic crisis. In northeastern Ontario the expansion of lumbering and mining attracted migrants from Quebec and Acadia. In the West, however, the population of French origin experienced not much more than natural increase.

TABLE 4.2: GROWTH AND DISTRIBUTION OF PEOPLE OF FRENCH ORIGIN, 1920–1960 [125]

	1920	1960
Acadians	189,590	354,604
French Canadians		
Quebec	1,889,269	4,241,354
Ontario	248,275	647,941
West	125,455	296,000

Nevertheless, the most striking feature of the period after the First World War was the urbanization of French Canadians. By 1920, a majority of Quebeckers lived in towns and cities, a trend that was clearly irreversible. Although Montreal and its suburbs accounted for an important segment of the urban population, smaller centres in areas connected with key industries such as pulp and paper and hydroelectricity also prospered. The number of Quebec towns with more than 2,500 inhabitants almost doubled in the first thirty years of the century. After the Second World War the rural population of Quebec declined rapidly. This time, it was the large urban centres—Montreal, its suburbs, and, to a lesser degree, Quebec City—that benefited from the massive shift of population away from the countryside. Large-scale urbanization affected all of Canada, not just Quebec, and French Canadians outside the province were also involved in this process.

The two wars stimulated urbanization and contributed significantly to the linguistic assimilation of people of French origin in provinces outside Quebec by inducing them to leave their compact rural settlements for ethnically mixed urban centres. As well, lack of access to French-language education in both urban and rural areas hastened the assimilation of school-age children. In the West, French was proscribed as a language of instruction by the end of the First World War. In the Maritimes and Ontario, education officials regarded bilingual instruction for their French-speaking populations as a transitional step facilitating the minority's acquisition of the majority tongue. Between 1931 and 1961, the proportion of people of French ethnicity retaining their language dropped from 62 per cent to 28 per cent in Nova Scotia and Prince Edward

Island, and from 76 per cent to 33 per cent in the Prairies.[126] In the West, French-Canadian communities that once boasted parishes, credit unions, and schools, even convents, became ghost towns after the Second World War.[127] The French fact remained a cultural reality in very few areas.

On the other hand, as Table 4.3 shows, by 1960 there were marginally more people in Quebec with French as their mother tongue than there were ethnic French Canadians. This discrepancy reflects the absorption into French-speaking culture of both Irish and Scots Catholics and the offspring of an earlier wave of Italian immigrants.[128] Although half a million new immigrants settled in the province between 1945 and 1965, only a tiny fraction of them were French-speaking (44,000 from France and an undetermined number of the 11,000 immigrants from Belgium). Of the 100,000 Italians who settled in Quebec in this period, the overwhelming majority sent their children to English schools.[129] Until the immigration of francophones from the Third World in the 1960s and 1970s and the National Assembly's adoption of the Charter of the French Language in 1977, the French-speaking population of Quebec remained remarkably homogeneous, in terms both of ethnicity and of religion.

TABLE 4.3:	DISTRIBUTION BY FRENCH MOTHER TONGUE (ETHNIC ORIGIN), 1960[130]	
Acadians	261,206	(337,428)
French Canadians		
Quebec	4,269,689	(4,241,354)
Ontario	425,302	(647,941)
West	166,954	(296,000)

THE FLUCTUATIONS OF FRENCH PROTESTANTISM

The 1931 census represented the first attempt in Canada to correlate statistics on religion and ethnicity.[131] In that year there were 76,738 Protestants of French origin in Canada, representing 2.6 per cent of the population of French extraction: 15.5 per cent (12,000) in Quebec, 43 per cent (32,925) in Ontario, and 30 per cent (22,300) in the West. Wherever they resided, the overwhelming majority (over 85 per cent) of French Protestants belonged to the major denominations: United, Anglican, Presbyterian, and Baptist, in descending order of importance. But significant regional variations in membership are evident in this census. Whereas Anglicans were evenly distributed in each region except Ontario, where they were twice as numerous, adherents of the Presbyterian and United churches were overwhelmingly concentrated in Ontario and the west (75 per cent and 80 per cent respectively). Baptists, on the other hand, were strongest in the Maritimes and Ontario (35 per cent in each region), with the rest of their members evenly divided between Quebec and the West.

What accounts for the increase in French Protestants? Their geographical spread seems to support the explanation that French Canadians were so intolerant of converts to Protestantism that these simply left Quebec. French-Canadian Baptists in the province, for example, numbered only 1,135 after almost a century of missionary and educational activity. Yet other factors cannot be discounted. While conversion may have led to emigration, the converse is also true. Indeed, the farther French Canadians and Acadians moved from the Catholic heartland of the country, the greater the proportion of Protestants in their midst became. One-third of Franco-Columbians were Protestant, as were 16 per cent of their compatriots in Alberta and 14 per cent in Nova Scotia, whereas the French Protestant presence in the rest of the Prairies and Ontario was closer to 10 per cent.

Urbanization and intermarriage were also related to the growth of Protestantism (see Table 4.4). Outside the Catholic heartland (including Ottawa) large cities all had much higher percentages of French Protestants than their respective provincial averages. The very high percentages of French Protestants in cities in southwestern Ontario (except for Windsor, which had a French Catholic hinterland in Essex and Kent counties) and British Columbia suggest connections between urbanization, intermarriage, and conversion. In this context, the figures from Kitchener are revealing: fully 44 per cent of French Protestants belonged to ethnic German churches (Lutheran, Evangelical, Mennonite, Brethren).

TABLE 4.4: PROTESTANTS AS PERCENTAGE OF FRANCOPHONE POPULATION, CITIES OF OVER 35,000 INHABITANTS (1931)[132]

City	%	City	%
Halifax	20%	Winnipeg	23%
Saint John	14	Regina	30
Toronto	41	Saskatoon	31
Brantford	57	Edmonton	23
Hamilton	44	Calgary	35
Kitchener	40	Vancouver	39
London	53	Victoria	45
Windsor	10		

Yet it would be simplistic to conclude that urbanization *per se* led to conversion. French-Canadian Catholics were just as urbanized as the overall Canadian population and marginally more so than their Protestant compatriots (see Table 4.5). Whereas Anglicans and Presbyterians were the most urbanized, Baptists were markedly more rural—a reflection, perhaps, of their strength in the Maritimes. On the other hand, members of the United Church, the largest French Protestant denomination, were less urbanized than the Canadian population as a whole. It appears, then, that urbanization outside the Maritimes and the Catholic heartland contributed to both religious slippage and linguistic loss among French Canadians.

TABLE 4.5: CHURCH MEMBERSHIP OF FRENCH CANADIANS ACCORDING TO URBAN/RURAL DISTRIBUTION (1931)[133]

	Rural	Urban
Anglicans	42%	58%
Baptists	53	47
Presbyterians	41	59
Roman Catholics	46	54
United Church	50	50

In Quebec, meanwhile, the institutional foundations of traditional French-Canadian Protestantism were weakening, especially in the field of education. Sabrevois College, the Anglican private school, was closed before the First World War. The consolidation of Protestant school boards on the island of Montreal in 1925 led to the elimination of parish schools and of French Protestant public education in an area where 38 per cent of the province's French Protestants resided. In the same year, church union forced the closing of one of the three private boarding schools in the Montreal area: students at the French Methodist Institute in downtown Montreal were transferred to the former Presbyterian Institute at Pointe-aux-Trembles on the eastern periphery of the island.[134] During the Second World War, the Feller Institute, a Baptist boarding school south of Montreal that already operated as an English-speaking high school,[135] was turned into a camp for German soldiers. Neither institution functioned as a properly French-speaking school in the post-war era, and both ceased operations in the late 1960s.[136] Since 1977, however, the Charter of the French Language, by making French the language of instruction for all but the English-speaking minority, has breathed new life into French Protestant public education.

French Protestant congregations also fared poorly in the inter-war years. The formation of the United Church of Canada led to the absorption of all

French Presbyterian ministers into the new body, leaving the almost 2,000 faithful who resisted union without spiritual leadership. As a result, French-language religious structures were badly undermined, although the infusion of Protestant immigrants from France, Switzerland, and Belgium after the war revitalized the Presbyterian community in Montreal. Elsewhere the church had two small congregations, one in Quebec City and the other in the Eastern Townships.[137] With large-scale urbanization in Quebec, older Baptist and United Church congregations in the Ottawa valley, the Laurentians, the Eastern Townships, and south of Montreal and Quebec City struggled to survive. Some became mission stations served from the larger centres that often received the emigrants from those areas.[138] By the late 1960s the Baptists had eight churches in Quebec, the United Church five, the Presbyterians three,[139] and the Anglicans two, in marked contrast with the sixty-five Protestant churches and mission stations of the early 1900s.[140]

These older denominations still lacked specifically French-Canadian administrative structures. Claude de Mestral noted that when he was installed as a United Church minister in the 1930s in Montreal suburb of Verdun, the ceremony was carried out entirely in English, except for the French hymns sung by the congregation. Only in the 1970s did the United Church create its first French-speaking consistory. Still, closer co-operation among the French Protestant churches became possible in the 1940s with the establishment of a federation of French evangelical pastors and the Inter-Church Committee on French Work in Canada.[141] De Mestral was an outstanding figure in this regard, fighting to break down denominational barriers of every kind and taking decisive stands on critical social questions affecting modern Quebec.[142]

The relative decline of older French Protestant churches has been ascribed to their forsaking active proselytism before the First World War. It is much more likely, however, that socio-economic factors, such as emigration, urbanization, and integration into English-speaking congregations, played the largest role. Nevertheless, another factor was the competition that these churches began to face from a number of sects starting after 1918 and especially 1945. Pentecostals, Evangelical (as distinct from Convention) Baptists, Adventists, Jehovah's Witnesses, and Brethren, as well as Mennonites, all made determined efforts to convert French-Canadian Catholics. Missionary workers were sent from western Canada, the United States, France, and Switzerland. Like nineteenth-century proselytizers, they targeted in particular the migrant workers attracted to areas of strong economic growth in the primary sector, such as Abitibi, Lac St-Jean, Chibougamau, the Trois-Rivières hinterland, and the North Shore, although they did not neglect older and larger urban centres. In some instances, as with the Jehovah's Witnesses, they were subjected to harassment by public officials because their literature was aggressively anti-Catholic.[143]

Colportage, which the older Protestant churches had come to see as futile and inimical to the spirit of ecumenism, was taken up with fresh fervour by these new evangelical churches. They also showed inventiveness in their use of the electronic media. At first broadcasts originated from outside the province, but gradually smaller radio and, later, television stations inside Quebec transmitted evangelical programming. In this way these new evangelicals reached most of Quebec and northern New Brunswick. Faced with the hostility of Catholics and many traditional Protestants, they opened their own schools, summer camps, and old-age homes. In 1948 they also set up an interdenominational evangelical establishment at Lennoxville, the Bethel Bible School, specifically to train French-Canadian proselytizers.[144]

THE TWILIGHT OF CATHOLIC TRIUMPHALISM

Continuity: Piety, institutional growth, ethnic conflict

In time, large-scale urbanization would have even more dramatic effects on French-Canadian Catholicism. But these effects were not immediately apparent. Until 1960, levels of popular piety were maintained and even surpassed. The faithful in a working-class parish of east-end Montreal went to communion almost weekly in the 1920s, in conformity with Pius X's directive.[145] Devotional fervour continued unabated. Membership in the third order of St Francis—more than a confraternity, since lay members followed the Franciscan rule under the direction of the order—increased to almost 100,000 in the mid-1930s and did not begin to decline until 1960.[146] The Sacred Heart of Jesus became a particularly powerful symbol; images of it could be found not only in private but in parks, factories, and even buses. This devotion led to the establishment of two new shrines. The cult of Mary expanded in the years immediately after the Second World War, culminating in 1950 with Pius XII's definition of the doctrine of her Assumption into heaven. Meanwhile, older shrines drew more devotees than ever before. In 1921 St Joseph's Oratory exceeded all records with one million pilgrims,[147] a number that would double within a few years. Smaller centres of devotion with local or regional followings proliferated up to about 1960.

As an antidote to an urban culture, a variety of church-sponsored societies were established in the early 1920s to foster good morals, Sunday observance, modest dress, and wholesome entertainment.[148] The clergy made use of plays, radio, and films, as well as specialized publications, to champion these causes. And although temperance crusades experienced a brief lull in the inter-war years, they resumed during the war. In Montreal the Franciscans were the chief strategists and general staff of these campaigns, which included retreats, triduums (three-day devotions preceding a feast day), and recruitment drives. It is estimated that 800,000 people heard their sermons between 1939 and 1945, of whom almost one-quarter joined temperance leagues.

Following on the success of the international Eucharistic Congress of 1910 in Montreal, which attracted 500,000 participants, other mass religious spectacles were organized, but none could match the national eucharistic congress held in Quebec City in 1938. Its instigator, Quebec's Archbishop Rodrigue Cardinal Villeneuve, took part in a number of diocesan religious spectacles across Canada. As a build-up to the main event, regional congresses were held at St-Norbert, Manitoba, for French-speaking Catholics in the West and at Hearst, Ontario, for Franco–Ontarians living in the North. Schools, hospitals, and other institutions throughout Quebec observed days of prayer, meditation, and renunciation, while seventy preachers hand-picked by Villeneuve held missions in the parishes of the archdiocese of Quebec.

Despite the difficult economic times, organizers managed to collect over $130,000 for the congress. Bell offered 'an ingenious system of communication' that allowed organizers to co-ordinate the never-ending processions and spectacles. Imperial Tobacco funded a loudspeaker system that brought prayers, sermons, and hymns to the remotest participant. The railways put on extra trains and even gave the faithful reduced prices on their tickets. The common folk were not the only ones to benefit, of course. General Motors provided a luxurious convertible for Villeneuve, named pontifical legate for the congress by Pius XI; the premier of Quebec, Maurice Duplessis, presented him with a gold and amethyst ring; and the Château Frontenac furnished a suite of rooms for the prelates sent by Rome to form the legate's court.

Spectacle was an essential component of the ceremonies. Dominated by a 130-foot tower, the historic Plains of Abraham, the focal point of the congress, became a huge open-air nave holding over 100,000 people. Twelve triumphal arches, reflecting diverse styles of modern architecture and representing the ecclesiastical provinces of Canada, marked the parade route between the episcopal palace in the old town and the Plains. Among the participants were the 55 archbishops and bishops of Canada, 3,000 clerics of various ranks and orders, Catholic political and judicial leaders, some holding knighthoods from the Holy See, members of pious societies and Catholic Action groups, schoolchildren, and tens of thousands of spectators. In addition, radio brought the event into the homes of many Canadians.

The purpose of this extravaganza was expressed in a sermon given at the mass inaugurating the four-day event. Georges Gauthier, coadjutor-archbishop of Montreal, denounced materialism for transforming people into commodities and encouraging them to seek change in 'chimeric' doctrines of equality. True change, the prelate emphasized, could come about only through personal commitment to transcendent religious values: 'Without conflict and without bloodletting [Jesus] effects a revolution that no form of communism has ever dreamed of.' Describing French Canadians as the bulwark of order and social stability, Gauthier implored God to keep them faithful to these values.[149]

The Marian congress held nine years later to commemorate the centenary of the diocese of Ottawa was a repeat performance. As a prelude to this event, the Oblates carried the miraculous statue from their Cap-de-la-Madeleine shrine in a triumphal procession along a 350-kilometre route to Ottawa. The congress itself took place on the grounds of the Coliseum and is estimated to have cost over $1-million. Attracting hundreds of thousands of participants, it included exhibitions and plays, as well as properly religious services.[150]

Commemorative publications recited litanies of statistics to indicate the impact and success of such events.[151] It was as if six- and seven-digit figures detailing participation rates, financial contributions, and the sheer size of facilities were magic talismans warding off the spectre that haunted the church: a rapidly expanding materialism, both practical and philosophical, that was undermining once-dominant religious values. Events such as the congresses in Quebec City and Ottawa were not new; they harked back to the mass movements of the Forbin-Janson missions and the temperance crusades of the 1840s. But in the early days of the church's ascending power, Bishop Bourget had looked to the future with confidence and expectancy. A century later, by contrast, Cardinal Villeneuve watched the horizon with a sense of foreboding as the spread of mass culture in the daily life of the people threatened to undermine the religious edifice so laboriously constructed over a century.

On the surface, at least, it was business as usual. As levels of popular piety increased, so too did the institutional commitments of male and female religious. The proportion of primary schools under their direction doubled between 1900 and 1930, although they still accounted for only 16 per cent of those in the Catholic public system of Quebec; the rest were in the hands of the laity. Over the same period almost 200 home-economics schools were founded, primarily for rural girls, as well as 20 teacher-training establishments. At the same time, four out of every five new hospitals and social-service institutions were set up under ecclesiastical auspices.[152] The St Vincent de Paul Society remained the main vehicle of poor relief in Quebec. In 1918 it distributed $100,000 provided by the city of Montreal to aid victims of the Spanish influenza epidemic. New forms of assistance were also offered in the following years: medical and legal aid, advocacy for young delinquents, and religious retreats for the homeless, the latter organized by a Grey Nun who provided her patrons with food, clothing, and spiritual help. In 1933 the first exclusively female St Vincent de Paul conference was established. Eight years later a central woman's council was formed out of the 17 such conferences in Quebec and New Brunswick.[153]

With the church's encouragement, unions of Catholic farmers and workers became solidly established in Quebec in the inter-war period. Inspired by Belgian and French Catholic models, a priest named J.B.A. Allaire had given impetus to the farm co-operative movement at the beginning of the century.

Soon province-wide co-operatives in specific sectors of agricultural production were created to serve essentially as marketing agencies. These were promoted by the Quebec ministry of agriculture, which hired Allaire as an organizer. At the end of the First World War, as farmers faced rising costs and falling revenues, an agricultural union movement emerged. But it was quickly co-opted by Quebec Liberals, who feared that this organization's attraction to the United Farmers, a Canada-wide political protest movement, would draw votes away from them. To prevent disastrous divisions among farmers, as well as their exploitation for party political purposes, the church intervened. The Union Catholique des Cultivateurs (UCC) was the result, with branches set up locally in the parish and regionally at the diocesan level. Although the organizers most closely associated with the United Farmers were shunned by the new movement, the UCC still became an effective instrument in the promotion of farmers' interests.[154]

The church also played a pivotal role in the early years of the 20,000-member Confederation of Canadian Catholic Labourers (CCCL), founded in 1921. Construction and typographical unions affiliated to the CCCL expanded because many episcopal corporations, parish councils, and religious congregations reserved lucrative contracts for their members. Dioceses also gave important financial contributions to the organization. The church's role was not always a positive one, however. During the 1930s a split occurred within the Quebec City local precisely over the question of church financing, with some union chaplains determined to impose their will on the workers. The confrontation abated, but not without the resignations of some dynamic union leaders, lay and religious alike. Behind the scenes, Cardinal Villeneuve actively supported the champions of clerical control. His mediation of the Dominion Textile strike later in the 1930s is seen by some historians as having led to the CCCL's defeat in this conflict and its subsequent loss of members throughout the province.[155]

The clergy were instrumental as well in the spread and operation of the *caisses populaires*, conceived as instruments for the economic emancipation of French Canadians. Inspired, like the co-operative movement of which they were a part, by Catholic social doctrine and patterned on French and Belgian models, these institutions made credit available in the many areas where chartered banks either were non-existent or used local savings to advance investment schemes elsewhere. In 1920 priests were managers or members of the board of 80 per cent of Quebec's credit unions. At Lévis, where the movement was born in 1900, the parish priest fought to maintain democratic principles in the running of the *caisse* and the availability of credit to all classes of society, not just the local élite. Increasingly, however, the *caisses* came to be managed by local entrepreneurs serving their own interests.[156]

At the same time clerics continued to play a leadership role in the ideological movements of the period. With the eclipse of Henri Bourassa, the nationalist leader whose influence peaked during the First World War, Abbé Lionel Groulx became the undisputed leader of the movement. A prolific figure, Groulx taught history at the Université de Montréal, wrote scholarly and literary works, including three novels, published journals, gave public lectures, and campaigned tirelessly for numerous causes. Although the nationalist themes he emphasized varied over time, his overriding aim was for French Canadians to flourish freely, untrammelled by the economic, social, political, and cultural constraints resulting from their historical domination first by the British and then by English Canadians: in short, to reconquer all aspects of French-Canadian life. At the end of the First World War, Groulx considered economic nationalism to be an important means of achieving this goal, but as a philosophical idealist he could not confine his aspirations to narrowly material parameters. The ultimate objective was eminently political: the creation of a French state in North America. Whether this happened inside or outside Confederation was of secondary importance to Groulx. Clearly, however, French Canadians could never achieve this goal if they ignored the spiritual (in the broadest sense of the word) dimension of their struggle. The sources of their collective being, their historical past, Catholic faith, and French culture, from which they had been progressively alienated, had to become their inspiration.[157] With these, they could fight for linguistic and denominational school rights outside Quebec, and for the use of French as a fully public language in Quebec and the federal civil service. An implacable social and political critic, Groulx had enemies both in the church hierarchy and among fellow clerics, and certainly did not speak for the Catholic Church. But he was unmistakably a central figure in the nationalism of the first half of the twentieth century.

Other churchmen articulated social philosophies that sought to remedy the evils of industrial capitalism and economic crisis. Under the auspices of the École Sociale Populaire and its founder J. Papin Archambault, thirteen clerics, including Jesuits, Dominicans, Sulpicians, and socially active seculars, came together in 1933 to study these problems. Rejecting the various proposals for social change spawned by the Depression as secular, subversive, and inimical to French-Canadian interests, they produced their own Catholic Action plan inspired by Pius XI's encyclical *Quadragesimo anno*, published in 1931. Their *Programme de restauration sociale* (plan for social regeneration) was a comprehensive package of social and political reforms whose ultimate goal was not to abolish capitalism, but to transform it. Among the measures it advocated were economic planning, state intervention, social-welfare legislation, protection of consumers, farmers, and workers against exploitation by monopoly capital, transparency in party financing, and conflict-of-interest rules.

These ideas were not new. They had been expressed by turn-of-the-century activists, including Bourassa, whose inspiration came from American progressivism, Catholic social thought, and European models of economic nationalism. It would be incorrect, then, to see the *Programme* simply as a reaction to the founding, the year before, of the English-speaking Co-operative Commonwealth Federation (CCF)—although the thirteen clerics and the Quebec hierarchy wasted no time in condemning the new party as socialist. In accordance with the religious and cultural values underlying them, the *Programme* and the CCF's Regina Manifesto differed significantly in approach. Yet their objectives were remarkably similar: the creation of a Christian co-operative society in which class conflict, though not class differences, would vanish and the common good would triumph through regulation and planning. In any event, the *Programme* led in 1934 to the creation of the Action libérale nationale, a group of dissident Liberals who were instrumental in bringing the 39-year-reign of their former party to an inglorious end.[158]

A number of studies have criticized this 'clerico-nationalist thought' as xenophobic (and especially anti-Semitic), anti-democratic, and reactionary, and several have held it responsible for the arrested intellectual and social development of French Canadians.[159] While it is beyond the scope of this chapter to offer a thorough critique of these interpretations, a few points may serve to suggest some of the flaws in such reasoning. First, it is clear that, despite the prominence of Bourassa, Groulx, and Archambault, nationalism was not the dominant ideology either of Quebec or of the Catholic Church.[160] Moreover, Bourassa's turn-of-the-century nationalism was socially and politically modern, as well as progressive: it did not seek to turn the clock back to some agrarian utopia, but to control the anti-social power of big business.[161] The nationalism of the Depression was a direct outgrowth of this movement. Its criticism of the party system and its cult of the leader (*le chef*) had less to do with the Fascism that was then becoming dominant in several European states than with frustration at the inability of traditional parties to defend French-Canadian interests. When, in the 1930s, Groulx held some Fascist leaders up as models for French Canada, as mistaken symbols of social consensus, he did so out of ignorance of their programs and practices;[162] like many Canadians who admired Mussolini for his resolute action, Groulx had a woefully poor understanding of events in Europe.

French-Canadian nationalism did seek to promote the interests of a historically oppressed ethnic group. But did this ethnically-based ideology encourage hostility toward 'the other'? In the emotionally charged atmosphere of English-French relations,[163] anti-British, anti-Irish, and anti-Jewish sentiments were certainly expressed both in Quebec and in the nationalist movement. It is also true that whereas some English-Canadian community leaders showed a commendable concern for the plight of Jewish and other refugees, French-Canadian nationalist intellectuals remained indifferent to them. But ethnic antagonism was by no means the essence of their movement. Except among the fringe elements sympathetic to Adrien Arcand's fascist party, the prime goals were not the achievement of racial purity or the denial of civil rights to those citizens who were not of French descent. French-Canadian nationalism was undoubtedly a product of its time and shared with contemporary doctrines a Eurocentric view of the world. However, it never championed the use of the repressive power of the state against minority groups, as in Nazi Germany and other Fascist regimes.

In any case, for the vast majority of those in religious life, social commitments took precedence over ideological debate. As the range of the church's social commitments expanded, so too did the numbers of women and men in religious life. In the peak year of 1965 Quebec had twice as many nuns and sisters (43,274), as well as female communities, as in 1931. Urban growth led to growth in those communities working in the fields of education and health. But those whose activities were non-secular or more strictly religious also increased. This overall rise was truly spectacular: in 1940 the ratio of nuns and sisters to the overall female population reached a high point of 18:1,000, a figure unsurpassed in any Catholic country. The increase in female religious was equally remarkable in French America outside Quebec. The total of nuns and sisters went from 7,671 in 1930 to 12,490 in 1965, and many were recruited locally. It is estimated that 5.7 per cent of all religious women in French America (including Quebec) came from Acadia (3 per cent) and Ontario (2.7 per cent).[164]

Two Acadian religious communities, both specializing in education, were established in the 1920s, bringing the total number of indigenous foundations to three. One was the first to offer postulants the opportunity of doing their teacher-training in French without having to leave Acadia; the other resulted from a split along linguistic lines within the Sisters of Charity. Meanwhile, older congregations expanded French schooling so that Acadian women could pursue professional or technical careers in the Maritimes.[165] In the West, French-Canadian sisters extended their missionary activities and increased the number of social-service institutions for the local French-speaking population. The Grey Nuns, for example, opened a mission in Aklavik and a hospital in the diocese of Gravelbourg, Saskatchewan, during the inter-war years.[166]

New female religious communities were established in French Canada well into the 1950s. They were fostered in part by the implementation in 1918 of the new code of canon law that, while centralizing power in Rome, gave religious orders a definite legal standing. Some of these communities quietly but effectively questioned the norms of conventional behaviour for women and sisters. Others reinforced traditional gender roles. Among the former were two foundations that shared a pronounced social commitment in favour of women. The first offered shelter to young working women irrespective of religious or national origin and provided evening courses in working-class districts of Ottawa. (This led to criticisms that sisters were roaming the streets of the capital after dark!) The other community was devoted to the self-realization of women and made available intellectual, technical, and material resources to that end. Founded by the remarkable Marie Gérin-Lajoie, the Institut de Notre-Dame du Bon Conseil sought to place lay and religious women on an equal footing. At first, Gérin-Lajoie wanted to establish a mixed group (her words) of laity and religious who would neither wear a habit nor submit to a formal novitiate. But she had to comply with the more orthodox expectations of her ecclesiastical superiors. Her community subsequently became involved in activities ranging from advanced courses in social science (the first in the province) and domestic arts to the promotion of the Girl Guide movement and the care of Catholic immigrants after the Second World War. The new but more conventional foundations included contemplative orders and those providing domestic service to secular priests and Catholic establishments, one of which originated in the archdiocese of St-Boniface.[167]

From 1930 to 1960 the number of priests (secular and regular) in Quebec increased from 4,274 to 7,908, giving a ratio of clergy to laity of 1:586. The high point seems to have been reached early in the 1950s, when it stood at 1:534. Regulars continued to grow faster than seculars, representing 32 per cent of the clergy at the start of the 1960s. The number of brothers also rose, from 4,740 to 7,647. Nevertheless, whereas in 1930 there were more than twice as many women in religious life as men, in 1960 the former were nearly three times more numerous.[168] Outside Quebec, French-speaking priests numbered approximately 1,050 in 1930. Regulars continued to predominate, representing 56 per cent of the total, and Oblates were by far the largest contingent in this category, accounting for well over half the regulars. They were followed far behind by the Jesuits and the Dominicans who, unlike the Oblates, concentrated their activities mainly in eastern and northern Ontario. With the addition of 450 brothers, the total of French-speaking men in religious life outside Quebec in 1930 came to 1,500. By contrast, nuns and sisters were five times more numerous outside Quebec in the same year.[169] Men in religious life doubled their numbers between 1930 and 1960, and this expansion seems to have peaked in 1965.[170]

One important aspect of church activity in this period was missionary work. Indeed, French Canadians formed the overwhelming majority of Canadian Catholic missionaries abroad in the half-century after the First World War. It was the irrepressible Délia Tétrault (founder of the Montreal community of missionary nuns) who saw the importance of establishing an indigenous training school so that Canadian clerics would not be mere auxiliaries in the missionary endeavours of other countries. For twenty years she tried to convince the episcopate of the soundness of her idea. Finally, with Rome's approval the bishops established a specialized seminary just north of Montreal in 1921. Already in 1934 French Canada had a number of prelates abroad, including seven bishops and three apostolic administrators. The Second World War interrupted recruitment and missionary work somewhat, but the end of hostilities heralded a new period of expansion, especially in Latin America and Japan. In 1950 French Canada ranked fourth (after Ireland, the Netherlands, and Belgium) in its proportion of missionaries to overall Catholic population. The apex was reached in 1971, when over 5,250 female and male religious were working in more than one hundred countries, with the largest contingents in French- and English-speaking Africa (2,245), Central and South America (1,894), and Asia (944); in the same year there were only 310 English-Canadian Catholic missionaries. Numbers fell by 30 per cent, however, in the next decade. Efficient and widespread organizations operating in parishes and primary schools sustained French Canadian missionary activity, particularly with money. Collecting almost $2.25 million in 1957 alone, French Canada was one of the leading contributors to the Catholic Church's proselytizing efforts.

With respect to missionaries' approach to their work, it would appear that in the era before decolonization most shared the Eurocentric perspective evident in missions to the First Nations. Westernization and Christianization were simply considered to go hand in hand. Hence little was done to prepare women and men in the formative years of their religious training to understand and interact with other cultures. In general, the missionaries' objective was for native cultures to adopt French-Canadian religion in its entirety. With the advent of the decolonization movement of the late 1950s and early 1960s, therefore, their convictions and goals were profoundly shaken. As colonized peoples took charge of their own affairs, missionaries had to redirect their efforts from institutional care in the social services to more properly pastoral activities.[171]

French Canadians remained the bastion of Canadian Catholicism. In 1930 they comprised two-thirds of the Catholic population. The remaining third was made up of equal portions of British/Irish and other origins, including Ukrainians, Poles, Germans, Italians, and First Nations. Thirty years later, French-speakers (as opposed to ethnic French Canadians) still accounted for 60 per cent of the 8.5 million Catholics, followed by those of 'other origins'. The British and Irish element fell to third place with less than 15 per cent. While French-speakers comprised 42 per cent of Maritime Catholics, their proportion of the Catholic population in Ontario and the Prairies declined to 23 per cent and 17 per cent respectively, reflecting the ravages of linguistic and religious assimilation.

The question of which group would occupy pride of place in the Canadian church was a continuing source of tension. The issues remained the same: episcopal and parish appointments, the linguistic character of Catholic educational institutions, and, more generally, the relative importance of French- and English-speakers within the church. Confrontations inevitably involved political and diplomatic manoeuvres at the highest levels, as ambassadors from Britain and France joined prelates from Canada and abroad in lobbying the Holy See on behalf of their favourite causes.[172] Unhappy with the fact that Canada's lone cardinal had always been a French Canadian, in the 1930s English-speaking bishops enlisted Prime Minister R.B. Bennett in a campaign to appoint one of theirs to the College of Cardinals. Their efforts were unsuccessful, and the eventual nomination of an English-speaking prelate after the Second World War was made in addition to, not in place of, a French-Canadian cardinal. However, the Vatican was still so sensitive to ethnic issues that it waited until 1956 before naming the archbishop of Quebec primate of the Canadian church.

In the Maritimes the inter-war years witnessed a more equitable distribution of episcopal power than had been the case in the past. By 1945 French-speakers held three of the four dioceses in New Brunswick, which from 1938 formed an an ecclesiastical province under an Acadian archbishop resident in Moncton, and their sees were now located in Acadian areas. In Nova Scotia the Acadian diocese of Yarmouth was carved out of the archdiocese of Halifax in 1953. The English-speaking Maritime clergy ardently resisted such changes, and Acadians outside these few dioceses still did not have a single national parish, even in areas where they were numerically significant, whereas their English-speaking co-religionists in Acadian areas did. Nevertheless, the ecclesiastical reorganization of New Brunswick gave impetus to the founding of *collèges classiques* and teachers' training schools for young men and women in each of the newly created dioceses. These efforts culminated in 1963 when the Université de Moncton, the first Acadian university, was established by the Eudist and Holy Cross fathers.[173] At last a true Acadian church existed, with fully developed institutions to see Acadians from the cradle to the grave.

In the eastern part of Ontario the inter-war years saw the emergence of a Franco-Ontarian church. Yet even here access to French-language education would begin to become a reality only in the late 1960s. In addition, the issue of episcopal nominations continued to sow discord among the province's Catholics. Through trial and especially error, the Holy See arrived at a more or less equitable territorial arrangement. Except for Pembroke, dioceses in the ecclesiastical province of Ottawa had French-Canadian incumbents. But outside this area the gains were minimal. Not until 1941 did a French Canadian become bishop of Alexandria, where his compatriots had been a majority since the turn of the century, and Sault Ste Marie continued to have English-speaking bishops until the mid-1980s even though French Canadians had comprised a plurality, if not a majority, of Catholics since the foundation of the diocese. There the issue of parish appointments had been particularly acute, with French Canadians complaining that since preference was given to English-speaking priests, the spiritual care they received was inadequate.

Meanwhile, the ongoing controversy over the University of Ottawa began to find a resolution as early as 1926. Following Rome's intervention, the Oblates in Canada abandoned their unitary structure and organized themselves in two linguistic sections. In so doing the order followed a path taken in the same period by other communities including the Redemptorists (1912), the Jesuits (1924), the Grey Nuns of the Cross of Ottawa (1926), and, as we have seen, the Sisters of Charity (1924). But the founding of St Patrick's College by the English-speaking Oblates in 1930 did not bring about a decline in the use of English at the University of Ottawa, to which it was affiliated. If anything, the addition, after the Second World War, of professional and scientific faculties operating exclusively in English strengthened its position, much to the dismay of French-Canadian nationalists who publicly accused the Oblates of fostering assimilation. However, the fierce confrontations that at the turn of the century had threatened the university's very existence became a thing of the past.[174]

In the Prairie provinces the drama over episcopal nominations had largely been played out in the 1910s, and the inter-war period simply consolidated earlier trends. Still, the death of Archbishop O.E. Mathieu of Regina in 1929 set off intense in-fighting that eventually led to a reconfiguration of the ecclesiastical map of Saskatchewan. Mathieu's successor was English-speaking, but in an attempt to appease wounded ethnic sensibilities, the new diocese of Gravelbourg, where French Canadians formed a plurality, was carved out of Regina's territory. Then, since two of Saskatchewan's three titular bishops were now French-Canadian, Rome divided the diocese of Prince Albert, giving the new see of Saskatoon to an English-speaker. Thus the province's dioceses were allotted equally to French- and English-speaking prelates. In 1948 it was the turn of Franco-Albertans to obtain their own diocese when St Paul was created from Edmonton's territory. Twenty years later, when the Holy See abolished the system of vicariates in the northern parts of Canada and established regular dioceses, there would be 27 bishops and nine archbishops across the country who were French-Canadian, compared with 19 bishops and eight archbishops who were English-speaking.

After years of conflict, by mid-century the Vatican had finally achieved a balance in episcopal nominations that largely reflected the linguistic composition of Canadian Catholicism. Gradually, the sense of grievance and despair with which French Canadians had met its decisions earlier in the century was dissipated. The sociological reality of Prairie Catholicism, in which French Canadians were no longer the main component and successive generations of non-British immigrants adopted English as their *lingua franca*, was sinking in. French Canadians might have lost their commanding position in the western church, but they still had at least one diocese in the settled areas of each Prairie province. Meanwhile Acadians made big gains in the 1930s and 1940s that reflected the ethnic reality of Maritime Catholicism: Acadians and English-speaking Canadians each had one archbishop and four bishops. In Ontario, French Canadians occupied a proportion of dioceses roughly equivalent to their share of the Catholic population, and these were situated in areas of the province where they formed compact and solid communities. Earlier pretensions to the diocese of London and calls for the creation of a see at Windsor had to confront the hard facts of linguistic assimilation, which had exacted its toll among French Canadians living in south and southwestern Ontario since the First World War.

Ethnic confrontation within the Catholic Church was being gradually but successfully contained. Prelates hostile to the cultural survival of Acadians and French Canadians outside Quebec were either unwilling or unable to act on the broader stage; the days when someone like Bishop M.F. Fallon of London could singlehandedly stir up ethnic strife, with devastating impact on provincial and federal politics, were over. (Fallon had been largely credited with spearheading the campaign that led to the Ontario government's adoption in 1912 of Regulation XVII, which abolished French as a medium of instruction in schools.) In 1944, the Canadian episcopate established a co-ordinating body, the Canadian Catholic Conference, that observed the principle of linguistic duality.[175] But the decline of ethnic confrontation was not primarily attributable to the new organizational and institutional structures within Canadian Catholicism, nor to Vatican policies. Rather, it reflected the fact that by the inter-war period issues affecting French and Catholic minorities outside Quebec were no longer the focus of controversy in Canadian public life.

In essence, French Canadians had lost the battle, begun at Confederation, for a pluralist vision of Canada in which Catholics and French Canadians could play an equal role with Protestants and English Canadians in shaping the new Dominion. Canada clearly emerged from the First World War as an Anglo-Protestant country in which Catholics and French Canadians occupied a minority status. After having clearly put its stamp on the country, the non-Catholic majority now regarded culture as an essentially private matter, peripheral to public life. Provisions relegating the teaching of religion to the end of the day; restrictions on the display of religious symbols; political deals concerning Catholic educational rights devised as temporary or informal arrangements; harassment by petty functionaries intent on demonstrating that Catholic schools flouted the letter of the law; inequitable funding for such schools—all gave substance to this homogeneous vision. The majority saw little point in protracting ethnic and religious hostilities. In Ontario academics and politicians founded the Unity League to promote understanding between French- and English-speaking Canadians, and in Ottawa Prime Minister Mackenzie King, who wished to be regarded as the champion of national harmony and reconciliation, began his long reign. This did not mean that minorities no longer had legitimate grievances or that Canadian ethnic relations were more harmonious. It was simply that the locus of conflict had been displaced.

In one sense, conflict became localized. French-speaking Catholics living outside the dioceses controlled by their compatriots had to fight for ethnically homogeneous parishes and schools, as well as services in their language. Similarly, in many provinces the struggle for French and Catholic education continued, often led by parish priests, teaching sisters, and militant editorialists of the Ottawa daily *Le Droit* and the Acadian *L'Évangéline*. It was in this context that the Ordre Jacques Cartier was born in 1926. This secret society, in which the clergy played a prominent part, was an effective lobby for French and Catholic interests throughout Canada until after the Second World War. But these struggles no longer had the resonance they had enjoyed before 1914; now they were regarded by the majority as no more than local skirmishes concerning local issues. The minority, for its part, could not get the attention of mainstream newspapers or political institutions to promote its interests. As we shall see, questions of greater import than minority rights were beckoning politicians. Hence agitation in favour of such rights was largely a private affair, carried on through secret societies and ethnic presses.[176]

Change: The rise of the interventionist state

In another sense, however, ethnic confrontation began to take a very different form in the inter-war years, coming to focus on the role of the state. This was the direct outcome of the evolution of capitalism towards corporate concentration in the early twentieth century. Examples of this phenomenon include the formation of joint-stock companies and of trusts resulting from ever more frequent mergers, and the growth of bigger units of production incorporating various stages of manufacturing. The emergence of large-scale capitalism meant that the state had to play a regulatory role in society because it alone had the means both to guarantee the smooth accumulation of capital and to dispense assistance to the increasingly numerous victims of economic downturns.[177]

Starting in the First World War, and especially during the Depression, the state took the first tentative steps towards helping the most vulnerable members of society to cope with economic restructuring by providing income security and labour-market stability. The state, in this instance the federal government, began to move into areas that in Quebec had traditionally been under the church's purview. Progressives in English Canada were even calling on Ottawa to extend its authority over the fields of health and welfare. As a result, the system that had ensured Quebec's distinctiveness since the Union was being undermined. Beyond the expansion of state authority, though, it was really the advent of corporate capitalism that was to determine both Quebec's evolution in the twentieth century and the church's position in that society. As we have seen, the church had adapted quite well to the urban-industrial environment of the nineteenth and early twentieth centuries.[178] In fact, many of the institutions that it founded flourished in towns and smaller cities throughout Quebec well into the 1950s. But the challenges posed by monopoly capitalism rendered these same institutions unsuited to large metropolitan centres.

The Depression made this glaringly obvious. As in the past, the St Vincent de Paul Society was the agency through which municipalities funnelled relief to unemployed Catholics in the form of money, clothing, food, and fuel. In 1932 the Montreal branch gave out $3 million to 228,000 people; according to one estimate, it handled upwards of $500,000 a month in goods and cash. This time-consuming work was done entirely on a volunteer basis, without book-keepers or offices. Clearly the system could not long endure. On the one hand, since it was paying the bills, the federal government demanded greater efficiency and accountability, especially after recipients complained of significant irregularities. On the other, the St Vincent de Paul Society was reluctant to abandon its time-honoured practices, and rejected outside interference, particularly from a government dominated by Protestants innately suspicious of any parish-based system. In the event, a 'professional bureaucracy' under the authority of the city of Montreal took over the distribution of relief from the Society in 1933. In the same year the Fédération des Oeuvres de Charité Canadiennes-Françaises was instituted, signalling the end of a system of poor relief that had been inaugurated in the previous century by the Sulpicians and carried forward by the St Vincent de Paul Society. Under the pressures of corporate capitalism, even Catholic agencies adopted centralized, bureaucratic, professional methods. In this new order, which stressed training over simple Christian virtues, the laity would not long accept being in a subordinate position to the clergy.[179]

Even before the Depression, however, the ability of church-centred institutions to meet the needs of a society undergoing economic restructuring had come into question. In the period after the First World War these establishments faced vastly increased demands and shrinking financial resources. From 1916 to 1931 the number of people receiving institutional care in Catholic facilities more than doubled, while those treated at home quadrupled.[180] In response to the recession that followed the First World War, the Taschereau government passed the Quebec law on public assistance in 1921. This allowed social-service institutions desperately short of funds, especially hospitals in rapidly expanding urban centres, to apply to Quebec City for subsidies. In return, they were required to account for how these monies were spent and to submit to regular government inspection. The legislation provoked stiff opposition from most bishops, who feared that the government was usurping their authority over the religious communities running such institutions. But it is significant that shortly after passage of the act, fifty of these establishments had already asked for financial relief from the province.[181] In the same decade, the government initiated reforms in education and provided subsidies to universities, *collèges classiques*, and school boards. In social services and education, the Taschereau administration sought to place institutions on a sounder financial footing, making them less dependent on the vagaries of private philanthropy, which was no longer a reliable source of funding. It also encouraged the same trends towards centralization, specialization, and laicization that would mark the changes in welfare assistance in the 1930s.[182]

After the Second World War, institutions run by the church had even heavier strains to bear as a new period of economic expansion stimulated greater urbanization. The Duplessis government responded to this situation by radically altering its spending priorities, moving away from transportation and natural resources in favour of health, education, and welfare.[183] The religious superiors of establishments in these fields increased their 'pilgrimages' to Quebec City to implore the premier's largesse. Duplessis delighted in the church's dependence on government, proudly proclaiming that the bishops ate out of his hands.[184] But whereas in the inter-war years the church had had the human, if not the financial, resources to meet expanding demand, now even these began to flag. The numbers of women and men in religion were still high, but recruitment began to drop at the war's end.

It was in the 1940s that, for the first time, the archbishops of Quebec City and Montreal publicly expressed concern over the numbers of religious vocations. Meanwhile, both rural and urban dioceses began to experience shortages of parish priests. In part, these shortages reflected clerical involvement in other activities. Not even half the seculars were doing parish work, while the rest were absorbed in teaching, administration, and chaplaincy. By contrast, only 20 per cent of seculars in Europe worked outside the framework of the parish. In addition, however, the numbers of men and women in religious communities were no longer increasing faster than the overall population.[185] In the 1950s the situation was not acute enough to force religious communities to withdraw from their many temporal commitments, but increasingly they called upon the laity to perform both service and managerial functions.[186] Clearly the institutional church was overstretching itself.

Why was the Catholic Church no longer attracting the large numbers of young women and men it had done in the past? Once again the answer is related to the economic structure of Quebec, particularly in the case of religious women. In the first two decades of this century the number of women in religious life was growing twice as fast as the overall female population. This ratio dropped in the inter-war years, but their growth rate was still higher than that of the female population as a whole. From 1910 to 1940 nuns and sisters occupied an important segment (between 12 and 14 per cent) of the female labour force.

But all that changed with the Second World War. Until then married women in Quebec had had few opportunities outside the home. While their proportion of the female workforce did increase between the two wars–by a scant 2 per cent, paralleling an equivalent drop among religious women–by 1941 there were still one-and-a-half times more nuns and sisters than married women in the labour market. This ratio was reversed in the next decade and it widened considerably thereafter, so that by 1971 married women comprised half the female workforce.[187] The withdrawal of religious communities from the fields of health, education, and welfare in the 1960s entailed a drop in the numbers of skilled female workers in the labour market. In 1961, 40 per cent of female managers were nuns and sisters.[188] During the Quiet Revolution, however, the managerial positions opened up by the enormous expansion of the public sector were filled mostly by men.

If the process of economic restructuring began to make itself felt in Quebec after the First World War, why was its impact on religious women not more immediate? In other words, why did communities continue to expand faster than the female population in the inter-war years? The answer is partly demographic, partly economic. First, a rapid rise in the overall birthrate in the first two decades of the century produced a surplus of marriageable women in the 1920s and 1930s, since the tendency was for them to marry older men. Second, the Depression postponed the opening of opportunities for women in the job market. Not only were the jobs of religious women sheltered from the caprices of the economic cycle that caused lay women such hardship, but life in the convent was healthier and women religious lived longer than their counterparts in the world. For all these reasons the convent was still an attractive alternative.

At the same time, however, the percentage of nuns and sisters coming from the city declined in every decade of this century, reflecting the progress of urbanization; the numbers of religious women from small towns peaked between the wars, while those of women from rural areas rose so dramatically that by 1951 they represented nearly half the population of nuns and sisters. In addition, religious women consistently came from families with more than six children, and over successive generations such families became an increasingly rural phenomenon: hence the segment of the population from which the overwhelming majority of nuns and sisters were recruited was an ever-diminishing one.[189] Through the effects it had on the family and the options it offered to urban women, then, corporate capitalism exercised a definite impact on the recruitment of religious women. In no way does this negate the individual convictions that impelled men and women to join religious communities. It does, however, elucidate the socio-economic context in which such motives existed and such choices were made.

The relative positions of religious and married women in the labour market may shed some light on the reasons why Quebec was the last jurisdiction in

North America to recognize civil and political rights for women. There is no doubt that the institutional church in general was adamantly opposed to such rights. Since Catholicism stressed the importance of preserving gender distinctions in the human personality and in society, any theory challenging its view of femininity and women's essentially private sphere of activity was to be opposed. Thus most—though not all—Quebec bishops obstructed attempts by the Catholic women's movement, the Fédération Nationale St-Jean-Baptiste (as distinct from the older nationalist organization, the Fédération St-Jean-Baptiste), to obtain the franchise in the 1920s. The auxiliary bishop of Quebec launched a huge petition against female suffrage. Nevertheless, when the head of the FNSJB, Marie Lacoste Gérin-Lajoie (mother of Marie Gérin-Lajoie), appealed directly to Rome over the heads of the Quebec bishops, she had the support of Archbishop Georges Gauthier, whose brother had been the chaplain of her organization. A prominent Dominican, Ceslas Forest, professor of philosophy at the Université de Montréal, also gave Gérin-Lajoie strong moral backing. But the Vatican, unwilling to go against the Quebec episcopate on what must have seemed to be an issue of peripheral importance, refused to endorse the FNSJB's position.[190] As a result, the suffrage movement became thoroughly laicized. Annual appeals to the Quebec legislature for the right to vote were met with counter-petitions from the clerically-inspired Ligue Catholique Féminine, a parish- and college-based organization dedicated to modest female deportment whose membership was 30,000 in 1929. Pointing to such petitions, politicians claimed that women themselves did not want the franchise.

With some exceptions, then, the church was generally hostile to women's rights. But was it the most important obstacle to their realization? It is striking that the significant gains made in this area from 1940 to 1960 coincided with the massive entry of married women into the paid labour force. Although its position on working mothers remained unaltered during this period, the supposedly omnipotent church was unable to halt this trend.[191] As long as housewives and working girls played an integral role in the family economy because of the inadequate wages paid to the principal breadwinner, recognition of their personal rights was bound to be difficult to achieve. In this context the church reflected prevalent negative attitudes.[192] Indeed, it did all it could as an institution to block the implementation of such rights. But when the context changed, as wages rose significantly during the Second World War and women's work both inside and outside the home became a matter less of family survival than of personal choice, the church was increasingly transformed into a spectator of reality, a role hardly befitting an institution still popularly perceived as the moving force of Quebec history.

In addition to the changing position of women, the church faced growing restiveness in the Catholic union movement. The 1920s and early 1930s were a period of crisis for all trade unions, with membership dropping significantly as workers suffered a series of reversals. Some CCCL militants came to the conclusion that the problem lay in certain aspects of the church's social teachings, particularly its objections to strikes and the union shop—job-security measures that, on the whole, the international unions more readily embraced. Nevertheless, the CCCL's own attempts to come to terms with these measures eventually forced the church's attitudes to evolve. In the same period, the CCCL challenged clerical attitudes by strongly advocating federally sponsored social-welfare legislation, even though such a program would inevitably undermine the church's role in Quebec society.[193]

After a period of torpor, Catholic unionism expanded rapidly from 1935 to 1945. During the Second World War, however, the overtly denominational character of its affiliates was seen as an obstacle to further growth as the CCCL faced stiff competition from the internationals. Significantly, the proposal to drop the term 'Catholic' from the names of CCCL locals came from Quebec's metropolis, Montreal, and was endorsed by two chaplains. The realities of industrial relations forced some affiliates to make these changes as early as 1943. But the issue would bitterly divide the church in Quebec for many years, and it was only with the founding in 1960 of the secular Confédération des Syndicats Nationaux (Confederation of National Trade Unions) that it was finally resolved. Meanwhile, the CCCL's leadership was transformed during the Second World War. The informal, decentralized structures of the past were gradually replaced as full-time, professionally trained laymen took over the day-to-day administration of the union. This development coincided with the decline in the influence of the union chaplain, whose suspensive veto over any union resolution considered to go against Catholic social doctrine was formally removed at the CCCL's 1943 convention.

In the aftermath of the war, the union movement spread to institutions controlled by the church. Teachers and nurses joined the ranks of organized labour not only to increase their wages but to protect and advance their positions in the face of competition from their lower-paid religious colleagues. Both male and female educators accused employers of favouritism in hiring brothers and sisters, while nurses showed a growing impatience with religious administrators whose views of hospital work and employee relations were rooted in notions of Christian charity and submission to spiritual authority.[194] This perspective was echoed in secular publications such as *Cité libre*, which argued that a Roman collar or a habit did not necessarily qualify someone for a position of responsibility.[195]

It would be simplistic, though, to characterize the period after 1920 as one in which a turf war between laity and clergy led to the progressive secularization of society. For one thing, clerics did not constitute a monolithic bloc. Those working closely with lay men and women in secular organizations such as co-operatives and labour and credit unions tended to be more open to lay initiatives and practices diverging from official church policies. Together with the laity, some learned through praxis, modifying their views to take account of social realities. On the other hand, those who were further removed from such activities were more inclined to proclaim notions of hierarchy, authority, and leadership that subordinated the laity to the clergy. Although some priests were violently opposed to the militancy of trade unions, Catholic or otherwise, for ideological, moral, social, or political reasons,[196] the official church was increasingly obliged to respond to initiatives taken by the Catholic laity.

The Asbestos strike of 1949 has been seen as a turning-point in the secularization of Quebec society. The four-month dispute involved 5,000 miners affiliated to the CCCL in three company towns in the Eastern Townships. Aware that the high incidence of industrial diseases such as asbestosis was caused by conditions in the mines, they were seeking not only wage increases but stricter health controls. The strike underlined the collusion between the American-owned companies and the provincial government headed by Duplessis, who called out the provincial police to protect scabs and intimidate the strikers and their families. Intellectuals and journalists of various ideological persuasions associated themselves with the workers' struggle. Among the latter was one in particular, Pierre Elliott Trudeau, who stressed the secular nature of the strike and its difference from earlier labour conflicts in Quebec.[197]

In fact, however, the clergy played an active role in the strike. The miners, led by their chaplain, paraded through the streets of Thetford Mines reciting the rosary. Their parish priest openly supported them, just as some ten years earlier the pastor of Sorel had championed the cause of shipbuilding workers in their struggle against the powerful Simard family. The Catholic press played the same role at Asbestos as in the Dominion Textile Strike of 1937, when it denounced working conditions, the employers' intransigence, and the government's collusion. On both occasions it refused to condemn, as the English-language newspapers had done, the use of violence by workers, seeing them rather as victims of provocation. The archbishop of Montreal, Joseph Charbonneau, personally identified himself with the cause of the Asbestos miners. In a now famous sermon, Charbonneau asserted: 'The working class is a victim of a conspiracy which seeks to crush it, and when there is a conspiracy to crush the working class, the Church has a duty to intervene.'[198] Parishes throughout the province provided material and moral support, just as parishes in the Quebec City area had assisted striking shoemakers in 1926.[199] It was Abbé Groulx himself who proposed that collections be held throughout Quebec to help out the families of workers deprived of their salaries for so long.[200] Finally, the archbishop of Quebec agreed to mediate, as his predecessors had done in earlier strikes.

Nevertheless, by the 1940s relations between the laity and the church were no longer as clearly defined as they had been in the past. Ambiguities in this relationship were also revealed in the development of the Catholic Action movement, which Pius XI's encyclical *Ubi Arcano Dei* formally encouraged in 1922. Supporting the laity in its efforts to re-establish Christian principles in the world, especially in the fight against Communism, the pope called on those Catholics who had allowed temporal commitments to supplant spiritual ones to rally around these higher values and incorporate them into daily life. What Pius XI did not make clear, however, was the relationship between the hierarchy and the laity in this process of re-Christianization. In French America before the Second World War, Catholic Action was essentially a rapidly expanding youth movement. Sections were organized along gender lines among students, workers, farmers, and professionals at parish and diocesan levels. In 1935, a branch of Catholic Action comprising young workers, the Jeunesse Ouvrière Catholique (JOC), had a newspaper, other publications, a credit union, summer camps, and 6,000 members in provinces from New Brunswick to Manitoba, as well as in New England. In Montreal there was a JOC section in 90 per cent of the parishes.[201]

The Second World War interrupted this spectacular development, but the movement took off again after 1945 and peaked during the 1950s, becoming particularly strong among students and young women from cities outside the Montreal metropolitan area. Yet its success masked a lack of consensus within the Quebec church about the nature of the movement. Was it one of many Catholic organizations, or did it stand above them as a co-ordinating body? Was its orientation temporal or spiritual? Did the laity have freedom of initiative, or were they subject to religious authority? It seems that every bishop, every religious community, and every chaplain involved with Catholic Action had a different perception of its role.

Despite these disagreements, the movement proved in some cases to be a very effective training-ground for young men and women. At its best, it encouraged members to explore various aspects of social reality, such as unemployment, housing, and issues related to youth. Stress was laid on empirical observation: members were discouraged from speaking about issues in which they did not have first-hand experience. Lacking a clear ideological orientation (which was in any case discouraged) they developed a strong practical and organizational sense. They learned to conduct surveys, write newspaper articles, prepare briefs, arrange conferences, travel, express and defend points of view in public debate—in other words, to take the initiative even in areas previously under the clergy's purview. Inevitably, the lay people involved in such activities developed a sense of their own importance within the church. A young woman of twenty, Simonne Monet Chartrand, bluntly told Joseph Charbonneau, who had just been appointed archbishop of Montreal: 'We will not be junior instructors parroting prefabricated sermons. We wish to be treated in the Church as full members with real responsibilities. Through our studies, our friendships, our loves, we want to take the risk of being true Christians while preserving our free will.'[202] Speaking in 1944, the student Gérard Pelletier asserted: 'Catholic Action must wholly belong to the laity or it will not be.'[203]

The development of Catholic Action also helped the spread of new perspectives in Quebec. Following the pope's denunciation of both radical nationalism in *Ubi Arcano Dei* and the right-wing nationalist Action Française movement in France (which prompted Henri Bourassa to renounce nationalism as a political philosophy in the early 1920s),[204] Catholic Action too worked to steer youth away from this ideology. In its commitment to social issues, it came to be seen as a rival organization to the Association Catholique de la Jeunesse Canadienne-Française, the nationalist youth movement in which Groulx played so prominent a part in the early years of the century. In fact, Groulx held Catholic Action responsible for the ACJC's demise in the 1930s.[205]

A young leader of the new movement, Jules Léger, a future governor-general of Canada, illustrated its anti-nationalist outlook in 1939: 'Nothing is more dangerous than for a minority to weaken itself in local conflicts which cause a narrowing of the mind. Catholicism itself becomes imbued with ideas that are too narrowly chauvinistic. At that point, Catholicism can no longer be a dominant force (*conquérant*).'[206] Three years later the 'local conflict' that was the conscription plebiscite, in which French Canadians voted massively against compulsory military service overseas, saw Catholic Action take a resolutely neutral position, faithful to its principled rejection of political involvement. Among the future leaders in Canadian public life who, moulded by Catholic Action, would maintain a life-long distrust of nationalism were the federal cabinet ministers Gérard Pelletier, Maurice Sauvé and Jeanne Sauvé (who later became governor-general), and the journalist Claude Ryan, leader of the Quebec Liberal party during the 1980 referendum on sovereignty-association.

A consensus was now no more to be found around Catholic social and political thought than around nationalism. When the young André Laurendeau (who would become the influential editor of *Le Devoir* and, in the 1960s, co-chair of the Royal Commission on Bilingualism and Biculturalism) asserted, in 1937, 'Too often we [French Canadians] find ourselves among those who believe that God belongs to the Right',[207] it was clear that the cocoon in which the Quebec mind had evolved since the mid-nineteenth century was breaking open. For his ultimate frame of reference Laurendeau looked not to Catholic thought, but to the ideological polarities of right and left. Some Catholics took social Catholicism beyond the limits others found acceptable. Archbishop Charbonneau and the Dominican Georges-Henri Lévesque were particularly controversial figures. Both regarded the denominational and ethnic barriers that the church had erected over time as no longer compatible with social realities. In fact, they held these barriers responsible for much of the misunderstanding and conflict in Canada. In their view, the church had become a fortress cut off from the world around it. They were convinced that the end of the Second World War would herald a radically different social order that, together with the rise of Communism, made the search for new approaches urgent. Thus Charbonneau publicly expressed warm sympathy for the CCF, when barely ten years earlier the Quebec episcopate had condemned it. Against the rest of the hierarchy, he argued in favour of a non-denominational nurses' union, and during the Asbestos strike he was the only prelate to proclaim that the interests of humanity stood above those of capital.[208]

With the support of his Canadian superiors, Lévesque questioned denominationalism as an organizing principle for socio-economic organizations such as co-operatives. Close associates at his Faculty of Social Sciences at Université Laval publicly denounced Duplessis's anti-labour policies and gave intellectual justification for advanced forms of union security, including closer co-operation with the international unions. The Jesuit periodical *Relations* published an exposé on French-Canadian workers, victims of unscrupulous foreign capital, who had died of an industrial disease called silicosis. Meanwhile, the Clerical Commission on Social Studies, created at the end of the war by the Quebec church hierarchy, advocated the democratization of industrial capitalism with workers sharing in the profits and the management of industry.

The bishops incorporated the Commission's ideas in their pastoral letter on the working-class problem released in 1950; but it is clear that the document masked strong disagreements within the clergy.[209] Although the decade that followed saw some important labour battles, the pastoral failed to rally the church to collective action. The tensions caused by the labour question during the 1940s had taken their toll. The editor of *Relations*, Jean D'Auteuil Richard, was removed on Archbishop Charbonneau's orders and sent 'into exile' in the West after businessmen and politicians threatened libel suits as a result of the periodical's stand on the silicosis issue.[210] Lévesque and his Dominican provincial were denounced to Rome and investigated for their unorthodox opinions. Charbonneau was deposed as archbishop of Montreal and, ironically, followed D'Auteuil Richard into exile. Despite his actions in the *Relations* affair, the prelate remains an icon for those who see those years as an epic struggle between the forces of progress and those of reaction. Finally, the Jesuit Jacques Cousineau was forced to resign as a member of the Clerical Commission and sent to teach in a *collège classique* in Quebec City. The Commission gradually became an empty shell.

The 1950s had a *fin d'époque* feel about them. The decade began with Pius XII's proclamation of the dogma of the Assumption and naming of Paul-Émile Léger, the rector of the Canadian Pontifical College in Rome, whom the pope knew and esteemed, to succeed Charbonneau as archbishop of Montreal. Only two years later Léger was raised to the College of Cardinals. On his return from Rome, the cardinal urged the city to make itself beautiful to receive its prince. Léger's triumphalistic tone was characteristic of the church in this period, but it sounded a jarring note in a metropolis where *Refus global*, an anticlerical manifesto that set the tone for a new Quebec, had been published in 1948;[211] where attendance at Sunday mass and observance of the church's precepts were noticeably declining; where public vice flourished and consumerism was replacing work as the driving force in the family.

Equally incongruous was the report of the Royal Commission on Constitutional Problems (Tremblay Commission), released in 1956. The Commission had been instituted by Duplessis three years earlier in response to pressure from nationalists preoccupied with Quebec's loss of autonomy in a federation that had become increasingly centralized since the Second World War. Georges-Henri Lévesque, for one, had vigorously supported this centralizing trend in his capacity as co-chair of the federally appointed Royal Commission on Arts and Letters (Massey Commission), while his former student, Maurice Lamontagne, in a book dedicated to his mentor, argued that only a strong federal government could guarantee equality of opportunity for all Canadians. By contrast, the Tremblay Report took a nationalist position, affirming that Canada comprised two very different cultures, Anglo-Protestant and French Catholic. This bicultural vision precluded Ottawa's claim to act as the national government of all Canadians, which was its justification for recent interventions in the fields of welfare, education, and culture, jurisdictions normally regarded as provincial under the Constitution. French Canadians, the report maintained, had a national government in Quebec City that needed a full range of fiscal and jurisdictional powers in order for their culture to flourish.

According to the commissioners, what made French-Canadian culture distinct was its essentially metaphysical character: in other words, the values that sustained and propelled it were transcendent, spiritual ones. Hence the church had been more important than the state in French Canada's development; and provincial autonomy had been merely the constitutional instrument through which the church had pursued its historic mission. As far as Quebec's past was concerned, this perspective had some validity. What was incongruous, on the other hand, was the place the Tremblay Report assigned to the church in contemporary French-Canadian life. In its view, the church was the only effective bulwark against the two powerful forces undermining French-Canadian culture: the industrial capitalism that was introducing antithetical values in large segments of the population, and the massive increase in federal power that was destroying provincial autonomy. Quebec City, the report insisted, had to reclaim the areas of jurisdiction it had lost to Ottawa, in order to allow the church to wage an effective campaign against the culture of monopoly capitalism.[212]

CONCLUSION

A century and a half ago, French Canada was experiencing a crisis. The year 1840 marked a turning-point for its people. The attempt to erect a secular liberal state, culminating in the insurrections of 1837–8, had been soundly defeated. Through the Union, the British fostered the development of a socially and ideologically conservative society in the Canadas. As well, they anticipated that the new arrangement would bring about the marginalization and eventually the disappearance of French-Canadian culture. The immediate threat to that culture came from Protestant proselytism and political efforts in London and in Canada to speed up assimilation. A mass movement of resistance led by political élites and the church in Quebec dissipated this threat. But the longer-term danger posed by industrialization and urbanization under the aegis of an English-speaking élite remained.

Though lacking a solid institutional foundation since the Conquest, the elements of a distinct Canadien identity had been sustained in Papineau's time by the struggle for popular sovereignty. After the crushing of the insurrections, however, these elements—language, religion, and law—were left dangerously exposed. The expansion of English-Canadian demographic and economic power in the Union period compounded the danger. French Canadians needed not only to develop new ways of expressing their distinctiveness, in line with the changed social and cultural realities, but also to give these forms strong institutional expression. Failure to do so might well mean their disappearance as a people. In this crucial context, the Catholic Church played a vital part.

Perceived by the British and Canadian authorities primarily as a socially conservative institution, the Quebec church was allowed to pursue its development after the Union. The socio-political context favoured the church because its program was seen to be compatible with the aims of the ruling élite. But the institution also had dynamic leaders, men and women with both a vision and the tenacity to achieve it. They were able to tap the wealth and the energies of French Canadians in building a unique culture in which for many years the church would provide both the form and the content. Whereas previously French Canada's character had been expressed largely through politics, now the vehicle would be religion. French-Canadian Catholicism became decidedly Roman during the years of the Union. In fact, this element set French Canadians apart not only from English Canadians but from Americans as well. Ultramontanism touched all aspects of life. For the clergy, it meant a new liturgy, catechism, style of dress, method of training, ideological discourse; for the laity, it denoted an Italianate piety and a symbolic universe revolving around a beleaguered pope who refused to compromise with the forces of modernity. French Canadians spontaneously identified with Catholic causes around the world not because they were imperialists in an age of imperialism,[213] nor because they were intellectually committed to the cause of reaction, but because such issues reinforced their sense of collective self. Even religious architecture, statuary, and painting were heavily influenced by the Baroque style that had flourished in Rome during the Counter Reformation, once again setting Quebec apart from Protestant North America's enthusiasm for neo-Gothic religious art. All these ingredients made for a distinct French-Canadian identity.

They were also an integral part of the Acadian national revival that took place shortly after Confederation. This rebirth found expression in a renewed commitment to language and faith, and a determination to develop economic, social, and community institutions, as well as a lay and religious leadership, that would be distinctly Acadian. Quebec clergymen played a conspicuous role in the rebirth of an Acadian consciousness, essentially through the private educational establishments that they controlled. And though the symbols eventually chosen to express the Acadian identity were different from those of Quebec, they too were profoundly religious ones: the feast of the Assumption became the Acadian national holiday; *Ave Maris Stella* became the anthem; and the star of Mary became a prominent emblem on the Acadian flag. The clergy were central to the definition of both the Acadian and the French-Canadian identity.

To survive in the new urban–industrial environment dominated by English-Canadian economic and political power, the new culture of French Canada needed an institutional framework. With its international connections, the Catholic Church had the structure, human resources, organizational ability, and access to financial support required to establish and run a whole range of educational and social-welfare institutions. As well, it played a crucial role in such home-grown economic organizations as the *caisses populaires*, co-operatives, Catholic farmers' and trade unions, and other professional associations. In effect, the establishment of a French-Canadian public culture was accomplished through private means. In other societies, social-service institutions depended directly on the state for direction and financial assistance, and socio-economic organizations such as trade unions were indirectly connected to the state through the political parties that usually controlled them. Catholic institutions in these countries were private and only supplemented services provided by the state. The establishments that in other societies were private, however, functioned as public ones in Quebec.

This was so because French Canadians did not exercise control over the state. Their relative lack of political power in Ottawa was confirmed after a series of bitter conflicts over denominational education and language in the fifty years after Confederation. This resulted in the dominance of an Anglo-Protestant culture throughout Canada outside Quebec. It is true that French Canadians were preponderant in the provincial legislature; but their power was circumscribed by a number of formal and informal mechanisms meant to safeguard and promote the interests of an economic élite that was overwhelmingly English-speaking. In reality, therefore, the state was hemmed in by Anglo-Protestant power. French Canadians did not necessarily reject the state as an instrument for the promotion of their collective well-being.[214] Rather, the historical context forced them to look elsewhere to secure the autonomous development of French-Canadian society and culture, to an institution that was entirely under French-Canadian control. The distinct society that we know today was primarily the creation not of the state, but of the Catholic Church.

Beginning in Montreal in the early years of the century, however, and completing its spread throughout the province with the Second World War, monopoly capitalism undermined both the established structures and the culture of French Canada. While the church had adjusted to urban and industrial life, it was unable to cope with the greater challenge of corporate capitalism. At the institutional level it lacked both the money and the human resources to maintain the wide range of services it had once offered. The advent of the Keynesian state, in direct response to the consolidation of monopoly capitalism, subverted the political-constitutional framework in which the church had functioned since the Union. French Canadians were soon confronted with a choice: the autonomous church-run institutions that largely defined their culture would have to come under the control of an English-speaking majority in Ottawa or a French-Canadian one at home. The decline of St James Street made the decision somewhat easier. *Désormais* ('henceforth'), the slogan of Duplessis's successor Paul Sauvé, signalled a change: from now on the provincial state would be the instrument through which French-Canadian culture would develop. The Catholic Church had fulfilled its historic mission in French Canada.

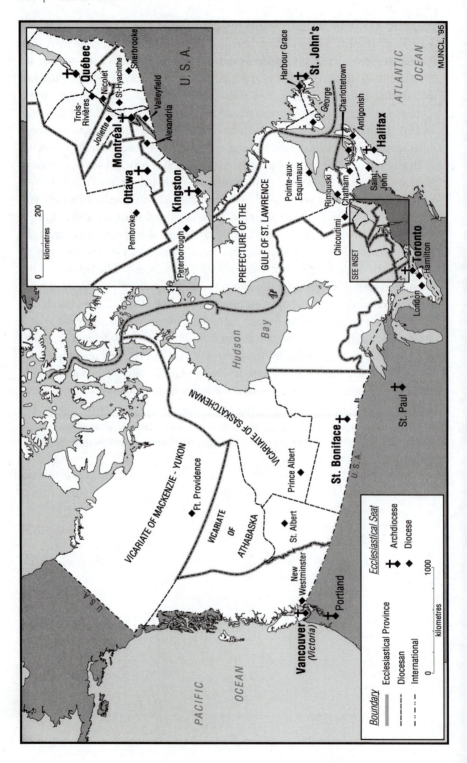

Five

English-Speaking Canada from 1854

B R I A N   C L A R K E

DISESTABLISHMENT AND THE NEW NATION, 1854–1914

THE STATE OF RELIGION: A STATISTICAL OVERVIEW

By the 1860s, the British North American colonies east of the Hudson's Bay territory were well on their way to becoming settled societies. Greater concentrations of population, improved transportation and communication, expanding commerce, the first steps towards an industrial economy, and the growth of mature social institutions combined to create increasingly stable and complex communities. Furthermore, despite wide regional variations, a significant portion of the population had by this time been born in British North America. In the 1860s, the first decade for which the birthplaces of the people in the colonies (PEI excepted) can be compared, the overwhelming majority of the people in Nova Scotia and Newfoundland had been born in British North America; fewer than one in ten came from the United Kingdom. In New Brunswick, over three-quarters of the population had been born and raised in North America, but immigrants from the UK accounted for about one-fifth of the population, and some three-quarters of these had come from Ireland. In Canada East, people born in British North America accounted for nearly 70 per cent of English-speakers, while in Canada West they comprised just over three-fifths of the anglophone population. Immigration was still an important factor in the growth of population, as the variety of accents constantly reminded contemporary observers, and some areas were still being settled: large-scale migration to the West did not begin until the end of the nineteenth

Opposite: ROMAN CATHOLIC DIOCESES OF CANADA, 1904.

SOURCE: R. Perin, *Rome in Canada* (Toronto: University of Toronto Press, 1990), 2.

century. Nevertheless, the vast majority of British North America's inhabitants had been born in the colonies.

Organized religion was growing faster than the society itself. The institutional expansion of Christianity, together with the impact of movements of religious renewal such as evangelicalism and Ultramontanism, had brought an ever-increasing number of people within the orbit of organized Christianity. This trend, already evident in the first half of the century, continued during the second half, as evidenced by the dramatic decline among those who reported to census-takers that they had no denominational ties. In Nova Scotia, the proportion declined from 7.7 per cent to 0.7 per cent in just one decade, from 1851 to 1861. In Ontario, the decline in the unaffiliated was equally dramatic, falling from 16.7 per cent of the population in 1842 to 4.5 per cent in 1851; by 1861 the figure had slipped to 1.8 per cent, and in the following two decades it would shrink to a mere 0.7 per cent. These figures suggest that in British North America, as in the United States, conformity in religion became the norm during the middle years of the nineteenth century.

What made the religious landscape of the British colonies unique in North America was that Protestant denominations did not monopolize the religious spectrum. The 'French fact', especially but not only in what is now Quebec, ensured a French-speaking Catholic presence so vibrant that the overall ratio between Protestants and Catholics remained at around 60:40 throughout the latter half of the nineteenth century despite the expansion of Canadian political frontiers and continued immigration from the United Kingdom (see Table 5.1). The French-Canadian presence had important consequences both for English-speaking Catholics and for Protestants. First, although anglophone Catholics typically outnumbered francophone Catholics outside Quebec (and although this predominance was not to last in New Brunswick), they were far out-

TABLE 5.1:   LEADING DENOMINATIONS IN CANADA, 1851-1911[1]

Year	Methodist	Presbyterian	Anglican	Baptist	Roman Catholic	Total
1851	258,157	310,512	303,897	92,489	983,680	2,303,919
1861	448,774	500,575	475,056	192,530	1,404,775	3,171,418
1871	567,091	544,998	494,049	239,569	1,492,029	3,485,761
1881	742,981	676,165	574,818	296,525	1,791,982	4,234,810
1891	847,765	755,326	646,059	303,839	1,992,017	4,833,234
1901	916,886	842,442	680,620	316,477	2,229,600	5,371,315
1911	1,079,892	1,115,324	1,043,017	382,666	2,833,041	7,206,643

numbered by the French-Canadian population of Quebec itself. Second, not only was the Catholic Church more than two and a half times larger than the largest Protestant denomination, but in Protestant eyes it represented the national church of a people who saw themselves as the country's co-founders. Thus even though Protestants vastly outnumbered Catholics outside Quebec, the French-Canadian face of Catholicism was a constant reminder of a religious, cultural, and linguistic presence that did not conform to their version of Canada as a British Protestant nation, and that challenged the Anglo-Protestant cast of the country's public institutions.

Protestant denominations were both vital and numerous at mid-century. Nearly 85 per cent of Protestants were distributed among four dominant traditions—Anglican, Presbyterian, Methodist, and Baptist—although Presbyterians and Methodists still encompassed a number of separate denominations and Baptists were divided between Regular and Free Will Baptists. Nationally, in 1871, all Methodists combined accounted for 28.5 per cent of Protestants, Presbyterians as a whole accounted for 27.3 per cent, and Anglicans accounted for 24.8 per cent: Baptists followed at a distance with 12 per cent (see Table 5.2). This national pattern, however, masks considerable regional differences in religious affiliation. In Nova Scotia, Presbyterians were far in the lead with

TABLE 5.2: PERCENTAGES OF PROTESTANT POPULATION IN LEADING DENOMINATIONS[2]

Place	Year	Methodist	Presbyterian	Anglican	Baptist
Canada	1871	28.5	27.3	24.8	12.0
Canada	1891	29.8	26.6	22.7	10.6
Canada	1911	25.8	26.6	24.9	9.1
Nova Scotia	1871	14.2	36.2	19.2	25.7
Nova Scotia	1891	16.5	33.2	19.6	25.3
Nova Scotia	1911	16.6	31.7	21.8	24.2
New Brunswick	1871	15.7	20.5	24.0	37.2
New Brunswick	1891	17.3	19.9	21.0	38.8
New Brunswick	1911	16.7	19.0	20.8	39.8
Ontario	1871	34.3	26.5	24.6	6.4
Ontario	1891	37.3	25.8	22.0	6.0
Ontario	1911	33.5	26.2	24.4	6.6
Newfoundland	1869	33.9	1.1	64.5	N/A

36.2 per cent of the Protestant population, followed by Baptists (25.7 per cent), Anglicans (19.2 per cent), and Methodists (14.2 per cent). In Newfoundland, Anglicans predominated with nearly two-thirds of the Protestant population, and Methodists made up most of the remaining third. In New Brunswick, Baptists were by far the largest group, with 37.2 per cent of Protestants; Anglicans made up 24 per cent and Presbyterians 20.5 per cent, with Methodists bringing up the rear at 15.7 per cent. In Ontario, Methodists accounted for over one-third of the Protestant population; Presbyterians (26.5 per cent) and Anglicans (24.6 per cent) vied for second place, and at 6.4 per cent the Baptists placed a distant fourth.

Between 1871 and 1911, both the Methodists and the Presbyterians experienced declines in their relative proportions of the overall Protestant population. The Methodists' share fell more rapidly than that of the Presbyterians, who took over the Methodists' former spot in first place. During the same period the Anglicans managed to hold on to their proportion of the Protestant population, while the Baptists' fell off sharply. Not all regions, of course, followed this pattern. While the Methodists led the way in Ontario, the Anglicans held a commanding lead in Newfoundland, and New Brunswick departed the most from general trend: there the Methodists and Baptists modestly expanded their shares of the population, while the Anglicans faced a significant decline.

All religious traditions were ethnically diverse. Although the published returns of the national census, which began collecting data on national origins in 1871, do not correlate national origin with religious affiliation, a random sample undertaken by A. Gordon Darroch and Michael D. Ornstein offers an invaluable snapshot of the ethnic composition of the main religious groupings in central Canada (see Table 5.3). Of particular note is the fact that, among the population of origins other than French, 85 per cent traced their roots to the United Kingdom. Not surprisingly, the national composition of denominations

TABLE 5.3: ETHNIC COMPOSITION AMONG ANGLOPHONES OF LEADING DENOMINATIONS, CENTRAL CANADA, 1871[3]

Religion	English	Scots	Irish	German	Other
Roman Catholic	4.6	12.5	76.0	3.9	3.1
Methodist	46.1	9.2	28.0	11.6	5.1
Presbyterian	7.2	65.0	24.0	2.2	1.6
Anglican	49.0	5.6	37.6	5.3	2.5
Baptist	54.7	14.2	15.2	8.3	7.6

in central Canada tended to reflect the relative strength of their counterparts across the Atlantic.

Two traditions were primarily associated with specific ethnic groups from the UK: Catholicism with the Irish and Presbyterianism with the Scots. Even so, both the Irish and the Scots were divided along religious lines. More than one-fifth of those of Irish origin were Presbyterian, accounting for almost one-quarter of that denomination's members. Similarly, though to a much lesser degree, the Scots were a significant minority in the Catholic Church. As for the Church of England, contemporaries commonly assumed that it catered primarily to people of English origin, an assumption as prevalent today as it was in the past; but while nearly half of the church's members did trace their roots to England, only about one-third of people of English background belonged to the Anglican Church, which also contained a strong Irish contingent. A higher proportion of Baptists than Anglicans were English by background, and many people of English origin also gravitated to the Methodists, the only denomination that managed to attract a sizeable following across the spectrum of national origins.

Aside from the French Canadians, there were only two significant groups who did not trace their origins back to the UK: those of German origin and the aboriginal peoples. People of German descent represented about 8.4 per cent of the non-French population in central Canada, and they tended to cluster in specific regions. As one would expect, given this pattern of settlement, many were Lutherans (in central Canada, about one-fifth according to Darroch and Ornstein), but even more were Methodists (in central Canada, three-tenths). The other significant group, the aboriginal peoples, who in the 1871 census numbered 23,035, were much more varied in their religious affiliations.[4] Over 95 per cent identified themselves as belonging to one of the five leading Christian traditions: 40 per cent Methodist, 25 per cent Catholic, almost 20 per cent Baptist, a little under 10 per cent Anglican, and 3.7 per cent Presbyterian.

Strong links between religion, national origin, and patterns of settlement created a regional mosaic of ethnic and denominational affiliations. Methodists generally made a poor showing in Atlantic Canada, but they were numerous in the Bay of Fundy watershed, particularly in Sackville, among settlers from New England, and in the English settlements of Cumberland county and Springhill.[5] The Baptists enjoyed a strong presence in both Nova Scotia and New Brunswick, especially among the settlers from New England who were concentrated around the Bay of Fundy.[6] The Presbyterians of Atlantic Canada were concentrated in Truro, Pictou county, and along the north shore of Nova Scotia and Cape Breton. In Canada West, Presbyterians clustered in the areas bounded by Hamilton, London, and Owen Sound in the west and Kingston, Brockville, and Almonte in the east.[7] Scottish Catholics were concentrated in three areas: Prince Edward Island, Cape Breton and eastern Nova Scotia, and around Glengarry and Stormont counties in the southeastern part of the future Ontario.[8] Large numbers of Irish Catholics were found in the urban centres of St John's, Halifax, Saint John, Quebec City, Montreal, Kingston, Toronto, and Hamilton. Still, unlike their cousins in the United States, most settled outside the cities; this was notably the case in Newfoundland, where numerous Catholics lived in the outports of the Avalon peninsula. Elsewhere in Atlantic Canada, Irish Catholics were concentrated in the area around Halifax, as well as in the Saint John River valley and the Miramichi region. Farther west, pockets of Irish Catholics could be found, especially in the Ottawa valley, but most were scattered throughout the region that is now southern Ontario.[9] German Lutherans settled in Nova Scotia around Halifax and Lunenburg, while in Canada West they were drawn to the Waterloo area. However, like the Scots of Nova Scotia's north shore, Germans who settled around Waterloo were divided along religious lines: both areas had large Catholic populations. Finally, low-church Anglicanism enjoyed a regional base in the southwestern part of Canada West, where Anglicans of American and Irish origin had tended to settle.

In Canada East the anglophone population, concentrated in the two main cities, Montreal and Quebec, was similarly divided along Protestant–Catholic lines. At mid-century, Montreal's Protestants and Irish Catholics were almost evenly matched, and together they outnumbered francophones by 5 per cent. But industrialization attracted a growing influx of francophones, with the result that by 1881 anglophones made up only 44 per cent of the population, and fewer than one-quarter of Montreal's Catholics were English-speaking. In Quebec City francophones were the dominant presence, with Irish Catholics a distant second, and anglophone Protestants an even more distant third. According to the 1871 census, francophones accounted for 68 per cent of the population, Irish Catholics just under 20 per cent, and Protestants 12 per cent. Finally, in rural areas, concentrations of Protestants could be found in the outports of Gaspé and in the Eastern Townships, whose founding families traced their roots to the British Isles and the United States.

THE FORMATION OF DENOMINATIONS

Denominations and the public sphere

The secularization of the clergy reserves and the end of church establishment in the Atlantic region were part of a long process that fundamentally changed the public status of religious bodies in British North America. In this process the Church of England lost its state support and special privileges, while other religious bodies were relieved of the last of the disabilities under which they had formerly existed. The transition signalled a major change in status for all of the churches. Although many had functioned all along as voluntary associations, they now shared that status with the Church of England, making each of them denominations in the strict sense of religious organizations independent of the state and depending on the support of their members.[10] While Anglicans accepted the change with considerable reluctance, most Protestants (especially evangelically-minded groups such as Free Church Presbyterians) embraced it with enthusiasm.

Besides placing all churches on the same legal footing, the triumph of voluntarism reinforced and accelerated their tendency towards independence from their parent bodies. At the same time that the British North American churches were seeking greater autonomy and self-reliance, however, they faced the immense challenges and opportunities posed by the formation of a new country. Canadian Confederation was driven by political and economic rather than religious factors, but the union of the British colonies in 1867, the acquisition of the former Hudson's Bay territory in 1870, and the entry of British Columbia in 1871 filled the imaginations of religious leaders with visions of Canada as the Lord's dominion reaching from sea to sea.[11] In order to rise to the challenge, the churches would have to surmount some formidable obstacles. Despite their considerable expansion over the preceding decades, they still lacked the financial and human resources to provide pastoral care across the country. Moreover, their ability to generate and organize such resources was seriously hampered by the fact that they were not national institutions. At best they were regional organizations, and some of the larger religious traditions remained divided into denominational branches.

All of the larger Protestant bodies responded to the new challenges by consolidating themselves into national bodies. This process of consolidation meant not only the development of national structures but also, in the case of those divided into separate branches, the overcoming of those divisions to produce single denominations. The example of political union among the British colonies helped to promote such mergers, as did the large measure of consensus that had already taken shape around evangelical principles. Members of separate denominations not only shared common assumptions but had already worked together in interdenominational organizations such as the Evangelical Alliance and the Sunday-school movement.[12] Evangelical zeal combined with nationalist sentiment and the prospect of sharing overtaxed resources to make the idea of church union very attractive.

The first to achieve a unified national organization were the Presbyterians, who at this stage were divided into three main groups: the Church of Scotland, Seceders, and the Free Church. The Secession and Free Churches united in Nova Scotia in 1860 and in the Canadas in 1861. In 1866, the Free Church in New Brunswick joined the union formed in Nova Scotia, and only one year later the Church of Scotland in those two provinces joined ranks. The fact that the new denominations formed through the union of the Free Church and Seceders embraced voluntarism and were staunch supporters of temperance made it difficult for the Church of Scotland to contemplate joining them. But the Kirk was in dire straits, depending heavily on aid from Scotland, chronically short of ministers, and with a membership that was not increasing. After protracted negotiations, in which promises to respect and tolerate diversity of opinion became a condition of reconciliation, union was eventually achieved in 1875. All four major Presbyterian bodies, two from the Maritimes and two from central Canada, came together to form the Presbyterian Church in Canada. Following the completion of the Canadian Pacific Railway in 1886, the Presbyterians of the Prairies and British Columbia joined the new denomination.[13]

The Methodists were not far behind in achieving a unified national organization. As we have seen, disputes within Methodism after the death of John Wesley in 1791 had led a number of splinter groups, such as the Primitive Methodists and Bible Christians, to separate from the Wesleyan Methodists. These groups established themselves alongside Wesleyan Methodists and the Methodist Episcopal Church in Canada, complicating even further an already complex picture. Each branch of Methodism had its own tradition and polity, but their methods of evangelization and modes of fellowship were similar, and they shared a commitment to establishing the distinctive Methodist version of the Christian life across the country. Economic considerations also played a crucial role in promoting union, not least the cost of training the professional clergy who had replaced saddle-bag preachers and of mounting a concerted missionary effort in the West. Two unions, in 1874 and 1884, brought together six branches of Methodism as the Methodist Church in Canada, leaving only two small bodies, the Free Methodists and the Evangelical Association, outside the mainstream.[14]

The Church of England had greater difficulty in developing national structures. With its episcopal form of church government, it was essentially a loose network of independent dioceses. Within these dioceses, synods comprising lay and clerical delegates had been introduced, beginning in 1854 when John Strachan called the first such gathering in Toronto. Diocesan synods, much like church societies, were initially a means of adapting to voluntarism and the need for Anglicans to become self-supporting. They achieved legal recognition in 1857, the same year in which they first elected a bishop. Diocesan synods strengthened local autonomy, and in this sense made the development of over-arching structures more difficult. The task was further complicated by the deep internal divisions between high- and low-church factions, each of which had regional or diocesan strongholds. In this conflict, which would last until the opening decades of the twentieth century, episcopal elections became highly charged partisan affairs, rival groups established competing theological colleges, and mission funds were all too often held hostage by the feuding factions.[15]

On the other hand, the formation of diocesan synods had set a precedent that could be followed at a higher level of organization. The dioceses of central

Canada led the way, forming the first interdiocesan synod in 1861. In 1874, the dioceses of Nova Scotia and Fredericton joined this Provincial Synod of Canada, and the following year witnessed the birth of the Provincial Synod of Rupert's Land. The economic incentives for co-operation were especially persuasive in the West, where eight dioceses had been established between 1874 and 1891, each one serving a huge but sparsely populated area. But eastern Canadian dioceses preferred to leave the burden of supporting Western missions to British agencies, especially the CMS and SPG. Only after the western dioceses applied heavy pressure was a General Synod for the whole of Canada finally formed in 1893. The General Synod comprised two houses, one consisting solely of bishops, the other of lay and clerical delegates from each of the dioceses. Included in its functions was the election of a primate. The Synod allowed Anglicans to address issues of national concern and provided a means of remaining in communion with Anglicans the world over, but it was a purely consultative body whose decisions were not binding. The centre of ecclesiastical authority remained firmly fixed in the local dioceses. Meanwhile, the Canadian church did not assume full responsibility for the West until the Second World War.

The Roman Catholic Church offers another example of a regionalized denominational structure. Roman Catholic, like Anglican, church government is episcopal in nature and rests on the territorial jurisdiction of bishops over their dioceses. The creation of ecclesiastical provinces in the Maritimes (1852), Ontario (1870), and the North-West (1871) brought the dioceses of these regions together under the nominal leadership of archbishops, but this step did not result even in effective regional government, let alone the emergence of a national body. In keeping with Roman Catholic canon law, bishops continued to exercise sole jurisdiction within their own dioceses, subject only to the authority of the pope, who rarely intervened in the affairs of the local church. Provincial synods, which unlike Anglican synods included only bishops, met infrequently, and could scarcely institutionalize episcopal co-operation or provide a basis for the emergence of a national leadership. The only means by which a bishop could exercise leadership beyond the borders of his diocese were thus *ad hoc*. Linguistic barriers and cultural divisions between French-speaking and English-speaking bishops made co-operation especially difficult. The hierarchy rarely acted as a body except in moments of crisis, and, as we shall see, such action often did little to ease the tensions between anglophone and francophone bishops.

While the immediate post-Confederation era witnessed attempts, some more successful than others, to create national denominational structures, it also saw the emergence of two exclusive communities in English Canada: the Protestant majority and the English-speaking Catholic minority. Religion was central to the ethos and collective identities of both groups, although it inspired them with quite different visions of society and set them on what in the short term would be a collision course.

Among Protestants the role of religious beliefs in society had in the past proved to be both politically and culturally divisive, not only in the early rivalry between evangelical and non-evangelical forms of Christianity but in the struggle over the Anglican establishment. With the settlement of the clergy reserves in the united Canada and the repeal of church establishment in the Maritimes, the way was clear for Protestants to shape a common vision of the destiny and purpose of their society under God. Already an evangelical consensus had begun to emerge that embraced most if not all Protestants, and now that an established church was no longer an option, the main Protestant churches collectively aspired to the role of a cultural establishment. Such a role could only be unofficial—formally, all religious bodies were equal before the law—but it was supported by a vision of the nation that cut across denominational lines, although it excluded Roman Catholics.

None of the elements of this vision was new, but in the context of the emerging Canadian nation they were formulated as principles for the country as a whole. In this national vision, evangelical piety combined with Victorian social values and British patriotism. The British people were seen as a new Israel, chosen to spread true Christianity over the globe, and through the imperial connection Canadians would participate in the great work of the empire to free humanity from ignorance and sin. Loyalty to Britain thus took on a religious aura, and Protestantism was conceived not only as the embodiment of religious truth but also as the agent of human progress. Only Protestantism could foster those moral and intellectual qualities, such as diligence, discipline, independent judgement, and self-reliance, that would usher in an age of improvement and prosperity. The fusion of religious aspirations and cultural expectations inherent in this view of the world rested on the widely held assumption that religion was the foundation of society.[16] While investing denominational spokesmen with cultural authority, it rose above particular denominational identities to create a broader sense of Protestant solidarity. In addressing public issues, Protestant leaders appealed to what they interpreted as the essentials of Christianity, a generic form of Protestantism that went hand in hand with civilization and progress.

The Catholic understanding of the public sphere, which differed sharply from the Protestant one, was informed by Ultramontanism. By mid-century this international movement of religious reform and renewal was having a profound effect on British North American Catholicism. According to the Ultramontane view, the Catholic Church was a society complete unto itself, embracing all aspects of the lives of the faithful. Public institutions such as schools, hospitals and orphanages were to come under the aegis of the church, the role of the state being simply to provide funding and generally to support the church in its social endeavours. To this end Catholics established a wide range of social agencies and institutions to care for their own from cradle to grave. These institutions ran parallel to those of mainstream society, which in Catholic eyes were tainted by the dominant Protestant ethos. Among Catholics, therefore, denominational identification entailed joining an enclosed subculture apart from the anglophone mainstream. Although many Protestants assumed that this cultural isolation was forced on the laity by their clergy, in fact it was self-imposed; and Catholic laity and clergy alike believed it to be necessary if they were to preserve their faith from the surrounding sea of Protestantism.

While erecting protective barriers against the dominant culture, however, Catholics felt that they were entitled to public support. If Protestants had their own institutions, paid for out of government funds, Catholics felt that they should enjoy the same right. Public funding thus became a subject of controversy in which two major issues were at stake. The first was the viability of Catholic social institutions; the second was the public recognition of the Catholic subculture that such funding would imply. English-speaking Catholics were determined to secure such recognition, even if the effort meant all-out conflict with the Protestant majority.

Alongside this conflict, but largely unnoticed by Protestants, was the linguistic and cultural divide within the Canadian Catholic Church between French- and English-speakers. Among anglophone Catholics, the Irish were by far the dominant group, and for them, as for French-Canadian Catholics, religion was the touchstone of both collective identity and community life. As John Moir has pointed out, Irish Catholics constituted a double minority: a religious minority in English-speaking Canada, and a linguistic minority in the Catholic Church.[17] In order to preserve their cultural distinctiveness, therefore, they found themselves battling on two fronts. Within the Catholic fold, they campaigned for control over the church outside Quebec, chiefly through the appointment of Irish bishops, on the grounds that as representatives of the English-speaking majority in the country they were entitled to such hegemony. Within the broader society, meanwhile, they struggled for recognition as a distinct and important component in the emerging Canadian mosaic. Besides public funding, they wanted to see their own lay and clerical leaders included in the country's political and cultural establishment. Not only did such leaders represent and promote Catholic interests, but in many cases they personified the collective aspirations of English-speaking Catholics.

Denominations and the formation of local communities
The formation of national denominations was a significant development, but for the laity denominational involvement centred on the local congregation. The congregation was an important social institution, and like other such

institutions it was substantially affected by the major changes taking place in Canadian society. With industrialization and urbanization, the decades after 1850 saw the growth of sizeable cities, as well as a proliferation of small towns whose prosperity depended on manufacturing and commerce, typically with their adjoining rural areas. In Ontario, for example, the number of towns with populations of between 1,000 and 5,000 doubled from 33 to 69 in the two decades after 1850.[18] At the same time class divisions became more obvious. Although social and economic disparities had certainly existed before, industrialization brought previously unimagined wealth to entrepreneurs, made possible an unprecedented expansion of the middle class, and attracted workers with the prospects of employment. These changes in turn led to the differentiation of neighbourhoods along class lines, a novel development at the time.

Partly because of the demand created by growing urban populations, and partly because of economic prosperity and the rapid expansion of the middle class, a church-building boom occurred in the towns and cities. Both the number and the size of churches increased rapidly, reflecting their dominant role in the community; the rate of construction actually exceeded population growth, and new or renovated churches were bigger and more imposing than their modest predecessors. Wooden frame structures gave way to brick and brick to stone as congregations adopted Gothic and, after the 1880s, Romanesque architecture.[19] Many churches could seat 1,000 people or more,[20] a figure comparable to major theatres, and in total capacity the churches vastly outranked these secular establishments.

Once a congregation built a large church, it put into play a dynamic with far-reaching consequences for its social, cultural, and religious life.[21] The size of churches to some degree embodied hopes for future growth, and congregations had to reach out beyond their original circle of members in order to fill the pews. In fact, their position was not much different from that of theatre-owners, who also had large mortgages and overhead expenses to pay. If they were to continue to operate, they would have to fill the house, and not just with a one-time sensation: what they needed was a star attraction who would keep the crowds coming back.

A large church therefore required a very particular kind of preacher. He would need an excellent voice, and would have to project a certain personal charisma. He would also (unlike most public figures today) need to be an effective writer, capable of producing distinctive material week after week. Among Methodists, these requirements contributed to the changing character of the ministry as itinerant preachers gave way to settled ministers, some of whom were assigned to a single congregation. The members of the leading Methodist congregations were people of wealth, substance, and education, who wished their clergy to have the attainments appropriate in such circles, including, if not a degree, at least some university education.[22] Settled ministry meanwhile enlarged the duties of the local pastor, who became responsible for supervising the congregation and co-ordinating its many activities, from the Sunday school to the woman's auxiliary. This expanding role, together with the increasingly professional status of ministers, enhanced their authority as community leaders.

One indication of the clergy's prestige was the growing popularity of evening services. Usually better attended than those offered in the morning, evening services tended to be less formal and to address a wider audience. Attendance at evening services was an important part of many people's Sunday recreation. Before and after church, people would promenade up and down the streets, and those attending the service expected to be entertained. Thus in many cases the minister of a large church became something of a local personality. In 1891, the Toronto *Daily Mail* even mounted a circulation campaign in which it invited readers to fill in ballots contained in each issue to nominate their favourite minister for a free return passage to England. That the winning minister, Joseph Wild of Bond Street Congregational Church, received 160,494 votes in a city of only 144,023 people gives some indication of the breadth—and enthusiasm—of his following.[23]

The nature of congregational worship also changed during this era. As church buildings grew in size, congregations sought to beautify their interiors. Richly carpeted front platforms and pulpits, tall stained-glass windows, walls panelled with well-oiled wood, vaulted ceilings decorated with tinted paper and elegant chandeliers created a dignified and imposing setting for worship. Even among evangelical Protestants, who in the past had championed plainness, worship became more elaborate. Perhaps the most visible innovation was the introduction of the organ, with its massive pipes soaring high above the pulpit. Such was the rage for organs that congregations frequently competed to secure the biggest and best instrument—not an insignificant endeavour when an organ could cost $2,000 or more. Even the Presbyterians, who had traditionally banned musical instruments of any sort from their sanctuaries, soon joined in. This allegedly unscriptural practice aroused considerable opposition, and some congregations split over the issue. But opposition eventually gave way to acceptance, as the case of Erskine Presbyterian Church in Montreal illustrates. In 1874, those who opposed the purchase of an organ felt so strongly that they walked out to form a new congregation on Stanley Street; two decades later, the Stanley Street church itself installed an organ.

Once organs were introduced, choirs and then musical directors soon followed. Unlike their Roman Catholic counterparts, where the organ and choir were in the back gallery, Presbyterian, Methodist, and Baptist churches usually placed their choirs in the front of the church, surrounding the pulpit. These innovations were accompanied by two major changes in ecclesiastical architecture, which made churches look more like auditoriums: the introduction of galleries wrapping around the front of the nave, and sloped floors, both of which gave congregations a better view of the pulpit. The design of new Anglican churches also tended to emphasize spectacle, although here the organ was placed along one side of the chancel, with the two halves of the choir on either side, facing one another.

Since professional organists and choir directors naturally wished to show their talents to advantage, choirs expanded their repertoires to encompass not only hymns but anthems and oratorios including parts for soloists. Performed music became a major element in congregational worship, in some cases over-shadowing the minister's sermon. To mark major festivals, such as Christmas and Easter, churches would present choral services that dispensed altogether with preaching, and as churches competed for audiences such events became major entertainments in their own right. So too did Sunday services, and some-times congregations—even among Methodists, who were forbidden to attend the theatre—would invite singers from troupes appearing locally to perform in their churches.

In building large, imposing churches, congregations made a social as well as a religious statement. These 'sermons in stone', to borrow William Westfall's evocative phrase,[24] proclaimed the grandeur of Christian truth and pointed the way to salvation. At a time when office and communication towers had yet to be imagined, church spires dominated the skyline, a visible expression of the churches' claim upon the Canadian city. The leading congregations of each denomination sought sites in the best parts of town, either in the central busi-ness district or in the newly fashionable suburbs. As a conspicuous display of wealth and substance, a well-located, imposing church affirmed the public sta-tus of the particular denomination as well as the social standing of individual church members. At the same time, the fact that church buildings were objects of civic pride—the larger and more numerous they were, the more apparent it was that a community had prospered and matured—made it easier to raise funds for church building, since few people wanted their communities to look second-rate in comparison with others.

Large churches required huge resources. Construction costs for the largest of them, such as Wesleyan Metropolitan in Toronto, could reach $150,000, an exceptional price at a time when many labourers earned no more than a dollar a day. Wesleyan Metropolitan was unusually expensive, but a cost of $40,000 was not atypical, and that price tag would leave even a prosperous congregation with a sizeable mortgage. Congregations also had to meet large overhead costs, not the least of which were the usual expenses for maintenance. A large congrega-tion would have to offer its minister an attractive salary, and in addition might support a salaried organist and musical director, as well as a secretary in the church office. A large church depended, therefore, on the support of the middle classes and, above all, the wealthy. One way of inducing such people to be gen-erous—and of obliging their peers to be generous too—was to get them involved in managing the church's affairs (a formula that fund-raisers have long relied upon). Thus the middle class dominated church management, and the wealthy were especially prominent among the leaders of most congregations.

One result of these developments was that in most large churches the prevailing ethos was unmistakably middle-class. As church membership and involvement became a means for middle-class people to affirm their status as respectable members of society, their churches became more distant, both geographically and socially, from the working class. And although some large congregations did set up branch churches for mission outreach in working-class areas, these tended to preserve and strengthen the middle-class character of the churches in more desirable locations. The determination of the well-off to make their churches the best that money could buy served only to emphasize the social gulf between those who had and those who had not.

As in so many other respects, Catholic congregations departed substantially from this Protestant pattern. The urban expansion of the Catholic Church was based on the influx of immigrants from Ireland, who for the most part augmented the ranks of the working class. Although the occasional wealthy benefactor did come forward, most parishes depended on regular contributions from ordinary working men and women. Their donations were necessarily small, perhaps a nickel or a dime a week, but they quickly added up, and many lay people were prepared to make extraordinary sacrifices to support their church. Bazaars, for example, could bring in $2,000 or more, even in small towns. With such generous donations Catholics could build churches that rivalled those of their Protestant neighbours, and the 'brick-and-mortar' priest dedicated to church building and expansion became a familiar figure.

In Hamilton, Ontario, where Catholics made up only 17 or 18 per cent of the population, property belonging to the Catholic Church accounted for nearly one-third (around $300,000) of the assessed value of all church property in 1895.[25] Much of this property, of course, represented the church's stake in social institutions such as homes for the aged and infirm, orphanages, and schools. This network of Catholic social institutions helps to explain why lay people contributed so generously to their church. But to build and run these institutions it was essential that the church use its resources efficiently. In Hamilton there were only four Catholic churches, compared with ten each for the Methodists and Anglicans. These churches served parishes that were as large as any Protestant congregation, even though the buildings themselves tended to be smaller. Catholic churches were able to manage with fewer seats because they re-used them, offering as many as three morning services on a Sunday, whereas most Protestant churches offered only one.

Early Catholic churches tended to be unobtrusive, plain structures with bare interiors. Not only did such buildings cost less to construct, but through the 1830s most Catholics still preferred to keep a low public profile, as they had done in the old country. As Ultramontanism gained influence in Canada, however, and Catholics became more self-assured, they adopted the more assertive styles of Gothic and, later, Romanesque architecture for their churches. This shift in architectural style reflected the Ultramontane emphasis on new forms of Catholic worship, stressing visual display. The more 'churchly' styles of the new Catholic architecture furnished the appropriate setting for the elaborate ceremonies that were to emerge as hallmarks of the new Catholic piety. Churches were transformed into houses of God, as exemplified in the custom of reserving the host permanently in the tabernacle, which became common only after the mid-1800s. No less anxious than their Protestant neighbours to beautify the interiors of their churches, Catholics commissioned not only stained-glass windows and massive paintings, but statues and other images considered idolatrous by most Protestants. Nevertheless, the focal point remained the altar. Candelabra and ornamental gas-jet lighting were strategically deployed in and around the chancel, while altarpieces became more elaborate and imposing, with intricate carvings and gilded surfaces surrounding and soaring above the tabernacle.

PIETY, LAY ACTIVISM, AND IDENTITY

By the middle of the nineteenth century many Victorian clergy and laity, convinced that sheer numbers of church-goers revealed the moral and intellectual progress achieved by society, feared that church attendance was on the decline. Yet the available evidence suggests that the opposite was true. Only two surveys measuring levels of church attendance appear to have been conducted, both of them in Toronto, and they show that church attendance rose appreciably over a decade and half, from 45 per cent in 1882 to a little more than 55 per cent in 1896.[26] In 1882 just over half the city's Presbyterian and Roman Catholic populations were in church on the February Sunday in question; among Methodists the figure was nearly half (45 per cent), and among Anglicans, one-quarter. In May 1896 the proportions had risen significantly across the board, and in some cases the increases were dramatic: almost three-quarters for Methodists, around three-fifths for both Roman Catholics and Presbyterians, and nearly one-third for Anglicans.

The nature of the surveys, moreover, indicates that their results were probably conservative. For one thing, no attempt was made to determine how many people were unable to attend church for reasons of health or age. The count was also limited to those attending services and evidently did not include those participating in other church activities. Among Anglicans, for instance, the group with the lowest rate of attendance, the survey results do not appear to include Sunday-school students; yet later reports to the Synod reveal that the usual turnout at Sunday school was not much less than that for morning services.[27] Finally, the surveys counted those attending worship on a single

Sunday, which would be lower than the number of people who might be fairly described as frequent or regular church-goers. If the surveys counted the number of people who had attended worship at least once in the previous month, for example, the percentages would have been higher than those in church on a given day. All these considerations suggest that the attendance figures establish only a floor level of participation.

People's involvement in and commitment to their local congregation varied enormously. At one end of the spectrum were those whose contact with any church was minimal, perhaps being limited to the major transitions in life—birth, marriage, death. At the other end were those whose calendars were filled with church activities and meetings of church-based organizations such as women's auxiliaries among Protestants or devotional organizations among Roman Catholics. Between these two poles one finds various combinations of participation and apathy. Some people who did not go to church themselves insisted that their children attend Sunday school faithfully; this was a common pattern in Anglican parishes. Others stopped short of joining a congregation, even though they regularly attended evening services.

Denominations defined membership in different ways. Among evangelical groups, such as Methodists and Baptists, it entailed a profession of faith (testifying to a conversion experience) and an undertaking to abide by the discipline and doctrines of the church. Among Anglicans and Roman Catholics, on the other hand, all those baptized are considered to be members. These denominational differences, especially in the emphasis placed on the conscious decision to affiliate oneself with a particular denomination, make meaningful comparisons difficult. Fortunately, though, there is a marker of affiliation for Anglicans and Catholics that roughly approximates membership in the evangelical churches. Both kept reliable statistics on communicants: those who conformed to the ecclesiastical regulation enjoining the faithful to receive the sacrament of the eucharist (and penance among Catholics) at Easter.

No doubt the single most important determinant of church membership was gender. In the broadest terms, women of all ages, single or married, Catholic or Protestant, were considerably more inclined than men to expressions of piety. This pattern reflected the roles that Victorian society assigned to the two sexes. The dependence on God, self-sacrifice, and service that Christianity asked of the faithful were thoroughly familiar to women in their social relationships, especially within the family. For men, on the other hand, the social ideal of virile self-reliance did not necessarily encourage religious observance. However, marital status and class produced variations in this broad picture, as the pioneering community studies of Lynne Marks and Doris O'Dell have shown.[28] Among Protestants, women dominated church membership rolls for two reasons. First, young single men from all classes stayed away from church. Second, whereas among middle-class men marriage typically led to church membership, this was not the norm in working-class families. Moreover, among the middle class most who regularly attended church were church members. By contrast, many working-class church-goers dispensed with formal membership.

Gender and class operated in different ways among Roman Catholics. While young Catholic men generally were no more likely to attend church than their Protestant counterparts, by the 1880s most did receive the sacraments of penance and communion at Easter. Levels as high as eight in ten were not unusual even in urban areas, where the vast majority of Catholics were working-class. Though women were the more avid church-goers, the observations of contemporaries suggest that the differences in church attendance between them and married men were not as marked as among Protestants; nor were significant differences evident between the social classes.

Besides strong religious convictions, there were many reasons why people joined a congregation. Especially among the middle class, to be known as a church member consolidated one's social position, and businessmen found that church connections helped to secure customers and obtain financial backing. Church-going was not only the fashionable thing to do, but a respectable form of recreation. As the novelist Sara Jeannette Duncan observed, the Sunday service 'was for many the intellectual exercise, for more the emotional lift, and for all the unfailing distraction of the week'.[29] Churches offered an opportunity to hear some of the best music and oratory available, an occasion to socialize with friends, and an approved setting for courtship. In addition, members of the middle class faced considerable social pressure for religious conformity. Not to attend church was at the very least a show of bad manners, which could undermine one's position in society, and at worst it could be taken as evidence of lack of character and moral sensibility.

Similar influences, positive and negative, were at work among the working class. Opportunities for courting, entertainment, and sociability could all be found at church, not to mention social connections that could prove helpful should one fall on hard times. Among the Protestant working class, however, such considerations were not always sufficient to induce people, especially men, to become involved with a congregation. A significant working-class minority, mostly women, did join a church. Many more attended church regularly but did not join a congregation, and here again women predominated, though to a lesser degree than was the case among church members. Finally, an abstaining hard core, mostly men, avoided church altogether.

There is little doubt that many working-class Protestants faced considerable obstacles to becoming involved with a church. Congregations preferred to locate their churches in the better parts of town, away from working-class areas, and as neighbourhoods increasingly reflected class differences after mid-century, the distance that working-class people had to travel to attend church was as much social as geographic in nature. Then too, it cost money to attend church, let alone to become a member. While, for many, simply to buy Sunday clothes required significant sacrifices, church members were expected to contribute to the collection plate and to rent pews, which even at the lower end of the fee scale could represent several days' earnings. Seating in most churches reflected the social hierarchy, with some churches charging as much sixty-five dollars a year—more than many working-class families paid in rent for their homes. Such high rents reflected the middle-class ethos of the Protestant congregation, which in itself would have tended to make people from the working class uncomfortable. Those who could spare a few dollars a year were relegated to the second worst seating in the church (the worst being reserved for those who paid no pew rent at all). In this way seating arrangements underlined disparities in wealth and status, and for many from the working class such emphasis was nothing less than an assault on their dignity and self-respect.

Such discrimination affected all people from the working class regardless of their gender. Nevertheless, one study indicates that its effect was far greater on men.[30] While Protestant working-class women were somewhat less likely than their middle-class counterparts to become church members, working-class men were half as likely as middle-class men to join a church. Why this was the case, and why congregational life was particularly attractive to women, may become clearer in the light of the patterns of lay piety and activism that emerged during the middle decades of the nineteenth century.

The word piety means different things to different people. For some it is primarily associated with the development of the interior life, what some would call spirituality. For others, piety is primarily a question of practice. Most would agree, however, that neither aspect should be emphasized at the expense of the other. Jerald Brauer has suggested that piety be examined as a 'way of becoming, being, and remaining Christian'.[31] This perspective has several advantages, not the least of which is that it helps us to see piety as a process with its own internal dynamics that give it structure and coherence. Thus Brauer's definition points as well to the importance of piety in creating and sustaining cultural identity.

In many ways nineteenth-century Roman Catholicism exemplifies how piety fostered both personal commitment and group identity. At mid-century, the prospects facing the Catholic Church outside Quebec were hardly encouraging. Rich in neither personnel nor resources, it ministered to a Catholic population that was growing rapidly and expanding into recently settled areas. Not only was the church struggling to keep up with this population growth, with the risk that many people would remain unchurched, but in some parts of the country a large proportion of the laity were first-generation immigrants, mainly from Ireland, whose Catholicism was more likely than not to be nominal, at least as measured by official standards.

Beginning in the Atlantic colonies during the late 1830s, Canada East in the 1840s, and Canada West in the following decade, a new generation of clergy had come to the fore that was inspired by the Ultramontane tenets then gaining dominance in the Catholic Church world-wide. As we have seen, Ultramontanism not only exalted the authority of the papacy but also promoted ecclesiastical reform and religious renewal. A variety of means were employed to achieve this end, but among the most successful was the parish mission. The Catholic equivalent of Protestant revival meetings, parish missions consisted of several consecutive days of intense worship and preaching under the leadership of visiting members of religious orders such as the Redemptorists, who specialized in such events.

In the course of such missions preachers liberally invoked the fires of hell and used all sorts of dramatic devices, including open coffins, to remind their audiences of human mortality and bring them to the moment of decision, following which the faithful would confess their sins and receive communion. At the same time, parish missions also helped to promote the new form of Catholic piety characterized by the performance of private and public devotions—such paraliturgical activities as the recitation of the rosary, or the Forty Hours Devotion to the Blessed Sacrament. Most of these devotions were Italian in origin, and many can be traced back to the medieval era, but their popularization through the Ultramontane revival was so effective as to create a new kind of Catholicism that may be aptly described as 'devotional'. The papacy played a central role in this development, systematically promoting devotional exercises in general as well as specific devotions, with the result that Roman practices became standardized the world over. To be considered a devout Catholic it was no longer sufficient to attend mass and to receive the sacraments regularly: one now had to perform a variety of devotions as well, some of them several times daily. Although exacting, these practices became extremely popular, strengthening the attachment of many people to the church and contributing to higher rates of attendance at worship.

Devotions became popular because they made the supernatural more accessible to lay people. In performing devotions the faithful developed relationships with figures such as Jesus, Mary, and the saints. Through the good offices of these figures, they could secure temporal favours, such as improved health or employment, and advance their salvation by gaining access to the church's spiritual treasury: the merit earned by others that they could now add to their own good works. Devotions made supernatural beings present in everyday life in an immediate and personal way, and the emotional bonds that people developed with their patrons were frequently described in sentimental terms. Such piety, which was highly demonstrative, was at once formalistic, in that it placed great stress on the correct performance of rituals, and deeply experiential.

Devotions supplemented but were not meant to replace sacramental worship; they were merely the daily exercises that kept the faithful in shape to make the most effective use of the graces imparted by the sacraments by cultivating those virtues most pleasing to God. Thus although devotional piety provided direct access to the divine, and so encouraged individuals to pursue their personal salvation, at the same time they underscored the Catholic Church's mediating role in the process of salvation. Devotions engendered a specific kind of piety, a form of sacramental nurture, in which salvation depended on the regular reception of the sacraments, which the clergy alone could administer. But they also had advantages for ordinary worshippers that the sacraments themselves did not offer. For example, unlike the mass, which was conducted in Latin, devotions were performed in the vernacular. As time went on, more and more lay people recited devotions when at mass, especially as relatively inexpensive editions of prayer books made them more easily available. Since most devotions typically focused on one or another aspect of the lives of Jesus and Mary, with the Lord's passion occupying a central place, they connected the laity to the events celebrated by the mass and thus helped to communicate the official teachings of the church. They also reinforced the priest's authority by drawing attention to his intimate association with Jesus through his celebration of the mass, in which he re-enacted the passion and transformed bread and wine into the body and blood of Christ.[32]

The clergy often encouraged lay people to practise devotions such as the rosary and the stations of the cross in their own homes. Accordingly, the faithful eagerly bought inexpensive lithographs of the Virgin Mary, the pope, and the like, as well as crucifixes and miniature altars or stations of the cross, with which to decorate and sanctify their homes. It was in the home, at their mother's knee, that children began to form emotional relationships with Jesus, Mary, and the saints, and many clergy urged men to spend their free time at home, under the beneficent spell of female influence. But if the home was associated with religion, both Catholic ritual and doctrine prevented it from rivalling the parish church as a religious centre. Domestic devotions could not equal the mass in importance, and the home could never replace the true house of God, where the real body and blood of Christ were to be found. The home became sacred because it served as an extension of the parish church—that haven in a heartless and sinful world whose ways, as the clergy frequently reminded the faithful, were at the very least Protestant, if not utterly godless.

Within a couple of generations after mid-century, the vast majority of Catholics not only attended mass regularly but also practised devotions. The key to this transformation was the parish church, which became the chief link in the chain of social institutions through which Catholics hoped to preserve their culture and religion. In effect, the parish church was not only a religious but a communal institution. Its success in the latter role reflected in part the fact that, in any given area, anglophone Catholics usually shared a common ethnic background, whether Irish or Scottish, and often settled in sufficient concentrations to support their own institutions. In both Quebec City and Montreal, for instance, Irish Catholics had their own national parishes, and in Montreal they supported an orphan asylum, a refuge for the poor, schools, and a hospital.[33] Yet even with the inexpensive work force composed of the men and women in religious communities,[34] parish life depended in large part on the efforts of lay people in a wide variety of voluntary organizations.

Parish women formed charitable associations known as sewing societies, while the most common outlet for such work among lay men was the Saint Vincent de Paul Society. Devotional organizations were by far the largest parish associations, and they gave the church immeasurable assistance in promoting the new piety. Throughout the nineteenth century, the overwhelmingly female membership of these groups reflected the fact that in general women were more assiduous in their religious practice than men, who were more likely to join temperance or literary societies. Yet even groups whose overt purposes were mainly secular often had a religious agenda as well. Temperance societies, for instance, deliberately appealed to working-class aspirations to social respectability while endeavouring to persuade their members that religious observance was not incompatible with the popular ideal of manly independence.

Shortly after 1900, devotional organizations began to recruit men on a large scale, and in this they largely succeeded: in Toronto the Holy Name Society for men became one of the church's most successful voluntary organizations. Among the factors that prompted men to take up devotions was the church's role as a communal institution. Even before devotional organizations became popular among men, however, Catholicism had exercised an appeal that transcended divisions of gender and class. Men and women alike thronged the churches on Sunday evenings, for the benediction of the Blessed Sacrament, and some public devotions, such as the processions marking the feast of Corpus Christi, became truly popular neighbourhood celebrations.

The church's network of voluntary associations and social institutions meant that it offered something for everyone, from every social background, at every stage of life. All were served by the church and, just as important, all had an equal claim to it. In providing outlets for lay activism and opportunities to exercise leadership, parish organizations also directed lay energies along church-approved channels. They taught their members to assist the parish priest in his ministry; lay leaders were to buttress the priest's authority, not to compete with him. And although the middle class played a disproportionate role in such organizations, the church did not become the property of any one class (in contrast to the tendency in Protestant congregations), in part because of the supreme rule of the parish priest.

The womb-to-tomb services provided by the church made possible the emergence of a distinct anglophone Catholic subculture within a generation as schools and other social institutions inculcated the outlook and practices of devotional Catholicism. The culture of piety that resulted enabled English-speaking Catholics to develop communities that were in many ways separate from those of their Protestant and French-Canadian neighbours. While their devotional practices set them apart from Protestants, the ethnic nature of their institutions set them apart from francophone Catholics, and the result was a powerful sense of cultural identity.

In contrast to Catholicism, with its emphasis on the sacraments, evangelical Protestantism fostered a revivalist form of piety based on personal conversion. Although they were not the only revivalist denomination, the Methodists were by far the largest, and they believed themselves to be the most consistent in both doctrine and practice. Like other evangelicals, Methodists believed they had a responsibility to announce the good news of salvation through faith in the redemptive work of Jesus. Unlike evangelicals of a Calvinist bent, however, they held that salvation was freely available to anyone who would respond to and co-operate with God's grace. Salvation was within humanity's grasp, for God had given humans free will and the ability to take the first step in the Christian life and renounce sin. Believing that people had a moral responsibility to save both themselves and others, Methodists developed a variety of techniques and institutions, of which the revival meeting, with its mass conversions, is the best-known, first to bring individuals to the moment of decision and then to sustain them in the Christian life.

Methodist piety was experiential in nature: through a new birth in Christ individuals repented their sins and placed their faith in the transforming power of the cross to save their souls. In this respect it was similar to other forms of revivalism, but Methodist piety was distinct on two counts. First, the instantaneous experience of conversion was accompanied by the assurance (known as the witness of the Holy Spirit) that one was forgiven. The second hallmark of Methodism was its emphasis on the quest for holiness, or entire sanctification. Holiness was the goal of the Christian, and all Methodists agreed on the need to avoid deliberate sin. They disagreed, however, on the way in which personal righteousness was attained. Some Methodists understood holiness as a process of gradual moral growth and improvement that began with conversion and continued for the rest of one's life. Others believed that conversion was followed some time later by another instantaneous experience, a second blessing of the Holy Spirit, and the achievement of Christian perfection. This latter approach gained a wide following as a result of a several 'holiness revivals' in the 1850s, and a number of prominent Methodists—including Nathanael Burwash, the chancellor of Victoria University in Toronto—made it a cornerstone of their preaching and teaching. In either case, however, growth in grace was the result of participation in the Christian community and the performance of good works.

Some historians have argued that after the 1850s Methodist revivalism went into decline.[35] It is true that, as they moved into the middle class, most Methodists came to disapprove of the emotional displays associated with camp meetings. Over the next couple of decades such meetings were gradually abandoned in favour of permanent Methodist campgrounds equipped with summer cottages and all the amenities expected by middle-class vacationers. At the same time, a new type of revivalism—urban-based, frequently (though not always) conducted by professional evangelists, and decidedly sober in character—became the norm. Typical of the new preachers who appealed to the intellect as well as the heart was James Caughey, who led several of the holiness revivals that were so successful in the 1850s. His sermons did not lack for melodrama as he singled out individuals and drew scenes from daily life to illustrate the tragic consequences of sin. But he spoke in a direct and colloquial style, and his contemporaries were struck by his quiet manner and plain reasoning. As in the past, revivalists continued to soften hearts and stir the emotions, but now they did so in the decorously sentimental fashion of which respectable Victorians approved.

Revivalism had long occupied a central place in the religious life of Methodists, Baptists, Congregationalists, and a substantial segment of Presbyterians, encouraging interdenominational competition and reinforcing denominational boundaries. By contrast, the new style of revivalism contributed to a growing consensus among Protestant denominations. Caughey's converts in central Canada, for instance, were accepted into Baptist as well as Methodist congregations, while the teachings of Phoebe Palmer, another leader of holiness revivals, received a warm response from Baptists in the Maritimes. In turn, this emergent consensus laid the groundwork for Protestant co-operation in the future. Following a continent-wide interdenominational revival in 1857–8, many Presbyterians who had previously looked askance at revival-based conversion embraced it, and by the 1870s low-church Anglicans were among the most enthusiastic supporters of the new revivalism. As a result of these developments, interdenominational revivals conducted by professional revivalists supported by the local Protestant clergy became common in many urban centres. Theological differences between Arminian Methodists and Calvinist Protestants (including Presbyterians, Anglican evangelicals, and some varieties of Baptists) became less important as all came to emphasize the practical consequences of conversion. Together with its emphasis on good works, the more subdued ethos of the new revivalism did much to make it respectable. True conversion would be manifested not in displays of emotion, but in how one lived one's life.[36]

To the extent that revivalism emphasized personal responsibility in the work of salvation, it was highly individualistic, as were the quintessential Victorian values—self-improvement, self-control, self-reliance—that it helped to promote.

At the same time, however, a revival was a public event, a ritual of community that brought people together, whether or not they were all affiliated with a particular denomination. In converting the faithless and renewing the faith of believers, the revival transformed individuals into people of God, brothers and sisters in Christ. At revivals the bonds of fellowship were made real, and one result was a sense of community that expressed itself in collective action.

Conversion remained the first step in the Christian's journey to heaven, and the usual place for conversions was the revival meeting. Even towards the end of the nineteenth century, informed observers believed that as many as three-quarters of all church members had been converted at revivals,[37] which were hugely popular, community-wide events. In the mid-1880s one month-long campaign in Toronto, led by Hugh T. Crossley and John E. Hunter, drew between 75,000 and 100,000 people.[38] But these meetings differed in one fundamental respect from earlier ones: now those who converted had more than likely grown up in Methodist homes where they were regularly exposed to Sunday-school lessons, sermons, Bible readings and, above all, parental example.

Nathanael Burwash recounted how his parents led their children in prayer every morning and evening, regularly read aloud passages from the Bible, and every Sunday evening offered religious instruction. Such household piety was typical among Methodists, and Burwash had no doubt that it had prepared his way to conversion.[39] Nurture, then, did not make conversion redundant, but rather laid the groundwork for it. The religious odyssey of Methodist children began at an early age—Burwash began at age seven to seek deliverance from his sins—but in most cases conversion, the one essential precondition for church membership, did not occur before early adulthood. The new birth and the pursuit of righteousness subsequent to it remained the distinguishing features of Methodism and the touchstones of the religious life. In its quest for righteousness, Methodism required periodic revivals not only to recruit new members but also to refresh the faith and moral tone of the rank and file. Thus revivalism continued to be central to Methodist piety and identity, and Methodists took pride in the fact that their methods and approaches to piety were adopted by others, most notably in the holiness movement.

The holiness movement changed the character of Methodist piety in at least two respects. First, the refound emphasis on holiness provided church members with a richer and more fulfilling spiritual life. Second, to the extent that this approach stressed the experiential basis of moral progress, the living presence of the Holy Spirit, this in turn galvanized people to dedicate themselves to the service of God. Under the influence of the holiness movement, moral reform, both personal and social, increasingly became the focus of evangelicalism, providing the impetus for many of the reform and humanitarian initiatives of the day. On the other hand, moral earnestness could easily degenerate into a rigid moralism, and middle-class conformity too often became the principal indication of an individual's sanctity.[40]

The institutional cast of Methodist revivalism also changed significantly in the latter part of the nineteenth century as itinerant preachers were replaced by settled ministers, and evangelism became the domain of specialists, particularly after 1870. Many of these professional revivalists were freelancers, however, operating without church approval, and it was widely feared that their teachings ran counter to Methodist doctrine. In response, the church began to commission its own evangelists. The demand for revival specialists steeped in Methodist traditions opened the way for a number of women to become full-time evangelists in the 1880s, some three decades after women had stopped serving in the pulpit. Though not admitted to the ministry, women would remain familiar figures on the revival circuit until the turn of the century.[41]

One of the reasons that Methodism thrived was its success in institutionalizing revivalism. Revival meetings may have yielded bountiful harvests, but they could not guarantee that converts would persevere in leading a holy life. Thus in addition to the extraordinary means of grace exemplified by the revival meeting, Methodists relied on a variety of ordinary means of grace to promote the work of the spirit. Among the most distinctive of these was the class meeting—originally established in the era when itinerant ministers made only infrequent visits—attendance at which was required of all members. Every week, members would discuss their religious experiences in groups of a dozen or so under lay leadership and direction. Class meetings were intended as nurseries for Methodist piety, where the converted could cultivate their life in grace in co-operation with other wayfarers on the path to salvation, and the unconverted could experience the love of their neighbours and through them find peace with God. How well they succeeded has been the subject of disagreement among historians.[42] Significantly, though, the most concerted attempt during the nineteenth century to remove class attendance as a condition of membership was overwhelmingly defeated in 1878. Most clergy were steadfast in their defence of the class meeting, but as the century wore on new voluntary organizations vied for the laity's attention.

The emergence of these voluntary associations was closely related to the activist impulse inherent in Methodism. If it was the central objective of evangelicalism to convert the world to Christ, and the personal responsibility of each Christian to pursue this task, the holiness movement in Methodism added a special impetus. Regeneration washed away sin, making it possible to consecrate oneself entirely to God, and it was His will that Christians lead a life of service to others. Love of God was to find its worldly expression in love of one's neighbour. The spiritual ethos of Methodism encouraged activism on the part of individuals and at the same time encouraged church members to band together and reclaim souls.

A prime example of the proliferation of voluntary organizations at the congregational level can be seen in the Sunday schools, which in addition to religious instruction and moral uplift offered reading lessons, exposure to literature, and entertaining pastimes for children. In many cases, the Sunday school was the nerve centre of the congregation; Sunday-school picnics, concerts, and rallies were major events in the community, and through them, along with their work in the classroom, Sunday-school activists formed important networks both among themselves and with the community at large. Equally important, a series of auxiliaries to the Sunday school developed, starting with the program of home visits to infants and their mothers known as the Cradle Roll. Quickly assuming its own identity as an organization, in larger congregations the Cradle Roll established separate divisions for the training of visitors and the promotion of mothers' meetings, which in turn took on lives of their own. These organizations point to the central role played by women in the Sunday-school movement. Of the more than 33,000 volunteers who worked in Methodist Sunday schools in 1902, four-fifths were women.[43] Their strength in numbers, however, was not reflected in the schools' leadership. In general, men predominated in supervisory positions, women in the teaching rank and file. This hierarchy of functions and responsibility reflected—and, of course, reinforced—the prevailing stereotypes according to which women's business was child care, while administration and finance were strictly male preserves.[44]

This imbalance was reproduced in the life of the congregation as a whole. Women may have been disproportionately represented among the general membership, but church officers were typically male. In most congregations the lay leaders were drawn from the ranks of the middle and, above all, upper classes. That prosperous men would enjoy the prestige associated with such positions is not surprising. Clearly it was also in any church's financial interest to fill positions of authority with people who could afford to show their gratitude with generous financial contributions. For most middle- and upper-class men, managing church affairs was simply an extension of their regular responsibilities in the business world. At the same time, many believed that by virtue of their social standing and prosperity—not to mention their religious convictions—they had an obligation to serve their community. Civic responsibility and religious service went together.[45] Both were affirmations of character, and in fulfilling such duties a man could help to advance the moral values that would improve the character of society in general.[46]

Effectively excluded from positions of power, women reacted by banding together and forming their own groups, the earliest of which were the ladies' aid societies.[47] Such organizations were strictly local in character, but they underline how important women were to the vitality, both social and financial, of the parish. Not only could no fund-raising drive be successful without their contributions, but the events they organized, such as strawberry socials, teas, and picnics, were essential to the social life of the congregation.⁴⁸ Yet these organizations rarely received their due from the church trustees who made the decisions and who often expected the ladies' aids simply to do their bidding. Just as wives were to be helpmates to their husbands and submit to them, so the ladies' aids were expected to assist and be subject to the male leadership of the congregation.⁴⁹ If the ladies' aids lacked official standing in the governance of the congregation, however, they could still influence the deliberations of the congregation's male leaders by retaining control over the funds they raised. In some cases the ladies' aids were even known to refuse requests for funds, but the usual tactic was to earmark funds for particular purposes, which most typically involved improving or beautifying the church's interior.⁵⁰

Nor were the ladies' aids the only organizations that offered women the opportunity to exercise a degree of power with the explicit sanction of their church. Beginning in the 1870s, a number of Protestant denominations established women's organizations for the promotion of missions, both at home and abroad. Baptist women led the way in 1870, followed by the Presbyterians in 1876. In the same year, the women of the Methodist Episcopal Church in the United States established a mission society, and in 1880 their counterparts in the Methodist Church of Canada (formed in the union of Wesleyan and New Connexion churches in 1874) launched their first mission organization, the Woman's Missionary Society (WMS).

Foreign missions had long been part of the evangelical enterprise to win the world for Christ, but the Methodist churches of Canada had never had the cash or the personnel to send missionaries into foreign fields. The precedent set by the American Methodists presented an obvious solution to this problem. Improved access to education and the emergence of a growing and increasingly prosperous middle class meant that there was a large group of women with both the means and the leisure to run a national organization capable of raising unprecedented amounts of money. These same developments also created a pool of women prepared to serve in the mission field under the auspices of the WMS.

First established as a local organization in Hamilton, Ontario, within a year the WMS had become a national body with branches in small towns as well as large urban centres. The WMS offered women a national stage on which to exercise leadership and develop their organizational talents, but at the same time it struck such strong roots at the local level that it became part of the fabric of congregational life. The routine of the missionary society meetings—hymn singing, prayers, readings from Scripture or missionary tracts, transaction of business, and the taking up of a collection—gave women a chance to take charge of their own social and associational life in the context of the congregation. In the missionary society, women could escape from their mundane routines in their homes and gather with other women to help reclaim the world for Christ as well as to socialize and share the news from the exotic places where missionaries were spreading the faith.

In all Protestant denominations, women's missionary societies were fund-raising auxiliaries to the central boards charged with directing each church's missionary endeavours. The degree of autonomy and authority they enjoyed varied greatly from denomination to denomination. At one end of the spectrum, a missionary society could receive practically no accounting from the denominational board in charge of missions for the funds it had raised, and the society could play only a minimal role in selecting the women missionaries that it was to sponsor in the field. The WMS deliberately placed itself at the other end of the spectrum. Not only did it retain control over its own funds, but in so doing it also secured a measure of independence from the church's central missionary board.[51] The power exercised by the national leaders of the WMS was real, and the connections that it members had with prominent clergy, through marriage or other family ties, gave the society additional clout.

The success of the WMS—over its forty-five years of existence, it raised more than six and a half million dollars—is an indication of the strength of Methodist women's commitment to the mission cause. In turn, that commitment suggests that WMS work held particular appeal for women. Like the activities of so many other women's groups, those of the WMS were frequently described in terms reminiscent of women's domestic roles and duties: nurture, self-denial, caregiving. Women were expected to take the leading role in the religious formation of their children, in part by making the home a sacred haven. Such idealization of female domesticity may at first glance seem unlikely to promote women's activism. Yet even as evangelicalism sacralized female domesticity, it encouraged women to become active outside the household and to band together to save pagan souls. That women should work on behalf of other women and their children seemed only natural; that they had a special obligation to serve those women and children who were in a less fortunate position, bound by the shackles of pagan superstition and ignorance, subject to the unbridled and brutish passions of their menfolk, appeared equally obvious. By contrast, Canadian Protestant women saw themselves as the beneficiaries of Christianity and its ethic of self-restraint; no religion had so improved the position of women. Christianity's blessings were many, and few doubted that social progress was among them.

This conjunction of female domesticity and evangelical dynamism was by no means unique to Methodism; a similar conjunction could be found in other Protestant denominations, as the proliferation of women's missionary societies illustrates. Church-based associations provided a respectable social space in which to meet outside the home, and the activities they offered, unlike more frivolous pursuits, were personally fulfilling and uplifting. The membership of these organizations, however, was largely drawn from middle-class women who had servants to take care of running their households. Daytime meetings were out of the question for women who had to work, whether inside or outside the home. Besides, fund-raising was the very *raison d'être* for these organizations; most expected their members to dip regularly into their purses, and this was not possible for many working-class women.

Why, then, did Methodism and evangelical piety in general appeal to women from all classes? The answer lies in the tendency of evangelical denominations, including Methodism, to invest women's social roles with religious significance. In the evangelical concept of womanhood, women were by nature spiritual beings possessed of moral qualities that uniquely fitted them for marriage and motherhood. In marriage women could fulfil their vocation as the guardians of the family, making the home a moral refuge and bringing the blessings of religion to their husbands and children. This idealization of womanhood strikes many today as quaint, to put it mildly. Yet it captured the imagination of women from across the social spectrum. For most women the role of wife and mother was the one they had been brought up to perform, and after marriage their place of work was the home; even working-class women tended not to work outside their homes if they could help it. Domestic labour was time-consuming and back-breaking in the days before home appliances, but production for home use, such as canning produce from a garden plot or raising chickens, was as important to most working-class families' survival as the wage income earned by men. In the eyes of many women, the call to godly motherhood, far from devaluing their role, recognized that their efforts contributed directly to both the material and the spiritual well-being of their families.

Evangelical mores also encompassed a definition of appropriate male attitudes and behaviour. The Christian man was to exercise self-restraint and sobriety, and to be diligent in fulfilling his responsibilities as *pater familias*. In short, the evangelical code of conduct spelled out how men were to demonstrate and affirm their masculinity. A real man spent his leisure time at home with his wife and children. As a loyal husband, he would support his wife in her efforts to make the home a sacred place in which cultural improvement was closely associated with religious uplift. Evangelical Christianity appealed especially to middle-class men because its conception of manhood conformed exactly to the norms and expectations of Victorian middle-class culture. Although later generations were to make much of that culture's hypocrisy, given the strictness of its conventions, perhaps hypocrisy was inevitable. Another way of coping with this rigid and exacting moral code, however, was through participation in fraternal associations. These predominantly middle-class organizations (with the exception of the Orange Order, which enjoyed a significant working-class following) offer a unique perspective on the values of middle-class men.

Fraternal organizations paid homage to middle-class propriety and its domestic ideal in various ways. Most offered insurance schemes, so that men could provide their families with economic security, and from time to time they included members' wives in their activities, most notably through 'mixed' socials. In addition, all such organizations identified themselves in one way or another with the Protestant faith. Local branches would invite Protestant clergymen to act as their chaplains, and the church parade was an annual event. The social ethos of these fraternal organizations was also redolent of Protestantism. Their rituals typically contained frequent allusions to and citations from Scripture, and the declared purpose of these rituals was to assist members in improving themselves morally and spiritually.

Fraternal organizations made much of their devotion to church and to home, but their chief attraction was that they offered men a night out with the boys. Although the man who made a virtual career of attending lodge meetings—and arriving home much the worse for wear—was a stock figure of fun, there was a good deal of truth behind that image. After the regular lodge business had been conducted, it was not at all unusual for members to consume large quantities of alcohol; in fact, the mixings for toddies were frequently an organization's largest expenditure. As a place for men to socialize away from their homes and the watchful gaze of their wives, the lodge celebrated male conviviality and autonomy, and it is no wonder many wives were concerned about it. The clergy too were uneasy, particularly since one of the most important features of any fraternal organization was the burial ritual, which frequently overshadowed conventional religious services.

But if the attitude of fraternal associations towards middle-class values was somewhat ambivalent during the middle decades of the nineteenth century, in one respect at least that attitude would soon change. By the 1890s most fraternal organizations—including the Orange Order, an association not always known for its genteel ways—had gone dry. Among the middle class the public display of sobriety conveniently telegraphed one's worth as a Christian, a decent citizen, and a good family man. And that was precisely what the members of fraternal organizations wished to affirm, even if they did also welcome the opportunity to have a night out socializing with their friends.

Victorians often distinguished between two sorts of people, the rough and the respectable. This fundamentally moral distinction could be used to judge a wide range of behaviour, including the pastimes that people engaged in. But opinions differed as to what was respectable. While middle-class moralists condemned a variety of pastimes as immoral, others celebrated them because they embodied other values of which they approved. Class was a crucial factor here, as the traditional model of manhood embraced by many, though hardly all, working-class men was one that pre-dated the appearance of evangelicalism. For many working-class men, evangelical injunctions to self-restraint and

sobriety ran directly counter to ideals of manly behaviour in which spontaneity (sometimes to the point of impulsiveness) and drinking (sometimes to
excess) figured prominently. The pastimes and conviviality of working-class
men were governed by a moral code quite different from that of the middle
class. Working-class pastimes were not family-centred: men and women often
led separate social lives, and for many working-class men, maintaining that
autonomy was fundamental to their honour and self-respect.

Thus while many working-class women found fulfilment in belonging to a
church, relatively few working-class men became church members. In contrast
to their Catholic counterparts, who strongly identified with their church,
Protestant working men tended to see the churches as alien institutions unwilling to accommodate the mores of their gender and class. Even so, a good many
must have attended church somewhat regularly at least, judging by the statistics collected for Toronto. As a religion, then, Christianity was important to a
significant number of working men; it was the moral and social obligations of
church membership and the social life associated with it that they rejected.

The same was even more true for young men from across the social spectrum. Very few became church members, and if many did attend evening services, it was for purposes of entertainment and meeting members of the
opposite sex. That young men just a few years out of Sunday school should so
distance themselves from the church troubled many contemporary observers.
Worse, the wasteful and idle fashion in which many spent their spare time—in
bars, billiard parlours, and dance halls, at least when they had money to
spend—were far from improving, either to themselves or to society. The sight of
working- or middle-class youths in fancy clothes lounging about the main
streets and smoking cheroots (all signs of a burgeoning consumer culture
among Canadian youth) induced countless apoplectic denunciations from
press and pulpit alike.

The most immediate responses to this situation were local in nature. In the
hope of inoculating young men against the influences of street and tavern,
some churches added special classes for them to their existing Sunday-school
programs; some, including a number of Methodist churches, started Young
People's Christian Associations; and some, such as Bridge St Methodist church
in Belleville, Ontario,[52] established reading rooms and libraries run under adult
supervision. It was only towards the end of the century that Protestant denominations began forming national voluntary associations devoted to youth,
among the first of which was the Methodist Epworth League, founded in 1889.
As time went on, voluntary organizations became increasingly specialized, tar-
geting people in specific age groups with particular interests. For example, the
Young People's Forward Movement (1896) was devoted to generating support
for foreign missions among Methodist youth, while the interdenominational
Student Volunteer Movement, affiliated with the Young Men's Christian

Association, went one step further: in joining it, members committed themselves to becoming missionaries. Such organizations did much to foster among young men a core of activists in the local congregation and beyond. But they did not succeed in their broader goal of reforming the vast majority of them[53] and enticing them to become full-fledged church members.

CONFLICT, COMPETITION, AND CONSENSUS

An emerging Protestant consensus: Religion and the social order
Even before disestablishment was achieved in 1854, education was a source of controversy over the relationship of church and state. These disputes did not end once the Church of England lost its official status; indeed, the role of the churches in education became an even more central issue. The main lines for university education had been laid down in the 1850s. Though the terms of legislation varied from colony to colony, in all cases the result was the same: denominational colleges were permitted to flourish. The question of public funding caused friction, and except in Nova Scotia and Quebec denominational colleges initially received none of the state support that secular institutions enjoyed. Yet this issue was eventually settled—in many cases to the benefit of the colleges—and at no time did it become nearly so contentious as the question of elementary schooling. Elementary schools became the focus of disputes for many reasons. Above all, however, they functioned as a lightning rod in a conflict between two competing cultural identities that understood the proper role of the state *vis-à-vis* religion in very different ways. Regarding elementary school as a central cultural institution, each of these groups was anxious that its schools should reflect its particular vision of society.

With the arrival of Ultramontanism in British North America, Catholicism had acquired a new militancy. No longer did the Catholic Church view denominational schools simply as protection in the event that public schools at the local level were not responsive to Catholic sensitivities. Now public support for Catholic schools was seen as matter of fundamental justice in which the civil rights of Catholics, both as individuals and as a group, were at stake. Since education was ultimately concerned with the religious formation of the child, to deny Catholic schools state funding was seen by Catholics as a denial of parents' right to educate their children as their conscience dictated. Accordingly, they called on the state to establish and support a full-fledged Catholic system of primary education. Many Protestants, on the other hand, objected vehemently to state funding for Catholic schools. Some of this opposition was rooted in loyalty to the principle of voluntarism, some in Protestant objections to Catholicism itself (to be explored below). At the same time, nondenominational public schooling embodied many Protestants' hopes and aspirations for themselves, their children, and their society. According to the proponents of public schooling, education was the key to both individual advancement and social progress, building character and contributing to the formation of productive and loyal citizens. In a society marked by diversity of class, ethnicity, and religion, public education would impart common values and thereby promote social stability and political order. An educational system designed to form character and instil morality could hardly dispense with religion. But denominational schools could only lead to discord and division. If it was to forge a social, cultural, and religious consensus, public schooling would have to promote a form of Christianity that was non-denominational, common to all. The problem was that the common Christianity championed by the defenders of public schools was overtly evangelical and as such unacceptable to high-church Anglicans and Roman Catholics. Ultimately, the type of school system that emerged depended upon the political power of Catholics in each colonial jurisdiction. The result was that school systems across the country were as diverse as the landscape itself, ranging from publicly supported denominational schools to a unified state school system that was non-denominational in character.

In the Maritimes the school systems were officially non-denominational, but in fact Catholic schools became part of the public educational system in both Nova Scotia and PEI. At the time of Confederation, Nova Scotia's schools were non-denominational both in law and in practice, despite periodic Catholic efforts to secure concessions during the 1850s and 1860s. After Confederation, matters took a different turn as local school boards worked out their own administrative arrangements. The type of teaching offered by rural schools came to reflect the populations they served, and in Catholic areas religious instruction was the norm. In urban areas, two different arrangements took root. In Halifax, Archbishop Thomas W. Connolly's quiet diplomacy bore fruit with the incorporation of Catholic schools into the otherwise non-denominational public school system. In most other towns, however, the public system remained non-denominational, and Catholic instruction was available only in church-supported schools that were not part of the public education system.[54]

Prince Edward Island, which entered Confederation in 1873, followed the example of Nova Scotia in two respects: in the rural areas, where Catholics were concentrated, the public schools were Catholic in all but name, and in both Summerside and Charlottetown Catholic schools were part of the public system. In New Brunswick, by contrast, Protestants made a concerted effort to establish public education on a non-denominational basis. At the time of Confederation, public denominational schools did not by law exist. In practice, however, they did, particularly in the case of Anglicans and Catholics.

This arrangement was not to last, and in 1871 the Protestant-dominated assembly cut off funding to denominational schools, establishing a non-denominational system in their place. After a protracted battle in the House of

Commons and in the courts, the Judicial Committee of the Privy Council ruled that as denominational schools were not by law established prior to Confederation, they did not fall under the protection of the British North America Act, which constitutionally entrenched only such educational privileges as had been granted by legislation prior to union.[55] The council's decision set a precedent that was to influence the outcome of later school cases in the West, but in New Brunswick it was soon outpaced by events.

In 1875 a dispute over the control of the local school in Caraquet led to a series of bloody riots resulting in the deaths of two people, one a Catholic francophone, the other a Protestant anglophone. The Caraquet riots shocked the province, and when a group of Catholics led by Bishop John Sweeny indicated that compromise was possible, the government eagerly grasped this opportunity to defuse religious tensions. In the compromise of 1875 Catholics did not obtain state-supported schools, but they did secure the right to gather together in the same schools (often in premises rented from religious orders), to have their children instructed by Catholic religious, and to receive religious education (usually after regular school hours).[56]

The pattern of elementary education in Newfoundland—a religious school system in which all denominational schools were equally eligible for state support—was altogether unique in British North America. Originally, however, the government of Newfoundland had attempted to educate both Protestants and Catholics in common schools, an arrangement that proved unworkable when each group boycotted those schools dominated by the other. In 1843, the government established a dual system for Protestants and Catholics. In addition, it agreed to provide small grants to schools supported by Newfoundland's two Protestant denominations, an arrangement that suited the Methodists but not the Anglicans. Over the next two decades, the Anglican Bishop Edward Feild single-mindedly campaigned for state-supported Anglican schools. Newfoundland politics—polarized, as always, along denominational lines—finally gave Feild the opening he was looking for. In 1875 Premier F.B.T. Carter needed Anglican support to shore up his pan-Protestant alliance, and to that end he brokered a deal between the Anglicans and Methodists. Newfoundland would have three denominational school systems—Catholic, Anglican, and Methodist—and in the twentieth century this system would be expanded as new denominations arrived.[57]

Central Canada offers yet another study in contrasts. The school act of 1841 permitted Protestants and Catholics to opt out of their local common schools and establish separate schools of their own in the united Canada. Thereafter, the two sections of the province were to go their different ways. In Canada East the school act of 1846 put in place a dual system of education for urban areas based on religion rather than language: one Roman Catholic, the other Protestant. In rural areas, by contrast, schools were to be common, open to all, although in practice the common schools were Catholic, and Protestants were free to establish their own schools if they wished. In any case, the government played a limited role in education. Although it supervised school finances and inspection, the establishment of the Council for Public Instruction in 1859 ensured that the Catholic Church controlled what was taught in its schools—a power that was bolstered in 1875 when every bishop in Quebec gained the right to sit on the council, which to all intents and purposes became independent of the government.

In Canada West, the school bill of 1841 established a system that was the reverse of that in Canada East: the public school system was to be non-denominational in character, but Catholics could establish schools of their own at public expense. Legislation in 1850, 1855, and 1863 completed the legal basis for a Catholic separate school system, and the 1850 school act, which left the establishment of denominationally specific Protestant schools (almost all of them Anglican) to the discretion of local trustees, meant the virtual disappearance of Anglican separate schools. While the school act of 1841 slipped by almost unnoticed, such was not the case for the separate-school legislation put forward in the 1850s. Each bill came under intense fire, and the Catholics of Canada West owed much of their success to the concerted pressure applied by the bishops and legislators from Canada East, but with the achievement of Confederation the Catholic separate school system became constitutionally enshrined under the terms of the British North America Act.[58]

PROTESTANT–CATHOLIC CONFLICT

State support for Catholic schooling was one of the most divisive issues facing the inhabitants of British North America during the middle years of the nineteenth century. To understand why this was so, it is essential to examine the anti-Catholic mind-set shared by many Protestants. This prejudice can be traced back to the Reformation, when Protestant England was beset by Catholic foes. Having survived Bloody Mary's persecution, the attempted invasion by the Spanish Armada, and the Gunpowder Plot to blow up parliament, English Protestantism had ultimately triumphed over Catholicism. But these episodes of persecution were not forgotten. Indeed, they were among the foundations of Britain's national mythology, and as such they offered British Protestants a key to understanding the present as well as the past. In this drama of national history, the stripes of Britain's antagonists remained unchanged. Almost three centuries later, Catholicism still threatened the British people and their Protestant faith.[59]

Those who objected to Catholicism did so on three grounds—religious, social, and political—each of which melded imperceptibly into the other. The religious objection to Catholicism dated back to the Reformation, but it gained much of its impetus from the resurgence of evangelicalism. In this view,

Catholicism usurped the divine authority of the Bible in favour of the human authority of the pope and his clergy. In placing itself between God and humanity, the Catholic priesthood arrogated to itself powers that properly belonged to God. Catholic beliefs and practices—most notably, the sacrifice of the mass, the adoration of the sacred host, the veneration of the saints, and the practice of confession—were patently idolatrous, clear evidence that Catholics were held in thrall to priestcraft and superstition.

Catholicism was seen as inimical to the well-being of society. If superstition flourished among the Catholic laity, it was because their clergy kept them in ignorance, not allowing them to think for themselves. In turn, ignorance and lack of initiative resulted in indolence and poverty, both of which were breeding-grounds for crime and disease. Moreover, Catholicism posed a direct political threat to the constitutional order of colonial self-government. 'This is a Protestant country,' insisted the *Nova Scotian*. 'Ours is a Protestant Queen.'[60] For the *Nova Scotian*, as for most Protestants, the connection between Protestantism and the British constitutional monarchy was hardly incidental. The civil and religious liberties guaranteed by British institutions were attributable to the enlightened and tolerant spirit of Protestantism. By contrast, priest-ridden Catholicism represented intolerance, tyranny, and coercion in both religious and political matters. Not only were Catholics dominated by their clergy, but they owed allegiance to a foreign ruler, the pope. Historical instances of papal designs on Britain and its monarchy were enough to convince many Protestants that the prospect of Catholic disloyalty was quite real.

Anti-Catholicism was a frame of mind, a cluster of beliefs and emotions, that organized people's perceptions of the world around them and imparted a cultural identity. In this sense, anti-Catholicism was an ideology, and from time to time it found expression in mass movements of anti-Catholic protest. As this ideology was part and parcel of the cultural baggage that British Protestants brought with them to Canada, it is not surprising that outbreaks of anti-Catholic sentiment often reflected events in the United Kingdom and the United States. During the 1850s, for example, the 'papal aggression' crisis in Britain and the 'know nothing movement' in the US stirred up anti-Catholic feeling in Canada West. Even when that was the case, however, anti-Catholic movements were closely connected to domestic developments and directed to domestic ends.[61]

An example was the wave of anti-Catholicism that swept over Canada West during the 1850s. This spell of anti-Catholic feeling was so intense and long-lasting that historians of Ontario have come to call the decade the 'fiery fifties'.[62] Although the 'papal aggression' controversy that erupted in England in response to the restoration of the Roman Catholic hierarchy was the spark that set things off in the fall of 1850, the tinder had been well prepared. The passage of the school act in early 1850 had already led to fears that the

Catholics of Canada East were intent on imposing their institutions on the good people of Canada West. In this volatile atmosphere, the English controversy captured the imagination of many Protestants in Canada West, who promptly found evidence of papal aggression closer to home when the French-born aristocrat Armand de Charbonnel arrived in the fall of 1850 to assume his title as bishop of Toronto.

The outcry that greeted Charbonnel's arrival set the tone for what was to be a controversial episcopacy. Charbonnel personified the new militant spirit of Catholicism, as his repeated and strident demands for separate schools were soon to demonstrate. His militancy, together with his French nationality, led Protestants to believe that he was the French-Canadian hierarchy's agent in an Ultramontane design upon Canada West. Although in time such fears began to subside, they were quickly revived by a new round of controversies. Two events in Canada East set off alarms among Canada West's Protestants: the public authorities' failure to bring to justice the Catholic rioters who in 1853 attacked the ex-priest and Italian nationalist Alessandro Gavazzi, with the loss of ten lives, in Montreal, and the acquittal of the Irish-Catholic gang who in late 1855 savagely battered to death the Protestant Robert Corrigan.

Bishop Charbonnel could hardly have chosen a less opportune time to champion separate schools. Earlier in 1855, Catholic legislators from Canada East had rammed through the legislature of the united Province of Canada a supplemental bill to facilitate the establishment of separate schools in the western section of the province, a measure that was sure to arouse Protestant ire in that region. Still not satisfied, Charbonnel issued a pastoral in January 1856 warning Catholics that failure to use their suffrage to advance separate schools was a mortal sin. That summer, in response to yet another separate-school bill, Protestants throughout Canada West deluged the legislature with petitions in protest. Tempers were to become even more heated in July, when a riot broke out between Orangemen and Irish Catholics near Guelph, which was followed by similar riots in Toronto during 1857 and 1858. A few years later, beginning in the fall of 1864, Canada West was periodically alarmed by rumours of an impending invasion by the Irish-American revolutionaries of the Fenian Brotherhood. During one such outbreak, the local militia in Toronto marched by the residence of the Roman Catholic bishop crying 'To Hell with the Pope', a sentiment that met with approval among a Protestant population increasingly vexed by Irish-Catholic cultural particularism and nationalist dreams for an independent Ireland.[63] Fortunately, when the Fenians did attack British North America, in 1866, popular opinion was remarkably restrained. But if bloodshed had been averted, relations between Protestants and Catholics were far from free of tension.

By contrast, in New Brunswick the 1850s saw the end of brawling and rioting between the Orange and the Green. Economic prosperity and the migration of Irish Catholics to the United States had considerably eased religious and ethnic tensions.[64] But such was not the case in Nova Scotia. In the latter part of the 1850s, a local version of the 'papal aggression' controversy polarized the political scene. Although Irish-Catholic immigration had largely ended by the late 1840s, its demographic impact endured. By the 1850s, Catholics of Irish extraction, largely concentrated in Halifax and its environs, accounted for over two-fifths of the city's population. Together with their Scottish co-religionists, they made up at least one-sixth of the population in the province as a whole, and many Protestants feared that they would threaten the distinctive character of their society.[65]

A similar dynamic was at work in Canada West, but local circumstances were to aggravate further the relations between Protestants and Catholics. Immigration from Ireland during the Great Famine had not appreciably altered the proportions of Protestants to Catholics. Nevertheless, the growing numbers of impoverished Irish Catholics in the towns and cities, together with the proliferation of Irish-Catholic communal and religious institutions, meant that Catholics were much more visible than they had been before. They were also becoming more aggressive in asserting their religious and national distinctiveness.

This in itself would have been enough to inflame Protestant tempers, but two features made the situation in Canada West even more heated than elsewhere in British North America. The political Union of 1841 had set the French-speaking Catholics of Canada East and the English-speaking Protestants of Canada West on a collision course as each group struggled to build a society that reflected its fundamental values. While francophones sought state support for their church in its mission to protect the religious and national particularity of the French-Canadian people, anglophone Protestants sought official equality among denominations in a society whose ethos was to be unmistakably Protestant. As the two halves of the united Province of Canada drifted further apart, the Catholics of Canada West came under increasing attack as an alien presence that threatened to subvert all that Protestants held dear.

One other factor that made the tensions between Protestants and Catholics particularly virulent in Canada West was the unique make-up of its Irish population. Not only did Irish Protestants outnumber Irish Catholics two to one, but they were a significant group in the province, comprising about one-fifth of the total population.[66] Not surprisingly, the traditional enmity between Irish Protestants and Irish Catholics quickly took root, and clashes between gangs of the Orange and the Green became common. More important, the ultra-Protestantism and staunch British nationalism of Irish Protestants appealed to and in turn reinforced the region's Loyalist traditions. By the 1850s, the Orange Order was well on its way to becoming a powerful social and political institution as it expanded beyond its traditional Irish-Protestant constituency to recruit a broad cross-section of the male Protestant population. The spirit expressed in the order's slogan—'No Surrender'—united all British Protestants in defence of their public institutions against the inroads of Catholicism. As Protestants grew even more convinced that the Catholics of Canada East sought to dominate them, that spirit became part of the region's identity. The sobriquet 'Orange Ontario' may have exaggerated the Order's influence, but it was not wide of the mark in describing the outlook of most Protestant Ontarians.

As political and religious conflict between Canada East and West became entrenched, many people came to believe that only a new constitutional arrangement could prevent it from escalating. The achievement of Confederation in 1867 released the two halves of the united Province from their unhappy union, but the new country was not to be the peaceable kingdom that many had hoped for. The increasingly Ultramontane character of Quebec society and, above all, the dominant role of the Catholic Church in the province's public institutions alarmed many of the country's Protestants, even though provincial autonomy in such matters (subject to the constitutionally entrenched protections for the Protestant minority in Quebec and the Catholic minority in Ontario) was what had made Confederation attractive in the first place both to the Catholics of Canada East and to Protestants elsewhere. As new territories to the west were incorporated, the question of Catholic rights again vexed the Protestants of British North America, and this time many Protestants were tempted to use their political muscle to preserve their dream of westward expansion.

The Métis uprising of 1869–70, led by Louis Riel, and his provisional government's execution of the Ontario Orangeman Thomas Scott ignited Protestant tempers. At public meetings throughout Ontario, Protestants invoked the spectre of Romanism and rebellion. That Catholic clergy in the West should support Riel was appalling enough; that Riel should escape justice was an outrage both to the memory of Scott and to the rule of British law. Predictably, the calls from Ontario for Riel's blood rallied Quebec's French-speaking people and eventually led them to launch a campaign seeking amnesty for Riel, which would be granted—on the condition of his exile—in February 1875. The Métis uprising aroused passions on both sides because both Ontario Protestants and Quebec Catholics realized that the future not only of the West but of the entire country hung in the balance. The terms under which the province of Manitoba was created in 1870, which appeared to entrench minority linguistic and religious rights, dismayed many Ontarians who believed that these concessions defeated their national mission to extend to the West the blessings of civilization, which to them was naturally British and Protestant.

Meanwhile, Protestants became exercised over events in Quebec. The Guibord affair, sparked when a member of the liberal Institut Canadien was refused burial in a Catholic cemetery, called forth further denunciations of priestly intolerance, while the emergence of Ultramontanism as a political force, signalled by the publication of the *Programme catholique* in 1871, raised new fears about Catholic designs on the political order. The alleged interference of the clergy in the provincial election in 1875 and the federal by-election in Charlevoix the following year so inflamed Protestant tempers in Toronto that a procession of Catholic pilgrims set off the worst disturbance in the city's history as over 8,000 people—a tenth of the total population—rioted in the streets. On 12 July 1877, Montreal was the scene of a clash between Orangemen and Irish Catholics, resulting in the death of a Protestant named Thomas Hackett, who was soon celebrated as yet another innocent victim of Catholic bigotry.

For the next few years tensions between Protestants and Catholics subsided, only to resurface in the mid-1880s. By then the mood among Protestants in central Canada had soured considerably. The National Policy had not brought the promised era of economic prosperity, and Canadians were flocking south to seek their fortunes in the United States. The Riel uprising of 1885 reopened old wounds, not least because Riel's execution sparked a resurgence of French-Canadian nationalism. While Quebec Protestants resented their provincial government's nationalist policies and close alliance with the Catholic Church, Ontarians chafed at French-Canadian influence in Ottawa, which they thought came at the expense of their own province. Ontario Protestants also regarded with alarm the rising tide of francophone immigrants from land-short Quebec who were moving into the Ottawa valley. In some districts francophones had migrated in such numbers that they had overtaken the older anglophone population. What made this development even more threatening in the eyes of many Protestants was that francophones settled in compact communities and so were able to turn local schools into French-language institutions. Both Quebec's evident political power in Ottawa and the Franco-Ontarians' determination to preserve their language and culture revived old fears of Catholic aggression. During the 1886 Ontario provincial election, the 'No Popery' campaign waged by newspapers allied with the Conservative party, a campaign in which the Toronto *Mail* took the lead, gave full vent to these pent-up grievances as they repeatedly attacked both separate and unilingual French schools.

The Jesuits' Estates Act, passed by the Quebec government in 1888 as a means of awarding compensation for lands that had devolved to the Crown during the temporary suppression of the Society of Jesus, further fuelled Protestant outrage.[67] The government's well-intentioned strategy of submitting the contentious issue to the pope for binding arbitration was seen not only as a violation of the separation of church and state but as an attempt to subordinate the authority of a British legislature to the papacy. The bid by a handful of members of parliament to have the federal government disallow the Act set in motion a broad-based protest movement, leading to the foundation of the Equal Rights Association (ERA) in 1889. With branches springing up in Montreal as well as Ontario, and with members drawn from business, the professions, and the clergy, the ERA represented a wide spectrum of Protestant opinion. When the time limit for disallowance of the Act ran out in August, the ERA had already broadened its attack to include separate and unilingual French schools in Ontario.

Meanwhile, in Manitoba, the government began over the summer to move against separate schools and the official use of French, both of which it formally abolished in early 1890. Although the Jesuits' Estates agitation in Ontario had created a favourable climate for this step, the government's campaign also had strong local roots. For many years the anglophone majority, many of whom had come from Ontario, had agitated to end linguistic dualism in the legislature and religious dualism in education. Rather than join in demands from Ontario for federal disallowance of the Jesuits' Estates Act, they demanded that their government invoke provincial sovereignty and use its powers to establish institutions that reflected the province's anglophone and Protestant character.

The Manitoba Schools Question, together with the equal-rights agitation, was to ensure that language and religion remained among the chief political issues for the next half-decade. In Ontario, William Meredith took up the banner of equal rights on behalf of the Conservative party in the 1890 provincial election. After much debate, the ERA itself took the plunge into electoral politics and fielded candidates of its own. In the particularly heated campaign that followed, the Liberals under Oliver Mowat won a decisive majority. The ERA's failure at the polls was due in part to internal divisions that had widened in the heat of the campaign, but in a sense the party was also a victim of its own success: all parties had taken up its slogan, including the Liberals who portrayed their modifications to separate and French-language schools as a matter of 'equal rights'.[68]

By the time of the 1891 federal election, the ERA was unable even to exercise influence as a pressure group. The Catholic minority in Manitoba focused their campaign on religious rather than linguistic rights, and instead of lobbying the federal government for disallowance of the Manitoba Schools Act, they sought redress through the courts. In taking this approach, Manitoba Catholics robbed the ERA of its best issue, and it disbanded shortly after the election. A few months later, in December 1891, the Protestant Protective Association (an offshoot of the American Protective Association) established its first branch in Ontario, but it never enjoyed the support of moderate Protestants, as the

ERA had done in its heyday. In early 1895, the courts tossed the Manitoba Schools Question back into the political arena.[69] The ruling Conservative party, rudderless since the death of John A. Macdonald in 1891, was likewise ill-prepared to handle the issue. After protracted debate in cabinet, the government finally ordered the government of Manitoba to restore separate schools. This Remedial Order set off a political fire-storm that badly divided the Conservative party, and the resulting uproar, whose spirit was aptly captured in the motto 'Hands Off Manitoba', contributed to the party's defeat in the federal election of 1896. In the aftermath of the election the new prime minister, Wilfrid Laurier, used his 'sunny ways' of conciliation to close the book on the Manitoba Schools Question. The agreement of 1896 between Laurier and Thomas Greenway, the premier of Manitoba, provided for both religious instruction after school hours and bilingual elementary instruction in other languages together with English. The Laurier–Greenway agreement made the public system somewhat more palatable to the Catholic minority, but it nonetheless represented a severe setback. Not only did the agreement confirm that the state educational system would be a unitary one, in which separate schools had no place, but it placed French schooling on a par with schooling in any language other than English, a provision eagerly embraced by immigrants recently arrived from Europe. In the eyes of the provincial government, Franco-Manitobans had become simply one ethnic group among many.

In the North-West Territories, the Catholic minority were also on the defensive. Although they enjoyed both separate and unilingual French schools, these privileges had been significantly curtailed during the 1880s and 1890s in response to Protestant complaints, and in 1892 French was stripped of its official status in the territory's courts and legislature. As the Laurier–Greenway agreement demonstrated, Catholic minorities could not depend on the federal government to defend their interests, and the situation remained unchanged when in 1905 the provinces of Saskatchewan and Alberta came into being.[70]

Throughout the turbulent nineties Atlantic Canada remained calm. The only discordant note was the campaign led by H.H. Pitts against Catholic schools in New Brunswick during the early years of the decade. Although the issue was extremely popular among the rank and file of the Orange Order, of which Pitts was Grand Master, among the electorate at large it soon fizzled out.[71] Apparently anti-Catholicism had limited appeal even at a time when the Acadian minority was growing so quickly that by the turn of the century Acadians would constitute nearly one-quarter of the province's population. What, then, accounts for the agitation in central Canada and the West?[72] One standard explanation is that both the Equal Rights campaign and the Manitoba Schools Question reflected the influence of nativism from the United States and the persistence of Protestant voluntarism. Certainly the latter was an important ingredient in both campaigns, but as the case of Atlantic Canada demonstrates, it was not a sufficient cause. Nor was the example of American nativism all that compelling, at least in the Atlantic region. In fact, the origins of both campaigns were indigenous to the regions affected.

As J.R. Miller has pointed out,[73] these campaigns were expressions of a coercive form of nationalism that responded to cultural diversity by insisting on cultural conformity. This form of anglophone nationalism was in fact Ontario regionalism writ large. Confederation had not lived up to Ontarians' hopes; political union had failed to create a new nationality common to all. Instead of promoting social uniformity and national unity, Confederation had laid the foundations for the resurgence of French-Canadian nationalism by enabling the francophones of Quebec to establish their own national government in the province. It was this national particularism, symbolized by the Jesuits' Estates Act, that many Ontario Protestants rejected as incompatible with their own national project. What is more, Protestant Ontario's aspirations were frustrated at both the federal and provincial levels. No party could hope to govern the country without the Quebec vote. Similarly, Ontario elections were decided by a slim margin, and here too the Catholic vote was crucial. Catholics were accused of acting as a special interest group, one that held the common good hostage to its own advancement. Using such illegitimate means, it was alleged, Catholic minorities had made linguistic and religious dualism part of the Dominion's social and cultural fabric. Although these minorities were themselves highly diverse—the traditions and history of Franco-Manitobans and Irish Catholics could hardly be more distinct—their attempts to secure recognition and public support for their institutions merely underscored the degree to which they were not British Canadians, and in that they were all alike.

The backlash against French-Canadian nationalism was one factor contributing to British-Canadian nationalist militancy. Another was the American continentalism that threatened the country's survival. In response to this threat, even nationalists could seek comfort and security in the British empire. British imperialism and Canadian nationalism were not incompatible: in fact, as Carl Berger has argued, they reinforced one another. As George Monro Grant, the principal of Queen's University, declared, 'we are Canadian, and in order to be Canadian we must be British'.[74] If Canadian imperialists sought closer ties with Britain, however, they also sought to transform the imperial framework so that Canada would play a vital role in the empire. This imperial vision had a messianic quality: Canada's destiny was to perfect British institutions, and the path to national fulfilment lay in its becoming a full partner with Britain in bringing the blessings of true civilization and religion to the rest of the world.[75]

Occupying a special place in this great mission was the Canadian West. One way to ensure that it became an extension of Ontario, rather than Quebec, was to insist that the West was untouched territory, a *tabula rasa*—a perspective that conveniently overlooked the undertakings made in the Manitoba Act of 1870 and the North-West Territories Act of 1875. Here in this virgin land the linguistic and religious dualisms that impeded social progress in the east could finally be jettisoned. Here in the great open spaces that inspired moral grandeur, British traditions and institutions could be purified. In this way, the West would point the way to a better civilization for Canada and, in time, the rest of the British empire as well.[76]

Nationalists in Ontario and the West often pictured Canada's imperial mission in racial terms. Many believed not only that Anglo-Saxons were biologically better fitted than other peoples for the task of governing and advancing civilization, but that their culture—the foundation of which, as the new science of linguistics purported to show, was language—stood above all others.[77] If cultural uniformity was the precondition for nationality, it stood to reason that any culture other than the British-Canadian one was an alien presence in the country; it was on this reasoning that D'Alton McCarthy, one of the instigators of the Equal Rights movement, denounced French Canadians as a 'bastard nationality'.[78] Another of the Orange Order's slogans—'One flag, one language, and one school'—captured the Protestant quest for national unity, and to this list many would have added religion.

The quest for homogeneity betrayed a severe lack of confidence in the country's future. In early 1893, Prime Minister John Thompson declared to an audience in Toronto, 'this country ought to be a nation, will be a nation, and please God we will and shall make it a nation'.[79] As a Roman Catholic, Thompson had little sympathy for the Equal Rights movement and other such Protestant nationalist crusades, but he did draw attention to a perpetual source of anxiety for the Protestants of Ontario and the West: the fact that their country was indeed not yet a nation, and that the lineaments of their Canadian nationality had yet to gain acceptance among the country's Catholic populations. The Protestant crusades of this era were efforts to allay this anxiety and make the Protestant national dream a reality. If many Protestant Ontarians and westerners believed that British-Canadian patriotism was pleasing to God, they also firmly believed that God helps those who help themselves. They were prepared to take their destiny in their own hands by combatting French-Canadian nationalism and, wherever possible, preparing the ground for the eventual assimilation of the country's francophone minorities.

When the Boer War erupted in 1899, Protestants demanded that Canadian troops come to Britain's aid, and in all some 7,000 Canadians fought in South Africa. There was no question of conscription—Canada's expeditionary force was composed solely of volunteers—yet many French Canadians still opposed any participation on Canada's part, fearing that imperial aggression abroad would lead to jingoism at home. Nor were their fears unjustified. During the course of the war leading anglophone newspapers regularly placed French-Canadian loyalty on trial and judged it severely lacking. In the spring of 1900 students from McGill nearly set off a riot when they attempted to place the Union Jack atop two francophone newspaper offices. This was an act of student bravado, no doubt, but it made plain the presumed right of anglophone Protestants to exact deference from their social subordinates even when the latter constituted a majority of the population. The controversies of the turbulent nineties had polarized the country, and the hostility and the resentment that they had fomented set the country on the road that would lead to the conscription crisis of 1917.

Catholicism: Language and religion

Anglophone Catholics, the vast majority of whom were of Irish extraction, also came under fire during the controversies that, beginning in the late 1880s, continued to rage throughout the next decade. Rallying to defend their schools, on two occasions English-speaking Catholics even joined forces with their francophone co-religionists: in Manitoba to appeal to the courts for redress, and in Ontario to vote for the political party most likely to resist ultra-Protestant pressure, the Liberal party. Such demonstrations of unity masked the degree to which language divided the Catholic fold. The major battles between anglophone and francophone Catholics would not erupt until early in the twentieth century, but by the closing decades of the nineteenth the groundwork for these conflicts had already been thoroughly laid.

Like their francophone counterparts, Catholics of Scots and Irish extraction looked to their church to preserve their ethnic group and perpetuate its identity. While these two anglophone groups were a linguistic minority in the Catholic Church as a whole, especially in the province of Quebec, they did predominate in the Maritimes and Ontario. In these regions they quite naturally believed they should control the church, and the key to securing control lay in capturing the hierarchy. The problem was that francophones still had their own regional bases in Ontario's Ottawa valley and on New Brunswick's north shore, where they constituted the bulk of the Catholic population. And in these areas the francophone population had been growing rapidly over the latter half of the nineteenth century.

At the time of Confederation, Acadians accounted for just under half of New Brunswick's Catholic population, but by the turn of the century that figure had grown to nearly two-thirds. The rapid growth in the Acadian population was accompanied by a national awakening that, taking hold during the 1870s and 1880s, developed into a movement to Acadianize their church. For many years the church had served as the cradle for Acadian nationalism, protecting and promoting Acadian language and culture. English-speaking Catholics, however, retained a firm grip on the episcopacy, and so controlled the church even in those areas where the Acadians made up the majority of the population. Beginning in the 1890s, Acadian nationalists turned their energies towards securing a French-speaking bishop in the region. When these first efforts met with failure around the turn of the century, the nationalists broadened their goals to include a new diocese specifically for the Acadians.[80]

In Ontario the growth of the francophone population was even more dramatic. Accounting for about a quarter of the province's Catholics at Confederation, by the turn of the century francophones composed two-fifths of that population. This growth was concentrated in the diocese of Ottawa, which straddled the Ontario–Quebec boarder, and in large part it was fed by the influx of French Canadians from adjoining territories in Quebec. Such migration enjoyed the blessings and support of the Quebec bishops, who saw to it that the diocese under the direction of the French-born Joseph-Eugène-Bruno Guigues was well supplied with French-speaking personnel.[81] In the rest of the province, however, diocesan personnel were overwhelmingly of Irish background, and by the late 1860s Irishmen headed every diocese in the province except that of Ottawa. Like their francophone co-religionists, Irish Catholics saw their religion as defining their sense of peoplehood, and that was the problem: both peoples laid claim to Catholicism as the touchstone for their national identity.

Although Irish bishops predominated in the civil province of Ontario, they were a minority in the ecclesiastical province of Quebec, of which they were still a part. Quite naturally, they wished to free themselves from the shadow of the French-Canadian hierarchy, but their quest for independence ran directly counter to Guigues's desire to see his diocese remain securely in the French-Canadian orbit. The French-Canadian bishops supported Guigues in the belief that only in this way could the assimilation of Franco-Ontarians be averted. As a result, when Rome raised Toronto to an archdiocese in 1870, the new ecclesiastical province did not include the diocese of Ottawa, whose bishop remained a suffragan of the archbishop of Quebec.

Instead of easing tensions between the two branches of the Catholic hierarchy in central Canada, the creation of the new ecclesiastical province of Toronto exacerbated matters by giving the bishops of Ontario an institutional power base of their own from which to conduct their campaign, which would continue well into the twentieth century. Ontario's bishops had always believed that the limits of their territory ought to coincide with those of the civil province; just as Quebec belonged to the French Canadians, so Ontario should belong to English-speakers. That it did not was, in their view, proof of French-Canadian designs upon their territory. The bishops therefore availed themselves of every opportunity to wrest territory from the diocese of Ottawa. Each attempt ended in failure, and each failure further convinced the bishops of Ontario that they were victims of French-Canadian aggression.

Still worse, while their efforts failed, Ottawa's efforts to consolidate its position succeeded. In 1882, the diocese carved out the vicariate apostolic of Pontiac (in 1898 the diocese of Pembroke) from its northern territories, and in 1886 Rome elevated Ottawa to an archdiocese, albeit one whose archbishop would have no suffragans.[82]

The religious and linguistic conflicts that dominated the political scene during the 1880s and 1890s caught the Irish Catholics in their vortex, even though the objects of Protestant antagonism were usually French Canadians. Despite ongoing conflict between anglophones and francophones at the episcopal level, Irish Catholics usually supported their co-religionists' rights in these crises, although at times they were less than enthusiastic. The trial and execution of Riel, the attack on francophone schools during the provincial election campaign of 1886, the Jesuits' Estates controversy, and the Manitoba Schools Question, all galvanized Irish-Catholic opinion. Significantly, the Irish-Catholic press defended these causes almost exclusively on religious rather than linguistic grounds. In Protestant bigotry anglophone and francophone Catholics faced a common foe, but the unity created by that fact would not endure. In the twentieth century, Catholics of Irish descent were not only to make their language a touchstone of their group identity but to see in it a badge of their superiority vis-à-vis French-speaking Canadians.

Intra-Protestant co-operation

Protestant bigotry was not the only spectre that alarmed Catholics of both linguistic groups: the Protestant penchant for social activism disturbed them as well, for it invariably resulted in proselytism. After the mid-nineteenth century, as revivalism became more respectable and the evangelical consensus broadened, this activist temper inspired Protestants from across the denominational spectrum to collaborate in various crusades to claim the country for God and so to transform its social ethos.

In itself, such collaboration was by no means new. For decades interdenominational Bible and tract societies had provided a forum for Protestants to work together in advancing the evangelical empire, and the Evangelical Alliance had attempted to create a united Protestant front against Romanism, Tractarianism, and other such threats to evangelical hegemony in public life. In transforming individuals into brothers and sisters in Christ, revivalism promoted a sense of community that naturally sought expression in collective action. What had changed was, first, that many more people had come to embrace the evangelical ethos, and, second, that as evangelicalism moved into the mainstream of Canadian society, growing numbers of its adherents had the time and the money to contribute to religious and philanthropic causes.

One of the most important ways in which Christians were to pursue their personal righteousness was by reclaiming their society for Christ. As the beneficiaries of God's love, Christians had a duty to extend compassion to those less fortunate than themselves: the poor, the sick, and, not least, the sinful. Thus soul-winning and humanitarianism went hand in hand. To improve others' material condition was a good in itself, but to transform their moral and spiritual life was even better. Besides, in practical terms, providing social services offered Christians an opportunity to reach people who might otherwise have little or no contact with organized religion.

Perhaps the most important outlet for activism within the churches was the Sunday school. The network of these schools extended throughout English-speaking Canada, and, as we have seen, it was made possible by a virtual army of lay volunteers. Sunday schools began as local institutions, often interdenominational in character, but as the nineteenth century progressed more and more of them became incorporated into denominational structures. One reason was that they were becoming an increasingly important source of new members. Among the Methodists, to take just one example, only 3 per cent of church members were recruited through Sunday schools in 1862, but by the early 1900s this figure had rocketed to 60 per cent.[83] The fact that Sunday schools had become instrumental in recruitment, however, did not prevent interdenominational co-operation in the adoption of the International Uniform Sunday School Lessons, first drawn up in 1872. As the century wore on, the emergence of inter-denominational Sunday school organizations and summer institutes created a common meeting-ground for Protestant activists. Not surprisingly, such co-operation served to standardize curricula and pedagogy across denominational lines.

After mid-century Protestants also began to co-operate in the formation of new organizations aimed specifically at the country's youth, notably the Young Men's Christian Association (introduced to Canada in 1853 and reorganized in 1864) and the Young Women's Christian Association, which established its first branches in Canada during the 1870s. Initially, the work of both organizations was highly focused: the YMCA offered meeting rooms for respectable young men to cultivate future church activists, and the YWCA ran hostels for young working women to protect them from the temptations of the city. As lay-dominated agencies free of ties to any particular denomination, these organizations typified the approach of many lay activists to religion, emphasizing Christian service and moral reform over doctrinal precepts. They also served as visible expressions of Protestant unity in the task of Christianizing the nation.

Lay men and women from diverse denominational backgrounds worked together in humanitarian organizations whose activities ranged from running old-age homes and orphanages to conducting poor relief and door-to-door visits. Together these organizations constituted a virtual empire of benevolent work. At a time when the state provided little in the way of social assistance, they were the major providers of social services, and as such did a great deal to impart an evangelical ethos to Victorian society. Non-evangelicals did, of course, participate in benevolent work, but evangelicals tended to predominate, largely because personal service to the poor was a way of bearing witness to their conversion.

Central to the evangelical social outlook was the view of poverty as essentially a moral and religious problem.[84] Some poverty, naturally, was inevitable. Personal misfortune, such as the illness or death of a family breadwinner, could strike even the most God-fearing and hard-working of people, and these deserved the assistance of those who were more fortunate. In most cases, though, poverty was considered to be the result of moral failings, most notably lack of self-discipline. Society, like everything else in the universe, came under God's providence and was so structured as to exemplify His system of rewards and punishments. On this view, generous social assistance would only encourage the undeserving poor to continue in their bad habits and disregard their responsibilities to both God and themselves. Furthermore, while such assistance might alleviate the immediate distress of poverty, its effects would be superficial without the aid of religion; only the transforming power of the cross could effect moral regeneration and thereby set individuals on the road to self-reliance and self-improvement. As a result, the social assistance offered by humanitarian organizations came with a strong dose of moralizing.

Evangelical concern for moral reform also manifested itself in the political arena. Fired with the conviction that they were entrusted to advance God's work in the world, evangelicals were determined to make Canada His dominion, and to that end they called on the state to use the compulsion of the law. In the decades between 1850 and 1880 evangelicals concentrated their energies on improving the tone of society in two areas, sabbath observance and temperance. The proper observance of the sabbath, evangelicals believed, signified society's recognition of God's dominion over the land. Over the years, evangelical lobbying resulted in a series of local ordinances and provincial laws closing down various business ventures and leisure activities that had formerly taken place on Sundays, many of which, such as excursion trains and taverns, were heavily patronized by workers. Sabbatarian laws ensured that, domestic workers aside, many would have at least one day of rest, but they did so at the cost of regulating both public and private behaviour.

Another area of public and private behaviour that evangelical agitation succeeded in regulating was the consumption of alcohol. That drinking was an extremely popular pastime was evident in the fact that in 1873 the city of Toronto boasted one tavern for every 120 inhabitants.[85] Even in most rural areas one would not have to travel far to enjoy a drink and partake of the entertainment—including cock-fights, gambling, and prostitution—that such establishments offered. Nor were such illicit pastimes the only evils associated with taverns: music and smoking were hardly innocent in evangelical eyes. Public drunkenness was common even in such august places as the House of Commons, where late-night sessions and inebriation were often inseparable, and in many trades 'Saint Monday' was widely observed—a testament to the effects of drink as workers took the day off to recover from a boozy weekend. More seriously, a Saturday-night spree would severely deplete a working man's wages, and if he were a breadwinner the family hardship that would result is not difficult to imagine. In addition, alcohol was often involved in family violence, as many Victorians learned from reading accounts of battered wives and children in their daily newspapers. It did not take a leap of faith to conclude, as evangelicals did, that drink was a blight on the common weal. Not only did it reduce productivity, but it undermined people's health, caused poverty, and led to violence and crime.

In response to these social evils, evangelicals sought to introduce local and provincial ordinances that would regulate the liquor trade and reduce the availability of alcohol generally. In this endeavour they largely succeeded. Under evangelical pressure many jurisdictions dramatically restricted the number of drinking establishments and reduced their hours of business, especially on weekends. During the 1870s a second wave of temperance agitation took hold among evangelicals, and like their counterparts at mid-century, they were not content to advocate voluntary abstinence: they wanted to legislate prohibition. Co-ordinated by the Dominion Alliance for the Total Suppression of the Liquor Traffic, this campaign succeeded in securing laws that provided the option for local prohibition, the most important of which was the Canada Temperance Act of 1878. One of the more influential organizations in the prohibition movement was the Woman's Christian Temperance Union. First introduced to Canada by Letitia Youmans in 1874 and organized on a national basis in 1883, the WCTU was to play a key role in the drive for first province- and later nation-wide prohibition.

Aboriginal peoples: Christianity and civilization

Missionary work caught the imagination of the public in the latter part of the nineteenth century. Yet both in English-speaking Canada and in Britain it was the exotic East, not the western and northern reaches of Canada, that attracted donations and recruits for Protestant missions. The situation for Catholic missions was somewhat different, since the availability of resources and personnel did not depend on popular preferences. Still, among English-speakers there was a serious shortage of vocations to the priesthood, whereas French-speaking priests were plentiful. Thus even in dioceses where the majority of the white population were anglophones, bishops were content to appoint francophone missionaries.

In addition to their perennial shortage of resources, Protestant missionaries working in the Northwest faced a significant obstacle in the form of the Hudson's Bay Company, whose writ ruled the land. Anxious to ensure that missionaries did nothing that would adversely affect the fur trade, the HBC endeavoured to limit the missionaries' contact with native people, preferring that they devote their energies to the company's white employees. Even so, the British-sponsored Methodist mission made a promising start, establishing four missions in 1840, at Rainy Lake, Norway House, Edmonton House, and Moose Factory. Although French-speaking Catholic missionaries frequently outpaced their Protestant rivals, Robert Rundle at Edmonton House had particular success with the Stoney people. Support for the Methodist effort was inadequate, however, and it soon declined. In 1854 the British turned over the remnants of the mission to the Canadian Wesleyans, but it never recovered from its earlier setback.

Anglican missions, whose roots reached back to 1820, were also British-sponsored, depending almost entirely on the Church Missionary Society. Although CMS recruits found other mission fields far more attractive, and volunteers from central Canada were few, by the mid-1860s the Anglicans had more than twenty ministers scattered across the plains and even into the Yukon. The Presbyterians were the last major Protestant denomination to send missionaries to the region, the first one arriving in 1851. They were never to become a major force among the native peoples, though, primarily because they devoted most of their attention to the growing population of white settlers.[86]

On the Pacific coast missionary work took hold during the 1850s, with the beginnings of white settlement. The Anglicans made converts among the Tsimshian around Fort Simpson and the Haida of the Queen Charlotte Islands. The Methodists entered the field following the Fraser River gold rush of 1858–9, although their efforts to serve both the Salish and white populations around Victoria, Nanaimo, and Chilliwack limited their effectiveness among the former. Nevertheless, their revivals did result in the conversion of some Tsimshian, and this led the Methodists in 1874 to establish a mission at Fort Simpson, in direct competition with the Anglicans. One reason for the success of revivals among aboriginal people was that natives played prominent roles in conducting them. The Methodists were not unique in this regard. The CMS regularly employed native catechists and readers, and in the opening stages of their missionary work both the Methodists and the Anglicans ordained aboriginal ministers, of whom several, such as the Methodist Henry B. Steinhauer and the Anglican Henry Budd, were lionized by natives and whites alike. The role of aboriginal people in the church changed dramatically, however, as the initial era of outreach came to a close in the 1870s. Not only did the churches stop ordaining native people, but they relied less on their contributions as catechists and readers, and the responsibilities and authority of those lay workers who remained on the rosters were significantly circumscribed. An early harbinger of these developments was the model village of Metlakatla, near Prince Rupert, established for Tsimshian converts by the Anglican missionary William Duncan in 1862.[87]

Like most missionaries of his time, Duncan believed that Christianity and civilization were inseparable: only if aboriginal converts adopted British habits and mores could they become true Christians. In part, Duncan and his colleagues were motivated by humanitarian considerations. The whole basis for the aboriginal way of life was disappearing with the spread of European settlement, and if native people were to survive they would have to acquire new skills. Yet the missionaries' approach to assisting in the process of adaptation was unmistakably paternalistic. Convinced that they alone knew where the native people's true interests lay, they were determined to eradicate what they saw as the indolence, dissipation, and idolatry of aboriginal societies and replace them with the godly virtues of hard work, thrift, and sobriety. To this end, Duncan began conducting classes in the central Christian teachings, reading, writing, and singing shortly after his arrival in Fort Simpson in 1857. But, like so many before him, he quickly discovered that the semi-nomadic life of the native people undermined any such attempt at acculturation. Fearing that the persistence of aboriginal customs would undo all his work, he proposed that the Christian Tsimshian establish a new community that would be a refuge from the corrupting influences of white society.[88]

In selecting the location for his model village, Duncan consulted the Tsimshian, who suggested the old native site of Metlakatla. This was the last time he would consult them on any question of importance. Duncan's purpose was to create a controlled environment in which Christian doctrine and British customs would be inculcated in equal measure, and among the customs on which he insisted was obedience to duly constituted authority. In practice that meant obedience to himself in all matters, whether secular or spiritual.

Metlakatla set the pattern for future missionary work. By the 1870s the federal government was beginning to settle the native peoples of the plains on reserves, as it had already done in eastern Canada. In 1879 it adopted Nicholas Flood Davin's recommendation, in his report on native education, that each reserve be assigned to a single denomination, which would then be responsible for both education and spiritual care. In the process, white missionaries became the state's principal agents of acculturation, and aboriginal mission workers found themselves shunted to the sidelines. Under the absolute rule of their white ministers, missions developed into highly regimented communities in which the church and the school were the two foci of life. The effort to create a controlled social environment was perhaps even more evident in the residential schools, where aboriginal children, isolated from their families, were

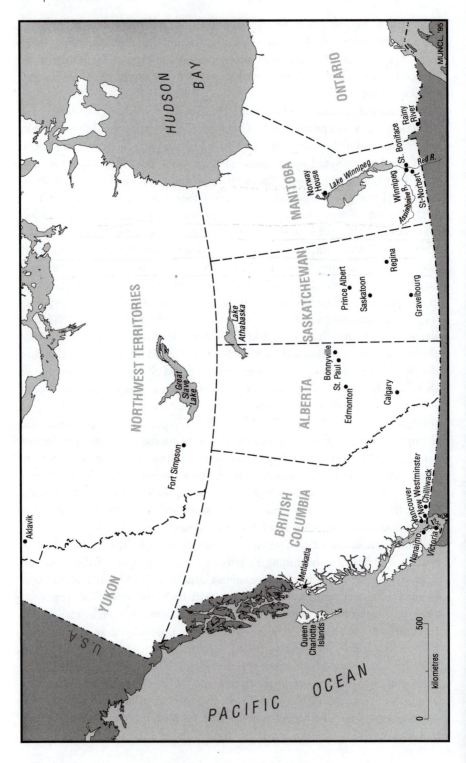

expected to lose their native identity and be thoroughly converted to white religion and culture. Under these circumstances, it is hardly surprising that in many respects some of these church-run establishments came closer to the Protestant ideal of the community as a worshipping congregation than any community in the outside world. Although from time to time a few people would wonder whether the Protestant churches could afford the huge expenses associated with this kind of mission work, only in the 1960s did they begin to question the methods and goals of this enterprise.[89]

NEW CHALLENGES

NEW INTELLECTUAL CURRENTS: DARWINISM AND HISTORICAL CRITICISM

The late nineteenth century was a time not only of rapid social change but also of intellectual ferment. New developments in science, above all Darwin's theory of evolution, and the application to the Bible of historical criticism posed new issues for the churches to confront. On the whole, the Protestant churches' leading thinkers quickly found ways of reconciling contemporary science and historical criticism with traditional beliefs, if only by interpreting the new ideas in a way that limited their potential damage to orthodoxy.

Adaptation was made easier by the firmly entrenched conviction that science and religion were not only compatible but mutually supportive. A mainstay of Protestant apologetics was William Paley's *Natural Theology*, first published in 1802. According to Paley, nature evinced order and harmony: everything in it served a purpose. The particular purposes manifest in the natural world were for Paley evidence that they were a product not of chance but of design. Such design, he insisted, required a designer who was both intelligent and benevolent. Just as the intricate mechanisms of a watch found on a deserted beach indicate that a watchmaker exists, so too creation is evidence of the existence of God.

Protestant thinkers from across the denominational spectrum invoked this tradition of natural theology to demonstrate that the findings of science were in harmony with the truths of religion. In addition, however, Methodists and in particular Presbyterians drew on another intellectual tradition that similarly promised to harmonize science with religion, known as Scottish Common Sense. In opposition to the philosophical scepticism of Hume, this school of philosophy maintained that the universal (or common) experience (or sense) of humanity assures us that reason provides a firm basis both for knowing the

Opposite: WESTERN CANADA.

world around us and for making moral judgements. For the most part, though, Canadian religious thinkers ignored the epistemological and ethical dimensions of Common Sense philosophy and appropriated only its inductive method, which went under the name of Baconianism. In adopting this method without its original philosophical underpinnings, they managed to keep the exercise of reason on a short leash. Instead of basing religion on the authority of reason, as Common Sense thinkers had typically done, they based it solely on revelation.[90] Regarding both Scripture and nature as vast storehouses of facts—the one containing God's words, the other His works—they insisted that the proper role of reason was merely to organize and classify these facts. Thus true science was simply an exercise in taxonomy, and those who indulged in hypotheses could be dismissed for straying from the facts. The conservative purpose of this reverence for facts was clear: science was to confirm established verities, not to discover new truths. In this way, theology exercised hegemony over science and determined how nature and human nature were to be understood.

Confidence in the harmony between science and religion was reflected in an almost devotional approach to the study of nature, evident both at the popular level and in the curricula of Protestant colleges. In the mid-1850s the study of natural history was a popular pastime; in an era when professional scientists were few and, even among them, generalists were the norm, many non-professionals contributed to the advancement of science by collecting specimens and writing reports on topics ranging from botany and zoology to geology and ethnology. The conviction of many middle-class Victorians that their diversions must be useful made such studies particularly attractive, for they promised to unlock the mysteries of nature, unleash the forces of intellectual and material progress, and provide a window on God's handiwork. 'The God of grace is also the God of nature,' exclaimed Egerton Ryerson; 'how delightful to trace his footsteps in the works and laws of the material universe, as well as in the pages of Revelation!'[91] Far from being a threat to religion, science was a form of piety, elevating the soul and refining the intellect and emotions.

Whatever uneasiness existed about attempts to separate the study of nature from religion was at first offset by the confidence that science revealed the glories of God's creation. This belief, however, rested on two comfortable assumptions: first, that the universe was static, and, second, that it was directed by divine purpose. The publication in November 1859 of Charles Darwin's *On the Origin of Species* shattered this world-view. Not only did Darwin argue that new species arose as a result of evolution, but he proposed natural selection as the explanation of how evolution occurred. On scientific grounds alone, Darwin's theory was revolutionary. Rejecting the long-standing assumption that species were immutable, he argued that differences between species and varieties within a species were of degree, not of kind, and offered a convincing hypothesis for how change occurs in the natural world.

But at the same time Darwin posed a severe challenge to traditional religious beliefs. On the basis of processes readily observable in nature, he proposed a naturalistic explanation for the development of all life, including human life. Though Darwin rarely mentioned humanity in the *Origin*, his theory of speciation had clear implications for humanity's position in nature, for it implied that there was no essential difference between human beings and other animals: natural selection could account for human origins as well as the emergence of humanity's apparently unique abilities, such as reasoning and moral judgement. Equally unsettling, Darwin's theory posited immense stretches of evolutionary time, and thus flatly contradicted the biblical account of humanity's creation, fall, and redemption.

In addition to overturning received opinion regarding human nature and its origins, Darwin's theory clearly called into question traditional beliefs concerning God's involvement in creation. One could hardly go further towards freeing science from its former tutelage to theology than to claim that natural causes, not divine intervention, brought new species into being. Darwin's theory did not exclude the existence of God, but the only deity it could accommodate was one remote from this world—a view that scarcely accorded with the experience of pious Christians. As Carl Berger has pointed out, Darwinism subverted the major tenets of the traditional view of God and nature:

> For a benevolent, supervising deity it substituted a blind, relentless, physical process; for adaptations deliberately designed, random adjustments; for harmony, abiding violence and conflict; for plan and economy, order and balance, a chaotic wasteful process.[92]

On this view, nature served no moral purpose, and next to Darwin's view of God as an absent deity it was this aspect of his theory that most preoccupied his contemporaries.

Today it is often thought that the controversy over Darwin's theory pitted science against religion. From this perspective, the victory of Darwin's theory represents the triumph of the forces of scientific enlightenment over those of religious obscurantism. The story is not so simple. Not all Darwin's opponents were churchly reactionaries, nor were all his supporters secular acolytes of progress. Responses in both theological and scientific circles hinged on whether individuals thought evolutionary theory could accommodate Christian understandings of God's providence. Many clergymen were soon convinced that it was possible to accept at least some aspects of Darwin's theory without jeopardizing faith.

Among Darwin's foremost critics in the international debate sparked by the *Origin* was William Dawson, the principal of McGill University. One of the leading geologists of his generation, a devout Presbyterian who saw the pursuit of science as a means of honouring God, Dawson was to become the only scientist to serve as president of both the British and the American Association for the Advancement of Science. His blistering attack on Darwin's theory was based partly on his assessment of the physical evidence and partly on his grave doubts about Darwin's daring new method of advancing a scientific hypothesis on the basis of probabilities.[93] Such an approach opened the floodgates to speculation, to the detriment of true science. In defending the conventions of the scientific establishment of his day, Dawson represented the old guard, and he was a man of the past in another respect as well, upholding the Baconian approach to science in which nature and Scripture were the two books of God's revelation. Although historians have debated whether Dawson's anti-Darwinism can be traced primarily to his religious or his scientific convictions, to frame the issue in this way would have made little sense to Dawson.[94] To deny the connection between God and nature, as Darwin had done, was simply bad science; and for religion to make any compromise with such a defective scientific theory would likewise result in bad theology.

Yet by the end of the 1870s Dawson had been shunted to the margins of the scientific establishment. Natural selection, Darwin's explanation of how evolution occurred, would not be widely accepted until well into the twentieth century, but the basic theory of evolution appealed to many Protestants.[95] As E.H. Dewart, editor of the Methodist *Christian Guardian* put it, 'every intelligent Christian will candidly admit that evolution is one of God's modes of working in the universe.' Before the 1870s were out, the Protestant clergy had successfully co-opted evolutionary science as support for their belief in divine providence and their faith in progress.[96]

Just a few months after the appearance of *On the Origin of Species*, another book was published that set off even more severe and long-lasting shock waves. Although its title could not have been more modest, *Essays and Reviews* was in fact a ringing manifesto for the historical study of the Bible. The last essay, by the pre-eminent classicist of the age, Benjamin Jowett, captured the general tone and message of the book. The Bible, Jowett affirmed, should be 'interpreted like any other book, by the same rules of evidence and the same canons of criticism'.[97] Not only should the books of the Bible be studied in the same way as any other historical document, but the results of historical scholarship should inform a re-evaluation of Christian doctrine and a re-formulation of Christian theology.[98]

The contributors to *Essays and Reviews*, all but one of whom were Anglican ministers, had hoped to demonstrate that the Christian faith had nothing to fear from the historical pursuit of the truth. But their essays did little to reassure their clerical colleagues or the public at large; instead, they reaped a whirlwind of outrage. The authors' emphasis on the poetic truth as opposed to the historical accuracy of the Bible, as demonstrated in their analysis of the creation stories in Genesis, and their questioning of biblical miracles and prophecies as proofs of the Scriptures' divine origin, struck many as reckless assaults on the Bible's divine authority. The Bible recorded God's relationship with humanity, and to question its reliability as history was to question its validity as revelation. Striking at the foundations of evangelical Christianity, the historical study of the Bible seemed to pose a much greater challenge to the faith than did evolutionary theory and the natural sciences.

The historical challenge to belief was pervasive, and it is one reason why Victorian debates over religion were so earnest and vehement. As a young pastor in Belleville, Ontario, during the early 1860s, Nathanael Burwash discovered that many local young professionals were so taken with historical criticism that they could not bring themselves to believe anything in the Bible, even though they had been raised in good Methodist homes. Burwash resolved to use the arguments he had recently learned in college as weapons in the battle with this new enemy. He soon discovered, however, that they were designed for an altogether different mode of warfare. Many years after the event, Burwash revealed that reading the historical critics of the Bible had sometimes left him feeling 'all certain ground sinking from under my feet'.[99]

Along with his evangelical colleagues of all denominational stripes, Burwash took a Baconian approach to Scripture that mirrored Dawson's approach to science. It began by assuming that the Bible was an inspired document and, as such, not only furnished a reliable account of God's action in history but disclosed the meaning and purpose of all history. In the Baconian view, theology was an inductive enterprise: just as scientists collected, classified, and interpreted the data found in the natural world in order to discover the laws of nature, so theologians collected, classified, and interpreted the facts contained in the Bible in order to explicate the divine plan for human redemption as the basis for Christian doctrines and moral principles. In this way, Baconian empiricism served to limit the scope and competence of reason in religious matters just as it did in the natural sciences, subordinating reason to revelation. The proper role of reason was to clarify the Bible's message and to justify its claims, not to question its teachings or its historical accuracy. Yet with the advent of historical criticism, it was precisely upon this latter point that the credibility of the Bible's religious message depended.[100]

Burwash weathered his spiritual crisis. Nevertheless, the experience was sufficiently troubling to send him on an intellectual odyssey in search of an adequate theological response to the challenges posed by the historical study of the Bible that was to continue for well over thirty years.[101] When, by the mid-1880s, Burwash came to accept historical criticism, it was because he now believed that a distinction should be made between the Bible's message and its manner of expressing that message. The writers of the Bible, in his view, communicated in the cultural idiom of their day. By shedding new light on their cultural outlook, historical investigation helped to clarify the divine message that they intended to convey and make it accessible to men and women living in the very different cultural milieu of the modern world.[102]

Burwash's approach to historical criticism can be found equally in the thought of leading Canadian Presbyterian educators, such as William Caven of Knox College and George Monro Grant of Queen's University. Under the aegis of such men, historical criticism was able to enter the classrooms of the Protestant colleges and become central to the theological curriculum for ministerial candidates. The reason that historical criticism gained acceptance lay in their re-casting of the historical study of the Bible as an unmistakably reverential discipline. Since the encounter between God and humanity remained at the core of the Bible, its divine authority intact, theology could continue to be an inductive process of recovering God's message from Scripture. The difference was that now the results of this retrieval came to be seen as progressive in nature. Advances in scholarship simply meant that Christians could now better understand the Bible and give its teachings more adequate expression.[103] In Burwash's view, historical study served to anchor the truths of the Bible in the certain bedrock of fact and the progress of science. Religion could safely embrace modern science and in so doing gain the respect of all those who sought the truth and admired intellectual candour.[104]

In some cases the Canadian Protestant clergy's efforts to absorb the new criticism gave rise to disputes, especially when progressive preachers or professors in theological colleges drew public attention to their views. Ideas that were common inside the classroom were still controversial outside them. Even so, these conflicts were mild compared with those provoked by similar issues in the United States, and except among the Baptists they produced no lasting divisions.

Debates of this kind typically started with a call for a formal investigation into a particular individual's teaching or preaching. The Presbyterians Daniel James Macdonnell and John Campbell, the Methodists George C. Workman and George Jackson, and the Anglican F.J. Steen were all charged with or investigated for heresy by their denominational authorities. Their alleged offences ranged from rejecting doctrinal standards such as those contained in the Westminster Confession of Faith to questioning the inerrancy of Scripture. These men were sometimes subjected to bitter attacks by leading denominational spokesmen, but with the exceptions of Workman and Steen, their cases usually ended either in complete exoneration or in compromises that respected their intellectual freedom. Macdonnell, who was required to reaffirm his adherence to the Westminster Confession, was permitted at the same time to acknowledge that he found some features of the confession perplexing. Campbell's conviction on charges of heresy by his own presbytery in Montreal was overturned amidst applause by the Synod of Montreal and Ottawa.

Workman was transferred from the divinity school to the Arts faculty of Victoria College and resigned in protest when the college's board asked him not to discuss historical criticism in public; it would take him twelve years to find another academic post. Jackson, supported by prominent Methodist laymen such as Newton Wesley Rowell and Chester Massey, had the charges against him dropped. Steen was fired from Montreal Diocesan College in 1901, but his dismissal had as much to do with his high-church sympathies as his advocacy of higher criticism. Elsewhere in Anglican circles, the teaching of historical criticism caused scarcely a ripple.[105]

By the early decades of the twentieth century, historical criticism was fast gaining recognition among most denominations as an essential component of any self-respecting program of theological study. The reasons for this rapid acceptance of new ideas lay largely in the convergence of intellectual currents and middle-class aspirations. Among evangelical Protestants, a new understanding of the religious life was emerging which recognized that if the churches were to succeed in transforming the lives of people familiar with modern currents of thought, they would have to update both their practice of piety and their approach to evangelism. Closely linked to this progressive outlook was the desire to expand the sphere of Christian service to include a stronger emphasis on social reform. According to this way of thinking, the measure of a Christian's religion was not so much doctrinal conformity as the kind of life it produced on both individual and collective levels.

Among Methodists, this approach entailed a new understanding of conversion. Formerly understood as an instantaneous, highly emotional experience, conversion was increasingly considered to manifest itself in a gradual quickening of one's moral life. The new stress on the development of character, rather than conversion, was reflected not only in the thought of Biblical scholars such as Jackson but also among leading Methodists such as Hart Massey and S.D. Chown. It reinforced the emphasis that Methodism already placed on service and prepared many middle-class Methodists to embrace social reform as a way of living out their faith, a perspective that was central to the emerging social-gospel movement.[106]

Presbyterians experienced a similar development in which service became the hallmark of the Christian life. Here, however, idealist philosophy, with its emphasis on the immanent presence of the divine in the world, played a much more formative role than among the Methodists. Like their Methodist counterparts, Presbyterian preachers used historical criticism to bring the Bible to life, in particular by emphasizing its call to serve God and love others.[107]

Baptists were the exception to the rule of easy acceptance of historical criticism. In 1909 Elmore Harris, a Toronto pastor and founder of the Ontario Bible College, charged McMaster University's professor of Hebrew, I.G. Matthews, with heresy for teaching historical criticism. The university's senate supported Matthews, as did the Baptist Convention of Ontario and Quebec the following year. Although Matthews was vindicated, the issue was merely the opening skirmish in what, in the 1920s, would become a concerted assault on McMaster led by Thomas Todhunter Shields.[108] Not only were controversies over Biblical criticism more bitter and prolonged among Baptists, but, as we shall see, they had more lasting effects in the form of enduring schisms in both central Canada and the West.

NEW RELIGIOUS MOVEMENTS AND DENOMINATIONS

While the mainstream Protestant churches were adjusting to new intellectual currents, they were also facing a challenge from new religious movements and denominations. The vast majority of prosperous Methodists and Presbyterians came to accept biblical criticism because it offered an intellectually respectable rationale for a form of piety that updated but did not repudiate evangelical traditions. This adjustment was one aspect of the broader process of accommodation with secular culture that characterized the major Protestant churches in the later nineteenth and early twentieth centuries. A significant minority were dissatisfied with such accommodations, however, with the result that protest movements embodying what they claimed to be traditional forms of Christian witness enjoyed considerable success.

One of the most significant manifestations of protest was the Salvation Army, which quickly gained notice for its energy and flamboyance. Founded in England by William Booth in 1878, the Salvationists made their first Canadian appearance in 1882, in Toronto, and the following years saw spectacular growth, centred mainly in Ontario; by mid-decade the Army had attracted 25,000 members, a number that it would not reach again until 1921. Unlike the country's leading Protestant denominations, the Army drew the great majority of its members from the working class, many of them women attracted by the unique opportunity to exercise leadership that the Army's officer corps afforded to them. Indeed, part of the Army's appeal lay in its biting criticism of the Protestant churches' condescension towards working people, and its inventive use of elements of popular culture such as band music and parades. Its greatest attraction, however, lay in its old-time revivalism.[109] In a sense, the Army functioned as a litmus test for middle-class evangelicals: conservatives were offended by the Army's displays of raw emotion, which they saw as evidence of bogus spirituality, but more progressive evangelicals were impressed by its work among the disadvantaged and saw its success as an indictment of their own churches' neglect of the working class. The leaders of the Methodist Church perhaps best embodied the ambivalence of many middle-class evangelicals towards the Salvation Army. Although they looked askance at the Army's boisterous style, they took pride in their own church's revivalistic heritage and its origins as a religion of the common folk. The

Salvationist invasion prompted them to defend that heritage by co-opting some of the Army's evangelistic methods; one conspicuous example was the formation of gospel bands for evangelistic outreach among Methodist youth.[110]

Rejection of the mainstream churches' new outlook and style of piety was also evident among the Plymouth Brethren, who came to notice after their British founder John Darby began paying regular visits to Canada in 1862. In contrast to most Protestant denominations, which took a post-millenialist view in which history was a story of progress, Darby taught that history consisted of a series of 'dispensations', or stages, each characterized by increasing tribulation, that would culminate in Christ's pre-millenial return to establish God's Kingdom on earth. According to this view, Scripture was the inerrant Word of God; even apparently minor details in the Bible could be the key to unveiling the future. Darby's biblicism, together with his emphasis on conversion, struck many notes characteristic of old-time revivalism. Although few joined the denomination, the Plymouth Brethren's influence extended widely, in part because they successfully infiltrated other denominations, especially the Presbyterians and the Baptists. Another reason for the Brethren's influence was their ability to forge pan-denominational networks, notably through the annual Bible and prophecy conferences introduced in 1878 and from 1883 to 1897 held at Niagara-on-the-Lake, Ontario. These 'Niagara Conferences' drew Protestants from both sides of the border and knitted them into a pre-millenialist alliance that transcended denominational boundaries.[111] Among the prominent Protestant clergy and laymen who embraced the Plymouth Brethren's teachings were the Baptist Elmore Harris; Maurice Baldwin, the Anglican bishop of Huron; Henry Parsons, the pastor of Knox Presbyterian Church in Toronto; and Toronto's Mayor William Howland, an evangelical Anglican.[112]

Yet another element stoking the fires of revivalism was the holiness movement. Introduced to the Canadian colonies in the 1840s and 1850s, holiness had many adherents within the Methodist Church, but towards the end of the nineteenth century it acquired an independent denominational base. In 1879 Nelson Burns had formed the Canadian Holiness Association as a ginger group to promote holiness both within and outside the Methodist Church in southern Ontario. Burns's idiosyncratic understanding of holiness, which led him to doubt Christ's divinity and to deny that Scripture was the sole authority for Christian belief, resulted in his expulsion from the church in 1894.[113] The following year, another Methodist holiness revival preacher, Ralph Horner, was expelled for having repeatedly refused to accept the postings assigned to him by his conference. The result was a new denomination, the Holiness Movement Church.[114] Preachers representing the Keswick movement from Britain also secured a wide audience for their brand of holiness as an alternative to Wesleyan holiness, but like the Plymouth Brethren they recruited few actual adherents.[115] Among the other denominations that espoused holiness were the Salvation Army, the Free Methodists (first introduced to Ontario in the late 1870s), the Mennonite Brethren in Christ (a union of Mennonite seceders formed in 1883), and the Reformed Baptists (formed in the Maritimes in 1888 after the expulsion of holiness proponents from the First Christian Baptists), but none of these had a large following.

Though each of these movements introduced innovations in doctrine, piety, and organization, all sought to conserve what they took to be the central verities of old-time religion. Only a handful of activists joined organizations associated with these movements, such as the Toronto Mission Union, or participated in international networks such as the one formed around the Niagara Bible Conferences, but they were highly influential. Recently described by one historian as 'proto-fundamentalists',[116] these activists were certainly in touch with those Americans who were to become the leading lights of the fundamentalist movement, and the networks they forged with these Americans were to become an important breeding ground for fundamentalism in Canada. Yet in the nineteenth century the boundaries between these particular activists and other evangelical Protestants were for the most part permeable. For this reason, even terms such as 'liberal' or 'conservative'—let alone the ones that came into vogue in the following century, 'modernist' or 'fundamentalist'—are scarcely apt. The absence of hard and fast boundaries was to continue in most mainstream denominations well after the controversy over fundamentalism that was to divide Canadian Baptists in the 1920s and 1930s. Fundamentalism was a descendant of these revivalist movements, but it was not the only one.

SOCIAL REFORM AND THE SOCIAL GOSPEL

As we have seen, moral crusading and social activism were central to the evangelical temper. With Canadian Confederation and the gradual emergence of a shared vision among the majority of Protestants, the quest to establish a righteous nation intensified. The late nineteenth century, however, also witnessed the profound social changes associated with industrialization. Canada was a relative late-comer to this process, since industrial manufacturing displaced commerce in importance only in the 1880s, but Canadians were already well aware of the social problems that the industrial economy had engendered in Britain and the United States. They were familiar as well with the new ideas developing among British and American religious leaders in response to industrialization. These new ideas hinged on an enlarged conception of sin and salvation that, without rejecting the necessity of individual regeneration, insisted that social institutions must also be redeemed in order to create an environment in which the individual could be healed and renewed.[117]

This new point of view, usually referred to as the 'social gospel' in North America and as 'social Christianity' in Britain, was both a school of theology and an active reform movement. But it was far from homogeneous, and therefore it resists precise definition.[118] Social gospellers took part in a wide variety of campaigns, including many, such as sabbatarianism and temperance, that were traditional to evangelicalism. But their efforts were informed by a greater appreciation of the social matrix of sin and a new sensitivity to questions of economic justice such as the rights of the working classes. This transformation of perspective was linked to the tempering of revivalism in the course of the nineteenth century; as the emphasis shifted from dramatic conversion to the cultivation and development of character, service was seen as the road to rather than the fruit of sanctification.[119]

Although the social gospel in Canada was inspired in part by British and American sources, it shaped Canadian Protestant churches and Canadian society in distinct ways. Christian social activists secured a much wider sphere of influence than their counterparts in the United States. Consensus among the major Protestant churches of Canada was deepened and reinforced by broad acceptance of the basic principles of the social gospel, and this convergence of opinion eventually paved the way to such uniquely Canadian developments as the formation of the United Church.

The social gospel's first and most important institutional bases were the theological colleges. At schools such as the Presbyterian Queen's University in Kingston, the Baptist McMaster University (then located in Toronto), and the Methodist Wesley College in Winnipeg, professors inspired by the social gospel reached a generation of students destined for the ministry and other professions. One of the best-known Methodist advocates of the social gospel, Salem Bland, offers a good example of how the social gospel made the transition from the classroom to the pulpit, and from there to the public domain. The influences that shaped Bland's social outlook were many, but the Queen's Theological Alumni Conference, in which he participated regularly when he held a pastoral charge in Kingston, did much to crystallize his views and turn him into a social gospeller.[120] After joining the faculty of Wesley College in 1903, Bland quickly became the movement's guiding spirit in the West. A charismatic teacher with, some said, the eyes of a prophet, he gained a large following among his students, who soon were proclaiming the social gospel from their own pulpits. In addition, Bland forged a strong network for the emerging social-gospel movement within the church. Almost as soon as he arrived in the West, Bland had become active in the Winnipeg Ministerial Association, and the programs he organized for it helped to recruit clergy to the movement and knit them into a cohesive group. Bland also generated popular support for the social gospel through regular speaking tours across the West for the YMCA, the YWCA, literary societies, and young people's groups.[121]

That Bland and other social-gospel ministers found receptive audiences was in part attributable to the wave of social-reform movements and moral crusades that swept Protestant Canada during the closing years of the nineteenth century. The new organizational bases that these created offered social-gospel ministers a unique opportunity to exercise leadership and shape public policy. One example was the crusade to preserve Sunday as the Lord's Day. The initial object of the Lord's Day Alliance, formed in 1888, was to ensure that existing laws against pleasure excursions, illicit tippling in bars, and other such violations of the sabbath were rigorously enforced. Though Presbyterians were its most ardent adherents, the Alliance enjoyed interdenominational support. That support remained diffuse, however, until Sunday streetcars began running in towns and cities across southern Ontario in the late 1890s. In response to this new threat, the Alliance put itself on a war footing in 1899, hiring as a full-time organizer a young Presbyterian minister named J.G. Shearer, whose many social-reform activities were soon to make him a pre-eminent leader of the social gospel and gain him wide regard as the social conscience of his church.[122] When, in 1903, the Privy Council struck down provincial Sunday legislation on the grounds that it infringed on the federal government's jurisdiction, the Alliance unleashed a campaign that culminated in the federal Lord's Day Act of 1906, which regulated business activities and public events on Sundays.

Many historians have viewed the passage of the Lord's Day Act as a hollow victory, a sign that religion had declined to the point that it was unable to resist the pressures of secularism.[123] As evidence they point to the bill's numerous concessions to business interests (notably the steel industry and others that relied on continuous manufacturing processes), concessions to which the Alliance agreed, and the fact that in the campaign for the bill the sabbath was promoted as a common day of rest rather than a Christian holy day. On both counts, though, the Alliance's stand might better be seen as reflecting a solid grasp of political realities. The concessions succeeded in neutralizing the business lobby against the bill, while the emphasis on the individual and social well-being that would result from the Act helped to gain labour support for its passage from the Trades and Labour Congress of Canada. This recognition of the interests of labour indicated a growing sympathy for social reform. But it did not mean that the Alliance and its supporters ignored religion or moral reform. As the francophone MPs who strenuously opposed the bill correctly observed, the overriding purpose of the Alliance's campaign was to enact legal protection for the evangelical sabbath. In this respect, the passage of the Lord's Day Act represented a significant victory for the evangelical vision of Canada.

The sabbatarian crusade also reflected the growing tendency of evangelical Protestants to rely on legislation and enforcement. As we have seen, they were able to advocate such coercive measures because they believed they were merely enacting into law what were already widely accepted principles of Christian morality. For evangelicals, the point of such measures was not simply to restrain sin, important as that goal was; they were also intended to set the country on a path to righteousness, so that it could become a truly Christian nation. Another of the great evangelical campaigns taken up by the social gospellers, the temperance movement, reflected the same assumptions. From the middle of the century the movement's leaders had shown an increasing inclination towards mandatory prohibition, and by 1900 prohibition had become established as an article of faith among evangelical Protestants. However, the social gospel extended to new areas of social and economic life the earlier idea that the state should be able to impose regulations for society's own good.

In calling for the state to suppress the liquor trade, prohibitionists made two claims: that drinking was a question not merely of private morality but of social ethics, and that this social problem could be adequately addressed only by state power; palliative measures were not enough. Thus prohibitionists promoted a new understanding of the state's role and responsibilities, and in so doing gained acceptance for the idea that the state had a duty to transform society by abolishing the conditions that produced misery and despair. This approach recognized that social problems were so multifaceted and interrelated that any attempt to address them must take into account the general environment in which they arose.

During the 1880s the Dominion Alliance and the WCTU intensified their campaign in the hope that communities would vote themselves dry under the local-option provisions of the Canada Temperance Act. But these provisions cut both ways, since communities that voted in favour of local prohibition could always revert. Recognizing this danger, the Dominion Alliance began to endorse political candidates who had pledged themselves to prohibition, and with the WCTU it deluged the federal and provincial legislatures with petitions in favour of total prohibition. Opinions on the subject were sharply divided along linguistic lines, as the national plebiscite of 1898 revealed. Although the measure passed with a paper-thin majority, Quebec voted solidly against it, and that, together with a weak voter turnout, persuaded Laurier and his Liberals that the safest course for Ottawa was not to enact legislation. In response, the Dominion Alliance and WCTU concentrated their energies at the provincial level. Their efforts were rewarded in 1900 when Prince Edward Island enacted the first province-wide prohibition. In 1916 British Columbia, Alberta, Manitoba, Ontario, and New Brunswick all went dry as well. By 1918 Quebec was the only province without prohibition, and in that year the federal government outlawed the sale of liquor for the duration of the Great War.

There is no doubt that the war contributed to the victory of the prohibitionists. They took advantage of the surge in patriotism in English-speaking Canada, deliberately equating support for prohibition with loyalty to country. As one advertisement asked, playing on the anxieties of the home front: 'Is the

Sacrifice made by our soldiers for us on the battlefield to be the only sacrifice? The Bar or the War? That is the Question of the Hour.'[124] The main pitch of this advertisement—its insistence that the moment of decision has come—underlines how much prohibition owed to evangelicalism. Not surprisingly, those denominations with the strongest evangelical heritages were the first to endorse the Dominion Alliance's campaign, with the Presbyterians taking the lead in 1888 and the Methodists following in 1890. By contrast, the Anglicans were deeply divided over the issue and managed to come out in united support of prohibition only after the federal government had presented the nation with a *fait accompli*.[125] Evangelicals remained the most fervent supporters of prohibition, and their activism was instrumental in the cause's eventual victory. A further key to prohibition's success was that, like sabbath observance, it was an issue on which traditional and progressive evangelicals could unite. Progressives could incorporate prohibition into their broad campaign for social reform and at the same time use the movement to introduce the larger public to new ways of looking at society, above all those championed by the social gospel.[126]

In addition to the familiar causes of sabbath observance and prohibition, a wide range of issues arising from rapidly changing social conditions engaged the attention of social gospellers. These issues included the impact of urbanization, class conflict, the repercussions of large-scale immigration from Southern and Eastern Europe, and the rights of women.

While English Canada's economic prosperity depended on an expanding population, industrialization and the rapid growth of the leading cities[127] unleashed forces that threatened the very fabric of society. Poverty and human misery now existed on a scale previously unimaginable, and the swollen slums in the city centres overwhelmed existing sanitary facilities and social services. In a nation that was still predominantly rural, many feared that the expansion of cities would undermine traditional values. The idealization of rural life, however, was coupled with a frank recognition that the cities were the nerve centres of Canada's social and economic life. As *The Missionary Outlook* of the Methodist Church observed, 'evangelize the cities and you evangelize the nation'.[128]

Class conflict also became increasingly visible as successive waves of labour militancy burst on the scene. Beginning with the Knights of Labor in the 1880s, a series of industry-wide strikes erupted, leaving communities divided throughout the southern parts of Ontario and Quebec. Around the turn of the century the American Federation of Labor launched a successful organizing drive, and soon more militant activists entered the political arena, establishing independent labour parties in towns and cities across Ontario and the West. The polarization of society only became more acute as family-owned companies were replaced by corporations traded on the stock exchange. In many cases such corporations were merely parts of interlocking empires controlled by financiers who did not hesitate to use the market advantages their conglomerates enjoyed to reap huge returns on their capital. As these corporate giants moved into the field of utilities, such as city tramways and electricity, their impact on everyday life became even more direct.

Middle-class Canadians felt beset by forces that they feared would soon be beyond control. But despite this sense of crisis, a certain optimism was widespread. Part of this optimism was rooted in people's faith in human ability: the material progress evident in the opening decade of the new century seemed testimony to the powers of human ingenuity. More important, most still had faith in the power of Christianity to redeem even the most hardened sinners. The message proclaimed by advocates of the social gospel was that sin was not only personal but structural in nature: society was organized to serve Mammon, and to that end it ruthlessly exploited the majority of people. It subordinated the many to the few, immiserated the masses so that the rich could profit, robbed the poor of their humanity, and, stripping them of all hope, deprived them of Christ's offer of salvation. Society itself was in need of redemption. Yet true Christianity could regenerate even the most deformed social structures and bring society back to God.

Given the severity of the social gospel's indictment and the sweep of its program for social reform, it may seem curious that middle-class Protestants rallied to it. Their reasons for doing so reveal the same mixture of altruism and self-interest that we have seen in earlier evangelical crusades. Many middle-class Protestants were genuinely moved by the human misery occasioned by social change. At the same time, reform was in their class interest, promising to ease working-class resentment and the threat of social conflict. In the eyes of middle-class Protestants, the social gospel was above all practical Christianity, and if aiding the disadvantaged would help to restore social harmony, many of them were prepared to do their part.

The social reformers' range of activity was astonishingly broad, and all of it was sustained by one voluntary association or another. Movements for the suppression of prostitution, the promotion of child welfare and the advancement of public health, for slum clearance and model housing, for public ownership of utilities, for city parks and urban beautification, all attracted activists and supporters. Although many of these objectives may appear to be wholly secular, reformers believed that improvements in the social environment would effect moral regeneration and spiritual transformation.[129] Not all who participated in these crusades were motivated by the social gospel. Mayor William Howland, for instance, an inveterate reformer who in his crusade against vice did more than anyone else to turn his city into 'Toronto the Good', was an old-style born-again evangelical. Nevertheless, social gospellers were instrumental in shaping the public's understanding of social problems and gaining acceptance for social reform. More traditional evangelicals such as Howland participated in the reform movements, but in the public mind these causes were closely identified with the social gospel and its ideals for society.[130]

As part of their campaign to promote social righteousness, social reformers also sought to advance civic righteousness, or good government. Governments at all levels resisted the pressure to enact much-needed social programs, and in the opinion of many people the reason was that corrupt professional politicians were in league with corporate interests. Movements to clean up city hall sprang up in towns and cities across Canada beginning in the mid-1880s, and in the countryside organizations such as the United Farmers of Alberta, the United Farmers of Ontario, and the Saskatchewan Grain Growers Association entered the political arena in the late 1910s, convinced that old-time politicians had sold them out to big business: while tariff protection kept manufactured goods dear and corporate profits high, farmers sold their produce cheaply on the open international market. Only new political parties and structures could liberate government from corporate interests and make it accountable to the people. If economic disparity fuelled farmers' resentment, however, the inspiration for their social vision can be traced to the social gospel. Agrarian manifestos were often nothing less than social-gospel sermons; as W.R. Wood, the secretary of the Manitoba Grain Growers, confided in a letter to Salem Bland, 'we are practically seeking to inaugurate the Kingdom of God and its righteousness.'[131] The supporters of the new agricultural organizations looked forward to the emergence of a new society based on co-operation rather than competition.

In urban and rural areas alike, another factor inspiring crusaders from across the Protestant spectrum was fear of the 'foreign peril'. The vision of Canada as a haven for immigrants who would transform the West into the bread-basket of the world had not been realized. Since Confederation, every census had recorded more people leaving than entering the country, and despite the completion of the CPR, most of the West remained unsettled. When immigration finally did pick up, beginning in the 1890s, the increase was dramatic; from 50,000 in 1901, the annual total quadrupled to 200,000 by 1906. Non-English-speakers comprised approximately one-quarter of the new arrivals, most of them from the predominantly Roman Catholic or Orthodox countries of Southern and Eastern Europe.[132] Each group developed its own settlement pattern. Italians established themselves in the urban areas of Central Canada and Ukrainians (known then as either Galicians or Ruthenians) largely in the West,[133] while Poles settled in the cities of central Canada as well as the agricultural regions of the West.

These newcomers would present significant challenges for the Catholic Church, as we shall see. Among Protestants, however, they were seen as posing an immediate threat to the British heritage that for most Protestants represented the highest form of civilization. In their eyes, it was bad enough that the new arrivals from Southern and Eastern Europe were unfamiliar with the

English language and Canadian customs; worse, their culture was morally debased, and their religion, whether Catholic or Orthodox, little more than superstition. Surely vice, squalor, and violence would flourish in the cities as never before, and the West, the region that many saw as the nation's best hope, would be overrun by the teeming foreign masses. 'We have to ask ourselves,' the Reverend W.D. Reid, the former superintendent of Presbyterian missions in Alberta, proclaimed, 'will the foreigner paganize us or shall we Christianize him?'.[134] As the Reverend Charles W. Gordon (widely known as the novelist Ralph Connor), put it, 'They must be taught our ways of thinking and living or it will be a mighty bad thing for us'.[135]

The initial response to the influx of immigrants was to evangelize them along traditional lines. After the turn of the century, though, the Methodist and Presbyterian churches, under the influence of the social gospel, adopted new approaches emphasizing the provision of social services. Providing immigrants with social services came to be seen as an inherently religious task, not simply a preliminary means to evangelization. It was assumed that improving the social environment in which immigrants lived would transform their culture, and that Protestantism would naturally take root.[136]

Whether or not they endorsed the social gospel, Canadians agreed that the new immigrants needed to be assimilated. For English-speaking Protestants, the country's constitutional connection to Britain defined their sense of nationhood: to be one hundred per cent Canadian was to be one hundred per cent British, and to be British was to possess those qualities—an attachment to freedom and democracy, a sense of decency and fair play—that made social progress and good citizenship possible.[137] The racism and religious bias in this approach are clear. But many Protestants were also genuinely moved by the newcomers' struggle to overcome poverty, loneliness, and the challenges of adapting to a different culture. In assisting the disadvantaged, they hoped to exemplify the social gospel's ideal of the brotherhood of humanity and so help to prepare the way for a better society where mutuality and harmony would prevail.[138]

Finally, another movement supported by both social gospellers and more traditionally-oriented evangelicals was the movement for women's rights. The evangelically-inspired Woman's Christian Temperance Union was one of the first organizations to agitate for women's suffrage, making this a central element in its broad reformist program during the late 1880s. For many evangelical women it was the WCTU that provided their first exposure to the currents of progressivism. Through their involvement in the prohibition movement they discovered that to address all the ills that beset society, the social environment itself would have to be changed. Taking as its motto 'do everything', the WCTU launched an astonishing array of initiatives on everything from dietary reform and the rehabilitation of ex-convicts to curfews for juveniles. Whatever the activity—education, social outreach, political lobbying—the WCTU's purpose remained constant: to effect a fundamental transformation in social mores.[139]

The WCTU's approach to women's public role reflected in part the traditional evangelical view of woman as the embodiment of domestic virtue. It justified women's entry into public affairs on behalf of issues such as temperance on the grounds that they had a special responsibility to protect the home and the family, and in presenting the case for women's suffrage it invoked the differences that, in the traditional view, distinguished the moral sensibilities of women and men. Agreeing in part with their more traditional opponents who claimed that politics was too dirty a business for women, they argued that precisely because they were different from men, women would be able to clean up the nation's political life. The idea that granting women the franchise would simply extend their domestic responsibilities into the political arena was reassuring to many people: for men it meant that their status and authority remained intact, while for women it suggested that femininity and fulfilment as a person were not antithetical.[140]

Yet at the same time the WCTU challenged the conventional evangelical view of women, particularly when men used it to argue that women should be satisfied with exercising influence rather than power. As the official journal of the Ontario WCTU, *The Canadian White Ribbon Tidings*, put it, the saying that ' "the hand that rocks the cradle moves the world" is a lie'; rather, 'the hand that holds the ballot is the hand that moves the political world.' Women's suffrage was not only a matter of allowing women to bring their special moral qualities to bear on political life; it was also an issue of natural justice.[141] Moreover, for at least one prominent member of the WCTU, the popular writer and social activist Nellie McClung, the franchise itself was merely part of a broader vision. As she put it, she hoped for a time 'when women will be economically free, and mentally and spiritually independent enough to refuse to have their food paid for men; when women will receive equal pay for equal work, and have all avenues of activity open to them; and . . . free men and free women will marry for love, and together work for the sustenance of their families'. According to one study, McClung regarded the social issues of the day, whether health care, living conditions, or employment opportunities, through the prism of gender, and for her true reform of society had to begin with reform of the relations between the sexes.[142]

The social-gospel movement had a profound impact on the conception of pastoral care and Christian outreach among the major Protestant denominations, especially the Methodists and Presbyterians, and this new outlook had many practical consequences. Existing interdenominational organizations were transformed under its influence, and new co-operative programs and initiatives came into existence. Fundamental reforms took place in religious education, as Sunday schools were re-organized under denominational control and entrusted to the supervision of professional religious educators.[143] New approaches to youth work were also introduced. Greater demands were placed on the financial and human resources of the churches, with the result that more elaborate bureaucracies developed to co-ordinate fund-raising and to supervise the ever-broadening range of outreach activities. Most of the Protestant churches established national committees to deal specifically with social questions. The Methodists were the first to do so (1894), followed by the Presbyterians (1907) and the Anglicans (1915). The Baptists, whose denominational structures were less centralized, did not form such a committee, but support for social-gospel principles was evident in the proceedings of regional Baptist conventions.[144]

A good illustration of the transforming influence of the social-gospel perspective can be seen in the changes that occurred among organizations whose work was directed towards adolescents. The activities of the YMCA and YWCA had initially reflected conventional evangelical outreach: the former offered boys and young men uplifting prayer meetings and edifying speeches, while the latter provided supervised lodging for young working women, many of whom were new to the city. Shortly after the turn of the century, however, the emphasis of these organizations shifted. Inspired in part by a new understanding of adolescence as a distinct stage in life (a view that reflected the theories of the American psychologist G. Stanley Hall) and in part by the social-gospel faith in the power of a wholesome environment to mould character, comprehensive recreational programs were drawn up, aimed at cultivating the physical, intellectual, and spiritual faculties of young people. One of the initiatives that grew out of this revised approach was the development of two standardized programs of leisure activities, tests, and awards to promote the physical, intellectual, social, and religious development of adolescents: Canadian Standard Efficiency Tests (CSET) for males and the Canadian Girls in Training (CGIT) for females. First devised by the Ys, these programs were later administered by the major Protestant denominations. While the CSET program soon faltered, the CGIT expanded rapidly. By 1925 it had 30,000 members in congregations from coast to coast, although membership numbers varied considerably from denomination to denomination.[145]

A new form of outreach that began under the influence of the social gospel was the downtown mission. In most cases, these establishments began as Sunday schools for the unchurched children of the poor, as was the case of the two best-known missions of the time, both of them Methodist: the Fred Victor Mission in Toronto and the All Peoples' Mission in Winnipeg. Over time, however, they branched out to offer other services. Some of these, such as free lodging and meals for the homeless, were quite in keeping with traditional charitable work, but a large part of what the missions did marked a new departure. Most housed clinics staffed by nurses, along with milk-stands, both of which reflected the burgeoning movement for public-health reform. They also mounted extensive educational programs: mothers' meetings to improve child care, kindergartens for young children, manual training and English-language instruction for men, and classes for girls and young women in sewing, gardening, and cooking. Recreational activities for children and youths likewise became a standard feature. After the turn of the century this aspect of mission work became even more extensive as some, such as the All People's Mission, erected new buildings complete with reading rooms, libraries, swimming pools, and gymnasiums.[146]

New forms of outreach inspired by the social gospel placed new demands on the resources of the denominations that sponsored them. When it came to personnel, for example, their requirements were very different from those of ordinary congregational life. Not only did their wide-ranging work need people in unprecedented numbers, but many of their activities also required personnel with specific skills. Although ordinary lay people doing volunteer work in their spare time could make important contributions, the new initiatives called for trained, full-time workers; but these were in short supply. One remedy was to create new professions within the churches, with their own specific training and certification programs. Among the best-known innovations of this kind was the introduction of deaconesses, of whom the largest contingent by far was found in the Methodist Church. First formally recognized by the church's General Conference in 1894, the same year its first training school opened in Toronto, the deaconess movement had by 1910 more than eighty workers in some twenty-four communities from coast to coast. By 1926, when they merged with their Presbyterian counterparts following church union, some 235 women had at one time or another served as deaconesses. Without these women, whom one historian has described as 'the foot soldiers of Methodist applied Christianity', the new forms of outreach favoured by the proponents of the social gospel would not have been possible. Yet deaconesses advanced from their status as unpaid workers only in 1910, when for the first time the church began paying them a salary.[147]

Among the most visible signs of the ascendancy of the social gospel were the progressive declarations of the major denominations on social questions. Typically, these declarations drew attention to systemic injustice in the economic order and endorsed such remedies as an eight-hour working day, a living wage for family breadwinners, old-age pensions, labour safety regulations, compulsory arbitration in industrial disputes, and public ownership of utilities. The most radical manifesto was the report approved by the General Conference of the Methodist Church in 1918, entitled 'Church Leadership in the Nation', which flatly rejected the capitalist system, calling for a complete reconstruction of the economy so that it would serve the needs of all, not just a select few.[148]

In 1907, under the joint leadership of J.G. Shearer, a Presbyterian, and T. Albert Moore, a Methodist, the interdenominational Social Service Council of

Canada was formed for the purpose of co-ordinating the activities of church-related reform bodies, the WCTU, and labour and farm organizations. The joint efforts of the members of this council culminated when it sponsored the first national council on social welfare. Social gospellers and other social reformers gathered in Ottawa to discuss the burning issues of the day. More important than the specific topics of discussion was the event itself. The fact that such a congress could be organized so quickly testified to the extensive networks that social gospellers had developed within and between denominations, as well as beyond the confines of their own movement. Public interest, reflected in extensive newspaper coverage, was also very high, showing that the social gospel enjoyed the sympathy of many people who were not active supporters. The mood of the conference was buoyant and optimistic, many of the participants being convinced that the individual social consciences were awakened as never before. With so many men and women living out the Gospel ethic, it seemed clear that a more Christian society was in the making.[149]

THE NEW ERA

THE FIRST WORLD WAR AND ITS AFTERMATH

The national conference on social welfare preceded by only a few months the declaration of war in August 1914. The First World War was the turning-point for the Canadian churches. While the optimism of the pre-war years remained initially intact, the passion and fervour that Canadian Protestants had hitherto devoted to social reform was redirected to fighting the 'war to end all war'. Believing that they were fighting not only to defend freedom, democracy, and justice against the brute force of Prussian militarism but to preserve Christianity itself, they saw the conflict as a holy war. Protestant clergy preached sermons urging young men to do their patriotic and religious duty by enlisting in the army; they threw their support behind conscription when the government introduced it in mid-1917; and, in the election that followed, they called on Canadians to vote for the wartime Union government in the name of God and Country.[150] Canadian Protestants were both intensely loyal to Britain and fervently nationalistic. They saw no conflict between Canada's fulfilling its duty to empire and working out its own destiny: the country's national interests were also at stake in the war, and by sending its own contingents to fight in Europe, it was taking a step towards claiming its place among the nations.[151]

However, this national vision, fusing British imperialism with Canadian nationalism, was to bring English-speaking Canadians into conflict with the country's francophone population. In fact, by 1914 simmering linguistic conflicts were already approaching the boiling point. In Ontario, the use of French in the schools attended by francophones in the Ottawa valley had been an ongoing source of friction since the 1880s. When, in 1910, Franco-Ontarians launched a campaign to establish French instruction on a firmer footing, anglophone tempers reached a flash point. Protestants saw in these demands a plot by French Catholic Quebec to extend its linguistic and religious institutions into British Protestant Ontario. Questions of language and religion overlapped in complex ways. Anglophone Catholics, most of whom were of Irish ancestry, were no more sympathetic to Franco-Ontarian aspirations than were Protestants. 'What is to become of us,' asked Bishop Fallon of London, Ontario, 'between the upper millstone of French Canadian nationalism and the lower millstone of Protestant bigotry?' Convinced that, constitutional guarantees notwithstanding, the existence of their separate schools depended on the good will of Protestant Ontarians, Fallon and his colleagues vehemently resisted Franco-Ontarian agitation for linguistic rights. In the event, the Ontario government took the position that only the religious rights of Catholics, not their linguistic rights, enjoyed protection under the law. Accordingly, in 1912 it issued Regulation XVII, which in effect abolished instruction in French in the province's schools.[152]

Four years later, francophone rights suffered another blow, this time in the West. The war had unleashed fears that newly arrived immigrants from Europe, many of whom sought to preserve their language and culture in the new land, were not sufficiently loyal. When they used the legal provisions available to them to secure bilingual education, in their native languages as well as English, English-speaking Protestants were only further alarmed. In the climate of xenophobic nationalism generated by the war, the Manitoba government in 1916 abolished all instruction in 'foreign' languages, a category that, as in 1896, was understood to include French.[153]

The introduction of conscription in 1917 and the election called by the federal government shortly afterward as a referendum on the issue split the country along linguistic lines. In the eyes of francophones, the war was a European issue with no bearing on North America. Conscription demonstrated that anglophones still put Britain's interests ahead of Canada's, and that all their talk of ideals was a flimsy mask for a colonial mentality. Meanwhile, as Canadian casualties mounted—more than 24,000 in the battle of the Somme alone—Protestant Canada became increasingly resentful of French Canada's failure to contribute its fair share to the war. That the bulk of the Canadians who enlisted were British-born made no difference. To oppose conscription and vote against the government was to give succour to the enemy and make a mockery of those who had already sacrificed their lives.[154]

The war was a milestone for English-speaking Catholics as well as Protestants. Hitherto much of the strength of the English-speaking Catholic community had come from its peculiar blend of religious commitment and ethnic consciousness. Irish nationalism had combined with Ultramontane

Catholicism to make anglophone Catholics a special component of the Canadian population who consciously distinguished themselves from both English-speaking Protestants and French-speaking Catholics. A recent study, however, reveals that English-speaking Catholics in Toronto viewed the war in much the same light as their Protestant fellow citizens, and that they enlisted for military service in the same proportion as the general population. Their response to the war seems to signal a closer identification with the prevailing outlook of the Protestant majority. Eager for acceptance as full-fledged Canadians, they were determined to demonstrate that they were no less British than the Protestants, and no less dedicated to the high ideals of sacrifice and service for the Christian cause.[155] But not all Protestants were ready to trust them as loyal citizens, as was demonstrated by the June 1918 raid on the Guelph novitiate of the Society of Jesus. Based on false rumours that the Jesuits were hiding draft dodgers, the raid, led by an over-zealous officer, resulted in the arrest of three innocent people. Fearing the prospect of an inquiry into the incident, the Orange Order launched a national campaign defending the honour of the military and of the minister in charge, the Orangemen Sam Hughes, while casting further aspersions on the patriotism of English-speaking Catholics.[156]

Social-gospel activists occupy a special place on the spectrum of responses to the war. Though a few stalwarts such as William Ivens and J.S. Woodsworth remained staunch pacifists, most of their colleagues embraced the prevailing view that the war was a sacred struggle for freedom and justice. Their attitude was influenced in part by their fervent nationalism, but in addition they believed that from the cauldron of war an age of international harmony would emerge. Only the bitter course of events showed how naïve this hope had been. At the same time, however, the war strengthened their cause by giving a new impetus to social reform. Many people interpreted the war's ravages as God's judgement and greeted the return to peace in 1918 as a unique opportunity to reconstruct Christian society. The war had shown how much remained to be done on the home front, but it had also demonstrated what could be accomplished and so shown the way to the future. The wartime regulation of industry, for example, opened new possibilities for the more efficient and equitable management of the economy through the use of state power. Social gospellers thought they had caught a glimpse of what society could be in another respect as well. In their view, the war had brought people together in a way that nothing had ever done before; Canadians had put aside their own immediate interests and, in whatever way they could, pitched in to support one another. This vision of the home front conveniently ignored the social and religious conflicts generated by the war, but it gave many Protestants a foretaste of a society where people could live in true community with one another, and in a society that had become reconciled to God.[157]

While the war had breathed new life into the social-gospel movement, it had also changed it fundamentally. The changes were most obvious in Methodism, the denomination where the social gospel had made the most headway. William Irvine, J.S. Woodsworth, and William Ivens had resigned from their positions, and Salem Bland had been dismissed from Wesley College. Although their precise circumstances and reasons for resigning varied, Irvine, Woodsworth, and Ivens each shared the belief that institutionalized Christianity had become part of the problem, not the solution. The church had become so closely identified with wealth that it was now incapable of reaching the working classes, and in their view the solution to that problem lay in forming a church independent of the middle class, a church exclusively for working people that embraced the cause of labour. The statement of faith drawn up by Ivens for one such independent congregation, the Labour Church of Winnipeg, which he founded in June 1918, affirmed that the church's first duty was to denounce the 'injustice and wrong' of the existing economic system and 'to blaze the way to a system that shall be essentially just and moral'. The establishment of the Winnipeg Labour Church underlined the close involvement of these social gospellers with the agrarian and labour movements. In the same period Irvine became the editor of a farmer's paper and Woodsworth toured the province on behalf of labour. Not surprisingly, some social gospellers, including Ivens, Woodsworth, and the Reverend A.E. Smith, then serving in Brandon, greeted the Winnipeg general strike of May 1919 as an unprecedented manifestation of human solidarity and mutuality that presaged the emerging new social order.[158]

Instead of inaugurating a new day of harmony and brotherhood, however, the Winnipeg strike drove a wedge between these men and the Methodist Church. For the former, the strike was a test of the churches' commitment to a cause that they themselves had upheld at considerable personal cost: both Ivens and Woodsworth were arrested when the federal government moved to suppress the strike. The leaders of the Methodist Church, on the other hand, among them S.D. Chown, feared the Winnipeg strike and the sympathy strikes it generated were signs that the labour movement had succumbed to worldly egotism and coercion. The prospect of class conflict, in their view, underscored the urgency of the need for reconstruction of the social order and demonstrated that the church's declaration of 1918, with its emphasis on co-operation and social harmony, was all the more relevant to the troubled times. Others feared that such pronouncements only encouraged the wild schemes of revolutionaries and abetted them in their attempts to divide and disrupt society. Nevertheless, over the summer the vast majority of local conferences endorsed the General Conference's report of 1918–a remarkable development, considering how much energy the federal government had devoted to portraying the general strike as merely a prelude to the establishment of a Bolshevik-inspired Soviet in Winnipeg. Even so, the strike revealed major fissures within the social-gospel wing of the Methodist Church. Very few were prepared to take an active part in this uprising of labour, and in the eyes of those who did, such reluctance was proof that the Methodist Church could never live up to the social teachings of Jesus. Instead, they looked to the labour movement to revive the true spirit of Christianity within the social order.[159]

When the Manitoba conference of the Methodist Church rejected requests from Ivens and Smith that they be free to develop their own ministries in labour churches, it put paid to any hope for reconciliation; the social-gospel wing was now clearly divided, and the two parts would go their own ways. Some radicals, such as Smith, ministered in labour churches for a time, but these would be their last pastoral charges. In 1925 Smith converted to communism, and although this was a singularly dramatic move, he was not the only social gospeller to find a new calling in politics; among the others was J.S. Woodsworth, who came to personify the social passion of the Co-operative Commonwealth Federation.[160] Their departure had significant consequences for the character and influence of the social gospel both in the Methodist Church and in its successor the United Church. More moderate social gospellers now had the field of social reform in the church largely to themselves, and with the radicals gone they would have an easier time gaining the support of those who saw themselves as occupying the middle ground between radicalism and reactionary conservatism.

Meanwhile, some 60,000 Canadians had died in the war. The sheer scale of carnage on the battlefields defied comprehension. Many of those who had served at the front returned home changed. E.H. Oliver, who was to become principal of Presbyterian College in Saskatoon and later moderator of the United Church, confided shortly after he was decommissioned as chaplain:

> I want to escape that utter depression of the soul that overwhelms me when I think of Ypres and Passchendaele, the hell of Lens, the mad ruin that stretches from Vimy and Arras to Cambrai and Valenciennes. The sheer havoc and appalling desolation of it all haunts me.[161]

Yet Oliver's faith remained intact. 'Redemption,' he declared in a sermon given in 1916, 'comes through a cross, life through death. We are learning to-day what sacrifice means, for the human race is marching to its Calvary.'[162] As a result of the war, the sacrificial death of Christ on the cross probably came to occupy a greater place in the thinking of social gospellers than it had before; certainly the war underscored their central conviction that sacrificial service on behalf of others was the basis of the Christian life. Progress could no longer be assumed to be inevitable; yet the fact that God had become incarnate for the sake of humanity and continued to act in history meant that even the most horrible sacrifices could lead to personal redemption and the eventual regeneration of society.[163]

Many clergy had hoped that the sacrifices of 1914–18 would inspire Christians to rededicate themselves to extending Christ's Kingdom with the same fervour that they had once given to the war effort. But the initial signs of religious renewal were disappointing, to say the least. Disturbing reports by military chaplains documented how little the wartime recruits had known of their religion.[164] Returning veterans generally suspected all established authority, including that of religion. Disenchantment had struck a new generation of students, who denounced the churches for their uncritical patriotism.

The 1920s soon came to be seen as an era of outright rebellion against religion and flight from the churches. In 1920, British Columbia repealed prohibition after holding a referendum that decisively favoured the move. Manitoba and Alberta followed suit in 1924, as did Saskatchewan a year later and Ontario two years after that. By 1930 prohibition had been repealed in every province except Prince Edward Island. One reason for prohibition's defeat was that its supporters had promised much more than they had been able to deliver. Instead of bringing prosperity, harmony, and freedom from crime, prohibition had created a whole new class of criminals; rum-runners, speakeasy operators, and corrupt government officials flourished to the point that the cure seemed worse than the disease. In addition, some of the most ardent supporters of prohibition, such as the WCTU, over-confident that that battle had been won, had shifted their attention to other reforms. They had failed to realize that once the hardships of wartime had passed, many people would be unwilling to sacrifice one of their pleasures in life.[165]

In the same period the impact of American mass culture was tremendous, above all in the cities. The undulating rhythms of the jazz club, the uninhibited flapper girls, and the automobile's promise of unprecedented freedom and privacy caught the imagination of English-speaking Canadians, particularly among the young. Many of these pleasures were well beyond the financial reach of ordinary people, but they could be experienced vicariously through the relatively inexpensive media of radio, films, and mass-circulation magazines. All these media depended upon advertising, which now hawked an unprecedented array of consumer products, from brand-name cosmetics to the latest fashions in clothing.[166]

On average, Canadians bought far fewer of these products than their American cousins: their incomes lagged behind, and unlike their neighbours to the south, they spent much of the roaring twenties mired in an economic recession. But even those who could not afford to buy gazed at the stores' display windows and dreamed of possessing such luxuries. As a result of their exposure to American media, Canadians began to acquire the outlook and orientation of a consumer culture. The free-spending, self-indulgent ethos of consumerism ran directly counter to the respectable Victorian values of thrift and self-restraint. For many clergy, these trends were clear indications of a nation adrift from its moral and religious moorings.[167]

INTERDENOMINATIONAL CO-OPERATION AND CHURCH UNION

The first few years after the war were a sobering experience for the clergy. Nevertheless, the mainstream churches showed their vitality in a number of new interdenominational initiatives aimed at stimulating lay involvement. One such initiative was the Inter-Church Forward Movement, a joint project of the Methodists, Presbyterians, Anglicans, and Congregationalists intended to raise funds for home and foreign missions and to promote the idea of social service among businessmen. Formally launched in 1918, it gave proponents of the social gospel an unprecedented opportunity to recruit the business class to their cause, and the response exceeded their wildest expectations. Businessmen flocked to volunteer their time to the ICFM, helping to raise some $15-million.[168] Another successful interdenominational initiative was the Student Christian Movement, founded in 1920 and aimed at promoting Christian service through study of the historical Jesus. So fruitful were the SCM's early efforts that it promptly gained the official support of the Methodist Church in the person of Ernest Thomas, then of that church's Department of Evangelism and Social Services.[169]

The most significant example of inter-church co-operation, and one of the most important developments in the history of the Canadian churches, was the formation in June 1925 of the United Church of Canada. The union, bringing together the Methodist and Congregational churches with the concurring majority in the Presbyterian Church, was the culmination of a long series of events. As we have seen, both the Methodist and Presbyterian churches in Canada had been formed through the consolidation of several smaller branches, the former in 1875 and the latter in 1884. These intra-confessional mergers inspired hopes among many clergy in the 1880s that their churches might go so far as to achieve trans-confessional union. While American churches pioneered inter-church co-operation with the formation of a federally-constituted council of churches in 1908 as a consultative body that respected the autonomy of its member denominations, Canadian Methodists, Presbyterians, and Congregationalists were to take the lead in the movement towards the achievement of organic trans-confessional union.[170] A merger was first officially proposed in 1886, when the Anglicans invited the Presbyterians and Methodists to discuss the possibility of union, but the effort foundered on the Church of England's insistence, underscored by the 1888 Lambeth Conference of world Anglicanism, that the 'historic episcopate' was a condition of union. Despite this setback, interest in co-operation and even organic union remained high, and both the Presbyterians and the Methodists kept standing committees prepared to discuss the possibility with other churches.

The particular series of events that led to the successful union of 1925 began in 1902 when the Presbyterian William Patrick, who as principal of Manitoba College had been selected as a fraternal delegate to the Methodist General Conference in Winnipeg, suggested that the Methodists consider joining forces with the Presbyterians. Unaware that Patrick had no authorization to make such an overture, the Methodists responded favourably. The following year, without consulting the church's lower courts or its congregations, the Presbyterian General Assembly agreed to enter into negotiations. In 1904, the Congregationalists, with a much smaller membership than either the Methodists or the Presbyterians, also joined the talks.

The 'Basis of Union' between the three churches took only four years to negotiate, largely because the ground for agreement had been well prepared by several decades of co-operation and commitment to common causes. The evangelical consensus that had been developing since the mid-nineteenth century had already promoted a meeting of minds among the majority of Protestants; and shared values had given rise to active co-operation in causes ranging from temperance to the evangelization of French Canadians.[171] This convergence of views and pooling of efforts had culminated in the social gospel, whose influence was rapidly ascending when the union talks began. All the parties to the discussion were heirs to a common revivalist tradition, which fostered a pragmatic approach to religion, emphasizing the importance of Christian life and service over doctrinal niceties.[172] This pragmatism was reflected in the ease with which the doctrinal portions of the Basis of Union were worked out. To the extent that obstacles were encountered, these generally had to do with reconciling different approaches to church government. But the polities of all three churches were non-episcopal, and the differences that did exist were amenable to compromise.

Thus a long history of co-operation and common commitments paved the way to union. What brought matters to a head, however, were the challenges posed by the future, especially on the western frontier. On the one hand, the opening of the West to large-scale settlement had inspired the evangelical churches with missionary zeal as they contemplated extending the Lord's dominion throughout so vast a territory; on the other hand, the project placed such strain on their resources that to compete among themselves seemed foolishly wasteful. Even more important, the fact that so many of the settlers were neither British nor Protestant was perceived as a threat to the very identity of Canada. For the churches that, despite their constitutional separation from the state, had come to see themselves as the guardians of the nation's soul, their duty was clear. Together with the practical demands of staffing so large a mission field, the spiritual task of ministering to so many newcomers and assimilating them into Canadian society made church union seem not merely desirable but imperative. So urgent was the need to join forces that the Canadian churches for once outpaced their counterparts in Britain and the United States: the Basis of Union for the United Church was accepted two years before the Edinburgh missionary conference of 1910, commonly regarded as the beginning of the international ecumenical movement, took place.[173]

The prospect of a new national church, embracing all regions, reconciling the diverse components of the population, and defining basic values for the country as a whole, had an almost irresistible appeal for the leaders of the three churches involved in the union negotiations of 1904–8. Yet when the negotiators finished their work, they encountered unexpected opposition from a number of Presbyterians who felt that the denominational leaders ought to have consulted church members before presenting them with a *fait accompli*. Not until a 1912 ballot of Presbyterians revealed opposition running at about one-third were Presbyterian leaders persuaded to negotiate further changes to the agreement. When the amended Basis was put to a vote in 1915, the opposition had increased to 40 per cent, and by then the dissidents had come to agree on what they were fighting for, not merely what they were against.[174]

The principal point on which they insisted was their right to opt out of the union and continue as the Presbyterian Church in Canada. When, in 1924, the proponents of union began to press for federal and provincial legislation that would dissolve the Presbyterian Church upon union and bar the opposition from using that name, the dissidents mounted a national lobbying campaign. Although it failed to achieve their main goal, this campaign did secure some important concessions, namely the establishment of a property commission to allocate assets and a provision allowing Presbyterian congregations to opt out, which about one-third of them did. On 9 June 1925, when the last General Assembly met in a Toronto church, the unionists passed a motion of adjournment, so that when the United Church of Canada Act took effect the next day, the church as a whole would enter the union. The dissidents, however, immediately reconvened the Assembly (an action that C.W. Gordon attempted to obstruct by having the organist play at full volume), and although it would take ten years to secure legal recognition of the claim they had thereby asserted, in 1935 the Supreme Court ruled that the United Church could not claim to be the Presbyterian Church in Canada. Since this ruling placed in jeopardy the bequests made to all the pre-union churches, in 1937 the United Church began negotiations to resolve the conflict; and finally, in 1939, an amendment to the United Church Act granted the dissidents the right to use the name of the Presbyterian Church in Canada.[175]

RELIGIOUS CROSS-CURRENTS

While the formation of the United Church was the most important institutional development of the inter-war years, Canadian Protestants were also caught up in a number of religious cross-currents, ranging from fundamentalism to the Oxford Group movement of Frank Buchman and the neo-orthodox theology inspired by the Swiss theologian Karl Barth. At the same time they were working out their responses to the social crisis caused by the Depression and the moral dilemma posed by the persecution of the Jews under the Third

Reich. Each of these developments caused new stresses and strains. Fundamentalist crusades, while largely unsuccessful in Canada, caused deep rifts among Baptists, the effects of which are still felt today. The hardships of the Depression inspired a new generation of Christian socialists with close links to the emerging Co-operative Commonwealth Federation party; but fear of social unrest also caused a backlash in the churches against attempts to link the Gospel to social reform.

From the opening decades of the twentieth century, fundamentalist influences made themselves felt to varying degrees in all denominations of evangelical background. Fundamentalists echoed many of the themes traditionally emphasized by evangelical Protestants, such as Christ's sacrifice to atone for humanity's sins, His bodily resurrection, and the divine authority of the Bible, but they marshalled these themes in support of militant opposition to modernity. Reacting against the churches' accommodation to Darwinism and biblical criticism, for instance, they invoked an understanding of Scriptural authority which insisted that the Bible was inerrant in every detail. As part of their rejection of prevailing cultural norms, fundamentalists encouraged the faithful to separate themselves from the ungodly and the unmilitant Christian alike.[176] Canadian fundamentalism bore many resemblances to its American counterpart, including its militancy and insistence on doctrinal purity, and there was extensive interaction between proponents of the movement in the two countries; nevertheless, the vast majority of fundamentalists in Canada were of British origin, and many of them ministered to overwhelmingly British congregations.[177]

Fundamentalism touched nearly all Protestant denominations in Canada, from the Anglicans to the Salvation Army, but its impact was greatest among the Baptists. That the latter should have been so deeply affected was due in large measure to the influence of Thomas Todhunter Shields, the British-born pastor of Toronto's Jarvis Street Baptist Church from 1910 until his death in 1955. Recognized as one of the most powerful preachers in the country, Shields was by both temperament and conviction an avid controversialist, whose no-holds-barred tactics galled his opponents and delighted his supporters. In 1925 he launched a virulent attack on McMaster University, a Baptist institution on whose board he served, that resulted eventually in the expulsion of Shields and his congregation from the Baptist Convention of Ontario and Quebec.[178] In the meantime, he had formed his own organization, the Union of Regular Baptists, which some thirty other congregations left the convention to join. But his tenure as leader was turbulent. In 1933 the majority of his followers left to form the Fellowship of Independent Baptist Churches, and in 1949 Shields was deposed from his office as president. In retaliation, he quit the union to start up the Conservative Baptist Association of Canada; by that time, however, his following had dwindled considerably, and only 1,500 accompanied him into the new organization. Shields also attempted to extend his personal leadership and the influence of fundamentalism to the Maritimes and the West. In the Maritimes, where he acted through his subaltern John James Sidey, his efforts were singularly unsuccessful. In the West, however, a campaign in which Shields played a crucial role led to a schism in 1925 between the existing Baptist Union of Western Canada and the newly-formed, fundamentalist Convention of Regular Baptists of British Columbia, which claimed nearly a third of the union's members.[179]

Despite Shield's limited success, fundamentalism was nowhere near as strong an influence among Canadian Protestants as it was among their American counterparts. Beginning in the 1920s, the radio preacher and future premier of Alberta William ('Bible Bill') Aberhart enjoyed some success promoting fundamentalist principles, building up an empire that included a church, a Bible school, and an impressive array of radio ministries, most notably the Sunday-afternoon 'Back to the Bible' program and the Radio Sunday School correspondence course.[180] For all his popularity as a broadcaster, though, Aberhart, like Shields, proved incapable of working with other conservative Protestants, and he was no more successful at building broad and enduring support for the fundamentalist cause. Canadian conservative Protestants differed from their American brethren in that they were not on the whole estranged from the mainstream of their country's culture, nor were they confronted by the very advanced views that characterized the progressive clergy of the American Protestant churches. As a result, most Canadian conservative Protestants felt no need to withdraw from their churches or adopt the Manichean outlook of fundamentalism, in which all other Christians appeared as traitors to the faith.[181]

More important than fundamentalism to the development of conservative Protestantism in Canada was the Bible-school movement, which enjoyed success in Ontario and especially the West. Supported by conservative Protestants from various denominations—many in fact had no specific denominational ties—these schools trained lay workers for service either in their home churches or in the missionary field. Their main purpose was to provide a solid background in biblical knowledge, but, like the mainstream Protestant theological colleges before the advent of historical criticism, they studied the Bible as revealed truth, with none of the qualifications required by modern scholarship. They also stressed the personal and moral development of students, to which end most Bible colleges enforced strict codes of conduct and required their students to gain practical experience in evangelizing.[182] Denominational Bible schools, many of which are still in existence, were founded by a wide range of conservative churches, including the Pentecostals, the Baptists, the Christian and Missionary Alliance, the Church of Christ, the Church of God, the Church of the Nazarene, and the Plymouth Brethren. An important subset of colleges identified with ethnic communities, such as German-speaking Mennonites and Scandinavian and German Lutherans, originally had the additional goal of preserving language and culture, though in time some adopted a more generic Bible-school curriculum that gave their students a point of entry into the broader world of conservative Protestantism. Bible schools without specific denominational ties, however, have usually attracted the largest enrolments. In the 1910s and 1920s the non-denominational Toronto (later Ontario) Bible College (founded in 1894) drew most of its students from the mainstream: Baptists and Presbyterians were prominent in the student body, which also included a good sprinkling of Anglicans and some Methodists as well.[183]

The fact that the large majority of Bible schools were located in the West reflected the strong growth experienced by conservative Protestant denominations in that region in the period when the newly formed United Church was struggling to establish itself and the Presbyterians were recovering from the turmoil caused by church union. Leaders of the country's mainstream churches hoped that a wave of religious renewal would revive their fortunes, and as economic conditions deteriorated with the advent of the Depression, they prayed that hard times would bring Canadians back to God. When a religious revival did occur, however, it was far different from what they had expected.[184] In the fall of 1932, the American-born Frank Buchman arrived in Montreal to launch his Oxford Group movement. Named after the student fellowship he had formed at Oxford University, it is not to be confused with the high-church nineteenth-century Oxford movement. The Oxford Group movement was decidedly revivalistic–though scarcely populist–in character. Buchman cultivated the favour of the wealthy and powerful, and as he travelled across Canada his public meetings were packed with leading citizens and clergy. These meetings were only the most visible aspect of the Oxford Group revival. The real work of 'life-changing' took place at so-called house parties: religious retreats devoted to prayer, Bible reading, and public confession, attendance at which was by invitation only. Inspired by Buchman's message that peace of mind could be attained through complete surrender to Christ, lay people formed their own meeting groups–some thirty in Toronto alone–and many, though by no means all, clergy gave his movement enthusiastic support. On his second tour, in 1934, Buchman set out to cure the ills of society as well as those of individuals, but here he was not so successful. Once the initial excitement wore off, the movement began to founder, and Buchman's plans for a God-centred civilization were soon largely forgotten.[185]

Meanwhile, the hardship caused by the Great Depression gave a fresh impetus to radical social thought among a small number of progressive Christians, especially in the United Church, where figures such as J. King Gordon (son of C.W. Gordon) and Eugene Forsey rose to prominence in the 1930s. At the same time, Christian socialism became one of the defining elements of the Co-operative Commonwealth Federation, the alliance of farmers' groups, labour organizations, and left-wing intellectuals formed in 1932. Yet many middle-class and wealthy people were coming to fear the threat posed by revolutionary agitation in a society already under severe stress. As a consequence, left-wing activists in the United Church found their position far from secure. When, in 1932, the church's United Theological College rid itself of the Christian social-ist J. King Gordon by eliminating his position in Christian ethics, the board's plea of financial exigencies did little to allay left-wing suspicions that Gordon had been targeted because of his political views. Suspicions deepened the fol-lowing year, when St Stephen's College in Edmonton refused to allow the Alberta School of Religion to hold its summer courses at the college after it made its socialist sympathies plain. Such attacks only served to galvanize the radicals into taking action.[186] In June 1933 John Line of Emmanuel College introduced a motion at the meeting of the Toronto presbytery declaring the socialization of banks, natural resources, and essential industries such as trans-portation, together with social insurance, old-age pensions, and unemployment insurance, to be indispensable for a Christian society. The application of Jesus' principles to economic life, Line pointed out, would mean the abolition of the capitalist system. Despite strong opposition, the motion passed. When Forsey and Gordon introduced a similar motion in Montreal, it also passed, but not until the two proponents had been told that the 'inexperience, impractical and idealistic minds' of university professors made them easy dupes for communist agitators.[187]

In the spring of 1934, the small group of left-wing churchmen who had been responsible for such measures formed the Fellowship for the Christian Social Order (FCSO), and that fall the United Church's Board of Evangelism and Social Service released a report entitled 'Christianizing the Social Order'. Although this document reflected the FCSO's influence in its recognition that the Depression was the result of economic dynamics peculiar to modern indus-trial society, the solution it proposed was the standard social-gospel remedy of Christian social service and an enlightened social conscience. For the FCSO that response did not go far enough: what the situation required was a sweeping reconstruction of the social order. Society itself stood under God's judgement, and for some FCSO members, such as R. Edis Fairbairn, that meant that indi-vidual salvation could not be achieved until society itself had been regener-ated. Riven by internal factions, the FCSO would dissolve in 1945; nevertheless, by then some of its members had gained such influence within the CCF that they came to be known as the party's brains trust. If the FCSO enjoyed more success outside than inside the church, at least it opened the door to a new the-ological critique of Canadian society and of the church's role in sanctioning the status quo.[188]

Finally, another new theological current of this period was the movement known as 'neo-orthodoxy' or the 'theology of crisis'. Closely associated with the Swiss theologian Karl Barth, this school of thought reflected a profound loss of confidence in human achievements occasioned by the appalling events of the First World War. It criticized the growing tendency among theologians to identify social progress with the advancement of God's Kingdom. Neo-orthodoxy has been aptly described as the theology of the Word of God, stressing as it did that the foundation of faith is God as revealed in Scripture. Without rejecting the principles and methods of modern science and historical scholarship, it reaffirmed both the absolute authority of God's word and the utter dependence of human beings on divine benevolence for their salvation. Neo-orthodoxy gained a strong following in the United States in the 1930s. In Canada, however, it touched only a few thinkers, most notably the Presbyterian theologian Walter W. Bryden, who was influenced by Barth, and J. King Gordon, who had studied with the American theologian Reinhold Niebuhr. On the whole, neo-orthodoxy and its rediscovery of the central teachings of the Reformation made little headway in the United Church until the 1940s, when Gordon Harland began teaching at United Theological College in Winnipeg. Nevertheless, the faith in progress that had been typical of men such as C.W. Gordon became harder to sustain as the Depression deepened. Increasing numbers of clergy, among them E.H. Oliver (moderator of the United Church from 1930 to 1935), discerned the judgement of God in the events around them and urged all to repent.[189]

ENGLISH-SPEAKING CATHOLICS: ADAPTATION AND SOCIAL REFORM

The first three decades of the new century were a period of profound change for Canada's English-speaking Catholics. By 1900 they had already begun to come of age as a community. The growth and integration of their ecclesiastical institutions, the launching of a wide range of educational and philanthropic ventures, and the spread of Ultramontane piety had all helped to create a cohesive and distinctive national identity. Having flourished in the past as a religio-ethnic subculture determined to safeguard itself against Protestant proselytism and ethnic assimilation, in the early part of the twentieth century English-speaking (largely Irish) Catholics began to move into the mainstream of English-Canadian society. The growing network of Catholic social institutions, originally established as a barrier against the dominant culture, facilitated collective self-improvement and paved the way for upward social mobility. Meanwhile, Irish nationalism declined as a driving force in the community, giving way to Canadian patriotism and attachment to the British Empire. The rising generation of clergy, much more likely than their predecessors to have been born in Canada, encouraged this trend. Although English-speaking

Catholics remained a distinctive component of the Canadian population, their distinctiveness no longer depended so heavily on the identification of Catholicism with ethnicity.[190]

An early sign of this transition was the response of Toronto's English-speaking Catholics to the First World War, when they had enlisted for military service at the same rate as the population as a whole. In embracing British imperialism, however, anglophone Catholics also embraced the ideology that accompanied it: belief in the superiority of English-speaking civilization.[191] This ideological shift did not improve their relations with their French-speaking co-religionists. It also ensured that the arrival of thousands of Catholic and Orthodox immigrants from Southern and Eastern Europe would mark a major turning-point in the development of the English-speaking Catholic community.

As we have seen, the influx of Italians, Hungarians, Poles, and Ukrainians, beginning in the 1890s, had been perceived by the mainstream society as posing a threat to the predominantly British and Protestant character of the country; in response, Protestants had mounted an aggressive campaign of evangelization and acculturation aimed at promoting conformity to their own norms and values. For the predominantly Irish hierarchy within the English-speaking Catholic Church, on the other hand, the challenge presented by these new arrivals was more complex. Clearly they had to protect the newcomers' Catholic heritage against Protestant efforts to undermine it. At the same time, the influx of immigrants threatened to erode the standing of 'old stock' English-speaking Catholics within the church. By 1931, Catholics of European background were as numerous as those of British and Irish background. Moreover, their presence meant that the Catholic Church was becoming increasingly diverse (see Table 5.4), especially in Ontario and the West, where the bulk of the newcomers settled. In response to this situation, the anglophone bishops were anxious not only to defend their hegemony within the anglophone community but to strengthen the English-speaking Canadian church by

---

TABLE 5.4:   ETHNIC ORIGINS OF CANADIAN CATHOLICS, 1931[192]

Ethnic origin	%
French Canadian	66.5
British and Irish	16.0
Ukrainian	3.6
Polish	2.9
German	2.5
Italian	2.1

ensuring that those immigrants who settled in the West were incorporated into their fold rather than that of their French-speaking colleagues. Among the strategies that the English-speaking hierarchy adopted to accomplish these goals were the creation of national parishes in Ontario and British Columbia, the launching of an ambitious program of home missions, and concerted efforts to wrest control of the church in the West from the hands of French-Canadians through the appointment of English-speaking bishops.

The first of these strategies met with qualified success. In Toronto, whose vibrant economy attracted many European immigrants, the diocese established its first national parishes in 1908 for the Italians, in 1910 for the Ukrainians, and in 1911 for the Poles.[193] For the newcomers, Canadian parishes were foreign territory not only linguistically but culturally, offering none of the celebrations of village saints and national patrons that in their homelands were central to both religious and national identity. The new national parishes sustained such cultural traditions, but for the anglophone hierarchy their ultimate purpose was not to institutionalize ethnic diversity; rather, it was to assimilate the immigrants and their Canadian-born children. Whether recruiting students for Catholic schools or encouraging people of all ages to join Canadian-based devotional organizations, the clergy were intent on teaching their parishioners to do things 'the Canadian way'. The results of their efforts were mixed. Most of the children did attend Catholic schools, and though they generally retained their ethnic allegiances, they became increasingly proficient in English. Nevertheless, the newcomers tended to prefer their own ethnic associations, and to preserve their culture, lay leaders insisted on taking an active part in parish affairs. As a result, conflict between lay people and clergy was fairly common in the national parishes, and in the case of the Poles it led to numerous defections from the Roman Catholic Church as congregations in such places as Toronto, Hamilton, Oshawa, Montreal, and Brandon, Manitoba, left to join the Polish National Catholic Church. For other groups, though, ethnic consciousness tended to reinforce lay attachment to the church, Catholicism becoming a central component of their ethnic identity. The consequence, contrary to the hierarchy's assimilationist plans, was that English-speaking Catholicism developed into an ethnic mosaic.[194]

Efforts to promote Canadianization through home missions also had mixed results, as the case of the Toronto-based Catholic Church Extension Society illustrates. Founded in 1908, this national agency for the promotion of home missions was sponsored by the anglophone hierarchy in Ontario and the Maritimes, and its policy of anglicization and acculturation was a key part in the strategy to enlist the newcomers who were heading west in large numbers. In response to this threat to francophone dominance, however, Archbishop Adélard Langevin of St-Boniface attempted to consolidate his hold on the Ukrainians in his flock.[195]

The vast majority of the Ukrainians who immigrated to Canada belonged to the Uniate Church, which recognized the authority of the pope but observed the Eastern rather than the Latin rite. When in 1894, in response to pressure from the American hierarchy, the Vatican barred married clergy from North America, it virtually closed the door to Ukrainian priests, more than 95 per cent of whom were married. To make up for their absence Archbishop Langevin transferred clergy from the Latin rite to the Eastern, but by 1916 he still had not managed to recruit more than twenty-one priests for his own diocese and that of St Albert—hardly enough to care for the region's 150,000 Ukrainians. Nor did the situation improve with the appointment in 1912 of Nykyta Budka as the Ukrainian bishop for all of Canada. Though formally independent of the Canadian episcopacy and accountable only to the apostolic delegate (the pope's representative in Canada), Budka depended on the support of the French-speaking hierarchy, for more than one-third of his clergy were francophones themselves, and their first loyalty lay with their former superiors. On the other hand, he also needed the support of the anglophone hierarchy, which through the Catholic Extension Society funnelled more than $250,000 to him between 1919 and 1927, built and funded English-language schools for the laity, and provided candidates for the priesthood with an English-language education at St Augustine's Seminary in Toronto.[196]

The object of this funding was to bring Budka and his flock into the anglophone Catholic orbit, but its effect was quite the opposite. The competition for influence aroused suspicions among many Ukrainian lay people who, only too familiar with efforts at Latinization by Austrian and Polish authorities in the old country, now came to suspect that both English- and French-speaking Catholics were intent on absorbing the Uniate Church. The main beneficiary of these suspicions was the Ukrainian Orthodox Church, formed in 1918 at a meeting of Ukrainian nationalists in Saskatoon. By 1931 the new church could claim almost 25 per cent of Ukrainian Canadians, while the Uniate Church's membership had dropped to roughly 58 per cent. Although Budka's successor as bishop, Basil Vladimir Ladyka (appointed in 1929), did develop an indigenous clergy, he did not succeed in rebuilding its membership. Three decades later, in 1961, only a third of Ukrainian Canadians would belong to the Uniate Church. The struggle for control of the Roman Catholic Church in the West was long over, but its legacy lived on.[197]

In the end, only the hierarchy's campaign to secure English-speaking bishops for the West was an unqualified success. The Oblates, the overwhelming majority of whom were French-speaking, had exercised a monopoly of pastoral care and episcopal oversight in the region for decades. But as settlers continued to arrive from Ontario, the British Isles, and Europe, it became increasingly obvious that the Oblates had neither the personnel nor the resources to serve the West's growing and increasingly diverse population. Moreover, the Vatican itself had come to share the anglophone hierarchy's view that English-speaking priests and bishops were essential if Catholicism was to have a future in the West.[198] The first attempt to arrange the appointment of an anglophone bishop, led by Bishop Fergus Patrick McEvay of Toronto in 1910, failed when the newly created diocese of Regina went to Olivier-Elzéar Mathieu, but a partial victory was achieved two years later, when the archdiocese of Edmonton was created. Although the new archbishop was also a francophone, the Holy See passed over the candidates proposed by the French-speaking bishops and for the suffragan see of Calgary selected an anglophone, John T. McNally. In 1915, when Rome divided the archdiocese of St-Boniface to create the archdiocese of Winnipeg, it appointed Arthur Alfred Sinnot as the city's first archbishop. Finally, by 1930 anglophones had replaced the francophone incumbents in Regina and Edmonton as well.[199]

The other major campaign of the anglophone bishops, to assimilate European Catholics, was not so successful. Although their children rapidly took up the English language, many of the newcomers remained strongly attached to their original cultures. Nevertheless, the bishops' efforts to assimilate these Catholics received extensive support from the anglophone laity, support that owed much to the collective identity that had taken hold during the First World War. No longer perceiving themselves as a struggling immigrant group, English-speaking Catholics had become part of the host society.

With respect to social issues, English-speaking Catholics began to adopt new approaches in the 1930s. These changes were in part a direct response to the suffering and dislocation produced by the Great Depression, but they also reflected the growing influence of Leo XIII's encyclical *Rerum Novarum* (1891) and, in particular, Pius XI's *Quadragesimo Anno* (1931), which advocated far-reaching structural reforms in capitalist societies. For decades, the church's preferred approach to the problems associated with industrial society had been for the faithful to help their own through the church-centred network of Catholic social institutions. According to this view, the only effective remedies for the ills of society were charity and spiritual renewal. With *Rerum Novarum*, however, a shift became evident in the papacy's approach to social issues, and it prompted many anglophone Catholics to embrace the cause of social reform. In keeping with the church's traditional teaching, these activists advocated a distinctly Catholic understanding of social justice, but at the same time they urged Catholics to work with people from other religious traditions to bring about social reform. In this respect, they not only promoted social reform but also encouraged Catholics to participate fully in the political and social life of English-speaking Canada. Like the war effort and missions to European immigrants, this stance reflected the growing conviction among anglophone Catholics, many of whom were by now solid members of the middle class, that they were assuming their place as charter members of the dominant culture.

Among the first members of the anglophone hierarchy to promote the approach to social problems advocated in *Rerum Novarum* was Neil McNeil, archbishop of Toronto from 1912 to 1934. To this end he hired an English journalist named Henry Somerville to conduct study sessions and write for the diocesan newspaper. With a background in British Labour politics and Christian socialism, Somerville emphasized the state's obligation to promote social justice and urged Catholics to become active in the labour movement. When he assumed the editorship of the *Catholic Register* in the fall of 1933, not long after the formation of the CCF, he declared that there was nothing in the party's program that would prevent Catholics from supporting it. On that point, however, francophone bishops were far less open than their anglophone colleagues.[200]

When the bishops met later that fall, the Quebec hierarchy had already declared itself resolutely opposed to socialism in all its forms. In the document approved at that meeting, English- and French-speaking bishops together enjoined Catholics to apply a litmus test to any new political party. Did it promote class warfare? Did it attack public property? Was its outlook materialistic? In the view of the Quebec bishops, the CCF clearly failed this test. But most anglophone bishops disagreed, and at their insistence the official statement did not specifically mention the CCF. They did not publicly clear the party of suspicion, however, and on the basis of the francophone bishops' statements most Catholics assumed that the party had indeed been condemned. Nevertheless, the way bishops had framed the issue enabled Somerville and others who sympathized with the CCF to declare that it had passed the test. So matters remained for a decade. Meanwhile, Murray Ballantyne, a lay convert to Catholicism whose social views had been greatly influenced by Eugene Forsey, was vigorously lobbying the Quebec bishops to reverse their position on the CCF. In 1943 he arranged a meeting between the party's leader, M.J. Coldwell, and Archbishop Joseph Charbonneau of Montreal, at which, in response to Coldwell's assurances, Charbonneau agreed to press the CCF's case. As a result, at their next plenary meeting the bishops freed Catholics to vote for the party.[201]

By far the most important experiment in social activism among anglophone Catholics was the Antigonish Movement. Through the extension department of Saint Francis Xavier University, Fathers J.J. Tomkins and M.M. Coady established study groups to promote consumer and producer co-operatives among the economically marginal farmers and fishermen of eastern Nova Scotia, many of whom were tied to processors and suppliers through a truck system of payment. The only way they could free themselves from this arrangement was to create their own co-operatives through which to sell their wares and purchase goods. The next step was to bring finance within the reach of these small producers through the establishment of credit unions. This practical approach reflected the social philosophy of the Antigonish Movement. The only

producers who could be truly free were those who controlled the means of production, and in Coady's view that could be the case only in a society of small
producers where no one business interest could dominate the others. The
Antigonish Movement had no effect on the Catholic hierarchy's position on
social issues, but it did succeed in making co-operatives a viable option for a
population that was among the most economically disadvantaged in the country, and its success inspired Catholics elsewhere to follow its example.[202]

FROM THE SECOND WORLD WAR TO THE POST-WAR 'BOOM'

As the 1930s drew to a close, Canada's Protestant clergy watched the rise of
Fascism with apprehension. Initially they had been preoccupied with the threat
of Bolshevism, but Mussolini's invasion of Ethiopia in 1935 alerted them to the
military threat posed by right-ring nationalism. At the same time, Protestant
leaders were increasingly alarmed by the Nazification of Germany and the
menace it presented to Christianity. Their response to the Nazi persecution of
the Jews, however, was ambivalent. Much as individual clergymen deplored
this outrage, it was not until February 1939 that the churches formally backed
a campaign to admit Jewish refugees to Canada, and even then Mackenzie
King's government refused to change its restrictive immigration policy.[203] By
contrast, the Roman Catholic clergy followed the Vatican's official policy of
defending Mussolini's invasion of Ethiopia. They were also slower than their
Protestant counterparts to raise the alarm over National Socialism, not protesting against the Nazi persecution of the churches in Germany until 1938, some
four years after the first attacks.[204]

When war began in September 1939, the churches rallied to support the
war effort, but with little of the fervour they had shown in 1914. As we have
seen, their uncritical patriotism during the First World War had later returned
to haunt the clergy, and they were anxious to avoid a replay of the linguistic
conflict over conscription that had so divided Canadians in the past. Among
the churches' efforts to promote good will, perhaps the most notable was the
pastoral letter of May 1942, in which the country's Catholic bishops demonstrated that, despite their differences, anglophones and francophones could still
co-operate and speak with a united voice in denouncing National Socialism as
pagan and anti-Christian. Such contributions helped, but the timing of events
played a greater part in avoiding outright confrontation. Discontent among
francophone Catholics and anglophone Protestants peaked at different times,
the former reaching its height during the conscription plebiscite of 1942 and
the latter in 1944, when it became obvious that the government was still reluctant to enact the measure despite the plebiscite's success. Expecting that conscription would come sooner or later, church leaders did their best to moderate
a volatile situation, and by the time it finally did take effect, the war was practically over.[205]

The end of hostilities inaugurated a period of religious revitalization. After nearly two decades of uncertainty and hardship occasioned by the Depression and the war, the return to peace brought renewed optimism as ordinary Canadians looked forward to leading normal lives. The economy flourished as a result of an export boom and a surge in capital investment; low unemployment, rapidly rising wages, and growing opportunities for social mobility fuelled a dramatic rise in consumer spending on new homes, cars, and appliances; and the new prosperity, together with the return of thousands from military service, encouraged young people to start families. Bright prospects also attracted large numbers of new immigrants: between 1951 and 1961 alone, Canada's population grew by 30 per cent. This population explosion was accompanied by increasing urbanization. While industry and commerce prospered, farm incomes declined and the rural population fell precipitously, continuing a trend already evident before the war. The country's general affluence made possible a vast expansion of the public sector as the federal government introduced new social programs such as old-age security and expanded the existing unemployment insurance plan, laying the foundations of the welfare state. Social welfare, once a prime area for Christian activism and engagement, was fast becoming the responsibility of the secular state. Nevertheless, the prevailing mood of the post-war years, especially the deep longing for a return to a secure, normal life, was conducive to a reawakening of religious commitment.

The most potent symbol of post-war values was suburbia. For all its novelty as a social reality, suburban life embodied the traditional values of home and family, in which religious nurture and observance played a prominent part. Bringing people together into self-contained communities, suburbia also introduced new pressures for social conformity, including a return to traditional gender roles as women lost their wartime gains in the labour market and again came to be identified almost exclusively with the domestic sphere. Like the emphasis on family values, compliance with prevailing norms and suburban notions of respectability and responsibility encouraged church attendance and involvement in church-sponsored activities.

Together, the post-war baby boom, immigration, and renewed commitment to certain traditional mores led to significant growth in church membership. Among the mainstream Protestant denominations, the Anglicans increased their rolls by close to 10 per cent between 1951 and 1961, while the United Church grew by well over one-quarter. Even the Presbyterians, after more than three decades of decline, enjoyed modest growth. The majority of Protestants (over 70 per cent) continued to be concentrated in these three denominations, with the balance distributed across a wide range of smaller denominations. Among the latter, the ranks of conservatives were bolstered by significant growth among Pentecostals and the arrival of Dutch immigrants belonging to the Christian Reformed Church.[206]

The Catholic Church also experienced substantial growth in this period, rising from just under 40 per cent of the total population in 1931 to 45 per cent thirty years later.[207] A high birth rate among francophones contributed to this increase, but so did immigration. By 1961, Catholics of British and Irish ancestry were slightly outnumbered by those of European backgrounds other than French, of whom the Italians, accounting for almost 5 per cent of the total, constituted the largest group.[208]

Increases in church membership were accompanied by a sharp rise in the construction of new facilities. The United Church, which provides an especially striking example of the general trend, erected more than 1,500 churches and 600 manses in the two decades after the war, mainly in the new suburban communities.[209] At the same time, congregational life showed a new vitality. Among Protestants, the baby boom, combined with the desire of many young parents to inculcate trusted values in their children, ensured growing Sunday-school enrolments. Many people contributed regularly and generously to their churches, despite the competing demands of mortgages and other household expenses; without their support, the massive church-building programs would not have been possible. Revivalism also enjoyed a resurgence, boosted by media coverage of movements such as Charles Templeton's Youth for Christ crusade. Church attendance was generally high: in 1946, pollsters estimated that 60 per cent of Protestants and 83 per cent of Catholics attended services on a given Sunday.[210]

Catholics maintained their level of church attendance throughout the 1950s; the rate was highest in Quebec (88 per cent in 1957), but even outside that province 75 per cent said they regularly attended Sunday worship. By contrast, a change was becoming apparent among Protestants as the end of the decade approached. For the total Protestant population, the rate of weekly attendance fell to 38 per cent, and even for conservative denominations it dipped to 51 per cent.[211] While the proportions of Protestants who regularly attended Sunday worship were still considerable, weekly observance had ceased to be the custom of the majority. On the other hand, it is worth recalling that, even in the later Victorian era, surveys done in Toronto showed that only about half the total population attended church on a given Sunday (45 per cent in 1882; 55 per cent in 1896), not including the large numbers of children who attended Sunday school.

Even so, this decline was a signal that the outward vitality of the churches in the post-war years masked the seeds of a fundamental change. Alongside the circumstances conducive to religious renewal, other forces were at work that tended to weaken people's ties to and involvement in the churches. The tension between the two tendencies became most apparent in the culture of suburbia. While the suburban lifestyle in some ways promoted traditional values, it also broke through a number of taboos and fostered a preoccupation with material comfort and success that undermined spiritual commitments. In practical terms, the change manifested itself in the rise of social drinking, still frowned on by most Protestant churches, and the growing popularity of Sunday sports and other amusements that disrupted older patterns of sabbath observance. Even for those who did not live in the suburbs, the affluent suburban lifestyle became a defining ideal, widely advertised with the advent of television.

Among Catholics, the gap between church teachings and popular mores had not yet emerged as clearly as it had among Protestants; but even they stood on the brink of change. The religious ethos of Canadian Christians, Catholic and Protestant alike, was rooted in a culture that made cardinal virtues of self-restraint and deferred gratification. But post-war prosperity and technology brought the promise of immediate comfort and pleasure. In English-speaking Canada, the worldly attractions of the consumer society overshadowed, if they did not entirely subvert, the forces of religious renewal.

CONCLUSION

By 1960, the influence of religion on Canadian culture was visibly waning. The decline in church attendance among the Protestant majority was the chief outward manifestation of this change, but underlying the transformation was a profound shift in outlook and behaviour. The two great movements of spiritual renewal that had dominated the religious lives of most Canadians for more than a century, the evangelical and Ultramontane revivals, no longer shaped the country's cultural life or informed its dominant social institutions.

Evangelicalism and Ultramontanism, despite their mutual antagonism, had shared many features. Both had engendered personal commitment to particular ways of living out the Christian faith: for Protestants, a new birth followed by a life of service; for Catholics, sacramental nurture, devotional observance, and a virtuous life within an all-embracing community. In both cases, personal commitment gave rise to social transformation as Protestants and Catholics sought to realize their ideals in the public sphere. While Protestants campaigned to have evangelical principles enshrined in the public life of English-speaking Canada, anglophone Catholics demanded public support for their own institutions and strove to maintain a thriving religious subculture with strong ethnic overtones. In taking these different approaches, each of these religious traditions advocated a particular interpretation of the nature and destiny of the nation.

The self-proclaimed mission of evangelical Protestants had been to make Canada God's dominion, and in some respects they achieved their goal. Once the disestablishment of the Church of England had removed the last vestige of a state church, the main Protestant denominations, bound together by common evangelical values, had formed a kind of collective cultural establishment, offering social and intellectual as well as moral and religious leadership.[212] Their claim to exclusive cultural authority, however, presupposed a homogeneous population, a population that Canada had never possessed and one that, given growing numbers of non-British immigrants, it was increasingly unlikely to attain. Nevertheless, in a bid to achieve uniformity in religion and culture, Protestants engaged in aggressive missionary crusades aimed at assimilating and converting those who were not blessed with a Protestant and Anglo-Saxon background. The role of the churches as agents of assimilation was openly acknowledged and extolled. It is not enough, said W.B. Creighton, editor of the United Church's paper *The New Outlook*, for newcomers to embrace our language and customs; they must also accept our moral standards and deepest ideals.[213]

The Protestant vision of Canada as the Lord's dominion ultimately collapsed for a combination of reasons, the most important of which was the country's changing ethnic composition. The growing diversity of the Canadian population made the homogenizing agenda of the Protestant churches impossible to sustain. By 1961, Protestants of British and Irish ancestry comprised only 35 per cent of the population; Catholics of French descent made up another 30 per cent; and the remaining 35 per cent belonged to neither of these two 'old stock' groups.[214] Anglo-Protestants were the largest single group in Canada, but their churches could no longer claim, as they had done since coming to terms with disestablishment, to embody the values and sensibilities of the majority of Canadians.

In addition to the transformation of the social environment, internal changes helped to change the course of the churches. Even before the 1940s, a few astute religious leaders, influenced by neo-orthodox theology, had begun to criticize familiar assumptions, especially the churches' tendency to identify the progress of Christianity with the advance of modern culture. Translated into the Canadian context, this critique rendered the alliance between Protestantism and British civilization highly suspect. Neo-orthodoxy challenged not only traditional evangelical beliefs but also the progressive principles of the social gospellers, who were no less inclined to seek the Kingdom of God on earth. The full impact of the new currents of thought was felt only after the war, however, by which time the dominant evangelical interpretation of Canadian nationality was already beginning to dissolve. The collapse of old assumptions was accelerated by the post-war dismantling of the British Empire, a development that led many to question the supposed superiority of English-speaking culture.

English-speaking Catholics had always rejected the Protestant vision of Canada, if only because it made no room for them. In response to Protestant hegemony, they developed an alternative world-view that initially rested on a close identification of Ultramontane principles with Irish ethnicity. These two ingredients of the anglophone Catholic subculture were so closely intertwined in the nineteenth century that Catholics of Irish ancestry could scarcely distinguish them. Around the turn of the century, however, this collective identity began to give way to a new one based on a mixture of Catholic faith, Canadian patriotism, and attachment to the British Empire, a self-understanding crystallized by the First World War. Whereas the old ethnic Catholicism had emphasized separation, this new identity signalled a desire to join the English-speaking mainstream and to be recognized not only as equals but as members of the charter society. Although it sacrificed little in the way of spiritual commitment, the new spirit of anglophone Catholicism embraced and incorporated the Protestant conviction that Canada was essentially an English-speaking country. As a result, it exacerbated the already tense relations between the English- and French-speaking hierarchies.

Throughout the 1950s, the network of church-centred social institutions continued to insulate the faithful from a society whose public ethos was becomingly increasingly secular. Nevertheless, innovative directions in post-war European Catholic theology were already calling into question the church's defensive or suspicious attitude towards the outside world. Thinkers such as Yves Congar in France and Karl Rahner in Germany were preparing the way for a massive reform of the Roman Catholic Church, the impact of which would be felt in Canada as elsewhere. While Canadian Catholics as yet showed little inclination to challenge traditional teaching, the walls with which they had surrounded themselves were about to come down.

MUNCL, '95

Epilogue

TERRENCE MURPHY

By the 1960s, social and cultural changes in Canada were outstripping the churches' capacity to adjust. The forces behind these developments were not new, but their impact was heightened as several tendencies seemed to converge and come to a head. Cities and suburbs grew rapidly as people continued to drift away from the countryside toward urban–industrial centres. Traditional customs and values declined, while the consumer lifestyle steadily gained ground. The quest for material success and instant satisfaction shaped growing numbers of lives, crowding out old-fashioned ideals of self-discipline and restraint. Rising rates of immigration from non-European countries, meanwhile, were making Canadian society ever more diverse, rendering plainly obsolete the already tenuous idea of a uniformly Christian nation. Amid these fundamental shifts, young people, who formed a disproportionate segment of the post-war population, began to question the shallowness of bourgeois culture. In this era of youthful rebellion and experimentation, established norms of all kinds were subjected to relentless criticism. Traditional authorities, including the churches, were rejected in favour of exotic alternatives ranging from drugs to oriental religions.

The general atmosphere of change that pervaded Canadian society took on added significance in Quebec, where the reform program that came to be known as the Quiet Revolution overturned the social order that had existed in essence since the failed rebellion of 1837 and the legislative union of Upper and Lower Canada in 1841. In the old order, the political power of French Canadians, even at the provincial level, was circumscribed by the privileges of the largely English-speaking economic élite, religion was the principal vehicle for the development and protection of French-Canadian culture, and the church supported and controlled the major educational and social-welfare

Opposite: CENTRAL CANADA, TWENTIETH CENTURY.

institutions. The Quiet Revolution restored politics as the means of advancing French-Canadian interests, gave French Canadians far greater control over their own affairs, and removed educational, health, and welfare institutions from the control of the church. While the roots of the change can be traced back as far as the early decades of the century, at least in Montreal, the actual transformation was inaugurated in 1960, when a Liberal government under Jean Lesage replaced the Union Nationale regime of Maurice Duplessis. The new government—whose efforts were foreshadowed during the very brief administration of Duplessis's successor, Paul Sauvé—intervened directly in economic life, nationalizing major industries such as hydroelectric power and paving the way for large-scale secular trade unionism. At the same time it assumed control over social-welfare and health institutions, created a ministry of education, and launched a sweeping reform of the school system. Religion was not excluded from hospitals and schools, but the administration of such institutions was removed from the hands of the clergy and religious orders.

Alongside the political modernization of Quebec and the re-organization of public institutions, the period of the Quiet Revolution saw a fundamental transformation of Quebec culture. Almost every index of religious commitment and observance pointed to a sudden and massive secularization of society. The number of practising Catholics dropped precipitously, to considerably less than half the total population. According to one study, the percentage of Roman Catholics attending mass weekly dropped from 88 per cent in 1957 to 41 per cent in 1975.[1] Religious vocations also declined dramatically; between 1967 and 1976, the numbers of priests dropped from 9,052 to 5,414, teaching brothers from 3,014 to 1,453, and nuns from 61,942 to 41,145.[2] The average age of clergy and religious rose in proportion to the decline in new recruits. Popular devotions, long a mainstay of the vernacular culture of Quebec, declined sharply. In the new Quebec, Catholicism was no longer the pre-eminent defender of French-Canadian culture nor the main source of the symbols of French-Canadian identity. The church had lost not only its control over Quebec's public institutions, but also its cultural hegemony.

Although initially resistant to some aspects of the Quiet Revolution, the Quebec clergy soon adopted a policy of pragmatic accommodation. As was noted above, the loss of administrative control over social institutions did not mean that religion was excluded from schools, hospitals, and welfare agencies, and the church focused much of its attention on ensuring that provisions for religious instruction and pastoral care were maintained within the new framework. Acceptance of the new order was made easier by a certain affinity between the modernizing agenda of the Lesage government and the new currents in Catholic thought that, as we shall see, were finding expression in the Second Vatican Council (1962–5). Some of the most sensational attacks on the old social order came from within the ranks of the clergy. In 1960, for example, the same year that the Liberal government came to power, a Marist Brother (later identified as Jean-Paul Desbiens) published an anonymous critique of Quebec society and the traditional church, under the title *Les Insolences du frère Untel* (*The Impertinences of Brother Anonymous*), that quickly became a bestseller.

The Quebec bishops meanwhile actively promoted change. In 1968, they appointed a commission on ecclesiastical reform, headed by the distinguished sociologist Fernand Dumont. The 1971 report of the Dumont commission, entitled *L'Église du Québec: Un héritage, un projet*, called for the democratization of the church. Though its recommendations were imperfectly implemented, the commission's work reflected a profound openness to new ideas. As Gregory Baum has pointed out, secularization in Quebec was achieved without the deep cultural schisms that occurred in some European Catholic countries, such as France and Italy.[3] Not only did the Quebec church adapt to new realities, but the province's political leaders showed no inclination to indulge in anti-clerical rhetoric or crusades. Anti-clericalism existed (as it does today) among Quebeckers who repudiated the church as an obstacle to personal freedom and social progress, but it never became public policy.

In the midst of the ferment of the 1960s and 1970s, the prevailing mood among the churches in the rest of Canada was similar to that in Quebec. Awareness of the need for fundamental adjustments grew rapidly, and most denominations entered a period of searching self-criticism and painstaking reassessment. The desire for reform was reflected at many levels as the churches reorganized ecclesiastical institutions, revised programs of religious education, updated modes of worship, and reconsidered patterns of church governance. A general shift occurred away from authoritarian or paternalistic leadership towards more consultative procedures for decision-making in which the laity, including young people, were encouraged to participate. In the meantime, many of the remaining barriers between denominations were falling as inter-faith dialogue and co-operation flourished.

The spirit of reform was manifested most dramatically in the Roman Catholic Church. For more than a century, the Catholic outlook had been characterized by resistance to modern ideas. But a remarkable change occurred in the 1960s, when the work of innovative theologians and progressive clergy culminated in the Second Vatican Council. In a concerted effort to promote *aggiornamento*—that is, to bring the church up-to-date with the contemporary world—this ecumenical council, convoked by Pope John XXIII, laid out a wide-ranging program of reform. The archaic Latin liturgy was replaced by simplified services conducted in the vernacular, traditional devotional practices gave way to new communal forms of piety, hierarchical approaches to church government were tempered by collegiality and lay involvement, and a much more open attitude was adopted towards other faiths, Christian and non-Christian. The consequences of these reforms were felt well beyond the confines of the Catholic Church. Ecumenism entered an entirely new phase as Catholics embraced the movement and as many Protestants responded positively to their overtures.

Yet beneath the optimism and enthusiasm that characterized Catholic renewal lay serious problems, which were not long in rising to the surface. In its zeal for modernization, the council cast doubt on old certainties and set in motion a profound process of re-examination. For some, this process meant a reformulation of traditional beliefs and a renewed commitment; for others, it brought a loosening of attachment to the church, if not a loss of faith. Rates of church attendance among Canadian Catholics, exempt from the downward trend that had affected Protestants in the 1950s, began to decline significantly in the 1960s.

The consequences of church reforms for Canada's Protestants were no less ambiguous than for their Catholic neighbours. In part, the problem was that these changes could not keep pace with those occurring in the broader society. Even the most progressive doctrinal statements, religious education programs, and liturgical expressions seemed outdated by the time they appeared. In some cases, attempts at modernization tended as much to highlight as to overcome the gap between Christianity and contemporary culture; in other cases, they seemed to indicate that the major churches had embraced that culture at the cost of their moral independence and distinctive spiritual message. Virtually every denomination contained a substantial contingent of committed and creative people who successfully promoted efforts at adaptation. Their work was carried out, however, in the context of an increasingly secular culture. Though a majority of Canadians continued to identify themselves as belonging to one or another Christian denomination, a dwindling minority remained actively committed to their churches.[4]

Empirical research on the behaviour of Canadians with respect to organized religion has yielded results that may at first seem surprising. In spite of common-sense assumptions about widespread secularization, the 1981 census revealed that almost nine in ten Canadians still claimed either Protestant or Roman Catholic affiliation,[5] and additional evidence shows that most of those included in this group identified with the denomination of their forebears.[6] Even more startling, 80 per cent of Canadians surveyed in a recent national poll affirmed their belief in God, and two-thirds said they believed in the death and resurrection of Christ.[7] On the other hand, all the major Protestant churches have experienced pronounced declines in membership, and rates of church attendance continue to drop among Protestants and Catholics, anglophones and francophones alike.[8] Many occasional church-goers limit their attendance to special occasions such as baptisms, marriages, and funerals. It has been estimated that only three in ten Canadians attend church on a weekly basis, although the figures vary somewhat by denomination and region.[9]

The gap between religious affiliation and church membership and attendance is not necessarily easy to interpret. Reginald Bibby, who has done much of the statistical research on the subject, takes the gap as evidence that religion has become a 'fragment' in Canadian society, not so much a life-defining commitment as a commodity or service to be consumed along with all the others.[10] But one of the problems with trying to interpret this pattern of behaviour by placing it within the context of the modern consumer society is the tendency to assume that relatively low rates of church attendance and selective participation in rites of passage are historical novelties. On the contrary, these have been recurring patterns in the religious history of many predominantly Christian countries; the clerical complaint about people who show up in church only for special occasions is a familiar refrain. Even in the Victorian era, when the major churches had succeeded in drawing most Canadians within the orbit of organized Christianity, weekly church attendance was by no means universal.

Nevertheless, an important change has taken place. The segment of the population that does not participate in religious life has become the majority, and it now includes groups such as Roman Catholics (especially in Quebec), women, and members of the middle class, the very groups whose active involvement in the past contributed most to high rates of observance. Not only are church attendance and membership dropping, but the proportion of Canadians who profess no religion has risen steadily, to nearly 20 per cent in 1991.[11]

Nor can we infer from the fact that a large majority still identify themselves as Christians and profess belief in basic Christian doctrines that Canadians are overwhelmingly religious, if alienated from organized Christianity.[12] Token identification and nominal adherence to traditional beliefs do not demonstrate the persistence of meaningful belief among the general population. What survey results reflect may be no more than residual attachment to traditions that no longer exercise any formative influence on people's attitudes or behaviour. The change that has occurred in Canada since 1960 is much more fundamental than these findings suggest.

If there has been a limited exception to the rule of declining commitment, it is to be found among Canada's conservative Protestant denominations. Some of these groups, such as the Pentecostals, the Christian and Missionary Alliance, and the Salvation Army, have grown faster than the population,[13] and their rates of membership and regular church attendance are significantly higher than those of the Anglican, United, and Presbyterian churches.[14] Contrary to popular assumptions, the relative strength of the conservative churches is not due to recruitment from mainstream denominations so much as to higher than average birth rates and success in retaining the children of members.[15] The conservative churches as a group have not significantly increased their share of the total population.[16] However, as rates of church attendance have dropped among mainstream churches, the percentage of

Canadian church-goers who belong to conservative denominations has risen accordingly. The proportion of Canada's rapidly declining body of active Christians who are conservative Protestants is even larger if that category is extended to include the evangelical members of denominations such as Anglicans and Presbyterians.[17]

While grappling with the problems of declining membership and rates of religious observance, the churches have by no means retreated from the public realm. But if secularization has not meant relegating religion to the purely private sphere, it has entailed giving up any notion that the churches in either French or English Canada can define a set of dominant beliefs for society as a whole. Accepting the pluralistic character of Canadian society, the churches have redefined their role in public life, raising their voices, alongside others, to speak out on issues ranging from economic justice through aboriginal rights to responsible use of natural resources, world peace, and reform of the criminal justice system. Official church policies on such matters have been made known in a stream of public declarations, briefs to government, and press releases. In most cases, the churches have shown a strong tendency to fight for the rights of those who lack power and prestige by challenging public policies that they deem unjust. One way of describing the shift in the roles they have defined for themselves is to say that they have exchanged their former function, in which they defined and legitimated prevailing norms, for a prophetic role, in which they challenge the status quo and call on those in authority to be faithful to their avowed principles.

Declarations on public policy often emanate from the national offices or headquarters of individual denominations. In the case of the Catholic Church, whose members comprise nearly half of Canadian Christians, such official statements are issued by the Canadian Conference of Catholic Bishops. Formed in 1943, the CCCB brought together for the first time the English-speaking and French-speaking hierarchies in a single national organization. While its initial focus was on diocesan pastoral work, the emphasis shifted after Vatican II to broader issues such as ecumenism, liturgy, and social justice. Among the most widely-discussed of the CCCB's many declarations on public policy was the 1983 statement of its Social Affairs Commission, *Ethical Reflections on the Economic Crisis*, which was followed later that year by a submission to the Macdonald Commission on the Economic Union and Development Prospects for Canada. More recently, the CCCB has published major statements on the reform of Canada's social programs (*Will the Poor Have the Most to Fear from Social Security Reform?*, 1994) and aboriginal rights (*Let Justice Flow Like a Mighty River*, 1993), the latter incorporating a brief to the Royal Commission on Aboriginal People. Within four days of the Quebec referendum of 30 October 1995, the Executive Committee of the CCCB had issued a statement on the outcome and its broad implications for the country.

Most Canadian churches have undertaken similar efforts to influence public policy in the areas of human rights and social justice, both individually and in collaboration with one another. Inter-church coalitions such as Ten Days for World Development, GATT-Fly (formed to influence Canadian aid and trade policies), and Project North (which provided a link between the First Nations of the north and southern advocates of aboriginal rights) have been among the chief vehicles for social action. On a number of occasions, church-based advocacy groups have also made common cause with secular organizations on matters of mutual concern.

The churches do not agree on all social issues. Abortion, to which Roman Catholics and conservative Protestant denominations remain implacably opposed, is one issue that divides them from more liberal-minded Protestant denominations such as the United Church. On certain key issues, sharp divisions exist within denominations as well. Attempts to adapt to changing social values by ordaining women and homosexuals have provoked lively, sometimes acrimonious debates. Whereas the United Church admitted a female candidate to ordination as early as 1936, the Anglican Church of Canada took this step only in 1976, amid considerable internal controversy, while the Catholic Church has assigned women to a number of pastoral roles but still does not admit them to holy orders. Questions of alternative sexuality have divided a number of the Protestant churches. The debate has been liveliest in the United Church of Canada, where the admission of gays to ordination and decisions by some congregations to recognize homosexual marriages[18] have occasioned deep rifts. In 1992, the year in which the first gay United Church minister was ordained, a gay Anglican priest was removed from a pastoral charge in the diocese of Toronto and a study commissioned by the Presbyterian Church in Canada re-affirmed the belief that homosexuality is contrary to God's will.

Evangelical Protestants have played a special role in advocating conservative social and religious values. The term evangelical, which in the nineteenth century applied to the overwhelming majority of Protestants, is now reserved for the conservative Protestant denominations, ranging from Baptists to Pentecostals, and those members of mainstream Protestant churches who still adhere to frankly evangelical principles. In recent years, evangelicals have become much more conspicuous in public life. Aware of the declining strength of the major churches, and convinced that these churches have compromised themselves through accommodation to an increasingly secular culture, the evangelicals have consciously attempted to articulate alternative values for the nation. In the process, they have developed a transdenominational network of evangelical denominations, congregations, and individuals across the country. This network, which has both formal and informal dimensions, culminated with the formation of the Evangelical Fellowship of Canada in 1964. Founded initially as an association of evangelical pastors, it has developed into a national body for the promotion and communication of evangelical principles.[19] The EFC was strengthened in the early 1980s by the appointment of a full-time executive director, and its agenda has gradually been expanded to include efforts to influence public policy, especially on moral issues such as abortion, pornography, and family life. This marks a very significant change, since conservative evangelicals have traditionally maintained a position of self-conscious estrangement from the society at large, interacting with it only in very limited ways, chiefly through efforts at evangelism. Today this estrangement expresses itself in the public articulation of an alternative moral vision. In attempting to bring moral direction to government, however, the EFC has for the most part eschewed party politics, and political parties have shown little inclination to form alliances with the EFC or other evangelical bodies. In this respect, Canadian evangelicals differ markedly from their American counterparts.

In recent years, almost all of Canada's churches have been shaken by revelations of past abuses by the clergy and religious communities. Shocking facts have come to light concerning physical and sexual abuse on the part both of individual clergymen and of groups working in institutions such as orphanages, reform schools, and residential schools for native children. Few if any churches have escaped painful disclosures of clerical misconduct, but the Roman Catholic Church has probably been most affected by revelations of abuse. Perhaps the most widely-publicized case is that of the Mount Cashel Orphanage in St John's, Newfoundland, where widespread sexual abuse of boys over several years by a number of the Christian Brothers working in the institution came to light in the late 1980s. While the events revealed in such cases have all occurred in the (sometimes recent) past, the trauma they caused is part of the contemporary experience of the churches. We are too close to the events to know what long-term effects such scandals will have on the religious commitment or affiliation of lay people, but there is no denying the profound feelings of revulsion and betrayal that accompany revelations of abuse. The churches have been compelled to engage in a painful examination of conscience and to seek ways both of making amends to victims and of preventing any recurrence of such crimes. In cases where these efforts have been judged less than adequate, the churches have been exposed to renewed criticism and denunciation.

An especially important aspect of their past with which the churches have been trying to come to terms is their historical involvement in the lives of Canada's aboriginal people. While continuing to believe that their missionary, educational, and philanthropic work brought positive benefits, the churches now admit that their entire approach was coloured and corrupted by assumptions of cultural and racial superiority. Accordingly, they have publicly acknowledged and repudiated their earlier attempts to destroy native cultures in the name of evangelization. Included in such confessions of guilt have been belated avowals of widespread physical and sexual abuse in residential schools and pleas for their victims' forgiveness. The churches have attempted, with varying degrees of success, to re-fashion their relationship with aboriginal people in terms of mutual respect and co-operation. Included in this new approach are both a recognition that Christians have much to learn from native spirituality and a commitment on the part of the major churches to the cause of aboriginal rights. Advocacy of native rights by the major churches reached a high point in 1987, with a pastoral statement by leaders of the Anglican, Roman Catholic, Christian Reformed, Evangelical Lutheran, Quaker, Presbyterian, Mennonite, and United churches on aboriginal rights and the Canadian constitution. Signed on the eve of the 1987 First Ministers' Conference, the statement, entitled *A New Covenant*, called unequivocally for the entrenchment of aboriginal rights, particularly the right to self-government, in the Canadian constitution.

It would be foolhardy to predict the future of organized Christianity in Canada. The downward trend in church membership and attendance has continued at an accelerated pace and now appears to be affecting even the conservative Protestant denominations. By 1990, weekly attendance at worship appears to have dropped to 23 per cent for the population as a whole and to 48 per cent for adherents of conservative Protestant churches.[20] But the influence of the churches has fluctuated in the past, and it may rise and fall again. One fundamental change, however, does seem to be irrevocable: the concept of 'Christendom'—that is, of a society where Christianity and culture are essentially integrated—is gone forever in Canada. The defining reality of contemporary Canadian society is pluralism, which includes not only cultural, racial, and religious diversity, but also the recognition of tolerance of differing beliefs and customs as a basic societal value. Whatever the fortunes of the Christian churches, they must live within a framework that precludes the sort of cultural authority they once enjoyed.

Notes

ABBREVIATIONS

AAQ   Archives de l'Archevêché de Quebec
ACAM   Archives de la Chancellerie de l'Archevêché de Montréal
APFR   Archivio della Sacra Congregazione 'de Propaganda Fide' (SC, Scritture
        Riferite in Congressi; NS, Nuova Serie)
ASQ   Archives du Séminaire de Québec
ASV   Archivio Segreto Vaticano (DAC, Delegazione Apostolica del Canadà)
CCHA   Canadian Catholic Historical Association
CHA   Canadian Historical Association
CHR   *Canadian Historical Review*
CSCH   Canadian Society of Church History
DCB   *Dictionary of Canadian Biography* (Toronto: University of Toronto Press, 1966–)
FCMS   French-Canadian Missionary Society
HCQ   Histoire du Catholicisme Québécois, ed. Nive Voisine (Montréal: Boréal
        Express, 1984–91)
JR   *The Jesuit Relations and Allied Documents*, Reuben J. Thwaites, ed., 73 vols
        (Cleveland: Burrows Brothers, 1896–1901)
MEM   *Mandements des Évêques de Montréal* (Montréal: J. Chapleau et Fils, Imprimeurs
        de l'Archevêché)
MEQ   *Mandements, lettres pastorales et circulaires des Évêques de Québec*, ed. Henri Têtu and
        C.-O. Gagnon, 9 vols (Québec: Imprimerie Générale A. Côté et Cie, 1887–98)
NAC   National Archives of Canada (AN, Archives Nationales [France])
RAQ   *Rapport de l'Archiviste de la Province de Québec* (Québec: R. Paradis, Imprimeur
        de Sa Majesté le Roi, various years)
RHAF   *Revue d'Histoire de l'Amérique Française*
RS   *Recherches Sociographiques*
SCHEC   Société Canadienne de l'Histoire de l'Église Catholique
UCCA   United Church Committee on Archives
USPG   United Society for the Propagation of the Gospel

CHAPTER ONE

1 H.P. Biggar, ed., *The Voyages of Jacques Cartier* (Ottawa: Public Archives of Canada, 1924), 64–6, 165–6, 206–7; *A Collection of Documents Relating to Jacques Cartier and the Sieur de Roberval* (Ottawa: Public Archives of Canada, 1930), 64–8, 165, 227, 235.

2 *Oeuvres de Champlain* (Montréal: Éditions du Jour, 1973), 709.

3 Norman Ravitch, *The Catholic Church and the French Nation 1589–1989* (London: Routledge, 1990) develops the implications of the confessional state for France. The Protestant presence in New France is analyzed in Marc-André Bédard, *Les Protestants en Nouvelle-France* (Québec: Société historique de Québec, 1978) and Cornelius Jaenen, 'The Persistence of the Protestant Presence in New France (1541–1760)', *Second Meeting of the Western Society for French History 1974* (1975): 29–40.

J.F. Bosher, *The Canada Merchants 1713–1763* (Oxford: Clarendon Press, 1987) underscores the importance of religious affiliations in creating trading networks.

4 James Axtell, *After Columbus: Essays in the Ethnohistory of Colonial North America* (New York: Oxford University Press, 1988). By the third quarter of the seventeenth century, 75 per cent of the objects buried with the Seneca were European in origin; Axtell, *The European and the Indian: Essays in the Ethnohistory of Colonial North America* (New York: Oxford University Press, 1981), 255.

5 Bruce G. Trigger, *Natives and Newcomers: Canada's 'Heroic Age' Reconsidered* (Montreal–Kingston: McGill–Queen's University Press, 1985), 97.

6 Marcel Trudel, *The Beginnings of New France 1524–1663* (Toronto: McClelland and Stewart, 1973), 123.

7 Rome's involvement in Canadian affairs is discussed in Lucien Campeau, *L'Évêché de Québec: Aux origines du premier diocèse érigé en Amérique française* (Québec: Société historique de Québec, 1974) and Luca Codignola, 'Rome and North America, 1622–1799', *Storia Nord Americana* 1 (1984): 5–33.

8 Marcel Trudel, *Histoire de la Nouvelle-France*, III, *La Seigneurie des Cent-Associés, 1627–1663*, I, *Les Événements* (Montréal: Fides, 1979), 108; Candide de Nant, *Page glorieuse de l'épopée canadienne: Une mission capucine en Acadie* (Montréal: Le Devoir, 1927); John G. Reid, *Acadia, Maine, and New Scotland: Marginal Colonies in the Seventeenth Century* (Toronto: Ontario Ministry of Culture and Recreation, 1981).

9 Olive P. Dickason, *Canada's First Nations: A History of the Founding Peoples from Earliest Times* (Toronto: McClelland and Stewart, 1992), 233.

10 Lucien Campeau, *La Mission des Jésuites chez les Hurons, 1634–50* (Montréal: Bellarmin, 1987), 221, 246.

11 Marie de l'Incarnation to her son, 1647, in [Marie Guyart], *Word From New France, The Selected Letters of Marie de l'Incarnation*, ed. and trans. Joyce Marshall (Toronto: Oxford University Press, 1967), 167.

12 Charles Frostin, 'Vogue canadienne et milieu métropolitain de soutien à la mission lointaine du XVIIe siècle', in Joseph Goy, Jean-Pierre Wallot, and Rolande Bonnain, eds, *Évolution et éclatement du monde rural: Structures, fonctionnement et évolution différentielle des sociétés rurales françaises et québécoises XVIIe–XXe siècles* (Montréal: Presses de l'Université de Montréal, 1986), 415–27. See also Claude Lessard, 'L'Aide financière de l'Église de France à l'Église naissante du Canada', in [n.a.], *Mélanges d'histoire du Canada offerts au professeur Marcel Trudel* (Ottawa: University of Ottawa Press, 1978), 162–81.

13 Quoted in François Rousseau, *La Croix et le scalpel: Histoire des Augustines de l'Hôtel-Dieu de Québec (1639–1989)*, I, *1639–1892* (Sillery: Septentrion, 1989), 125.

14 Marie de l'Incarnation to a lady of rank, 3 September 1640, *Word from New France*, 70.

15 *JR*, VII, 272–3.

16 Quoted in James Axtell, *The Invasion Within: The Contest of Cultures in Colonial North America* (New York: Oxford University Press, 1985), 80.

17 *JR*, XXXII, 209–11.

18 *JR*, X, 19–21. Brébeuf worked from more than one of the several French translations of [Jacques] Ledesma, *Dottrina Christiana* (1593). See Gilles Raymond, 'Le

Premier Catéchisme de la Nouvelle-France: Celui de Jean de Bréboeuf', in Raymond Brodeur and Jean-Paul Rouleau, eds, *Une inconnue de l'histoire de la culture: La Production des catéchismes en Amérique française* (Québec: Presses de l'Université Laval, 1986), 17–55.

19 Indeed, aboriginal women were sometimes the fiercest opponents of departing from traditional ways; John W. Grant, *Moon of Wintertime: Missionaries and the Indians of Canada in Encounter since 1534* (Toronto: University of Toronto Press, 1984), 41–2. Concerning native women's responses to Christianity, contrast Karen Anderson, *'Chain Her by One Foot': The Subjugation of Women in Seventeenth Century New France* (London: Routledge, 1991) with Eleanor Leacock, 'Montagnais Women and the Jesuit Program for Colonization', in Mona Etienne and Eleanor Leacock, eds, *Women and Colonization: Anthropological Perspectives* (New York: Praeger, 1980), 25–41, and Carol Devens, *Countering Colonization: Native American Women and the Great Lakes Missions, 1663–1900* (Berkeley: University of California Press, 1992).

20 Trigger, *Natives and Newcomers*, 294, is most adamant in rejecting the legitimacy of conversions, but C.J. Jaenen, *Friend and Foe: Aspects of French-Amerindian Cultural Contact in the Sixteenth and Seventeenth Centuries* (Toronto: McClelland and Stewart, 1976), 41–83, is also critical of the syncretism that crept into Indian Catholic expression. Axtell, 'Were Indian Conversions *Bona Fide?*', in his *After Columbus*, assumes the opposite view, as does Campeau, *La Mission des Jésuites*, 221, 246.

21 Marie de l'Incarnation to her son, October 1661, *Word from New France*, 267–8.

22 Bruce G. Trigger, *Children of the Aataentsic: A History of the Huron People to 1660* (Montreal–Kingston: McGill–Queen's University Press, 1976), 710–24, and *Natives and Newcomers*, 264–5, argues that Christianity weakened the Huron response to Iroquois aggression.

23 Nicolas Denys, *The Description and Natural History of the Coasts of North America (Acadia)*, ed. William F. Ganong (Toronto: Champlain Society, 1908), 603.

24 *JR*, XXII, 67.

25 *JR*, XXIX, 33–5.

26 The lives of these and other individuals like Marie Forestier, Marie-Catherine Simon de Longré (Catherine de Saint-Augustin), and Marie Maillet can be followed in the first two volumes of the *DCB*. For natives conforming to this pattern, see Léon Pouliot, 'États mystiques chez les Convertis Indiens dans la Nouvelle-France', SCHEC, *Rapport (1939–40)*: 99–106.

27 Trudel, *La Seigneurie des Cent-Associés*, 336. André Vachon, 'The Administration of New France', *DCB*, II, xv–xxv, outlines these and other developments succinctly.

28 An *arpent* is slightly less than an acre.

29 Fernand Ouellet, 'Proprieté seigneuriale et groupes sociaux dans la vallée du Saint-Laurent (1663–1840)', *Mélanges d'histoire*, 182–213; R.C. Harris, *The Seigneurial System in Early Canada: A Geographical Study* (Madison: University of Wisconsin Press, 1966), 42; Trudel, *Beginnings*, 246–56.

30 *Word From New France*, 193. The writings of Max Eastman, *Church and State in Early Canada* (Edinburgh, 1915) and William A. Riddell, *The Rise of Ecclesiastical Control in Quebec* (1916; repr. New York: AMS, 1968) were influential only among anglophone historians, many of whom did not read French, but they were reinforced by

clerico-nationalist historians in French Canada; see Serge Gagnon, *Québec et ses historiens de 1840 à 1920* (Québec: Presses de l'Université Laval, 1978).

31 Joseph Bergin, 'Between Estate and Profession: The Catholic Parish Clergy of Early Modern Western Europe', in M.L. Bush, ed., *Social Orders and Social Classes in Europe Since 1500: Studies in Social Stratification* (London: Longman, 1992), 78.

32 Noël Baillargeon, *Le Séminaire de Québec sous l'épiscopat de Mgr de Laval* (Québec: Presses de l'Université Laval, 1972), 4–5. See also Pierre Hurtubise, 'Ni janséniste, ni gallican, ni ultramontain: François de Laval', *RHAF* 28 (1974): 3–26.

33 NAC, AN (France), Colonies, C11A, II, file 1, 332ff, Voyer D'Argenson à son frère (automne 1660).

34 The British also appointed clergy to judicial positions. When the first civil council began in Nova Scotia in 1720, Governor Richard Philipps appointed one of the garrison chaplains as a member. Anglican priest John Jago was appointed as one of three justices of the peace in Newfoundland in 1723.

35 See Lucien Campeau, 'Le Commerce des clercs en Nouvelle-France', *Mélanges d'histoire*, 27–35.

36 ASQ, Lettres R, 179A: 91, Antoine Gaulin à Tremblay (1701).

37 Raphael N. Hamilton, 'Who Wrote *Premier Établissement de la Foy dans la Nouvelle France*?', *CHR* 57 (1976): 265–88. Louis Hennepin, the Récollet who accompanied La Salle to the upper Mississippi in 1679–80, assumed an anti-Jesuit position in his publications, as did the military officer Louis-Armand de Lahontan in subsequent decades.

38 Two-and-a-half centuries later, when the Canadian government placed Dollard and his band on its posters to promote military enlistment during the First World War, Quebec's foremost clerico-nationalist historian, Abbé Lionel Groulx, would reclaim him as the 'saviour' of New France and a lay exemplar of Catholic virtue and leadership for twentieth-century youth to emulate. See John Dickinson, 'Annaotaha et Dollard vus de l'autre côté de la palissade', *RHAF* 35 (1981): 163–78, and Terry Crowley, ed., *Clio's Craft: A Primer of Historical Methods* (Toronto: Copp Clark Pitman, 1988) for the primary sources surrounding this event and the historiographical controversies it has generated.

39 Marie de l'Incarnation, *Word From New France*, 312. See Jack Verney, *The Good Regiment: The Carignan-Salières Regiment in Canada* (Montreal–Kingston: McGill–Queen's University Press, 1991).

40 François Dollier de Casson, *A History of Montreal, 1640–1672*, ed. and trans. Ralph Flenley (London: J.M. Dent, 1928), 301.

41 Hubert Charbonneau, André Guillemette, Jacques Légaré, *Naissance d'une population: Les Français établis au Canada au XVIIe siècle* (Montréal: Presses de l'Université de Montréal, 1987), 21.

42 The debate over the relationship between religion and magic since 1500, which began with Keith Thomas, *Religion and the Decline of Magic* (New York: Scribner, 1973), is reviewed in the introduction to Richard Godbeer, *The Devil's Dominion, Religion and Magic in Early New England* (New York: Cambridge University Press, 1992), 9–10.

43 Albert Jamet, ed., *Les Annales de l'Hôtel-Dieu de Québec, 1636–1716* (Québec: Hôtel-Dieu, 1939), 148.

44 Marie de l'Incarnation to Gabrielle de l'Annonciation, 1663, *Word from New France*, 299–300, 306. The practice was predicated on Corinthians 2:14–16, and Ephesians 5:2.

45 *Catéchisme du diocèse de Québec* (Paris: U. Coustelier, 1702; repr. Montréal: Éditions franciscaines, 1958), 431. See Marie-Aimée Cliche, *Les Pratiques de dévotion en Nouvelle-France: Comportements populaires et encadrement ecclésial dans le gouvernement de Québec* (Québec: Presses de l'Université Laval, 1988).

46 *Word from New France*, 312; *JR*, IV, 36–8.

47 *Word from New France*, 287–8; *JR*, IV, 36–8.

48 Matthew 24: 1–34; Mark, 13: 3–27, Revelation 11: 1–19. See David Hall, *Worlds of Wonder, Days of Judgment: Popular Religious Belief in Early New England* (New York: Knopf, 1989), 74–83, and William Christian, Jr, *Apparitions in Late Medieval and Renaissance Spain* (Princeton: Princeton University Press, 1981). The theme of fear is explored in Jean Delumeau, *La Peur en Occident, XIVe–XVIIe siècles* (Paris: Fayard, 1978).

49 Cliche, *Les Pratiques de dévotion*, 69–72. See also *Word from New France*, 264–5 and 'Gadois, Pierre', *DCB*, II, 233–4. Marcel Trudel, *La Seigneurie des Cent-Associés*, 317–19, ended a long controversy and repeated misinterpretations by sorting out the Vuil affair.

50 Godbeer, *Devil's Dominion*, 235–7.

51 *Catéchisme du diocèse de Québec*, 320; *MEQ*, 268, 280, 285, 374, 409.

52 *Word from New France*, 366; Paul Ragueneau, *La Vie de Mère Catherine de Saint-Augustin* (Paris: Florentin Lambert, 1671).

53 Confraternities are examined extensively in Cliche, *Les Pratiques de dévotion*, and Brigette Caulier, 'Les Confréries de dévotion à Montréal du 17e au 19e siècles' (Ph.D thesis, Université de Montréal, 1986).

54 Denis Delâge, 'Les Iroquois chrétiens des 'réductions', 1667–1770', *Recherches amérindiennes au Québec* 21 (1991): 59–70. See also K. Richter, 'War and Culture: The Iroquois Experience', *William and Mary Quarterly* 40 (1982): 528–59; and Richter, 'Iroquois Versus Iroquois: Jesuit Missions and Christianity in Village Politics, 1642–86', *Ethnohistory* 32 (1985): 1–16.

55 Lucien Campeau, 'The Catholic Missions in New France', in Wilcomb Washburn, ed., *Handbook of North American Indians*, IV (Washington, DC: Smithsonian Institution, 1988), 464–71. On Marquette see *DCB*, I, 490–3 and Joseph P. Donnelly, *Jacques Marquette, S.J. 1637–1675* (Chicago: Loyola University Press, 1968).

56 Jean-Baptiste de la Croix Chevrières de Saint-Vallier, *Estat présent de l'église et de la colonnie françoise dans la Nouvelle-France* (Paris, 1688; repr. 1965), 92–111; Lettre circulaire aux curés de l'Acadie (20 avril 1742), *MEQ*, II, 15–17; 'Moireau, Claude', *DCB*, II, 477–8; Noël Baillargeon, *Le Séminaire de Québec de 1685 à 1760* (Québec: Presses de l'Université Laval, 1977), 249–50; Axtell, *Invasion*, 248.

57 Baillargeon, *Le Séminaire de Québec de 1685 à 1760*, 46.

58 W.J. Eccles, *Canada Under Louis XIV 1663–1701* (Toronto: McClelland and Stewart, 1964), 228–9, 233; Guy Frégault, *Le XVIIIe Siècle canadien: Études* (Montréal: Fides, 1968), 126; *MEQ*, I, 395–6.

59 See W.J. Eccles, 'Social Welfare Measures and Policies in New France', *Essays on New France* (Toronto: Oxford University Press, 1987), 38–49 and André Lachance,

'Le Bureau des pauvres de Montréal, 1698–1699: Contribution à l'étude de la société montréalaise de la fin du XVIIe siècle', *Histoire sociale/Social History* 2 (1969): 99–110.

60 Jamet, *Les Annales de l'Hôtel-Dieu de Québec*, 296–7.

61 Eccles, 'The Role of the Church in New France', *Essays*, 26–37; Henri Têtu, *Les Évêques de Québec: Notices biographiques* (Québec: N.S. Hardy, 1889), 149. On the Quebec asylum, see Micheline D'Allaire, *L'Hôpital-Général de Québec 1692–1764* (Montréal: Fides, 1971) and Marguerite Jean, *Évolution des communautés religieuses de femmes au Canada de 1639 à nos jours* (Montréal: Fides, 1977), 39–44.

62 Roger Magnuson, *Education in New France* (Montreal: McGill–Queen's University Press, 1992), 66, 82.

63 See Guy Plante, *Le Rigorisme au XVIIe siècle: Mgr de Saint-Vallier et le sacrement de pénitance* (Gembloux, 1971) and Cornelius J. Jaenen, *The Role of the Church in New France* (Toronto: McGraw-Hill Ryerson, 1976), 54–6, 124–6. When a Jansenist Benedictine named Georges-François Poulet appeared at Quebec, Bishop Saint-Vallier tried to expel him, an order the governor refused to execute. After a bout of illness during which the bishop refused absolution, Poulet left the colony of his own accord in 1718.

The catechism is analyzed in Benoît Boilly, 'Le Premier *Catéchisme du diocèse de Québec* (1702)', in Brodeur and Rouleau, *Une inconnue*, 123–42.

64 NAC, AN, Colonies, F3 (Collection Moreau-St Mery), 95: 35, Reglements faits par les chefs sauvages de l'Isle Royale et M. de Bourville (9 juillet 1739); C11B, 22: 118, de Bourville au Ministre de la Marine (26 octobre 1740).

65 NAC, AN, Colonies, C11A, 75: 141, Beauharnois au ministre (1741).

66 See Charles O'Neill, *Church and State in French Colonial Louisiana: Policy and Politics to 1732* (New Haven: Yale University Press, 1966).

67 ASQ, Lettres R: 37, Saint-Cosme à Tremblay, 4 mai 1704.

68 Marest à Germain (9 novembre 1712), *JR*, LXVI, 263–5. Bergier had died of natural causes, most likely stomach ulcers.

69 André Vachon's influential article, 'L'Eau de vie dans la société indienne', CHA, *Annual Report 1960*: 22–32, argued this thesis, one similar to that expounded by missionary François Vachon de Belmont, whose own study had been published in the nineteenth century as 'Histoire de l'eau-de-vie en Canada', *Collection de Mémoires et de Relations sur l'histoire de l'ancienne Québec* (Québec, 1840). J.R. Miller, *Skyscrapers Hide the Heavens: A History of Indian–White Relations in Canada* (Toronto: University of Toronto Press, 1989), 48, 58, is inconsistent, claiming that religion was a scourge akin to epidemics but then claiming that its long-term impact should not be exaggerated. Contrast Nancy Bonvillain, 'The Iroquois and the Jesuits: Strategies of Influence and Resistance', *American Indian Culture and Research Journal* 10 (1986): 29–42.

70 ASQ, Lettres R, 33: 3, Saint-Cosme à Tremblay (7 décembre 1701); same, 35: 2 (19 avril 1702). And the following: Lettres R, 87, Le Loutre à _____ (1 octobre 1738); Lettres R, 179A: 1, Gaulin à Tremblay (1702). See also Micheline Dumont Johnson, *Apôtres ou Agitateurs? La France missionaire en Acadie* (Trois-Rivières: Boréal Express, 1970), 58–70; L.F.S. Upton, *Micmacs and Colonists: Indian-White Relations in*

the Maritimes, 1713–1867 (Vancouver: University of British Columbia Press, 1979); and Olive P. Dickason, *Louisbourg and the Indians: A Study in Imperial Race Relations* (Ottawa: Department of Indian Affairs and Northern Development, National Historic Parks Branch, 1976).

71 NAC, AN, CllA, 6: 185, de Meulles à Colbert (4 novembre 1683). Statistics are provided in Frégault, *Le XVIIIe Siècle canadien*, 99–101; Louis Pelletier, *Le Clergé en Nouvelle-France: Étude de la démographie historique et répertoire biographique* (Montréal: Presses de l'Université de Montréal, 1993), 23, 32–4; Government of Canada, *Census of Canada, 1871*, 4: 61. Priest-to-people ratios in France varied enormously during the seventeenth and eighteenth centuries.

72 NAC, AN, CllD, 2: 20, Rapport de François-Marie Perrot (9 août 1686). On the high rate of geographical mobility away from Port-Royal, see Gisa Hynes, 'Aspects of the Demography of Port Royal, 1650–1755', *Acadiensis* 3 (1973): 3–17.

73 'Procès verbaux sur la commodité et l'incommodité dressés dans chacune des paroisses de la Nouvelle-France par Mathieu-Benoît Collet (janvier 1721)', *RAQ, 1921-2*, 262–362; Dale Miquelon, *New France 1701–1744* (Toronto: McClelland and Stewart, 1987), 233.

74 Louise Dechêne, *Habitants and Merchants in Seventeenth-Century Montreal* (Montreal: McGill–Queen's University Press, 1992), 265–6; Louis Lavallée, *La Prairie en Nouvelle-France 1647–1760* (Montréal–Kingston: McGill–Queen's University Press, 1992), 133; Charles Lippy, Robert Choquette, and Stafford Poole, *Christianity Comes to the Americas, 1492–1776* (New York: Paragon, 1992), 213.

75 Magnuson, *Education in New France*, 169.

76 Hynes, 'Aspects of the Demography of Port-Royal', and for what follows, Magnuson, *Education in New France*, 89–91; David H. Fischer, *Albion's Seed: Four British Folkways in America* (New York: Oxford University Press, 1989), 344–9, 718. The higher literacy rates at Louisbourg, observed by A.J.B. Johnston, *Religion and Life at Louisbourg* (Montréal–Kingston: McGill–Queen's University Press, 1984), 107–8, should be interpreted in light of that port's thriving commerce and connections with France.

77 *Word From New France*, 259–61; Dechêne, *Habitants and Merchants*, 271, 276–7; Pelletier, *Le Clergé en Nouvelle-France*.

78 However, in most places, fewer women than men could sign their names on official documents. See Micheline D'Allaire, *Les Dots des religieuses au Canada français, 1639–1800: Étude économique et sociale* (Montréal: Fides, 1986), 57–9; D'Allaire, *L'Hôpital-Général*, 130–1: Yvon Desloges, *A Tenant's Town: Québec in the 18th Century*, trans. Department of the Secretary of State (Ottawa: Department of the Environment, National Historic Parks and Sites Branch, 1991), 33; Johnston, *Religion and Life at Louisbourg*, 107. Elizabeth Rapley, *The Dévotes: Women and Church in Seventeenth-Century France* (Montréal–Kingston: McGill–Queen's University Press, 1990) 146, corrects the proclivity of the former to read nineteenth-century pedagogy back into the two preceding centuries.

79 This paragraph is based on Rousseau, *La Croix et le scalpel*, especially vol. I, 16, 106, 122-2. Demographics are provided in Pelletier, *Le Clergé en Nouvelle-France*. See also [n.a.] *L'Hôtel-Dieu de Montréal 1642–1973* (Montréal: Hurtubise HMH, 1973).

80 Rapley, *The Dévotes*, 170; Terry Crowley, 'The Inroads of Secularization in New France: Church and People at Louisbourg', CCHA, *Study Sessions 1984*: 5–27. The choices made by Christianity in its earliest years are brought out by Elaine Pagels, *The Gnostic Gospels* (New York: Random House, 1979). See also Marina Warner, *Alone of All Her Sex: The Myth and the Cult of the Virgin Mary* (New York: Knopf, 1976) and Peter Burke, *Popular Culture in Early Modern Europe* (New York: Harper and Row, 1978), 207–43.

81 More general male attitudes towards women can be found in Nelson Dawson, 'Les Filles du roi: Des pollueuses?' La France du XVIIe siècle', *Historical Reflections/Réflections historiques* 12 (1985): 9–38, as well as in Rapley, *The Dévotes*, and Anderson, 'Chain Her By One Foot'.

82 Leslie Choquette, '"Les Amazones du Grand Dieu": Women and Mission in Seventeenth-Century Canada', *French Historical Studies* 17 (1992): 627–55.

83 NAC, AN, Collection Beauharnois, Lettre pastorale de Vachon de Belmont (1704), 388–9; *MEQ*, II, 22–3. See Terry Crowley, '"Thundergusts": Popular Disturbances in Early French Canada', CHA, *Historical Papers 1979*: 11–31.

84 Quoted in Colin Coates, 'Authority and Illegitimacy in New France: The Burial of Bishop Saint-Vallier and Madeleine de Verchères vs. the Priest of Batiscan', *Histoire sociale/Social History* 22 (1989): 65–90.

85 The restraints placed on young people led some to marry themselves—a custom referred to as *à la gaumine*, after the first supposed to have perpetrated the sacrilege. See Christopher Moore's lively account of the marriage of Marie-Louise Cruchon in *Louisbourg Portraits* (Toronto: Macmillan, 1982), 55–117, and [n.a.] 'Les Mariages à la gaumine', *RAQ*, *1920–21*, 366–407.

86 Rousseau, *La Croix et le scalpel*, 117; D'Allaire, *L'Hôpital-Général de Québec*, 231; Baillargeon, *Le Séminaire de Québec de 1685 à 1760*, 271–6. The only thorough analysis of the church's finances as a whole is Frégault, *Le XVIIIe Siècle canadien*, 104–22.

87 NAC, AN, Colonies, F5A, 3: 62–77, La Manche à Pontchartrain (1713).

88 *Édits, ordonnances royaux, déclarations et arrêts du conseil d'état du roi concernant le Canada* (Québec: Assemblée legislative, 1854), 528–9, 576–81. See also Gustave Lanctôt, 'Situation politique de l'Église canadienne sous le régime français', SCHEC, *Rapport 1940–1941*, 35–56, and Cornelius Jaenen, 'Church and State Relations in Canada, 1604–1685', CHA, *Historical Papers 1967*: 20–40.

89 'Une autobiographie de l'abbé Jean Loutre', *Nova Francia*, 3 (1931): 1–34; *Collection de manuscrits contenant lettres, mémoires, et autres documents historiques relatifs à la Nouvelle-France* (Québec, 1883–5), I, 477–81.

90 Contrast the interpretations in Crowley, 'The Inroads of Secularization', and 'Religion in New France: Church and State at Louisbourg', *Proceedings of the Tenth Meeting of the French Colonial Historical Society, April 12–14, 1984*, 139–60, with Johnston, *Religion and Life at Louisbourg*.

91 Paul Hazard, *The European Mind 1680–1715* (New York: World, 1963), xvii-xviii; Peter Gay, *The Enlightenment: An Interpretation* (New York: Knopf, 1967), 338.

92 [Louis-Armand de Lom d'Arce] Baron de Lahontan, *New Voyages to North America. . . .* ed. R.G. Thwaites, 2 vols (Chicago: Mcclurg, 1905) and *Oeuvres complètes*, ed. Réal

Ouellet, 2 vols (Montréal: Presses de l'Université de Montréal, 1990); Thomas Pichon, *Lettres et mémoires pour servir à l'histoire naturelle, civile et politique du Cap Breton*. . . . (London, 1760; repr. [n.p.]: S.R. Publishers, 1966).

93 Cliche, *Les Pratiques de devotion*, 82–123, 273; Lavallée, *La Prairie*, 42, 133. In interpreting the voluntary parish revenues provided by Cliche in Table 20 (105), I have excluded parishes in which a new church was built, as construction occasioned greater offerings in the short term; this was also evident at La Prairie in the Montreal district.

94 Lorraine Gadoury, Yves Landry, Hubert Charbonneau, 'Démographie différentielle en Nouvelle-France: Villes et campagnes', and Réal Bates, 'Les Conceptions prénuptiales dans la vallée du Saint-Laurent avant 1725', *RHAF* 38 (1985): 357–78, 40; (1986): 253–72. Of the towns, Quebec City was lowest in premarital conception rates. Figures for rural areas should be interpreted with caution as they represented places in which churches and parish priests were available. The lower illegitimacy rates observed by Hynes at Annapolis Royal are difficult to interpret, although they may be partially attributable to the frequent movements of the Acadian population.

95 France, Archives Départementales, Finistère, Series 23H14, Remarques concernant la dispensation pour Daccarrette (Joseph Deny) (1726); Michel Le Duff à Saturin Dirop (3 novembre 1727). On these questions, see also André Lachance, *Crimes et criminels en Nouvelle-France* (Montreal: Boréal Express, 1984) and *La Vie urbaine en Nouvelle-France* (Montreal: Boréal, 1987).

96 ASQ, Lettres M, 30: 42, Tremblay aux directeurs du Séminaire de Québec (12 mars 1704). Petr Kalm noted later that the seminary accepted young men of middling capacity. Priests rattled off services in incomprehensible Latin and could not converse in that language; Adolphe B. Benson, ed., *Peter Kalm's Travels in North America*, 2 vols (New York: Wilson-Erickson, 1964), II, 451–3, 541–2.

The school of arts and crafts at Saint-Joachim, once acclaimed by historians as a major contribution to artistic development by Quebec's seminary, was essentially a summer camp where students helped to farm and acquired skills from local craftspeople. See Peter N. Moogk, 'Réexamen de l'École des arts et métiers de Saint-Joachim' and Lucien Campeau, 'A propos de l'École de Saint-Joachim', *RHAF* 29 (1975–76): 3–29, 567–76; Baillargeon, *Le Séminaire de Québec de 1685 à 1760*, 233–4.

97 ASQ, Manuscrit C–18, 24, Tremblay à Maizerets (juin 1706).

98 Quoted in Emilia Chicoine, *La Métairie de Marguerite Bourgeoys* (Montréal: Fides, 1986), 77.

99 Archives de l'Archidiocèse de Québec, 10B, Registre du Chapitre de Québec, 1: 425/1, Acte de sépulture de François-Elzéar Vallier (17 janvier 1747).

100 Quoted in Jean, *Évolution des communautés religieuses*, 54.

101 The Frères Charon disappeared, and Marguerite d'Youville was canonized in 1990 by Pope John Paul II.

102 Quoted in Marcel Trudel, *L'Église canadienne sous le Régime militaire, 1759–1764*, I, *Les Problèmes* (Québec: Presses de l'Université Laval, 1956), 71.

CHAPTER TWO

1 M. de Tonnancour to the Abbé de La Corne (15 September 1760), quoted in Dom Guy-Marie Oury, *Mgr Briand, évêque de Québec et les problèmes de son époque* (Solesmes/Québec: Éditions de Solesmes/Éditions La Liberté, 1985), 64–5. A wealthy Trois-Rivières merchant, de Tonnancour was a government official during the French regime.

2 'Mandement pour des prières publiques à l'occasion de la dispersion des Acadiens' (15 February 1756), *MEQ*, II, 105.

3 In the absence of any exact census, we are relying on the estimate of Marcel Trudel, *L'Église canadienne sous le Régime militaire, 1759–1764*, 2 vols (Québec: Presses de l'Université Laval, 1956–7), I, 359.

4 Murray to Amherst (November 1759 [?]), quoted in Alfred Leroy Burt, *The Old Province of Quebec* (Toronto: Ryerson Press, 1933), 17.

5 Guy Frégault, *La Guerre de la Conquête, 1754–1760* (Montréal: Fides, 1955), 455.

6 Quoted in Claude Galarneau, *La France devant l'opinion canadienne (1760–1815)* (Québec: Presses de l'Université Laval, 1970), 88–9.

7 Ibid., 89.

8 Ibid.

9 Trudel, *L'Église canadienne*, I, 335, 340–1, 358–61.

10 The chapter to Dean La Corne (Autumn 1764), ibid., 348.

11 The Jesuits would disappear in 1800, the Récollets in 1813.

12 These statistics are provided by Trudel, *L'Église canadienne*, I, 36, 40.

13 Lucien Lemieux, *Les Années difficiles*, vol. I, *1760–1839*, of HCQ, II (Montréal: Boréal, 1989), 76.

14 Adam Shortt and Arthur G. Doughty, eds, *Documents Relating to the Constitutional History of Canada, 1759–1791* (Ottawa: King's Printer, 1911), I, 169, 191. These instructions referred to the original law passed by the Westminster parliament on 25 January 1559 and signed by Elizabeth I.

15 Michel Brunet, *Les Canadiens après la Conquête, 1754–1760* (Montréal: Fides, 1955), 140.

16 Murray to Shelburne (14 September 1763), ibid., 122.

17 Born in Brittany in 1715, Jean-Olivier Briand had arrived in New France in 1741. For nineteen years he was Bishop de Pontbriand's secretary and close collaborator before becoming his grand vicar in September 1759.

18 Murray to Shelburne (22 July 1763), in Auguste Gosselin, *L'Église du Canada après la conquête*, 2 vols (Québec: Imprimerie Laflamme, 1916–17), I, 69.

19 Murray to Shelburne (14 September 1763), in Trudel, *L'Église canadienne*, I, 313.

20 Murray to Briand (20 June 1766), *RAQ, 1929–1930*, 65.

21 *La Gazette de Québec*, 29 juin 1766.

22 AAQ, 941 CD, I, 92–3, *Registre du Chapitre de Québec (1684–1773)*.

23 Brunet, *Les Canadiens après la Conquête*, 127.

24 This is especially true of Trudel in *L'Église canadienne*, I, 221, 309–34.

25 See ibid., 82.

26 Letter (13 November 1759), quoted in Brunet, *Les Canadiens après la Conquête*, 32.

27 Pastoral letter from Bishop Briand to the Acadians of Île Saint-Jean (Prince Edward Island), Cape Breton, Nova Scotia and the Gaspé (16 August 1766), *RAQ, 1929–1930*, 66. Later, in 1818, Bishop Plessis also blamed the Acadians for 'their contacts and secret relations with the French' which led to the Deportation; *MEQ, III, 143.

28 'Mandement de Mgr Briand pour faire chanter un Te Deum en action de grâce pour le bienfait de la paix' (4 June 1763), ibid., II, 169–70.

29 Briand to Abercromby (1762 [?]), *RAQ, 1929–1930*, 50.

30 'Mandement de Mgr Briand pour faire chanter un Te Deum en action de grâce du mariage du roi George III' (14 February 1762), *MEQ, II, 160–1.

31 This point is emphasized in Brunet, *Les Canadiens après la Conquête*, 34.

32 See ibid., 279.

33 See ibid., 244.

34 This is particularly true of his 'Mandement du jubilé pour la ville de Québec' (5 March 1771), *MEQ, II, 222–34.

35 Brigitte Caulier, 'Bâtir l'Amérique des dévots: Les Confréries de dévotion montréalaises depuis le Régime française', *RHAF* 46, 1 (été 1992): 45–6.

36 Lemieux, *Les Années difficiles*, 308.

37 See Guy Laperrière, 'Religion populaire, religion de clercs? Du Québec à la France, 1972–1982', in Benoît Lacroix and Jean Simard, eds, *Religion populaire, religion de clercs?* (Québec: Institut québécois de recherche sur la culture, 1984), 35.

38 Jean-Charles Falardeau, 'Religion populaire et classes sociales', ibid., 286.

39 See Pierre Hurtubise, 'La Religiosité populaire en Nouvelle-France', ibid., 56.

40 Ibid., 61.

41 'Lettre pastorale aux habitants de Repentigny' (9 December 1769), *RAQ, 1929–1930*, 83.

42 'Mandement pour le jubilé accordé par notre Saint-Père le pape Clément XIII' (26 January 1767), *MEQ, II, 192, 196.

43 'Mandement à l'occasion de l'élection d'un coadjuteur' (1771), ibid., 243.

44 'Mandement pour la visite des paroisses du diocèse en 1775', (22 May 1775), ibid., 260.

45 Lemieux, *Les Années difficiles*, 127.

46 Ibid.

47 See ibid., 133.

48 'Mandement du jubilé pour la ville de Québec' (5 March 1771), *MEQ, II, 225.

49 Briand to M. de La Corne (6 June 1774), *RAQ, 1929–1930*, 106.

50 Brunet, *les Canadiens après la Conquête*, 126–7.

51 Briand to P.G. Saint-Onge (1766), ibid., 235.

52 See Lemieux, *Les Années difficiles*, 237–8.

53 See Léon Thériault, 'L'Acadianisation de l'Église catholique en Acadie, 1763–1953', in Jean Daigle, ed., *Les Acadiens des Maritimes: Études thématiques* (Moncton: Centre d'études acadiennes, 1980), 303. The British government stopped its financial support for the missionaries in 1838. See Lemieux, *Les Années difficiles*, 253.

54 See Lemieux, *Les Années difficiles*, 235, and Thériault, 'L'Acadianisation', 303.

55 It seems that the instructions given to Governor Prevost on this matter in 1811 were generally not carried out. See Lemieux, *Les Années difficiles*, 250.

56 See ibid., 238–9.

57 'Mémoire sur le diocèse de Québec', *MEQ*, II, 481.

58 Quoted in Lemieux, *Les Années difficiles*, 241.

59 See ibid., 247.

60 Plessis to Jonathan Odell (31 August 1816), quoted in ibid., 238.

61 Quoted in ibid., 240.

62 Dosquet was the last bishop of Quebec to assert that this would always be a case reserved for the bishop; 'Mandement contre la traite des boissons aux Sauvages' (26 November 1730), *MEQ*, I, 536.

63 Bailly to Briand (23 May 1769), quoted in J. Wilfrid Pineau, *Le Clergé français dans l'Île du Prince Edouard, 1721–1821* (Québec: Éditions Ferland, 1967), 45.

64 'Mandement aux sauvages du Sault-Saint-Louis' (6 March 1784), *MEQ*, II, 306.

65 Hubert to Cardinal Antonelli (14 June 1788), ibid., 351.

66 These are the figures given by Raymond Roy ('La Croissance démographique en Acadie, 1671–1763' [Master's thesis, Université de Montréal, 1975], 149) for the Acadian region; by contrast, Robert G. LeBlanc ('The Acadian Migrations, 1775–1785' [M.A. thesis, University of Minnesota, 1961], 41) estimates the Acadian population at this time to be 2,336. Roy's figures are more accurate, according to Muriel K. Roy, 'Peuplement et croissance démographique en Acadie', in Daigle, ed., *Les Acadiens des Maritimes*, 166.

67 See Thériault, 'L'Acadie, 1763–1978: Synthèse historique', in Daigle, ed., *Les Acadiens des Maritimes*, 53; and his 'L'Acadianisation', ibid., 298.

68 Quoted in Pineau, *Le Clergé français*, 43.

69 Bailly to Briand (24 April 1771), quoted in ibid., 46–7.

70 Thériault, 'L'Acadianisation', 301.

71 Ibid.

72 Lemieux, *Les Années difficiles*, 56.

73 Thériault, 'L'Acadianisation', 302.

74 Bailly de Messein to Briand (24 April 1771), quoted in Pineau, *Le Clergé français*, 46.

75 Briand to Father Bocquet, missionary at Detroit (3 September 1768), *RAQ, 1929–1930*, 75.

76 Briand to Father Sebastien Meurin, missionary to the Illinois (February 1767), ibid., 69.

77 'Mandement de Mgr Briand au sujet de la proclamation publique qu'il fit de Mgr de Dorylée, son coadjuteur, le jour anniversaire de sa consécration' (14 March 1774), *MEQ*, II, 254.

78 Josiah Quincy, Jr, *Memoir of the Life of Josiah Quincy* (New York: Da Capo, 1971), 184–5.

79 Alexander Hamilton, *Works* (St Clair's Shores, Mich.: Scholarly Press, 1971), 38–9.

80 See Marcel Trudel, *La Révolution américaine, 1775–1783* (Québec: Boréal Express, 1976), 66.

81 'Mandement de Mgr Briand' (June 1776), *MEQ*, II, 275.

82 'Mandement de Mgr Briand au sujet de l'invasion des Américains au Canada' (22 May 1775), ibid., 264–5.

83 'Circulaire au sujet du rétablissement des milices' (13 June 1775), ibid., 265–6.

84 Briand to Abbé Saint-Onge (May 1775), quoted in Laval Laurent, *Québec et l'Église aux États-Unis sous Mgr Briand et Mgr Plessis* (Montréal: Librairie St-François, 1945), 37.

85 Briand to the de Pontbriand sisters (27 September 1776), ibid., 39.

86 Trudel, *La Révolution américaine*, 117.

87 Briand to P.-L. Bédard, parish priest of Saint-François-du-Sud (30 August 1776), *RAQ, 1929–1930*, 113.

88 Briand to Montgolfier (5 November 1775), ibid., 112.

89 AAQ, CL, IV, 589–92, Briand à Jean-Baptiste Maisonbasse dit Petit (25 octobre 1775).

90 'Mandement de Mgr Briand aux sujets rebelles durant la guerre américaine' (May 1776), *MEQ*, II, 274, 276–7.

91 See Galarneau, *La France devant l'opinion canadienne*, 49.

92 'Mémoire de Mgr Bailly au juge Smith' (5 April 1790), quoted in Louis-Philippe Audet, *Le Système scolaire de la Province de Québec*, 6 vols (Québec: Éditions de l'Érable, 1950–6), II, 166.

93 'Mémoire concernant l'admission des prêtres européens dans le diocèse de Québec' (20 May 1790), *MEQ*, II, 430.

94 Gravé to M. Hody of the Foreign Missions Seminary in Paris (25 October 1791), quoted in Galarneau, *La France devant l'opinion canadienne*, 133.

95 *La Gazette de Montréal*, 15 janvier 1786, quoted in Jean-Paul de Lagrave, *Fleury Mesplet, 1734–1794: Diffuseur des lumières au Québec* (Montréal: Patenaude Éditeur, 1985), 234.

96 Marcel Trudel, *L'Influence de Voltaire au Canada*, 2 vols (Montréal: Fides, 1945), I, 122.

97 'Mandement de Mgr Briand pour le jubilé universel accordé par Clément XIV' (28 January 1771), *MEQ*, II, 220.

98 Hubert to the prefect of the Congregation for the Propagation of the Faith (26 October 1792), quoted in Galarneau, *La France devant l'opinion canadienne*, 133.

99 The historian Claude Galarneau maintains that, far from being a partially closed peasant society, isolated from the major movements that influenced the historical development of other nations, Quebec always remained in contact with its former mother country with respect to cultural matters.

100 Galarneau, *La France devant l'opinion canadienne*, 118.

101 *La Gazette de Montréal*, 2 décembre 1790, quoted in Lagrave, *Fleury Mesplet*, 244.

102 Quoted in Michel Brunet, 'La Révolution française sur les rives du Saint-Laurent', *RHAF* 11, 2 (septembre 1957): 159.

103 'Circulaire à Messieurs les curés à l'occasion des rumeurs de guerre' (9 November 1793), *MEQ*, II, 471–2.

104 Hubert to James Jones (29 March 1794), *RAQ, 1930–1931*, 298–9.

105 Report from Dorchester to Dundas (25 May 1794), in Michel Brunet, 'Les Canadiens et la France révolutionnaire', *RHAF* 13, 4 (mars 1960): 469.

106 Ibid., 468.

107 Quoted in Lionel Groulx, *Notre maître le passé*, 3 vols (Montréal: Librairie Granger Frères, 1944), III, 137.

108 Report of the Attorney General to the Executive Council (30 October 1796), in Brunet, 'Les Canadiens et la France révolutionnaire', 472.

109 Prescott to Portland (24 October 1796), ibid.

110 Denaut to Plessis (12 October 1796), quoted in Lemieux, *Les Années difficiles*, 33–4.

111 'Circulaire de Mgr Hubert recommandant la fidélité au gouvernement' (5 November 1796), *MEQ*, II, 501–2.

112 Quoted in Brunet, 'Les Canadiens et la France révolutionnaire', 474.

113 Jean-Pierre Wallot, 'La Révolution française au Canada, 1789–1838', in Michel Grenon, ed., *L'Image de la Révolution française au Québec, 1789–1989* (Montréal: Hurtubise HMH, 1991), 72.

114 Denis-Benjamin Viger, 'Considérations', *Oeuvres politiques* (Montréal: Réédition-Québec, 1970), 18.

115 'Projet de mandement de Mgr Plessis' (December 1798), quoted in Groulx, *Notre maître le passé*, III, 139.

116 The report of Charles Morgan, who was sent to Canada in 1785 to investigate the situation, is explicit on this point. See James H. Lambert, 'Montmollin, David-François de', *DCB*, V, 601.

117 J.H. Lambert, 'Veyssière, Léger-Jean-Baptiste-Noël', *DCB*, IV, 753.

118 Ibid.

119 Ryland to (?) (23 December 1804), quoted in Jean-Pierre Wallot, *Un Québec qui bougeait: Trame sociopolitique au tournant du XIXe siècle* (Québec: Boréal Express, 1973), 179.

120 Milnes to Portland (1 November 1800) in Arthur G. Doughty and Duncan A. McArthur, eds, *Documents Relating to the Constitutional History of Canada, 1791–1818* (Ottawa: King's Printer, 1914), 253.

121 Portland to Milnes (6 January 1801), ibid., 259.

122 AAQ, RL, IV, 50, Denaut à Plessis (8 septembre 1800).

123 Sewell to Milnes (29 May 1801), quoted in Wallot, *Un Québec qui bougeait*, 172.

124 Plessis to Roux (3 June 1805), quoted in Gilles Chaussé, *Jean-Jacques Lartigue, premier évêque de Montréal* (Montréal: Fides, 1980), 51.

125 Thomas R. Millman, 'Mountain, Jacob', *DCB*, VI, 524.

126 Craig to Lord Liverpool (1 May 1810), in Doughty and McArthur, eds, *Documents, 1791–1818*, 389.

127 *MEQ*, III, 71.

128 Millman, 'Mountain, Jacob', 527.

129 'Mandement pour la visite du diocèse' (19 April 1787), *MEQ*, II, 327.

130 'Mémoire sur le diocèse de Québec' (1794), ibid., 487–8.

131 Lemieux, *Les Années difficiles*, 283.

132 'Mandement qui permet de travailler à certains jours de fêtes' (15 April 1791), *MEQ*, II, 438.

133 Tabeau to Bishop Plessis (10 January 1818), quoted in Lemieux, *Les Années difficiles*, 320. For the Montreal area, only one new confraternity (Notre-Dame Auxiliatrice) is known to have been established between 1760 and 1840.

134 'Mémoire sur le diocèse de Québec' (1794), *MEQ*, II, 488.

135 AAQ, SM, I, 92, Brassier à Hubert (7 septembre 1791).

136 Ibid., RL, II, 65, Hubert à Cherrier (13 juillet 1793).

137 Lemieux, *Les Années difficiles*, 136.

138 Bishop Briand wrote to the residents of Sainte-Rose on 26 September 1768: 'I have worn many cassocks turned inside out, I do not have a piece of bread or a glass of wine to offer a friend. I am quite happy for the seminary to support me'; *RAQ 1929-1930*, 75.

139 Briand to P.-A. Porlier (24 March 1762), ibid., 51.

140 The 'Lettre de Mgr Hubert aux archiprêtres sur les moyens à prendre pour secourir les pauvres' (19 March 1789) is quite revealing on this point; *MEQ*, II, 377.

141 Quoted in Pierre Savard, *Aspects du catholicisme canadien-français au XIXe siècle* (Montréal: Fides, 1980), 28.

142 'Mémoire sur le diocèse de Québec' (1794), *MEQ*, II, 479.

143 Lemieux, *Les Années difficiles*, 132-5.

144 Second meeting of Craig and Plessis (27 May 1811), *MEQ*, III, 65.

145 AAQ, RL, VII, 81, Plessis à Roux (4 décembre 1809).

146 Ibid., 131-2, Plessis à Roux (22 mars 1810).

147 ACAM, RLL, II, 129-30, Lartigue à William Poynter, vicaire apostolique de Londres (12 janvier 1823).

148 *Le Canadien*, 18 décembre 1822.

149 Lartigue to the editor of *Le Canadien*, signed 'A Canadian priest', published 17 November 1837.

150 Edgar McInnis, *Canada: A Political and Social History* (New York–Toronto: Holt, Rinehart and Winston, 1967), 215–16.

151 ACAM, RLL, IV, 256, Lartigue à Keller, curé de Sorel (25 août 1827).

152 Ibid., 294–5, Lartigue à Panet (1 décembre 1827).

153 *La Minerve*, 30 juillet 1827.

154 Lemieux, *Les Années difficiles*, 215–16.

155 Plessis to the prefect of the Congregation for the Propagation of the Faith (26 July 1818), quoted in Lemieux, *L'Établissement de la première province ecclésiastique au Canada, 1783-1844* (Montréal: Fides, 1968), 85.

156 These are three separate titles. A vicar-general is not necessarily a bishop, but assists the bishop in his diocese. An auxiliary bishop assists his superior, who is charge of the diocese; he is also a suffragan if he is responsible for a district within the diocese.

157 These are the figures provided by Bishop Plessis in a report delivered to the Congregation for the Propagation of the Faith. See Lemieux, *l'Établissement*, 112. Cape Breton Island was incorporated into the district of Prince Edward Island on 1 February 1820.

158 Thériault, 'L'Acadianisation', 308.

159 Ibid., 309.

160 G. Edward MacDonald, 'MacEachern, Angus Bernard', *DCB*, VI, 448. MacEachern's relations with the bishops of Quebec would later turn sour.

161 On these questions, see Thériault, 'L'Acadie, 1763–1978', 53–6, and 'L'Acadianisation', 298–9.

162 See ibid.

163 Antoine Bernard, *Histoire de la survivance acadienne, 1755–1935* (Montréal: Les Clercs de Saint-Viateur, 1935), 247.

164 See Thériault, 'L'Acadianisation', 310, 311. During the final years of his episcopate Bishop Plessis seems to have changed his view of this situation and endeavoured to provide French-speaking bishops for the Acadians.

165 Panet to H.-J. Tétreau, missionary in Richibouctou (14 April 1830), quoted in ibid, 311.

166 Gagnon to Plessis (31 March 1822), quoted in ibid.

167 One case is known: in 1785 Jean Doucet of Rustico was allowed by the bishop to carry out certain functions normally reserved for priests. See Pineau, *Le Clergé français*, 57.

168 Thériault, 'L'Acadianisation', 315.

169 See Gérald C. Boudreau, 'Sigogne: Artisan de la soumission religieuse et civile', in Boudreau, ed., *Une dialectique du pouvoir en Acadie: Église et autorité* (Montréal: Fides, 1991), 184.

170 Boudreau, *Le Père Sigogne et les Acadiens du sud-ouest de la Nouvelle-Écosse* (Montréal: Bellarmin, 1992), 77.

171 Lucien Lemieux, 'Provencher, Joseph-Norbert', *DCB*, VIII, 720.

172 Papineau to Julie Papineau (27 February 1821), *RAQ, 1953–1955*, 199.

173 Provencher to Plessis (16 January 1821), quoted in G. Dugas, *Monseigneur Provencher et les missions de la Rivière-Rouge* (Montréal: C.O. Beauchemin et Fils, 1889), 104.

174 These figures are provided by *Le Spectateur canadien*, which used statistics furnished by the Legislative Assembly in 1820. See Lemieux, *Les Année difficiles*, 188.

175 *Le Canadien*, 18 avril 1821.

176 Audet, *Le Système scolaire*, V, 63.

177 ACAM, RLL, V, 55, Lartigue à Mgr Panet (24 mars 1829).

178 'Mandement de Mgr Lartigue' (12 March 1839), *MEM*, I, 49.

179 AAQ, RL, IX, 170, Plessis à Roux, supérieur du Séminaire de Saint-Sulpice à Montréal (27 juin 1817).

180 ACAM, 901.114, 817–11, Roux à Plessis (2 septembre 1817).

181 Ibid., RLL, IV, 180, Lartigue à Panet (25 novembre 1826).

182 Plessis to Jean-Baptiste Saint-Germain, parish priest of Terrebonne (25 January 1822), quoted in Lemieux, *Les Années difficiles*, 207.

183 Ibid., 193–4.

184 ACAM, RLL, VIII, 133, Lartigue à Mgr Turgeon (28 février 1836).

185 Ibid., 183, Lartigue à Signay (1er mai 1836).

186 Ibid., VI, 167–8, Lartigue à Provencher (13 décembre 1831).

187 Quoted in a letter (signed 'idem') from Lartigue to the editor of the Quebec *Gazette*; ACAM, 780.034, 832–1.

188 NAC, FM, 24, B-6, III, 1405, Lartigue à Denis-Benjamin Viger (5 juin 1832).

189 Quoted in Fernand Ouellet, *Papineau* (Québec: Presses de l'Université Laval, 1970), 46.

190 Speech by L.-J. Papineau, reported in *La Minerve*, 21 janvier 1833.

191 Ibid., 4 décembre 1834.

192 ACAM, RLL, VI, p. 228, Lartigue à Panet (18 février 1832).

193 Quoted in Chaussé, *Jean-Jacques Lartigue*, 194.

194 ACAM, 295.103, 837-2, Blanchet à Bourget (25 octobre 1837).

195 'Premier mandement à l'occasion des troubles de 1837', *MEM*, I, 16.

196 Claude Bressolette, *L'Abbé Maret: Le Combat d'un théologien pour une démocratie chrétienne, 1830-1851* (Paris: Beauchesne, 1977), 495.

197 *La Minerve*, 30 octobre 1837.

198 ACAM, 901.106, 838-4, Letter from a group of political prisoners to Bishop Lartigue (6 juin 1838).

199 ACAM, RLL, VIII, 445, Lartigue à Signay (2 novembre 1837).

200 *L'Ami du Peuple*, 31 octobre 1837.

201 Proceedings of the meeting on 4 November 1837, recorded by the superior of the Seminary of Saint-Hyacinthe, cited in C.-P. Choquette, *Histoire du Séminaire de Saint-Hyacinthe depuis sa fondation jusqu'à nos jours*, 2 vols (Montréal: Imprimerie de l'Institut des sourds-muets, 1911-12), I, 203.

202 ACAM, 295.101, 837-44, Signay à Lartigue (14 novembre 1837).

203 *MEM*, I, 23-4.

204 Ibid., 24-9.

205 Archives du Séminaire de Saint-Sulpice à Montréal, S. 24, T. 73, no. 43, p. 26, Pierre Rousseau, 'Notes biographiques et historiques sur J.-J. Lartigue'.

206 ACAM, RLL, IX, p. 47, Lartigue à G.-A. Belcourt, missionnaire à la Rivière-Rouge, (24 avril 1838).

207 Ibid.

208 ACAM, RLB, II, 73, Bourget à Manseau (2 avril 1840).

209 Michel Brunet, 'L'Église catholique du Bas-Canada et le partage du pouvoir à l'heure d'une nouvelle donne', *Rapport de la Société historique du Canada* (1969): 45.

210 Archives du Séminaire de Saint-Sulpice à Paris, 99-37, Quiblier à Carrière (1er août 1838).

211 René Hardy, 'Odin, Henriette (Feller)', *DCB*, IX, 609.

CHAPTER THREE

1 Gillian T. Cell, *English Enterprise in Newfoundland, 1577-1660* (Toronto: University of Toronto Press, 1969); and Gillian T. Cell, ed., *Newfoundland Discovered: English Attempts at Colonisation, 1610-1630* (London: Hakluyt Society, 1982).

2 Louis B. Wright, *Religion and Empire: The Alliance Between Piety and Commerce in English Expansion, 1558-1625* (Chapel Hill: University of North Carolina Press, 1943), 134-49.

3 Hans Rollmann, 'Puritans', *Encyclopedia of Newfoundland and Labrador*, IV, 481-2.

4 Luca Codignola, *The Coldest Harbour of the Land: Simon Stock and Lord Baltimore's Colony in Newfoundland, 1621-1649*, trans. Anita Weston (Kingston–Montreal: McGill–Queen's University Press, 1988), 43-7, 53-4. See also Raymond J. Lahey, 'The Role of Religion in Lord Baltimore's Colonial Enterprise', *Maryland Historical Magazine* 72 (1977): 492-511; and Raymond J. Lahey, 'Avalon: Lord Baltimore's Colony in Newfoundland', in G.M. Story, ed., *Early European Settlement and*

Exploitation in Atlantic Canada (St John's: Memorial University of Newfoundland, 1982), 115–37.

5 Hans Rollmann, 'Anglicans, Puritans, and Quakers', unpublished paper, 4.

6 John Reid, *Sir William Alexander and North American Colonization: A Reappraisal* (Edinburgh: Centre of Canadian Studies, University of Edinburgh, 1990), 6.

7 Hans Rollmann, 'Quakers', *Encyclopedia of Newfoundland and Labrador*, IV, 487–8.

8 Ruth M. Christensen, 'The Establishment of SPG Missions in Newfoundland, 1703–1783', *Historical Magazine of the Protestant Episcopal Church* 20 (1951); 207–29.

9 Fred Crabb, 'The Church in the North', in Richard C. Davis, ed., *Rupert's Land: A Cultural Tapestry* (Waterloo, Ont.: Wilfrid Laurier University Press, 1988), 213.

10 Glyndwr Williams, 'Highlights of the First 200 Years of the Hudson's Bay Company', *The Beaver* (Autumn 1970): 10–11.

11 Arthur S. Morton, *A History of the Canadian West 1870–71*, 2nd ed., ed. Lewis G. Thomas (Toronto: University of Toronto Press, 1973), 102.

12 Philip Carrington, *The Anglican Church in Canada: A History* (Toronto: Collins, 1963), 31, 36. Charles Bruce Ferguson, 'Harrison, John', *DCB*, 11, 274–5; James Lambert, 'Brooke, John', *DCB*, IV, 103–5.

13 It is impossible to determine the exact population of Newfoundland at this date. For reliable estimates, see Grant Head, *Eighteenth Century Newfoundland: A Geographer's Perspective* (Toronto: McClelland and Stewart, 1976), esp. 82–4; and W. Gordon Handcock, *So Longe as there comes noe women: Origins of English Settlement in Newfoundland* (St John's: Breakwater Books, 1989), esp. 97. The figure of >10,000 for the 1780s is a conservative one, as the total 'wintering' population may have been greater than 15,000 by the end of the decade. An additional 10,000–15,000 people remained only for the annual summer fishery. The only sources of information that purport to survey all areas of settlement are the reports of the governors. These have been tabulated by Alison Earle, and the figures for 1786 show a total population of 16,427; see Alison Earle, 'Distribution of Roman Catholics and Protestants', unpublished report.

14 Barry Gough, *Canada* (Englewood Cliffs, NJ: Prentice-Hall, 1975), 38–9.

15 John S. Moir, *Enduring Witness: A History of the Presbyterian Church in Canada* (Toronto: Presbyterian Church in Canada, n.d.), 47.

16 Ronald Rudin, *The Forgotten Quebecers* (Ville Saint-Laurent, Quebec: Institut québécois de recherche sur la culture, 1985), 57–9.

17 John Webster Grant, *A Profusion of Spires: Religion in Nineteenth-Century Ontario* (Toronto: University of Toronto Press, 1988), 21.

18 For a concise description of these conditions, see Phillip Buckner, *English Canada— The Founding Generations: British Migration to British North America, 1815–1865* (London: Canadian High Commission, n.d.), 18. See also Phillip Buckner, 'The Peopling of Canada', *History Today* 43 (November 1993): 53.

19 USPG, Series B, vol. 6, fol. 179 rv: Laurence Coughlan to USPG (13 October 1769); and ibid., fol. 213 r: Governor Richard Edwards to Charles Garland and Robert Gray, Justices of the Peace for Conception Bay (31 August 1779).

20 The first SPG missionary was John Jackson; see Christensen, 'The Establishment of SPG Missions', 211. The first Methodist preacher was Laurence Coughlan; see

John Webster Grant, 'Methodist Origins in Atlantic Canada', in Charles H.H. Scobie and John Webster Grant, eds, *The Contribution of Methodism to Atlantic Canada* (Montreal–Kingston: McGill–Queen's University Press, 1992), 32–52. The first Presbyterian clergyman in the Atlantic region was James Lyon; see Moir, *Enduring Witness*, 38. The first English-speaking priest in the Maritimes was James Jones; see Terrence Murphy, 'James Jones and the Establishment of Roman Catholic Church Government in the Maritime Provinces, 1785–1801', CCHA, *Study Sessions* 48 (1981): 26–42. The priest who regularized Roman Catholic church government in Newfoundland was James Louis O'Donel; see Raymond J. Lahey, *James Louis O'Donel in Newfoundland, 1784–1807: The Establishment of the Roman Catholic Church* (St John's: Newfoundland Historical Society, pamphlet no. 8, 1984). The first Lutheran minister in Upper Canada was Samuel Schwerdeferger; see Grant, *Profusion of Spires*, 39. The first Dutch Reformed clergyman in Upper Canada was Robert McDowell; see John S. Moir, 'Robert McDowell and the Dutch Reformed Mission to Canada', *de Halve Moen* 53, 2 (Summer 78): 4–14.

21 For a detailed account of this group of merchants, see Allen B. Robertson, 'John Wesley's Nova Scotia Businessmen: Halifax Methodist Merchants, 1815–1855', (Ph.D. thesis, Queen's University, 1990), 198.

22 Allen B. Robertson, 'Barry, Robert', *DCB*, VII, 52; G.S. French, 'Man, James', *DCB*, V, 573; D.A. Sutherland, 'Marchinton, Philip', *DCB*, V, 574–5; C. Bruce Fergusson, 'Perkins, Simeon', *DCB*, V, 664–5; E. Arthur Betts, *Bishop Black and His Preachers* (Halifax: Maritime Conference Archives of the United Church of Canada, Pine Hill Divinity College, 1976), 30–6.

23 [St David's Presbyterian Church Bicentennial Committee], *The Dissenting Church of Christ at St. John's, 1775–1975* (St John's: St David's Presbyterian Church, 1975), 1–39.

24 Juw fon Wearinga, 'The First Protestant Ordination in Canada: The Story of Bruin Romkes Comingo, 1723–1820', *The Bulletin*, United Church Committee on Archives (1958): 19–32; Ronald Rompkey, 'Comingo, Bruin Romkes', *DCB*, V, 199–200.

25 James W. StG. Walker, 'George, David', *DCB*, V, 340–2.

26 Mark A. Noll, *A History of Christianity in the United States and Canada* (Grand Rapids, Mich.: William B. Eerdman's Publishing, 1992), 108.

27 J.M. Bumsted, *The Peoples of Canada*, 2 vols (Toronto: Oxford University Press, 1992), I, 172.

28 Stephen Davidson, 'Burton, John', *DCB*, VII, 122–4.

29 Grant, *Profusion of Spires*, 42.

30 Goldwin French, *Parsons and Politics: The Role of the Wesleyan Methodists in Upper Canada and the Maritimes from 1780 to 1885* (Toronto: Ryerson Press, 1962), 33.

31 J.M. Bumsted, 'Highland Emigration to the Island of St John and the Scottish Catholic Church, 1769–1774', *Dalhousie Review* 58, 4 (1978–9): 511–27; Bumsted, 'The Scottish Catholic Church and Prince Edward Island, 1770–1810', in Terrence Murphy and Cyril J. Byrne, eds, *Religion and Identity: The Experience of Irish and Scottish Catholics in Atlantic Canada* (St John's: Jesperson Press, 1987), 18–33.

32 John Webster Grant, *Moon of Wintertime: Missionaries and the Indians of Canada in*

Encounter since 1534 (Toronto: University of Toronto Press, 1984), 71–2. See also C. Thomas, 'Wood, Thomas', *DCB*, IV, 775–6.

33 L.F.S. Upton, *Micmacs and Colonists: Indian-White Relations in the Maritimes, 1713–1867* (Vancouver: University of British Columbia, 1979), 154; K. Brooks, 'The Effect of the Catholic Missionaries on the Micmac Indians of Nova Scotia, 1610–1986', *Nova Scotia Historical Review* VI, 1 (1986): 107–15.

34 Judith Fingard, 'The New England Company and the New Brunswick Indians, 1786–1826: A Comment on the Colonial Perversion of British Benevolence', *Acadiensis*, 1, 2 (Spring 1972): 29–42.

35 Grant, *Moon of Wintertime*, 72–3. See also Douglas Leighton, 'The Ethnohistory of Missions in Southwestern Ontario', *Journal of the Canadian Church Historical Society* 26, 2 (October 1984): 52–3.

36 L.F.S. Upton, 'The Extermination of the Beothuks of Newfoundland', *CHR* 58, 2 (June 1977): 133–53.

37 Ibid.

38 W.H. Whiteley, 'The Establishment of the Moravian Mission in Labrador and British Policy, 1763–83', *CHR* 45, 1 (March 1964): 29–50.

39 Ibid., 45.

40 James K. Hiller, 'The Foundation and the Early Years of the Moravian Mission in Labrador, 1752–1805' (M.A. thesis, Memorial University of Newfoundland, 1965), 159 ff.

41 Ibid., 163.

42 Whiteley, 'The Establishment of the Moravian Mission', 48.

43 A.H. Young, 'The Revd John Langhorn, Church of England Missionary at Fredericksburgh and Ernesttown, 1787–1813', *Ontario Historical Society Papers and Records* XXIII (1926): 553, 558. See also Curtis Fahey, *In His Name: The Anglican Experience in Upper Canada, 1791–1854* (Ottawa: Carleton University Press, 1991), 14.

44 Fahey, *In His Name*, 15.

45 Hans Rollmann, 'John Jones, James O'Donel, and the Question of Religious Toleration in Eighteenth-Century Newfoundland', *Newfoundland Quarterly* 80, 1 (Summer 1984): 23–7.

46 H.W. Baker, 'The History of the United Church Archives', UCCA, *The Bulletin*, 1 (1948): 15–16.

47 Thomas R. Millman, *Jacob Mountain, First Lord Bishop of Quebec: A Study in Church and State, 1793–1825* (Toronto: University of Toronto Press, 1947), 85–6.

48 Ibid., 135.

49 United Church Archives, Wesleyan Methodist Church (Great Britain), Foreign Missions, Box 1, file 16, William Bulpitt to Mr Smith (n.d.; copy).

50 Terrence Murphy, 'The Emergence of Maritime Catholicism, 1781–1830', *Acadiensis* 13, 2 (1984): 29–49; Grant, *Profusion of Spires*, 22. The suggestion by Alexander Macdonnel, cited by Grant, that the Protestants had profit in mind is not supported by evidence.

51 Edmund Burke, *Letter of Instruction to the Catholic Missionaries of Nova Scotia and Its Dependencies, by the Reverend Mr. Burke* (Halifax: A. Gay, 1804), 3.

52 Since Nova Scotia at this time included New Brunswick, the act extended to the latter as well. The Assembly of Prince Edward Island passed an act establishing the Church of England in 1802.

53 Judith Fingard, *The Anglican Design in Loyalist Nova Scotia, 1783–1816* (London: Society for the Promotion of Christian Knowledge, 1972). See also Judith Fingard, 'Inglis, Charles', *DCB*, V, 444–8. For a much more favourable judgement of Inglis, see Brian Cuthbertson, *The First Bishop: A Biography of Charles Inglis* (Halifax: Waegwoltic Press, 1987).

54 Charles Inglis, *Steadfastness in Religion and Loyalty Recommended, in a Sermon preached before the Legislature of His Majesty's province of Nova Scotia in the Parish Church of St. Paul at Halifax, on Sunday, April 7, 1793* (Halifax: J. Howe, 1793), as quoted in Fingard, *The Anglican Design*, 30.

55 Hans Rollmann, 'Laurence Coughlan and the Origins of Newfoundland Methodism', in Scobie and Grant, eds, *The Contribution of Methodism*, 53–78. See also Arthur E. Kewley, 'The First Fifty Years of Methodism in Newfoundland, 1765–1815: Was It Authentic Wesleyanism?', *Journal of the Canadian Church Historical Society* 19, 1–2 (March/June 1977): 6–26; and Grant, 'Methodist Origins in Atlantic Canada', in Scobie and Grant, eds, *The Contribution of Methodism*, 32–52.

56 John Wesley to Lawrence Conghlan, 27 August 1768, *The Works of John Wesley*, 3rd ed. (Grand Rapids, Mich.: Baker Book House, 1966), III, 340–1.

57 The literature on Alline is very extensive. The most important works include Maurice Armstrong, *The Great Awakening in Nova Scotia: 1776–1809* (Hartford, Conn.: American Society of Church History, 1948); J.M. Bumsted, *Henry Alline, 1748–1784* (Toronto: University of Toronto Press, 1971; repr. Hantsport, NS: Lancelot Press, 1984); Gordon Stewart and George Rawlyk, *A People Highly Favoured of God: The Nova Scotia Yankees and the American Revolution* (Toronto: Macmillan, 1972); J.M. Bumsted, 'Alline, Henry', *DCB*, IV, 16–20. G.A. Rawlyk, *Ravished by the Spirit: Religious Revivals, Baptists, and Henry Alline* (Kingston–Montreal: McGill–Queen's University Press, 1984); James Beverley and Barry Moody, eds, *The Life and Journal of The Rev. Mr. Henry Alline* (Hantsport, NS: Lancelot Press, 1982); George A. Rawlyk, ed., *The Sermons of Henry Alline* (Hantsport, NS: Lancelot Press, 1986).

58 On Payzant, see B. Cuthbertson, 'Payzant, John', *DCB*, VI, 573–4; and Brian Cuthbertson, ed., *The Journal of the Reverend John Payzant, 1749–1834* (Hantsport, NS: Lancelot Press, 1981).

59 George A. Rawlyk, 'From Newlight to Baptist: Harris Harding and the Second Great Awakening in Nova Scotia', in Barry M. Moody, ed., *Repent and Believe: The Baptist Experience in Maritime Canada* (Hantsport, NS: Lancelot Press, 1980), 1–26; reprinted in George A. Rawlyk, *Wrapped Up In God: A Study of Several Canadian Revivals and Revivalists* (Burlington, Ont.: Welch Publishing Co., 1988), 76–95. For older studies of Maritime Baptist origins, see E.M. Saunders, *History of the Baptists of the Maritime Provinces* (Halifax: J. Burgoyn, 1902); and G.E. Levy, *The Baptists of the Maritime Provinces, 1753–1946* (Saint John, NB: Barnes-Hopkins, 1946).

60 Betts, *Bishop Black*; G.S. French, 'Black, William', *DCB*, VI, 62–7; and Grant, 'Methodist Origins in Atlantic Canada', in Scobie and Grant, eds, *The Contribution of Methodism*.

61 Kewley, 'The First Fifty Years'; and Hans Rollmann, 'The Origins of Newfoundland Methodism: 1766–1791', unpublished manuscript.

62 On Garretson's role in Nova Scotia, see Rawlyk, *Wrapped Up in God*, 55–75; and Rawlyk, 'Garretson, Freeborn', *DCB*, VI, 275–7.

63 French, *Parsons and Politics*, 54.

64 John Carroll, *Case and His Cotemporaries*, 5 vols. (Toronto: Rose, 1867–77), I, 8. See also John S. Moir, *The Church in the British Era: From the British Conquest to Confederation*, vol. II in John Webster Grant, ed. *A History of the Christian Church in Canada* (Toronto: McGraw-Hill Ryerson, 1972), 85.

65 Carroll, *Case and His Cotemporaries*, I, 7–8. See also Grant, *Profusion of Spires*, 45.

66 On Dunham, Ryan, and Case see Carroll, *Case and His Cotemporaries*, I, *passim*. See also G.S. French, 'Ryan, Henry', *DCB*, VI, 670–6; and French, 'Case, William', *DCB*, VIII, 132–4.

67 On Bangs, see Carroll, *Case and His Cotemporaries*, I, 27–9; and G.S. French, 'Bangs, Nathan', *DCB*, IX, 26–7.

68 Rollmann, 'Coughlan and the Origins of Methodism', in Scobie and Grant, eds, *The Contribution of Methodism*.

69 Stewart and Rawlyk, *A People Highly Favoured of God*, *passim*.

70 Elizabeth Gillan Muir, *Petticoats in the Pulpit: The Story of Early Nineteenth-Century Methodist Preachers in Upper Canada* (Toronto: United Church Publishing House, 1991).

71 Carroll, *Case and His Cotemporaries*, I, 224.

72 See, for example, Charles Inglis to William Morice, 16 August 1799: 'The New Lights are, almost to a man, violent Republicans and Democrats'; PANS, Copies of Inglis Letters (1798–1811), as quoted in Judith Tulloch, 'Conservative Opinion in Nova Scotia during an Age of Revolution, 1789–1815' (M.A. thesis, Dalhousie University, 1972).

73 William Black to Francis Asbury, as quoted in M. Richey, *A Memoir of the Late Rev. William Black* (Halifax: W. Cunnabel, 1839), 310.

74 Murphy, 'The Emergence of Maritime Catholicism', 42.

75 Hans Rollmann, 'Religious Enfranchisement and Roman Catholics in Eighteenth-Century Newfoundland', in Murphy and Byrne, eds, *Religion and Identity*, 34–52.

76 John Garner, 'The Enfranchisement of Roman Catholics in the Maritimes', *CHR* 34, 3 (1953): 203–18.

77 For a detailed analysis of this contrast in Upper Canada, see William Westfall, *Two Worlds: The Protestant Culture of Nineteenth Century Ontario* (Kingston–Montreal: McGill–Queen's University Press, 1989), esp. 19–49.

78 Great Britain. Parliament. House of Commons. Sessional Papers. 1863 (430), XXXVIII, 21.

79 R. Cole Harris and John Warkentin, *Canada Before Confederation* (Toronto: Oxford University Press, 1974), 180.

80 Ibid. See also *Statistics of Canada, IV: Censuses of Canada, 1665–1871* (Ottawa: Government of Canada, 1876), 132.

81 Harris and Warkentin, *Canada Before Confederation*, 180. See also J.B. Brebner, *Canada: A Modern History* (Ann Arbor: University of Michigan Press, 1960), 193.

82 Harris and Warkentin, *Canada Before Confederation*, 180; *Censuses of Canada, 1665–1871*, 94, 125.

83 Gerald M. Craig, *Upper Canada: The Formative Years, 1784–1841* (London and New York: McClelland and Stewart and Oxford University Press, 1963), 262.

84 Robert Gourlay, *Statistical Account of Upper Canada: Compiled with a View to a Grand System of Emigration*, 2 vols. (London: Simpkin, Marshall, 1822), I, 139; *Censuses of Canada, 1665–1871*, 83, 134.

85 Buckner, *English Canada*, 18. See also Buckner, 'The Peopling of Canada', 53.

86 *Censuses of Canada, 1665–1871*, 135.

87 Grant, *Profusion of Spires*, 79–80.

88 Ibid., 83.

89 W. John McIntyre, *Children of Peace* (Kingston–Montreal: McGill–Queen's University Press, 1994); Albert Schrauwers, *Awaiting the Millenium: The Children of Peace and the Village of Hope, 1812–1889* (Toronto: University of Toronto Press, 1993).

90 D.G. Bell, ed., *Newlight Baptist Journals of James Manning and James Innis* (Hantsport: Lancelot Press, 1984), and D.G. Bell, 'The Allinite Tradition and the New Brunswick Free Christian Baptists, 1830–1875', in Robert S. Wilson, ed., *An Abiding Conviction: Maritime Baptists and Their World* (Hantsport, NS: Lancelot Press, 1988).

91 For background information, see Leigh Eric Schmidt, *Holy Fairs: Scottish Communions and American Revivals in the Early Modern Period* (Princeton, NJ: Princeton University Press, 1989).

92 Laurie Stanley, *The Well-Watered Garden: The Presbyterian Church in Cape Breton, 1798–1860* (Sydney, NS: University College of Cape Breton Press, 1983), 133 ff; David E. Weale, 'God's Exiles: A Theology for Immigrants', *Canadian Society of Church History Papers* (1977): 27–40; John Webster Grant, 'Burning Bushes: Flames of Revival in Nineteenth Century Canadian Presbyterianism', *Canadian Society of Church History Papers* (1991): 97–112; Marguerite Van Die, 'The "Double Vision": Evangelical Piety as Derivative and Indigenous in Victorian English Canada', in Mark A. Noll, David W. Bebbington, and George A. Rawlyk, eds, *Evangelicalism: Comparative Studies of Popular Protestantism in North America, the British Isles and Beyond* (New York: Oxford University Press, 1994), 253–74.

93 French, *Parsons and Politics*, 54–67.

94 Ibid., 203.

95 Ibid., 73.

96 Ibid., 77.

97 For a discussion of developments among both Methodists and Newlights, cast in terms of the transition from 'sect' to 'free church' types, see S.D. Clark, *Church and Sect in Canada* (Toronto: University of Toronto Press, 1948).

98 Rawlyk, 'From New Light to Baptist', in Moody, ed., *Repent and Believe*, 1–26.

99 For the ideal conceptualization of womanhood, see Barbara Welter, 'The Cult of True Womanhood', *American Quarterly* 18 (Summer 1966): 151–74.

100 The notion of 'separate spheres' for men and women has recently been subjected to criticism. See, for example, Linda Kerber, 'Separate Spheres, Female Worlds, Woman's Place: The Rhetoric of Women's History', *Journal of American History* 75, 1 (June 1988): 9–39.

101 I am indebted for many of the points which follow to Marguerite Van Die, '"A Women's Awakening": Evangelical Belief and Female Spirituality in Mid-Nineteenth-Century Canada', unpublished paper delivered to the annual meeting of the Canadian Historical Association, 1991.

102 Allen B. and Carolene E.B. Robertson, eds, *Memoir of Mrs. Eliza Ann Chipman, Wife of the Rev. William Chipman, of Pleasant Valley, Cornwallis* (Hantsport, NS: Lancelot Press, 1989).

103 Ibid., 3.

104 Ibid., 45.

105 Ibid.

106 Fahey, *In His Name*, 39.

107 Ibid., 103–7.

108 French, *Parsons and Politics*, 73.

109 Harry A. Renfree, *Heritage and Horizon: The Baptist Story in Canada* (Mississauga, Ont.: Canadian Baptist Federation, 1988), 76.

110 Ibid., 76–7; and Theo T. Gibson, *Robert Alexander Fyfe: His Contemporaries and His Influence* (Burlington, Ont.: Welch Publishing, 1987), 45.

111 Frank S. Boyd, 'Preston, Richard', *DCB*, VIII, 968–70.

112 Grant, *Profusion of Spires*, 110–11.

113 Murphy, 'The Emergence of Maritime Catholicism', 46; Grant, *Profusion of Spires*, 84.

114 D.C. Masters, *Protestant Church Colleges in Canada: A History* (Toronto: University of Toronto Press, 1966), 73; French, *Parsons and Politics*, 77.

115 Millman, *Jacob Mountain*, 186–92; and T.R. Millman, *The Life of the Right Reverend, the Honorable Charles James Stewart* (London, Ont.: Huron College, 1953), 93–4. See also Fahey, *In His Name*, 39.

116 Masters, *Protestant Church Colleges*, 82. Of 37 residents Anglican clergymen of Nova Scotia who gathered in Halifax in 1846 for a convocation, 26 had been educated at King's. See Judith Fingard, 'Inglis, John', *DCB*, VII, 435.

117 Grant, *Profusion of Spires*, 49.

118 Ibid., 70.

119 Ibid.

120 Levy, *Baptists of the Maritime Provinces*, 131.

121 Grant, *Profusion of Spires*, 71–2.

122 For what follows, see Muir, *Petticoats in the Pulpit*.

123 Ibid., 133.

124 A.A. Johnston, *History of the Catholic Church in Eastern Nova Scotia*, 2 vols (Antigonish, NS: St Francis Xavier University Press, 1960–1971), II, esp. parts 1 and 2.

125 For what follows, see Stanley, *The Well-Watered Garden*.

126 Ibid., 99–101.

127 T.C. Boon, *The Anglican Church from the Bay to the Rockies* (Toronto: Ryerson, 1962); J.E. Foster, 'The Anglican Clergy in the Red River Settlement, 1820–1826' (M.A. thesis, University of Alberta, 1966).

128 Richard A. Willie, 'West, John', *DCB*, VII, 900–3.

129 S.M. Johnson and T.F. Bredin, 'Jones, David Thomas', *DCB*, VII, 454–5; J. E. Foster, 'Cockran, William', *DCB*, IX, 134–7.

130 Foster, 'Cockran, William', 134–5.

131 Frits Pannekoek, 'The Anglican Church and the Disintegration of Red River Society, 1818–1870', in R. Douglas Francis and Howard Palmer, eds, *The Prairie West: Historical Readings* (Edmonton: Pica Press, 1985); Frits Pannekoek, *A Snug Little Flock* (Winnipeg: Watson Publishing, 1991).

132 Grant, *Moon of Wintertime*, 87.

133 Upton, *Micmacs and Colonists*, 140; Judith Fingard, 'English Humanitarianism and the Colonial Mind: Walter Bromley in Nova Scotia, 1813–25', *CHR* LIV, 2 (June 1973): 136–42.

134 Upton, *Micmacs and Colonists*, 159.

135 Grant, *Moon of Wintertime*, 99.

136 Ibid.; and Foster, 'Cockran, William', 134–7.

137 Grant, *Moon of Wintertime*, 88.

138 On Jones, see Donald B. Smith, 'Jones, Peter', *DCB*, VIII, 439–43; and Donald B. Smith, *Sacred Feathers: The Reverend Peter Jones (Kahkewaquonaby) and the Mississauga Indians* (Lincoln and London: University of Nebraska Press, 1987).

139 Elizabeth Graham, *Medicine Man to Missionary: Missionaries as Agents of Change among the Indians of Southern Ontario, 1784–1867* (Toronto: Peter Martin Associates, 1975), 14–17.

140 Smith, *Sacred Feathers*, 90.

141 Ibid., 96.

142 Grant, *Moon of Wintertime*, 94.

143 James R. Miller, *Skyscrapers Hide the Heavens: A History of Indian-White Relations in Canada* (Toronto: University of Toronto Press, 1989), 111–12.

144 Grant, *Moon of Wintertime*, 93–4.

145 Terrence Murphy, 'Priests, People, and Polity: Trusteeism in the First Catholic Congregation at Halifax, 1785–1801', in Murphy and Byrne, eds, *Religion and Identity*, 68–80; Terrence Murphy, 'Trusteeism in Atlantic Canada: The Struggle for Leadership among the Irish Catholics of Halifax, St. John's, and Saint John, 1780–1850', in Terrence Murphy and Gerald Stortz, eds, *Creed and Culture: The Place of English-speaking Roman Catholics in Canadian Society, 1750–1930* (Montreal–Kingston: McGill–Queen's University Press, 1993), 126–51. The best available treatment of the O'Grady affair at York is found in Curtis Fahey, 'O'Grady, William John', *DCB*, VII, 661–5, but see also J.E. Rea, *Bishop Alexander Macdonell and the Politics of Upper Canada* (Toronto: Ontario Historical Society, 1974), 97–112; and Grant, *Profusion of Spires*, 81–2.

146 Grant, *Profusion of Spires*, 108.

147 The literature on the British North American temperance movement includes James J. Talman, 'Pioneer Drinking Habits and the Rise of the Temperance Agitation in Upper Canada Prior to 1840', in F. Armstrong, ed., *Aspects of Nineteenth-Century Ontario* (Toronto: University of Toronto Press, 1974); J.K. Chapman, 'The Mid-Nineteenth-Century Temperance Movement in New Brunswick and Maine', *CHR* XXXV (March 1954): 43–60, repr. in J.M. Bumsted, ed., *Canadian History Before Confederation: Essays and Interpretations* (Georgetown, Ont.: Irwin-Dorsey, 1972); James M. Clemens, 'Taste Not: Touch Not: Handle Not: A Study of the Social Assumptions of the Temperance Literature and Temperance Supporters in Canada West between 1839 and 1859', *Ontario History* LXIV, 3 (September 1972): 141–60;

G. Hildebrand, 'Les Débuts du mouvement de tempérance dans le Bas-Canada, 1828–1840' (M.A. thesis, McGill University, 1975); F.L. Barron, 'The Genesis of Temperance in Ontario, 1828–1850' (Ph.D. thesis, University of Guelph, 1976), and F.L. Barron. 'The American Origins of the Temperance Movement in Ontario, 1828–1850', *Canadian Review of American Studies* 11, 2 (Fall 1980): 131–50; T.W. Acheson, *Saint John: The Making of a Colonial Urban Community* (Toronto: University of Toronto Press, 1985), 138–59; Sandra Barry, ' "Shades of Vice . . . and Moral Glory": The Temperance Movement in Nova Scotia, 1828 to 1848' (M.A. thesis, University of New Brunswick, 1986); Jane Virginia Noel, 'Temperance and a New Social Order in Mid-Nineteenth Century Canada and Red River' (Ph.D. thesis, University of Toronto, 1987); Jan Noel, *Canada Dry: Temperance Crusaders before Confederation* (Toronto: University of Toronto Press, 1995).

148 Barron, 'Genesis of Temperance', 135–6.

149 Acheson, *Saint John*, 144.

150 Ibid., 140–1.

151 Ibid., 141–3.

152 Ibid., 144.

153 Ibid.

154 Barron, 'American Origins of the Temperance Movement', 138.

155 For a critical discussion of this interpretation of the temperance movement in American historiography, see Leonard I. Sweet, ed., *The Evangelical Tradition in America* (Macon, Ga.: Mercer University Press, 1984), 1–86. In Canada, the 'social control' interpretation is reflected mainly in Clemens, 'Taste Not: Touch Not: Handle Not', but see also Hildebrand, 'Les Débuts du mouvement de tempérance'. Barron, 'The American Origins of the Temperance Movement', ties the phenomenon to the requirements of emergent capitalism.

156 Acheson, *Saint John*, 145; Barron, 'The American Origins of the Temperance Movement', 141.

157 Allan Greer, 'The Sunday Schools of Upper Canada', *Ontario History* LXVII, 3 (September 1975): 169.

158 Neil Semple, ' "The Nurture and Admonition of the Lord": Nineteenth-Century Canadian Methodism's Response to "Childhood" ', *Histoire sociale/Social History* XIV, 27 (May 1981): 174–5.

159 Greer, 'The Sunday Schools', 169.

160 Semple, ' "The Nurture and Admonition of the Lord" ', 173.

161 For contrasting interpretations of the social function of Sunday schools in England, see E.P. Thompson, *The Making of the English Working-Class* (London: V. Gollancz, 1963), and Thomas Walter Laqueur, *Religion and Respectability: Sunday Schools and Working Class Culture, 1780–1850* (New Haven: Yale University Press, 1976).

162 The literature on Strachan is extensive. Among the items that may be consulted are G.M. Craig, 'Strachan, John', *DCB*, IX, 751–66; Sylvia Boorman, *John Toronto: A Biography of Bishop Strachan* (Toronto and Vancouver: Clarke Irwin, 1969); David Flint, *John Strachan: Pastor and Politician* (Toronto: Oxford University Press, 1971); and J.L. Henderson, *John Strachan, 1778–1867* (Toronto: University of Toronto Press, 1969).

163 R. Gidney, 'Ryerson, Egerton', *DCB*, XI, 784.
164 C.B. Sissons, *Egerton Ryerson: His Life and Letters*, 2 vols (Toronto: Clarke Irwin, 1937–47), I, 24–6.
165 Masters, *Protestant Church Colleges*, 23–5. See also Craig, 'Strachan, John', 758.
166 Masters, *Protestant Church Colleges*, 26; Craig, 'Strachan, John', 759.
167 Statutes of Upper Canada, 9 George IV, cap. 2.
168 Statutes of Upper Canada, 1 William IV, cap. 1.
169 Thomas R. Millman, 'Stewart, Charles James', *DCB*, VII, 827.
170 Craig, 'Strachan, John', 760–2.
171 Ibid., 760.
172 Masters, *Protestant Church Colleges*, 30; Grant, *Profusion of Spires*, 92–3.
173 Gidney, 'Ryerson, Egerton', 786.
174 Ibid.
175 Grant, *Profusion of Spires*, 93.
176 Statutes of Great Britain, 3 and 4 Victoria cap. 78. See John Moir, ed., *Church and State in Canada, 1627–1867: Basic Documents* (Toronto: McClelland and Stewart, 1967), 193–5.
177 Grant, *Profusion of Spires*, 100.
178 Buggey and Davies, 'McCulloch, Thomas', *DCB*, VII, 534.
179 Ibid.
180 Ibid.
181 Ibid., 536.
182 Masters, *Protestant Church Colleges*, 19.
183 Statutes of Nova Scotia, 9 George IV, cap. 6.
184 Moir, ed., *Church and State*, 57.
185 For the course of Catholic emancipation in the Maritimes, see John Garner, 'The Enfranchisement of Roman Catholics in the Maritimes', *CHR* XXXIV (September 1953): 203–18. See also Murphy, 'The Emergence of Maritime Catholicism', 41–2.
186 Hans Rollmann, 'Religious Enfranchisement and Roman Catholics in Eighteenth-Century Newfoundland', in Murphy and Byrne, eds, *Religion and Identity*, 34–52.
187 Raymond J. Lahey, 'Catholicism and Colonial Policy in Newfoundland, 1779–1832', in Murphy and Stortz, eds, *Creed and Culture*, 49–78.
188 Ibid.
189 Judith Fingard, 'Inglis, John', *DCB*, VII, 434; Craig, 'Strachan, John', 759–62; Grant, *Profusion of Spires*, 99–100; and Fahey, *In His Name*, 132–51.
190 Thomas R. Millman and A.R. Kelley, *Atlantic Canada to 1900: A History of the Anglican Church* (Toronto: Anglican Book Centre, 1983), 71.
191 Ibid.
192 Ibid., 94.
193 Monica Marston, 'Mountain, George Jehoshaphat', *DCB*, IX, 580.
194 Fahey, *In His Name*, 224.
195 Fingard, 'Inglis, John', 435.
196 These rough calculations are based on the following census figures: for Newfoundland, 96,295 in 1845 and 122,638 in 1857 (27% increase); for Nova Scotia, 202,575 in 1838 and 276,854 in 1851 (36% increase); for New Brunswick,

156,162 in 1840 and 193,800 in 1851 (34% increase); and for Prince Edward Island, 47,045 in 1841 and 62,678 in 1848 (34% increase). See *Censuses of Canada, 1665–1871*, 160, 246; 125, 232; 129, 224; 132, 174.

197 Rudin, *Forgotten Quebecers*, 61.

198 *Censuses of Canada, 1665–1871*, 131, 178.

199 Buckner, *English Canada*, 10.

200 Grant, *Profusion of Spires*, 152–3.

201 The figure varies according to region, but it was in all cases under 10% by mid-century. In Upper Canada, it had been 16% in 1842 but dropped to 4% by 1851–2. In Lower Canada, with its large French-speaking Catholic population, it was a mere 2% in 1844 but had declined to less than 1% in 1851–2. In Nova Scotia, the category of no specific affiliation was included for the first time in 1861, when it amounted to 7% of the total. No figures are available for New Brunswick. Only in Prince Edward Island did the number with no identifiable affiliation increase in absolute terms, but it jumped from 126 in 1841 to 434 in 1848, in both cases less than 1% of the total.

202 Grant, *Profusion of Spires*, 167.

203 Grant, *Moon of Wintertime*, 100–2; Gerald M. Hutchinson, 'Evans, James', *DCB*, VII, 275–8.

204 W.L. Norton, 'Introduction' to E.E. Rich and A.M. Johnson, *London Correspondence Inward from Eden Colville, 1849–1852* (London: Hudson's Bay Record Society, 1956), 1i.

205 Acheson, *Saint John*, 147.

206 Fahey, *In His Name*, 99–100.

207 Christopher Headon, 'Developments in Canadian Anglican Worship in Eastern and Central Canada: 1840–1868', *Journal of the Canadian Church Historical Society*, XVII, 2 (June 1975): 26–37.

208 Ibid.

209 Gregg Finley, 'Stained Glass and Stone Tracery: The Gothic Revival and the Shaping of Canadian Sensibilities', *British Journal of Canadian Studies* V, 1 (1990): 78–98; Gregg Finley, 'The Gothic Revival and the Victorian Church in New Brunswick: Toward a Strategy for Material Culture Research', *Material History Bulletin* 32 (Fall 1990): 1–16; Alan Gregg Finley, '"Habits of Reverence and Awe": Bishop John Medley and the Promise of Ecclesiology', *Journal of the Canadian Church Historical Society* XXV, 1 (April 1993): 3–22.

210 Robert L. Watson, *Christ Church Cathedral, Fredericton: A History* (Fredericton: Bishop and Chapter of Christ Church Cathedral, 1984).

211 Finley, '"Habits of Reverence and Awe"', 10.

212 Richard W. Vaudry, *The Free Church in Victorian Canada, 1844–1861* (Waterloo, Ont.: Wilfrid Laurier University Press, 1989).

213 Grant, *Profusion of Spires*, 124.

214 Richard A. Vaudry, 'Peter Brown, the Toronto Banner, and the Evangelical Mind in Victorian Canada', *Ontario History* LXXVII, 1 (March 1985): 5.

215 Moir, *Enduring Witness*, 104–5.

216 Westfall, *Two Worlds*, 50–81.

217 Ibid., 72–3.

218 Greer, 'The Sunday Schools', 180.

219 Phyllis D. Airhart, *Serving the Present Age: Revivalism, Progressivism, and the Methodist Tradition in Canada* (Montreal–Kingston: McGill–Queen's University Press, 1992), 6–7; Marguerite Van Die, *An Evangelical Mind: Nathanael Burwash and the Methodist Tradition in Canada, 1839–1918* (Kingston: McGill–Queen's University Press, 1989), 25.

220 Neil Semple, 'The Decline of Revival in Nineteenth-Century Central-Canadian Methodism: The Extraordinary Means of Grace', *Canadian Methodist Historical Society Papers* 2 (1977–80): 6–8; Robert J.A. Samms, 'Revivalism in Central Canadian Wesleyan Methodism, 1824–1860' (Ph.D. thesis, McGill University, 1984).

221 Semple, 'The Decline of Revival'; Neil Semple, 'The Quest for the Kingdom: Aspects of Protestant Revivalism in Nineteenth Century Ontario', in David Keane and Colin Reade, eds, *Old Ontario: Essays in Honour of J.M.S. Careless* (Toronto: Dundurn Press, 1990); Westfall, *Two Worlds*, 72.

222 On college revivals, see Van Die, *An Evangelical Mind*, 22–3, 50; Grant, *Profusion of Spires*, 154–5; Michael Gauvreau, 'Protestantism Transformed: Personal Piety and the Evangelical Social Vision', in George Rawlyk, ed., *The Canadian Protestant Experience, 1760 to 1990* (Burlington, Ont.: Welch Publishing Co., 1990); and A.C. Chute, *The Religious Life of Acadia* (Wolfville, NS: Acadia Alumni Association, 1933), 161, 171–2, 183, 187. I am indebted to Barry Moody for drawing my attention to this last source.

223 Westfall, *Two Worlds*, 73. P. Bush, 'The Rev. James Caughey and Wesleyan Methodist Revivalism in Nineteenth Century Canada', *Ontario History* 74, 3 (September 1987): 231–50.

224 Van Die, *An Evangelical Mind*, 25.

225 Phillip McCann, 'Culture, State Formation, and the Invention of Tradition: Newfoundland 1832–1855', *Journal of Canadian Studies* 23, 1 & 2 (Spring/Summer 1988): 86–103; reprinted in J.M. Bumsted, *Interpreting Canada's Past*, 2 vols, 2nd ed. (Toronto: Oxford University Press, 1993), II, 608–22.

226 N.G. Smith, 'Religious Tensions in Pre-Confederation Politics', *Canadian Journal of Theology* IX (1963): 250.

227 A.J.B. Johnston, 'Popery and Progress: Anti-Catholicism in Mid-Nineteenth Century Nova Scotia', *Dalhousie Review* LXIV, 1 (Spring 1984): 149.

228 Johnston, 'Popery and Progress', 159.

229 Acheson, *Saint John*, 105.

230 Hereward Senior, *Orangeism: The Canadian Phase* (Toronto: McGraw-Hill Ryerson, 1972); Cecil J. Houston and William J. Smyth, *The Sash Canada Wore* (Toronto: University of Toronto Press, 1980).

231 Acheson, *Saint John*, 113.

232 Smith, 'Religious Tensions', 252–3.

233 J.R. Miller, 'Anti-Catholic Thought in Victorian Canada', *CHR* LXVI, 4 (December 1985): 474–94.

234 Miller, 'Anti-Catholic Thought', 483.

235 Moir, *Church in the British Era*, 178.

236 Ibid., 179.

237 Grant, *Profusion of Spires*, 80–1, 114.

238 Westfall, *Two Worlds*, 159–77; Grant, *Profusion of Spires*, 73–5, 161.

239 Westfall, *Two Worlds*, 177–85; Grant, *Profusion of Spires*, 167.

240 Grant, *Moon of Wintertime*, 113.

241 Ibid., 113–4.

242 John Webster Grant, 'Missionaries and Messiahs in the Northwest', *Studies in Religion/Sciences religieuses* 9, 2 (1980): 125–36.

243 Norman James Williamson, 'Abishabis the Cree', *Studies in Religion/Sciences religieuses* 9, 2 (1980): 217–45.

244 Grant, 'Missionaries and Messiahs', 134.

245 Bruce Peel, 'Hunter, James', *DCB*, XI, 436–7.

246 Grant, *Moon of Wintertime*, 111–12.

247 Ibid., 112.

248 Olive Patricia Dickason, *Canada's First Nations: A History of Founding Peoples from Earliest Times* (Toronto: McClelland and Stewart, 1980), 250–1.

249 John S. Moir, *Church and State in Canada West: Three Studies in the Relationship of Denominationalism and Nationalism, 1841–67* (Toronto: University of Toronto Press, 1959), 130–2; Phillip McCann, 'The Politics of Denominational Education in the Nineteenth Century in Newfoundland', in W.A. McKim, ed., *The Vexed Question: Denominational Education in a Secular Age* (St John's: Breakwater Books, 1988), 31–7; Ian Ross Robertson, 'The Bible Question in Prince Edward Island from 1856 to 1860', *Acadiensis* 5, 4 (Spring 1976): 6–25.

250 John S. Moir, 'The Origin of the Separate School Question in Ontario', *Canadian Journal of Theology* V (1959): 105–18.

251 McCann, 'Politics of Denominational Education', 38, 40–2.

252 Grant, *Profusion of Spires*, 157.

253 Ibid., 166.

CHAPTER FOUR

1 Alexis de Barbézieux, *L'Église catholique au Canada* (Québec: Éditons de l'Action sociale catholique, 1914), 14, 17, 68–9, 77.

2 Richard Chabot, 'Côté, Cyrille-Hector-Octave', *DCB*, V, 208–11; Amand Parent, *The Life of the Rev. Amand Parent, the First French Canadian Ordained by the Methodist Church* (Toronto: William Briggs, 1887); J.B. Boucher-Belleville was also converted to Protestantism in these circumstances, although, oddly, this fact is not mentioned in Louis-Philippe Audet, 'Boucher-Belleville, Jean-Baptiste', *DCB*, X, 75–6.

3 René Hardy, 'La Rébellion de 1837–8 et l'essor du protestantisme canadien-français', *RHAF* 29, 2 (septembre 1975): 163–89. The British government, Hardy maintains, believed that it was necessary to uphold Catholicism in order to achieve political stability in Quebec. It therefore never gave financial support to these proselytizing campaigns. What Hardy seems to ignore, however, is the fact that London would never have provided funds for activities unconnected in some way with the established church. In addition, tactical support for the Catholic Church

in Quebec was not incompatible with a long-range strategy of linguistic and religious assimilation of French Canadians.

4 The FCMS was mainly aided by the Foreign Evangelical Society, another non-denominational organization. See Philippe Sylvain, 'Aperçu sur le prosélytisme protestant au Canada français', *Mémoires de la Société Royale du Canada* LV (1961), 3e série, sect. I, 65–74; Robert Merrill Black, 'Different Visions: The Multiplication of Protestant Missions to French-Canadian Roman Catholics', in J.S. Moir and C.T. McIntyre, eds, *Canadian Catholic and Protestant Missions* (New York: Peter Lang, 1988), 49–73. American support for the FCMS is disputed by Glen Scorgie; see his 'The Early Years of the French Canadian Missionary Society, 1838–50' (Master of Christian Studies thesis, Regent College, University of British Columbia, 1982).

Rivalry between Presbyterian and Baptist evangelists soon led the latter to seek separate funding from private American patrons; J.N. Cramp, *A Memoir of Madame Feller* (London: Elliott Stock, n.d.). [published in 1874]; W.N. Wyeth, *Henrietta Feller and the Grande Ligne Mission* (Philadelphia: 1898). Wyeth claims that the Baptist Home Missions gave Grande-Ligne $28,899 from 1849 to 1860. The Rockefellers gave $5,000 on one occasion and $10,000 on another to promote Baptist evangelization among the French Canadians. See David-Thiery Ruddel, *Le Protestantisme français au Québec, 1840–1919: 'Images' et témoignages* (Ottawa: National Museum of Man, 1983).

For support of Anglican proselytism, see John Irwin Cooper, *The Blessed Communion: The Origins and History of the Diocese of Montreal 1760–1969* (Montreal: Archives Committee of the Diocese of Montreal, 1960); Robert Merrill Black, 'A Crippled Crusade: Anglican Missions to French Canadian Roman Catholics in Lower Canada, 1835–1868' (Th.D. dissertation, Trinity College, University of Toronto, 1989).

5 See Claude Gilbert, 'Une communauté protestante de langue française dans l'Outaouais au XIXe siècle: Le Cas de Namur', *Cultures du Canada français* 7 (automne 1990): 79–87; Claude Gilbert, 'Le Protestantisme canadien-français en Outaouais au XIXe siècle: Namur, mission française de l'Église presbytérienne du Canada', *Outaouais* 3: 29–40.

6 Hardy, 'La Rébellion de 1837–8', 179.

7 See Ruddel, *Le Protestantisme français*, which reproduces the diary of a French colporteur working in the region north of Montreal in the 1840s.

8 The Presbyterians set up a school at Pointe-aux-Trembles in 1847 that eventually accommodated 250 students per year. The Baptists founded the Feller Institute at Grande-Ligne in 1855, although schooling was offered from the very beginning of the mission station. The Feller Institute housed as many as 190 students per year. The Anglicans instituted a normal school at St-Jean, south of Montreal, which was later moved to Sabrevois and finally to Montreal in 1882: 3,000 students were on the roll of this institution. The French Methodist Institute was established in 1878; located in downtown Montreal, it was later moved to Westmount and accommodated 90 students. It must be stressed, however, that not all the youngsters in these boarding schools were French Canadians. A sizeable proportion of the students at the Methodist Institute were English Canadians, while a certain number of Syrians and

Italians also attended. These statistics are drawn from Paul Villard, *Up to the Light: The Story of French Protestantism in Canada* (Toronto: United Church of Canada, 1928).

9 Parent, *The Life of the Rev. Amand Parent*; Louis-Georges Harvey, 'Parent, Amand', *DCB*, XIII, 809–10. Anglican missionaries working among the Amerindians in the lumber districts of the Ottawa valley apparently ministered to them in French. See Cooper, *Blessed Communion*, 157.

10 E.A. Therrien et al., *Baptist Work in French Canada* (Toronto: American Baptist Publication Society, n.d.), published around 1925; J.E. Duclos, *French Bi-Lingual Work in Alberta* (n.p. n.d.), pamphlet published around 1918.

11 Sylvain, 'Aperçu sur le prosélytisme protestant'; entries on *Le Semeur canadien* and *L'Aurore* in André Beaulieu et Jean Hamelin, eds, *La Presse québécoise des origines à nos jours* (Québec: Presses de l'Université Laval, 1973); United Church Archives, Toronto, *Missionary Work* (n.p. n.d.). This was a talk given under the auspices of the James Robertson Memorial Committee and probably delivered by Joseph E. Boucher, principal of the school at Pointe-aux-Trembles; Robert Lindsey, 'Evangelization of the French Canadians by the Presbyterian Church, 1863–1925', Presbyterian Church of Canada Archives (B.D. thesis, University of Toronto, 1956).

12 Marcel Trudel, *Chiniquy* (Trois-Rivières: Éditions du Bien Public, 1955). This work has not aged well; it is an excellent example of pious historical writing. See also Paul Laverdure, 'Charles Chiniquy: The Making of an Anti-Catholic Crusader', CCHA, *Historical Studies* 54 (1987); Yves Roby, 'Chiniquy, Charles', *DCB*, XII, 189–93. On Bracq, see Ruddel, *Protestantisme français*.

13 René Hardy, 'Odin, Henriette', *DCB*, IX, 607–10. Normandeau's words are cited in Joseph Boucher, 'Le Protestantisme français au Canada', in Hervé Fines, *Album du protestantisme français en Amérique du Nord* (Montréal: L'Aurore, 1972), 27. A description of Feller's activities is found in Cramp, *Memoir*.

14 For a discussion of tactics employed by peasants to enforce community standards, see Allan Greer, *The Patriots and the People: The Rebellion of 1837 in Rural Lower Canada* (Toronto: University of Toronto Press, 1993), 69–86, *passim*; René Hardy, 'Le Charivari dans la sociabilité rurale québécoise au XIXe siècle', in *De la sociabilité: Spécificité et mutations* (Montréal: Boréal, 1990), 59–72.

15 R.P. Duclos, *Histoire du protestantisme français au Canada et aux Etats-Unis*, 2 vols (Lausanne: Georges Bridel et Cie, 1912), I, 293. Duclos seems to suggest that the institutional link with English-speaking Protestantism made French-Canadian Protestantism less credible among the general population. See I, 219–20, 281.

16 E.A. Therrien is cited in Villard, *Up to the Light*, 75. Although the early converts Narcisse Cyr, Théodore Lafleur, and Rieul Duclos were sent to receive their theological instruction in Switzerland, this was the exception rather than the rule. Baptists and Methodists tended to be trained in the United States, Ontario, or English-language institutions in Quebec. The Frenchman Daniel Coussirat held the French Chair at the Presbyterian College, McGill, and taught Hebrew and Semitic languages.

17 Calvin Amaron, *The Future of Canada: The Extraordinary Privileges of the Roman Catholic Church in Quebec* (Montreal: n.d.).

18 Quoted in E.A. Therrien, *Baptist Work*, 48.

19 Jacques Monet, *The Last Cannon Shot: A Study of French Canadian Nationalism 1837–1850* (Toronto: University of Toronto Press, 1969).

20 Roberto Perin, 'Nationalism and the Church in French Canada, 1840–1880', *Bulletin of Canadian Studies* I, 1 (1977); Marta Danylewycz, *Taking the Veil: An Alternative to Marriage, Motherhood and Spinsterhood in Quebec, 1840–1920* (Toronto: McClelland and Stewart, 1987), 28–38.

21 René Bouchard, 'Calvaires et croix de chemin en Beauce', in Jean Simard et al., *Un patrimoine méprisé: La Religion populaire des Québécois* (Montréal: Hurtubise HMH, 1979).

22 Philippe Sylvain and Nive Voisine, *Réveil et consolidation*, vol. II, *1840–1898*, of HCQ II (Montréal: Boréal Express, 1991), 356–7. In 'Luc Désilets et la fondation du centre de pèlerinage de Notre-Dame-du-Cap', in Pierre Boglioni and Benoît Lacroix, eds, *Les Pèlerinages au Québec* (Québec: Presses de l'Université Laval, 1981), 116, Voisine recounts that Désilets's meditated recitations of the rosary lasted two-and-a-half hours!

23 René Hardy questions the notion of revival, preferring instead that of religious renewal. He doubts that religious practice underwent a sudden and dramatic change in the 1840s. Rather, this change was the culmination of two decades of activity on the part of clerical leaders. See his 'A propos du réveil religieux dans le Québec du XIXe siècle: Le Recours aux tribunaux dans les rapports ente le clergé et les fidèles (district de Trois-Rivières)', *RHAF* 48, 2 (automne 1994): 187–212.

24 Léon Pouliot, *La Réaction catholique de Montréal, 1840–1841* (Montréal: Imprimerie du Messager, 1942), 38. An excellent examination of these missions in the Montreal area is found in Louis Rousseau, 'Les Missions populaires de 1840–42: Acteurs principaux et conséquences', SCHEC, *Sessions d'étude* 53 (1986): 7–21; see also his 'Crise et réveil religieux dans le Québec du XIXe siècle', *Interface* (janvier-février 1990): 24–31; and, with Frank Remiggi, 'Le Renouveau religieux au XIXe siècle: Une analyse spatio-temporelle de la pratique pascale', *Studies in Religion/Sciences religieuses* 21, 4 (1992): 431–54, which suggests that the revival took place at the same rate and with the same intensity in the diocese of Montreal. See also Claude Galarneau, 'Mgr Forbin-Janson au Québec en 1840–1841', in Jean Hamelin et Nive Voisine, eds, *Les Ultramontains canadiens-français: Études d'histoire religieuse présentées en hommage au professeur Philippe Sylvain* (Montréal: Boréal Express, 1985), 121–42.

25 Sylvain and Voisine, *Réveil et consolidation*, 22.

26 Jan Noel, 'Dry Patriotism: The Chiniquy Crusade', *CHR* LXXI, 2 (June 1990): 189–207; Nive Voisine, 'Mouvements de tempérance et religion populaire', in Benoît Lacroix and Jean Simard, eds, *Religion populaire, religion de clercs?* (Québec: Institut québécois de recherche sur la culture, 1984), 65–78.

27 APFR, SC, America Settentrionale, 1862–5, Bourget au cardinal Barnabò (17 mars 1863), 563. A description of the deposition of the bones of St Janvière illustrates the sensuousness of these religious ceremonies and may be found in Danylewycz, *Taking the Veil*, 35.

28 Sylvain and Voisine, *Réveil et consolidation*, 356.

29 René Hardy, *Les Zouaves: Une stratégie du clergé québécois au XIXe siècle* (Montreal: Boréal Express, 1980), 189–202.

30 On Marquis, see Jean Roy, 'L'Invention du pèlerinage de la Tour des Martyrs de St-Célestin (1898–1930)', *RHAF* 43, 4 (printemps 1990): 487–507. On the cult of St Philomena, see Pierre Savard, 'La Dévotion à Sainte-Philomène', in *Aspects du catholicisme canadien-français au XIXe siècle* (Montréal: Fides, 1980), 173–96. See his 'L'Italie dans la culture canadienne-française au XIXe siècle', in Voisine and Hamelin, *Les Ultramontains*, for the connection between Quebec and Italian art; on the same subject, see Laurier Lacroix, 'Italian Art and Artists in Nineteenth-Century Quebec: A Few Preliminary Observations', in Roberto Perin and Franc Sturino, eds, *Arrangiarsi: The Italian Immigration Experience in Canada* (Montreal: Guernica Editions, 1989), 163–78.

31 See Roy, 'L'Invention du pèlerinage', 488 and Danylewycz, *Taking the Veil*, 39–46.

32 Voisine associates the devotional upsurge at Notre-Dame-du-Cap with the person of Désilets, an authoritarian cleric who exploited his rural parishioners' fears of the elements in order to promote Ultramontanism, especially the causes of his bishop, Louis-François Laflèche. See his 'Luc Désilets et la fondation du centre de pèlerinage de Notre-Dame-du-Cap', 115, 121–2. In a similar vein, Danylewycz suggests that the emerging cult of Mary projected the image of a nurturing, selfless, motherly figure meant to uphold a feminine ideology undermined by the process of industrialization. See her *Taking the Veil*, 38–46.

33 Lucia Ferretti, *Entre voisins: La Société paroissiale en milieu urbain: Saint-Pierre-Apôtre de Montréal, 1848–1930* (Montréal: Boréal Express, 1992); Lucia Ferretti, 'Mariage et cadre de vie familiale dans une paroisse ouvrière montréalaise: Sainte-Brigide, 1900–1914', *RHAF* 39, 2 (automne 1985): 233–51; Clermont Trudelle and Pierre Fortier, eds, *Toronto se raconte: La Paroisse du Sacré Coeur* (Toronto: Société d'histoire de Toronto, 1987). For religious life in a rural parish, see Gilles Laberge, 'La Vie religieuse dans la paroisse de la Nativité de La Prairie, 1854–1877: Religiographie historique' (M.A. thesis, Religious Studies, Université du Québec à Montréal, 1987).

34 Raymond Breton, 'Institutional Completeness of Ethnic Communities and the Personal Relations of Immigrants', *American Journal of Sociology* LXX (September 1964).

35 Micheline Dumont, 'Des garderies au 19e siècle: Les Salles d'asile des soeurs Grises à Montréal', in Nadia Fahmy-Eid and Micheline Dumont, eds, *Maîtresses de maison, maîtresses d'école: Femmes, famille et éducation dans l'histoire du Québec* (Montréal: Boréal Express, 1983), 272; D. Suzanne Cross, 'The Neglected Majority: The Changing Role of Women in 19th Century Montreal', in S.M. Trofimenkoff and A. Prentice, eds, *The Neglected Majority* (Toronto: McClelland and Stewart, 1977); Bettina Bradbury, 'The Fragmented Family: Family Strategies in the Face of Death, Illness, and Poverty, Montreal, 1860–1885', in Joy Parr, ed., *Childhood and Family in Canadian History* (Toronto: McClelland and Stewart, 1982), 109–28.

36 Sylvain and Voisine, *Réveil et consolidation*, 296–7. On Bourget's reaction to the *Petit catéchisme*, see APFR, SC 1862–65, Mémoire Bourget au Cardinal Barnabò sur le catéchisme (11 novembre 1864). For parish priests' insistence on school attendance,

see Serge Gagnon and René Hardy, eds, *L'Église et le village au Québec 1850–1930* (Ottawa: Leméac, 1979).

37 ASV, DAC, box 179, Rapport de Mgr Duhamel sur les écoles élémentaires du diocèse d'Ottawa (2 novembre 1901).

38 René Bouchard, 'Calvaires et croix', 36.

39 ASV, DAC 179, Rapport de l'école Notre Dame de Lourdes (Filles de la Sagesse) (28 août 1901); Rapport du Couvent St-François du Lac (Soeurs Grises) (27 juillet 1901); Rapport des Soeurs Grises d'Aylmer (25 juillet 1901); Rapport des Frères des Écoles Chrétiennes (25 juillet 1901); Rapport de l'Académie Notre Dame (27 juillet 1901); Rapport de l'Académie de Notre Dame de Gloucester (9 août 1901); Report of Rideau Street Convent (27 July 1901); see Micheline Dumont et Nadia Fahmy-Eid, eds, *Les Couventines: L'Éducation des filles au Québec dans les congrégations religieuses enseignantes 1840–1960* (Montréal: Éditions du Boréal, 1986).

40 Claude Galarneau, *Les Collèges classiques au Canada français* (Montréal: Fides, 1978), 210–15.

41 Laurier Renaud, 'La Fondation de l'ACJC', in Fernand Dumont, ed, *Idéologies au Canada Français 1900–1929* (Québec: Presses de l'Université Laval, 1974), 173–91; Michael Behiels, 'L'Association catholique de la jeunesse canadienne-française and the Quest for a Moral Regeneration, 1903–1914', *Journal of Canadian Studies* 13, 2 (Summer 1978): 27–41. On the basis of the writings of various members of the ACJC, Behiels maintains that the association had a clerical and anti-democratic structure and that it championed a 'volkish' ideology. Hélène Pelletier-Baillargeon argues instead that the *cercles d'études* were egalitarian and democratic; they gave a wide degree of latitude to the laity, and their chaplains played a self-effacing role; see her *Marie Gérin-Lajoie* (Montréal: Boréal Express, 1985). Certainly Behiels' use of the word 'volkish' seems excessive, since the ACJC did not promote an ideology based on racial supremacy or blood ties. The anti-Semitism of some ACJC members was religious, not racial.

42 Nicole Laurin, Danielle Juteau, Lorraine Duchesne, *A la recherche d'un monde oublié: Les Communautés religieuses de femmes au Québec de 1900 à 1970* (Montréal: Le Jour Éditeur, 1991), 183.

43 Huguette Lapointe-Roy, *Charité bien ordonnée: Le Premier Réseau de lutte contre la pauvreté à Montréal au 19e siècle* (Montréal: Boréal Express, 1987). See the interesting article by Shelley Horstein, 'The Architecture of Montreal Teaching Hospitals in the Nineteenth Century', *Journal of Canadian Art History* XIII, 2 and XIV, 1 (1990, 1991), 12–24, where she contrasts the divergent architectural styles of a Catholic and a Protestant hospital in Montreal, the first reflecting the organizing principle of religion, the second, that of secular science. See also Bettina Bradbury, 'Mourir chrétiennement: La Vie et la mort dans les établissements catholiques pour personnes âgées à Montréal dans la première moitié du XXe siècle', *RHAF* 46, 1 (été 1992): 143–75, an innovative article that goes beyond the social-control theory regarding institutional care.

44 Danylewycz, *Taking the Veil*. See especially chap. 5.

45 APFR, SC 24, Rapport décennal de Mgr Duhamel (6 avril 1886), 803–31; Léon Pouliot, 'Berthelet, Antoine-Olivier', *DCB*, X, 52–3.

46 Robert Rumilly, *La Plus Riche Aumône: Histoire de la Société St-Vincent de Paul au Canada* (Montréal: Éditions de L'Arbre, 1946).

47 Alfred Charpentier, *Ma conversion au syndicalisme catholique* (Montréal: Fides, 1946); Jean Hamelin and Nicole Gagnon, *Le XXe Siècle*, vol. I, *1898–1940*, HCQ (Montréal: Boréal Express, 1984), 215–31.

48 Rousseau, 'Les missions populaires', 20. At Notre-Dame-du-Cap, only a handful of the more than 3,000 parishioners failed to do their Easter duty in the 1910s. In Champlain, the Forty Hours devotion drew 900–950 communicants out of a total population of 1,500 inhabitants, and pilgrimages attracted one-third of this population. These figures are drawn from Gagnon and Hardy, *L'Église et le village*.

49 APFR, SC 23, Smeulders à Domenico Jacobini (23 octobre 1883); ibid., NS, 195, rubrica 154, Falconio a Ledochowski (6 giugno 1900).

50 This judgement was supported by Archbishop Gaetano Bedini, a Roman envoy who visited Canada in 1853. See Matteo Sanfilippo, 'L'Image du Canada dans les rapports du Saint-Siège, 1622–1908', *International Journal of Canadian Studies* 5 (1992): 9–24.

51 ASV, DAC, 157 (2), Rapport du Frère Colomban Marie sur la propagande protestante (5 décembre 1900).

52 This is the case in the parish of Notre-Dame-du-Cap. See Carmen Rousseau, 'Les Oblats et l'encadrement paroissial au Cap-de-la-Madeleine', in Gagnon and Hardy, *L'Église et le village*, 126.

53 François Alary, 'Vocation et vision du monde au XIXe siècle: Le Cas de Mgr Édouard-Charles Fabre (1839–1846)', SCHEC, *Études d'histoire religieuse* 59 (1993): 43–64.

54 ASV, DAC, 157, Bégin à Falconio (29 novembre 1900). Archbishop Bégin insisted, however, that although frequent, such clashes rarely resulted in outright defections from the church.

55 Normand Séguin, *La Conquête du sol au 19e siècle* (Montréal: Boréal Express, 1977), chap. 6, on relations between the laity and clergy in a rural parish. For a description of the pre-industrial laity's behaviour in the face of a weak episcopal authority, see Gilles LeBlanc, 'La Révolte de Grand-Digue en 1848: Contestation au sein de l'Église acadienne au XIXe siècle', in Gérald C. Boudreau, *Une dialectique du pouvoir en Acadie: Église et autorité* (Montréal: Fides, 1991). In Manitoba, Archbishop Adélard Langevin (1895–1915) encountered resistance from some diocesans over support for Catholic schools. They were primarily concerned with the double taxation that such support entailed. Archbishop Thomas Duhamel (1874–1909) had similar problems in Ottawa. See ASV, DAC 50; the file is entitled 'Question scolaire de la paroisse de St-Joseph d'Orléans 1901–1902'. Examples of ethnic conflict may be found in ASV, DAC, 58, London, la paroisse de St-Alphonse de Windsor (1900); DAC 13, St. John paroissiens de Grande Digue contre Mgr. Sweeney (1900); DAC 88, Alexandria Canadiens Français contre l'Evêque (1902). See as well Robert Choquette, *L'Église catholique dans l'Ontario français du dix-neuvième siècle* (Ottawa: Presses de l'Université d'Ottawa, 1984).

56 ASV, DAC, 13, (1900–02) in the Acadian parishes of Little Bras d'Or, Tracadie, Lourdes, and Heatherton; DAC 69, *passim* for Manitoba. On the Charlevoix

by-election, see Noel Bélanger, 'Une introduction au problème de l'influence indue, illustrée par la contestation de l'élection de 1876 dans le comté de Charlevoix' (thesis, licence-ès-lettres, Laval, 1960).

57 Guy Laperrière, 'Religion populaire, religion de clercs? Du Québec à la France, 1972–1982', in Lacroix and Simard, eds, *Religion populaire*, categorically rejects the notion of an autonomous popular religion in opposition to the official clerical religion in Quebec. Citing a study done on beliefs and popular practices in the Lower St Lawrence area, René Hardy seems more inclined to speak of the existence of a syncretic religion based on magical formulas of pagan origin overlaid with the miraculous and mysterious elements of Christianity. See Gagnon and Hardy, eds, *L'Église et le village au Québec*, 31.

58 Claire Dolan, 'Jalons pour une historiographie des pèlerinages au Québec', in Boglioni and Lacroix, eds, *Les Pèlerinages*, 82.

59 This is also seen in the wills of nineteenth-century French Canadians, which indicate a high degree of personal spirituality. See Marie-Aimée Cliche, 'L'Évolution des clauses religieuses traditionnelles dans les testaments de la région de Québec au XIXe siècle', in Lacroix and Simard, *Religion populaire*, 367–88.

60 The Ladies of the Sacred Heart looked after the education of young women; the Jesuits and the Holy Cross Fathers, that of young men. The Sisters of St Anne and Sisters of the Holy Names were Canadian foundations. The Sisters of Wisdom originated in France.

61 These were the Sisters of Providence and the Sisters of Mercy (Miséricorde). The Good Shepherd Sisters of Angers came from France.

62 Sylvain and Voisine, *Réveil et consolidation*, 48–51, criticize Bourget for being precipitate and for leaving newer congregations in the lurch in their first years of operation. The early period of their Canadian establishment was undoubtedly one of trial and error. Mistakes were certainly made. In retrospect it may seem strange that the bishop at first established some of these communities on the outskirts of the island of Montreal. But this was where Protestant proselytism had made a breakthrough. Once the situation there stabilized, once regular parish and school life existed, these communities could go on to play a more dynamic role elsewhere. Sylvain and Voisine reflect the negative treatment that Bourget has generally received from historians who have focused on his failings. Even in his own lifetime, he was accused of being dogmatic, intolerant, imperious, impulsive, and quarrelsome. This perspective, however, has diminished the bishop's real achievements.

63 Guy Laperrière, ' "Persécution et exil": La Venue au Québec des congrégations françaises', *RHAF* 36, 3 (décembre 1982): 389–411.

64 These statistics are in Danylewycz, *Taking the Veil*, 17, 47.

65 Bernard Denault and Benoît Lévesque, *Éléments pour une sociologie des communautés religieuses au Québec* (Montréal: Presses de l'Université de Montréal, 1975), 43.

66 Georgette Desjardins, 'Le Rôle des religieuses Hospitalières de Saint-Joseph dans l'éducation au Madawaska depuis 1873', SCHEC, *Sessions d'Études*, 48 (1981): 57–66; A.J. Savoie, 'Les Communautés religieuses et l'enseignement au Nouveau-Brunswick depuis 1872', ibid., 67–77; Léon Thériault, 'The Acadianisation of the Catholic Church in Acadia, 1763–1953,' in Jean Daigle, ed., *The Acadians of the*

Maritimes: Thematic Studies (Moncton: Centre d'Études Acadiennes, 1980), 293–369.

67 Estelle Mitchell, *Les Soeurs Grises de Montréal à la Rivière Rouge, 1844–1984* (Montreal: Éditions du Méridien, 1987); P.-J.-B. Duchaussois, *Les Soeurs Grises dans l'Extrême-Nord: Cinquante ans de missions* (Ottawa: Imprimerie Le Droit, 1916); Henri Bourassa, *Le Canada apostolique* (Montréal: Bibliothèque de l'Action française, 1919), 91–9.

68 A.G. Morice, *History of the Catholic Church in Western Canada*, 3 vols (Toronto: Musson, 1910); Marguerite Jean, *Évolution des communautés religieuses de femmes au Canada de 1639 à nos jours* (Montréal: Fides, 1977), 151–6. Langevin detached the Canonesses Regular of the Five Wounds of the Saviour from their French mother house and was co-founder of the Oblate Missionaries of the Sacred Heart and the Immaculate Conception.

69 Bourassa, *Le Canada apostolique*, 120–37. The Sisters of Providence went to Chile and the Sisters of the Good Shepherd of Montreal, to Peru, Ecuador, Bolivia, Columbia, and Nicaragua. Sisters of the General Hospital of Quebec went to Natal, while Sisters of Jesus and Mary (Sillery) were in India.

70 Denise Helly, *Les Chinois à Montréal 1877–1951* (Québec: Institut québécois de recherche sur la culture, 1987), 163–5.

71 Jean, *Évolution des communautés religieuses*, 160–5; Hamelin and Gagnon, *Le XXe Siècle*, I, 161–3. Tétrault founded the Missionary Sisters of the Immaculate Conception, while Gervais established the Missionary Sisters of Our Lady of the Angels.

72 See Yolande Pinard, 'Les Débuts du mouvement des femmes', in Marie Lavigne and Yolande Pinard, eds, *Les Femmes dans la société québécoise* (Montréal: Boréal Express, 1977), 61–87; this view is also implicitly expressed by Cross, 'The Neglected Majority', 66–86.

73 Micheline Dumont, 'Une perspective féministe dans l'histoire des congrégations des femmes', SCHEC, *Études d'histoire religieuse* (1990): 29–35.

74 Danylewycz, *Taking the Veil*, has become a classic statement of this position.

75 ASV, DAC 13, Hôtel-Dieu de Tracadie (1902–3). On the sisters of the Hôtel-Dieu of Montreal, see André Lavallée, *Québec contre Montréal: La Querelle universitaire, 1876–1891* (Montréal: Presses de l'Université de Montréal, 1974).

76 Pelletier-Baillargeon, *Marie Gérin-Lajoie*, 122–5.

77 Elizabeth de Moissac, 'Les Soeurs Grises et les événements de 1869–70', SCHEC, *Sessions d'étude* (1970): 215–28.

78 Jean, *Évolution des communautés religieuses*, 143–7.

79 Laurin, Juteau, Duchesne, *A la recherche d'un monde*, 157–8. The original contention about class divisions appeared in Danylewycz, *Taking the Veil*, chap. 3.

80 Louis-Edmond Hamelin, 'Évolution numérique séculaire du clergé catholique dans le Québec', *RS* II, 2 (avril-juin 1961): 189–241; Louis Rousseau, 'Morphologie des carrières cléricales dans le Sud-Ouest québécois', in *Le Bas-clergé catholique au XIXe siècle: Approche comparative d'une population pastorale en voie de changement* (Québec: Presses de l'Université Laval, 1994), Introduction.

81 APFR, NS 51, Fabre à Ledochowski, n.d. (received in Rome 21 May 1892), 329–30.

82 Sylvain and Voisine, *Réveil et consolidation*, 274.

83 Lucien Lemieux, *L'Établissement de la première province ecclésisastique au Canada 1773–1844* (Montréal: Fides, 1968); Roberto Perin, 'Mgr Bourget and the Dream of a Free Church in Quebec' (Ph.D. dissertation, History, University of Ottawa, 1975); Jean-Pierre Asselin, *Les Rédemptoristes au Canada: Implantation à Sainte-Anne-de-Beaupré* (Montréal: Bellarmin, 1981), chaps 9–10; Nive Voisine, *Les Frères des Écoles chrétiennes au Canada*, vol. I of *La Conquête de l'Amérique 1837–1880* (Québec: Éditions Anne Sigier, 1987); Paul Desjardins, *Le Collège Sainte-Marie de Montréal*, II (Montréal: 1945).

84 These figures are approximations based on *Le Canada ecclésiastique* (Montreal: Librairie Beauchemin, 1921). Figures were also checked against Denault and Lévesque, *Éléments pour une sociologie*, 42. See Raymond Huel, ed., *Études oblates de l'Ouest*, I, *Actes du premier colloque sur l'histoire des Oblats dans l'Ouest et le Nord canadiens/Western Oblate Studies*, I, *Proceedings of the First Symposium on the History of the Oblates in Western and Northern Canada* (Edmonton: Institut de recherche de la Faculté de Saint-Jean/Western Canadian Publishers, 1990).

85 Alexandre Taché, *Esquisse sur le Nord-Ouest de l'Amérique* (Montreal, 1869), cited in Claude Champagne, *Les Débuts de la mission dans le Nord-Ouest canadien: Mission et église chez Mgr Vidal Grandin, o.m.i. (1829–1902)* (Ottawa: Presses de l'Université d'Ottawa, 1983), 77. Descriptions of Oblate missions may be found in Gaston Carrière, 'The Oblates and the Northwest: 1845–1861', CCHA, *Study Sessions* (1970): 35–65; Morice, *History of the Catholic Church*; Margaret Whitehead, ed., *'They Call Me Father': Memoirs of Father Nicolas Coccola* (Vancouver: University of British Columbia Press, 1988); Whitehead, *The Cariboo Mission: A History of the Oblates* (Victoria: Sono Nis, 1981); David Mulhall, *Will to Power: The Missionary Career of Father Morice* (Vancouver: University of British Columbia, 1986).

86 Champagne, *Les Débuts de la mission*, 189.

87 Ibid., 175–7.

88 Rodney Arthur Fowler, 'The Lemert Thesis and the Sechelt Mission', CCHA, *Historical Studies* (1990): 51–63, 51. See as well Jacqueline Gresko, 'Roman Catholic Missions to the Indians of British Columbia: A Reappraisal of the Lemert Thesis', *Journal of the Canadian Church Historical Society*, 24 (Octobre 1982): 51–62.

89 Champagne, *Les Débuts*, 179–84; Raymond Huel, 'The Oblates, the Métis, and 1885: The Breakdown of Traditional Relationships', CCHA, *Historical Studies* (1989): 9–29.

90 Jacqueline Gresko, 'Creating Little Dominions with the Dominion: Early Catholic Indian Schools in Saskatchewan and British Columbia', in Jean Barman, Y. Hébert, and Don McCaskill, eds, *The Legacy: Indian Education in Canada*, I (Vancouver: University of British Columbia Press, 1986).

91 Morice, *History of the Catholic Church*.

92 Champagne, *Les Débuts de la mission*, 196, cites various writings of Bishop Grandin.

93 Kerry Abel, 'Prophets, Priests and Preachers: Dene Shamans and Christian Missions in the Nineteenth Century', CHA *Historical Papers* (1986): 211–24.

94 Mitchell, *Les Soeurs Grises de Montréal*; Duchaussois, *Les Soeurs Grises dans l'Extrême-Nord*.

95 Zonia Keywan, *A Turbulent Life: The Biography of Joseph Jean OSBM (1885-1972)* (Verdun: Clio Editions, 1991); Andrii Krawchuk, 'Between a Rock and a Hard Place: Francophone Missionaries among Ukrainian Catholics', in Lubomyr Luciuk and Stella Hryniuk, eds, *Canada's Ukrainians: Negotiating an Identity* (Toronto; University of Toronto Press, 1991), 206–17; Roberto Perin, *Rome in Canada: The Vatican and Canadian Affairs in the Late Victorian Age* (Toronto: University of Toronto Press, 1990), chap. 6.

96 Adolphe Proulx, 'Histoire du diocèse de Sault-Sainte-Marie', SCHEC, *Rapport* (1960): 71–82; David Nazar, 'Anishinabe and Jesuit 1840–1880: Nineteenth-Century Missiology on Manitoulin Island', *Église et théologie* 22 (1991): 157–76.

97 Savoie, 'Les Communautés religieuses et l'enseignement au Nouveau Brunswick'; Anselme Chiasson, 'Le Clergé et le réveil acadien (1864–1960)', *Revue de l'Université de Moncton* 11, 1 (1978): 29–46; Emile Lauvrière, *La Tragédie d'un peuple: Histoire du peuple acadien de ses origines à nos jours* (Paris: Librairie Henri Goulet, 1924); Clarence Lebreton, *Le Collège de Caraquet* (Montréal: Éditions du Fleuve, 1991).

98 The census of 1921 underestimates the number of Catholics in Canada because Ukrainian Catholics are listed together with Orthodox Christians as belonging to the Greek Church, whose membership is given as 170,000. I have estimated Ukrainian Catholics as numbering 105,000, of whom 15,000 were residents of Ontario and Quebec and 90,000 lived in the Prairie provinces. As a result, the total number of Prairie Catholics would rise from 418,687 to 508,687 and the proportion of French Canadians in the Catholic population would drop accordingly.

99 Lemieux, *L'Établissement de la première*, especially chap. 7.

100 Jacques Grisé, *Les Conciles provinciaux du Québec et l'Église canadienne* (Montréal: Fides, 1979).

101 Thériault, 'The Acadianisation of the Catholic Church'; Martin Spigelman, 'Race et religion: Les Acadiens et la hiérarchie catholique irlandaise du Nouveau Brunswick', *RHAF* 29, 1 (juin 1975): 69–85; Neil Boucher, ' "Il faut que l'Acadie nous soit rendue": La lutte pour la nomination du premier évêque acadien', in Boudreau, *La Dialectique du pouvoir*.

102 Robert Choquette, *Language and Religion: A History of English-French Conflict in Ontario* (Ottawa: University of Ottawa Press, 1975); Robert Choquette, *L'Eglise catholique dans l'Ontario français*; Chad Gaffield, *Language, Schooling, and Cultural Conflict: The Origins of the French Language Controversy in Ontario* (Montréal–Kingston: McGill–Queen's University Press, 1987); Roger Guindon, *Coexistence difficile: La Dualité linguistique à l'Université d'Ottawa, 1848–1898* (Ottawa: Presses de l'Université d'Ottawa, 1989); D.G. Cartwright, 'Ecclesiastical Territorial Organization and Institutional Conflict in Eastern and Northern Ontario, 1840–1910', CHA, *Historical Papers* (1978): 176–99; John Moir, 'The Problem of a Double Minority: Some Reflections on the Development of the English-Speaking Catholic Church in Canada in the Nineteenth Century', *Histoire sociale/Social History* (April 1971): 53–67.

103 Gilbert Comeault, 'Les Rapports de Mgr L.-P.-A. Langevin avec les groupes ethniques minoritaires et leurs répercussions sur le statut de la langue française au Manitoba, 1895–1916', SCHEC, *Sessions d'étude* (1975): 65–85. Robert Painchaud, 'Les Exigences linguistiques dans le recrutement d'un clergé pour l'Ouest canadien,

1818–1920', ibid., 43–64; Robert Choquette, 'Adélard Langevin et l'érection de l'archidiocèse de Winnipeg', *RHAF* 28, 2 (septembre 1974): 187–207; Raymond Huel, '*Gestae Dei per Francos*: The French Canadian Experience in Western Canada', in B.G. Smilie, ed., *Visions of the New Jerusalem* (Edmonton: NeWest Press, 1983); Raymond Huel, 'The Irish French Conflict in Catholic Episcopal Nominations: The Western Sees and the Struggle for Domination Within the Church', CCHA, *Study Sessions* (1975): 51–70.

104 Giovanni Pizzorusso, 'Un diplomate du Vatican en Amérique: Donato Sbarretti à Washington, La Havanne et Ottawa (1893–1910)', *Annali accademici canadesi* IX (1993): 5–33; Matteo Sanfilippo, 'Diomede Falconio et l'Église catholique en Amérique du Nord', *Rivista di Studi Canadesi* 5 (1992): 43–7; Matteo Sanfilippo, 'La Question canadienne-française dans les diocèses de la Nouvelle Angleterre, 1899–1922', *Canada ieri e oggi, 2, II, Sezione storica e geografica* (Selva di Fasano: Schena Editore, 1990), 55–76; Matteo Sanfilippo and Monique Benoit, 'Sources romaines pour l'histoire de l'Église catholique au Canada: Le Pontificat de Léon XIII (1878–1903)', *RHAF* 44, 1 (été 1990): 85–96.

105 R. Perin, 'Clerics and the Constitution: The Quebec Church and Minority Rights in Canada', CCHA, *Historical Studies* (1989): 31–47.

106 Perin, *Rome in Canada*; Choquette, *Language and Religion*.

107 Mason Wade, *The French Canadians* (Toronto: Macmillan, 1955); Marcel Bellavance, *Le Québec et la Confédération: Un choix libre? Le Clergé et la constitution de 1867* (Québec: Septentrion, 1992). Practically every book on Wilfrid Laurier deals with this question. See H.B. Neatby, *Laurier and a Liberal Quebec* (Toronto: McClelland and Stewart, 1973), chaps 1, 5. For discussion of this issue in the twentieth century, see Bernard Vigod, *Quebec Before Duplessis: The Political Career of Louis-Alexandre Taschereau* (Montréal–Kingston: McGill–Queen's University Press, 1986).

108 Philippe Sylvain, 'Libéralisme et ultramontanisme au Canada français: affrontement idéologique et doctrinal (1858–1865)', in W.L. Morton, ed., *The Shield of Achilles* (Toronto: McClelland and Stewart, 1968), 11–38, 220–55; M. Ayearst, 'The *Parti Rouge* and the Clergy', *CHR* XV, 4 (December 1934): 390–405.

109 English versions of the *Programme catholique* and the 1875 joint pastoral are found in H.D. Forbes, ed., *Canadian Political Thought* (Toronto: Oxford University Press, 1985), 93–106. Bourget's 1876 pastoral is found in Adrien Thério, ed., *Ignace Bourget écrivain* (Montréal: Éditions Jumonville, 1975), 183–95; see also Nadia Fahmy-Eid, 'Les ultramontains et le *Programme catholique*', in Hamelin and Voisine, *Les Ultramontains*, 161–81. Paul Benoit, 'On the Defeat of the *Programme* of 1871', *Studies in Religion* 1, 2 (Spring 1982): 163–71, presents a conservative perspective on the question and challenges Eid's interpretation of the *Programme* as trying to achieve the dominance of the church over the state.

110 This point is discussed more fully in Perin, *Rome in Canada*, Introduction and chap. 4.

111 Bourget à F.X.A. Trudel (6 juin 1871), cited in Robert Rumilly, *Histoire de la Province de Québec*, vol. I (Montréal: Éditions Fides, 1971), 158. The issue is complicated by the fact that in French the names of political parties are not capitalized. Thus 'le vrai parti conservateur' may refer to the Conservative party or to all those who support conservative principles.

112 R. Perin, 'Clercs et politiques au Québec, 1865–1876', *Revue de l'Université d'Ottawa* 50, 2 (avril-juin 1980): 168–90.

113 Paul Crunican, *Priests and Politicians: Manitoba Schools and the Election of 1896* (Toronto: University of Toronto Press, 1974). For the North-West Schools Question, see Manoly Lupul, *The Roman Catholic Church and the North-West School Question: A Study in Church-State Relations in Western Canada* (Toronto: University of Toronto Press, 1974).

114 Sylvain and Voisine, *Réveil et consolidation*, chaps 7–12; Jean-Roch Rioux, 'Gonzalve Doutre et l'Institut canadien', in P. Hurtubise et al., eds, *Le Laïc dans l'Église canadienne-française de 1830 à nos jours* (Montreal: Fides, 1972), 129–44. As a result of Bourget's actions, some historians accused the church of trying to institute a theocracy in Quebec; Nadia Fahmy-Eid, 'Ultramontanisme, idéologie et classes sociales', *RHAF* 29, 1 (juin 1975): 49–68; Nive Voisine, *Louis-François Laflèche: Deuxième évêque de Trois-Rivières* (St-Hyacinthe: Edisem, 1980).

115 Léon Pouliot, *Monseigneur Bourget et son temps*, vol. IV, *Affrontement avec l'Institut canadien, 1858–1870* (Montréal: Bellarmin, 1976)

116 Lovell Clark, ed., *The Guibord Affair* (Toronto-Montreal: Holt, Rinehart and Winston, 1971); Jean de Bonville, 'La liberté de presse à la fin du XIXe siècle: Le cas de *Canada-Revue*', *RHAF* 31, 4 (1978): 501–23; Jean Laflamme et Rémi Tourangeau, *L'Église et le théâtre au Québec* (Montréal: Fides, 1979); Ramon Hathorn, 'Sarah Bernhardt and the Bishops of Montreal and Quebec', CCHA, *Historical Studies* 53 (1986): 97–120; Lise Saint-Jacques, 'Mgr Bruchési et le contrôle des paroles divergentes: Journalisme, polémique et censure (1896–1910)' (M.A. thesis, History, Université du Québec à Montréal, 1987).

117 Giovanni Pizzorusso, 'Le Fonds Benigni aux Archives Secrètes du Vatican', *Annali Accademici Canadesi* VIII (1992): 107–1.

118 Fernand Dumont, 'Idéologies au Canada français (1850–1900): Quelques réflexions d'ensemble', *RS* X (1969): 145–56; Jean-Paul Bernard, 'Définition du libéralisme et de l'ultramontanisme comme idéologies', *RHAF* 25 (septembre 1971): 244–46; Perin, 'Nationalism and the Church in French Canada'.

119 Marcel Lajeunesse, *Les Sulpiciens et la vie culturelle à Montréal au XIXe siècle* (Montréal: Fides, 1982).

120 William Ryan, *The Clergy and Economic Growth in Quebec, 1896–1914* (Québec: Presses de l'Université Laval, 1966); J.W. Lapierre and M. Roy, *Les Acadiens* (Paris: Presses Universitaires de France, 1983); Chiasson, 'Le Clergé et le réveil acadien'; Alphonse Deveau, 'La Religion et l'économie dans les milieux acadiens', *Revue de l'Université Sainte-Anne* (1983): 18–26.

121 Brian Young, *In Its Corporate Capacity: The Seminary of Montreal as a Business Institution* (Montréal-Kingston: McGill-Queen's University Press, 1986); *Promoters and Politicians: The North-Shore Railways in the History of Quebec, 1854–85* (Toronto: University of Toronto Press, 1978), chap. 2; *George-Étienne Cartier: Montreal Bourgeois* (Montréal-Kingston: McGill-Queen's University Press, 1981).

122 Séguin, *La Conquête du sol*, chap. 9.

123 Bouchard, 'Les Prêtres, les capitalistes'.

124 Ferretti, *Entre voisins*, 133–9.

125 Alexis de Barbézieux, *L'Église catholique au Canada: Précis historique et statistique* (Montréal: Librairie Franciscaine, 1934), 16–18; Federation of Francophones Outside Quebec, *The Heirs of Lord Durham: Manifesto of A Vanishing People* (Ottawa: Burns and MacEachern, 1978), 23; Paul-André Linteau, René Durocher, Jean-Claude Robert, and François Ricard, *Quebec Since 1930* (Toronto: Lorimer, 1986), 430.

126 Richard Joy, *Languages in Conflict: The Canadian Experience* (Toronto: McClelland and Stewart, 1972), 34–5.

127 For a poignant evocation of this process, see *Enchantment and Sorrow: The Autobiography of Gabrielle Roy* (Toronto: Lester and Orpen Dennys, 1987).

128 Joy, *Languages in Conflict*, 59, Table 26, shows the French language's attraction among four non-British, non-French ethnic groups in Quebec in 1960.

129 Jeremy Boissevain, *The Italians of Montreal: Social Adjustment in a Plural Society* (Ottawa: Queen's Printer, 1971), table IV-1, shows 75 per cent of children attending English schools in 1962–3. This figure would rise to 90 per cent before the adoption of Bill 22 by the Quebec National Assembly in 1974. For the broader context to this question, see Paul-André Linteau, 'The Italians of Quebec: Key Participants in Contemporary Linguistic and Political Debates', in Perin and Sturino, *Arrangiarsi*, 179–207.

130 Canada, *Report of the Royal Commission on Bilingualism and Biculturalism*, book I (Ottawa: Queen's Printer, 1967), 28.

131 The following statistics have been calculated on the basis of Canada, Dominion Bureau of Statistics, Seventh Census of Canada, 1931, bulletin no. XXXV, *Religious Denominations by Racial Origins 1931* (Ottawa, 1933).

132 Ibid., 17–36.

133 Ibid., 15–16.

134 Fines, *Album du protestantisme français*. This information is found in the section dealing with the United Church.

135 Therrien et al., *Baptist Work in French Canada*, chap. 6.

136 Fines, *Album du protestantisme*, chap. on Grande-Ligne.

137 Ibid., section on Presbyterians.

138 For example, a majority of the French Protestant families from Belle-Rivière, northwest of Montreal, had migrated to the metropolis and were members of l'Église Béthanie in Verdun; Claude de Mestral, *Mémoires d'un homme libre* (Montréal: Éditions du Méridien, 1986), 77.

139 Ibid.

140 Archives of the United Church of Canada, Anonymous (probably J.E. Boucher), 'Missionary Work,' the text of a talk given in the churches under the auspices of the James Robertson Memorial Committee, n.d.

141 De Mestral, *Mémoires*, 81, 86–7.

142 Ibid., 78–80, for his position on the 1937 textile strike in Valleyfield and on the question of industrial diseases in the Asbestos mines in the immediate post-war era.

143 The Witnesses published a pamphlet in 1946 entitled 'La Haine ardente du Québec pour Dieu, pour Christ (*sic*), et pour la liberté, est un sujet de honte pour tout le Canada'. This led to the famous Roncarelli affair, which was finally decided in the Supreme Court of Canada. See Michel Sarra-Bournet, *L'Affaire Roncarelli:*

Duplessis contre les Témoins de Jéhovah (Québec: Institut québécois de recherche sur la culture, 1986). As a result, the Civil Liberties Association of Montreal was formed with the United Church pastor Claude de Mestral as secretary-treasurer; De Mestral, *Mémoires*, 79.

144 Fines, *Album du protestantisme*; Henry Warkentin, 'A History of the Protestant Church in Quebec' (B.D. thesis, Waterloo Lutheran University, 1963), chap. 3.

145 Ferretti, *Entre voisins*, 180. On average, parishioners went to communion 32 times in 1923, 35 times in 1924, and 39 times in 1926.

146 Brigitte Caulier, 'L'Ordre franciscain séculier (tiers-ordre)', in Hamelin, *Les Franciscains au Canada*, 99–121.

147 Hamelin and Gagnon, *Le XXe siècle*, I, 345–7; Laperrière, 'Religion populaire', 25. In 1932, stone-cutters at St-Marc-des-Carrières near Quebec City erected a statue of the Sacred Heart in order to save their jobs threatened by the Depression. See also his 'Les Lieux de pèlerinage au Québec: Une vue d'ensemble', in Boglioni and Lacroix, *Les Pèlerinages*, 37–8, where the author points out that 10 shrines were established from 1947 to 1955, compared with 12 in the period 1873–83.

148 N. Voisine, 'De *La Tempérance* à *La Famille* 1906–1954', in Hamelin, *Les Franciscains*, 157–79.

149 Francis Goyer, *Le Premier Congrès eucharistique national du Canada* (Québec: Secrétariat des oeuvres eucharistiques, 1939), 101–6.

150 *Le Congrès marial d'Ottawa* (Ottawa, 1948); Jean Hamelin, *Le XXe siècle*, vol. II, *De 1940 à nos jours*, HCQ (Montreal: Boréal Express, 1984), 102–8.

151 Goyer, *Le Premier Congrès eucharistique*, for example, noted that across Canada events leading up to the national eucharistic congress netted 4,971,447 masses, 3,903,428 communions, 3,000,500 rosaries, 1,659,972 stations of the cross, 1,091,893 adorations, 3,380,434 visits to the Blessed Sacrament, 34,462,998 prayers of various kinds, 27,094,657 ejaculations, 21,345,661 abnegations, and 1,726,197 works of various kinds, for a grand total of 12,637,247 (p. 21).

152 Hamelin and Gagnon, *Le XXe siècle*, I, 240–58; Nicole Thivierge, *Écoles ménagères et instituts familiaux: Un modèle féminin traditionnel* (Québec: Institut québécois de recherche sur la culture, 1982).

153 Rumilly, *La Plus Riche Aumône*, 129–221.

154 P.A. Linteau, René Durocher, and Jean-Claude Robert, *Quebec: A History, 1867–1929* (Toronto: James Lorimer, 1983), 422–6; Hamelin and Gagnon are critical of the clergy's efforts to remove the radical elements from the UCC. See their *Le XXe siècle*, I, 278–84; Jean-Pierre Kesteman et al., *Histoire du syndicalisme agricole: UCC-UPA, 1924–1984* (Montréal: Boréal, 1984).

155 Jacques Rouillard, *Histoire de la CSN 1921–1981* (Montréal; Boréal Express, 1981), chaps. 2–3; Michelle Lapointe, 'Le Syndicat catholique des allumettières de Hull, 1919–1924,' *RHAF* 32, 4 (mars 1979): 603–28; J.P. Lefebvre et al., *En grève! L'histoire de la CSN et de ses luttes de 1937 à 1963* (Montréal: Éditions du Jour, 1963); Hamelin and Gagnon, *Le XXe siècle*, I, 285–91, 406–12.

156 Yves Roby, *Les Caisses populaires: Alphonse Desjardins, 1900–1920* (Quebec: 1975); Ronald Rudin, 'In Whose Interest? The Early Years of the First Caisse Populaire, 1900–1945', CHA, *Historical Papers* (1987): 157–77.

157 Jean-Claude Dupuis, 'La Pensée religieuse de l'Action Française (1917–1928)', SCHEC, *Études d'histoire religieuse* 59 (1993): 73–88.

158 Jacques Cousineau, *L'Église d'ici et le social, 1940–1960*, I, *La Commission sacerdotale d'études sociales* (Montréal: Bellarmin, 1982); Gregory Baum, *Catholics and Canadian Socialism: Political Thought in the Thirties and Forties* (Toronto: James Lorimer, 1980), chaps 3 and 6. Although Baum sees the *Programme* as a progressive document, he is still heavily influenced by the liberal historiography of Pierre Trudeau and André-J. Bélanger in his negative assessment of French-Canadian nationalists.

159 See, for example, Pierre Elliott Trudeau, *The Asbestos Strike* (Toronto: James Lewis and Samuel, 1974), chap. 1; André-J. Bélanger, *L'Apolitisme des idéologies québécoises: Le Grand Tournant de 1934–36* (Québec: Presses de l'Université Laval, 1974). Michael Oliver, *The Passionate Debate: The Social and Political Ideas of Quebec Nationalism* (Montreal: Vehicule Press, 1991), while agreeing that nationalist thought was dominant in Quebec, is less inclined to see it as monolithic. Esther Delisle, *The Traitor and the Jew: Anti-Semitism and the Delirium of Extremist Right-wing Nationalism in French Canada from 1929–1939* (Montreal: Robert Davies Publishing, 1993) provides an even more extreme interpretation of French-Canadian nationalism.

160 Fernande Roy, *Progrès, Harmonie, Liberté: Le Libéralisme des milieux d'affaires francophones à Montréal au tournant du siècle* (Montreal: Boréal Express, 1988), argues that liberalism was a mainstream ideology in Quebec at the turn of the century. My own *Rome in Canada* has argued that French-Canadian nationalism was resisted not only by the Holy See, but by an increasingly influential portion of the Quebec clergy.

161 Joseph Levitt, *Henri Bourassa and the Golden Calf: The Social Program of the Nationalists of Quebec/1900–1914* (Ottawa: University of Ottawa Press, 1972).

162 Robert Arcand, 'Les Catholiques du Québec et le fascisme italien' (M.A. thesis, History, Université de Sherbrooke, 1986); Clinton Archibald, *Un Québec corporatiste? Corporatisme et néo-corporatisme: Du passage d'une idéologie sociale à une idéologie corporatiste* (Hull: Asticou, 1984).

163 One need only think of works such as Robert Sellars, *The Tragedy of Quebec* (Toronto: University of Toronto Press, 1974), with its racist stereotypes regarding French Canadians.

164 Figures for the number of religious women are taken from Denault and Lévesque, *Éléments pour une sociologie*, 43. Another methodology produced different results in Laurin et al., *A la recherche d'un monde oublié*, 170; but numerical trends are similar in both methods. Laurin provides statistics on the highest ratios of religious women to the female population. These were 12 per thousand in Belgium, 7 per thousand in France, 6 per thousand in Italy (171). Estimates of religious women coming from Acadia and Ontario are extrapolated from figures provided by Laurin et al. (297–8). See Barbara Jane Cooper, 'In the Spirit: Entrants to a Religious Community of Women in Quebec, 1930–1939' (M.A. thesis, History, McGill University, 1983).

165 The two new communities are the Daughters of Mary of the Assumption and the Sisters of Our Lady of the Sacred Heart. See Thériault, 'The Acadianisation of the Catholic Church', 361–2; Savoie, 'Les Communautés religieuses et l'enseignement,' 72; Desjardins, 'Le Rôle des religieuses Hospitalières de St-Joseph', 64–5;

Jean, *Évolution des communautés religieuses de femmes*, 156–60; Neil Boucher, 'Un exemple du nationalisme de l'Église de l'Acadie: Les French Sisters chez les Soeurs de Charité, 1914–1924', SCHEC, *Études d'histoire religieuse* 60 (1994): 25–34.

166 Mitchell, *Soeurs grises*.

167 Jean, *L'Évolution des communautés religieuses*, 167–84. The Jeanne d'Arc Institute was an Ottawa foundation. Marie Gérin-Lajoie founded the Institute of the Sisters of Good Counsel. See Pelletier-Baillargeon, *Marie Gérin-Lajoie*, part IV; Danylewycz, *Taking the Veil*, 150–4; Julien Harvey, 'L'Église catholique et l'accueil des immigrants au XXe siècle', SCHEC, *Études d'histoire religieuse* (1993): 89–103; N. Laurin et al., *A la recherche d'un monde*, provides a chart showing the expansion of religious communities by category from 1902 to 1971 (251).

168 These figures are extrapolated from Denault and Lévesque, *Éléments pour une sociologie*, 42; Hamelin and Gagnon, *Le XXe Siècle*, I, 123–5; Hamelin, *Le XXe siècle*, II, 162.

169 These figures are based on *Le Canada ecclésiastique*. (Montréal; Librairie Beauchemin, 1930) and are at variance with the statistics given in Denault and Lévesque, *Éléments pour une sociologie*, 42. The number of regulars and brothers cited in the latter is 1,214, whereas my total comes to 1,040.

170 Denault and Lévesque give the number of regulars and brothers as 2,452 in 1960 and 2,772 in 1965 (42).

171 Henri Goudreault, 'Les Missionnaires canadiens à l'étranger au XXe siècle', SCHEC, *Sessions d'étude* (1983): 361–80; Hamelin, *Le XXe siècle*, II, 189–205.

172 F.J. McEvoy, 'Religion and Politics in Foreign Policy: Canadian Government Relations with the Vatican', CCHA, *Study Sessions* (1984): 121–44; Huel, 'The Irish French Conflict in Catholic Episcopal Nominations'.

173 Thériault, 'The Acadianisation of the Catholic Church'; Micheline Laliberté, 'Un exemple de la trilogie langue, nationalisme et religion: La Création du diocèse de Yarmouth', in Boudreau, *La Dialectique du pouvoir*, 67–103; Chiasson, 'Le Clergé et le réveil acadien'.

174 Choquette, *La Foi gardienne de la langue en Ontario*; Guindon, *Coexistance difficile: La Dualité linguistique à l'université d'Ottawa*, II, *1898–1936* (Ottawa: Presses de l'Université d'Ottawa, 1993).

175 Hamelin, *Le XXe Siècle*, II, 48–52.

176 On the the formation of a society called the Unity League to promote goodwill between French and English Canadians, see Choquette, *Language and Religion*, chap. VIII. For the Ordre Jacques Cartier, see his *La Foi gardienne de la langue*, chap. 8. See also Raymond Huel, 'The Anderson Amendments and the Secularization of Saskatchewan Public Schools', CCHA, *Study Sessions* (1977): 61–76.

177 Linteau, Durocher, Robert, *Quebec: A History*, chap. 20.

178 Despite opinions to the contrary in William Coleman, *The Independence Movement in Quebec* (Toronto: University of Toronto Press, 1984), chap. 2, and implicitly in Michael Behiels, *Prelude to Quebec's Quiet Revolution* (Montréal–Kingston: McGill–Queen's University Press, 1985), chap. 3.

179 Terry Copp, 'Montreal's Municipal Government and the Crisis of the 1930s', in Alan Artibise and Gilbert Stelter, eds, *The Usable Urban Past* (Toronto: Macmillan, 1979), 12–29; Rumilly, *La Plus Riche Aumône*; Wendy Johnston, 'Keeping Children

in School: The Response of the Montreal Catholic School Commission in the Depression of the 1930s', CHA, *Historical Papers* (1985): 193–217.

180 Hamelin and Gagnon, *Le XXe Siècle*, I, 257.

181 Lucie Deslauriers, 'Histoire de l'hôpital Notre-Dame de Montréal' (M.A. thesis, History, Université de Montréal, 1984).

182 Antonin Dupont, *Les Relations entre l'Église et l'État sous Louis-Alexandre Taschrereau 1920–1936* (Montréal: Guérin, 1973), chap. 2; Vigod, *Quebec Before Duplessis*; Ruby Heap, 'Urbanisation et éducation: La Centralisation scolaire à Montréal au début du XXe siècle', CHA, *Historical Papers* (1985): 132–55. See also her 'Les Relations Église-État dans le domaine de l'enseignement primaire public au Québec: 1867–1899', SCHEC, *Sessions d'étude* 50 (1983): 183–99.

183 Daniel Latouche, 'La vraie nature de . . . la Révolution tranquille', *Canadian Journal of Political Science* VII (September 1974).

184 See Conrad Black, *Duplessis* (Toronto: McClelland and Stewart, 1977), chap. 16.

185 Hamelin, *Le XXe Siècle*, II, 161–74.

186 Hubert Guindon, 'The Social Evolution of Quebec Reconsidered', in Marcel Rioux and Yves Martin, eds, *French Canadian Society* (Toronto: McClelland and Stewart, 1964), 137–61.

187 Laurin et al., *A la recherche d'un monde oublié*, chaps 6–7.

188 Ibid., 235.

189 Laurin, et al., chaps 10–12.

190 Luigi Trifiro, 'Une intervention à Rome dans la lutte pour le suffrage féminin au Québec (1922)', *RHAF* 32, 1 (juin 1978) ; 3–18; the Clio Collective, *Quebec Women: A History* (Toronto: Women's Press, 1987), chap. 9. Denyse Baillargeon, *Ménagères au temps de la crise* (Montréal: Remue-ménage, 1991), shows that the church was not monolithic on the issue of birth control, and that a number of Franciscan confessors turned a blind eye to such practices during the Depression.

191 See Bettina Bradbury, 'The Family Economy and Work in an Industrializing City: Montreal in the 1870s', CHA, *Historical Papers* (1979): 71–96; Gail Brandt, '"Weaving It Together": Life Cycle and the Industrial Experience of Female Cotton Workers in Quebec, 1910–1950', in Alison Prentice and Susan Mann Trofimenkoff, eds, *The Neglected Majority*, vol. II (Toronto: McClelland and Stewart, 1985), 160–83.

192 Jennifer Stoddart, 'Quebec's Legal Elite Looks at Women's Rights: The Dorion Commission 1929–31', in David Flaherty, ed., *Essays in Canadian Legal History*, (Toronto: University of Toronto Press, 1981), I, 322–57; Andrée Lévesque, 'Mères ou malades: Les Québécoises de l'entre-deux-guerres vues par les médecins', *RHAF* 38, 1 (Été 1984): 23–37.

193 Suzanne L'Espérance-Morin, 'Les débats concernant la loi des pensions de vieillesse au Québec de 1927 à 1936' (M.A. thesis, History, Université de Montréal, 1981).

194 Hamelin, *Le XXe siècle*, II, 178–84.

195 Roberto Perin, 'Monolithism and Modernization: *Cité libre: première série* and its emergence from the Quebec intellectual milieu' (M.A. thesis, History, Carleton University, 1970), 94–10.

196 Hamelin, *Le XXe Siècle*, II, 82–102, 140–52.

197 Trudeau, *The Asbestos Strike*, 346.

198 Cited in Linteau et al., *Quebec Since 1930*, 224.

199 Lefebvre et al., *En grève!* chaps 1–2; Rouillard, *Histoire de la CSN*, chaps 2–3; Cousineau, *L'Église d'ici et le social*, chap. 12; Hélène David, 'La Grève et le bon Dieu: La Grève de l'amiante au Québec', *Sociologies et sociétés* 1, 2 (novembre 1969): 249–76; Hamelin, *Le XXe Siècle*, II, 97–100, is correct in challenging David's conception of the strike as a conflict between church and state. He points out that the bishops were very discreet in their disagreement with Duplessis and that they based their position on Christian charity, not on the substance of the workers' conflict; Frank Isbester, 'Asbestos 1949', in Irving Abella, ed., *On Strike: Six Key Labour Struggles in Canada 1919–1949* (Toronto: James Lorimer, 1975), 163–96.

200 Lionel Groulx, *Mes mémoires* (Montreal: Fides, 1974), IV, 270.

201 Gabriel Clément, *Histoire de l'Action catholique au Canada français* (Montréal: Fides, 1972), 17: Jean-Pierre Collin, 'La Ligue ouvrière catholique et l'organisation communautaire dans le Québec urbain des années 1940', *RHAF* 47, 2 (automne 1993): 163–91.

202 Simonne Monet Chartrand, *Ma vie comme rivière: Récit autobiographique, 1939–1949* (Montréal: Éditions Remue-Ménage, 1982), 69.

203 Cited in André Bélanger, *Ruptures et constantes* (Montréal: Hurtubise HMH, 1977), 36.

204 Susan Mann Robertson, 'Variations on a Nationalist Theme: Henri Bourassa and Abbé Groulx in the 1920s', CHA *Historical Papers* (1970): 109–19.

205 Groulx, *Mes mémoires*, IV, 145, 219–20.

206 Cited in Pierre Savard, 'Pax Romana, 1935–1962: Une fenêtre sur le monde', *Cahiers des Dix* 47 (1992): 279–323, 288.

207 Article in *L'Action nationale* 10, 3 (novembre 1937), cited in Ramsay Cook and Michael Behiels, eds, *The Essential Laurendeau* (Toronto: Copp Clark, 1976), 50. On the ideological transition in the Quebec of the thirties, see Christian Roy, 'Le Personnalisme de *l'Ordre Nouveau* et le Québec, 1930–1947', *RHAF* 46, 3 (hiver 1993): 463–84.

208 Groulx, *Mes mémoires*, IV, chap. 2; Cousineau, *L'Église d'ici et le social*, chap. 2.

209 Ibid., chap. 13.

210 Robert Rumilly, *Maurice Duplessis et son temps* (Montréal: Fides, 1973), II, 218–20.

211 P.E. Borduas, 'Refus Global', in Ramsay Cook, ed., *French Canadian Nationalism: An Anthology* (Toronto: Macmillan, 1969), 276–83.

212 David Kwavnick, ed., *The Tremblay Report* (Toronto: McClelland and Stewart, 1973); Coleman, *The Independence Movement in Quebec*, chap. 3.

213 Arthur Silver, 'Some Quebec Attitudes in an Age of Imperialism and Ideological Conflict', *CHR* LVII, 4 (December 1976): 440–60.

214 Michel Brunet, 'Trois dominantes de la pensée canadienne-française: L'Agriculturalisme, l'anti-étatisme et le messianisme', *La Présence anglaise et les Canadiens* (Montréal: Beauchemin, 1958). An abridged English version appeared in Dale Miquelon, ed., *Society and Conquest: The Debate on the Bourgeoisie and Social Change in French Canada, 1700–1850* (Toronto: Copp-Clark, 1977).

CHAPTER FIVE

1 Source: *Census of Canada*, 1851–1911.

2 Source: *Census of Canada*, 1871–1911.

3 Source: Figures calculated from Table 1 in A. Gordon Darroch and Michael D. Ornstein, 'Ethnicity and Occupational Structure in Canada in 1871: The Vertical Mosaic in Historical Perspective', *CHR* 61 (1980): 312.

4 Ibid.

5 T.W. Acheson, 'Methodism and the Problem of Methodist Identity in Nineteenth-Century New Brunswick', in Charles H.H. Scobie and John Webster Grant, eds, *The Contribution of Methodism to Atlantic Canada* (Montreal–Kingston: McGill–Queen's University Press, 1992), 112.

6 Peter Toner, 'Ethnicity and Regionalism in the Maritimes', in Robert Garland, ed., *Ethnicity in Atlantic Canada* (Saint John, NB: Division of Social Sciences, University of New Brunswick, 1985), 6.

7 Ruth Compton Brouwer, *New Women for God: Canadian Presbyterian Women and India Missions, 1876–1914* (Toronto: University of Toronto Press, 1990), 56.

8 J.M. Bumsted, 'Scottish Catholicism in Canada, 1770–1845', in Terrence Murphy and Gerald Stortz, eds, *Creed and Culture: The Place of English-Speaking Catholics in Canadian Society, 1750–1930* (Montreal–Kingston: McGill–Queen's University Press, 1993), 79.

9 Cecil J. Houston and William J. Smyth, *Irish Emigration and Canadian Settlement: Patterns, Links, and Letters* (Toronto: University of Toronto Press, 1990), 169–80, 188–235; Glenn J. Lockwood, 'Success and the Doubtful Image of Irish Immigrants in Upper Canada: The Case of Montague Township, 1820–1900', in Robert O'Driscoll and Lorna Reynolds, eds, *The Untold Story: The Irish in Canada* (Toronto: Celtic Arts of Canada, 1988), 319–40; various essays in Peter M. Toner, ed., *New Ireland Remembered: Historical Essays on the Irish in New Brunswick* (Fredericton: New Ireland Press, 1988).

10 Sidney E. Mead, *The Lively Experiment: The Shaping of Christianity in America* (New York: Harper and Row, 1963), 103–4. Discussion draws on material from pp. 115–26 and 129–33.

11 John Webster Grant, 'Canadian Confederation and the Protestant Churches', *Church History* 38 (1969): 331, 334.

12 John S. Moir, *Enduring Witness: A History of the Presbyterian Church in Canada* (Toronto: Presbyterian Publications, 1974), 128.

13 Ibid., 129–31, 134–42.

14 J. Warren Caldwell, 'The Unification of Methodism in Canada, 1865–1884', UCCA, *The Bulletin* 20 (1968): 6–7, 9–11; John Webster Grant, *The Church in the Canadian Era* (Toronto: McGraw-Hill Ryerson, 1972), 41.

15 Richard E. Ruggle, 'The Canadianization of the Church of England', CSCH, *Papers* (1981): 81–4, 86.

16 This discussion of the public role of religion is based on W.L. Morton, 'Victorian Canada', in Morton, ed., *The Shield of Achilles: Aspects of Canada in the Victorian Age* (Toronto: McClelland and Stewart, 1968), 314–18, 320–23 (quote at 315); Goldwin French, 'The Evangelical Creed in Canada', ibid., 15–22, 19–31, 33–4;

French, 'The Impact of Christianity on Canadian Culture and Society before 1867', *McMaster Theological Bulletin* 3 (1968): 33–5; French, 'Egerton Ryerson and the Methodist Model of Upper Canada', in Neil McDonald and Alf Chaiton, eds, *Egerton Ryerson and his Times: Essays on the History of Education* (Toronto: Macmillan, 1978), 53–7; J.M.S. Careless, 'Mid-Victorian Liberalism in Central Canadian Newspapers, 1850–67', *CHR* 31 (1950): 231–4.

17 John S. Moir, 'The Problem of a Double Minority: Some Reflections on the Development of the English-speaking Catholic Church in Canada in the Nineteenth Century', *Histoire sociale/Social History* 7 (1971): 55.

18 J.M. Bumsted, *The Peoples of Canada: A Pre-Confederation History* (Toronto: Oxford University Press, 1992), 345.

19 William Westfall, *Two Worlds: The Protestant Culture of Nineteenth-Century Ontario* (Kingston–Montreal: McGill–Queen's University Press, 1989), 129, 131–3.

20 *Globe*, 7 February 1882.

21 The discussion of large churches in Ontario's towns here and in the following paragraph owes much to the studies of Doris Mary O'Dell, 'The Class Character of Church Participation in Late Nineteenth-Century Belleville, Ontario' (Ph.D. dissertation, Queen's University, 1990), 134–5, 206, 265–9, and Lynne Sorrel Marks, 'Ladies, Loafers, Knights and '"Lasses": The Social Dimensions of Religion and Leisure in Late Nineteenth Century Small Town Ontario' (Ph.D. dissertation, York University, 1992), 132–7.

22 Neil Semple, 'The Impact of Urbanization on the Methodist Church of Canada, 1854–1884', CSCH, *Papers* (1976): 41–8; R.D. Gidney and W.P.J. Millar, *Professional Gentlemen: The Professions in Nineteenth-Century Ontario* (Toronto: University of Toronto Press, 1994), 120–1.

23 John Webster Grant, *A Profusion of Spires: Religion in Nineteenth-Century Ontario* (Toronto: University of Toronto Press, 1988), 175.

24 Westfall, *Two Worlds*, 151.

25 Peter F.M. Hanlon, 'Moral Order and the Influence of Social Christianity in an Industrial City, 1890–1899', (M.A. thesis, McMaster University, 1984), 30.

26 The surveys are reported in the *Globe*, 7 February 1882, and *Telegram*, 4 May 1896. Both enumerated every place of worship in the city, but the *Globe*'s survey adjusted its figures to take into account those who attended church twice by subtracting one-third from the total attendance for morning and evening. I have recalculated the *Telegram*'s returns using this formula.

27 *Journal of the Incorporated Synod of the Church of England in the Diocese of Toronto* (1884), 150–1.

28 This discussion is based on O'Dell, 'Class Character', 74–5, 141–5, 173–6, and Marks, 'Ladies', 64–81, 89.

29 Quoted in O'Dell, 'Class Character', 310.

30 Marks, 'Ladies', 74–5.

31 Jerald C. Brauer, 'Conversion: From Puritanism to Revivalism', *Journal of Religion* 58 (1978): 227–43; Brauer, 'Revivalism and Millenarianism in America', in Joseph D. Ban and Paul R. Dekar, eds, *In the Great Tradition: Essays on Pluralism, Voluntarism, and Revivalism* (Valley Forge: Judson Press, 1982), 147–59.

32 Jay P. Dolan, *The American Catholic Experience: A History from Colonial Times to the Present* (Garden City, NJ: Doubleday, 1985), 225.

33 D.S. Cross, 'The Irish in Montreal, 1867–1896' (M.A. thesis, McGill University, 1969), 95–126, 180–3.

34 By 1895, more than 660 religious women were working in the relatively small diocese of Peterborough, Ontario, compared with fewer than fifty priests; Edgar J. Boland, *From the Pioneers to the Seventies: A History of the Diocese of Peterborough 1882–1975* (Peterborough: Maxwell Review, 1976), 29.

35 Neil Semple, 'The Decline of Revival in Nineteenth Century Central-Canadian Methodism: The Extraordinary Means of Grace' Canadian Methodist Historical Society, *Papers* 2 (1977–80): 1–2, 5–8, 14, 17–18; David B. Marshall, *Secularizing the Faith: Canadian Protestant Clergy and the Crisis of Belief, 1850–1940* (Toronto: University of Toronto Press, 1992), 34.

36 Marguerite Van Die, '"Double Vision": Evangelical Piety as Derivative and Indigenous in Victorian Canada', in Mark A. Noll, David W. Bebbington, and George A. Rawlyk, eds, *Evangelicalism: Comparative Studies of Popular Protestantism in North America, the British Isles, and Beyond, 1770–1990* (New York: Oxford University Press, 1994), 257–61; Peter Bush, 'The Reverend James Caughey and Wesleyan Methodist Revivalism in Canada West, 1851–1856', *Ontario History* 89 (1987): 243–5; George A. Rawlyk, 'The Holiness Movement and Canadian Maritime Baptists', in Rawlyk and Mark A. Noll, eds, *Amazing Grace: Evangelicalism in Australia, Britain, Canada, and the United States* (Montreal–Kingston: McGill–Queen's University Press, 1994), 299–301; John Webster Grant, 'Burning Bushes: Flames of Revival in Nineteenth-Century Canadian Presbyterianism', CSCH, *Papers* (1991): 99–100; D.C. Masters, 'The Anglican Evangelicals in Toronto, 1870–1900', *Journal of the Canadian Church Historical Society* 20 (1978): 63–4; Marguerite Van Die, 'In Search of Piety', *Touchstone* 11 (1993): 10.

37 Phyllis D. Airhart, *Serving the Present Age: Revivalism, Progressivism, and the Methodist Tradition* (Montreal–Kingston: McGill–Queen's University Press, 1992), 21.

38 Ibid., 35.

39 Marguerite Van Die, *An Evangelical Mind: Nathanael Burwash and the Methodist Tradition in Canada, 1839–1918* (Kingston–Montreal: McGill–Queen's University Press, 1989), 23.

40 Neil Semple, ' "The Nurture and Admonition of the Lord": Nineteenth-Century Canadian Methodism's Response to "Childhood"', *Histoire sociale/Social History* 14 (1981): 168, 172, 174.

41 Marilyn Färdig Whiteley, 'Modest, Unaffected, and Fully Consecrated: Lady Evangelists in Canadian Methodism', in Elizabeth Gillan Muir and Marilyn Färdig Whiteley, eds, *Changing Roles of Women within the Christian Church in Canada* (Toronto: University of Toronto Press, 1995), 186–7, 189, 195–7.

42 Compare Semple, 'Impact of Urbanization', 25–7, 33–6, and Airhart, *Serving the Present Age*, 30–2.

43 Mary Anne MacFarlane, 'Gender, Doctrine and Pedagogy: Women and "Womanhood" in Methodist Sunday Schools in English Speaking Canada, 1880 to 1920' (Ph.D. dissertation, University of Toronto, 1992), 169–78.

44 Mary Anne MacFarlane, 'Educating, Sanctifying and Regulating Motherhood: The Cradle Roll Department in Methodist Schools', *Canadian Methodist Historical Society, Papers* 9 (1991/92): 167–91; MacFarlane, 'Gender, Doctrine, and Pedagogy', 144.

45 Marks, 'Ladies', 121.

46 Hanlon, 'Moral Order', 162–4.

47 Marilyn Färdig Whiteley, ' "Doing Just About What They Please": Ladies' Aids in Ontario Methodism', *Ontario History* 82 (1990): 289–304.

48 Marks, 'Ladies', 177.

49 Whiteley, ' "Doing Just About What They Please" ', 292.

50 Ibid., 298–9; Marks, 'Ladies', 146, 155, 158.

51 Rosemary R. Gagan, *A Sensitive Independence: Canadian Methodist Women Missionaries in Canada and the Orient, 1881–1925* (Montreal–Kingston: McGill–Queen's University Press, 1992), 20, 94; Brouwer, *New Women for God*, 15–16, 68–78.

52 O'Dell, 'Class Character', 193.

53 Semple, ' "Nurture and Admonition" ', 172, 174.

54 C.S. Sissons, *Church and State in Canadian Education: An Historical Study* (Toronto: Ryerson Press, 1959), 315–34; William B. Hamilton, 'Society and Schools in Nova Scotia', in J. Donald Wilson, Robert M. Stamp, and Louis-Philippe Audet, eds, *Canadian Education: A History* (Scarborough: Prentice Hall of Canada, 1970), 102–5.

55 Peter M. Toner, 'The New Brunswick Schools Question', CCHA, *Historical Papers* 37 (1970): 85–95.

56 George F.G. Stanley, 'The Caraquet Riots of 1875', *Acadiensis* 2 (1972): 21–38.

57 F. Jones, 'Religion, Education and Politics in Newfoundland, 1836–1875,' *Journal of the Canadian Church Historical Society* 12 (1970): 64–76; Philip McCann, 'The Politics of Denominational Education in the Nineteenth Century in Newfoundland', in William A. McKim, ed., *The Vexed Question: Denominational Education in a Secular Age* (St John's: Breakwater Books, 1988), 30–59.

58 For two different perspectives on this development see Franklin A. Walker, *Catholic Education and Politics in Upper Canada* (Toronto: English Catholic Education Association of Ontario, 1955), and John S. Moir, *Church and State in Canada West: Three Studies in the Relation of Denominationalism and Nationalism, 1841–1867* (Toronto: University of Toronto Press, 1959).

59 On anti-Catholicism in Britain see G.F.A. Best's pioneering work 'Popular Protestantism in Britain', in Robert Robson, ed., *Ideas and Institutions of Victorian Britain: Essays in Honour of George Kitson Clarke* (London: G. Bell & Sons, 1967), which is still the standard work in the field. Best's portrait has been filled out by two more recent works. See John Wolffe, *The Protestant Crusade in Great Britain, 1829–1860* (Oxford: Clarendon Press, 1991), especially chapters 1 and 4 ('The Roots of Anti-Catholicism' and 'The Anti-Catholic Frame of Mind') and D.G. Paz, *Popular Anti-Catholicism in Mid-Victorian England* (Stanford: Stanford University Press, 1992), especially chapter 2 ('Cultural Images'). For the Canadian scene see J.R. Miller, 'Anti-Catholic Thought in Victorian Canada', *CHR* 66 (1985): 474–94; 'Bigotry in the North Atlantic Triangle: Irish, British, and American influences on Canadian anti-Catholicism, 1850–1900', *Studies in Religion* 16 (1987): 289–301, and

'Anti-Catholicism in Canada: From the British Conquest to the Great War', in Murphy and Stortz, eds, *Creed and Culture*, 24–48. Also useful is Franklin Walker's 'Protestant Reaction in Upper Canada to the "Popish Threat"', *CCHA Report* (1951): 91–107, which covers anti-Catholic attitudes from the 1830s through to the 1850s in that part of the country.

60 2 November 1857; cited in Miller, 'Anti-Catholic Thought', 478.

61 On this point I disagree with J.R. Miller, who emphasizes the derivative nature of Protestant–Catholic tensions at mid-century. See his 'Bigotry in the North Atlantic Triangle', 290, 292–4.

62 Moir, *Church and State in Canada West*, 16, and Susan E. Houston and Alison Prentice, *Schooling and Scholars in Nineteenth-Century Ontario* (Toronto: University of Toronto Press, 1988), 279.

63 John S. Moir, 'Toronto's Protestants and their Perceptions of their Roman Catholic Neighbours', in Mark George McGowan and Brian P. Clarke, eds, *Catholics at the 'Gathering Place': Historical Essays on the Archdiocese of Toronto 1841–1991* (Toronto: CCHA, 1993), 317.

64 Scott W. See, 'The Orange Order and Social Violence in Mid-Nineteenth Century Saint John', *Acadiensis* 13 (1983): 90–2.

65 A.J.B. Johnston, 'Popery and Progress: Anti-Catholicism in Mid-Nineteenth-Century Nova Scotia', *Dalhousie Review* 64 (1984): 146–63.

66 See D.H. Akenson's estimates based on the 1851 census in his *The Irish in Ontario: A Study in Rural History* (Kingston–Montreal: McGill–Queen's University Press, 1984), 18–19, 42–3 re. 1871 census.

67 The definitive account of the controversy is J.R. Miller's *Equal Rights: The Jesuits Estates Act Controversy* (Montreal: McGill–Queen's University Press, 1979).

68 Ibid., 159–60, 187–9.

69 Paul Crunican, *Priests and Politicians: Manitoba Schools and the Election of 1896* (Toronto: University of Toronto Press, 1974), 23–5; Miller, *Equal Rights*, 171–2.

70 Manoly R. Lupul, *The Roman Catholic Church and the North-West School Question: A Study in Church–State Relations in Western Canada 1875–1905* (Toronto: University of Toronto Press, 1974), 12–14, 46–7, 72–9.

71 Michael Hatfield, 'H.H. Pitts and Race and Religion in New Brunswick Politics', *Acadiensis* 4 (1975): 49–51, 56–8.

72 Miller, *Equal Rights*, 175–201, offers a cogent explanation for the outbreak of the Equal Rights agitation, which I have largely followed here.

73 Miller, 'Anti-Catholicism', 40.

74 Robert Craig Brown and Ramsay Cook, *Canada 1896–1921: A Nation Transformed* (Toronto: McClelland and Stewart, 1974), 28.

75 Carl Berger, *The Sense of Power: Studies in the Ideas of Canadian Imperialism 1867–1914* (Toronto: University of Toronto Press, 1970), 1, 32, 217, 226, 260.

76 Doug Owram, *Promise of Eden: The Canadian Expansionist Movement and the Idea of the West, 1856–1900* (Toronto: University of Toronto, 1980), 144, 148.

77 J.R. Miller, ' "As a Politician He is a Great Enigma": The Social and Political Ideas of D'Alton McCarthy', *CHR* 63 (1977): 413.

78 Miller, *Equal Rights*, 108.

79 P.B. Waite, *The Man from Halifax: Sir John Thompson, Prime Minister* (Toronto: University of Toronto Press, 1985), 357.

80 Léon Thériault, 'The Acadianization of the Catholic Church in Acadia (1763–1953)', in Jean Daigle, ed., *The Acadians of the Maritimes: Thematic Studies* (Moncton: Centre d'études acadiennes, 1982), 305–11.

81 Robert Choquette, *L'Église catholique dans l'Ontario français du dix-neuvième siècle* (Ottawa: Éditions de l'Université d'Ottawa, 1984), 139–40, 237–41.

82 D.G. Cartwright, 'Ecclesiastical Territorial Organization and Institutional Conflict in Eastern and Northern Ontario, 1840–1910', CHA, *Historical Papers* (1979): 183–8.

83 Grant, *Profusion of Spires*, 171.

84 Stephen A. Speisman, 'Munificent Parsons and Municipal Parsimony: Voluntary vs Public Poor Relief in Nineteenth Century Toronto', *Ontario History* 65 (1973): 33–4.

85 P.B. Waite, 'Sir Oliver Mowat's Canada: Reflections on an Un-Victorian Society', in Donald Swainson, ed., *Oliver Mowat's Ontario* (Toronto: Macmillan, 1972), 20.

86 John Webster Grant, *Moon of Wintertime: Missionaries and the Indians of Canada in Encounter since 1534* (Toronto: University of Toronto Press, 1984), 104, 107, 148–9; Kenneth Coates, 'Send Only Those Who Rise a Peg: Anglican Clergy in the Yukon, 1858–1932', *Journal of the Canadian Church Historical Society* 28 (1986): 5; John H. Archer, 'The Anglican Church and the Indian in the Northwest', ibid., 25; Moir, *Enduring Witness*, 159.

87 Grant, *Moon of Wintertime*, 132–3; J.H. Riddell, *Methodism in the Middle West* (Toronto: Ryerson Press, 1946), 35–8; Kerry Abel, 'Bishop Bompas and the Canadian Church', in Barry Ferguson, ed., *The Anglican Church and the World of Western Canada 1820–1970* (Regina: Canadian Plains Research Centre, 1991), 122; Winona Stevenson, ' "Our Man in the Field" ': Charles Pratt, a CMS Catechist in Rupert's Land', *Journal of the Canadian Church Historical Society* 33 (1991): 68, 71, 73.

88 This discussion is based on the definitive work on Duncan's career, Jean Usher's *William Duncan of Metlakatla: A Victorian Missionary in British Columbia* (Ottawa: National Museums of Canada, 1974). See also Robin Fisher, *Contact and Conflict: Indian–European Relations in British Columbia, 1774–1890* (Vancouver: University of British Columbia Press, 1977), 128–36.

89 Grant, *Moon of Wintertime*, 158, 162, 173–84, 192–6, 224–5.

90 Mark A. Noll, *A History of Christianity in the United States and Canada* (Grand Rapids, Mich.: William B. Eerdmans Publishing, 1992), 154; Noll, 'Common Sense Traditions and American Evangelical Thought', *American Quarterly* 37 (1985): 220–4; Michael Gauvreau, *The Evangelical Century: College and Creed in English Canada from the Great Revival to the Great Depression* (Montreal–Kingston: McGill–Queen's University Press, 1991), 16–19, 28–9, 38–9; Marguerite Van Die, *An Evangelical Mind: Nathanael Burwash and the Methodist Tradition in Canada, 1839–1918* (Kingston–Montreal: McGill–Queen's University Press, 1989), 42–3.

91 A.B. McKillop, *Matters of Mind: The University in Ontario, 1791–1951* (Toronto: University of Toronto Press, 1994), 105.

92 Carl Berger, *Science, God, and Nature in Victorian Canada* (Toronto: University of Toronto Press, 1983), 54.

93 Charles F. O'Brien, *Sir William Dawson: A Life in Science and Religion* (Philadelphia: American Philosophical Society, 1971), 103–7, 119; A.B. McKillop, *A Disciplined Intelligence: Critical Inquiry and Canadian Thought in the Victorian Era* (Montreal: McGill-Queen's University Press, 1979), 100–2; Robert John Taylor, 'The Darwinian Revolution: The Responses of Four Canadian Scholars' (Ph.D. dissertation, McMaster University, 1976), 58–9.

94 Gauvreau, *The Evangelical Century*, 128; James R. Moore, *The Post-Darwinian Controversies: A Study of the Protestant Struggle to Come to Terms with Darwin in Great Britain and America, 1870–1900* (Cambridge: Cambridge University Press, 1979), 205; O'Brien, *Dawson*, 183–5.

95 Peter J. Bowler, *Charles Darwin: The Man and His Influence* (Oxford: Basil Blackwell, 1990), 128, 139–41, 148; Van Die, *An Evangelical Mind*, 67.

96 McKillop, *Matters of Mind*, 119–20; David B. Marshall, *Secularizing the Faith: Canadian Protestant Clergy and the Crisis of Belief, 1850–1940* (Toronto: University of Toronto Press, 1992), 54–9 (quote at 57); Phyllis D. Airhart, *Serving the Present Age: Revivalism, Progressivism, and the Methodist Tradition in Canada* (Montreal–Kingston: McGill-Queen's University Press, 1992), 54–5; Barry Moody, 'Breadth of Vision, Breadth of Mind: The Baptists and Acadia College', in G.A. Rawlyk, ed., *Canadian Baptists and Christian Higher Education* (Kingston–Montreal: McGill-Queen's University Press, 1988), 25–8.

97 Quoted by Claude Welch, *Protestant Thought in the Nineteenth Century* (New Haven: Yale University Press, 1972), I, 169.

98 Owen Chadwick, *The Victorian Church*, 2nd ed. (London: A. and C. Black, 1972), part 2, 76–7.

99 Van Die, *An Evangelical Mind*, 59, 93.

100 Gauvreau, *The Evangelical Century*, 42–4, 46–7, 57–8, 77, 79, 84, 90.

101 Van Die, *An Evangelical Mind*, 59–60.

102 Ibid., 102–3, 107.

103 Ibid., 150–3; Gauvreau, *The Evangelical Century*, 152–60; Barry Mack, 'Of Canadian Presbyterians and Guardian Angels', in George A. Rawlyk and Mark Noll, eds, *Amazing Grace: Evangelicalism in Australia, Britain, Canada, and the United States* (Montreal–Kingston: McGill-Queen's University Press, 1994), 280.

104 Van Die, *An Evangelical Mind*, 110.

105 Joseph C. McLelland, 'The Macdonnell Heresy Trial', *Canadian Journal of Theology* 4 (1958): 273–84; Mack, 'Of Canadian Presbyterians', 274–6; Marshall, *Secularizing the Faith*, 39–45, 76–80; Gauvreau, *The Evangelical Century*, 158–9; John S. Moir, *A History of Biblical Studies in Canada: A Sense of Proportion* (Chico, Cal.: Scholars Press, 1982), 9–12, 35–6; McKillop, *Matters of Mind*, 207–8; Tom Sinclair-Faulkner, 'Theory Divided from Practice: The Introduction of the Higher Criticism in Canadian Protestant Seminaries', CSCH, *Papers* (1979): 43–6; Van Die, *An Evangelical Mind*, 104, 111–12.

106 Airhart, *Serving the Present Age*, 95–100, 105–7, 111.

107 Brian Fraser, *The Social Uplifters: Presbyterian Progressives and the Social Gospel in Canada, 1875–1915* (Waterloo, Ont.: Wilfrid Laurier University Press, 1988), 4–5, 11–12; Gauvreau, *The Evangelical Century*, 184–6.

108 Charles M. Johnston, *McMaster University: The Toronto Years* (Toronto: University of Toronto Press, 1976), 102–12.

109 Lynne Marks, 'The Knights of Labor and the Salvation Army: Religion and Working-Class Culture in Ontario, 1882–1890', *Labour/Le Travail* 28 (1991): 111–15.

110 Airhart, *Serving the Present Age*, 73–4; S.D. Clark, *Church and Sect in Canada* (Toronto: University of Toronto Press, 1948), 409–13.

111 Ron Sawatsky, ' "Looking for That Blessed Hope": The Roots of Fundamentalism in Canada, 1878–1914' (Ph.D. dissertation, University of Toronto, 1985), 39–55, 76; Ernest R. Sandeen, *The Roots of Fundamentalism: British and American Millenarianism 1800–1930* (Chicago: University of Chicago Press, 1970), 134, 142.

112 Grant, *Profusion of Spires*, 162, 215; Airhart, *Serving the Present Age*, 41–3.

113 Ron Sawatsky, ' "Unholy Contentions About Holiness": The Canadian Holiness Association and the Methodist Church, 1875–1894', *CSCH, Papers* (1982): 12, 18.

114 Brian R. Ross, 'Ralph Cecil Horner: A Methodist Sectarian Deposed 1887–1895', *Journal of the Canadian Church Historical Society* 19 (1977): 99, 101.

115 Airhart, *Serving the Present Age*, 52.

116 Sawatsky, ' "Looking for That Blessed Hope"', 4.

117 James C. Livingston, *Modern Christian Thought: From the Enlightenment to Vatican II* (New York: Macmillan, 1972), 266.

118 Airhart, *Serving the Present Age*, 104–5.

119 Ibid., 108, 109–11.

120 Richard Allen, *The Social Passion: Religion and Social Reform in Canada 1914–28* (Toronto: University of Toronto Press, 1973), 9–10.

121 Richard Allen, 'Salem Bland and the Spirituality of the Social Gospel: Winnipeg and the West, 1903–1913', in Denis L. Butcher, Catherine Macdonald, Margaret E. McPherson, Raymond R. Smith, and A. McKibbon Watts, eds, *Prairie Spirit: Perspectives on the Heritage of the United Church of Canada in the West* (Winnipeg: University of Manitoba Press, 1985), 221, 223.

122 Christopher Armstrong and H.V. Nelles, *The Revenge of the Methodist Bicycle Company: Sunday Streetcars and Municipal Reform in Toronto, 1888–1897* (Toronto: Peter Martin Associates, 1977), 50–1; Paul Laverdure, 'Canada's Sunday: The Presbyterian Contribution, 1875–1950', in William Klempa, ed., *The Burning Bush and a Few Acres of Snow: The Presbyterian Contribution to Canadian Life and Culture* (Ottawa: Carleton University Press, 1994), 84–5.

123 Marshall, *Secularizing the Faith*, 137–8; A.M.C. Waterman, 'The Lord's Day in a Secular Society: A Historical Comment on the Canadian Lord's Day Act of 1906', *Canadian Journal of Theology* 11 (1965): 108–23; Paul Laverdure, 'Sunday Secularism? The Lord's Day Debate of 1906', CSCH, *Papers* (1986): 85–107.

124 Robert Craig Brown and Ramsay Cook, *Canada 1896–1921: A Nation Transformed* (Toronto: McClelland and Stewart, 1974), 300.

125 Edward Pulker, *We Stand on Their Shoulders: The Growth of Social Concern in Canadian Anglicanism* (Toronto: Anglican Book Centre, 1986), 58–9.

126 E.R. Forbes, 'Prohibition and the Social Gospel in Nova Scotia', *Acadiensis* 1 (1971): 11, 14–15; Phyllis D. Airhart, ' "Sweeter Manners, Purer Laws": Women as Temperance Reformers in Late Victorian Canada', *Touchstone* 9 (1991): 22.

127 Between 1881 and 1911, Montreal, by far the largest city in Canada, grew from approximately 155,000 inhabitants to some 490,500; Toronto, from 96,900 to 381,000; and Winnipeg, from 7,900 to 136,000. Municipalities that had not even existed in 1881 now had sizeable populations, with Vancouver counting roughly 100,000, Calgary 43,700, and Edmonton 31,000; Alan F.J. Artibise, 'Divided City: The Immigrant in Winnipeg Society, 1874–1921', in Gilbert A. Stelter and Alan F.J. Artibise, eds, *The Canadian City: Essays in Urban History* (Toronto: McClelland and Stewart, 1977), 310.

128 Marilyn Barber, 'Nativism, Nationalism, and the Social Gospel: The Protestant Response to Foreign Immigrants in Western Canada, 1897–1914,' in Richard Allen, ed., *The Social Gospel in Canada* (Ottawa: National Museum of Man, 1975), 218.

129 Mariana Valverde, *The Age of Light, Soap, and Water: Moral Reform in English Canada, 1885–1925* (Toronto: McClelland and Stewart, 1991), 45.

130 Barber, 'Nationalism, Nativism, and the Social Gospel', 222; Michael Owen, ' "Keeping Canada God's Country": Presbyterian Perspectives on Selected Social Issues 1900–1915' (Ph.D. dissertation, University of Toronto, 1984), 19; Sawatsky, ' "Looking for That Blessed Hope"', 81–2.

131 Richard Allen, 'The Social Gospel as the Religion of the Agrarian Revolt,' in Carl Berger and Ramsay Cook, eds, *The West and The Nation: Essays in Honour of W.L. Morton* (Toronto: McClelland and Stewart, 1976), 175.

132 Owen, ' "Keeping Canada God's Country"', 44.

133 John Webster Grant, 'The Reaction of Wasp Churches to Non-Wasp Immigrants', CSCH, *Papers* (1968): 1–2.

134 Owen, ' "Keeping Canada God's Country"', 44.

135 Grant, 'Reaction', 4.

136 Barber, 'Nationalism, Nativism, and the Social Gospel', 220–3; John Webster Grant, 'Presbyterian Home Missions and Canadian Nationhood', in Massimo Rubboli and Franca Farnocchia Petri, eds, *Canada Ieri E Oggi 2: Atti Del 7 Convegno Internazionale di Studi Canadesi* (Fasano: Schena Editore, 1990), 151.

137 Mary Vipond, 'Canadian National Consciousness and the Formation of the United Church of Canada', UCCA, *The Bulletin* 24 (1975): 9–10.

138 Barber, 'Nationalism, Nativism, and the Social Gospel', 190, 208–10, 222.

139 Phyllis D. Airhart, 'Sobriety, Sentimentality, and Science: The WCTU and the Reconstruction of Christian Womanhood', Canadian Methodist Historical Society, *Papers* (1988/90): 126, 131–2; Sharon Anne Cook, ' "Continued and Persevering Combat": The Ontario Woman's Christian Temperance Union, Evangelicalism, and Social Reform' (Ph.D. dissertation, Carleton University, 1990), 196, 210.

140 Wendy Mitchinson, 'The WCTU: "For God, Home and Native Land": A Study in Nineteenth-Century Feminism' in Linda Kealey, ed., *A Not Unreasonable Claim: Women and Reform in Canada, 1880–1920s* (Toronto: Women's Press, 1979), 155, 159, 163–4; Airhart, 'Sobriety, Sentimentality, and Science', 121, 123; Airhart, ' "Sweeter Manners, Purer Laws"', 24.

141 Cook, ' "Continued and Persevering Combat"', 210–12 (quote at 212); Veronica Strong-Boag, ' "Ever a Crusader": Nellie McClung, First Wave Feminist', in Strong-

Boag and Anita Clair Fellman, eds, *Rethinking Canada: The Promise of Women's History* (Toronto: Copp Clark Pittman, 1986), 181.

142 Randi R. Warne, 'Nellie McClung's Social Gospel', in Elizabeth Gillan Muir and Marilyn Färdig Whiteley, eds, *Changing Roles of Women Within the Christian Church in Canada* (Toronto: University of Toronto Press, 1995) 339–40, 344–5, 348–9 (quote at 345).

143 Patricia Dirks, 'Finding the "Canadian" Way: Origins of the Religious Council of Canada', *Studies in Religion/Sciences religieuses* 16 (1987): 311–12, 315–16.

144 George A. Rawlyk, 'The Champions of the Oppressed? Canadian Baptists and Social, Political and Economic Realities', in Robert E. VanderVennen, ed., *Church and Canadian Culture* (Lanham, Md: University Press of America, 1991), 105–6, 108–11, 116–18.

145 Diana Pedersen, ' "Keeping Our Good Girls Good": The YWCA and the "Girl Problem", 1870–1930', *Canadian Woman Studies/Les cahiers de la Femme* 7 (1986): 21, 23; Wendy Mitchinson, 'The YWCA and Reform in the Nineteenth Century', *Histoire sociale/Social History* 12 (1979): 381; David Macleod, 'A Live Vaccine: The YMCA and Male Adolescence in the United States and Canada 1870–1920', *Histoire sociale/Social History* 11 (1978): 14, 20–2; Margaret Prang, ' "The Girl God Would Have Me Be": The Canadian Girls in Training, 1915–39', *CHR* 66 (1985): 157–8, 160–1, 163–6; Patricia Dirks, ' "Getting a Grip on Harry": Canada's Methodists Respond to the "Big Boy" Problem 1900–1925', Canadian Methodist Historical Society, *Papers* (1989): 73–7.

146 Allan Irving, Harriet Parsons, and Donald Bellamy, *Neighbours: Three Social Settlements in Downtown Toronto* (Toronto: Canadian Scholars' Press, 1995), 13–15; G.N. Emery, 'The Methodist Church and the "European Foreigners" of Winnipeg: The All People's [sic] Mission, 1889–1914', Historical and Scientific Society of Manitoba, *Transactions*, series 3, no. 28 (1971–2): 86, 93–4; William Magney, 'The Methodist Church and the National Gospel, 1884–1914', UCCA, *The Bulletin* 20 (1968): 22–3.

147 John D. Thomas, 'Servants of the Church: Canadian Methodist Deaconess Work, 1890–1926', *CHR* 65 (1984): 371, 377, 379–80, 394.

148 Allen, *The Social Passion*, 71–6.

149 Ibid., 18–20, 24–5, 27, 29, 31–2.

150 Michael Bliss, 'The Methodist Church and World War I', in Carl Berger, ed., *Conscription 1917* (Toronto: University of Toronto Press, n.d.), 43–4, 46–7; Moir, *Enduring Witness*, 208–9.

151 Beth Profit, ' "The Making of a Nation": Nationalism and World War I in the Social Gospel Literature of Ralph Connor', CSCH, *Historical Papers* (1992): 131–7, which offers a number of examples in addition to Connor.

152 Margaret Prang, 'Clerics, Politicians, and the Bilingual Schools Issue in Ontario, 1910–1917', in Craig Brown, ed., *Minorities, Schools, and Politics* (Toronto: University of Toronto Press, 1969), 106 (quote); Marilyn Barber, 'The Ontario Bilingual Schools Issue: Sources of Conflict', ibid., 79–81; Robert Choquette, *Language and Religion: A History of English–French Conflict in Ontario* (Ottawa: University of Ottawa Press, 1975), 77–8, 87, 90, 251–2.

153 W.L. Morton, 'Manitoba Schools and the Canadian Nationality, 1890–1923', in Brown, ed., *Minorities, Schools, and Politics*, 15–16.

154 Brown and Cook, *Canada 1896–1921*, 263–4, 273–4; Elizabeth Armstrong, *The Crisis of Quebec, 1914–1918* (1937; repr. Toronto: McClelland and Stewart, 1974), 121, 178, 221.

155 Mark G. McGowan, ' "To Share in the Burdens of Empire": Toronto's Catholics and the Great War, 1914–1918', in McGowan and Clarke, eds, *Catholics at the 'Gathering Place'*, 179–80, 182–3, 189–90.

156 Brian Hogan, 'The Guelph Novitiate Raid: Conscription, Censorship and Bigotry during the Great War', CCHA, *Study Sessions* 45 (1978): 64–6, 68, 73–4, 76–7.

157 Allen, *The Social Passion*, 34–6, 40–5; Bliss, 'The Methodist Church and World War I', 53, 57, 59.

158 Allen, *The Social Passion*, 46, 61, 97–8, 101–2; Vera Fast, 'The Labour Church in Winnipeg', in Butcher et al., eds, *Prairie Spirit*, 241 (quote).

159 Allen, *The Social Passion*, 97–8, 101–2, 109, 113, 119, 124–6, 130–1; Ramsay Cook, *The Regenerators: Social Criticism in Late Victorian Canada* (Toronto: University of Toronto Press, 1985), 222–3, 225.

160 Allen, *The Social Passion*, 114–19, 132, 167.

161 Marshall, *Secularizing the Faith*, 183.

162 Gauvreau, *The Evangelical Century*, 260–1.

163 Robert Wright, *A World Mission: Canadian Protestantism and the Quest for A New International Order, 1918–1939* (Montreal–Kingston: McGill–Queen's University Press, 1991), 15; Gauvreau, *The Evangelical Century*, 260–2; Airhart, *Serving the Present Age*, 110–11; Marshall, *Secularizing the Faith*, 164.

164 Marshall, *Secularizing the Faith*, 171, 173–5, 177–8; Wright, *A World Mission*, 17–18.

165 John H. Thompson, 'The Voice of Moderation: The Defeat of Prohibition in Manitoba', in S.M. Trofimenkoff, ed., *The Twenties in Western Canada* (Ottawa: National Museums of Canada, 1972), 173, 179–81; Forbes, 'Prohibition and the Social Gospel', 35; Cook, ' "Continued and Persevering Combat" ', 112, 137.

166 John Herd Thompson and Allen Seager, *Canada 1922–1938: Decades of Discord* (Toronto: McClelland and Stewart, 1985), 175–84; Veronica Strong-Boag, *The New Day Recalled: Lives of Girls and Women in English Canada, 1919–1939* (Toronto: Penguin, 1988), 85–6, 128–9.

167 Marshall, *Secularizing the Faith*, 197–8; Wright, *A World Mission*, 19–20.

168 Allen, *The Social Passion*, 137–40.

169 Ibid., 220–1.

170 John Webster Grant, *The Canadian Experience of Church Union* (London: Lutterworth Press, 1967), 19–20.

171 Ibid., 26.

172 John Webster Grant, 'Blending Traditions: The United Church of Canada', in Grant, ed., *The Churches and the Canadian Experience* (Toronto: Ryerson Press, 1963), 134–5, 136; Grant, 'The United Church and its Heritage in Evangelicalism', *Touchstone* 1 (1983): 7–8, 13; Van Die, *An Evangelical Mind*, 146, 157–9, 168–9; Airhart, *Serving the Present Age*, 111; Gauvreau, *The Evangelical Century*, 260.

173 Grant, *The Canadian Experience of Church Union*, 21; Vipond, 'Canadian National Consciousness and the Formation of the United Church', 6, 8, 11, 16, 20.

174 N. Keith Clifford, *The Resistance to Church Union in Canada* (Vancouver: University of British Columbia Press, 1985), 13–14, 28–9, 58, 79–81.

175 Ibid., 163, 179, 189–91, 220–2, 232–4.

176 John G. Stackhouse, Jr, *Canadian Evangelicalism in the Twentieth Century: An Introduction to Its Character* (Toronto: University of Toronto Press, 1993), 9–10, 41–2; George M. Marsden, *Understanding Fundamentalism and Evangelicalism* (Grand Rapids, Mich.: Eerdmans, 1991), 1–4; Martin E. Marty and R. Scott Appleby, *The Glory and the Power: The Fundamentalist Challenge to the Modern World* (Boston: Beacon Press, 1992), 10–12, 15–18.

177 Ian Rennie, 'Fundamentalism and the Varieties of North Atlantic Evangelicalism', in Noll, Bebbington, and Rawlyk, eds, *Evangelicalism*, 342–5.

178 W. Gordon Carter, 'Controversy in the Baptist Convention of Ontario and Quebec, 1908–1928', *Foundations* 1 (1973): 355–7, 362–73; C. Allyn Russell, 'Thomas Todhunter Shields, Canadian Fundamentalist', *Ontario History* 70 (1978): 270–2.

179 Robert K. Burkinshaw, *Pilgrims in Lotus Land: Conservative Protestantism in British Columbia* (Montreal–Kingston: McGill–Queen's University Press, 1995), 77–8, 80–91; Margaret E. Thompson, *The Baptist Story in Western Canada* (Calgary: Baptist Union of Western Canada, 1974), 155–8.

180 David R. Elliott and Iris Miller, *Bible Bill: A Biography of William Aberhart* (Edmonton: Reidmore Books, 1987), 74, 79–80, 191.

181 Russell, 'Thomas Todhunter Shields', 262, 272, 276–7.

182 Ronald G. Sawatsky, 'The Bible School/College Movement in Canada: Fundamental Christian Training', CSCH, *Papers* (1986), 7–8, 11; W.E. Mann, *Sect, Cult, and Church in Alberta* (Toronto: University of Toronto Press, 1955), 84–5, 101, 104–5; Stackhouse, *Canadian Evangelicalism*, 59–60, 73, 82–3.

183 Ben Harder, 'The Bible Institute/College Movement in Canada', *Journal of the Canadian Church Historical Society* 20 (1980): 31–3, 35–6; Bruce L. Guenther, 'The Origin of the Bible School Movement in Western Canada: Towards an Ethnic Interpretation', CSCH, *Historical Papers* (1993): 146–8, 151–2; Stackhouse, *Canadian Evangelicalism*, 55, 68.

184 Marshall, *Secularizing the Faith*, 206–12.

185 N. Keith Clifford, 'Religion in the Thirties: Some Aspects of the Canadian Experience', in R.D. Francis and H. Ganzevoort, eds, *The Dirty Thirties in Prairie Canada* (Vancouver: Tantalus Research, 1988), 128–31; Marshall, *Secularizing the Faith*, 218, 220, 223–4.

186 Clifford, 'Religion in the Thirties', 125–7; Roger Hutchinson, 'The Fellowship for a Christian Social Order', in Harold Wells and Roger Hutchinson, eds, *A Long and Faithful March: 'Towards the Christian Revolution' 1930s/1980s* (Toronto: United Church Publishing House, 1989), 22.

187 Clifford, 'Religion in the Thirties', 126; Roger Hutchinson, 'The Canadian Social Gospel in the Context of Social Ethics', in Allen, ed., *The Social Gospel in Canada*, 296–8.

188 Phyllis D. Airhart, 'Christian Socialism and the Legacy of Revivalism in the 1930s', in Wells and Hutchinson, eds, *A Long and Faithful March*, 34; Brian J. Fraser, 'From Anathema to Alternative: The Gordons and Socialism', in ibid., 46–7.

189 Clifford, 'Religion in the Thirties', 132–3; Gordon Barnhart, 'The Prairie Pastor–
E.H. Oliver', *Saskatchewan History* 37 (1984): 89–91.

190 Brian Clarke, *Piety and Nationalism: Lay Voluntary Associations and the Creation of an Irish-Catholic Community in Toronto, 1850–1895* (Montreal–Kingston: McGill–Queen's University Press, 1993), 249–53; Mark G. McGowan, 'The De-Greening of the Irish: Toronto's Irish Catholic Press, Imperialism, and the Forging of a New Identity, 1887–1914', CHA, *Historical Papers* (1989): 126–7, 135–6, 139.

191 Mark McGowan, 'Toronto's English-Speaking Catholics, Immigration, and the Making of a Canadian Catholic Identity, 1900–30', in Murphy and Stortz, eds, *Creed and Culture*, 209–11.

192 Source: *Census of Canada*, 1931, Table 45.

193 McGowan, 'Toronto's English-Speaking Catholics', 213.

194 Zofia Shahrodi, 'The Experience of Polish Catholics in the Archdiocese of Toronto', in McGowan and Clarke, eds, *Catholics at the 'Gathering Place'*, 145–7, 150; Enrico Carlson Cumbo, ' "Impediments to the Harvest": The Limitations of Methodist Proselytization of Toronto's Italian Immigrants', in ibid., 168; Henry Radecki with Benedykt Heydendorn, *A Member of a Distinguished Family: The Polish Group in Canada* (Toronto: McClelland and Stewart, 1976), 145–50; John E. Zucchi, *Italians in Toronto: Development of a National Identity, 1875–1935* (Kingston–Montreal: McGill–Queen's University Press, 1988), 138–9; McGowan, 'Toronto's English-Speaking Catholics', 214–15, 218.

195 McGowan, 'Toronto's English-Speaking Catholics', 219–25.

196 Mark G. McGowan, ' "A Portion for the Vanquished": Roman Catholics and the Ukrainian Catholic Church', in Lubomyr Luciuk and Stella Hryniuk, *Canada's Ukrainians: Negotiating an Identity* (Toronto: University of Toronto Press, 1991), 221–2, 227–9.

197 Paul Yuzyk, 'Religious Life', in Manoly Lupul, ed., *A Heritage in Transition: Essays in the History of Ukrainians in Canada* (Toronto: McClelland and Stewart, 1982), 155–7; McGowan, ' "A Portion for the Vanquished"', 233.

198 Roberto Perin, *Rome in Canada: The Vatican and Canadian Affairs in the Late Victorian Age* (Toronto: University of Toronto Press, 1990), 227–8.

199 Raymond Huel, 'The Irish-French Conflict in Catholic Episcopal Nominations: The Western Sees and the Struggle for Domination within the Church', CCHA, *Study Sessions* (1975): 54–5, 57, 59–60; Huel, 'Gestae Dei Per Francos: The French Catholic Experience in Western Canada', in Benjamin G. Smillie, ed., *Visions of the New Jerusalem: Religious Settlement on the Prairies* (Edmonton: NeWest Press, 1983), 49; McGowan, 'Toronto's English-Speaking Catholics', 228–30.

200 Jeanne R. Beck, 'Contrasting Approaches to Catholic Social Action During the Depression: Henry Somerville the Educator and Catherine de Hueck the Activist', in McGowan and Clarke, eds, *Catholics at the 'Gathering Place'*, 214–17; Gregory Baum, *Catholics and Canadian Socialism: Political Thought in the Thirties and Forties* (Toronto: James Lorimer, 1980), 98.

201 Baum, *Catholics and Canadian Socialism*, 122, 126, 129–30, 140; Murray G. Ballantyne, 'The Catholic Church and the CCF', CCHA, *Report* (1963): 39–42.

202 Baum, *Catholics and Canadian Socialism*, 192, 195–6; R. James Sacouman,

'Underdevelopment and the Structural Origins of the Antigonish Movement Co-operatives in Eastern Nova Scotia', *Acadiensis* 8 (1977): 68–72, 76–8, 82; Brian F. Hogan, CSB, 'Ivory Tower and Grass Roots: The Intellectual Life and Social Action in the Congregation of St Basil, Archdiocese of Toronto, 1930–1960', in McGowan and Clarke, eds, *Catholics at the 'Gathering Place'*, 266–8.

203 Wright, *A World Mission* 216–17, 221–6, 228–9, 248.

204 Luigi G. Pennacchio, 'The Torrid Trinity: Toronto's Fascists, Italian Priests and Archbishops during the Fascist Era', in McGowan and Clarke, eds, *Catholics at the 'Gathering Place'*, 242, 251n.54.

205 Ibid., 248; Charles Thompson Sinclair Faulkner, ' "For Christian Civilization": The Churches and Canada's War Effort, 1939–1942' (Ph.D. dissertation, University of Chicago, 1975), 38–9, 231.

206 *Census of Canada*, 1961, vol. 7: 11–4, 11–5.

207 Ibid.

208 Ibid., 11–4, 11–6.

209 Grant, *The Church in the Canadian Era*, 161.

210 Reginald W. Bibby, *Fragmented Gods: The Poverty and Potential of Religion in Canada* (Toronto: Irwin Publishing, 1987), 17.

211 Reginald W. Bibby, *Unknown Gods: The Ongoing Story of Religion in Canada* (Toronto: Stoddart, 1993), 6.

212 John Webster Grant, 'The Impact of Christianity on Canadian Culture and Society, 1867–1967', McMaster Divinity College, *Theological Bulletin* 3 (1968): 42–3.

213 N. Keith Clifford, 'His Dominion: A Vision in Crisis', *Studies in Religion/Sciences religieuses* 2 (1973): 320.

214 Figures calculated from *Census of Canada*, 1961, vol. 7, 11–16.

EPILOGUE

1 Reginald Bibby, *Unknown Gods: The Ongoing Story of Religion in Canada* (Toronto: Stoddart, 1993), 6.

2 'Religion in Quebec: Present and Future', *Pro Mundi Vita: Dossiers* (Nov.-Dec. 1977), 6.

3 Gregory Baum, 'Catholicism and Secularization in Quebec', in *The Church in Quebec* (Ottawa: Novalis, 1991), 30.

4 Reginald Bibby, *Fragmented Gods: the Poverty and Potential of Religion in Canada* (Toronto: Irwin, 1987), 11–23, 46–52.

5 Ibid., 47.

6 Ibid., 47–51.

7 'Special Report: The Religion Poll. God is Alive', *Maclean's* (12 April 1993): 32–7.

8 Bibby, *Fragmented Gods*, 14, 16–17, 20.

9 Bibby, *Unknown Gods*, 10.

10 Bibby, *Fragmented Gods*, 91–6, 233.

11 *Census of Canada 1991: Religions in Canada* (Ottawa: Statistics Canada, 1993), 1.

12 'Special Report: The Religion Poll', 32, where *Maclean's* claims that 'The Religion Poll portrays Canada as an overwhelmingly Christian nation, not only in name, but in belief.'

13 Bibby, *Fragmented Gods*, 27.

14 Bibby, *Unknown Gods*, 6–8.

15 Bibby, *Fragmented Gods*, 28–31.

16 Ibid., 28.

17 John G. Stackhouse, *Canadian Evangelicalism in the Twentieth Century: An Introduction to its Character* (Toronto: University of Toronto Press, 1993), 5.

18 For more on the Canadian churches and homosexuality, see James Ferry, *In the Courts of the Lord: A Gay Minister's Story* (Toronto: Key Porter, 1993), and Michael Riordon, *The First Stone: Homosexuality and the United Church* (Toronto: McClelland and Stewart, 1990).

19 Stackhouse, *Canadian Evangelicalism*, 165–73.

20 Bibby, *Unknown Gods*, 6.

Index